Date Due

APR 13 '70	OCT 27 '80		
NOV 8 '71	MAY 14 '85		
NOV 22 '71	OCT. 1 1988		
DEC 13 '72			
JUN 18 '73	MAY 1 1994		
JUL 28 '75	APR 05 1995		
SEP 30 '75			
MAY 27 '76			
JUN 9 '76			
SEP 12 '78			
DEC 14 '78			

ŚRĪ PRAKĀŚA,

(B. A., LL. B., Honors, Cantab., Bar-at-Law, Member of the Central Legislative Assembly of India), Honorary Principal, Secretary, and Superintendent of the Publication Department, of the Kāshi Vidyā Pītha.

THE ESSENTIAL UNITY OF ALL RELIGIONS

COMPILED

BY

BHAGAVAN DAS

(M. A., Calcutta University; D. Litt., *hon. causa*,
Benares University; D. Litt., *hon. causa*,
Allahabad University.)

Published under a grant from The Kern Foundation

THE THEOSOPHICAL PRESS
WHEATON, ILLINOIS

First Edition, 1932.
Second Edition, greatly enlarged, 1939.
REPRINT (U. S. A.) 1966.

FOREWORD

(to the first edition)

"The first World Conference on Education was held in San Francisco in July, 1923. Out of this Conference, the World Federation of Education Associations was born. The Constitution of the Federation provided the following article regarding Conferences. 'The World Conference shall meet in full session at such place and time as may be determined by the directors; but a meeting of sections, one in Europe, one in America, and one in Asia, may be held in the intervening years.' "[1]

The first All-Asia Education Conference was held at Benares, from 26th to 30th December, 1930.

The conveners[2] desired the undersigned to write a paper on "The Unity of Asiatic Thought". The subject took shape in his mind as "The Essential Unity of All Religions". Asiatic thought is deeply tinged with Religion. Asia has given birth to all the great living religions. He read the paper to the Conference on December 30.

---

[1]Foreword to the Report of The First All-Asia Education Conference.

[2]Through their Secretary, Shrī Rāma Nārāyaṇa Mishra, then Head Master of the Central Hindū School, on the grounds and in the buildings, (donated by the Maharaja of Benares), of which, the sessions of the Conference and its Committees were held. The C. H. School was founded, in 1898, by Dr. Annie Besant and colleagues, as part of the Central Hindu College of Benares, which has now been developed, by Pt. Madan Mohan Malaviya and colleagues, into the Benares University.

Members of the audience, belonging to several religions and sects, very kindly expressed approval, and also desire for separate publication. The General Secretary[1] of the Indian Section of the Theosophical Society, generously printed and distributed free over four thousand copies of it, in a revised and enlarged form, with *Theosophy in India,*[2] the monthly organ of the I.S.T.S. It was reproduced serially in the *Theosophist* of Adyar, Madras, in the South, and the *Vedic Magazine* of the Arya Samaj, Gurukula, Kangri, near Hardwar, in the north. A brother wrote from Burma, asking consent to reprint. But the Theosophical Publishing House of Adyar had already arranged to publish it in book form.

It has been revised again, in the time left by many other distracting demands, and enlarged greatly by addition of many more parallel passages, in the hope of making it more serviceable, because of the encouragement received. Even so, a good many passages remain in a note-book, which the writer has not been able to incorporate, for lack of the needed freedom from distractions.[3] There is also a rough draft of a glossary of over five hundred Arabic-Persian words, pertaining to religion, especially Islāmic Sūfī mysticism, with Samskṛt and English equivalents, (a good many of which will be found in the book, scattered all over, but which are arranged in alphabetical order in the glossary). He wished very much to append it. But it requires careful revising and fairing, and therefore has had to be put off till more favorable times, lest the publication of the book be delayed indefinitely.[4]

---

[1]Shri D. K. Telang.

[2]Since then re-named *The Indian Theosophist.*

[3]This has been done now, in the present edition.

[4]It has been put in now, with many additions.

If this book is so fortunate as to succeed in giving a taste to readers for discovering identities of thought in the great records of the deepest human experience in different languages, they will be able to see such identities at almost every step, in their further readings in such records, to their great joy, and to the perpetual expansion of their sympathetic appreciation of others.

Some learned scholars essay to prove that the religions of later birth have copied from the earlier. The question, whether it is so, may have an intellectual historical interest for the learned few. A far deeper, more vital, more human interest is possessed, and for all mankind, by the question, why they have done so, if they have copied from one another at all. Is it not because there is only One Eternal Truth for all to copy ? New generations are born from old, new nations grow out of colonies from old, new lamps are lighted from old, but the Life, the Light, the Might, which is only embodied in and expressed by the ever-changing forms, is beyond them all, is common to them all, is originated by none of them, but originates them all. It is an honor and a duty to copy—if what is copied is Truth ; it were a disgrace to be original—if what is originated be False. And there can be 'originality' in only the 'fleeting', therefore the False. There can be no originality in Truth ; for only the Eternal can be the Truth ; and it can only be, and ought to be, copied, in the large sense, diligently ; there can be no 'copy-right' in Truth. But there is no need to 'copy', 'in the small sense'. The River of Life is ever flowing ; whoever feels thirsty can dip his bucket directly into it. The same Truth wells up independently in the heart of Seer after Seer, Seeker after Seeker.

While compiling the book and revising it again and again, the compilor has prayed constantly to the Great

Masters of all the living Religions, Manu, Kṛshṇa, Vyāsa, *Z*oroaster, Moses, Isaiah, Laotse, Confucius, Buḍḍha, Jina, Christ, Muhammad, Nānak, and the Spiritual Hierarchy to which they all belong, for guidance of his very feeble fingers in this humble effort to serve his fellow men and women and children of all countries.

He should inform his dear readers that he has no knowledge of Arabic and but a smattering of Persian. But he has a profound conviction that Truth is one and the same, and that all the Great Lovers of Mankind cannot but have said the same true things. He has, therefore, from time to time, asked Maulavī friends to give him texts from the Qurān and the Haḍīs (Sayings of the Prophet Muhammad), parallel to the Samskṛṭ texts whose purport he placed before them. As the Qurān is a comparatively small-sized book, and many good Maulavīs know it by heart, they were able to supply the needed texts without much difficulty; in some cases readily. The Persian and Urḍū texts are, most of them, quoted from famous and venerated Sūfī-s, like Maulānā Rūm, Hāfiz, Jāmī, Sā'ḍī, Fariḍuḍḍīn Aṭṭār, and some others. Much helpful information about Sūfism, and many valuable Arabic and Persian texts, have been found in the excellent, very learned and very thoughtful, books of Khān Sāhib Khājā Khān (of Madras), *viz.*, *Studies in Tasawwuf*, *The Secret of An-al-Haq*, *Philosophy of Islam*, *and The Wisdom of the Prophets*. Because of the present writer's ignorance of Arabic and slight acquaintance with Persian, there are probably many mistakes in the Roman transcript and the English translations. Of course, he has based the English renderings of the Arabic texts on the explanations kindly supplied by the Maulavī friends, and on the published translations regarded as standard. Still he may have failed to be accurate. Readers learned in Arabic and Persian will kindly correct. The original texts also have been reproduced here, in Roman transcript; translations by themselves do not command complete confidence; and the work of correction by learned readers will be made easier.

The compiler shall be very happy if friends learned in their respective Scriptures will approve this kind of work and will take it up themselves. Indeed, what is very much needed is that representatives of all the great living religions, large-hearted, broad-minded, copiously-informed, philanthropically-motived, may come together in a small and active Committee, and prepare a series of graded text-books of Universal Religion, expounding the main points systematically, and illustrating them amply, for ready reference and obviation of doubts, with parallel passages, in the original, from the scriptures of the several religions. Such text-books would be authentic and authoritative, carry great weight with all communities, open their eyes to the utterly common essentials of all religions, and be introduced and studied with pleasure and profit, in private homes as well as public educational institutions, by students and readers of various ages and capacities—to the sure and certain promotion of peace on earth and good will among men.

It will make the compiler rejoice, and will repay him a thousandfold for such labor as he has been privileged to bestow upon this compilation, if Universities and other educational institutions make it their own; and issue their own editions of it at cost-price, or free, for the use of their students, after making improvements in it, by omissions or alterations, and, particularly, additions of many more parallel passages, (on the broad principles, as well as on the details of observances, rites and ceremonies, customs and practices), through the learned scholars on their staff who may be specially conversant with the subject, and who may form, in each University, a Committee of Representatives of the several Faiths, such as has been desiderated above—for where else should large hearts, broad minds, and richly stored intellects be found, if not in Universities? If a single such Committee could be formed, of members contributed by different Universities—that were best of all; its work would carry the greatest weight and be the most convincing.

The undersigned should record here his gratitude to the Theosophical Publishing House (Adyar, Madras), for having undertaken the publication of the work, on the condition of copyright limited to three years; and to the Vasanṭa Press, (of the Theosophical Society, Adyar, Madras) for bearing patiently with his incorrigible habit of making too many alterations and additions in the proofs—greatly aggravated in the present instance by the large use of diacritical types for the Roman transcript.

AUM! ĀMĪṄ! AMEN!

Benares,
17-11-1932.

BHAGAVAN DAS

A LETTER TO THE READER

as

PREFACE TO THE SECOND EDITION.

Dear Reader,

This book is not by a scholar with any the least pretensions to accurate learning. It has been compiled by a mere seeker, a would-be servant of his kind, and, withal, one who, all his life, has been drawn from within, by inclination, towards study and thinking, and dragged from without, by circumstances, towards executive and miscellaneous work of various kinds. It is, therefore, full of manifold imperfections.

There are printing defects and mistakes, due to inefficient correction of proofs; old eyes lack keenness. Sentences are probably often dull and obscure, instead of bright and attractive; command over the language was insufficient, and ability was wanting to express difficult thought lucidly. The presentation of ideas is often discursive and inconsecutive; an old mind wanders. To many readers, many of the paragraphs, in larger type, which link up the texts quoted from the scriptures will probably give the feeling of a car running over a road strewn with boulders; unfamiliar Samskṛṭ and Arabic-Persian words have been put in, too lavishly, perhaps, side by side with English equivalents. The compiler can only plead, in exculpation, that the very purpose of the book, (see pp. 67–73, 525-526, *infra*), is, by means of such juxtapositions of the technical words of the three most widespread living religions, Christianity, Islām, Véḍism (or 'Hinḍuism', including Buḍḍhism and

Jainism, which use many the same Samskṛt words), to throw into relief, the identities and similarities of their thoughts, aspirations, practices. To those who are acquainted with all the three languages, the collocations will, it is hoped, bring the pleasure of gatherings of friends from distant lands, nations, races, meeting and greeting each other with beaming smiles.

And there is much repetition. An old man, at seventy-one years of age, is weak of memory, and garrulous of speech. He forgets what he has just said; so repeats, over and over again. But that is the way of the very old Scriptures also! And this book is just a compilation of their utterances; nothing else. Even the thread, on which those precious pearls are strung, is spun out of material supplied by the Scriptures themselves. There is nothing new in the book; except, may be, error, here and there, in the interpretation of the Great Sayings. It may be said, then, that when the spiritual food is good and wholesome, it is, indeed, worth while to repeat it, day after day, even like healthy and pleasant material food. Not too often, of course; nor in very large quantities; for then it palls; nor to be taken too quickly, without leisurely 'mastication', reflection, turning over and over in the mind, as food in the mouth; for then it does not yield its full sweet taste, and is not duly assimilated.

There are, quite likely, errors in the translations of the many passages quoted from many Scriptures. But not many, it is hoped. The original texts, in roman, will enable the reader to rectify the errors; himself, or with the help of friendly scholars. The versions are seldom literal. Such, word for word, done with the help of a lexicon, often ruin the real sense. The principle followed here is, that the translator should absorb the 'spirit' of the original 'letter', and reproduce that 'spirit' faithfully in the 'letter' of the new language.

The renderings have all been done in blank verse, with very rare exceptions in rhyme, here and there. It seemed that the 'emotional' constituent of religion, now the devoutness, then the solemnity, again the earnestness, or the injunctional impressiveness, and, throughout, the 'holiness', of scriptural utterances, most of which are themselves in verse or rhythmic prose—it seemed that this would be more truly reflected in verse than in prose. This too has necessitated some deviation from literality. It is trusted, nevertheless, that the *intention* of the original has always been correctly expressed. At times, the version has been expanded a little, in the light of the original context of the text actually quoted.

This whole attempt, to bring together parallel texts of the several scriptures, to prove identities and similarities, may, perhaps, fail to satisfy some critics, who would insist that minute differences should be at least as clearly brought out and emphasised as, if not more than, the resemblances. They would, no doubt, be quite right, from their own standpoint, and for the purposes of, accurate intellectual scholarship. The compiler's plea is that the 'intellectual' interest is not the only interest of the book; that the 'emotional' and the 'practical' interests are of at least as great concern in it; that the minute differences are already far too much stressed and acted on, to the great harm of mankind; that the resemblances are far too much ignored, to their great loss; that even intellectually, what varies with each, deserves to be regarded as of the surface, as *non*-Essential, and what runs through and is common to all, to be regarded as of the core and the Essence; and that, therefore, the essential points, on which all religions agree, should be given far more prominence than they have been hitherto, and be regarded as the very heart of all, religions, as the very core of the Truth ; on the 'democratic principle' of 'majority vote' ; and for the very important and truly practical purpose of promoting mutual Good Understanding and Peace all over the earth.

There may be critics of another class, the persons of strong belief, of sincere and intense faith. They naturally feel, each, his own particular creed to be unique, 'the one and only,' the best. The wish to be thought 'original', 'the first', 'unprecedented', 'unrivalled', is a Nature-ordained and unavoidable preliminary ; in all aspects of human life, instinctual, nutritive, acquisitive, conjugal, military, financial, even literary and scientific. It is so, in every course of action, where ambitious competition is involved. And where is it not ? All embodied life seems to be incessant love-and-war, both concentrated in 'jealousy', of greater and lesser degree. This is patent in the worldly 'life of pursuit' of the things of the senses ; it is also present, though ever diminishingly, in the 'life of renunciation,' until the very end. We may therefore say that the wish to be *individually* 'unique' is the first of the two main aspects, egoist-altruist, of the Duality which runs through all Life and Nature ; as the wish to be *Universally* 'Unique', All-One, identified with All, is the second. The preliminary *Egoist* wish, therefore, invades the regions of Religion also, and very powerfully ! "My creed is the best ; and wholly original ; different from all others ; utterly new ; nothing like it ever before ; has borrowed nothing from any previous one ; and is the final one too ; there can never be another equally good, much less better"; even as "My race, color, caste, sex, is the best ; I belong to a chosen people, a divinely privileged caste, a fundamentally superior race, a solar or lunar dynasty; my nation rules the waves; my nation is *uber alles*; my country has the tallest skyscrapers, the largest purse, the vastest hoard of gold, is superlative in everything; on my empire the sun never sets; I am sprung directly from the mouth of Brahmā; I am the son of the Sun"; and so on. It requires much sad experience, before such egoism comes under control; before it is recognised that, while a certain amount of competitive egoism is necessary for the growth of the young animal or the young nation, more than that amount is a hindrance, is even positively destructive; before the soul turns to genuine *Altruism*, patient tolerance, understanding sympathy, the Truth of All in All; before it realises that, though, no doubt, distinctions of superior and inferior, senior and junior, stronger and weaker, are facts in nature, yet that they are relative and must not be over-emphasised, that strength must not be boasted too much, nor weakness be too much despised.

No one can say that his physical body is made of matter created out of nothing, originally, for the first time, for him alone; has borrowed nothing from anyone; differs from all other matter. It is fairly obvious that each atom of every 'body' has passed through countless bodies in the past, and will pass through countless bodies in the future; though it is also true that each body is somewhat different in make-up from all others. So too, every thought, emotion, volition, of every 'mind', (or 'soul', whichever word is preferred), has passed, and will pass, through countless other minds; though also with some difference in the grouping and the manifesting; whereby each 'mind' becomes as 'distinctive' or 'individual' as each body. Let us recognise such differences, which constitute the 'personal' element or 'personality', by all means; but let us regard them as of less importance, as changing, passing, therefore non-essential; and let us recognise more fully, the 'idealities', the 'impersonal' or 'all-personal element, and regard them as of greater importance, persisting through changes, permanent, and therefore essential. In other words, we should value, but not over-value, the 'individual', the 'personal'. We should value at least a little more, the 'universal', 'the common consciousness' belonging to all individuals; whereby 'each is for all, and all are for each'; whereby alone, social life, collective existence, the feel and fact of the unitive 'we', as distinguished from, and at the same time inclusive of, the feel and fact of separative and exclusive 'I's', is made possible.

Unhappily, most of us are at that stage of 'youth' (of mind) in evolution, in which we take greater delight in feeling 'peculiar', 'uniquely individual', 'original' than in feeling 'common', 'universal', 'eternal'. Yet the craving for the latter is there, always, in every heart. It is there, consciously, but not understandingly. No one wants to feel 'uniquely individual' in solitude, away from all fellow-creatures, 'away from the haunts of men', 'far from the madding crowd'; but wants to do so *amidst* other individuals; otherwise *his* 'peculiarity', which is wholly dependent on contra-distinction from *others*, would disappear. Thus does he tie himself to others unavoidably. The craving is present in every heart supra-consciously also; for the reason that every individual self *is* the Universal Self, and yearns in the depths of the heart, to recover consciously its forgotten and lost high status.

Of course, we must not futilely try to abolish wholly, this preliminary wish to feel separate and peculiar, in respect of religions, any more than in respect of individuals. It too has an obvious and necessary place in the evolutionary Scheme of God's Nature, the Universal Self's Nature. But we have to moderate it, reconcile it with, slowly transmute it into, its opposite; more and more. This is not impossible; rather, it too is equally ordained by that same Nature.

In the work of reconciling religions, it is very easy to avoid hurting sensitiveness on the subject of originality; by studiously eschewing all attempt to derive any one religion out of any other. It is not necessary at all to make such attempt, so far as the general public is concerned. Scholars who wish to study religions comparatively and historically, may of course do so for themselves, i.e., for their own refined recreation; and also for the enrichment of scientific knowledge regarding human *psychical* evolution, even as biologists trace *physical* evolution. But controversial propaganda should be avoided, in the interests of peace.

Also, if the task of tracing the ancestry of religions is pursued stringently and diligently, with open mind, it must obviously prove to be one without possibility of completion and termination. It will be like endeavouring to answer the question: 'Is the tree first, or the seed first?' "Veil after veil will lift, but there must be veil upon veil behind". Who can trace the atoms-and-mentations of any individual body-mind through ancestor before ancestor, up to a really first beginning? Metaphysic tells us that there can be no such absolute beginning, in the strict sense. Even if we could go right up to the beginning of our solar system, in primal nebula or invisible 'ether' or 'radiant matter', that would require to be derived from the corpus of a yet earlier system; and so on, ad infinitum. Why not then promote religious brotherhood and peace among the general public, by saying at once, what is utterly true also—that all atoms and all mentations and all religions, of all the countless generations of living beings, past, present, future, not only of this earth, but of all the orbs of heaven, (each of which has, presumably, its own types of living beings), and all visible and invisible planes of matter, are all equally derived from the Universal, Eternal, Body-Mind, Matter-Spirit, God-Nature, the One Omnipotent, Omnipresent, Omniscient Self, in whose Consciousness "all things live and move and have their being," which pervades them all?

It is better to understand, appraise, appreciate, than to ridicule, belittle, depreciate; better to see the good points more than the bad; better to see the agreements more than the differences; better to make peace than war.

Some students of comparative religion, of a tendency opposite to that which claims unique originality for the creed it favors, may say: "Since there is so much similarity, or even identity in some respects, between all, therefore, each later must have borrowed from an earlier; and, therefore, the 'democratic' test of validity, majority of votes, consensus of opinion, proffered in the book, in respect of 'religion', which test is not a test in 'science' at all, does not hold good. The consensus is not independent. We have only one vote, repeated over and over again, flowing down the river of time; and it may have been given to a falsehood in the beginning."

The reply to this would be: "Even in Science, the method of *concomitant* variations, used for testing the truth of hypotheses and conclusions, is only a way of proving 'unanimity' through uniformity, or, at least an overwhelming 'majority', of votes. Secondly, we have the right to ask, What is the cause of the initial falsehood, if any? And *why* has mankind given its vote to, and put faith in, *such* a falsehood; a falsehood of this particular kind; and generation after generation?" No sufficient answer has ever been offered to this query.

Yet again, some thinkers endeavour to explain away a religion or a philosophy by the peculiar psychological constitution of the individual who started the religion or formulated the philosophy, or by the 'environment', or 'historical accident', or 'economic', or 'geographic', or 'physiographic' circumstances. Such explanations may, no doubt, be justified in respect of variable 'peculiarities'; which, however, ought to be regarded as 'non-essential', for the reasons mentioned before. They cannot explain the invariable fundamental 'generalities'. Also, the question arises again, and always: *Why* and *how* the peculiar individual constitutions, the historical accidents, the economic and other circumstances?

Every law and fact requires further laws and facts to explain it; these, yet others; *ad infinitum*; until we come to the Infinite Self, Total Consciousness (including the Sub-, Supra-, and Un-Conscious; waking, dreaming, slumbering), Universal Mind, Anima Mundi, and to Its Will-and-Imagination; which works by Eeonic Plan of Integration and Disintegration of Forms; according to Its own Meta-physical (including physical) Laws of Nature. In this All-pervading All-including Mind and Its infinite Ideation, all Religion, Philosophy, Science, Law, Art, meet and merge; and from It they all emerge; in endless repetition. When we come to That, all questions are answered; all doubts are set at rest; the Final Synthesis is achieved; the Final Peace of Mind is gained.

Without achieving such synthesis, the human world cannot attain Happiness, here or hereafter. The 'religious' and other wars of the past (see pp. 368, 559, *infra*), the communal riots and pogroms of the present, between Hindus and Muslims, between different castes of Hindūs, between Shīā Muslims and Sunnī Muslims, in India, (see pp. 565-566, *infra*), Jews and Arabs in Palestine, Jews and Germans in Germany, the vast politico-economic 'riots', wars, of the recent past, the war by Japan upon China now going on for two years and more, since July, 1937, (indeed, since 1931), the European war which started on 1st September, 1939, as the inevitable consequence of the tremendous armings of all the 'Great Powers' (see pp. 569-585, *infra*) —all these are due, ultimately to the lack of such Synthesis (see pp. 32-33, 478-489, 599-601. *infra*).

After such maniacal accumulation of murderous explosives, a war of titans is inevitable. The bursting energies forcibly imprisoned in those explosives must find release. They cannot be kept locked-up thus, for ever. The worst, most powerful, most destructive, most elementary, primary, terrible explosives are the *psychical* explosives, the crassly egoistic evil human passions, lust, hate, greed, pride, fear, jealousy. It is these which manufacture all the secondary *material* explosives. After the monstrous amassing of both has exhausted itself, now that the war has begun in Europe; after it has left the human world in ruins, in Europe, and in many other countries (and few, scarcely excepting Russia and the two Americas, are likely to escape being slowly dragged into the maelstrom)[1]; after that, the need for reconstruction will arise, and be felt acutely by the broken nations.

---

[1]As this is being written, the papers (18th September, 1939) announce that the Russian army has also marched into Poland, "to safeguard Russian interests in eastern Europe," and "to take under their protection, the lives and property of the population in western Ukraine and western White Russia."

It is possible yet that wiser counsels may prevail, the war which has begun, may not drag in other nations, may not be fought out to the bitter end; but cease early. May the Mystery which has fashioned and maintains the Universe ordain it so! Thus we must pray, though from Its standpoint of Infinity, the birth and death of whole human races and civilisations can be of no greater import than the growth and destruction of ant-hills. But even if the war ceases early, new adjustments of human relations, on a world-wide scale, will be necessary. Otherwise, if conditions and causes, armaments and social structures, are left as they have been so far, the corresponding effects must follow again; in the shape of unappeasable discords, jealousies, hatreds; out of which, worse and worse wars must recur, inevitably, again and again; until the armaments have all perished, in one way or another, and the war-madness has been all purged and bled-out of the body-politic of the Human Race.

For such re-adjustment, after complete dispersal and exhaustion, either by mutual sincere and far-sighted agreement, or by mutual slaughter, of this vast mass of psychical and physical explosives; a Great Synthesis, a Comprehensive Integration, of all aspects, Spiritual and Material, Individual and Collective, of the Life of the Human Race, will be indispensable.

If the Russian experiment be thought successful, in all respects, it will naturally be imitated everywhere. If it fail, as is likely, (see pp. 619-620, *infra*), in important respects. because of the lack of Spiritual, 'anti-toxic', trust-breeding, sincerity-and-sympathy-producing, integrative and constructive nourishment; then the alternative will be, (1) a Universal Religion, which will be the Head-and-Heart of all religions, will unite them all; will provide and promote that Spiritual nourishment, in the shape of the ever-growing accumulation, and ever wider spread, of those most powerful cohesives, anti-explosives, anti-disruptives, the domestic and social affections and strong trusts; and, will also provide, as part of that Universal Religion, (2) a rational Scheme of Individuo-Social Organisation, which would be in accord with all sciences, and especially with the Science of Human Nature, i. e., Psychology.

Such Universal Religion has been provided for us, by the Scriptures of the Nations; and such a Scheme of Socio-Individual Organisation, by the Vẹdic Scriptures in particular, as fundamental part of Religion; because Religion, to justify itself, must be of help and service everywhere, must secure, for the human being, the maximum possible, of Happiness *Here* as well as Hereafter; (see pp 478-516, 618-620 *infra.*)

Everywhere, today, the 'rulers' of the nations which are regarded as the 'Great Powers', (rulers in the shape of presidents, dictators, kings, premiers, cabinets, influential capitalist and militarist cliques and coteries), are striving to capture yet more 'power' of all kinds than they have already got; and the 'leaders' of weaker or subjugated peoples, which are struggling to win back political freedom, are striving to recover the 'power' which their predecessors have lost. But neither those 'rulers', nor these 'leaders', anywhere, (except, perhaps Russia, in a lopsided, 'half-truth', fashion, see pp. 582-583, 620, *infra*), are willing to think about *how* 'power' can and should be *used*, so as to *Organise for Peace*, systematically, each nation, each people, and thereby the whole Human Race. They are all intensely and immensely busy with *Organising for War* or for political struggle. 'Let us snatch power, and more power, and yet more power, first; we shall do afterwards, at our sweet will, all the thinking that it may suit us to think.' The result of this attitude is—wars, in the one case; internal dissensions, jealousies, mutual thwartings, and failures, in the other.

The 'Great Powers' possess 'Self-government'; at least each one says it does. The 'leaders', of the peoples who are struggling for freedom from subjection and serfdom, proclaim that they want 'Self-government.' But, apparently, nowhere is any real effort being made by anyone to think out and expound *what exactly* Self-government *means*, and *how* Self-government can be made Good-government also, at the same time; to consider and explain whether Self-government means, and should mean, 'government *of* the people, *for* the people, (a) *by all* the people, (which is obviously impossible), or (b) *by a few* of the *worst* of the people (who may manage, as happens not rarely, to get themselves elected by the now well-known devices of 'electioneering, racketeering, propaganding, intimidating, deceiving, gerrymandering, disciplining, gagging, grafting, boodling, bribing, etc.,') or (c) *by a few* of *mixed* and *doubtful quality*, (which is the most frequent fact), or (d) *by a few* of the *best and wisest* of the people, (which is very, very, rarely the case in known history). In other words, no one who counts in the world's affairs, today, is (a) actively realising and proclaiming to the world, the fact that Self-government and Good-government can *coincide* only when the governing 'Self' is, *not* the *lower* and baser 'Self' of the People, *but* their *Higher*, nobler, genuinely philanthropic 'Self.' Nor is any such person (b) explaining *how* such government by the Higher Self, 'the kingdom of heaven on earth', may be achieved, i. e., *how* it may be managed that *only* the *best* and the *wisest* are *elected*. It is plainer and more self-evident than any axioms of geometry, that only good and wise laws can promote the happiness of mankind; that good and wise laws can be made and administered by only good and wise men and women, who constitute the Higher Self of the people; and that only such persons should be entrusted with powers of legislation and administration. Yet these so self-evident truths are so very difficult for mankind to learn, that it has not learnt them yet, after many thousands, probably hundreds of thousands, of years of the most bitter experience of the consequences of not acting in accord with them.

The result is that all these warring 'rulers', as much as the struggling 'leaders', actuated, not by far-sighted humanism, but by narrow and very short-sighted nationalism, or even by mean and sordid personal ambitions and motives, are wandering in the dark, 'blind leaders of the blind', causing only very grievous harm and hurt to those whom they profess to wish to help.

They cannot say that the Right Way is hidden from them. They are themselves turning their eyes away from it. The Sun of Scriptural Wisdom is flaming, and radiating Light upon it from the heavens, all the time. The rulers and leaders have only to remove from their own eyes, the thick bandages of egoism and nationalism, and put on the glasses of Humanism. They would all, then, see at once, clearly laid out for them, the Path to Peace and Prosperity for all. The Scriptures are telling us, all the time, *how* society can and should be *Organised for Peace*; *how* the *best* and *wisest* of the people can be *recognised*; *how* they and they alone should be *elected* to the places of legislative power.

Problems of 'Organising for War', and for political struggle, may seem more *urgent*; but, surely, in any case, they are not more *important* than the problem of '*Organising for Peace*'. The former are passing; they are concerned with temporary means and passing aims. The latter is the *Permanent Problem*, concerned with the *Permanent End*. To the far-sighted view, it is much the more *urgent* also, as well as more *important*. For, if it is solved satisfactorily, the former will abate and disappear automatically.

Let us all, then, engage in the work of promoting: firstly, by helping to spread right knowledge on the subject; and, secondly, in every other way possible; the Organisation of the Human Race for Peace and thence Prosperity.

Dear Reader, I pray you, unless you have found, and made sure of, a better way, to read about an Ancient Way, leisurely, in this book. Endeavour is made here, albeit very imperfectly, to expound, no new way, but the Way of the Ancients, a Way which is time-tested also to some extent. If you feel satisfied that that Way is worth experimenting with, then I pray you to do all you can to spread, as widely as may be possible for you, this Essential Message of all the Scriptures, as preparation for the great Readjustment and Synthesis.

Benares,
19-9-1939.

Your respectful and sincere
Well-wisher,
BHAGAVĀN ḌĀS.

NOTE

On the Texts gathered in this book, and certain other matters.

Eleven religions are usually regarded as living and current at present. These, proceeding from east to west, are: (2) Shintoism born in Japan; (2) Taoism (or Laotsism), and (3) Confucianism, in China; (4) Véḍism (or Vaiḍika Ḍharma, or Sanāṭana Ḍharma, or Arya Ḍharma, or Mānava Ḍharma, now commonly called 'Hinḍuism'), (5) Buḍḍhism, (6) Jainism, and (7) Sikhism, in India; (8) Zoroastrianism (or Pārsism), in Īrān (or Persia); (9) Judaism (or Hebraism, or Israelitism, or the Jewish religion), and (10) Christianity, in Palestine; (11) Islām (or Mohammedanism), in Arabia. Parallel passages have been gathered in this work from the universally recognised Scriptures, and also from some other generally and highly honored writings, of these eleven.

The well-known scriptures of Véḍism are the four *Véḍa-s* with their *Upanishaṭ-s*, *Manu-smṛṭi*, *Gīṭā*, *Mahā-bhāraṭa*, *Rāmāyaṇa*, *Bhāgavaṭa*, and several of the *Purāṇa-s*. Texts have been taken from these, principally. They are regarded as sacred and authoritative in the order mentioned. But the first four are practically of equal authority, and *Manu*, because of its compact conciseness, its comprehensive completeness, its high and austere tone, and its terse and clear language, is the most frequently referred to, in discussions over matters of religious practice. Véḍism is not connected with any one name as founder's; but the Véḍic socio-religious polity of India has been based, from time immemorial, on 'The Institutes, or Laws, of

Manu'. Manu is regarded as the Primal Patriarch and Law-giver of the Indian Aryans; and as having embodied, in his Laws, all that substance and quintessence of the Véḍa-s, which bears upon the orderly planning and conducting of individual and collective human life. The latest version of these Laws, in some 2700 couplets, is current under the name of *Manu-Smṛṭi.* It is said by critical Orientalist scholars, to be between 2000 and 2500 years old now. But all are agreed that it is based on, and includes large portions of, much earlier texts, *Mānava-Ḍharma-Sūṭra*, *Vṛḍḍha-Manu*, and others. These are not now extant, and are known only through quotations and references in available later works. The four *Véḍa-s*, the Scriptures proper of Véḍism, on which Manu and all subsequent expounders base themselves, are said, by unanimous Indian tradition, to have been collected, edited, and given their present shape, by Kṛshṇa Ḍvaipāyana Vyāsa, famous as Véḍa-Vyāsa, some 5000 years ago, i. e., about 3100 B. C.; just before the beginning of the Kali-Yuga era. But the Orientalists say that the oldest hymns belong to about 1500 B.C. New researches and fresh findings are, however, steadily pushing the period further and further back. Véḍa-Vyāsa is also the author of the *Mahā-ḃhāraṭa*, in which *Manu* is often referred to and quoted from. Where excerpts are taken from works other than the seven above-mentioned, the names of these are given in full.

The scriptures of Islām, from which passages have been taken, are, principally, the *Qurān* and the *Haḍīs*, in Arabic, and, in the next place, the writings of the great Sūfis, mostly in Persian. These have been already referred to in the Foreword to the first edition. The founder of Islām, the Prophet Muḥammad, was born in 570 A.C., and died in 632 A.C.

Texts of Shintoism, Taoism, and Confucianism, the compiler had no access to, in the original. But there is one exception. A pasage from the *Analects* of Confucius, transcribed in roman, was very kindly supplied by Prof. Tan Yun Shan, (see foot-note to p. 299, *infra*). All the others have been taken from various published English translations, of that primary scripture of Taoism, the *Tao Teh King*, ascribed to Laotse; and of the *Shu King*, *Shi King*, *Analects*, and other works of Confucius; many from that marvel of learned industry, *Treasure-House of Living Religions*, by Robert Ernest Hume, (pub: 1933, by Charles Scribner's Sons, New York and London). Like Vẹdism, Shinto is not connected with the name of any one person as founder. Lao-tse and Kung-fu-tse, i. e., Confucius, (as also Pythagoras, of Magna Graecia), were older and younger contemporaries of the Buḍḍha. The 6th century B. C. is remarkable for a great influx of religious thought and aspiration, in many countries, far apart from each other, but, as historical and archeological research is establishing more and more clearly year by year, not without communication with each other.

Buḍḍhist texts have been drawn, in the original Pālī, (a 'dialect' or popular form of Samskṛṭ), current among the people in the time of Buḍḍha, mostly from two small books, the *Khuḍḍaka Pātha* and the *Ḍhamma-paḍa.* They are collections, in Buḍḍha's own words, of his most important teachings. The *Ḍhamma-paḍa* is to Buḍḍhists what the *Gīṭā* is to Vẹdists (Hinḍū-s). A few texts in Samskṛṭ have been derived from other works, authoritative in the next degree, like those of Nāgārjuna and Asanga. The former is specially famous for his Dialogues with the Greek King Menander of the 2nd century B. C. These *Dialogues* are known as *Milindu Panho*. Of such works, the full names are given. The years of Buddha s birth and death are given variously, as 624 and 544 B. C. or 568 and 488 B. C.

Jaina texts have been derived, in the original Samskṛt or Prākṛt, (a variant of, and contemporaneous with, Pālī), from works regarded as authoritative, whose names have been given in full, after the texts quoted. No teachings of the founder, viz., Mahāvīra Jina, also known as Vardhamāna Svāmī. (b. 599 B. C., d. 527 B. C.; or, b. 549 B. C., d. 477 B. C) definitely known to be in his own words, are extant. The earliest collections are by Bhadra-bāhu, of the 4th century B. C.[1]

---

[1]A valuable text, the Jaina form of the Golden Rule, has come to hand, as this 'Note on Texts' is being written, after the Addenda have been printed off. The section on the subject, in the body of this book, (pp. 297-303), lacks in a Jaina text. Therefore, to supply that lack, the text is quoted here even though the place is not very appropriate. It belongs to one of the earliest available sacred books of the religions.

"Vayam puṇa évam āikkhāmo, évam bhāsāmo, évam parūvémo, évam paṇṇavémo—savvé pāṇā, savvé bhūyā, savvé jīvā, savvé saṭṭā, ṇa hantavvā, ṇa pari-ghéṭṭavvā, ṇa pari-yāveyavvā, ṇa uḍḍaveyavvā; āriya-vaya ṇam éyam": (*Āchāra-aṅga-sūtra*, 'Samaṭṭa', chaturtha Adhyayana, Uḍḍéshaka dvitīya). "Ṭumam si nāma ṭam ch-éva jam hanṭavvam ti mannasi. Ṭumam si nāma ṭam ch-éva jam ajjāvéyavvam ṭi mannasi. Ṭumam si nāma ṭam ch-éva jam pari-yāveyavvam ṭi mannasi. Ṭumam si nāma ṭam ch-éva jam pari-ghéṭṭavvam ṭi mannasi. Evam ṭumam si nāma ṭam ch-éva jam uḍḍavéyavvam ṭi mannasi". (*Ibid.*, 'Loga-Sāra', panchama Adhyayana, Uḍḍéshaka panchama).

The Samskṛt form of the above Prākṛt is : "Vayam punah évam āchakshmahé, évam bhāshāmahé, évam pra-

Texts of Sikhism, whose tenets are practically the same as those of the Gīṭā, have been taken mostly

---

rūpayāmah, évam prajñāpayāmah—Sarvé prāṇāh, sarvé bhūṭāh, sarvé Jīvāh, sarvé saṭṭvāh, na hanṭavyāh, na ājñā-payiṭavyāh, na pari-grahīṭavyāh, na pari-ṭāpayiṭavyāh, na upa-ḍroṭavyāh ; Ārya-vachanam éṭaṭ. Ṭvam asi nāma ṭaḍ éva yaḍ hanṭavyam...yaḍ ājñāpayiṭavyam...yaṭ pari-ṭāpayiṭavyam...yaṭ pari-grahīṭavyam...yaḍ upa-ḍroṭavyam iṭi manyasé.

(Thus we enjoin on you, thus do we say,
Thus we believe, thus we proclaim to all :
No living things should be slain anywhere,
Nor ordered forcibly this way or that,
Nor put in bonds, nor tortured any way,
Or treated violently otherwise ;
Because you are that same which ye would slay,
Or order here and there against his will,
Or put in prison, or subject to pain,
Or treat with violence ; *ye are that same* ;
The Self-same Life doth circulate in all.)

Of course this is the extreme ideal, for renunciant axcetics. It has had to be modified, in practice, for 'householders', in Jainism as in all other religions, on the incontrovertible principle, that 'Duty varies with circumstance'. An outstanding example of this, in Jaina history, is the case of King Kumāra-pāla of Gujerāt (12th century B. C.) who was a Jaiṇa, and under the guidance of his preceptor Héma-chanḍra Āchārya, almost the most famous 'doctor' of the Jaina Law, punished many offences with death strictly, and battled with and slew invaders. "Do your duty ; do it as humanely as you can"—was his interpretation of a-h i m s ā, non-violence. Jainism expressly upholds the *four* (*not hereditary but*) *vocational classes* and their *functions* (including the defender-soldier's and the punishing judge's); just as does Buddhism ; only the innocent must not be hurt, much less slain ; and animal-sacrifice and animal-food are forbidden by both.

from its chief scripture, the *Guru Granṭha Sahab*, in which are collected the hymns and teachings of the ten Sikh Gurus. Guru Nānak, the founder and first Guru, was born in 1469, fourteen years before Martin Luther; Guru Govind Singh passed away in 1708. The hymns and teachings are in a language which may be described as the Panjābī form of Hindī or Hindusṭānī.

Prof. R. E. Hume's remarkable book has been referred to. He tells us, in his Preface, that he has gathered in it, "3074 passages...selected...with the utmost care...(from) various alternative translations,... the total number of pages actually handled in the preparation of the volume amounting to 106,423." He has classified them into 4 Parts, sub-divided into 51 sections, without any comment of his own. Elaborate Reference Notes, Bibliography, Table of Citations, and Topical Index have been appended, which greatly facilitate use of the volume.

The subjects treated are: Part I, FAITH IN THE PERFECT GOD—(1) The One Supreme God, (2) The Divine Power and Wisdom, (3) The Divine Goodness and Wonder, (4) The Divine Omnipresence and Inner Presence, (5) Invocations and Calls to Worship, (6) Worship and Prayer, (7) Adoration and Praise, (8) Trust and Guidance, (9) Faith and Faithfulness, (10) Sin and Evil, (11) Confusion and Repentance, (12) Hope, (13) Salvation, (14) Rewards and Punishments, (15) Future Life and Immortality. Pt. II, MAN AND HIS PERFECTING—(16) What is Man?, (17) The Wise and the Foolish, (18) The Perfect Man, (19) Humility, (20) Unselfishness, (21) Self-examination and Self-Control, (22) Patience and Steadfastness, (23) Fearlessness and Courage, (24) Purity, (25) Simplicity, (26) Thought and Meditation, (27) Thankfulness, (28) Sincerity and Earnestness, (29) Truth and Truthfulness,

(30) Temperance, (31) Happiness and Joy, (32) Righteousness and Virtue, (33) Duty, (34) Self-dedication and Divine Benediction. Pt. III, MAN AND HIS SOCIAL RELATIONS—(35) Anger and Hatred, (36) Work and Deeds, (37) Wealth and Prosperity, (38) Giving and Helping, (39) Justice and Judgment, (40) Obedience, (41) The Golden Rule, (42) Good for Evil, (43) Forgiveness, (44) Love, (45) Serving Others, (46) Friendship and Brotherhood. (47) Associates. (48) Home and Family Relations, (49) Peace and War, (50) Summary Duties. Pt. IV, A PROGRAM OF JOINT WORSHIP, arranged as a Responsive Reading.

Another very noteworthy book is Dr. Frank L. Riley's *The Bible of Bibles*, (pub: 1929, by J F. Rowny Press, Los Angeles). The author says in his Foreword: "It is the concentrated essence of the Bibles of the world, extracted during nineteen years of study from sixty Sacred Books dating back, according to some authorities, 13000 years". Dr. Riley has included, in his researches, Ṭaoism, Vēḍism, Judaism, Zoroastrianism, Buḍḍhism, Christianity, and Islām, of the living and the Babylonian-Chaldean, Egyptian, and the Mithraist religions, of the past. He does not seem to have dealt with Shintoism, Confucianism, Jainism, and Sikhism. He does not tell us the total number of passages he has extracted. They cover 343 pages of fine large print. A rough calculation gives 1400. These are divided into 12 chapters, which cover 387 topics, listed in a table of contents, (which is named Index), at the beginning. The chapters are: (1) God, (2) The Beneficence of God, (3) Creation, ( ) The Origin and Constitution of Man, (5) The Problem of Evil, (6) The World, Matter, the Unreal, (7) The Works of the Flesh, (8) The Kingdom of Heaven, (9) The Fruits of the Spirit, (10) The Straight and

Narrow Way, (11) Prayer and Healing, (12) Peace-Brotherhood-Heaven on Earth. An Introduction gives brief accounts of the sixty Bibles of the several religions studied. "A digest, or terse account, of the excerpts from the Sacred Books which appear in" each chapter, averaging about a page and a half in length, is prefixed to it.

The present writer could not make such use of Dr. Riley's book as it deserved ; he came across it rather late ; the absence of an alphabetical Index, and of page-references in the table of contents, hampered utilisation; preparation of copy, for the new edition of the present work, from the notes previously gathered, on the margins and pasted-in slips of a copy of the first edition,[1] was begun in January, 1939, after resigning membership of the Central Legislative Assembly of India ; the first batch of copy was sent to press in March, 1939 ; thereafter, the compiler had not leisure and vitality to spare, nor peace of mind enough, for hunting up the originals of a score or more of translated passages, quoted in Dr. Riley's book, which appeared very relevant ; for throughout that whole month, and the first week of April, a very serious communal riot, a small 'civil war', raged in Benares ; between bands of Hindūs and Muslims, misguided and incited by evil-minded self-seeking politico-religious misleaders, despite all the endeavours of a joint Hindu-Muslim Peace Committee, of which the present writer had been elected Chairman, to his great unhappiness and

[1] The compiler should record here his gratitude to a young friend, Pandit Bhavānī Shankar, B. Sc., LL. B., (of Bareilly, U. P.) who faired out these notes neatly, and thereby very considerably lightened his labor over e preparation of copy.

helpless worry; the riots resulted in some 50 to 60 deaths, many more cases of serious and light hurt, very many cases of arson, loot, wanton destruction of property; the Spirit of Hatred, which has been stalking more and more proudly all over the human world, since the beginning of the 20th century, made its horrible presence felt acutely thus, in Benares; and showed that the 'Forces of Good, of Light, of Truth', have to struggle longer and harder against the opposite forces, of the 'Enemy of Mankind', the 'Forces of Evil, of Darkness, of Falsehood', before the latter will be checked effectively. It is very necessary, for many workers, in all countries, to take up the task of establishing religious peace and good-will; for, from it, and not without it, will come economic and political peace and good-will.

The works of Dr. Riley and Prof. Hume possess not only outstanding merit in respect of scholarly industry, but are very praiseworthy for the philanthropic spirit of all-conciliating all-embracing Human Brotherhood and Solidarity which breathes all through them. Because of lack of knowledge of any European language other than English, and of very limited reading in even that, this writer has not come across any other works using a similar method; except those which will be mentioned presently. It is to be hoped there are others; for such, and many such, in every language, are greatly needed to promote Human Brotherhood, true Spiritual Liberty and Fraternity, and Material Equitability. No doubt, a number of books have been written and published, whose purpose also is liberal-minded reconciliation of creeds. A fine recent work of the kind is *World-Fellowship*, edited by C. F. Weller (pub: 1935, by Liveright Publishing Corporation, New York).

But its nature and method are very different. And even such works are too few.

Dr. Riley and Prof. Hume do not give any texts in original; only translations; though these are from the works of recognised scholars. The present work, in the first edition, had only about 450 parallel passages from the scriptures of the several religions; and practically none from the three indigenous religions of China and Japan, nor from the Zoroastrian *Zend-Avesṭā*. The present edition brings together 1150 passages, in round figures, and gives the originals, in roman, as well as translations, with the exceptions mentioned before.

Dr. Riley and Prof. Hume do not make it their purpose to trace out and supply any scientific and *organic* Scheme of Universal Religion, Religion in general, running through all religions. All the topics dealt with by them, are dealt with here too; also many others; but they are arranged in a different way; not as a collection of comparatively un-jointed parts, but as forming a system, a single organism, with all its members livingly articulated together, in accordance with the Science of Psychology. Whether the arrangement is successful or not, the reader will decide for himself. The great majority of the topics dealt with by Dr. Riley and Prof. Hume, would be assigned to the chapter on 'The Way of Devotion, or the Emotional (or Ethical) Constituent of Religion', in this work; and they do not touch many of the topics treated here in the chapters on 'The Way of Knowledge, or the Intellectual Constituent of Religion', and 'The Way of Works or the Volitional (or Actional) Constituent of Religion'; (see pp. 85-89, *infra*, on 'The Three Aspects of Religion').

The present work endeavours to provide, for the parallel passages, a setting of elucidative and connective comment, in the way of interpretation and illustration, so as to interlink them and make of them, all together, a continuous organic entity; a Universal Religion with a definite frame-work; not artificially eclectic, but a natural living growth; which may be readily discerned as present within the outer garments of every religion; even as the main features, the general outlines, of the human form, can be discerned in every human individual. This Scheme is based on the psychological triad of knowing, desiring, acting, (see pp. 80-90, *infra*).

THE EVOLUTION OF THE PRESENT WORK.

This tripartite Scheme of Religion, based on Philosophy or Metaphysic, and Psychology, is fundamental part of Indian tradition from time immemorial; (see pp. 270, 420-422, *infra*). It was first utilised in the new way, required by the times, some forty years ago, for the preparation of a series of Text-Books of Hinḍuism, for use in the Central Hindu College and School of Benares, (see footnote on p. v., *supra*).

The first idea was to start a Theosophical College, in accord with the three objects of the Theosophical Society (see pp. 571-572, *infra*), in which the students would be taught the principles of Universal Religion, and be brought up in the atmosphere of a nucleus of Universal Brotherhood. But active workers in sufficient numbers were not forthcoming from the folds of other denominations. So it was decided to begin with a 'Hinḍū' College, which would endeavour to liberalise and rationalise at least 'Hinḍuism', and re-convert it into the ancient Upanishaḍic ('philosophical') and **Mānava** ('human') Vėdism ('scientific religion'); and would restore to it the main characteristics of 'Universal Religion'; whereby rapprochement with the other religions inhabiting the country would be facilitated.

Very shortly after the founding of the College, the need for systematic compendious Text-Books of Hinḍuism was felt, inevitably, for teaching purposes. Mrs. (later Dr.) Annie Besant, "that high-souled woman"[1], "the mother of Mother India,"[2] "whose radiant spirit rekindled India's faith in her own ideals and destiny,"[3] "the memory of the magnificent services rendered by whom to India will live as long as India lives",[4] was President of the Board of Trustees and the Managing Committee of the Institution; and the present writer had the high privilege and great good fortune of working with her as honorary Secretary of the two bodies. "If Annie Besant had not been, Mahāṭmā Gānḍhī could not be"[5]; "if any three or four of the other great people in India were named, the sum of their achievements, the aggregate of the benefit that they had rendered to this country, would not exceed what stood unquestionably to her credit."[6] The Board of Trustees appointed a Committee, with us two, as Chairman and Secretary, to prepare the Text-Books. They gave us general directions to the effect that the religious and ethical training, given to the students, should be of

---

[1]This is how Prof. William James, the renowned philosopher of U.S.A., speaks of her in his famous book, *Varieties of Religious Experience.*

[2 3 4 5 6]These words were respectively said, in paying tribute to her, after her passing away, in September, 1933, by Dr. Alam (a Muslim), by the famous orator and poetess Mrs. Sarojini Naidu, by Mahāṭmā Gānḍhī, again by Mrs. S. Naidu, and by the Rt. Hon'ble Shrī V. S. Shrīnivāsa Shāsṭrī, P. C. (Hinḍūs).

"a wide, liberal, and unsectarian character,...inclusive enough to unite the most divergent forms of Hinḍū thought;...must be directed to the building up of a character, pious, dutiful, strong, upright, righteous, gentle, and well-balanced—a character which will be that of a good man and a good citizen; such as can be formed only by the fundamental principles of religion, governing the general view of life and of life's obligations. That which unites Hinḍū-s in a common faith, must be clearly and simply taught; all that divides them must be ignored. Lastly, care must be taken to cultivate a wide spirit of tolerance, which not only respects the differences of thought and practice among Hinḍu-s, but which also respects the differences of religion among non-Hinḍu-s, regarding all faiths with tolerance, as roads whereby men reach the Supreme."

The Secretary placed before the Chairman, a Syllabus based on the ancient tradition as to the three parts or Constitnents of Religion. She agreed. That Syllabus, with some slight later modifications, appears as the Table of Contents of the Text-Book.

The Contents, as published, are: INTRODUCTION. Pt. I, BASIC HINDU RELIGIOUS-IDEAS: (ch. I) The One Existence, (2) The Many, (3) Rebirth, (4) Karma, (5) Sacrifice, (6) The Visible and Invisible Worlds. Pt. II, GENERAL HINDU RELIGIOUS RITES AND CUSTOMS, (ch. 1) The Samskāras (Sacraments), (2) Shrāḍḍha (Oblations to the Departed), (3) Shaucham (Hygiene and Purification), (4) The Five Daily Sacrifices (Acts of Service), (5) Worship, (6) The Four Stages of Life, (Planning of the Individual Life, (7) The Caste-system (Social Organisation). Pt. III, ETHICAL TEACHINGS, (ch. 1) Ethical Science, What is it ?, (2) The Foundation of Ethics, as given by Religion, (3) Right and Wrong, (4) The Standard of Ethics, (5) Virtues and their Foundation, (6) Bliss and Emotions, (7) 'Self-Regarding' Virtues, (8) Virtues and Vices in Human Relations; those in relation to Superiors, (9) Virtues and Vices in relation to Equals, (10) Virtues and Vices in relation to Inferiors, (11) The Reaction of Virtues and Vices on each other.

With this Syllabus we set to work on "An Advanced Text-Book of Hindu Religion and Ethics", in Shrinagar (Kashmir), in the summer of 1901. The Secretary and some other members supplied Dr. Annie Besant with Samskṛṭ texts; the present writer's book, *The Science of the Emotions*, the first edition of which was published in 1900, supplied the bulk of the material for the third part of the work. She herself gathered some texts from the English translations in the *Sacred Books of the East Series*; and, great worker that she was, drafted, in English, within two months, the whole of the Text-book, amounting, as subsequently printed with some additions and alterations, to over 400 pp., Cr. 8vo.

After approval by the Committee, a hundred copies of the draft were printed and sent to leaders of the Hinḍū community, Pandits famous for Samskṛṭ learning, and heads of the principal sects, in all parts of the country; and suggestions for additions and alterations were requested. Those that were received were carefully considered by the Committee and duly incorporated. Then the *Advanced Text-Book* was printed off, and introduced in the College classes, in 1904. Shortly after, an *Elementary Text-Book* was prepared by the Chairman and the Secretary, for use in the upper School classes This was a simplified abridgment of the Advanced; but a large number of illustrative stories from the *Mahā-bhāraṭa* and the *Purāṇas* were added in the 3rd Part. Then a very small Catechism was drawn up by the Chairman for use in the small children's classes. All these were in use in the C. H. College and School till 1914, after which the Institution was converted into the Benares University and passed into the hands of a new and elaborately constituted management, consisting of Court, Council, Senate, Syndicate, Faculties, etc. The graded series of Text-books was welcomed all over India, after publication; translations of the Catechism were published in eleven provincial tongues; and of the Elementary also in two or three.

In 1910-1911, Dr. Annie Besant, as President of the Theosophical Society, published two small volumes, entitled *The Universal Text-Book of Religion and Morals*, on the lines of Part I and Part III of the *Text-Books of Hindu Religion and Ethics*. She says, in the Foreword, that she is doing so "at the wish of the Theosophical Convention of December, 1909;...many friends, all the world over, have helped in the collection of illustrative verses;...the book is sent out with the earnest hope that it may contribnte to the recognition of the Brotherhood of Religions, and may be useful as offering the material out of which may be drawn lessons for religious and moral instruction in schools where the scholars are of different faiths." The illustrative texts are in translations, not in the original words.

The contents of Vol. I are: Introduction. (ch. 1) The Unity of God; (2) The Manifestation of God in a Universe; (3) The Great Orders of Living Beings; (4) The Incarnation of Spirit; (5) The Two Basic Laws; (6) The Three Worlds of Human Evolution;

(7) The Brotherhood of Man. Of vol. II : (1) The Object and Basis of Morality; (2) The Relation between Morality, Emotion, Virtues and Vices. (3) Classification of Virtues and Vices, (4) Virtues and Vices in Relation to Superiors, (5) Virtues and Vices in Relation to Equals; (6) Virtues and Vices in Relation to Inferiors; (7) Interaction between Virtues and Vices.

These two small books are admirably suited for the purpose intended. It is much to be regretted that they have not been circulated and used much more extensively, not been reprinted over and over again, and not been translated into all the more widely-spoken languages.

After the introduction of the *Text-Books of Hinduism* in the C. H. College, for six or seven years, till 1914, the Secretary of the Institution, the present writer, was also honorary Lecturer in Hinḍū Religion, in the College Department. With the experience gathered as such, he published a series of articles, on *The Science of Religion, or the Principles of Sanāṭana Vaiḍika Ḍharma,* in the C.H.C. Magazine, during 1914-1915. These were published as a small book with that title, in 1917. It is a sort of supplement to the Text-Books, going over the same ground, in a fresh manner, with many other Samskṛṭ texts in original; more exposition of the underlying psychological principles; and greater endeavour to interlink all parts; as may be seen from the titles of the 4 chapters of the work.

These are :(1) The Nature and Constituents of Sanāṭana Vaiḍika Ḍharma, ('The Permanent Scientific Religion'); (2) The Jñāna-kānda, the Science and Philosophy, or the Rationalism, of Religion, (3) The Bhakṭi-Kānda, the Ethics and Morals, or the Mysticism, of Religion,

(4) The Karma-Kānda, the Sociology (including Eugenics, Economics, and Politics), or the Practicalism, of Religion.

The sections of the chapters need not be repeated here. It will be noted that Part II of the *Text-Book of Hindu Religions* and Ethics, becomes ch. IV, and Part III becomes ch. II of the above.

In October, 1923, the Annual Provinçial Political Conference (of the Indian National Congress) was held in Benares. In view of the growing tension and also riots here and there, between Hindus and Muslims, the present writer, as Chairman of the Reception Committee of the Conference, gave an address in which he stressed the Unity, in Essentials, of the two religions, and quoted parallel texts from their Scriptures, in original. The address was well received. A public-spirited friend, Shri Ghana-shyām Ḍās Birlā, had ten thousand copies of it printed, in Hinḍī as well as Urḍū characters, page facing page, and distributed free all over the country. The address was subsequently incorporated in a colleetion of the Hinḍī writings of the compiler of this book, which was published in 1928, under the title of *Samanvaya.*

In October, 1924, a Hindu-Muslim Unity Conference was held in Delhi, in consequence of violent communal riots. engineered by political and politico-religious mis-leaders, which had been breaking out, for some time, in scores of places, all over the country. At that Conference, the present writer proposed that a Committee should be appointed, of learned and at the same time large-hearted, broad-minded, and philanthropic, not narrow, bigoted, fanatic, representatives of all the main religions of India, i. e. eight out of the eleven mentioned at the outest of this Note; (see also pp. 560-562, *infra)* ; to draw up a graded series of Text-Books of Universal Religion, with parallel passages from all Scriptures, which would be taught in all the educational institutions of India, be spread broadcast, and brought to every home in the land in every way possible. The proposal was not considered feasible. The Conference contented itself with appeals for the undefined, unexplained, word 'Unity', without any mention of the 'contents' of the word, its denotation and connotation and significance in concrete terms ; as is the case with the words 'Sva-rāj' and 'Self-government ; (see pp. xxiii-xxiv, *supra*, 591, *infra*). The communal riots have continued to grow worse and worse in India, as the politico-economic hatreds and war-'riots' in Europe, and indeed all over the world, in this 'Age of Discord', Kali-Yuga.

The next effort, of the present writer, on these lines, apart from articles in Hindī and English newspapers, was made at the All-Asia Educational Conference, at the close of 1930. The Foreword to the first edition gives the rest of the story of the genesis and developement of this work.

Two other books ought to be mentioned here, which have helped this compiler greatly in understanding something of the obscure, mysterious, puzzling legends in the Samskṛṭ Iṭihāsa-Purāṇa regarding the nature of other worlds and planes of matter, and their denizens, and the eonian course of the cyclical, cosmic, inorganic, organic, human and other involutions, evolutions, dissolutions. These matters are just touched in the present work ; because the compiler's knowledge of them is very far from sufficient ; general public is probably not deeply or scientifically interested in them ; the extant scriptures do not supply clearly intelligible and parallel passages about them; and finally, because, though precise and correct knowledge of their details is highly important for the specialist and advanced student of what has been called 'occult science', Yoga, *Sulūk*, yet the features of Religion which are the vitally most important for the average human being, are those which are dealt with plainly, by all the scriptures, and therefore here, in Chs: II and III.

The two books, above referred to, are Madame H.P. Blavatsky's monumental works, *Isis Unveiled* (2 vols., 1500 pages), and *The Secret Doctrine* (latest Adyar edition, 6 vols, 2200 pages, plus a sixth volume of Indices, 500 pages). The two parts of this last work are appropriately entitled 'Cosmogenesis' and 'Anthropogenesis' respectively. They supply an immense amount of out-of-the way information about the 'dead' religions; about the 'occult', 'super-physical', side of Religion, connected with other worlds and planes, and the 'subtle' body and 'finer' faculties latent in the normal man, but capable of being developed and made patent by 'mystic' disciplines and special 'education'; and about the details of cosmic and human evolution, through vast eons and cycles, (See p. 617, *infra*). Two passages from these two works are reproduced below. Members of the Theosophical Society, which she founded, and which now has branches in almost all civilised countries of the world, will readily see that the present work is only a popular and extended commentary on those two passages, in keeping with the second object of the T. S., (See p. 571-572, *infra*).

"Kapila, Orpheus, Pythagoras, Plato, Basilides, Marcian, Ammonius, and Plotinus, founded schools and sowed the germs of many a noble thought, and, disappearing, left behind them the refulgence of demigods. But the three personalities of Kṛṣhṇa, Gauṭama (the Buḍḍha), and Jesus appeared like true gods, each in his epoch, and bequeathed to humanity, three religions built on the imperishable rock of ages. That all three...have in time become adulterated, is no fault of...the noble Reformers. It is the priestly self-styled husbandmen of the 'vine of the Lord' who must be held to account by future generations. Purify the three systems of the dross of human dogmas, the *pure essence* remaining will be found to be *identical*": (*Isis Unveiled*, II, 536).

"Esoteric Philosophy reconciles all religions, strips every one of its outward human garments, and shows the *root of each* to be *identical* with that of *every other* great religion :" (*The Secret Doctrine*, I. 45.).

"Every Scripture inspired of God is profitable,
for teaching, for reproof, for correction,
for instruction which is in righteousness,
that the man of God may be complete,
furnished completely unto every good work.

(*B.*, 2 Timothy, 3. 16-17., *THR.* p. v.)

"We believe in what hath been revealed to us and revealed to you. Our God and your God is One and to Him are we Self-surrendered." (*Q.*, 29., 45.).

SYSTEM OF PRONUNCIATION

THE system of pronunciation followed in the Roman transcript confines itself to the simple differences. The more nice and subtle ones have not been taken account of. Thus, there are three shades of 's' in Arabic-Persian; they are all transcribed by 's' here. So four kinds of '*z*,' two of 'h,' two of soft 'ṭ,' are rendered by one '*z*,' one 'h,' one 'ṭ'. So two kinds of 'sh' in Samskṛṭ are both transcribed as 'sh'. Arabic gutturals of e, i, o, u, have also not been marked; that of 'a' has been, as a'.

Samskṛṭ letters are rendered as below:

a, as in similar, solar; *i.e.*, the sound of u in fur, cut, shut.

ā, far, car.

i, fit, sit.

ī, elite; the sound of ee in meet, feet, sheet.

u, put; the sound of oo in foot.

ū, flute; the sound of oo in shoot, hoot.

ṛ, somewhat as in iron.

e, as in get, jet, fetch.

é, as the 'a' in fate.

ai, somewhat like i in might, fight, right.

o, go.

au, somewhat as in how, cow.

aṁ, like um in jump, hump, bumper.

k, king, ken.

kh, buckhorn, inkhorn.

g, get, gain.

gh, big-horn, fog-horn, Birmingham.

ng, bring, sing.

ch, churn, chaste.

chh, rich-house, fetch-him.

j, joy, jam.

jh, bridge-head.

ñ, cañyon.

t, tit, talk.

th, get-home.

d, daughter, dame.
dh, madhouse.
ṇ, (n and d combined in a click-sound).
ṭ, petit, (soft t).
ṭh, think (without the sibilance).
ḍ, there, that (minus the sibilance).
ḍh, bid-him (soft d).
n, nephew, niece.
p, pan, pass.
ph, lip-homage.
b, bless, beam.
bh, hobhouse, abhor.
m, musk.
y, yes, you.
r, run.
l, lamb.
v or w, win.
sh, shine.
s, sun, son.
h, hand, heaven.

The special sounds of Arabic-Persian are:

kḥ, aspirate of k, like the German ach, or Scottish loch.
a', guttural of a.
gḥ, guttural of g.
f, fun.
q, guttural of k.
z, zephyr.

LIST OF ABBREVIATIONS.

(*B.*), *Bible.* (*O. T., Old Testament,* Hebrew ; *O. T.* and *N. T., New Testament,* Christian).

(*BB.*), Dr. F. L. Riley's *The Bible of Bibles*, published in 1929, by J. F. Rowny Press, Los Angeles. (See pp xxxii-xxxiii, *supra*).

(*Bh.*), *Bhāgavaṭa,* one of the 18 *Purāṇa-s,* sacred books of legends and traditional histories of the Cosmos and of the Human Race, which form part of the Scriptures of Vaidika Ḍharma, or Véḍism ('Hinḍuism').

(*Bu.*), Buḍḍhist Sacred Books

(*C.*), Confucian Works.

(*Dh.*), *Ḍhamma-paḍa,* a Buḍḍhist Scripture.

(*ERE.*), *Encyclopedia of Religion and Ethics,* in 13 vols., edited by Dr. Hastings.

(*G.*), *Gīṭā,* i. e., *Bhagavaḍ-Gīṭā,* the most widely known of the Véḍist Scriptures.

(*Gr.*), *Guru-Granṭha-Sāhab,* the Scripture of Sikhism.

(*H.*), *Haḍīs,* the Sayings of the Prophet Muhammad.

(*J.*), Jaina Sacred Books.

(*Ju.*), Sacred writings of Judaism, Hebraism, or the Jewish Religion, like the *Ṭalmūḍ* or Commentaries on the *O. T.*, and the Qabbālāh or Kabbala, a compilation of the writings of Jewish Mystics.

(*K.*), Kabbala, i. e., Qabbālah.

(*M.*), *Manu-Smṛṭi,* the oldest living law-book of the world, revered by Hinḍū-s like the Véḍa-s.

(*Mbh.*), *Mahā-bhāraṭa,* the 'Great Epic' of the 'Great War' between the Pāndava-s and the Kaurava-s, which ranks with *Manu-smṛṭi* in Hinḍū estimation.

(*Q.*), *Qurān*, often written in English as *Koran*; the chief Scripture of Islam or Mohammedanism.

(*R.*), *Rāmāyaṇa*, the 'Epic' of the War of Rāma and Rāvaṇa, which is ranked, by Hinḍū-s, with the *Mahābhāraṭa* and the *Purāṇa-s*. These three make up the 'Iṭihāsa-Purāṇa'.

(*S.*), Sūfī writings.

(*SBE.*), *Sacred Books of the East Series*, edited by Max Muller.

(*Sh.*), Shintoism.

(*Si.*), Sikh writings, among which the *Guru-Granṭha-Sāhab* is the chief Scripture.

(*T.*), The Scriptures of Taoism, among which the *Tao-Teh-King* of Lāo-tse is the chief.

(*THR.*), *Treasure-House of the Living Religions*, published in 1933, by Charles Scribner's Sons, New York and London). (See pp. xxxi-xxxii, *supra*).

(*U.*), *Upanishaṭ-s*, the philosophical and psychological parts of the *Véḍa-s*.

(*V.*), *Véḍa-s*; four, *Ṛg-Véḍa*, *Yajur-Véḍa*, *Sāma-Véḍa*, *Aṭharva-Véḍa*; the chief Scriptures of the *Hinḍū-s*.

(*Z.*), Zoroastrian Scriptures; the *Zend-Āvesṭā* in particular, of which the chapters known as the *Gāṭhā*, are regarded as the direct utterance of the Prophet Zaraṭhusṭra.

CONTENTS

(If the reader will glance through the 600 page-headings, he will find a much fuller table of contents in them.)

CHAPTER IV

A SUGGESTION

If the reader will please make a note, on the margin of the page, and at the line, concerned, of the page of the Addenda (pp. 609-621) on which an addition, for that page and line, is printed, before he begins reading the book, he will be sure not to miss the addition. The 'corrections' (pp. 622-623) may be made beforehand, similarly.

FURTHER ADDENDA

On p. xxviii, before line 1, insert:

Texts of Zoroastrianism have been taken from J. M. Chatterji's and A. N. Bilimoria's edition of the *Gatha*; (see foot-note on p. 45).

On p. 491, after 'mazdur', in l. 26, insert:
Abul-Fazl, the famous minister of Akbar, in the Introduction (***Muqaḍḍamah***) to his work, ***Āīn-i-Akbarī***, names these as (1) Ahl-i-qalam, 'the men of the pen', the learned, (2) Mubārizān, the 'warriors', (3) Pésha-warān wa Bāzar-gānān, 'the men of trade and business' and 'the men of the market-place' (bāzār), and (4) Barzagarān wa kishā-warzān, 'peasants and tillers of the soil.' And he expressly recognises and affirms the ***universal vocational character*** of this four-fold classification. Thus: Jahāniāṅ az chahār garoh burūṅ na bāshanḍ; i. e., "No human being, in all the world, falls outside of these four classes".

No man liveth unto himself....We are all parts of one another....God hath made of one blood all nations that dwell upon the face of the earth. (Bible).

All creatures are members of the one family of God. (Qurān).

Human beings, all, are as head, arms, trunk, and legs unto one another. (Véḍa).

THE ESSENTIAL UNITY OF ALL RELIGIONS

Invocation of the One Supreme Spirit of Unity

AUM-ĀMĪN-AMEN

Éko Ḍévah sarva-bhūṭéshu gūdhah
  Sākshī chéṭā sarva-bhūṭ-āḍhi-vāsah,
Ṭam Āṭma-sṭham yé-nu-pashyanṭi ḍhīrāh,
  Ṭéshām sukham shāshvaṭam, n-éṭaréshām.

Sarva-vyāpī sarva-bhūṭ-ānṭar-Āṭmā,
  Ékam rūpam bahu-ḍhā yah karoṭi,
  am Āṭma-sṭham yé-nu-pashyanṭi ḍhīrāh,
  Ṭéshām sukham shāshvaṭam, n-éṭaréshām.

Niṭyo niṭyānām, Chéṭanash chéṭanānām,
  Éko bahūnām yo vi-ḍaḍhāṭi kāmān,
Ṭam Āṭma-sṭham yé-nu-pashyanṭi ḍhīrāh,
  Ṭéshām shānṭih shāshvaṭī, n-éṭaréshām.

Éko A-varṇo, bahu-ḍhā shakṭi-yogāḍ
  Varṇān an-ékān nihiṭ-ārṭho yo ḍaḍhāṭi,
Vi-chaiṭi ch-ānṭé vishvam āḍau, sa Ḍévah,
  Sa no buḍḍhyā shubhayā sam-yunakṭu. (*U.*)[1]

(The One God hidden in all living beings,
  The Living Witness biding in all hearts—

---

[1] Please see the foregoing 'List of Abbreviations'; also the note on the 'System of Pronunciation', as regards the use of diacritical marks and accented types.

The Wise who seek and find Him in them-Self,
  To them, and None Else, is Eternal Joy.

The all-pervading Inner Self of all,
  Who from His Formlessness creates all Forms—
The Wise who see that One within them-Self,
  To them alone belongs Eternal Joy.

Eternity of aeons, Life of lives,
  The One who all the Many's wishes sates—
The Wise who Him within them-Self behold
  Theirs, and None Other's, is Eternal Peace.

The Colourless, who from His secret store
  Exhaustless, countless colours draws, to paint,
Efface, repaint the worlds upon the face
  Of Empty Space with Mystic Potency—
May He endow us with the lucid mind !)

Ṭurfa Bé-rangī ke ḍāraḍ
  rang-hā-é saḍ hazār !
Ṭurfa Bé-shaklī ke ḍāraḍ
  shakl-hā-é bé-shumār !

Ba nāmé Āṅ ke Ū nāmé na ḍāraḍ,
  Ba har nāmé ke kẖwānī sar bar āraḍ,
Ba nāmé Āṅ ke Wāhiḍ ḍar Kasīr asṭ,
  Ke anḍar wahḍaṭ-Ash kasraṭ asīr asṭ ! (*S.*)

(What marvel ! that a Being Colourless
  Displays a hundred thousand hues, tints, shades !
What wonder ! that a Being Void of Form
  Enrobes in forms beyond all numbering !—
May we behold Him in all hues and forms !

Thus, in the name of Him who hath no name,

Yet lifts to every name an answering head,
The name of Him who is the Changeless One
Amidst the changing Many, and within
Whose Oneness all this Many is confined,
May we begin our loving work of Peace.)

Aum ! Ṭaṭ Saviṭur-varéṇyam bhargo Ḍévasya ḍhīmahi, ḍhiyo yo nah prachoḍayāṭ. Agné !, naya su-paṭhā rāyé asmān, vishvāni, Ḍéva !, vayunāni viḍvān. Yuyoḍhy-asmaj-juhurāṇam énah. Bhūyishthām Ṭé nama-ukṭim viḍhéma. (*V.*)

(Father of all !, may Thy supernal Light
Inspire, illuminate, and guide our minds !
We open them to let Thy Glory in.
Supreme Director ! Lord of Warmth and Light,
Of Life and Consciousness, that knowest all !
Guide us by the *Right Path* to happiness,
And give us strength and will to war against
The sins that rage in us and lead astray !
We bow in adoration unto Thee !)

Bismillāh-ir-Rahmān-ir-Rahīm. Al-hamḍu lillāhi Rabb-il-ālimīn ! Ar-Rahmān-ir-Rahīm ! Mālik-i-yaum-iḍ-ḍīn ! Iyyāka na'buḍu, wa iyyāka nasṭa'īn. Ihḍi-nas-sirāṭ-ul-musṭaqīm. Sirāṭ-allazzīna ana'mṭa a'laihim, ghair-il-maghzub-i-a'laihim wa lā-azzālīn. Āmīn. (*Q.*)

(Lord of Compassion ! All praise unto Thee !
Creator and Protector of the worlds !
Lord God ! Beneficent and Merciful !
Master Supreme of the great Judgment Day !

Thee do we serve and Thee beseech for help ;
Show us the Path on which Thy blessings rest ;
The *Straight Path* ; not of those who go astray,
On whom descend Thy wrath and punishment).

Apāno ḍaryo jyāīṭīm, ā kshaṭhrém vanghéush manangho, ashāṭ ā éréjush paṭho, yaéshū Mazaḍāo Ahuro shaéṭi. (*Z.*, Gāṭhās)

(Grant us long life, Great Lord !, and fortitude,
And the right mind, and show us the *Straight Path*,
Oe'r which Thou broodest, and which leads to Thee !)

Hear, O Lord !, my cry, give ear unto my prayer, that goeth not out of feigned lips. Hold up my goings in Thy *Paths*, that my footsteps slip not. Show me Thy *Ways*, O Lord !, teach me Thy *Paths*; and lead me in Thy Truth. Thou art the God of my salvation. Open Thou mine eyes that I may behold wondrous things out of Thy Law. Quicken Thou me according to Thy word. Remove from me the way of lying. (*B.*, O.T.)

Our Father which art in heaven !, hallowed be Thy name. Thy Kingdom come. Thy will be done in earth as it is in heaven. Give us this day our daily bread. And forgive us our debts as we forgive our debtors. And *lead us* not into temptation, but deliver us *from evil*; for Thine is the kingdom, and the power, and the glory, for ever. Amen. (*B.*, N.T.)

O far great Heaven ! We call Thee,
Our Father and our Mother ! (*C.*, *THR.*, 19.)

(Ocean of Mercy ! Ever, in our hearts,
Dwell Thou, and so illuminate our minds
That we may love, serve, worship Thee, Our God !,
Ever Thy Presence may we feel near us !
Thou art our Father, Mother, Teacher, all !
Si., Grantha, *THR.*, 31).

DEAR FRIENDS, SISTERS, BROTHERS !

In accord with the time-old traditions of the East, let us begin our work of love thus, in the words of the venerable Scriptures of the several religions; of the *Vēḍas* and *Upanishaṭs*, the most ancient available records of passionately yearning and deeply searching human thought; of the *Qurān*, and of the Sūfis, the most poetical and beautiful exponents of that thought; of the *Zenḍ-Āvesṭā*, the *Bible*, the *Guru Granṭh Sāhab*; begin with ardent invocation of, and fervent prayer to, the One Supreme Spirit of Life. That Supreme Spirit, out of its Unity, creates the infinite Many-ness of Nature; and, at the same time, It imposes Its all-pervading, all-embracing, Unity upon that countless Multitude. By that Unity, It binds atoms and cells into tissues, organs, bodies; bodies into species, genera, kingdoms; ties these to planets; planets to suns, in solar systems; these to larger systems; chains these into vast star-galaxies; and makes of all the infinite World-process a Uni-verse. It enters into these dead dolls of bone and blood and flesh that we otherwise are, and endows us with the mind that can encompass all these countless systems. That Spirit, indeed, dwelling hidden in the hearts of all, makes it possible for these dolls to understand, and sympathize with, and help each other, in the difficulties of life. It is the One sole source of whatever Unity there is in all human thought. The realization of It alone, as eternally present, in one-Self and in all-selves, brings deathless happiness and peace, as nothing else can do. May that Universal Life and Light vivify and illuminate our hearts and minds! May It show to us the Right Path, and give to us the firm and Righteous Will to walk on it unwavering! Only after opening our hearts to It, may we commence all work with hope of full success!

Next, let us reverently salute the Ṛshis, Prophets, Buḍḍhas, Messiahs, Nabis, Rasūls, Messengers, Avaṭāras, Ṭīrṭhan-karas, Arhaṭs, Gurus, the Spiritual Hierarchs of all times; who have given Scriptures, age after age, to race after race, in order to keep alive the light of the consciousness of that Unity in the heart of humanity; and who brood over the Human Race and guide its progress, as benevolent parent-teachers watch over children in an educational home, leading the minds and bodies of the pupils onwards, from class to upper class, along the path of ever upward evolution.

Let us also offer tribute of deep gratitude to all Societies, Associations, Leagues, Parliaments of Religions, World-Fellowships of Faiths, which have been endeavouring to hold up before the world, the need and the possibility of reviving the sincere worship of that Spirit of Unity, (1) by educing more and more clearly, through sympathetic, deep, large-hearted and open-minded, comparative study of the Sacred Books of all religions, the essential unity running through all these religions, past and present, (2) by directing attention to the need for the study of the inner nature, as much as the outer, of the human being as such, and (3) by reuniting the peoples of all countries, without distinction of creed, caste, colour, race, or sex, in a Universal Brotherhood, which alone can give sincerity and real life and fulfilment to the work of the League of Nations. Such Universal Brotherhood alone can do so, by supplying the Spiritual half of that Whole, of which the League of Nations represents only the Material (hence useless) half; by creating a League of Religions, and linking it with the League of Nations.

CHAPTER I.

Religious Science and Scientific Religion

ASIATIC THOUGHT AND EUROPEAN THOUGHT. It is common knowledge that Asiatic thought is eminently coloured by religion; as modern European thought is by science. All the great living religions are of Asiatic origin; also almost all the historical great dead religions. The personal, domestic, and social life of the Hindū is largely governed by the rules of what he regards as his religion. So is that of the Musalmān. So of the Jew. So of the Confucian. So was, and to a considerable extent still is, that of the Christian belonging to the Roman Catholic form of Christianity. Such also is the case with the followers of the other forms and reforms of the Vedic religion, known as the Zoroastrian, the Buddhist, the Jaina, the Sikh; though perhaps the element of ritual is less prominent, and that of ethics more, in the later of these, in accordance with the very principle of reform.[1] Laotsism is mostly a profound philosophy, the same in essence as Vedānta-Yoga and

[1] "A religion which holds possession of our lives, which directs us at each step which we take, becomes part of our own souls. Unless, in some shape or other, it prescribes a rule of conduct, it inevitably loses its hold. The Catholic System *scarce leaves an hour* without its stated duties; such and such forms to be gone through; such and such prayers to be repeated.

Ṭasawwuf; its practical side is Confucianism. Shintoism, nobly regarding man as naturally virtuous, teaches ritual mostly[1]. In all these,

---

Night and day, morning and evening, at meals and in the intervals between meals, the Catholic is reminded of his creed by a set form. Calvinism superseded these formal observances by yet more noble practical observances. It was ever present with its behests in fixing the scale of permitted expenditure, in regulating the dress, the enjoyments, the hours of sleep and labor, sternly cutting short all idle pleasure and luxury; sternly insisting on the right performance of all practical work, the trade, the handicraft, or whatever it might be, as something for every thread and fibre of which a man would one day be called to account....Religion is the wholesome *ordering* of human life; the guide to furnish us with our daily duties in the round of common occupation; the lamp to light us along our road and to show us where to place our steps:" Froude, *Short Studies in Great Subjects*, III, pp. 154, 198.

All religions endeavour, suitably to the conditions amidst which they take their birth and grow, to fulfil this ideal duty; but unfortunately, bye and bye, the custodians of each and every religion begin to do the '*ordering*' too much, become over-conservative, rigid, narrow, domineering, greedy, immoral, despotic, lose elastic touch with changing times, forget the essentials, insist over-much on non-essentials, and thus corrupt the religion by their own excesses. Then 'politics' and 'science' begin to do the 'ordering', and go to perhaps even worse excesses and extremes.

[1] "There is a teaching which, if not confined to Shinto, is at least most emphasised in it, and that is the innate goodness of man...Shintoists...consistently uphold

the feeling is prominent, that the human being is under the ever-present influence of Something, is always in relation with Something, which is other than what is perceptible to the outer senses; that the life of the physical body is subordinate to the life of a Mysterious Something, the Soul, Spirit, which has a life beyond this life. Indeed, the tendency to what has been called other-worldliness has, in some communities, grown over-pronounced, even to the extent of becoming a disease.[2]

---

the theanthropic doctrine of *Kan-nagara*, of man being essentially divine:" Inazo Nitobe, *Japan*, (pub: 1931; The Modern World Series), p. 321.

[2]Incidentally, it may be noted that this excessive other-world-li-ness, (in the sense of neglect of this world), with which India is debited, (and not wholly wrongly either, by foreign as well as indigenous writers), has been prominent mostly only during those periods in which political and economic oppression and exploitation have been rampant. Subjected to cruel misery in this world, the people sought hope of relief from the next. Otherwise, India has always been sufficiently "this-world-ly" to have won the reputation of the land *par excellence* of silver and gold and jewels, wealth and plenty and luxury of all kinds, flowing with milk and honey, filled with corn and cotton and cattle, fruits and silk and wool, tanks and temples and palaces of stone and of marble inlaid with gems—the country whose enterprising merchants supplied, by sea as well as land, the requirements of Persia, Palestine, Egypt, and Rome, in the west, and exchanged things of art with China, Siam, Burma and Japan, in the east. Indeed, it was

Contrary to this, in the West, advanced thought was, until very recently, cutting itself off, more and more, from all concern with the possibility of things beyond the reach of our physical senses; excepting, of course, some very meta-physical 'abstract concepts', which, somehow, indispensably constitute the very roots of the various most positive sciences, and are a perpetual reminder, to the thoughtful, of the inseparable connection between the physical and the meta-physical; concepts like the arithmetical 'one, two, three, etc., and zero'; the geometrical 'point, line, surface'; the dynamical 'force, energy, attraction, repulsion'; the physical 'atom, electron'; the chemical 'affinity'; the biological 'life'; the psychological 'ego, I, we, will, memory, expectation, space, time'; and so on. That western thought, going to the other extreme, from excess of other-worldliness to excess of

---

this wealth and luxury, and this reputation, which led to her degradation, brought invasions, oppression, exploitation, and worse than all else, despiritualisation and demoralisation. In happier times, India's other-worldliness only illumined and softened, as with moonlight, her this-worldliness, transfigured it, filled it with reverence for God's Nature in all Its manifestations, and made her People see, not the things of the Spirit with the eyes of the flesh, but the things of the flesh with the eyes of the Spirit. To recover those days of peaceful and prosperous happiness, she must first recover her soul by realising anew the Essence of Religion and the Essential Unity of all Religions.

this-worldliness, brought about the greater disease of mind which resulted in the greatest of historical wars and continues to threaten a still worse.

To find out, then, whether there is or is not any substantial unity in Asiatic thought, we have mostly to concern ourselves with religious thought; as, if we had to investigate whether there is or is not unity in European thought, we would chiefly compare the views of those who have devoted their lives to the various branches of science, mathematical, physico-chemical, astronomical, biological, sociological.

To the cursory view, of the person of one kind of temperament, it might seem that the unity of Western scientific thought is patent; that the whole of what is known as science is a consistent body of theory and practice; that the unity of Eastern religious thought is an equally obvious myth; and that religions are born only to try to annihilate one another, and to induce their respective followers to plague and murder each other.

So, to the hasty sight of another, it would appear that, *e. g.*, in such a vitally important science as that of medicine, doctors disagree very much; that the more expert and scientific they are, the more intensely they differ; and that radically conflicting systems of treatment kill and cure, with much the same average of results, on the whole. In the system which regards itself as most scientific and up-to-date, theories as to the nature and cause of disease, the methods of treatment, and the drugs in favour and fashion, change from year to year. In almost all other sciences, pure and applied, old views and appliances are being daily scrapped in favour of new; the greater and more rapid the scrapping, the louder the vaunt of progressiveness; even in a rock-bottom science like mathematics, self-evident axioms are now in peril of their lives from the attacks of new theories; and in sociological sciences especially, the war of ideas, of words, of "isms," is maddening and internecine.

Indeed, Science has its ritual, its etiquette, its sacrosanct formalities, its mysterious technicalities, its sanctums, its oracular pomposity and superior stand-offishness, its popish infallibility, its expertcraft, its jingoism and fanaticism, as much as Religion; its controversial animus as bitter as the *odium theologicum*; and, becoming religionless and Godless, it has, as the debased servant of imperialism, statecraft, ruthless diplomacy, caused far more slaughter than Religion, becoming scienceless and reasonless, and degenerating into priestcraft, has done. But all such things are the fruit, neither of true science, nor of true religion, but of the evil in human nature. That evil falsifies and misuses them both, for its own selfish purposes.

THE UNITY UNDERLYING BOTH. Here as elsewhere, the wish is father to the thought. Those who, for temperamental or other and more substantial and permanent reasons, wish to see

Unity, will see Unity. Those who wish to see Discord, will see Discord only. Those who wish impartially to examine both sides of the question, will see both justly. They will discern the Truth, which always stands in the mean between opposite extremes; *viz*., the Truth of essential Unity in superficial Diversity, in religious as well as in scientific thought. Such Unity is established by the mediation of Philosophy; and the use of Philosophy, as such mediator, has begun to be recognized, more and more, latterly, by the more thoughtful and widely cultured scientists themselves, as well as by the more thoughtful religionists also. No two faces, no two bodies, no two voices, manners, gaits, are exactly similar. Even so, no two minds coincide completely. The Principle of Multiplicity in Nature sees to that. But, all the same, there is a broad general similarity too, between all human faces, figures, voices, feelings, thinkings, actings also. This alone makes it possible for human beings to understand one another, and to live together as a civilised society. The Principle of Unity, which governs Nature, is the source of such civilised association and sympathy. To recognise that Unity in the Essentials of all Religions, is to promote the cause of Civilisation.

THE ONE WAY TO PEACE ON EARTH. Those who thus discern the Truth, will always make it their duty, as lovers of the mankind of East and West alike, to do their best to maximize and glorify the Spirit of Unity, and subordinate (not abolish, which is impossible) the principle of Multiplicity to It. Such Spirit of Unity, in Europe, is witnessed by common science and culture; and, in Asia, by the fact that our brothers and sisters come from Tibet, Siam, Burma and distant China and far-off Japan, to worship the memory of the Buḍḍha Gauṭama at the Deer-Park in Benares, (which ancient-most of living towns is the most holy place of Pilgrimage for all Hinḍus) and at the Temple in Buḍḍha-Gayā; while pilgrims from all the countries of Asia, and from many parts of Africa, gather at Mecca annually, in obedience to the command of the great Prophet Muhammad.[1] The truth-seeing lovers of humanity will always work with all their might, to minimize the spirit of disunion and discord. Such spirit of discord, in Europe, has been and is proved by the Great War, and by the intense political, national, and racial jealousies and hatreds that continue there, in worse and more intense form, even after the awful bloodshed and agony of that War; and in Asia, especially in India, it is evidenced by the too well-known caste and creed dissensions, which keep it under all sorts of subjection, domination, and exploitation; whence arises, surely, great material as well as spiritual harm to the exploited, now, and to the exploiter, in the end. The best means of promoting this so desirable

[1] Jerusalem, Rome, Lourdes, Kiev, and other towns are similar gathering Centres of Pilgrimage for European Christians also, still.

peace, harmony, and unity, between all countries of both East and West, between all sections of their populations, is the proving, and the bringing home to all, of Unity between Science and Religion, and between religion and religion; and, secondly, the placing, before the world, of a Religio-Scientific scheme of Social Organisation and Planned Individual Life, which will secure, for the different temperaments, and the different ages in each lifetime, appropriate occupations, and means of livelihood, and the necessaries of life at least, for all. Thus only can indispensable Spiritual Bread, as well as Material Bread, be provided to all.

Some persons, disgusted with religious conflict, speak hastily of abolishing religion to allay that conflict. As well kill the body to cure disease. To uproot religion successfully, they must first exterminate Pain and Death. So long as human beings experience and fear these, they will not cease to crave the consolations of religion. Also, so long as men and women are left, are encouraged, are even positively taught, to believe that religions *differ*, even in *essentials*, so long will they, as the followers of such *different* religions, also necessarily continue to *differ*, to quarrel, to fight, to shed each other's blood. If, on the contrary, they are led to see that *all religions are one and the same, in essentials*, they will also assuredly become one in heart, and feel their common humanity in loving Brotherhood.

Scientific Religion. The bringing about, the proving, the establishing, of such union, between religion and religion, and between science and religion, in place of the conflict which has been raging between them so far, will make the beginning of a new and beneficent era, an era guided and governed by Scientific Religion and Religious Science.

The signs are hopeful. Slowly the artificial barriers are breaking down between science and science, between science and religon, between religion and religion. It is beginning to be recognized and said that sciences are not many, but that Science is one. It is to be hoped that before very long, with the help of that same completely unified science, it will soon come to be recognized that religions, too, are not many, but that Religion is one; and, finally, that Science and Religion are but different aspects of, or even only different names for, the same great body of Truth and its application which may be called the Science or Code of Life. If, formerly, every act was done in the name and under the guidance of religion, and, latterly, has tended to be done in the name of science, there is reason to hope that, in future, it may be done in the name of Spiritual or Religious Science.

History shows that new religions and their characteristic civilizations have taken birth, grown, and decayed, side by side. We may well regard the two as cause and effect. But what is regarded as the birth of a new religion, is really only a re-proclamation, and re-vivi-fication even more, by the extra-ordinary personality, the intense fervour, 'divine fire', en-*thusi*-(*Theos*)-asm, 'God-filledness', ṭapas, *jazbah*, self-sacrifice, high heart-compelling example, of the re-proclaimer. It is a fresh declaration, in new words, and a fresh en-live-ning thereby, of the *essential* eternal Universal Religion; and it is made necessary by the fact that the earlier proclamation had become covered up, beyond recognition, with non-essential, lifeless, misleading, harmful formalisms.

The fresh proclamation, needed for the present time, seems likely to take the form of Scientific Religion in a pre-eminent degree. And it apparently has to be made on the somewhat socialist and democratic, rather than individualist, lines; such lines as the Oversoul of the Human Race is taking in the other departments of its vast life; that is to say, it has to be made, and, indeed, is being slowly, gradually, almost imperceptibly, made, by the large body of scientific and religious thinkers in co-operation as a whole, rather than by a single individual; though leaders are needed even by the most democratic movements.[1]

---

[1] Associations form, now and then, with such religio-scientific objects as those indicated on p. 6, *supra*. Unfortunately, owing to inherent human weaknesses, they repeatedly stray away from principles to personalities, from humanitarianism to sectarianism and to all the dangers and mischiefs of 'priestcraft' which that implies. They do not keep the main objects steadily

Thus some scientists are working at psychical research. Sir Oliver Lodge, venerable veteran of world-wide fame in the realm of science, has said :[1]

in view, as beacon-light to guide all their efforts; do not work single-mindedly and whole-heartedly for the unification of the world's thought and practice in a Universal Scientific Religion, and a sincere League of *all Religions* as well as of *all Nations.* Varying the proverb, "Man proposes and God disposes", we may say, "God proposes, and Satan opposes, and, but too often, successfully disposes."

But there is no cause for excessive regret, much less despair. Instead, there is cause for greater effort in behalf of the Impersonal, and therefore All-personal, Truth. For the Principle of Good always re-composes and re-disposes. Schisms, due to 'personalities', due to over-emphasis, with much animus, on the personal element, on *meum* and *tuum*, and consequent violent disputes between followers, as well as violent opposition by persons outside the special fold, have been the experience, in their own life-times, of Kṛshṇa, Moses, Zoroaster, Confucius, Buḍḍha, Christ, Muhammad, Nānak—all. This is but another proof to the peaceful and discerning eye, of 'the *Unity* of all Religions', instead of the opposite, in respect of such unhappy experience too! We also see plainly, that such schisms do not at once destroy all the good work of the main religion. When, bye and bye, they do succeed in undermining it wholly, then the Principle of Good brings about a re-proclamation and re-viv-al of the Fundamental Truths in new ways. The believers in and servants of Unity must therefore always keep their hearts high.

[1] At Bristol, on 7 Sep., 1930.

The time will assuredly come when these avenues into unknown regions will be explored by science; and there are some who think that the time is drawing nigh when that may be expected to happen. The universe is a more *spiritual* entity than we thought. The real fact is that we are in the midst of a *spiritual* world which dominates the material. It constitutes the great and ever-present reality whose powers we are only beginning to realize. They might indeed be terrifying had we not been assured for our consolation that their tremendous energies are all controlled by a Beneficent Fatherly Power whose name is Love.

Some other older, as also more recent, declarations of faith by eminent front-rank scientists of the time may be cited.

Sir James Jeans, mathematician and astronomer, Cambridge and Princeton, secretary for many years to the Royal Society of Great Britain, says: "The Universe begins to look more like a great *Thought* than a great *Machine*." And again, "The apparent objectivity of things is due to their subsisting in the Mind...We reach...the concept of the universe as a world of pure Thought...Mind no longer appears as an accidental intruder in the realm of Matter. We are beginning to suspect that we ought rather to hail it as the creator and governor of the realm of Matter. Not, of course, our individual minds, but the Mind in which the atoms, out of which our individual minds have grown, exist as Thought." The same scientist, in *The New Background of Science* (1933), dealing with "the new knowledge", and surveying "the whole ground, from relativity, continuum, least interval, curved space, to quanta, wave-mechanics, waves of probability, indeterminacy and events,—*all concepts which we can neither picture, imagine, nor describe*", says: "The law and order which we find in the universe are most easily described and...explained in the language of *idealism*...At the farthest point Science has so far reached, *much, and possibly all, that was not mental has disappeared, and nothing new has come in that is not mental.* The final direction of change will probably be away from the materialism and strict determinism which characterised...nineteenth century physics." Again, in the last paragraphs of his book, *The Mysterious Universe*, (1937), he says: "The new knowledge compels us to revise our first hasty impressions...The old dualism of Mind and Matter...seems likely to disappear...through substantial Matter resolving itself into a creation and manifestation of Mind."

Prof. Eve, at p. 65 of *The Great Design*, a symposium edited by F. Mason (1936), says: "Most men today are engrossed in some one particular profession or occupation...It is doubtful if any group of men, except perhaps a few philosophers, is engaged in fitting together the jig-saw or patchwork puzzle of the multitudinous discoveries and theories of all our diverse branches of knowledge; thought is thus divided into water-tight compartments, between which the communications are blocked."[1]

---

[1]The philosophical, religious, and at the same time scientific *principles*, by means of which all possible, even contradictory-seeming, views and things were reconciled by ancient Indian Seers, and 'scientific determinist causation' as well as 'free-will' explained and combined in 'auto-matism'—these principles, of the ancient Indian thought, are attempted to be set forth in the present writer's *The Science of the Self* (1938; pub. by The Indian Book Shop, Benares).

Another scientist of note, Prof. Sir A. S. Eddington, has very recently confessed: "Something Unknown is doing we don't know what—that is what our theory amounts to." Elsewhere he says, "Modern physics has eliminated the notion of substance...Mind is the first and most direct thing in our experience...I regard Consciousness as fundamental. I regard Matter as derivative from Consciousness." The venerable Herbert Spencer said, towards the close of the last revised edition of his *First Principles* (pub. 1900, when he was eighty years of age), that his 'Unknowable' in no way conflicts with, but rather supports, religion. The Teacher-founders of the great religions have all taught, and many philosophers, ancient and modern, Western and Eastern, have perceived, that this Unknown and Unknowable, is our very Self, the all-pervading, Universal, Supreme Principle of Consciousness or Life.

The equally venerable Alfred Russel Wallace, co-discoverer with H. Spencer and Charles Darwin, of the Law of Evolution, has, in his book, *Social Environment and Moral Progress*, written when he was nearly ninety years of age, expressly declared his faith in Spirit as governing Matter.

In *The Great Design* (1934), edited by F. Mason, with an Introduction and a concluding chapter by Sir J. A. Thomson, great biologist, fourteen renowned scientists have written short articles summing up their life's researches. *All* agree that the world is not a soulless mechanism, and is not the work of blind chance; that there is a Mind behind the veil of Matter, give it what name we will. The scientists are: R. G. Allen, Director of Lick Observatory, astronomer; J. A. Crowther, professor of physics, University of Cambridge; A. S. Eve, professor of physics, McGill University; Baillie Willis, professor of geology, Johns Hopkins

University and University of Chicago ; C. Lloyd Morgan, professor of psychology, University of Bristol ; E. W. McBride, professor of geology, Imperial College of Science, London ; C. S. Gayer, Director, Brooklyn Botanical Gardens ; H.E. Armstrong, emeritus professor of chemistry, City College, London ; M. M. Metcalf, emeritus professor of zoology, Oberlin College, and research associate, Johns Hopkins University ; Sir Oliver Lodge (born 1851), emeritus professor of physics, Oxford and Cambridge ; Sir Francis Younghusband, retired General, traveller, humanist ; D. S. Fraser-Harris, emeritus professor of physiology, Dalhousie University, Nova Scotia : Hans Driesch, Professor of Philosophy, Leipzig; and Sir J. A. Thomson, Emerities Professor of Natural History, Aberdeen.

The following extracts, of other famous living scientists' opinions are taken from J. T. Sunderland's article, "Is Modern Science outgrowing God ?", in *The Modern Review* (of Calcutta), for July, 1936.

Albert Einstein, Mathematician, world-famous originator of the Theory of Relativity : "I believe in God...who reveals Himself in the orderly harmony of the universe. I believe that Intelligence is manifested throughout all Nature. The basis of scientific work is the conviction that the world is an ordered and comprehensible entity and *not* a thing of Chance."

J.B.S. Haldane, physicist, Oxford and Birmingham Universities : "The Material world, which has been taken for a world of blind Mechanism, is in reality a Spiritual world seen very partially and imperfectly. The *only real* world is the Spiritual world...The truth is that, not Matter, not Force, not any physical thing, but Mind, personality, is the central fact of the Universe."

Sir Arthur S. Eddington, astronomer, Cambridge: "The old atheism is gone...Religion belongs to the realm of Spirit and Mind, and cannot be shaken."

Kirtley F. Mather, geologist, Harvard: "The nearest approach we have thus far made to the Ultimate, in our analysis of Matter and of Energy, indicates that the Universal Reality is Mind."

Arthur H. Compton, physicist, Chicago University: "An examination of the evidence seems to support the view that there is *no* very close correspondence between brain-activity and consciousness. It seems that our thinking is partially divorced from our brain, a conclusion which suggests, though it does not prove, the possibility of consciousness after death." (As said in a theosophical scripture, *The Mahatma Letters*, p. 267: "The flame is distinct from the log of wood which serves it temporarily as fuel.")

Robert A. Millikan, physicist, Institute of Technology, Pasadana: "God is the *Unifying Principle* of the universe. No more sublime conception has been presented to the mind of man, than that which is presented by Evolution, when it re-presents Him as revealing Himself, through countless ages, in the age-long inbreathing of life into constituent Matter, culminating in man with his Spiritual nature and all his God-like powers."

The sentences with which Sir J. A. Thomson closes the book above referred to, viz. *The Great Design*, may be quoted here: "Throughout the World of Animal Life there are expressions of something akin to the Mind in ourselves. There is, from the Amœba upwards, a stream of inner, of subjective, life; it may be only a slender rill, but sometimes it is a strong current. It includes feeling, imagining, purposing, as well as occasionally thinking. It includes the Unconscious.

Whether in the plant it dreams, or is soundly asleep, or has never awakened, who can tell us ?...The omnipresence of mind in animals gives us a fellow-feeling with them. With Emerson we see 'the worm, stirring to be a man, mount through all the spires of form.' We see the growing emancipation of mind, and this gives Evolution its purpose...In a continuous process, there can be nothing in the end which was not also present in kind in the beginning; we are led from our own mind, and the story of its enfranchisement, back and back to the Supreme Mind 'without Whom there was nothing made that was made.' Facing, every day, things in the World of Life, around which our scientific fingers will not meet, what can we do but repeat what is carved on the lintel of the Biology Buildings of one of the youngest and strongest of American Universities : 'Open Thou mine eyes that I may behold wondrous things out of Thy Law'."

The (monthly) *Indian Theosophist* (Benares), for April, 1937, quoting from the (daily) *Leader* (Allahabad) reported : "The Court of the London University, after much discussion, has recently accepted a very valuable library, of Psychical and Magical books, collected by Mr. Harry Price, from all over the world, which is almost unique, and is one of the most comprehensive of its kind. In giving it to the University, Mr. Price, long keenly interested in the subject, said he hoped to stimulate a desire on the part of University authorities for a fully equipped department of Psychical Research to be installed in the new London University Buildings...It is a fact that a number of individual scientists, in many parts of the western world, have been for years past making serious investigations of *psychic phenomena*, and that the Universities of Bonn, Leyden, Leipzig—to name only a few on the

Continent—are taking a serious interest in the subject. It is stated that in Leyden, a recognised department dealing with psychical research is already established. If the phenomena are proved to be facts—and only the ignorant will deny their occurrence—then as facts they must be studied...The new series of evening University Extension Lectures...comprise a course of ten lectures on 'The Literature of the Occult'. They start with the main principles involved in occult study, and roam over the subject from the Egyptian 'Book of the Dead,' and medieval Chinese occult lore, to Yoga and modern spiritualism."

Thus is modern Science, which was fathered in its infancy, and persecuted in its youth, by Religion, in Europe, now endeavouring to repay the kindness, after having retributed the injury, by renovating Religion in what, let us hope, will be a finer, scientific, non-superstitious form.

With the breaking of the fences between science and religion, and by fuller scientific thought, will come the breaking of the hedges between religion and religion; then it will be possible for the artificial boundaries which now separate country from country to be obliterated, and the barriers to be cast aside which divide nation from nation in head and in heart. Then may the new civilization dawn, dreamt of by the poet and the socialist, and idealized and also practicalized by Manu; then may be realized the Parliament of Man and the Federation of the World, the Organization of the whole Human Race in one vast Joint Family and Brotherhood, of which the League of Nations is the first small, step today, and very feeble, because not yet quite sincere, not yet endowed with a soul in the shape of a League of All Religions integrated with it.

THE DUTY OF EDUCATIONISTS. Educational institutions can and ought to take a leading part in the ushering in of this new proclamation of Scientific Religion and of the consequent new era of human history.

If the daily Press reports at all correctly, at least many, if not yet all, of even the statesmen and the generals who were busiest in promoting and conducting the Great War, are now feeling that war is not a glorious business at all, but, besides being horrible, is also something very useless, senseless, mean, sordid, shabby, and shameful, altogether due to the most evil motives. A Field-Marshal of England, one of the prominent figures in the Great War, said in a public speech [1]:

War as a means of settling international disputes is now more universally condemned as a failure than ever before, and every day it becomes more evident that there are really no foreign nations, but that the interests of all are so closely interwoven that if one nation suffers all will suffer to some extent. Undoubtedly, the maintenance of great and costly armaments is not the first essential measure required to prevent war. By far the most important requirement is *less Jealousy* and *less Selfishness* in the conduct of international affairs. That spirit is, we may hope, now gradually appearing,

[1] Sir William Robertson, at Leeds, on 10th Dec., 1930.

and when it is adequately forthcoming, and not till then, disarmament will follow rapidly and easily enough, and the nations will be at last on the road to peace and goodwill.

These are the words of a war-worn veteran of to-day. *Jealousy* and *Selfishness* are the important words in his speech. Kṛishṇa, who had probably more personal experience of war than even a modern Field-Marshal, said long ago that: "Lust, Hate, and Greed form the triple gateway into hell." There can be no worse hell than war.[1] In accordance with the realization

---

[1] Another soldier, Brig.-General F. P. Crozier, C.B., C.M.G., D.S.O., trying to inaugurate a movement called *The Imperial Peace Crusade*, in 1929, wrote: "The World is slowly moving towards the desired goal of substitution of methods of Peace for methods of War...The future prosperity of the World depends on the formation of a World-opinion which will enable people to form a habit of always thinking in terms of Peace instead of in terms of War. Having studied the matter very closely, it is my desire to encourage and stimulate this mode of thought. Having spent most of my life in War, or preparing for war, I desire to devote the remainder of my life to the service of Peace." Miss Muriel Lester, philanthropist worker, of London, visiting India in January, 1939, spoke to press interviewers, in Calcutta, to the effect that "the present calamitous state of the world, when all the Powers are running a mad race in armament, preparing feverishly for a far worse World-War, is due to its ignoring the fact of God; that fact of God is the foundation which kept the world together. When it

of this fact, which is indeed obvious to eyes not blinded by those same evil motives, youth movements have been afoot for sometime in many western countries. They are intended to bring up the new generation in the purer moral and spiritual atmosphere of internationalist and humanist feeling, in place of nationalism. This 'nationalism,' useful while simply defensive and self-helping, and while duly subordinated to humanism, has now degenerated into something very offensive and aggressive and other-harming. Indeed it is now nothing else than vulgar bullyism on a large scale, inherently barbarous and unregenerate, and provocative of more and more murderous conflicts. Because this fact has come home to them, it is being suggested, very rightly, very wisely, by

---

was knocked away, the peoples floundered. They recognised nothing, no power greater than themselves; there was nothing left by which to regulate their lives. They had only themselves to please. They became bored with themselves; afraid of solitude and quietness. Many became obsessed with sex; and self-indulgence made them sick. They turned to any sort of dictatorship, the stricter the better, as a relief from self. There is also the evil of the present economic system." As some western writer has said: "If God did not exist, we should have to invent Him, for our own safety." God, or belief, sincere belief, in God, is man's only saviour from mutual destruction. Fortunately Science and Philosophy are combining to show anew to man that *God does exist, within him* even more than *without*.

influential persons in that same West, that the tone and the nature of the teaching given in schools and colleges should be changed ; that war-glorification and national boasting, self-conceit, contempt and decrial of other nations, and expression of triumph over them should all be eliminated from that teaching ; that, instead, there should be diligently inculcated the more truly refined and civilized spirit of 'humanism,' which has bigun to manifest itself in the higher thought and feeling of the best and wisest persons of all nations, as a reaction against the horror of the senseless butchery of the Great War. Moral disarmament must precede physical disarmament. War can be abolished or reduced only in direct ratio to the abolition or reduction of war-mentality. This is possible only by systematic cultivation of peace-mentality and 'organising for peace.'[1] That can be done only through diligent right education, of youth as well as the general public. Right education is the foundation of all well-being, all good.

Educational institutions should not be subservient to political jingoism. Instead, they should aspire to direct politics into the path of righteousness. The scientist-priest, the custodian of the spiritual power, ought to guide, nay, to command,

[1] As regards 'Organising for Peace,' see the present writer's *Ancient Solutions of Modern Problems*, *The Science of Social Organisation*, and *Ancient vs. Modern Scientific Socialism*,(Theos: Pubg: House, Adyar, Madras).

and compel, the ruler-soldier, the repository of the temporal power, into the right uses of all civil, military, political power. All such institutions, therefore, should regard it as a sacred duty to help forward, to the best of their ability, this most desirable change of tone and teaching. Here comes the use of *well-planned religious instruction* as the *most potent instrument* for the *moral regeneration* of mankind. Humanism, inter-nationalism, inter-religionism, go together, are only aspects of each other.

Men, according to their temperaments, may, with their head, their intellect, either admire great military heroes and conquerors of history, or condemn them as predaceous marauders and butchers; probably none will offer the reverence of their heart to them. But there are few who will not offer reverent homage, with their heart, to those truest and greatest educators of mankind, by precept and by example, whom we know as the Founders of the great Religions; who have ever reproclaimed the One Eternal *Truth* of the Unity of all; who have illustrated by their lives, the *Beauty* and the *Goodness* of the concomitant Love and Sympathetic Self-sacrifice of human beings for one another.

Genuine educators, who realize that it is their high spiritual duty to be the missionaries of the Supreme Spirit on this earth; who spend themselves in constant endeavour to uplift their fellowmen to the plane of righteousness, and help to usher in anew, and maintain, the era of peace on earth and goodwill among men ; such cannot do better than give to the teaching of the Essentials of Universal Religion, by example as well as by precept, a foremost place in their courses of instruction to the younger generation, and inculcate in their hearts the habit of seeking and practising 'In Essentials, in Principles, in great things—Unity ; in non-essentials, details, small and superficial things—Liberty ; in all things—Charity'.[1]

---

[1] Viscount H. Samuel, President of the British Institute of Philosophy, in his lectures, in the Senate House, Calcutta, on 9.1.1938, and in the University Buildings, Allahabad, on 15.1.1938, said ; "Bernard Shaw has declared that Civilisation needs Religion, as a matter of life and death...We all recognise that the mind of man, in our times, is confused The present generation is beset by anxieties and perils. Our escape, our rescue, from these, depends upon our finding a new *Synthesis* between *Philosophy* and *Science* and *Religion* ...Philosophy, coming out of its phase of classicism, Science coming out of its phase of materialism, Religion freeing itself from its servitude to dogmas that are outworn, may join in constructing a spiritual and intellectual framework for the future...Hegel said that ideas had hands and feet. There should be some Philosophy which would *guide the nations*....Conflict of religions could be solved by appeal to Philosophy... The philosopher could go to the different creeds, one by one, and ask them to *emphasise the common points* and not the differences. Philosophy would help to bring the religions together. The World Fellowship of Faiths is working in this direction. Its first Conference

was held (in Chicago, in 1933, its second) in London, in 1936, then in Oxford in 1937...We must *emphasise the points of agreement between the religions*, rather than the points of difference....What the world needs today, above all, is a Synthesis of Philosophy, Science, and Religion."

Véḍ-ānṭa, 'the final knowledge', Brahma-viḍyā, 'God-Science', Āṭma-viḍyā, 'Self-knowledge', the traditional Ancient Wisdom of India and of all countries, *is* just such a Synthesis. For a very brief but comprehensive presentation of it in modern terms, the reader may, if he is interested, see the present writer's *The Science of the Self*. The present work may also be regarded as such a Synthesis, though indirectly. Its main and direct purpose is to 'emphasise the points of agreement between the religions'.

The dining-hall of the great Feeder supplies edibles suited to all tastes; sweets for those who love sweets, salts for those who like salts, acids for those who want acids. Let all satisfy their tastes, each his own. Why quarrel with another for not having the same taste as mine, when his taste does not interfere with my enjoyment of mine? But we all have to drink water and breathe air in order to dissolve and assimilate our respective special foods. Even so are the *common essentials* necessary for even the due enjoyment of the *separate non-essentials*.

THE GOLDEN MEAN BETWEEN THE TWO EXTREMES. In the minds of some individuals, among some sections of some communities, or even perhaps in a large portion of a whole nation, there may be revolt against religion. If newspaper reports be true, the governing power in Russia has set itself to abolish religion from the face of that country. But this is sometimes denied also. It was recently reported that great masses of the people are clinging to their ikons and their churches, and refuse to part with them despite grievous persecution. The latest reports are that the Soviet Government has decided to 'let alone', to 'let be'. All this only means that revolt against religion, as commonly understood and practised, may be local and temporary, due to special causes, as reaction against priestcraft and abuse, but that permanent eschewal of Religion is impossible.

The poet complained that "the world is too much with us night and day." Thoughtful Asiatics have good reason to complain that so-called religion has been interfering with our lives, private and public, far too much. But we also see that law, and science often misapplied by law, are now trespassing excessively upon our daily life and into our very homes, from birth to death ; and that almost greater horrors are being perpetrated in the names of science, art, and law, than ever were in the name of religion.

Especially is so-called 'law' much too much with us, in private as well as public life. There are far too many laws already, and more are being manufactured every day by legislators who feel they must justify their existence thus. Every human being in a 'civilized' country to-day (and the more 'civilized' it is, the more is this the case) goes about in constant fear for his pocket and his liberty, through fines and jails, if not also for his life through the gallows, as a consequence of a chance infringement of any one of a thousand local, special, general, municipal, sumptuary, social, fiscal, executive, procedural, substantive, civil, criminal, etc., laws, which envelope his life as the tentacles of an octopus its victim. And the 'public servants', ('servants' forsooth !, 'masters' and 'monarchs of all they survey' rather !), of a hundred departments of the 'benevolent' state are ever on the watch to grab a victim, with, and quite as often without, even the merest technical cause. The behaviour of the 'myrmidons of the law' is now much more arrogant and troublesome than that of the 'myrmidons of religion'. A western statistician has calculated that one out of every ten, another that one out of every seven, human beings in a country like England, passes through the clutches of one penal law or another, and pays a fine or serves a term in jail. Surely this cannot be a mark of health in a civilization. Too much religion kills God, the God in Man; enslaves him to superstition, instead of bringing him Freedom from all fear. Too much law kills peace of mind and body; enslaves man to bureaucraft and expertcraft, instead of giving him ordered liberty.

All this only means that excess of even a good thing is bad. Indeed, excess is the one sin of all sins; and the following of the middle course, the one virtue ; in all the concerns of life. The way that the Buḍḍha taught is expressly and particularly known as the *Majjhima Pati-paḍā*, the Middle Path. One of the treatises of his contemporary, Confucius, is entitled, *The Doctrine of the Mean*, (the actual compilation of which is ascribed by tradition to his grandson, Kung Kei). A Samskṛṭ proverb says :

Āshrayén maḍhyamām vṛṭṭim aṭi sarvaṭra varjayéṭ.
(Follow the middle course ; avoid extremes.)

Kṛshṇa expounds it thus :

N-āṭy-ashnaṭas ṭu yog-osṭi, na cha-ikānṭam an-ashnaṭah,
Na ch-āṭi-svapna-shīlasya, jāgraṭo n-āṭi ch-Arjuna !
Yukṭ-āhāra-vihārasya yukṭa-cheshtasya sarvaḍā,
Yukṭa-svapn-āva-boḍhasya yogo bhavaṭi ḍuhkha-hā. (*G.*)

(He who avoids extremes in feed and fast,
In sleep and waking, and in work and play,
He winneth yoga, balance, peace, and joy.)

Ṭasmāḍ viḍvān bhavaṭi n-āṭi-vāḍī. (*U.*)
Aṭi-vāḍāns-ṭiṭikshéṭa. (*M.*)

(The wise man ever studiously avoids
Extremes in speech and act, himself ; and when
Others press to extremes in heated speech,
He passes by, in quiet, answering not.)

Lao-tze says :

Continuing to fill a pail after it is full, the water will be wasted. Continuing to grind an axe after it is sharp, will wear it away. Excess of light blinds the eye. Excess of sound deafens the ear. Excess of condiments deadens the taste. He who possesses moderation is lasting and enduring. Too much is always a curse, most of all in wealth. (*T.*, *Tao Teh King.*)

Confucius says :

Commit no excess ; do nothing injurious ; there are few who will not then take you for their pattern. ...The will should not be gratified to the full ;

pleasures should not be carried to excess. (*C.*, *Shi King*; *Li-ki.*)

The Bible says:

Be not righteous over much; neither make thyself over wise...Be not over much wicked; neither be thou foolish. (*B.*, Eccles.)

Give me neither poverty nor riches; feed me with food sufficient for my wants; lest I be full and deny thee, and say, who is Jahveh?; or be poor, and steal, and profane the name of my God. (*B.*, Proverbs.)

Shintoism embodies the same principle:

It has ever insisted on *ma-gokoro*, by which it means freedom from inordinate passions...All appetites are natural, hence divine gifts; and the *temperate* enjoyment of them is a divine power. If man oversteps the limits of *moderation*, he pollutes his body and mind. To be god-like is to be natural; to be natural is to follow Nature...(i. e. to keep) within the limits set by instinct and reason...This is the fundamental conception of *Due Measure*. (*Sh.*, Inazo Nitobe, *Japan*, 321, 32).

As the teaching of Buddha is known as the *Majjhima Patipaḍā*, so the Jaina way, taught by Mahāvīra Jina, is known as the *An-ék-ānṭa-vāḍa*, the Doctrine and the Way of Non-ex-tremism.

Ékén-ākarshanṭī, shlaṭhayanṭī vasṭu-ṭaṭṭvam iṭaréṇa,
Anṭéna, jayaṭi Jainī nīṭir, manṭhāna-néṭram iva gopī.
(AMṚTA CHANḌRA SŪRI).

(E'en as the dairy-maid, pulling and slacking
The two ends of the churning-string by turns,
Churns out the golden butter from the milk,
E'en so the sage, working alternately
At both the two inevitable sides
Of every question, finds the perfect Truth.)

Muhammad enjoins the same :

Lā ṭa'ṭaḍu inn-Allāhā lā yohibbul ma'ṭaḍin. (*Q.*)
(God loves not those who go beyond due bounds.)
Khair-ul-umūré ausaṭohā. (*H.*)
(All acts are good but in the mid degree).

A Greek philosopher has said : "Strive to acquire proper balance—courage without rashness; caution without timidity; mercy without weakness; justice without vindictiveness ; silence without deceit ; shrewdness without cunning ; courtesy without fawning ; firmness without obstinacy ; deliberation without dilatoriness ; patience without carelessness ; friendship without favoritism ; ambition without selfishness."

The *Mahā-bhāraṭa*, Shānṭi-parva, ch. 70, says : "Be religious, not bigoted ; virtuous, not self-righteous ; devout, not fanatical ; gather wealth, not cruelly ; enjoy, without elation ; speak gently, not insincerely; be brave, without boasting ; be generous, not wasteful; give, not indiscriminately ; speak boldly, not harshly ; make friends, not with the ignoble; fight, not with friends ; seek information, not from the unreliable ; serve your interest, without hurting others'; ask advice, not from the unwise ; praise virtues, not your own ; trust, but not the evil ; punish, not thoughtlessly ; love and guard the spouse, without jealousy; be refined, but not supercilious ; feed delicately, not unwholesomely ; enjoy conjugal pleasure, not overmuch ; honor the worthy, not proudly ; serve, without deceit ; propitiate, without fawning ; be clever, not out of season ; be angry, not without strong cause ; be gentle, not to the mischievous ; worship Deity, without display."

Every question has two inevitable sides. Wisdom consists in reconciling the two, by just compromise between them, in accord with the requirements of time-place-circumstance.

THE DUALITY OF GOD'S NATURE. There are these two sides to every question, because:

Sarvam ḍvam-ḍva-mayam jagaṭ.
Śarvāṇi cha ḍvam-ḍvāni. (*U.*)
Ḍvam-ḍvair-ayojayaṭ ch-émāh
Sukha-ḍuhkhā-ḍibhih prajāh. (*M.*)
(The world is made of pairs of opposites;
All things occur in pairs of two and two;
The Maker fused Duality in all;
Sorrow and Joy foremost of all these pairs.)
Kḥalaqna min kulle shayīn zaujain. (*Q.*)
(I, the Supreme and Universal Self,
Have made all things in pairs of spouse and spouse).
Male and female created He them. (*B.*)
Ishq-bāzī mī kunaḍ bā kḥwésh-ṭan;
Shuḍ bahānā ḍar-miyāné marḍ o zan. (*S.*)
(To play at Love the better with Him-Self
He put on separate masks of man and wife.)
Sa Ékākī n-āramaṭa; Sa Aṭmānam ḍvé-ḍhā-pāṭayaṭ; Paṭish cha Paṭni ch-ābhavaṭ; āpayaṭo vai ṭāv-anyo-nyasya kāmān sarvān. (*U.*)
(Lonely He felt, and all unsatisfied;
So into Two He did divide Him-Self,
To have a Play-mate; Man and Wife He was;
All wishes of each other they fulfil.)

Chiṭṭa-naḍī nām-obhayaṭo vāhinī; vahaṭi kalyāṇāya, vahaṭi cha pāpāya. (*Yoga-bhāshya*).

(The mind-stream in two rival currents flows,
Heading to virtue and to vice it goes.)
Bahr-e-ṭalkḥ o bahr-e-shīrīn ham-enān,
Ḍarmiyān 'shān barzakḥ-é lā-yubghiyān. (*S.*)

Qāyaman bil qisṭ. (*H.*)
(Oceans of Sweet and Bitter surge abreast ;
Between them rests the razor-line of Rest.
The Being of Godhead rests amidst the Pairs,
Maintaining even justice over all.)

Yaṭhā shīṭ-oshṇayor maḍhyé
n-aiv-aushṇyam na cha shīṭaṭā,
Taṭhā sṭhiṭam paḍam shānṭam,
Maḍhyé vai sukha-duhkhayoh. (*Mbh.*)

(There is a middle point, nor hot nor cold,
On the two sides of which spread cold and heat ;
So, of the Middle point, where there is Peace,
On the two sides, surge seas of Pain and Joy.)

Ichchhā-ḍvésha-samuṭṭhéna
ḍvam-ḍva-mohéna, Bhāraṭa !,
Sarva-bhūṭāni sam-moham
sargé yānṭi, paran-ṭapa !.

Yéshām ṭv-anṭa-gaṭam pāpam,
janānām puṇya-karmaṇām,
Ṭé ḍvam-ḍva-moha-nir-mukṭā
bhajanṭé Mām ḍṛdha-vraṭāh.

Nir-māna-mohāh, jiṭa-sanga-ḍoshāh,
aḍhy-āṭma-niṭyāh, vini-vṛṭṭa-kāmāh,
Ḍvam-ḍvair-vimukṭāh sukha-ḍuhkha-sañjñair-
Gachchhanṭy-amūdhāh paḍam Avyayam Ṭaṭ. (*G.*)

(They only who love Me with steadfast mind
Can cross this glamour of Duality ;
And they who rise above this Dualness
They only know Me as the One Sole Truth.
Crossing beyond this ever-battling Pair
Of Joy and Sorrow, mind now Proud now Low,
Elation and Depression, they attain
The state of Peace that knows not any change.)

Nir-ḍvam-ḍvo niṭya-saṭṭva-sṭho
nir-yoga-kshéma-Aṭma-vān ;
Jñéyah sa niṭya-sannyāsī
yo na ḍvéshti na kānkshaṭi ;
Nir-ḍvam-ḍvo hi, mahā-bāho !,
sukham banḍhāṭ pra-muchyaté.
Samah siddhā-va-siḍḍhau cha,
ḍvam-ḍvā-ṭīṭo vi-maṭsarah,
Yaḍ-ṛchchhā-lābha-san-ṭushtah,
kṛṭv-āpi na ni-baḍhyaṭé. (*G.*)

(Who is content with what lot brings to him,
Who is not envious, who has passed the Pairs,
Who in success and failure stands the same,
His acts, being only duties, bind him not.
Renunciation endless is his, who
Neither desireth aught nor hateth aught.
He who flings off the ever-wrestling Twins,
With ease he breaketh all his bonds of soul.
The Duads that take birth with Love-and-Hate
Intoxicate with these, all beings pass
Into the whirlings of this wheeling world.
They who with Virtues balance up their Vice,
They leave them Both behind, and pass beyond
Into the restful realm of deathless Peace.
They who have cast aside all Pride and Fear,
Conquered lusts of the flesh, its Loves and Hates,
And tied their hearts to Me, the Self of All,
They thrust aside the glamourous warring Pairs,
Whose primal name and form is Pleasure-Pain ;
They come to Me, the Universal.Self,
And enter into My eternal Peace).

To *realise in mind*, that the very nature of the world-process, of all life, of separate individuality, is *necessarily*, unavoidably, inevitably, a mixture of joy and sorrow, good and evil, that we *cannot* have gains without pains, nor pains without gains, so long as we feel identified with separate bodies; and, thus realising, to experience and bear both joys and sorrows with 'equable' mind, with 'peace' at the heart; and to go on discharging duties without craving for selfish recompense; this is to transcend the Duality, "to fling off the Twins," and the three g u ṇ a - s, triple functions of the mind, cognition, desire, action, in which the primal Duality is inherent and which in turn are inherent in that Duality.[1]

Yasmin vi-ruḍḍha-gaṭayo hy-anisham paṭanṭi
Viḍyā-ḍayo vi-viḍha-shakṭaya ānu-pūrvyā
...Ṭasmai sam-un-naḍḍha vi-ruḍḍha-shakṭayé
Namah Parasmai Purushāya Véḍhasé. (*Bḥ.*)
(In whom opposéd Forces ever swirl
Against each other, whirling the whole world
Unceasingly, Him we adore in heart.)
Prakṛṭih ubhaya-koti-sparshīnī;
Purushah madhyasṭhah. (*Bhāva-Prakāsha*).

[1] An English poet has caught the idea well:

Joy and woe are woven fine,
A clothing for the soul divine;
Under every grief and pine
Runs a joy with silken twine,
It is right it should be so;
Man was made for joy and woe;
And when this we rightly know,
Safely through the world we go.

(WILLIAM BLAKE)

(Nature doth ever swing between Extremes,
Holding the Balance, stands midway, Her God.)[1]

Zaraṭhusṭra says :

Aṭ ṭā maīnyū po-uruyé Yā yémā khafenā asravāṭém manahi chā vachahi chā shya-oṭhano-ī. Hī vahyo akém chā, āos-chā huḍā-onghaho. Érésh vīshyāṭā no īṭ duzhaḍā-ongho.

Aṭ chā hyaṭ ṭā hém maīnyū jasa-éṭém paurvīm ḍazḍé ga-ém chā ajyā-īṭīm chā. Yaṭha chā anghaṭ apémém anghush achishṭo drégvaṭām aṭ ashā-ūné vahishṭém mano.

Hamém ṭaṭ vahishṭā-chīṭ yé ūshurayé syas-chīṭ dahmahyā, kshayāṅs, Mazhaḍā Ahurā !, yéhyā mā ā-ithīsh chīṭ ḍva-éṭhā ; hyaṭa a-énanghé ḍrégvaṭo é-é-ānū īshyéng anghahyā. (*Z.*, Gāthā, 30. 3, 4 ; 32. 16).[2]

---

[1] "The two inscriptions on the Delphic Temple, (in Greece)—'Nothing too much' and 'Know thyself'—were complementary. If you have too much of anything, you cannot know yourself....The moral equipoise—the Golden Mean—is the attainment of god-head. Freedom and restraint, the 'Do-s' and the 'Don't-s' in the moral world, act like the centripetal and centrifugal forces in the physical, to keep a balance :" Inazo Nitobe, *Ibid.*

[2] The Samskṛṭ form of these, in prose order, is :

Aṭha yau paurvyau [purāṇau] manyū yamau svaphaṇau [sva-ṭanṭrau iva] ashrūyéṭām ṭau manasi cha vachasi cha syoṭhané [sāḍhané, karmaṇi] cha [sṭah]. Ṭau vahīyas [varīyas, puṇyam] cha, agham [pāpam] cha. Anayoh su-ḍhāh [su-ḍhīh] ṛsh [ṛṭam, saṭ, saṭyam] vīkshaṭī, no iṭ ḍur-ḍhāh [ḍur-ḍhīh].

Aṭha cha yaḍā ṭau manyū paurvīm samajaséṭām (sam-asajaṭām or sam-ajasaṭam, taḍā) gayam cha.

(These two Primordial Principles in One,
Of Light and Darkness, Good and Ill, that seem
Apart from one another, yet are bound
Inseparably together, each to each—
In Thought, in Word, in Action, everywhere
Are they in operation; and the wise
Walk on the side of Light, while the unwise
Follow the other until they grow wise.
These ancient Two, in mutual wrestle-play
Give birth to Twin-Desires, high and low,
That shape as Hate-Mentality in some,
In others as the Better Mind of Love.
O Mighty Lord of Wisdom, Mazaḍā!,
Supreme, Infinite, Universal mind!,
Ahūrā!, thou that givest Life to all!,
Grant me the power to control this mind,
This Lower Mind of mine, this egoism,
And put an end to all Duality,
And gain the reign of One—as is desired

---

ajyāṭim cha (? cf. rayim cha prāṇam cha, vāk cha prāṇah cha) ḍaḍhé (ḍaḍhaṭé). Yaṭhā (yaḍā) cha asoh apamam (? asu-bhṛṭsu, jīvéshu up-aitām, ṭaḍā ṭau) ḍrug-vaṭām (ḍhrug-vaṭām, ḍroha-vaṭām) achisṭam (an-ishtam), ashāvaṭī (ashā-vaṭām, ? shubh-āshā-vaṭām, ushā-vaṭām, jyoṭish-maṭām) vahisṭam (vasishtham, varishṭhām) manah āsaṭ (āsṭām).

Hé Kshayan Ahura Mazḍa!, (? A-kshaya, asūn prāṇān rāti ḍaḍāṭi īṭī Asurah; Mahaṭ, Buḍḍhi-ṭaṭṭvam, Bṛhaṭ, ṭam Mahānṭam ḍaḍhāṭi, iṭi Mahā-ḍhāh), samam ṭaṭ chiṭ (syāṭ) Vahisṭam, yat swasya ḍambhasya (aham-kārasya) īshwarah chiṭ (syam), yaṭra mé ḍvaiṭasya aṭih (iṭih, anṭah, syāṭ); yaṭ énasā ḍruga-vanṭah (api) asunā (prāṇéna, hṛḍayéna) evam éva ishyanṭi (ichchhanṭi).

Unconsciously, by e'en the graceless ones,
The evil sinners, in their heart of hearts.)[1]

The fact of this all-permeating Duality is signified pre-eminently by the very Names, in opposed Pairs, given to God in Islām as well as Vaiḍika Ḍharma. He is Al-Awwal and Al-Ākḫir, Āḍi and Anṭa, First and Last, Alpha and Omega; He is Al-Bāṭin and Az-Zāhir, Avyakṭa and Vyakṭa, Inner and Outer, the Un-manifest and the Manifest, the Uni-versal Un-Conscious, Sub-Conscious, Supra-Conscious, and the Individual and Particular Conscious, the seed of the tree and the tree of the seed; He is Al-Bāḍī and Al-Jāmi, Srashtā and Samharṭā, the Spreader-out and the Gatherer-in; He is Al-Muhiyy and Al-Mumīṭ, Bhava and Hara, the Giver of Life and the Giver of Death; Al-Muzil and Al-Hāḍī, Māyī and Tāraka, the Mis-Leader, Mis-Di-Rector, Tempter, Degrader, Tester, and also the Guide, Leader, Teacher, Rector, True-Di-Rector, Cor-Rector; Al-Qahhār and Ar-Razzāq, Ruḍra and Shiva, the Angry Overwhelmer and

---

[1] All the *Gāṭhā* texts have been taken from the very painstaking and illuminative edition of the *Gāṭhas*, with Samskṛt, English, Gujrāṭi translations and notes, by J. M. Chatterjee and A. N. Bilimoriya; (Cherag Office, Navsari; pub: 1932).

[2] The words within square brackets, in the Samskṛṭ version above, have been added by the present writer, as suggestions; the English translation is a free version of that by J. M. Chatterji, but care has been taken to preserve the same sense.

the Auspicious Nourisher; Al-Ghazzāb and Al-Ghaffār, Yama and Kshamā-vān, the Punisher and the Forgiver; Al-Jabbār and Al-Karīm, Ghora and Ḍayālu, the Severe and the Compassionate; Al-Jalīl and Al-Jamīl, Shāsṭā, Prabhu, Ishvara, and Maḍhu, Maḍhura, Sunḍara, Kānṭa, the Lord, Ordainer, Sovereign, Awesome, Terrible, and the Beautiful, the Beloved, the Friend of All.

The vibhūṭis, glories, guṇas, attributes, *sifāṭ*, of the Supreme are all in pairs of opposites, classifiable under the two main categories of aishvarya and māḍhurya, *jalālī* and *jamālī*, lordliness and sweetness, awesomeness and beauty, majesty and mercy, sovereignty and parentity.[1]

---

[1] In the Jewish Kabala (Qabbālah), the attributes of the Supreme Being, which correspond to the types or aspects or kinds of creation, are called the ten Sephiroth, the emanations of Adam Kadmon (Āḍam Qaḍīm), the Ancient Man, the Eternal and Infinite Macrocosm. The ten are: The Crown, Wisdom, Prudence, Magnificence, Severity, Beauty, Victory, Glory, Foundation, Empire. Wisdom is called Jeh or Jāh; Prudence, Jehovah; Severity, Elohīm; Magnificence, El; Victory and Glory, Sabaoth; Empire or Dominion, Adonai. Other names and aspects are mentioned, as, Sephira, the Androgyne (Arḍha-nārī-shvara, in Skt.); Hakama, Wisdom; Bīnah, Intelligence; Hesed, Mercy; Geburah or Eloha, Justice; Tiphereth, Beauty; Netzah, Firmness; Hod, Splendor; Jesod, Foundation. Hakama, Hesed,

Confucius says:

Yang and Yin, male and female, strong and weak, rigid and tender, heaven and earth, sun and

---

Netzah are the three male Sephiroth, known as the Pillar of Mercy; Bīnah, Geburah, Hod, are feminine, and named the Pillar of Judgment; the four Sephiroth of the Centre, Kether, Tiphereth, Jesod, and Malkuth, are called the Middle Pillar. (H. P. Blavatsky, *Isis Unveiled*, II, 205, 213, 215).

From the Zoroastrian scriptures, especially the Ahura Mazaḍa Yasht, the learned have made up lists of twenty, fifty-three, eighty-one, and one hundred and one, names of Ahurā Mazaḍā, which is the most famous name; as Allah is the most famous of the hundred names of God given in the Qurān. Some of the more eminent names are: Frakshṭya, the Sustainer, (cf. Vedic Su-pṛksh); Avi-ṭanya, All-pervading, (*V.* Abhi-ṭanya); Vīspa-vohu, All-Good; Asha-vahishṭa, Supreme Truth; Khraṭu, Supreme Knowledge, (*V.* Kraṭu, Persian Khiraḍ); Chishṭi, Supreme Wisdom or Consciousness, (*V.* Chiṭ); Spāna, Supreme Holiness; Sévishṭa, Almighty; Avanémna, Invincible; Vīspa-hishas, All-seeing; Ḍāṭā, Creator (Skt., Ḍhāṭā); Ṭhrāṭā, Preserver (Skt., Ṭrāṭā); Ḍūrae-ḍarshṭā, Far-seeing; Spashṭā, Watcher; Pāṭā, Saviour; Znāṭā, All-knowing; Isé-Kshathroyoṭéma, Omnipotent Ruler; Vīspa-van, Conqueror of All; Vīspa-ṭash, Architect of the Universe; Ahurā, Lord of Life (*V.* Asu-rah); Mazaḍā, Lord of the Great Creation, Lord of Ideation and Wisdom (*V.* Mahaṭ-ḍhā); and so on. These Zoroastrian names, corresponding Samskṛṭ words, and English explanations, have been kindly supplied to me by Dr. Irach J. S. Taraporevala, Principal of the M. F. Cama Athorvan Institute, Anḍheri (near Bombay).

moon, thunder and lightning, wind and rain, cold and warmth, good and evil, high and low, righteousness and humaneness,...the interplay of Opposite Principles constitutes the universe[1]...The final principle of an undivided One is Tai Chi, 'the great ridge-beam; out of it develope Yang and Yin.'[2]

Ri is reason or law, Ki is matter; the two give rise to all phenomena, physical and spiritual...There are two phases of Ki—Yin and Yo (Chinese Yang). The latter is light, positive, active, male; the former dark, negative, passive, female. All phenomena owe their origin to the action, reaction, interaction, and counter-action of these forces...Sometimes Yin is spoken of as water, Yo as fire;"[3] in Skt., agnī-shomīyam jagaṭ, 'the world is made of fire and water, heat and moisture.'

Laotze says:

Tao is divided into a *principal Pair of Opposites*, Yang and Yin. Yang is warmth, light, masculinity; also heaven. Yin is cold, darkness, femininity; also earth. From the Yang force arises *Schen*, the celestial

---

All these names, that have been given to the Supreme Spirit, the Mystery which runs the Universe, by the various scriptures, are mentioned here to draw attention to the identity of thought of all the religions, as to the attributes of that Mystery, the Eternal, Infinite, Universal Principle of all Life and Consciousness, give it what name we may.

[1] Suzuki, *History of Chinese Philosophy*, 15, 16, (pub: 1914).

[2] Wilhelm and Jung, *The Secret of the Golden Flower, a Chinese Book of Life* (1931), 12, 13.

[3] Inazo Nitobe, *Ibid.*, 345.

portion of the human soul; from the Yin force arises Kwei or Poh, the earthly part. As a micro-cosm, man is in some degree a *reconciler* of the Pairs of Opposites. Heaven, earth, man" (God-Nature-Man, Īshvara-Jada-Jīva) "form the three chief elements of the world, the *San-tsai*" (Samsāra, World-process).[1]

The Greek philosopher Heraclitus says:

God is Day-Night, Winter-Summer, Love-Hate, War-Peace, Repletion-Want, Heat-Cold, Death-Life, Youth-Age, Waking-Sleep, Creation-Destruction.

Har kamālé rā zawālé, wa har zawālé rā kamālé.
(Persian proverb).

(Every virtue has its vice;
Every vice its virtue, too.)

Subūṭ-i-shay ba ziḍḍ-i-shay. (Persian philosophical maxim).

(Each thing is proven by its opposite.)

Omnis determinatio est negatio.

(All determination is negation of the opposite.)

---

[1] C. G. Jung, *Psychological Types*, 267, quotes this from Lao-tse's *Tao-te-king*. He also quotes Goethe's *Faust*, to illustrate the familiar idea of man's dual nature, his two selves, higher and lower, altruist and egoist:

Two souls, alas!, within my bosom dwell;
The one doth hanker after love's delights,
And clings with clutching organs to the world;
The other, mightily, from earthly dust
Would mount on high to the ancestral fields.

Many other Eastern and Western poets have expressed the idea more powerfully. The *Upanishaḍs* speak of ḍvā suparṇā..., '*two* birds dwelling in this *tree* of life,' the human body.

Sarv-ārambhā hi ḍoshéṇa
dhūmén-āgnir-iv-āvṛṭāh. (*G.*)
N-āṭy-anṭam guṇa-vaṭ kin-chiṭ,
n-āṭy-anṭam ḍosha-vaṭ ṭaṭhā. (*Mbh.*)

(As fire doth carry smoke within itself,
So every action carries a defect;
Naught is there wholly good or wholly bad.)

Life is a perpetual choice between endless pairs of 'rival ills.' Right choice, which will, in any given time, place, and circumstance, bring most happiness and least pain, which will reconcile antagonisms, is the choice inspired by the Spirit which stands permanently in the Middle between the two extremes of Nature; which impartially 'tastes and tests all things, and holds fast that which is good,' most good, *viz.*, It-Self; which always avoids excess, excessive attachments, by loves or by hates, to the objects of the senses, things other than the Universal Self. Such seems to be the teaching of all religions as well as all sciences.[1]

THE NEED FOR SCIENTIFIC RELIGION. Religion is as necessary as science. As said before,[2] so

[1] If the reader cares to pursue the question, *Why* and *How* Duality, Trinity, etc., arise within the One; Multiplicity in Unity; Change within the Changeless; he may look into the present writer's *The Science of Peace*, or, for briefer statement, into the second and third chapters of *The Science of the Self*. Endeavour is made there to expound the ancient teachings, on the subject, in the terms of modern western philosophy and psychology, as far as possible.

[2] See pp. 16, 34, *supra*.

long as human beings suffer from and fear pain and death, and look before and after, and think about such things, so long will the human heart and head demand, and will not be denied, the solace that only religion can give. When anguish wrings the heart, then we overwhelmingly realize that it shall not profit a man anything if he gain the whole world but lose his own soul. If they are not given true and scientific religion by the philanthropic and the wise, men will inevitably swallow the false and superstitious religion given to them by priestcraft.

Only those who cannot 'look before and after', cannot think, at all, about such things, as the animals, have no craving for religion. Also those who have thought very deeply and very far; examined all the before and all the after; seen all there is to see; found the Eternal Now and the Infinite Here, the Ever-present and the Omni-present, between the Before and the After; found the secret in their own Infinite Self—they also no longer crave religion. They have achieved the purpose of Religion. The perfection of Religion can alone abolish the need for it. At the present stage of human evolution, such perfected souls are not many. The vast mass of mankind feel that need acutely, intensely, perpetually. That is why Religion survives. If it decays and dies in one form, it forthwith takes a new birth.

Yas-ṭu mūdha-ṭamo loké,
yash-cha buḍḍhéh param gaṭah,

Ḍvā-vimau sukham éḍhéṭé,
klishyaṭ-yanṭariṭo janah.

(He who is wholly dull, without a mind;
He who has gone beyond the reach of mind,
And found that which gives being to the mind,
And is established in the Mid twixt Pairs;
These two are well; those restless, 'tween, are ill.)

As a western writer has observed, "mankind has one innate, irrepressible, craving, that *must* be satisfied....the yearning after the proof of immortality."

The end of Religion is to transcend Religion. When the end has been found, the means are dropped:

Nis-ṭrai-guṇyé paṭhi vicharaṭo
ko viḍhih ko nishéḍhah. (SHANKAR-ĀCHĀRYA).
(The soul which finds the path that goes beyond
The 'three' that bind, knowledge-desire-and-act,
It hath no further need for 'Do-s' and 'Don't-s').
Rab ras Rab shuḍ, ṭamām Rab rā Rab nīsṭ;
Har jā khurshéḍ asṭ, āṅ-jā shab nīsṭ.
Sūfī shuḍ nīsṭ, nīsṭ rā mazhab nīsṭ;
Bā Yār raṣīḍah ḍīgar maṭlab nīsṭ. (*S.*)
(Who findeth God becometh wholly God;
And unto God there is no other God.
Where the sun shines, can there be any night?
The 'knower' is *non-est*; his lower self,
Of low desires, has been effacéd now;
To such 'non-est', Religion is 'non-est.'
He who hath found the Loved One, hath no more
Craving or need for any object left.)

If it be true, as it obviously is true, that the human heart has an ineradicable conviction that there *is* something beyond this life, and yearns to know about it and its relation with this life; if it be true, as it evidently is true, that science is for life, and not life for science; then surely man cannot and will not accept as final, the view that the present conflict between science and religion is incurable. Such a view means that Truth is self-contradictory, that science is not consistent in all its parts. But this cannot be. It must not be. Truth, Science, V é ḍ a, *Haqīqaṭ, Mā'rifaṭ*, Gnosis, J ñ ā n a, (all meaning the same thing), must be all-inclusive, all-explaining, all-reconciling. Otherwise, it is not Truth. This common conviction shows forth from behind the most hostile-seeming words.

The man of modern style piques himself on eating, drinking, bathing, sleeping, dressing, housing, travelling, doing all things in short, in the name of science and law. The man of older style has been trying to do all these same things in the name of God and religion.[1] Yet the two modes are not antagonistic, not even really different. 'In the name of God' means, among other things, 'In the name of God's Nature'; and, therefore, of the *laws* of that Nature in *all* its departments, physical as well as superphysical or psychical; whereas 'in the name of science and law' means, at present, 'in the name of the laws of only the physical department of Nature as recognised and utilised in man-made law'. Science, in the limited sense of physical science, is imperfect religion, is one part of religion. Religion, in the full sense, is larger science, is the whole of science. We owe debts and duties not only to our own and our fellow-creatures' physical bodies, but also to the 'souls', the 'superphysical bodies'. The rules of religion, *i. e.*, of the larger science, enable us, at least ought to enable us, to discharge all these wider debts and duties. They should also secure to us, all sinless joys which are rightly due to us.

Yaṭo Abh-yuḍaya-Nis-shréyasa-siḍḍhih, sa Ḍharmah.
(*Vaishéshika Sūṭra*).

(Religion, Ḍharma, is that which brings Joy,
In the Life Here, and the Hereafter, too.)

Religion has been described as 'the command or revelation of God'. This only means, in other words, 'the laws of God's Nature,' as revealed to us by the labours, intellectual, intuitional, inspirational, of the seers and scientists of all religions and all nations. The obeying of these should obviously bring happiness in this life as well as the life beyond this life.

THE UNIVERSAL RELIGION—THAT IN WHICH THERE MAY BE UNIVERSAL AGREEMENT. We have heard of the three R's long enough. This fourth R', of genuine Universal Religion, is more important than them all, and ought to be added to them everywhere, in every school and college. But it has to be carefully discovered and ascertained first. It behoves all sincere educators to help in this work by applying the scientific method of ascertaining 'agreements amidst differences.' What are the elements common to the great living religions? What are the agreements between them?

We may also call that method, in terms of the democracy in vogue at present, the method of majority-rule. Those truths which all the great living religions vote for—they should be prominently taught to the younger generation.

IMPERATIVE DUTY TO TEACH SUCH UNIVERSAL RELIGION. Some people, bewildered by the rival bigotries, fanatic cries, and bitter hostilities, indulged in by misguided persons, in the name of religion, ask: What right have we to impose upon our children, such evil things, such religions as create enmity between man and man, darken and make foolish the minds, and blind the eyes, of all? If religion were dispensable, the question might be answered readily in the negative: We have no right. But it is not dispensable, as indicated before.[1] We have therefore to answer the question by saying that we have as much right, nay, as much imperative *duty*, to teach religion, as we have to teach arithmetic, geography, history, science. Nay, more right and duty; for these other things, however desirable, however useful, are not so indispensable for comfort of soul. We teach these other things to our children for their good, out of our love for them. And we try to teach what we have ascertained, by our best lights, to be good and true and useful for them. If we make mistakes, it is because

[1]See pp. 16, 34, 51, *supra*.

we are human and liable to err. Because food now and then disagrees, we cannot stop all eating. We must make only greater efforts to ensure its healthiness of quality and quantity. So in Religion we must make the greatest efforts to ascertain what is most indubitable, most in accord with the best science, and, more than all else, is most approved and agreed in by all concerned, and most likely to promote good-will and active sympathy between all human beings. This is the very and only way to allay those dazing and amazing cries and bigotries and hostilities.

Let us examine the matter in another fashion. It is indisputable that the vast majority of human beings are born into their religions, inherit them, and cling to them exactly in the same way and for the same reasons as they do to inherited property. If a new-born Muslim child and a new-born Hinḍū child were exchanged and brought up, the one in Hinḍū, the other in Muslim, surroundings, they would grow up and feel and think and behave as Hinḍū and as Muslim respectively, and not as Muslim and Hinḍū. The same would be the case if the landholder's baby were exchanged with a banker's or a peasant's. At the same time, it is equally indisputable that anyone and everyone can withdraw his faith from any religion and put it in any other, whenever he likes, can put off one and put on another at will. Yet also, the vast majority of human beings crave, indeed everyone in the secret depths of his heart somewhere yearns, for religion in its deepest sense—of contact with, assurance of, support by, refuge and rest in, the Immortal. All this clearly signifies that Religion is necessary to man; that no *particular form* of religion is indispensable; that there are two alternatives open to us, either to reject all religions or to accept all religions; that both are impracticable; and that, therefore, the only practical, as also the best, most satisfying, and wise course, is to sift out the elements of *Essential Religion* from the non-essential (though, for their time, place, and circumstances, useful) forms, of all the great particular religions extant, and feed the younger generation with those vital grains, instructing them that the husks are useful only for preserving and storing the grains in, and not for eating and assimilating.

Some others hold that the work that Religion did, or was supposed to do, in the past, and did badly, if at all, has been taken up and is now being done by Philosophy, Science, Law, and also Art, in three or four separate departments of life; and, therefore, no Religion, old, reformed, or new, is needed any longer. The reply to this is that man is not a trinity only, in three separate parts, but is essentially a Unity; something is needed to coordinate, to unify, to organise, to articulate with each other, Philosophy, Science, Law. That is Religion, '*re*' and '*legere*', to bind together anew, again, the hearts of all to each other and *back* again to God, from Whom the temptations of the earth cause those hearts to stray away. Vedānta-Ṭasawwuf-Gnosis is all three; it is a Religion which includes the essentials of Philosophy, Science, Art; or, if we prefer it so, a Philosophy which synthesises Religion, Science, Art. We should call to mind again, here, that the latest speculation of the most renowned scientists tends to reduce all matter to atoms and super-atoms, param-āṇus, electrons, protons, neutrons, plutons, positrons, etc.; these to electrical energy; that, finally, to Mind-force.

The most passionate advocate of the utmost possible 'liberty' for the younger generation, who urges that it should be allowed to grow up according to its own 'free-will', its own 'inner promptings, inclinations, likes and dislikes', still unavoidably, helplessly, actively, *teaches something* to the young; and that something is necessarily what *he* thinks best and most useful for them to learn! The Bolshevik Communists of Russia are teaching 'Communism' to their young, most intensively; the Fascists of Italy, 'Fascism'; the Democratists of Britain, U.S.A., France, 'Democratism'. Each, in words, professes 'liberty' for youth; but largely relies for its success, on imbuing youth with its own ideas! The element of truth, in the plea that 'the younger generation should be allowed to grow up, in liberty, freely, according to its own inner promptings, inclinations, likes and dislikes'—the truth in this, and a *very* important truth it is, is that, *each* individual of the new generation, should be not only allowed, but carefully educated and trained, for the *vocation* which is most in accord with its particular temperament, its likes and dislikes, its tastes and interests.[1] But over and above this *special* education, there should always be, for *all* the individuals of the new generation, the *general essential* cultural education in the four R's. Of course, after the new generation has attained its majority, and stands on its mental as well as physical feet, it will be at liberty to change, modify, discard, forget, replace with something else, any or every part, essential or non-essential, general or special, which it has been taught during its minority. As a fact, we see hundreds of persons changing their religions everyday; as they change their 'minds' and 'parties' and 'schools of thought', in politics, history, science, philosophy, art, etc. Indeed, the changes have become so numerous and so frequent that we have a maddening welter of 'isms' today. The reason is that, in all these departments of thought and life, clear and definite, deliberate, knowledge of the *essentials*, of the psychological and philosophical basic *principles*, the fundamental facts, laws, needs of *human nature*, has been largely lost sight of. To revive memory of the Essentials is the only cure everywhere.

AGREEMENT OF RELIGIONS. It has been said before that the new proclamation, of Universal Religion has to be made on 'democratic' lines,

---

[1] Fuller exposition of this subject is attempted in *The Science of Social Organisation*, by the present writer.

i. e., the lines of 'majority-rule,' speaking broadly and generally, (though not quite fully and with scientific exactitude, which will be attempted later). On these lines, those truths and practices which receive, not only the greatest number of, but unanimous, votes from the living religions, those beliefs and observances on which all are agreed, should obviously be regarded as constituting Universal Religion. That there is agreement between the great religions, that all teach the same essential truths, their promulgators themselves are all agreed. We have their clear assurances on this point.

The *Upanishaṭs* say:

Gavām anḙka-varṇānām
  kshīrasy-āsṭy-ḙka-varṇaṭā;
Kshīra-vaṭ pashyaṭḙ Jñānam,
  linginas ṭu gavām yaṭhā. (*U.*)
(Cows are of many different colours, but
The milk of all is of one color, white;
So the proclaimers who proclaim the Truth
Use many varying forms to put it in,
But yet the Truth enclosed in all is One.)
Jāma-é saḍ-rang z-āñ khumm-é safā
Sāḍa-o yak-rang gashṭah chūñ ziyā. (*S.*)
(Jesus put many cloths of many hues
Into one jar. and out of it they came
With all their hues washed off, all clean and white,
As seven-colored rays merge in white light.)

Kṛshṇa says, and not once but twice:

Mama varṭm-ānu-varṭanṭé
  manushyāh, Pārṭha!, sarvashah. (*G.*)

(To but One Goal are marching everywhere,
All human beings, though they may seem to walk
On paths divergent; and that Goal is I,
The Universal Self, Self-Consciousness.)

This is "the one far-off," yet also always very near, "divine event to which the whole creation moves" perpetually. Zoroaster teaches:

And we worship the former religions of the world devoted to righteousness. (*Z.*, Yasna, XVI. 3).

Aṭ ṭoī anghén Saoshyanṭo ḍasyūnam. (Gāṭhā, 48. 12)
(Even the ḍasyus, tribes uncivilised,
Will have Saoshyanṭas, apostles, sent
To give them teaching and look after them).

Kung-fu-tse (Confucius) was a younger contemporary of Lao-tse. Buḍḍha lived and taught in India, the younger sister of China, in those same days. China has adopted Buddha together with Lao-tse and Confucius as her trinity of great Teachers. Confucius says:

I only hand on; I cannot create new things.

Buḍḍha and Jina speak of past and future Buḍḍhas (i. e., the Enlightened Ones) and Ṭīrṭhan-karas (i. e. 'the makers of the fords or bridges' by which men may cross safely to salvation) who reveal the same fundamental truths, again and again, for the benefit of humanity, only revivifying, confirming, enforcing them by the fire and fervour of their lives.

Is there anything whereof it may be said, See, this is new? It hath been already of old time, which was before us...There is no new thing under the sun. (*B.*, Eccles.)

Christ (i e., 'the anointed with Divine Wisdom') says :

I come not to destroy the law or the prophets, but to fulfil them. (*B.*)

The great teachers confirm, at most supplement, not supplant, one another.

Kṛshṇa says that the teaching he is giving to Arjuna was given by Vivasvān to Manu, by Manu to Ikshvāku, and then by many Ṛshis, age after age. All is always present in the Memory of God, the Omni-scient, Omni-potent, Omni-present Universal Self, the One Principle of all Life and Consciousness.

Muhammad (the Paighạm-bar, the Rasūl, *i.e.*, the 'message-bearer', 'sent' by the Spirit) says:

Innahū la-fī zubūr il-awwalīn ;
Le kullé qaumin hād̤ ;
In min ummaṭīn illā kḥalā fī hā nazīr.
Lā nofarriqo bainā ahaḍim min rusuleh.
Wa mā arsalnā min qablikā mir-rasūlin lllā nūhi ilaihé annahū, lā ilāhā illā Anā, fa'-buḍūn. (*Q.*)

(This that I am now uttering unto you,
The Holy Qurān—it is to be found
Within the ancient Seers' writings too ;
For Teachers have been sent to every race.
Of human beings no community
Is left without a warner and a guide.
And aught of difference we do not make—
For disagreement there is none 'twixt them—
Between these Prophets. All that have been sent,

Have been so sent but One Truth to proclaim—
"I, verily the I Al(l)-One, am God,
There is no other God than I, [the Self,
The Universal all-pervading Self],
And I alone should be adored by all".)

The Qurān makes this further quite unmistakeable:

Wa mā arsalnā mir-rasūlin bi-lessāni qaumehī.

Wa kazālika auhainā ilaika Qurānan A'rabi-yal leṭunzera umm-al-qorā wa man haulahā......Wa lau ja-a'lnaho Qurānan a'jamiyal la qālū lau la fussilaṭ āyāṭohu. (Q.)

(Teachers are sent to each race that they may
Teach it in its own tongue, so there may be
No doubt as to the meaning in its mind.
An Arabic Qurān is thus revealed,
That Macca and the cities round may learn
With ease the Truth put in the words they know.
For had we made them in a foreign tongue
They surely would have made objection thus—
"Why have not these revealings been made clear?")

The obvious significance of this remarkable text is that the essentials are common to all religions: that Truth is universal and not the monopoly of any race or teacher; that non-essentials vary with time, place, and circumstance; that the same fundamental truths have been revealed by God in different scriptures, in different languages, through different persons born in different nations.

And the Prophet adds the positive counsel:

Kul ṭā'lau elā kalemaṭin sawāim bain-anā wa baina-kum. (Q.)

(Let all of us ascend towards, and meet
Together on, the common ground of those
High truths and principles which we all hold.)

(Verily, all who faithfully believe
In God, and Day of Judgment, and do good,
Whoe'er they be, Jews, Christians, Sabians,
They shall have their reward from the Lord God.
There is no fear for them, nor shall they grieve.)
(*Q.*, ii, 62)

Wa ṭasému ba hubba Ilāhī jamīyan,
wa lā ṭafarraqu. (Q).

(Cling, all, to the strong rope of Love Divine
—Love for each other, and of the One God—
And do not think of separation ever.)

So too does the Veḍa enjoin on all:

Samānī va ākūṭih, samānā hṛḍayāni vah,
Samānam asṭu vo mano, yaṭhā vah
su-sahā-saṭi.

Samānī prapā, saha vo anna-bhāgah,
Samāné yokṭré saha vo yunajmi,
Samyancho Agnim saparyaṭa,
Arā nābhim iv-ābhiṭah.
San-gachchhaḍhvam, sam-vaḍaḍhvam,
Sam vo manāmsi jānaṭām. (*V.*).

(Your heart, mind, object—may all these be One,
So shall you prosper, all, and live in peace;
In common be your food and drink and work;
God harnesses you all to the same yoke;
The sacrificial Fire of Spirit tend
Ye all with one intent, as spokes the nave.
Walk ye together on the Path of Life,
And speak ye all with voice unanimous,
And may your minds all know the Self-Same
Truth.)

Seek to be in harmony with all your neighbours; live in amity with your brethren. (*C.*, *Shu King.*)

Be ye all like-minded, compassionate, loving as brethren, tender-hearted, humble-minded, not rendering evil for evil, or reviling for reviling, but contrariwise blessing...Be of one mind, live in peace. (*B.*, Corinthians.) God is no respecter of persons. But in every nation he that feareth Him, and worketh righteousness, is accepted with Him. (*B.*, Acts.) There is neither Jew nor Greek, there is neither bond nor free, there is neither male nor female; for ye are all one in Christ Jesus. (*B.*, Galatians.)

Christianity, through the mouth of Justin the Martyr, declares:

> Whatever things have been rightly said, among all men, are the property of us Christians.[1]

Faqaṭ ṭafāwaṭ hai nāma hī kā
Daṛ asl sab éka hī haiṅ, yāro!
Jo āb-i-sāfi ke mauj méṅ hai
Usī kā jalwā habāb mén hai.

(But the names differ, beloved!
All in Truth are only one!
In the sea-wave and the bubble
Shines the lustre of one Sun!)
Rūh bā a'ql o i'lm ḍānaḍ zīsṭ,
Rūh rā Ṭāzī wa Ṭūrkī n-īsṭ. (*S.*, AṬṬĀR).
Rūh bā a'ql-asṭ o bā i'lmasṭ yār,
Rūh rā bā (Hinḍu o Muslim) che kār. (*S.*, RŪMI)
(By loving wisdom doth the soul know life.
What has it got to do with senseless strife
Of Hinḍū, Muslim, Christian, Arab, Turk?)

---

[1]Quoted by J. E. Carpenter, *The Place of Christianity in the Religions of the World.*

The Vedic scriptures repeatedly reiterate that the soul has no creed, caste, color, race, or sex.

Indeed only the names, the words, differ. The thing meant is the same. Allāh means God, Akbar means greatest; Īshvara or Ḍéva means God, Parama or Mahā means greatest; Allāh-Akbar literally means Param-Éshwara or Mahā-Ḍéva. The Zoroastrian Ahura-Mazḍāo (equivalent to the Samskṛṭ Asura-Mahaḍ-ḍhā), also means the 'wisest' and the 'greatest' God. Rahīm and Shiva both mean the (passively) Bene-volent and Merciful; Rahmān and Shaṅkara both mean the (actively) Bene-ficent. Ḍāsa and Abḍ both mean the servant; Qāḍir and Bhagavān both mean Him who is possessed of *Quḍraṭ*, Bhaga, Aishvarya, Might, Lord-liness; Bhagavān Dās is absolutely the same as Abḍul-Qāḍir, the Servant of God the Almighty.

Such is a preliminary illustration of the fact that differences between religions are differences only of words, names, languages; or of non-essential superficial forms; and sometimes of emphasis, on this aspect of the Truth, or of Virtue, or of Duty, rather than another; never, of Essential Ideas. The Founders of Religions, *i. e.*, the Re-proclaimers, in new forms, of the One Universal Religion, have laid greater stress, now on this, now on that other, aspect of the One Religion, as needed by the special times, places, circumstances, in which they lived. The essential Religion, vidyā, *irfān*, Wisdom, is eternal, universal, im-personal, all-personal, unchanging, in *substance*—like geometry ; the ṭ a p a s , 'fire and fervour', 'blazing heart-energy', 'passionate compassion', 'ascetic glow and inspiration', of the 'magnetic personality' of each Re-proclaimer, is new, is his fresh 'personal' contribution, and gives a new *form* to the eternal *substance*.

THE JOY OF AGREEMENT. To some minds at least, the work of pursuing and discovering and clasping to their heart such agreements is a great joy, and the opposite process of dwelling upon the differences alone, a sheer pain.

> Khush-ṭar āṅ bāshaḍ ke sirré ḍil-barāṅ
> Gufṭa āyaḍ ḍar haḍīse ḍīgarāṅ. (*S.*)
> (It is a great delight to find
> One's own thought in another mind—
> The secret of the Lovely One,
> Disclosed in others' narration,
> Giving Him meed of highest praise
> In delicately worded ways).

> Iṭi nānā pra-sankhyānam
> ṭaṭṭvānām kavibhih kṛṭam ;
> Sarvam nyāyyam yukṭi-maṭ-ṭvāt,
> viḍushām kim asāmpraṭam. (*Bh.*)

> (In varying ways the sages have described
> The same unvarying and essential truths ;
> There is no real conflict twixt them all ;
> The knowers know the way to reconcile.)

The most beautiful face cannot see and appreciate its own beauty until it looks into a mirror. As the Sūfis say, God had to look into the mirror of Non-being, *a'ḍam*, a-s a ṭ, s h ū n y a, in order to behold and realise the infinitely varied beauties that lay hidden in Him-Self. *A'yniyaṭ-i-haqīqī*, Ā ṭ m-ā ḍ v a i ṭ a-s a ṭ ṭ ā, the Truth of the Self's Oneness, Ownness, is realised only by means of *Ghairiyaṭ-i-éṭabārī*, I ṭ a r-ā b h ā s a, Ḍ v a i t a-m i ṭ h y ā ṭ v a, the Falsehood, the Illusion, of hypothetical, suppositional, Otherness which has no *real* existence.

Ḍar āyīna gar-che khuḍ-numāī bāshaḍ,
Paiwasṭa ze khwésh-ṭan juḍāi bāshaḍ,
Khuḍ rā ba libās-i-ghair ḍīḍan a'jab asṭ,
K-īn b-ul-a'jabī kār-i-Khuḍāī bāshaḍ. (*S*).

(The vacant looking-glass doth show the Self,
Yet in that Self there is an Otherness !
Marvel ! In mask of Other to see Self ;
This shining miracle of miracles
Than God's Own Self None-Other can achieve !).

The Play, Krīdā, *Laīb* and *Lahw*, of God is an Inter-play of love, *Ishq-bāzī*, Rāsa-līlā, between God's Self and His reflected image, an-Other, the same yet not the same, indeed reversed. We cannot realise the full significance of our own thoughts until we see them reflected in another mind. That is why speakers wish to be heard, authors wish to be read, artists wish to be appreciated, by others. To cognise an idea through the veil of one language only, is to see it with one eye only, as it were, from one standpoint, in one perspective only. To see it through another language also, is to see it with both eyes, from many angles of vision, through a stereoscope. A new fullness of meaning breaks out from the two sets of words, and stands forth in clear relief, almost independent of all words. Communion between two friends brought up in two different cultures, but able to realise the underlying identity of the spirit of refinement and enrichment of life, is more interesting than that between friends brought up in the same culture. It has the charm of a more diverse-sided novelty, of travel in a new country, full of friendly hospitality, with scenes, foods, drinks, dresses, manners, flowers, fragrances, as beautiful, as tasteful, as delicious, as gracious, as those of one's own, yet also different. That is why God's L-one-ly Self, to vary the mono-tony, broke forth into infinite multi-tony.

To be able to recognise the Dearest of Friends only if He is clothed in one dress and no other, is not to know the Friend at all, but only the Dress. Beloved! I will dress you in many dresses; in the kimono of Japan, the mandarin coat of China, in the ava-sīya and uṭṭarīya, the golden shāta-pata, of India, in the shawls of Kashmere, in the *abā* and *choghā* of Persia, in the *burnous* of Arabia, in the multiform hats, blouses, jackets, coats, petticoats, gowns, shirts, shorts, trousers, kilts, of the several countries of Europe, in the plumes of the Amer-indian, the toga of the departed Roman, the mail of the medieval knight of Asia and Europe! Beloved! will you not be able to recognise your own True Self, your own Beautiful Face, your own Gracious Goodness, in all these disguises, when a mirror is placed before you each time your garments are changed? Beloved! you must recognise your own voice and your own meaning, surely, whether you speak in Samskṛṭ, or Arabic, or Hebrew, or Greek, or Latin, or Chinese, or Japanese, or Zend, or Pāli, or Prākṛṭ, or Gurmukhi, or any of the thousands of languages you yourself are always inventing, and forgetting from time to time, in order to fashion newer others for your Infinite Play and Pas-time!

Underneath, soaked through and through, permeating, pervading, holding fast together, all Multitude, remains ever the Unity. This is the One Fact to be remembered always.

Pots, pans, jugs, jars, tumblers, decanters, kettles are many and of many shapes; the water in them all is one. Lamps and lanterns are many and of many shapes; the light is one. Wood, coal, oil, fuels are many and of many shapes; the fire is one. Living organisms are many and of many shapes; the life in all is one. Religions are many and of many forms and formalities; the Universal Religion is One.

"In China, when strangers meet, it is the custom for each to ask his neighbour, 'To what sublime religion do you belong?' The first is perhaps a Confucian, the second a Taoist, the third a disciple of the Buḍḍha. Each then begins a panegyric on the religion *not* his own; after which they repeat in chorus, 'Religions are many, reason is one, we are all brothers'."[1] The critic of one temperament will exclaim, "Hypocrites !" ; of another, may burst out, "Old fogeys, marionettes, idiots !" ; of a third, unfortunately rarer perhaps, to-day, would say, "Just, wise, and courteous !". Experts of different sciences, of different arts, wedded and loyal and faithful each to his own favorite, can yet admire, nay, reverence, if they are real and thoughtful experts and not bumptious quacks, the same common factor of genius, skill, unremitting application, manifesting in all.

The saintly statesman, Prince Regent Shotoku of Japan, "one of the best known figures in Japanese history, for whom, when he died in 621 A. D., the old wept as if they had lost a child, and the young as if they had lost a parent," reconciled the indigenous religion Shintoism, and the newly come Buddhism and Confucianism, when conflict between the priests threatened to fill the land with dissensions, in this wise: "Shinto is the source and root of the Way, and, shot up with the sky and the earth, teaches man the primal Way; Classicism (Confucianism) is the branch and foliage of the Way, and, bursting forth with man, it teaches him the Middle Way; Buddhism is the flower and fruit of the Way, and, appearing after man's mental powers matured, teaches him the final Way. Hence, to

[1] J. Estlin Carpenter, *The Place of Christianity in the Religions of the World*, p. 60.

love one in preference to another, only shows man's selfish passion....The introduction of another foreign system of faith will add a new cubit to the stature of the Nation's mind, without depriving its predecessors of their authority; indeed each new creed enlightens the old."[1]

The poet has well said:

Mockery is the fume of little hearts,
And noble manners come from noble minds.

And again,

Let knowledge grow from more to more
But more of reverence in us dwell,
For fear divine philosophy
Should shoot beyond her mark and be
Procuress to the lords of hell. (TENNYSON.)

"'The teaching of sects,' said Lu Shun Yan, a distinguished Buddhist scholar, 'is not different. The large-hearted man regards them as embodying the same truths. The narrow-minded man observes only their differences'....The wisdom in all ages, entering into holy souls, maketh them friends of God, and prophets".[2]

Ṭafraqā ḍar nafs-i-haiwānī buwaḍ;
Rūh-i-wāhiḍ rūh-i-insāni buwaḍ. (*S.*)

(Separatism, difference, exclusiveness,
Characterise at once the animal mind:
The soul of Oneness is the soul of man,
The soul of all-inclusive Sympathy,

---

[1] Dr. Inazo Nitobe, *Japan*, 61, 370 (pub: 1931, The Modern World Series); and *Enc. Brit.*, 14th edn., art: Japan, 930c.

[2] J.E. Carpenter, *ibid*, 66, 67.

Of Unity and of non-separateness.)

The Arabic-Persian word for man, ***insān***, (from *ins*, *uns*, sympathy), means etymologically 'the friend of all,' 'the lover of his kind,' the 'gentle-man'. So the Samskṛṭ word ā r y a (from ṛ, to go) means 'the person to whom others, when trouble befalls them, go for relief,' 'he who is approached for help'.

Sarva-bhūṭéshu yen-aikam
bhāvam avyayam īkshaṭé,
A-vi-bhakṭam vi-bhakṭéshu
ṭaj-jñānam sāṭṭvikam smṛṭam.
Pṛṭhakṭvéna ṭu yaj-jñānam
nānā-bhāvān pṛṭhag-viḍhān,
Vèṭṭi sarvéshu bhūṭéshu
ṭaj-jñānam viḍḍhi rājasam. (*G.*)
Nivāraṇ-ārṭham arṭīnām arṭum yogyo bhavéṭ ṭu yah,
Aryaṭé saṭaṭam ch-ārṭaih, sa Ārya iṭi kaṭhyaṭé.
(Through all forms whatsoever runs One Life,
Immortal, making indivisble
All those that seem divided endlessly—
The higher, *sāṭṭvik*' wisdom seeth thus.
But that which takes the separate-seeming many
As many only, separate for ever—
That sight is of the lower *rājas*' mind.)
(He who is worthy to go to, for help,
For persons in distress, and unto whom
Such ever do resort—true Ārya, he).

THE ESSENTIAL AND THE NON-ESSENTIAL. That all the creeds and practices, all the parts, of any religion, are not equally important, not essential, is patent. All religions themselves make distinctions between the obligatory and the optional, the *mohkamāṭ* and the *mushābihāṭ*, the niṭya and the kāmya. That duty varies with time, place, and circumstance, is also plain, and is plainly stated too in all religions.

Ḍésha-kāla-nimiṭṭānām
bheḍair-ḍharmo vibhiḍyaté;
Anyo ḍharmah sama-sṭhasya
vishama-sṭhasya ch-āparah. (*Mbh.*)

(Changes of time and place and circumstance
Always cause changes in the duties too.
The law for men is one in time of peace
And quite another in calamity.)

Anyé Kṛṭa-yugé ḍharmās-Ṭréṭāyām Ḍvāparé-paré,
Anyé Kali-yugé nrīṇām, yuga-hrāsā-nu-rūpaṭah. (*M.*)

(As men change character and ways of life,
So change the laws their elders make for them;
Both vary, side by side, from age to age.
One law is for the Golden Age of Truth,
And ready 'doing' of loved Elders' words;
Another for the Age when Sin is born;
Yet other for the Age when equal Strife
Is waged twixt Vice and Virtue; and a fourth
Is needed for the Time when Discord reigns).

To everything there is a season, and a time for every purpose under heaven...a time to be born and a time to die; to plant, and to pluck up; to kill, and to heal; to break down, and to build up; to weep, and to laugh; to keep silence, and to speak; to love, and to hate; a time of war, and a time of peace. (*B.*, Eccles.)

Inna-kum fī zamānin man ṭaraka min-kum
a'shra mā omera behī halaka; summā yāṭī
zamānun man ā'mela min-hum be-a'shra
mā omera behi naja. (*H.*, Ṭirmizī.)

(Ye now are in an age in which if ye

Shirk even one-tenth of what is ordained
Ye will be ruined. After this will come
A time when he who will do e'en one-tenth
Of what is ordered now will be redeemed.)

The greatest of all Sūfī writers, Maulānā Jalāl-uḍ-ḍīn Rūmī, has used strong language in distinguishing between the essentials and the non-essentials, pradhāna and gauṇa amsha, *asl* and *furū'*, of religion. Describing the purpose of his work, the famous *Masnawī*, which is accepted by the Muslim world generally as next to the Qurān itself in holiness, he says:

Man ze Qur-āṅ maghz rā bar-ḍāshṭam,
Usṭukhāṅ rā bar sagāṇ anḍākhṭam. (*S.*)
(The marrow from the Qur-ān have I drawn
And the dry bones unto the dogs have cast.)

As regards the profound respect in which the *Masnawī* is held among the learned divines of Islām, a verse is current among them:

Man che goyam wasf-i-āṅ ā'lī janāb,
N-īst paigham-bar walé ḍaraḍ kiṭāb.
(How may we well describe this great soul's greatness!
He is not called a Messenger from God,
Yet in his hands he holds a Holy Script.)

Jesus has a saying, similar to Rūmi's, about "casting pearls" before those as yet unable to appreciate them. Kṛshṇa condemns in very plain terms those who are always harping upon outer ritual and neglecting inner wisdom.

Yām imām pushpiṭām vācham
pra-vaḍanṭ-ya-vipash-chiṭah,

Véḍa-vāḍa-raṭāh, Pārṭha !,
n-ānyaḍ-asṭ-īṭi vāḍinah. (G.)
(They who are always praising Vedic rites
And ceremonies, saying there' s naught else
Worth thinking of, are very foolish men.)

Even the benevolent Masters have, now and then, to use strong, almost harsh, language, when it is necessary to shake very heavy inertia !

From another standpoint, for the purpose of gradually leading on the child-soul from the in-essential to the Essential, from the symbol to the meaning, we are advised to "Give milk to babes and meat to the strong", (*B.*). Even Moses and Muhammad are scarcely able to look on the *Nūr-i-Qāhir*, 'the blinding effulgence of the Face of God wholly unveiled.' Even Arjuna trembles when his eyes are opened for the briefest instant to 'That Glory greater than a thousand suns' (*Gīṭā*), the Glory of the Universal Self, on beholding which, all small individual self-hood and self-ishness shrivel into nothingness. Therefore,

Apsu ḍévā manushyāṇām,
ḍivi ḍévā manishinām,
Bālānām kāshtha-loshtéshu,
buḍhasy-Āṭmani Ḍévaṭā. (*Purāṇa.*)

(Child-souls may find their gods in wood and stone ;
More grown-up souls in sacred lakes and streams ;
The older-minded in the orbs of space;
The wise see Him in all-pervading Self.)

We speak wisdom among the perfect or initiated, not the wisdom of this world, nor of the archons of this world, but divine wisdom in a mystery, secret—which none of the archons of this world know. (*B.*, Paul).

Jesus says:

To you it is given to know the mysteries of the Kingdom of Heaven, but to them it is not given. For whosoever hath (the key) to him shall be given, and he shall have more abundance, but whosoever hath not (and is likely to misuse), from him shall be taken away even that (which) he hath. (*B.*)[1]

THE NATURE OF RELIGION. But in order to make our investigation, very brief and merely suggestive as it must be here, somewhat systema-

[1] In the minor Eleusinian Mysteries of Greece, a sow was washed to typify the purification of the neophyte, as her return to the mire indicated the superficial nature of the work that had been accomplished: H. P. Blavatsky, *Isis Unveiled*, II, 493. See the articles 'Mystery' and 'Eleusis' in the *Enc. Brit.* The rites and ceremonies of the Vedic y a j ñ a may be regarded as an earlier form of such 'mystery-initiations'.

These minor and major Eleusinian Mysteries, into which only the select were initiated, are constantly referred to in Greek literature. All the great dead religions had their 'mysteries' and their ceremonial initiations of the worthy into them. They were dramatic ceremonies, symbolising the psychical, moral, and also physical trials and tests of the progress of the soul from stage to stage in real evolution, through which the person under initiation was passed. The intention seems to have been to prepare for the real life's trials and tests. Sometimes, this preparation was so severe that nothing in real life could be more so; as, today, in the case of the physical 'endurance' and other tests and rehearsals of athletes, racers, aviators, swimmers, film-thrillers.

tic, we should try first to ascertain, even though only rapidly, the nature of what is called Religion.

The word 'religion,' which is in use in the Christian world, is derived from Latin words (*re* and *legere*, or *ligare*) which mean 'to bind back' ; that is to say, it means that which binds human beings to each other in the bonds of love and sympathy and mutual rights and duties; binds them all also to God; endeavours to lead them back to that World-Soul, from Whom their lower nature makes them stray away again and yet again, in too eager following of the objects of the senses; and keeps tbeir minds fixed on that Supreme Principle of Unity amidst the press of all their daily work, in order to enable them to do that work with proper balance, righteously. The power to bind together the hearts of men to one another, by the common bond of God, the All-pervading Self, is the power to give birth to, and to nourish and maintain, a high civilization. It is noteworthy that every historic civilisation has had, and has today, its specific religion, its worshipped ideal. Indeed, the birth of a new religion, i.e., a fresh re-viv-al of the *spirit* of religion, whence united co-operation, has invariably preceded and given birth to a new civilisation.

The corresponding Veḍic word is Ḍharma, from Ḍhṛ, to hold and bind together, which has exactly the same significance.

The 'holding together' of human beings in a 'society' is not possible without perpetual 'give-and-take', 'right-and-duty', incessant little or great acts of *self-sacrifice*, yajña, *qurbānī*. The self-assertion of any one individual is not possible without corresponding self-denial on the part of some other or others. And *vice versa*. More; each individual, to secure selfish self-expression, must impose upon himself some unselfish self-repression, self-restraint, self-denial, also. Egoism and altruism make each other possible. Each disappears without the other. Such is the Law of Duality, which pervades the Multiplicity of the world-process, in subordination to the supreme Law of Unity. Hence, we have the Law of Sacrifice, yajña, *qurbānī*, of one's own smaller self's lower desires, in ever-growing degree, from birth to death of body.

Sah yajñāh prajāh sṛshtvā
pur-ovācha Prajā-paṭih—
Anéna pra-savishyaḍhvam,
ésha vo-sṭ-vishta-kāma-ḍhuk. (*G.*).

(By sacrifice of His own Perfect Being,
His Else-denying 'Singleness of Self,'
The Lord created countless Progeny
Of 'Many selves,' together with the Law
Of Sacrifice, and gave them this command:
"By Mutual Sacrifice, by Mutual Help,
Shall ye all grow, prosper, and multiply;
This is the cow will milk you all rich things.")

The self-sacrifice of each *smaller* self for the sake of the *larger* Self, which is *felt* to be embodied in Society as a *whole*; and the corresponding self-sacrifice of that *larger* Self or Society for the sake of each *smaller* self, which is *felt* to be integral *part* of the *whole*—this mutual self-sacrifice, though internally motived by all-wise Philanthropic Love, has yet to be externally regulated by all-loving Wisdom; through Laws which lay down rights-and-duties, which bind rights with duties, and all human beings with the bonds of both. The *feeling*, and the implicit and explicit *recognition*, of the omni-presence of the larger Self; and of one's particular smaller self being a part of, and subordinate to, It, as a cell or a tissue in an organism; this feeling, this recognition, may be said to be the quintessence of 'religion' or 'religiousness'. The conscious *conviction* that every 'finite' is created, ideated, maintained, 'held together', and periodically manifested and in-drawn, by the Infinite; this, and corresponding *philanthropic desire* and *action*, may be said to make up the whole of Religion.[1]

The word *Islām* has a profound and noble meaning which is, indeed, by itself, the very essence of religion. Derived from *salm*, peace, shānṭi, it means the 'peaceful acceptance' of God; the calm resignation and 'surrender', pra-ṇi-ḍhāna, pra-paṭṭi, of the small self to the Great Self; the letting out of egoism and the letting in of Universalism; na-mas-kāra, na-mama, kinṭu ṭava īhā, "Thy will be done,

[1]The idea is more fully expounded in the other works of the present writer, *Ancient vs. Modern Scientific Socialism*, *The Science of the Self*, *The Science of Social Organisation*, and *The Principles of Sanāṭana Vaiḍika Dharma, or The Science of Religion.*

Lord !, not mine" ; whence only the mind, the heart, at peace with itself and with all the world.

The significance of 'Ḍharma' is the same; for what else can 'hold together' living beings than mutual 'du(e)-ti-fulness', mutual rights-and-duties, through common 'submission' to the Will of the Divine Self ? The very important question arises here at once: How may human beings ascertain what the Will of the Divine Self is, generally, and, even more, in particular cases. The answer, in brief, is: (a) The Universal Essential Religion, Scientific Religion, Spiritual Science, tells us what that Will is, generally ; (b) *particularly*, *good-and-wise* laws, defining rights-and-duties, made by *good-and-wise* legislators, who know, love, fear God, i. e., the Supreme Universal Self of All ; who therefore disinterestedly wish well to all just interests of all sections, classes, vocations ; who, as far as is humanly possible, are 'near God', are 'Sons of God', are embodiments of the Higher, Better, Nobler, Wiser, Philanthropic Self of the People, and who are sincerely trusted, honored, and duly selected and elected by the People to make laws ;—such laws will represent the Divine Will, as nearly as possible for human beings. It is obvious that only good-and-wise laws can promote the general welfare ; and that such laws can be made by only *good-and-wise* persons. Legislation and administration by *such* only can establish 'the kingdom of heaven on earth.[1]

[1] For fuller exposition, the reader may see Ch. VII

The essence of Christianity is the same as that of Ḍharma. 'Christos' means the 'anointed,' the 'bathed in Divine Wisdom,' whence only the replacement of the small self by the Great Self.

So 'Vaiḍika-Ḍharma' etymologically means the Religion of *Knowledge*; 'Sanāṭana-Ḍharma' means the Nature, the Way, of the *Eternal* Self; 'Mānava-Ḍharma', the Religion of *Humanity* and *Humanism*; 'Bauḍḍha-Ḍharma,' the Religion of Buḍḍhi, *Wisdom*; 'Ārya-Ḍharma', the Religion of the Good. The other Islāmic name for religion is *Mazhab*, which means the 'Way,' *i. e.*, the Way of Righteousness, the Path to God and Happiness.

'Ḍharma' is also a *triple* Way, sub-divided into three intertwining Mārgas or Paths, of Knowledge, of Devotion, of Works. Buḍḍhism, as we have already seen, also describes itself as the Middle Path, and, again, in greater detail, as the Ashtānga Ārya Mārga, 'the Noble Eightfold Path.' But, always the One and only Path is the Path of Non-Egoism, of Unselfishness, *Ṭark-i-khuḍī*, Asmiṭā-ṭyāga, whence True Knowledge, Right Love, Righteous Action; and the only Light on the Path is the Light within, "the Light that lighteth every one," the Light of the One Self.

Jyoṭir-Āṭmani, n-ānyaṭra,
sarva-janṭushu ṭaṭ samam. (*Bh.*)

---

of *The Science of the Self*, and the other works of the present writer, referred to there.

Christ has said: "I am (i. e., is) the Way, the Truth, and the Life." To know that (the) I (is) am all selves is to know the Truth. To love all selves as my-Self is the right Life. To do unto all selves as to my-Self is the righteous Way.

Shinto, (the word is said to be Chinese), the ancient religion of Japan, now practically merged into Buḍḍhism, is *Kāmi-no-michi,* (in the Japanese language), 'the Way of the Spirits,' 'the Divine Way,' 'the Way of God'. *Kāmi* are the indwelling spirits—all sparks of the One Spirit. The name of the religion given by Lao-tse to China is *Ṭāo*, which, again, means the 'Way'.[1]

[1] "The idea of the middle path, that lies between the opposites, is found in China, in the form of Tao... The meanings of Tao are (1) Way, (2) Method, (3) Principle, (4) Nature-force or Life-force, (5) the Regulated processes of Nature, (6) the Idea of the World, (7) the Primal Cause of all phenomena, (8) the Right, (9) the Good, (10) the Eternal Moral Law. Some even translate Tao as God...Lao-tse, (born 604 B. C.), in *Tao-te-king,* says: Tao seems to have existed before God...It is indefinable, perfected,...formless, al-one, unchanging, inexhaustible, beyond reasoning, unseizable, nameless, existing and non-existing also....Dwelling without desire, one perceiveth its essence; clinging to desire, one seeth only its outer form...The kinship with the basic Brahmanic ideas is unmistakeable—which does not necessarily imply direct contact...The primordial image underlying both the Ṛṭa-Brahma-Āṭmā and Tao conceptions is as universal as man,

In every case what is meant is the Way which leads to happiness, to peace, to freedom from bondage to Egoism and thence to doubts; freedom from fear of pain and death; by leading to the God within, *i. e.*, to the realisation of the identity of the individual with the Universal Self, whence illumination and assurance of Immortality. We have seen before that so long as men fear pain and death, so long will they necessarily crave religion. It is the climax of religion itself which, by proving that all our

---

appearing in every age, among all peoples, whether as Energy-concept, or Soul-force, or however else it may be designated...The knowledge of Tao has therefore the same redeeming ('freedom'-giving, 'salvation'-bringing, 'moksha-bestowing) and uplifting effect as the 'knowing' of Brahman...The complete one (The perfected 'son of God', *kāmil*, m u k ṭ a) is beyond intimacy or estrangement, profit or injury, honor or disgrace...Being one with Tao resembles the spiritual condition of a child; (compare the verses of the *Gīṭā*, to the *same* effect):" C. G. Jung, *Psychological Types*, 264-266. What else can the Essential Concept be than 'as universal as man', when it is the Essence of Man him-Self, is his very Self! What in the Veḍa-mantras is named Saṭya and Ṛṭa, is mostly called Brahma and Ḍharma in the Upanishaḍs and Smṛṭis, or Purusha and Prakṛṭi or Sva-bhāva in some of the Ḍarshanas. The words Brahma and Ḍharma include all the meanings, ascribed above to Tāo; it will be readily noticed that they are all closely allied as aspects of the same thing, and shade off into one another.

pain is self-inflicted, (since it comes only as consequence of our own selfish desire), and by annihilating the fear of annihilation, can abolish the need for religion. When man has found God, his own Eternal and Infinite Self, and has thrown away his smaller self, he has himself become the Truth, the Life, the Way, and no longer needs any other way to God.

Whichever track we try, we always come round to the one and only way—of merging the small self in the Eternal Self.

THE THREE ASPECTS OF RELIGION. We may distinguish three main parts or aspects in all the great religions. In the Vaiḍika Ḍharma, they are expressly mentioned: the Jñāna-Mārga, the Bhakṭi-mārga, the Karma-mārga. Generally corresponding to these are, the *Haqīqaṭ* or *Aqāyaḍ*, the *Ṭarīqaṭ* or *Ibāḍāṭ*, and the *Sharīyaṭ* or *Mā'milāṭ*, of Islām. *Gnosis*, *Pietas*, and *Energeia*; the (a) Way of Knowledge, Illumination, Gnosticism, (b)the Way of Devotion,

---

Dr. Michiji Ishikāwā, in his paper on 'Shinto Theology', (*The Religions of the World*, I, 371-377; pub: by the Ramakrishna Mission Institute of Culture, Calcutta, 1938), says: "Shinto is the All-pervading Universal Way...According to Shinto mythology Ame-no-mi-na-ka-nushi (Heaven-centre-ruling Deity) is the *Absolute Universal Self*, from which both Kankai (visible) and Yukai (invisible) worlds have come into existence through the activities of the three deities of Musubi, Principle of Creation, Completion, and the Controlling Bond between; (cf., Brahma-Shiva-Vishṇu)."

Pietism, Mysticism, (c) the Way of Rites and Ceremonies and Works of self-denying Charity, Activism, Energism, Practicalism—these seem to be similarly distinguished in Christian theology, and to have the same significance. In the Buḍḍhist Eightfold Path, the three most important, under which the other five may be classified, are Right Knowledge, Right Desire, and Right Action—Samyak-ḍṛshti, Samyak-sankalpa, and Samyak-vyāyāma; which are the same things as the three Vaiḍika Mārgas. The Jaina teaching is the same:

Samyag-ḍarshana-jñāna-chāriṭryāṇi Moksha-mārgah.
(UMĀ-SWĀMI, *Taṭṭv-ārṭha Sūṭra*)
(The way to Liberty is Right Desire,
Right Knowledge, and Right Conduct–thtee in one).

Ḍarshana here stands for ichchhā or bhakṭi, and chāriṭrya for kriyā or karma.

I am the (*a*) Truth, (*b*) the Life, (*c*) the Way. (*B.*)
Sharīa'ṭ rā shaār-e-kh̤wésh sāzaḍ,
Ṭarīqaṭ rā wisār-e-kh̤wésh sāzaḍ,
Haqiqaṭ khuḍ maqām-e-zāṭ-e-Ū ḍāṅ,
Buwaḍ ḍāyam miyān-e-kufr-o-īmāṅ.
(*S.*, Gulshan-i-Rāz.)
(His outer garment woven is of Works;
His inner, of Devotion's ecstasy;
Him-Self, Knowledge of Truth, that wears the two
Standing between belief and unbelief.)
Yogās-ṭrayo mayā prokṭāh,
Jñānam, Bhakṭish-cha, Karma cha. (*Bh.*)
(Three Yoga-ways have I declared to men—
Of Knowledge, of Devotion, of right Deed).

Vāg-ḍando-(a)ṭha mano-ḍandah
kāyā-ḍandas-ṭaṭha-iva cha,
Yasya-iṭé nihiṭā buḍḍhau
ṭri-ḍandī-ṭi sa uchyaṭé. (*M.*)
Kāyéna samvaro sāḍhu, sāḍhu vāchāya samvaro,
Manasā samvaro sāḍhu, sāḍhu sabbaṭṭha samvaro,
Sabbaṭṭha sambuṭo bhikkhū sabba-dukkhā
pamuchchaṭi. (*Ḍh.*)
(Good is it to control the thought, the speech,
The act ; the wise man who will thus restrain
All these, he will, for sure, cast of all pain ;
He is the true thrice-self-ruled san-nyāsī.)

In these three words, knowledge—desire—action, j ñ ā n a—i c h c h h ā—k r i y ā, or *ilm,—khwāhish—fa'l*, or *a'rf—irāḍa—a'mal*, we find indicated, in terms of psychological science, the reason why all religions have this threefold nature. The human mind has three aspects. Human life is one incessant round of conscious or subconscious knowings, wishings, and doings. Only if we know rightly, wish rightly, and act rightly, can we secure happiness here and hereafter, for ourselves and our fellow-creatures. Religions teach us what are the most important items under each of these three heads, and how we may secure them.

A triad almost more frequently met with, is that of right thoughts-words-deeds ; m a n o - v ā k - k a r m a ; *khayāl-qaul-fa'l* ; *humaṭa-hukhṭa-huvarshṭa*, (*Z.*)[1] Here, 'words' stands for 'desire'.

---

[1] Humaṭa is, in Skṭ, su-maṭam, right-thought, well-

Manasy-ékam, vachasy-ékam,
karmaṇy-ékam mah-āṭmanām,
Manasy-anyaḍ, vachasy-anyaḍ,
karmaṇy-anyaḍ ḍur-āṭmanām. (*Mbh.*)

(In the great soul, thought, word, and deed are one;
In th' evil, all are diff'rent, each from each.)

Civilizations are also, correspondingly, made up of (a) bodies of knowledge, science, learning, (b) of special tastes, aspirations, ideals, ruling passions, and (3) of characteristic ways of living, behaviour, forms of enterprise. The larger, the more varied, the more carefully ascertained the knowledge; the nobler, the more aesthetic, artistic, philanthropic, the ideals, tastes, aspirations, emotions; the more refined the ways of living and the more humanitarian and wide-reaching the enterprises and activities—the greater and higher the civilization.

Thus does the quality of every civilization

---

thought; hu-khṭa is su-ukṭam, right-words, well-spoken; hu-varshta is su-vṛshṭam, su-varhiṭam, su-vṛdham, su-kṛṭam, well-done, well-worked, well-rained, right-deeds).

Compare the Upanishaḍ verse:
Éshā ḍaivī vāg anu-vaḍaṭi sṭanayiṭnur, ḍa-ḍa-ḍa
iṭi, ḍāmyaṭa-ḍaṭṭa-ḍayaḍhvam. (*U.*)
(Heaven, with voice of thunder, counsels us
'Ḍa-ḍā-ḍā'—Do deny your lower self,
Do deeds of charity, and do take ruth
On all the weak and frail and innocent.)

depend upon its working out of the threefold principles of its religion.[1]

THEIR RELATION TO EDUCATION. Educationists in particular should always bear in mind the fact that the pupil is a unity of intellect, emotion, and physical body, and that that education only is good which informs the intellect with true and useful, cultural as well as vocational, knowledge,

[1] Various religions and sects, philosophies and schools, civilisations and epochs, *emphasise* various aspects, facets, parts of the same One Universal Way and Life and Truth; though all necessarily expound, implicitly, if not explicitly, all the aspects; for these are all inseparable. Thus, one emphasises knowledge more; another, devotion; another, action; one stresses (comparatively changeless) Rest; another, changeful effort, Evolution, progress; another, cyclicity and periodical balancing: one, the Shiva-aspect of the Absolute, Peace, repose, abstention from restlessness; another, the Shakṭi-aspect of the same, Power, Libido, Elan Vital; another the inclusion of the latter within the former; one more prominently embodies and expresses Law and Order; another Beauty, Music, Fine Arts generally; another Trade, Enterprise, Colonial activity; another, Martial ardour. Which religion or civilisation express and embodies which aspect most—opinion as to this will, again, at least partly depend upon the personality of each observer. Thus, one person may think Buddhism mainly philosophical, rationalist, Intellectual; another as compassionate, benevolent, philanthropic, hence Emotional; another as renunciant of comforts for the bhikshus themselves, but ministrant towards the general public, hence Actional.

disciplines the emotions and the will into a strong, fine, righteous character, and trains the body into hardy health, active strength, handsome shape and occupational skill.

This trinity is also good, nay, very necessary, for educationists to bear in mind for another vital purpose, if the indications in the old books be right. In modern educational theory and practice, while, no doubt, some valuable additions have been made, in the way of tests of *degrees* and kinds of *intelligence*, attention does not seem to have been equally given to the testing of the *kinds* of *temperaments;* i. e., whether the element of knowledge predominates in the pupil, or of action, or of desire. Yet without such testing, the secret of the discovery of the vocational aptitude of the student, and of appropriate education and subsequent proper fitting into society, is not likely to be found.[1] Expert details too often swamp vital principles, in science as well as in religion. So, the wise priest, minister of soul and keeper of conscience, will discriminately guide each parishioner along the way of either works, or devotion, or knowledge, according to his inner requirement. So, the wise physician, minister of body, will prescribe only after ascertaining the patient's temperament, constitutional peculiarity, personal idiosyncracy, diathesis.

---

[1]For fuller exposition, the reader may see *The Science of Social Organisation.*

CHAPTER II.

The Way of Knowledge; i. e., The Intellectual Constituent of Religion

THE WAY OF KNOWLEDGE. The *Haqāyaq*, basic 'truths,' *Ḍaqāyaq*, 'deep' things, *Ma'arifāṭ*, the 'knowledges,' *A'qāyaḍ*, 'beliefs,' which form the object of the Jñāna-kānda of Religion are but few. Nay, there is but one ultimate Truth. The errors are numberless. There is but one straight line, the shortest distance, between two points. The curved lines between them are beyond count. All that is true and right in knowledge, in feeling, in conduct, is but corollary of the one Truth. The whole of geometry is pre-contained in the definitions, the postulates, the axioms. A Samskṛṭ verse says that the whole of arithmetic is contained in the Rule of Three.

Sarvam ṭrai-rāshikam pāṭī.

And the whole of religion, the whole of philosophy, the whole of science, is contained in the 'Rule of Three' also, the Trinity-in-Unity, God-Nature-Man. God includes Nature and Man.

1. GOD. The one basic Truth of truths is that Man is in essence one with God; that Nature is God's Nature, the unchanging Self's ever-changing garment; that the meaning and purpose of life is that God has forgotten himself

into man, and man should remember himself into God again; that Spirit has entered into, put on body of, more and more dense Matter, along the Path of Pra-vṛtti, (Pursuit of sense-objects, Av-āroha, *Qaus-i-Nazūl*, the Arc of Descent), and has to rise again to It-Self along the Path of Ni-vṛtti, (Renunciation, Ā-roha, *Qaus-i-Urūj*, the Arc of Ascent); that Allah, the Universal Self, has individualised It-Self, has superimposed upon Its true Pure Selfness (or Ownness, Oneness, Pure Being, That-ness, Ṭaṭ-ṭvam, Thing-in-Itself, Self-in-Itself, Pure Identity, *Ayniyaṭ-i-haqīqī*, Shuddh-āḍvaiṭam), an illusive Supposititions Other-ness, (False Hetereity, Pure Nothing, Asaṭ-ṭvam, *Ghairiyaṭ-i-éṭabārī*, Miṭhyā-iṭaraṭā); that Brahma, (Param-Āṭmā, *Khuḍā-i-murakkab*, 'All-including God), has imagined Itself by Māyāvic Will-and-Imagination, (Kāma-Sankalpa, Shuyūnāṭ), into Jīva, (Jīv-āṭmā, *Khuḍā-i-muayyan*, 'particularised god'), and has to realise Itself as Universal Self again. All the religions state this Truth, in different ways. They also say that it is very simple, yet very difficult, too, to realize—because we are too strongly interested yet in *selfish* 'errors', and do not *wish* to turn to the *un-selfish* Truth of the All-One-Self.

As the Sūfis say:

Chīsṭ ḍunyā? Az Khuḍā ghāfil shuḍan;
Nai ke mā'sh o nuqra o farzanḍ o zan.
Na gum shuḍ ke rūy-ash ze ḍunyā be-ṭāfṭ,
Ke gum-gashṭaé Khwésh rā bāz yāfṭ.

Na koi parḍā hai Us-ke ḍar par,
Na Rūye raushan naqāb méṅ hai,
Ṭū āp apnī khudī se, ai ḍil !,
Hijāb méṅ hai, hijāb méṅ hai ! (*S.*)
(The 'world' is but forgetfulness of God ;
It is not spouse and child, silver and gold.
Who from this world did turn his face away,
He was not lost ; indeed, instead, he found
His long-forgotten and lost Self again.
No bar guards His palace-gateway,
No veil screens His Face of Light—
Thou, my heart !, by thine own self-ness,
Art enwrapped in darkest night.)

Laotse says :

Knowing the Eternal means enlightenment ; not knowing the Eternal causes passions to arise, and that is evil. (*Tao-te-king*).

Kṛṣhṇa says the same :

Manushyāṇām sahasréshu
kashchiḍ yaṭaṭi siḍḍhayé,
Yaṭaṭām cha sahasrāṇām
kashchin mām véṭṭi ṭaṭṭvaṭah.
Shraḍḍhā-mayo-yam purushah,
yo yaṭ-shraḍḍhah sa éva sah. (*G.*)
(One here, one there, from among myriads, setteth
Forth on the quest of Me, hidden in all !
And, of the few that seek, fewer find Me ;
For many do not seek Me steadfastly.
But he who seeketh Me with heart resolved,
He surely findeth Me, his inmost Self !)

Ye cannot serve God and Mammon both...
Strait is the gate that leadeth unto
Life, and few there be that find it...
Few are chosen though many come. (*B.*)

Ham Khuḍā kẖwāhī wa ham ḍunyā-i-ḍūṅ ;
ıṅ kẖayāl-asṭ o muhāl-asṭ o junūṅ ! (*S.*)
(That thou shouldst seek for God and this world too—
Vain is the wish, futile insanity !)

Samsāra-vāsanā-yukṭam
mano baḍḍham viḍur-buḍhāh ;
Ṭaḍ-éva vāsanā-ṭyakṭam
mukṭam iṭ-yabhi-ḍhī-yaṭé. (*U.*)

(Bound by mundane desire, the mind is bound ;
Freed from that same desire, the Spirit is free.)

But,

If ye attain to God and His kingdom of righteousness, all things else shall be added unto you. (*B.*)

Eṭaḍ-éva viḍiṭvā ṭu yo yaḍ-ichchhaṭi ṭasya ṭaṭ. (*U.*)
(Knowing the Truth, whate'er ye wish ye find.)

Kẖuḍā ko pāyā ṭo kyā na pāyā
Sabhī milā jo milā Khuḍā hai !
Zarā ṭū sochai, kabhī bhi Khāliq
Sé Us-kī khilqaṭ huī juḍā hai ?
Sabhī ṭo Maiṅ hūṅ, sabhī ṭo Mérā,
Hamésha āṭi yahī niḍā hai !
Ṭuhī hai Khāliq, ṭujhī meṅ khilqaṭ,
Kẖayāl-i-kẖāyal, ṭuhī Khuḍā hai ! (*S.*)

(If ye find God then ye have found all things !
Just think ! if the Creator thou dost find,
Can His creation still remain behind ?
Is the One ever separate from the Other ?
'Indeed I am this All, All This is Mine'—
This Word resoundeth ever from within !
Thou art Thy-Self the Thinker, and this world
But Thine own Thought, and God but thou thy-Self!)

The greatness of learning which constitutes expert medical science is very imposing and commands great respect. The simple counsel to use pure air, pure drink, pure food, does not. Yet, at the best, the former can only cure disease; and, at the worst, creates new diseases. The latter will promote health and prevent disease always. But pure air, pure drink, pure food, simple though they be, are not easy to obtain under artificial conditions of life.

So, as the religions say, man having emerged from God, wanders round and round for long before he thinks of going back again to "God who is our home," nay, who is our very Self. And knowledge, of many kinds, is needed before we can 'recognise' God, the God 'within'. The prophet Muhammad said: "He dieth not who giveth his life to learning. (*H.*) Ali said: "Philosophy is the lost sheep of the faithful: take it up again; even if from the infidel": (*ERE.* IX., 878).

> Ke bé-ilm na ṭawāṅ Khuḍā rā shinākhṭ. (*S.*, SĀḌI.)
> (Without right learning God may not be known.)

That the Véḍ-ānṭa, the crown of the Veḍa, 'the final knowledge,' teaches this, is well known. But the Christian Scriptures also say to men:

> Behold, the man has become as *one of us.* (*B.*, Genesis.)

> I have said, ye are gods; and all of you are children of the most High. (*B.*, Psalms.)

Is it not written in your laws, 'I said, *ye* are gods'? ...I am the son of God. (*B*., John.)

Behold, the Kingdom of God is within you.

Know ye not that ye are the temple of God, and the Spirit of God dwelleth in you ? (*B*.)

He is not far from every one of us. For in him we live and move and have our being...We are the off-spring of God....The Spirit of God dwelleth in you... God is One...His Spirit in the inner man...One God and Father of all, who is above all and through all and in you all. (*B*.)

Maṭ-ṭah para-ṭaram N-Ānyaṭ
kin-chiḍasti, Ḍhanan-jaya ! (*G*.)
(There is No-Other-thing-than-I, in truth !)[1]

The word 'U p a n i s h a ṭ', which designates the last portion of the Veda, wherein the final knowledge is imparted to the *earnest seeker* only, etymologically means, "sitting very close to the teacher," who solemnly ***whispers*** the sacred secret knowledge into the year of the ardent, earnest, intense listener; for unless listened to with reverent and rapt mind, the 'psychic miracle' will not occur, the words will fail to convey their profound significance, even if trumpeted forth from tower-tops. The purport of the Arabic-Persian phrase, *ilm-i-sīnah*, 'knowledge which is

---

[1]For the metaphysical significance of 'I-Not-Another', the reader may look into the present writer's *The Science of Peace*, or *The Science of the Self*, if he wishes to pursue the subject further.

passed from heart to heart,' 'the doctrine of the heart,' is the same.[1]

---

[1] In all times and climes, within the fold of every religion, "a group here, a group there, has gathered together with no other motive than that of gaining a greater hold on the spiritual life than was prevalant in the ordinary circles of the people...They seem to have lived on the borderland of an unusual ecstasy, experiencing extraordinary invasions of the Divine, hearing mystic sounds and seeing mystic visions..." Among the Jews the 'Essenes' were such. They "were in possession of certain esoteric teachings, of which, those outside their ranks were uninformed..." They laid "great stress on fellowship, amounting to a kind of communism"; were apart "from the general people by reason of their sanctity"; were devoted "to the knowledge of the existence of God and the beginning of all things"; loved "allegorical interpretation."..."Silence or secrecy was frequently employed by the early Rabbis in their mystical exegesis of Scripture. A typical illustration is the following, from *Midrash Rabba* (a Hebrew commentary) on Genesis, iii (*B.*): '...The sage said this in a *whisper*...The other asked, Why dost thou tell this in a *whisper*, seeing that it is clearly taught in a scriptural verse? The sage replied, Just as I have myself had it *whispered* unto me, even so have I *whispered* it unto thee'...": J. Abelson, *Jewish Mysticism*, (1913), 18-23. The meek, the pure in heart, the earnestly and intensely seeking, alone can see God; not the flippant, the noisy, the disputatious. The laws of God's Nature are written on Nature's face; but it takes whole lifetimes of intense research by the ablest scientists to decipher one now, one again. Only the *receptive open* mind can *receive*. Even the Sun's light

The *Qurān* also says :

Wa fi anfusekum a-fa-lā-ṭubserūn. (*Q.*)
(I am in your own souls ! Why see ye not ?
In every breath of yours am I, but ye
Are blind, without true eye, and see Me not.)

Sūfis have sung :

Bā wujūdé ke muzhḍae ṭérā 'nahno aqrab,'
Safhe Masahaf pai likhā ṭhā, mujhe mā'lūm na ṭhā.
(Although the great glad news of Thee is writ
Plainly upon the *Qurān's* holy page :
'Nearer am I to thee than thy throat-vein'—
My eyes blinded with selfishness, saw not !)

The well known *Kalemā* of faith, the *Mahāvākya*, the Logos-word, of Islām, is in terms of the third person, *viz.*,

(Lā ilāh il-Allāh, (*Q.*)
(There is no god but God).

---

cannot come in through closed windows. Pre-occupied, pre-judiced, minds, closed by vibrant resistant active 'other'-ward, 'matter'-ward, thoughts, cannot perceive the things of the Spirit.

Incidentally, it may be noted that the derivation and meaning of the word 'Essenes' is in doubt ; see *Enc. Brit.*, art. 'Essenes'. 'Buddhist influence' is mentioned ; also 'gymno-sophists' ; but no western scholar seems to have thought of 's a n-n y ā s ī-s' in this connection. 'Gymno-sophists' were met with, and some taken away also, by Alexander ; one named Kalanos, (Kalyāṇa) is specifically mentioned by Greek writers. The word seems compounded of 'gymnast' and 'sophist', meaning h a t h a-y o g ī plus r ā j a-y o g ī, 'holy men' versed in various bodily as well as mental disciplines. Jesus is said to have lived and studied among the Essenes.

Sūfis declare that it is meant only for the younger souls who are not yet ready for the inner teaching; and that the real *Kalemā* is in terms of the first person:

Wa mā arsalnā min qablikā mir
rasūlin illā nūhi ilaihé annahu—
'Inni An-Allāhu lā ilāha illā Anā.' (*Q.*)
(The prophets, all, that ever have been sent,
Have been so sent by Me, the Supreme Self,
For but one purpose, namely, that they teach,
That 'Men should serve the Supreme Self Al-one',
That 'Verily the I, the Self, am God;
None other than the Supreme Self is God'.)

Aham éva, na maṭ-ṭo-(a)nyaḍ
Iṭi buḍḍhyaḍḍhvam anjasā. (*Bh.*)

('I, only I, Naught-Else-than-I at all'—
This is the whole truth, understand it well).

Iṭi ṭé jñānam ākhyāṭam
guhyāḍ guhya-ṭaram mayā;
Sarva-guhya-ṭamam bhūyah
shṛṇu mé paramam vachah:
'Man-manā bhava, Maḍ-bhakṭo,
Maḍ-yājī, Mām namas-kuru;
Mām év-aishyasi, saṭyam ṭé
praṭi-jāné, priy-osi mé;
Sarva-ḍharmān pari-ṭyajya
Mām Ékam sharaṇam vraja;
Aham ṭvām sarva-pāpébhyo
mokshayishyāmi; mā shuchah!' (*G.*)

(The Ancient Wisdom have I taught to thee,
Highest, most secret, sacred; yet again,
Hear thou the secret-most of mysteries,

The Final Word of all that 'I' can speak:
Place thy whole mind in Me, the Supreme Self,
And place Me, in thy mind, (and Nothing-Else);
Love Me, the Universal I, al-one;
Perform all acts as sacrifice to Me,
As Duty done for All-pervading Self;
Make salutation and submission, full,
Unqualified, of all thy heart and will,
To Me, the Self in Whom all selves unite.
Give up all other ways. Come unto Me.
'I' is the one sole Refuge of all beings.
The 'I' will save and salve thee from all sins,
All sorrows, prisonments of finitude,
By giving thee Its own Infinity.)

This is the one teaching of all the prophets, ṛshis, *nabis, rasūls*, avatāras, messiahs. It is given to the earnest and seeking souls, the *ahl-i-ḍil*, 'the men of heart,' the genuine hermits, anchorites, bhikshus, *faqīrs*, sannyāsis, *ḍurvéshas*, ḍīkshiṭas, initiates, *miskīns*; to the souls, that are ready to receive. It is the *ilm-i-sīnā*, 'the doctrine of the heart,' *ḍaqāyaq*, the esoteric doctrine of the Mysteries, the parā-viḍyā, 'the higher Knowledge,' rahasya, guhya, 'the Secret,' āḍhyāṭmika arṭha, the 'spiritual meaning', as it is variously named in the Vedic Scriptures. Distinguished from this is the *ilm-i-safinā*, 'the doctrine of the page,' 'the doctrine of the eye', 'the letter', the aparā-viḍyā, 'the lower knowledge;' this only, as yet, the younger souls, the *ahl-i-ḍaul*, 'the men that seek worldly wealth,' shrāvakas, 'lay disciples,' upāsakas, gṛha-sṭhas, householders, ordinary family-men-and-women, can apprehend and utilise.[1]

---

[1] In Christian writings, sometimes, 'prophets' are contrasted with 'priests'; as in Islam, 'sūfī auliyās' with 'shara'ī mullās'; and in Vaiḍika Ḍharma, jñānī-bhakṭas with karma-kānḍīs. Jesus rebuked and cursed the latter, whom he called the 'lawyers', i. e. priests of the 'ritualistic law': "Woe unto you, lawyers !, for ye have taken away the *key of knowledge*; ye entered not in yourselves, and them that were entering in, ye hindered": (*B.*, Luke, xi, 52). Buḍḍha distinguished between true Brāhmaṇas and false self-styled Brāhmaṇas, (as indeed does *Manu-smṛṭi*) ; and gave out, to the public, some of the ancient secret wisdom ; and thus aroused hostility. Among Christians it is believed that "the Apocalypse gives the key to the divine Gnosis, which is the same in all ages, and superior to all faiths and philosophies—that *secret* science which is in reality secret only because it is hidden and locked in the inner nature of every man... and none but himself can turn the key :" J. M. Pryse, *The Apocalypse Unsealed*, p. 5. Muhammad said : "I am the city (of occult knowledge), and Ali is the gate into it." Among Muslim Sūfis, the tradition is that Alī first declared to the 'select', who were qualified and ready for it, the Ancient Wisdom, *Ilm-i-Rūhānī*, Ṭasawwaf, Ḍivya-jñāna, 'Theo-sophy' proper, 'God-Wisdom', 'Soul-Science', 'Divine Knowledge', 'Spiritual Science'. H. P. Blavatsky's *Isis Unveiled* and *The Secret Doctrine* contain a vast amount of astonishing information and profound instruction on the whole subject ; but it is not easy reading. This Occult Science, Gupṭa-Viḍyā, *Ilm-i-Sīnā*, Ancient Wisdom, had to be kept secret, for long, (and the danger

We speak wisdom among them that are perfect.... To you is given to know the mysteries of the kingdom of God, but to them (*the polla*, the worldly-minded mass) it is not given...Therefore speak I to them in parables and allegories; because, they, seeing, see not, and hearing, they hear not, neither do they understand." (*B.*, Mat. xiii. 11, 13.)

Hear ye, indeed, but understand not, and see indeed, but perceive not. (*B.*, Isaiah, vi. 9).

Āshcharya-vaṭ pashyaṭi kashchiḍ-Énam,
Āshcharya-vaṭ ch-Ainam anyah shṛṇoṭi,
Āshcharya-vaḍ vaḍaṭi ṭaṭh-aiva ch-ānyah,
Shruṭvā-py-Énam véḍa na ch-aiva kashchiṭ. (*G.*)
(Men see, and hear, and speak of It also,
But seeing, hearing, speaking, they see not;
They simply wonder, and not understand.)

Shṛnvanṭo-pi na shṛnvanṭi,
jānanṭo-pi na jānaṭé,
Pashyanṭo-pi na pashyanṭi,
Pashyanṭi jñāna-chakshushah. (*U.*)
(Hearing, they hear not; knowing, they know not,
Seeing, they see not; the enlightened ones
Alone do see with wisdom-illumed eyes.

Truly the Self is sun-clear, ever near, nay nearest of all, is our very Self, yet we see not!

As the Sūfis say:

Ghāyab jo ho Khuḍā sè, ālam hai usko hū kā,
Anāniyaṭ hai jis-méṅ, mauqā nahīṅ hai ṭū kā.

---

is not over yet), because, as Jesus said: 'Give not that which is holy unto the dogs, neither cast ye your pearls before swine, lest they trample them under their feet, and turn again *and rend you*;" (*B.*, Matthew, vii. 6). Such is the Law of Duality. God proposes, Satan opposes, and often disposes.

Zāhiḍé gum-rāh ké maiṅ kis ṭarah ham-rāh hūṅ ;
Woh kahé Allāh hai, au maiṅ kahūṅ Allāh hūṅ ! (*S.*)

(He who is absent far away from God—
His heart can only say: 'God is,' somewhere;
He who has found the Loved One in him-Self—
For him God is not He, nor Thou, but I.
How may I take for guide upon the Way
One who himself away from it doth stray?
He is content to say "God is,' while I
Am desolate till I 'God am' can say!)

This is only an expanded and more poetical version of the Samskṛṭ verse:

Asṭi Brahm-éṭi chéḍ véḍa,
parokshanı jñānam éva ṭaṭ;
Asmi Brahm-éṭi chéḍ véḍa,
aparoksham taḍ uchyaṭé. (*U.*)

(Who says only 'God is'—he sees a screen;
He who can say 'God am'—he, sure, hath seen.)

A gāṭhā of Zaraṭhusṭra enjoins, in words which are the equivalent of the Qurānic Kalemā:

Mazaḍāo sakhāré mairisto.[1] (*Z.*, Gāṭhā, 29. 4.)
(The Great God only is to be adored.)

As the Upanishaṭs say:

Āṭmā ev-āré shroṭavyo, manṭavyo, niḍiḍhyāsiṭavyah
...N-ānyo-ṭo-ṣṭi vijñāṭā. (*U.*)
(The Self Alone is to be pondered on;
None Else is there who knows or should be known.)

With reference to the distinction between *paroksha* and *a-paroksha*, direct knowledge

[1](Skt: Mahā-ḍhāh, 'the Great All-Wise Creator' Mahā-ḍévah, 'the Great God', Sakṛṭ, Ékalah, Kévalah, 'One and Only', 'once for all', saḍā, 'always,' smarṭavyah, 'should be remembered', 'borne in mind'.)

and indirect knowledge, Arabian philosophers have said :

Al ilmo ilmān, maṭbū'un wa masmū'; lā yan-fa al-masmū' ezā lam yakum il-maṭbū'. (Phil: maxim.)
(Knowledge is of two kinds, that which is heard,
And that which is felt direct in the heart ;
The heard yields not full fruit until it comes
Home to the soul by some experience.)
Har ke rā ḍar jāṅ Kẖuḍā bi-nihaḍ mahak
Har yaqīṅ rā bāz ḍānaḍ ū ze shak. (*S.*)
(A touchstone God hath placed in every heart ;
It separates, with surety, False from True.)
The Great God has conferred a moral sense even on the lowliest people. (*C.*, *Shu-king.*)

The Christian world knows this touchstone as Conscience, Intuition, the Inner Monitor, the still small Voice of God, etc. The Vaiḍika (now called Hindū, or better Ārya) Ḍharma refers to it as Anṭar-yāmī, 'Inner Monitor, Watcher, Ruler, Endo-censor'; and in such expressions as:

Hṛḍayén-ābhy-anu-jñāṭah ; Manah-pūṭam samācharéṭ; Swasya cha priyam Āṭmanah ; Parito-sh-onṭar-Āṭmanah ; Svasy-aiv-ānṭara-Pūrushah; Āṭmanas-ṭushtir-éva cha ; Kshéṭra-jño n-ābhishankaṭé ; Yamo...ḍévo...hṛḍi sṭhiṭah. (*M.*)

Saṭām hi sanḍeha-paḍeshu vasṭushu
Pramāṇam-anṭah-karaṇa-pra-vṛṭṭayah.
(KĀLI-ḌĀSA, *Shakunṭalā.*)

(That which the 'Heart' permits ; which the 'Soul' likes ;
The 'God within' approves; the 'Mind' holds pure ;
Th' 'Eternal Witness' sees as free from doubt,
Without misgiving, as straightforward course ;

Which brings pure satisfaction to the 'Self';
That is the course to follow, for good men.
In matters wrapped in doubt, 'to do or not'—
The 'Inner Organ' of the good is guide.)

Sākshiṇam baṭa kalyāṇam Āṭmāṇam ava-manyasé !...
Na hṛṭ-ṣhayam véṭsi Munim purāṇam !...
Hṛḍi sthiṭah karma-sākshī Kshéṭra-jño nāsya ṭushyaṭi,
Ṭam Yamah pāpa-karmāṇam nir-bharṭsayaṭi pūrusham.
(*Mbh.*, Āḍi-parva, ch. 98.)

(He who ignores and does not satisfy,
But disobeys, the One, auspicious, pure,
Perpetual 'Inner Witness', the 'Own-Self',
The 'Ancient Sage', all-knowing, who abides
In every heart, recording every act,
Him Yama doth award dire punishment.)

Isṭafṭeh qalab-ak. (*H.*)
(Consult thine own heart, if thou art in doubt).

In every heart there dwelleth a Sajin (Sage); only man will not steadfastly believe it—therefore hath the whole remained buried. (WANG-YANG-MING)[1]

Our knowledge is obviously of two sorts, (1) that derived from personal first-hand experience, a very small portion, but the most certain, and (2) that based on the testimony of others, far the larger portion. In Samskṛṭ philosophy, the two are called p r a ṭ y - a k s h a 'immediately before the senses', 'directly cognised,' and s h ā b ḍ a or ā g a m a, that which has been described in 'words' by, has 'come' from, others;

---

[1]Quoted from the Confucian-Laotsian writings of Wang-Yang-Ming, "the Chinese father of Japanese philosophy", by Jung, *Psychological Types*, 269.

in Arabic-Persian, *maṭbū'* and *masmū'*; also, with a slight difference, *mā'qūlāṭ* and *manqūlāṭ*; in European, direct and traditional, first-hand and second-hand.

> L'Illāhé al-annāsi hujjaṭain, zāhiraṭun wa bāṭinah; hujjaṭ-uz-zāhira he-al-ambiyā w-ar-rasūl; hujjaṭ-ul-bāṭina he-al-u'qūl.
> (Two proofs are there of Deity, for men;
> The outer is the prophets' witnessing,
> The inner is our own rational mind.)

In the case of one's own intelligence and praṭy-aksha or direct observation, again, two kinds (or rather degrees) are recognised by all. Christians speak of intellection and instinctive perception or intuition; Vaiḍikas, of sāḍhāraṇa-jñāna (ordinary knowledge) and yoga-ja-jñāna or samāḍhi-ja-jñāna or prāṭibha-jñāna (knowledge born of yoga, or samāḍhi, or praṭi-bhā); Musalmāns, of *ilm-i-laḍunnī*, or *ilm-i-wahbī*, or *-wajḍānī*, or *-ilhāmī*, or *-kashfā*, or *-ishrāqī*, (*i. e.*, sudden, inspirational, illuminational, risen like the Sun), and *ilm-i-kasabī*, or *-ikṭisābī*, or *-nazārī*, or *-isṭiḍlālī*, or *-mashhāyī*, (*i. e.*, labored, argumentative, inferential, pedestrian).

All kinds of cognition, as also of desire and of action meet and merge in the Self. It is Self-luminous and Illuminator of all others. It senses It-Self, perceives It-Self, infers It-Self, intuites It-Self, desires and loves and lives It-Self, 'acts,' wills, maintains, asserts It-Self—eternally.

The well-known Sūfī exclamations, *An-al-Haq, Haq-ṭu-ī, Qalab-ul-insān baiṭ-ur-Rahmān,* are exact equivalents of the Upanishaṭ utterances, Aham Brahma, Ṭaṭ ṭvam asi, Êsha ma Āṭmā anṭar-hṛḍayé, Hṛḍi ayam ṭasmāḍ hṛḍayam; 'I am the True, the Real, Brahma; That thou art, too; the heart of man is the abode of God'; and of the Biblical declaration: "Ye are the temple of God." Khalīfā Ali declared:

> Qalab-il-momin a'rsh-Illāhī.
> (The heart of him who knows, and so believes
> With full assurance, is the throne of God.)

Christ said: "I and my Father are one." The *Old Testament* of the Jewish faith, especially the Book of Isaiah, also utters this same great *kalemā,* this mahā-vākya, logion, ten times and more, *viz.,* "I am (*i.e.,* the Self is) God and there is None-Else".[1]

Zoroastrian scriptural utterances, with the same significance are:

> Ajém ṭoī āish pouruyo fravoīvīḍé; vīspéng
> anyéng manyéush spasyā ḍvaéshanghā.
> Na échīm ṭém anyém Yūshmaḍ vaéḍā.

---

[1]This is the Hebrew form of the Arabic *Kalemās,* '*Lā-ilāh il-Allāh*' and *Inni an-Allāhu, lā ilāhā illā Anā,* 'There is no god other than Allāh', and 'Verily I am (i.e., is) God; there is no God but (the) I'; and also the Zoroastrian logion, 'Mazaḍāo sakhāre mairisto', 'Mazaḍāo alone is to be always ever contemplated and adored.' For an attempt at a philosophical exposition of the

Ṭém né yasnāish ārmaiṭoish mimaghjo,
Yé ānménī Mazaḍāo srāvī Ahuro.
Paré vāo vīspāīsh paré vaokhémā.
(*Z.*, Gāṭhās, 44.11 ; 34.7 ; 45.10 ; 34.5)
(Thee only do I know to be Supreme!
All others I dismiss from this my mind!
I know Him to be none except Thy-Self!
He who is known as Ahurā-Mazaḍā—
With duteous deeds we worship Him alone.
We know Thee as Supreme above all lives.)

That the teachings of Buḍḍhism and Jainism, on this essential point, are identical with those of Veḍānṭa, goes almost without saying, for those who do not revel in discovering minute differences. In one of his u ḍ ā n a s (*shuṭṭahiyāṭ*, as the Sūfis call them, or, in Vedic literature, y o g ā-r ū d h-o k ṭ i s), ecstatic utterances of overflowing joy, joy of realization of identity with the Supreme Self of all—the Buḍḍha, arising from s a m ā ḍ h i - trance, uses words which are the words of the Upanishaṭs, but in their Pālī form :

Véḍānṭa-gū, vushiṭa-brahma-chariyo, ḍhamména sa Brāhmaṇo Brahma-vāḍarn vaḍeyya. (*Uḍāna.*)
(He who successfully fulfils his vow
Of continence in body and in mind,
And has achieved the final knowledge, he
Acquires the right, high Brahma to declare
To others who would walk the Path ; he may
Give to himself the name of Brāhmaṇa.)

---

full significance of this m a h ā-v ā k y a, 'A h a m-E ṭ a ṭ-n a', see the present writer's *The Science of Peace*' and '*Praṇava-Vaḍa*, or *The Science of the Sacred Word*.'

In a similar mood of exaltation, Ashtāvakra, long before the Buḍḍha, cried out: Aho Aham! namo Mahyam!, and, long afterward, Bāyazīḍ Busṭāmi re-echoed him, *Subhāni ma āzama shānī*, 'How wonderful am I!, Salutation unto Me!, How great is my glory!' The *Upanishaṭs* reiterate, over and over again, Aham Brahm-āsmi, Yas-ṭvam-asi So-ham-asmi, Idam sarvam asi, Aham év-éḍam Sarvam, 'I am the Infinite; What thou art that same am I; Thou art all This; I am all This'. I, *the* 'I', the Self, the Principle of Consciousness', of Self-Existence, of 'I am', is the basis, the cause, of all 'This' too, of all this Not-Self, Other-than-I, of all the Object-World, the whole World-Process.

The *Ormazd Yasht*, of the Zoroastrian religion, declares: "My first name is *Ahmi*, (Samskṛt, Asmi, 'I am'); the last is *Ahmi yaḍ Ahmi*". The Vedic *Shaṭapaṭha Brāhmaṇa* has the same significant words, Yoham asmi so-smi, 'I am what I am', i. e. 'I am' ever the Changeless One, ever the same Self, at the end as at the beginning, for 'I have', *i.e.*, the 'I' has, no beginning and no end. The Bible too says: "I am that I am . . . I am hath sent me unto you": (*Exodus*). The words "*I am hath* sent me" are very noteworthy.[1]

[1] "Then spoke Zaraṭhushṭra: Tell me thou, O pure Ahura-Mazḍā, the name which is thy greatest, best, fairest, and which is the most efficacious for prayer.

The sayings of *Veḍānṭa* and *Ṭasawwuf* are so similar as to be almost indistinguishable when translated into a third language. Thus:

(O pilgrims for the Shrine! Where go ye, where?
Come back! come back! The Beloved is here!
His presence all your neighbourhood doth bless!
Why will ye wander in the wilderness!
Ye who are seeking God! Yourselves are He!
Ye need not search! He is ye, verily!
Why will ye seek for what was never lost?
There is Naught-Else-than-ye! Be not doubt-tost!)
(The wise see in their heart the face of God,
And not in images of stone and clod!
Who in themselves, alas!, can see Him not,
They seek to find Him in some outer spot.)

Thus answered Ahura-Mazḍā: My first name is Ahmi (I am),...and my twentieth is Ahmi Yaḍ Ahmi Mazḍao (I am that I am, Mazḍā):" Haug's *Essays on the Parsis*, 195. "In the *Hurmuzḍ-Yashṭ* of the Zenḍ-avesṭā, Ahura-Mazḍāo enumerates twenty of his names. The first is *Ahmi* (Skṭ., A s m i), 'I am'. The last is *Ahmi Yaḍ Ahmi* (Skṭ., A s m i Y a ḍ A s m i, Y o-s m i s o-s m i, Y o-h a m So-h a m, 'I am what I am'). Both of these phrases are also names of Jehovah in the Bible: And God said unto Moses, 'I am that I am', *Ehyeh ashar yehyeh*. And he said, 'Thus shalt thou say unto the children of Israel: *I am* hath sent me unto you'." (Gangā Prasāḍ, *The Fountain-Head of Religion*, p. 47.) "In the Egyptian *Book of the Dead*, 'I am he who I am' is applied to a god"; M. Yearsley, *The Story of the Bible*, p. 79.) Jesus says: "Before Abraham was *I* am", (*B.*); which can mean only that 'I am', the Self, the Principle of Consciousness, was 'before Abraham' and everything Else.

The originals of this translation are :

Ai Qaum ! ba hajj rafṭah ! kujā éḍ, kujā éḍ !
Māshūq hamīṅ jā-sṭ, bi-āyéḍ, bi-āyéḍ !
Māshūqe-ṭo hamsāya-ṭo, ḍīwār ba ḍīwār ;
Ḍar bāḍiyah sar-gashṭah cherā éḍ, cherā éḍ !
Ānāṅ ke ṭalab-gār-i-Kẖuḍā éḍ, Kẖuḍā éḍ !
Hājaṭ ba ṭalab n-īst, shumā éḍ, shumā-éḍ !
Chīzé ke na garḍīḍ gum az bahre che joyéḍ ?
Kas gẖair-i-shumā ṅ-īsṭ, kujā éḍ, kujā éḍ !

(SHAMS ṬABREZ)

Shivam Āṭmani pashyanṭi,
praṭimāsu na yoginah ;
Āṭma-sṭham yé na pashyanṭi,
ṭīrṭhē mārganṭi ṭē Shivam !

(*Shiva Purāṇa.*)

Sarvasya-iva janasy-āsya
Vishṇur-abhy-anṭaré sṭhiṭah
Ṭaṃ pariṭyajya yé yānṭi
bahir Vishṇum nar-āḍhamāh.

(*Yoga Vāsishtha*, 5. 34. 26)

(The 'All-pervading' Self, 'Who bindeth all',
'Knits them together', bides in every heart—
Who turn from Him, the Inmost Deity,
Seeking outside, their eyes are yet thick-veiled.)

Sarva-bhūṭéshu yah pashyéḍ
Bhagavaḍ-bhāvam Āṭmanah,
Bhūṭāni Bhagavaṭy-Āṭman-
yasau Bhāgavaṭ-oṭṭamah. (*Bh.*)

(Whoso 'in-sees' Divinity everywhere,
Godhead in every living thing, and all
In God—he only is true devotee
And servant of the Omni-present Lord.)

The Upanishaṭ-expression, Ékam éva A-ḍviṭīyam, "One—not a Second," is to be found in the Bible (*Ecclesiastes*) also, and is echoed in *Ṭasawwuf* exactly:

Har giyāhē ke bar zamīn royaḍ,
Wahḍahū lā sharīk-i-lah goyaḍ. (*S.*)
(Each single blade of grass that sprouts from earth,
Proclaims His word that 'I Al-One am He,
There is No-Other anywhere than I,'
That he, you, I, are all *One* I, One Life.)

The words of the Zoroastrian Scriptures are:

Na échīm ṭém anyém Yūshmaṭ vaéḍā. (*Z.*, Gāthā, xxxiv. 7).
(None Other do I know than Thee.)
Mazaḍāo sakhāré mairisto. (*Z.*, Gāṭhā.)
(Mazaḍa, the One Alone, we bear in mind.)

That only is True, Real, *Haq*, Saṭ, Sure, Certain, which holds true and abides the same in all three times, past, present, future, and in all three spaces, behind, here, before, unchangingly. That which *is not*, but is imagined or said to *be*, *as if it is*, that is unreal. That which at one time *is* and at another *is not*, or *was not* and now *is*, or *is* and *will not be*—is half-true and half-false. That which *always is*—such alone is True, Real, wholly. Naught-Else than I is such. I is I, in all times, all spaces, all conditions.

Mās-ābḍa-yuga-kalpéshu
gaṭ-āgāmishv-an-ékaḍhā,
N-oḍéṭi n-āsṭam-éṭy-éshā
Samviḍ-ékā Svayam-prabhā.
Samviḍo vyabhichāras-ṭu
n-aiva ḍrsht-osṭi karhi-chiṭ;

Yaḍi ḍṛshtas-ṭaḍā ḍrashtā
shishtah Samviḍ-vapuh svayam. (*Purāṇas.*)
(In all the months, years, ages, eons, cycles,
Past and to come, countless, infinitely,
What doth not ever rise nor ever set
Is this Self-lit Self-Consciousness al-one.
Break of this Consciousness was never seen.
If it was ever seen, then he who saw,
The witness, he him-Self remains behind
Embodied as that Self-same Consciousness.)[1]

---

[1] "I find my boy still hardly able to grasp the fact that there was a time when he *did not exist*; if I talk to him about the building of the Pyramids or some such topic, he always wants to know what he was doing then, and is merely puzzled when he is told that he did not exist." This is what Mr. Bertrand Russell writes of his son and himself in his book, *On Education*, p. 171. He is reputed to be a brilliant philosopher and also a great mathematician; yet he told the dear boy that he (the boy) "did not exist" a few years earlier! The child's soul, his Self, knew better, as did Wordsworth, in his *Ode to Immortality.* Consciousness, Self-consciousness, the Self, simply *cannot* be *conscious* of a time when it, the Self, it-Self, *Consciousness,* is not, was not, will not be. It is a contradiction in terms. Immortality is indelibly stamped on the face of Consciousness, the face of God. When 'I' say that the solar system was born so many hundreds or thousands of millions of years ago and will last so many more—the whole system with all its thousands of millions of years of life-time and all its thousands of millions of miles of body-space is *in* 'My' Consciousness, *'now'* and *'here'*; otherwise, my statement were wholly meaningless. As the Sūfī Sarmaḍ well says:

N-Āṭmā jajāna na marishyaṭi n-aiḍhaṭé-sau. (*Bh.*)
(The Self is never born nor dies nor grows.)
Lam yaliḍ wa lam yulaḍ . . .
Kullu shayīn hālikun illā Wajh. (*Q.*)
(Neither begetter nor begotten He . . .
All things are mortal but the Face of God,
His Self, the primal moveless Cause of all.)
Yaḍ-apariṇāmi ṭaḍ-akāraṇam (*Nyāya maxim.*)
(What changes never, never has a cause.)
What is incorruptible must also be ungenerable.
(*Western Scholastic philosophical maxim.*)

This Self is Self-luminous because, clearly, nothing else can illumine It. It illumines all else. Eyes see sights and ears hear sounds; but who sees the eyes and who hears the ears? They obviously do not see and hear themselves. *I* am conscious of the eyes and of their objects, of the ears and their objects. Indeed *I* see and hear, rather than the eyes see and the ears hear. They are only the instruments I use.

Lā ṭuḍrikul-absār, wa Huā yuḍrikul-absār. (*Q.*)
(Eyes do not see Him, but He sees the eyes.)
Shroṭrasya shroṭram, manaso mano yaḍ,
Vācho ha vācham, Sa u prāṇasya prāṇash,
chakshushah-chakshuh. (*U.*)
(Hearer of ear and Speaker of all speech,
Seer of eye and Mentor of the mind,
The Self is verily the Life of life.)

Mullā goyaḍ ki bar falak shuḍ Ahmaḍ;
Sarmad goyaḍ ki falak ba Ahmaḍ ḍar shuḍ.
(The mullā—learned in the Scripture-word
But not its sense—says Ahmaḍ went to Heaven;
But Sarmaḍ says that Heaven came into Ahmaḍ.)

Kunṭu sama'h-ul-lazī yasma'n bihī,
Wa bisārah-ul-lazī yubsiru bihī. (*Q.*)
(I do become the ear by which he hears;
And I become the eye by which he sees.)

Yo véḍ-éḍam shrṇavān-īṭi sa Āṭmā shravaṇāya shrōṭram; ḍarshanāya chakshuh; ganḍhāya ghrāṇam...(*U*).

(The Self, wishing the wish to hear, became
The ear; to see, the eye; to smell, the nose...)

Na ṭaṭra vāg-gachchhaṭi, na chakshur, no mano, na viḍmo, na vijānīmo, yaṭh-aiṭaḍ anu-shishyāḍ; anyaḍ-éva taḍ viḍiṭāḍ-aṭh-āviḍiṭāḍ-aḍhi. (*U.*)

(Speech reaches not the Self, nor eye, nor mind;
We know not how we may describe the Self;
It is not known, nor is it yet unknown,
The Knower nor unknown nor known can be.)

N-āham manyé su véḍ-éṭi
No na véḍ-éṭi véḍa cha;
Yo nas-ṭaḍ véḍa ṭaḍ véḍa,
No na véḍ-éṭi véḍa cha.
Yasy-āmaṭam ṭasya maṭam,
Maṭam yasya na véḍa sah;
Avijñāṭam vijānaṭām,
Vijñāṭam avijānaṭām. (*U.*)

(Who thinks he knows It, he does know It not;
While he who thinks he knows It not, knows It.
We do not know whether we know or not;
We know the Self; and yet what do we know!
Then do we know it not?. But, sure, we know!
How can we say we do not know our-Self!
Indeed It is the only Thing we know
Most positive, most doubtless, here and now!)

Iyam vi-sṛshtir yaṭa-ā-babhūva,
Yaḍi vā ḍaḍhé, yaḍi vā na,

Yo asy-Āḍhyakshah paramé Vyoman,
So-anga !, véḍa, yaḍi vā na véḍa !
(*Ṛg-Véḍa*).

(This vast-spread emanation, measureless,
Filling the infinite expanse of Heaven,
From Whom has it come into being ? Who
Maintains it going ? Or doth none maintain it ?
Who is its Ruler ? Doth it rule it-Self ?
He only knows ! Perchance He too knows not
Quite wakefully, and only dreams it all !)
Cognoscendo ignorari, ignorando cognosci.
(ST. AUGUSTINE).

Ai bar-ṭar az khayāl o qayās o gumān o wahm
W-az har che gufṭa-ém o shanīḍ-ém o kẖwānḍa-ēm.
(*S.*)

(Thou art beyond all thought, conception, guess,
Imagination, yea, and far beyond
All we have spoken, heard, or read in books ;
These deal with Objects—Thou, Subject of all !)
Ashrayaṭva-vishayaṭva-bhāginī
Nir-vibhāga-Chiṭir-éva kevalā.
(*Sankshépa-Shārīraka*).

(This marvellous Unique Self-consciousness
Al-one is Subject-Object both at once.
It knows It-Self and knows all-Else also.)

The Universal I, the Supreme Self, God, is indeed Unique, Al(l)-one, One-without-a-second, A-dviṭīya, *Lā-sāni*. There is No-thing Else like It, or beside It, or except It, nothing *mā-siwā-Allāh*, *gẖair-az-Kẖuḍā*, Aṭmanah iṭaraṭ, Brahmaṇah anyaṭ, 'other than God,' 'else than the Self'. It is *Majmua'-i-ziḍḍain*, Sarva-viruḍḍha-dharm-āshrayah, 'locus, focus, reservoir, of all contradictions, all opposites'.

Êkam éva Aḍviṭīyam. (*U.*)
(One only, always secondless, am I.)
Lā ilāh il-Allāh. (*Q.*)
(There is no god in truth other than God.)
Lā īlāhā illā Anā. (*Q.*)
(There is no God other than I my-Self.)
Aham éva na maṭ-ṭo-(a) nyaḍ-
iṭi buḍḍhyaḍḍhvam anjasā. (*Bh.*)
(Know well—There is no-other-than-My-Self.)

I am the Lord, and there is none Else; There is no God beside me...I am the first and I am the last: and beside me there is no God...(*B.*, Isaiah.)

To Ahura Mazaḍā, the Secondless...I sing the song of Glory. (*Z.*, Ahunavaḍ Gāthā, xxxvii. 3.)

There is One alone and there is not a second; yea, He hath neither child nor brother; yet is there no end of all His labor: (i. e. the World-Process is unending). (*B.*, Eccles., iv.)

Ṭasmai sam-un-naḍḍha-viruḍḍha-shakṭayé
Namah parasmai Purushāya Véḍhasé. (*Bh.*)
(To Him who wieldeth, in th' eternal Play
Of the World-Drama, mighty, turbulent,
Opposed, and ever-battling wondrous powers
—We offer salutation to that Self.)
Aham Āṭmā, Guḍā-késha!,
sarva-bhūṭ-āshaya-sṭhiṭah,
Aham Āḍish-cha, Maḍhyam cha,
bhūṭānām Anṭa éva cha. (*G.*)
(I am the Self abiding in all hearts,
I the Beginning, Middle, End of all.)

Hu-wal-Awwal, Hu-wal-Ākhir, Hu-waz-Zāhir, Hu-wal-Bāṭin, wa Hu-wā be kulle shayīn Alīm. (*Q.*)
(He is the First, He is the Last also,
He is the Outer, He the Inner too,
The Manifest and yet Unmanifest,

The Lord, Ordainer, knower of all things.)

I am (is) the first and the last...I am the alpha and the omega. (*B.*)

I am (is) the Light which lighteth every man... without Me (the Supreme Self in all) thou canst do nothing. (*B.*)

The Lord, before and beyond whom there is no other. (*Z.*, Yasna, xxviii. 3.)

My name is He who hath shaped everything. (*Z.*, Ahura-Mazḍa Yasht, 14.)

Aṭ hoi ḍāmām, ṭhvahmī āḍām, Ahurā !
(*Z.*, Gāṭhā, 48.7)
(Ahura ! the Beginning Thou, and End !).

All these great words describe, befittingly, the I, the Self, the Principle of Consciousness Al-one, and No-thing Else.

'I' is the *Ahaḍ*, of which nothing can be predicated, not even existence or non-existence, *Zāṭi-i-sāḍij*, *Zāṭ-i-muṭlaq*, *Munqaṭa'-ul-ishāraṭ*, *Lā-ba-sharṭ-i-shay*, Shuḍḍha, Nir-guṇa, Nir-vi-shésha, Nir-ava-chchhinna, the Absolute, Pure Being (the same as Pure No-thing), Aṭtribute-less, Un-particularised, Un-conditioned.

N-Āsaḍ-āsīn-no-Saḍ-āsīṭ. (*Ṛg Véḍa*).
(Neither Non-being was, nor Being then.)
Na San na ch-Asan na ṭaṭhā na ch-ānyaṭhā,
Na jāyaṭé, vyéṭi, na ch-āvahīyaṭé,
Na varḍhaṭé, n-āpi vishuḍḍhyaṭé punar,
Vishuḍḍhyaṭé Ṭaṭ Param-ārṭha-lakshaṇam.
(*Bu.*, ASANGA.)

A-niroḍham, an-uṭpāḍam,
an-uchchéḍam, a-shāshvaṭam,
An-ék-ārṭham, a-nān-ārṭham,
an-āgamam, a-nirgamam,

Na san, n-āsan, na saḍ-asan,
Na ch-āpy-anubhay-āṭmakam,
Chaṭush-koti-vi-nir-mukṭam
Taṭṭvam Māḍhyamikā viḍuh.
(*Bu.*, NĀGĀRJUNA, ***Māḍhyamika-Kārikā.***)

(It is not non-existent, nor existent,
It is not thus, nor is it otherwise,
It takes not birth, nor grows, decays, nor dies,
It has no stain to purify away,
It is the ever Pure—such is the mark
Of that which hath no mark, the One Supreme.
It cannot be suppressed, nor yet expressed,
It cannot die, nor yet be brought to birth,
Nor is it slayable, nor everlasting,
It means not any one thing, nor yet many,
It cometh not, nor ever doth It go.
Not being, nor non-being, nor yet both,
Nor free from both ! This wondrous Mystery,
Void of these four conditions, is the Truth
Which those that tread the Middle Path declare.)

Syāḍ asṭi, syān n-āsṭi, syāḍ asṭi cha n-āsṭi cha, syāḍ a-vakṭavyah, syāḍ-asṭi ch-āvakṭavyah, syān-n-āsṭi ch-āvakṭavyah, syāḍ-asṭi cha n-āsṭi ch-āvakṭavyah.
(*J.*, ***Syāḍ-Vāḍa.***)

(Perhaps It is ; or may be It is not ;
Or it may be that It both is and not ;
Or It is only Indescribable ;
Or though unspeakable It perhaps is ;
Or It both is not and unspeakable ;
Or, seventhly, it may be that It is
And is not and unspeakable also !)

Ṭaḍ-ējaṭi, Ṭan-n-aijaṭi,
Ṭaḍ-ḍūrē, Ṭaḍ u anṭiké,
Ṭaḍ anṭar-asya sarvasya,
Ṭaḍ u sarvasy-āsya bāhyaṭah. (*U.*)

(It moveth and It moveth not at all,
It is the farthest of the far, It is
The nearest of the near, It is within,
And yet it is without all that we know.)
Alone It standeth and It changeth not ;
Around It moveth, and It suffereth not ;
The Mother of the World It may be called.

(T., Tao-ṭeh-king, THR., 6)

I am the Lord, I change not.   (<i>B.</i>, Malachi.)
An-Éka māṅhi Éka rājai, Éka māṅhi an-Éka-no,
Ék-Ānék kī nahīṅ saṅkhyā ! namo Siḍḍha
Niranjano ! (J., Bʜūḍʜᴀʀᴀ.)

(That which is One in Many, Many in One,
Yet Neither One nor Many—I bow to That !)

The Tao hath no beginning and no end. (<i>BB.</i>, 88.)
Ai ! ke ḍar héch jā na ḍārī jā !
Bu-l-a'jab māṅḍah am ke har-jā-ī !
Ba-jahān ḍar hamésha paiḍā-ī !
Lék ḍar chashm-i-man na mī āyī !

(S., Sāḍɪ, Mā-muqīmān.)

(O Thou that hast no place in any place,
And yet, what wonder !, art in every place !
That art appearing perpetually,
In every place within this wheeling world,
Yet cannot be encompassed by my eyes !)

(The Tao cannot be heard ; what can be heard
Is not the Tao ; the Tao cannot be seen ;
What can be seen is not the Tao at all.
By words the Tao may not be well expressed;
What can be thus expressed is not the Tao.
The formless gives to every form that form ;
Can we know It as else than Void of Form ?
The Nameless gives to every name that name ;

It-Self may not be named but by all names.)
(*BB.*, 87 ; *SBE.*, vol, 40, p. 69.)

Chakra, chihna, aru varṇa, jāṭi,
aru pāṭi nahina jihu,
Rūpa, ranga, aru rékha, bhékha,
koi kahi na sakaṭa jihu,
A-chala-mūraṭi, Anu-bhava-prakāsa,
Amriṭ-oja kahijai !
Koti Indra-Inḍrān Shāha-
shāhāna ganijai !
Ṭri-bhuvana Mahī-pa ! sura nara asura,
N-éṭi, N-éṭi, vana ṭrna kahaṭ,
Ṭava sarva nāma kathai kavana,
karama nāma varnaṭa sumaṭ !
Éka mūraṭi an-éka ḍarshana,
kīna rūpa an-éka,
Khéla khéla a-khéla khélana
anṭa ko phira Éka !
(*Si.*, GURU GOVINDA SINHA, *Jāp.*)

(O Thou ! that hath no mark, sign, caste, or creed,
No clan, tribe, form, or color, or outline,
No special shape or dress ! Thou Movelessness !,
Self-luminosity eternally !,
Measureless, fathomless, All-Potency !,
Lord of the three worlds—Waking, Dreaming,
Sleep !—
Angels, men, titans, forests, grasses, all,
Only 'Not-This', 'Not-This', of Thee declare !
Who may recite Thy Names and Works in full,
Since every name and every work is Thine !
One art Thou, countless yet Thy Multitude !
All forms are Thine through which Thou makest
Play ;
All merge back into Thee at End of Day !)

A-nir-vachanīyam. (Vḗḍānṭa.)
(This Self indeed is indescribable
In words, though indefeasibly Self-known.)

Whom else can all these 'descriptions' which are 'non-descriptions', proclamations of inability to describe, fit, except the Self? This so indescribable 'I' cannot be proved by anything else. The 'I' proves whatever else is provable. Nobody saw the 'I' being born or dying. *Bodies* are seen being born and dying; never an 'I,' the 'I'. 'I' only can see 'I' being born or dying; Consciousness only can be conscious of consciousness originating or ceasing; which is a self-contradiction. '*Another's* consciousness,' 'another-consciousness', cannot be conscious of '*My* consciousness,' of 'I-consciousness', beginning or ending; that again is a self-contradiction. The fact is that the Principle of Consciousness, the Self, is One, Universal, all-pervading, a Plenum without parts, without break. The appearance of separate individual selves, of separateness, *ṭafraqā*, b h é ḍ a, is an illusion, is the great *jā'l* of the *Jā'el*, the m ā y ā of the M ā y ī; as the appearance of countless bubbles, ripples, waves, billows, in the ocean, separate-seeming yet inseparate from the ocean and each other. There is no 'Another-consciousness.' 'Consciousness' is always only '*I*-consciousness', '*My*-consciousness'; never 'an-other-consciousness'. One Consciousness only animates all material forms. The methods, the degrees, the kinds of manifestation are infinitely different in the infinite forms. That One Consciousness appears as now sleeping, now waking, in this form; or as giving up that form; or as taking up another. It never can conceive itself as beginning or ceasing. Whatever the point of time, in the past, or in the future, a few seconds away, or trillions and quadrillions of years distant, at which it may try to conceive itself as ceasing or beginning—it is already present *beyond* and *before* that point of time; it *includes* that point of time, with all the intervening period, *within* its vast embrace, and reaches infinitely farther still, beyond, on both sides. Truly is this Self-consciousness Unique, vaster than the vastest, smaller than the smallest.

Universal Being, *Hasṭī-i-muṭlaq*, Saṭṭā-sāmanya, is the logician's *summum genus*, *jins-i-ā'lā*, parā-jāṭi. At the other end are the smallest particles, atoms, electrons, protons, ions, super-atoms, param-āṇus, or whatever else they may be called, (—and neither the largest nor the smallest can ever be reached in any given time and space, for the infinitesimal is also infinite—), aṇu, *zarra*, the *summum individuum*, *ṭashakkhus-i-aḍnā*, para-vishésha. This I is both Universal Being and, ultimately, finally, particular in-divis-ible In-divid-ual. It is Infinite as well as Infinitesimal. What is the proof of Universal Being, of "Is," *est*, *hast*, asṭi? Is it not I, My Consciousness, 'Am'? Am I not present everywhere and everywhen? Whatever significance, smallest or vastest, can be assigned to these two words, is already *within* My Consciousness. 'Am' is the proof of 'Is'; not 'Is' of 'Am'. The only Being that we know, for certain, without a possibility of doubt, is My Being, 'Am'; all other beings, all other existences, have only such and so much existence as My Consciousness of them gives to them. What is the proof of the most utterly 'particularised' being? Again, nothing else than 'Am,' 'I am'. For, obviously, nothing is more 'a-*tom*-ic', in-divis-ible, more immediately, positively, definitely other-repudiating, nothing more completely distinguishes itself off from all 'others', than 'I,' my feel of 'personality,' here and now. Yet this so extremely compressed and limited 'here and now and thus' is infinitely expansible to 'anywhere and anywhen and also anyhow'. Whatever stretch of space or time or wealth of experiences I bring into my consciousness, my imagination, I *envelope* it all.

> Wasea' Rabbonā kulle shayīn ilmā...
> Huā alā kulle shayīn muhīṭ...
> Huā mākum yanama kunṭum. (*Q.*)
> (God's Consciousness envelopeth all things...
> He doth pervade, include, all things and beings...
> Wherever you may be, He is with you.)
> Aṇor-aṇīyān, mahaṭo mahīyān. (*U.*)
> (Greater than greatest, than smallest more small).

So-yam Āṭmā...ésha ma Āṭmā...sarva-karmā, sarva-kāmah, sarva-ganḍhah, sarva-rasah, sarva-gaṭah, sarva-prém-āspaḍah, sarvaṭo-mukhah, sarva-jñah, sarvaṭah-pāṇi-pāḍah, sarv-ānana-shiro-grīvah, sarvaṭ-okshi-shiromukhah, sarvaṭah-shruṭi-mān, sarva-bhūṭa-sṭhah, sarva-bhūṭa-guhā-shayah, sarva-bhūṭa-ḍamanah, sarva-bhūṭ-ādhi-vāsah, sarva-bhūṭ-ānṭar-Āṭmā, sarva-bhṛṭ, sarva-vyāpī, sarv-ājīvah, sarva-samsṭhah, sarva-sṛk, sarva-smṛṭ, sarva-harah, sarv-āḍhi-shṭhānah, sarv-ānu-syūṭah, sarv-ānu-bhūh, sarv-ānṭarah, sarv-āparah, sarv-āshī, sarv-éshvarah, sarv-Āham-mānī, sarv-ābhi-ḍhānah Aham-iṭi, sarva-mayah. (*U.*)

(This Self, My-Self, does *all* acts that are done;
Feels all desires that are felt anywhere;
Smells, tastes, sees, hears, and touches everything;
All heads, eyes, ears, arms, legs, mouths, hands, and feet,
Are Mine, My Self's, *the* Self's; It dwells in all;
Creates, pervades, preserves, destroys all;
All life of every living thing is drawn
From Its infinite life; all death—Its sleep;
Whoever knows, and whatsoe'er he knows,
Is known by It, by Me, by the One Self;
It is the Lord of All; Its Final Name
Is 'I', the Universal Name of All,
That *every* living 'one' gives to 'one-Self.')

I say, 'I am a human being'; I become identified in interest and sympathy with the whole of the human race, some two thousand million individuals. 'I am an Indian'—my consciousness at once contracts to three hundred and fifty million. 'I am Bhagavān Ḍās *alias* Abḍul Qāḍir"—it shrinks immensely with immense rapidity to a single lump of a few score pounds of bone and flesh and blood. 'I am a living being'—it suddenly expands infinitely to embrace all the universe, for there is not an atom of matter that is not alive, not pervaded by the Spirit, by Consciousness, by Life.[1]

---

[1] How it expands the consciousness, broadens the mind, enlarges the heart, and promotes science and philosophy, if we look for similarity amidst diversity, and unity amidst similarity; and how it contracts the outlook, narrows the intelligence, warps the sympathy, hinders appreciation of rational knowledge, if we look for differences rather than agreements, dividing features instead of unifying ones; may be illustrated thus. A greatly esteemed Maulavī friend writes to me that the 'essentials' of Islam are, (a) Belief in (1) Allah, (2) Muhammad as His Chief Prophet, and other prophets, (3) the Qurān as God's word, (4) the Day of Judgment, (5) God's omniscience, and (b) Practice of (6) *salāṭ* or *namāz*, (7) *saum* or *rozā*, (8) *zakāṭ*, (9) *hajj*, (10) *jehāḍ*, (11) the three festivals, Īḍ-ul-fiṭr, Iḍ-uz-zohā, Muharram. An equally worthy Pandit says the 'essentials' of Hinḍuism are, (a) Belief in (1) Param-éshvara, (2) Kṛshṇa as His Chief *Avaṭāra*, and other *avaṭāras*, (3) the Véḍa as God's word, (4) the Judgment of Yama, in accordance with the Laws of Karma and Re-incarnation, (5) the omniscience and accuracy of Yama's recorder, Chiṭra-Gupṭa, and (b) Practice of (6) *sanḍhyā*, (7) *vraṭa-upavāsa*, especially on *ekāḍashī*, (8) *ḍāna*, (9) *ṭīrtha-yāṭrā*, (10) *ḍharma-rakshā*, (11) a number of seasonal and historical festivals, *e. g.*, Holī (spring), Nir-jalā (summer), Ḍeva-shāyanī (beginning of rains), Shrāvaṇī (middle of rains), Dev-oṭṭhāna (end of rains), Ḍīpāvalī (autumn), Makara-snāna (winter), etc., and Rāma-nawamī (the birthday of Rāma), Kṛshṇ-āshtamī (the birthday of Kṛshṇa), etc., and (12) Varṇ-āshrama-ḍharma (the system of four 'class-castes and four stages of life). Here are two sets of 'essentials'. And there are

The sense of the 'separateness' of each personality, 'Ego-ism', the sense that 'I am I' and 'you are you', is so strong; this b h é ḍ a-

---

two ways of interpreting them. If we see them with the eye of difference, which sees particulars only—the stage is set for a mutual breaking of heads and feuds descending from century to century. But if we see them with the eye of agreement, which discerns the common features, the genera, behind the particulars, clearly—then we have irresistible inducement for hand-shakings and embracings and rejoicing of hearts.

Sarvaḍā sarva-bhāvānām
sāmānyam vṛḍḍhi-kāraṇam ;
Hrāsa-heṭur-visheshas-ṭu ;
pravṛṭṭir-ubhayasya cha. (*Charaka.*)
(If we look at the common elements,
Which make the genus, then all entities
Expand from more to more ; but if we look
Exclusively upon the differences,
Then all things shrink to ever narrower limits.
Both tendencies are ever at their work.
The wise man sides with the inclusive one.)

The prophet Muhammad has been quoted before as appealing to all to meet on high common ground. We have only to translate the *two* sets of 'essentials' into gener-al terms to see the essential *unity* of them. Thus: (a) Belief in (1) the Supreme Being, (2) highly advanced philanthropic souls, appearing from time to time in various races, as great teachers and lovers of mankind, (3) sacred scriptures, embodying knowledge which is of most help to mankind, (4) the law of cause and effect, of action and reaction, whereby sin unfailingly meets punishment, and virtue reward, in

buddhi, *ghairiyat*, created by the separateness of the bodies, is so overpoweringly ascendant; that the concept, the feeling, the sense, of a *common* I, a single I, running through all the bodies, and vitalising and energising and moving them all—is very, very, difficult to apprehend at first. Yet it is the very heart, the foundation, of all Religion. Like lesser but also difficult concepts, in all sciences, it becomes more and more clear, by dwelling upon, reflection, meditation. Analogies, as always, are very useful. My toes and fingers, my limbs, my sensor and motor

---

its own proper time, here or hereafter, (5) the omniscience and impartial justice of the Supreme Being; and (b) Practice of (6) prayer, (7) self-denying restraint of the senses, especially of the tongue, (8) discriminate charity, (9) pilgrimage and travel in the spirit of reverence for all manifestations of God's Nature, (10) defence of the right against wrong, (11) disciplines, festivals, public rejoicings and mournings for expression and promotion of fellow-feeling, (12) a rational Social Organisation, with a just division of the social labor, of the means of living, and of the necessaries, the comforts, and the luxuries or prizes of life, in accordance with the vocational temperaments of the different types of men, as indicated by the principles of psychology. Incidentally, Yama is the same as Al Qābiz, the Regulator, Judge, Punisher; and Chiṭragupṭa is Al-Muhsiy, the Recorder, the Counter, the Accountant, the 'Hidden Picture,' the Lauh-i-Mahfūz, the 'Preserved Tablet' of *Hāfizā*, Memory, Universal Mind, in which all is ever recorded and preserved, past, present, and future; Skṭ., *Chiṭ* or *Chiṭi*.

organs, the billions of living cells, which make up the 'I' or 'me' that is my living body, are all separate from each other, and have independent lives. Yet, are they separate? Have they independent lives? My 'I' runs through them all, holds them all together. The word 'we'; the feel 'sympathy'; the fact 'common interest'; the thing 'common property', 'public property'—all these would be impossible, if there were no unity, running latent, through the patent diversity and multiplicity of the world.

To make this latent Unity less latent, to make human beings more conscious of it, is the main purpose of Religion; and to make it fully patent, v a i-r ā g y a, *mujānibaṭ*, v i-s h ā ḍ a, *bé-zārī*, m a h ā-k a r u ṇ ā, *rahm*, change of heart, altruism, disgust with our own egoism and egoism in general, dis-illusion-ment, world-weariness, world-sadness, satiety, surfeit, n i r-v é ḍ a, *sérī-az-ḍuṇyā*, *dil-barḍāshṭagī*, and great compassion for the world, a craving, yearning, that all these other helpless souls as well as our own, wandering in the dark, may see light, may find the way out of this terrible labyrinth—all these are needed. They create the state of mind, the condition of soul, in which the finite dissolves into the Infinite, emotional and intellectual egoism is broken by emotional and intellectual altruism, and leaves behind Universalism. Some prefer to call this mood as Spiritual Consciousness, Super-mind, y o g a-j a-j ñ ā n a, a state transcending ordinary Intellect, a peculiar state of exaltation and realisation, like the rising of the sun upon a world of darkness; though, bye and bye, the exalted glories of the many-hued splendours of the dawn settle down into the steady light of day, and are utilised for the word's work, are made 'integral for life', are 'integrated into the daily life', as some would say.

In a sense, it is perfectly true that there is a special descent of the 'supra-mental' Divine, in such a condition; that God comes in, because ego-ism has gone out and made room; and the whole life is transformed. But it is also true that in the case of the 'lower knowledge' of any special science, the same process of 'yoga', though on a lower level, always takes place. Every discovery and invention is followed by an elation and exaltation in the inventor's and discoverer's being. 'Yoga is performed in all states and stages, on all planes of mind': thus declares the *Yoga-sūṭra*. 'Change of Heart', from hard to soft, from s ā-r ā g y a to v a i-r ā g y a, from k r ū r a-ṭ ā to k a r u ṇ ā, from *ṭakabbur* to *hilm,* from *g̣harrah* to *inkisār*, is absolutely neccessary, before God can come into it. Sympathy, Fellow-feeling, is of, from, by, Love Spiritual; and such Love is God.

God is very near the simple, innocent, guileless, unselfish, loving child—unconsciously; or, better, supra-consciously. He is very near the wise man in his second childhood—who has become as children, 'simple of heart'; but deliberately so, because he has realised the evils consequent on crookedness; 'natural' again, because he has experienced and put aside artificial ways; 'un-sophisticated', by voluntary de-sophistication.

Except ye be converted and become as little children, ye shall not enter into the kingdom of heaven. (*B.*)

Brāhmaṇah pāndiṭyam nir-viḍya bālyéna ṭishthāséḍ; bālyam cha pāndiṭyam cha nir-viḍya aṭha munih; a-maunam cha maunam cha nir-viḍya aṭha brāhmaṇah. (*U.*)

(The learned priest—let him feel sick of all
That load of arid learning, argument
Endless, and bitter odious debate;
Let him become again as simple child;
Next let him take to ways of silent thought,
Prolonged communing with him-Self, within;
And, finally, let him pass from that too,
And be the natural duteous Man of God.)

Such are the stages on the 'return-journey' of the soul 'back to God', on the *Qaus-i-Urūj*, or the *Safar-i-abḍ*, as also the Sūfis call it; i.e., 'the journey of the servant' back to 'Godhead'; while the opposite journey, of the *Qaus-i-Nazūl*, is correspondingly called the *Safar-i-Haq*, 'the journey of God' towards 'servanthood'. Briefly, the hard in heart cannot see God because they cannot feel Love which is an integral essential aspect of God. Ego-ism hardens the heart; altruism softens it. This mood of altruism, *bé-khuḍī*, n i s-s v-ā r ṭ h a-ṭ ā, n i r-a h a m-k ā r a, comes to every soul, in its own good time, in the course of evolution.[1]

[1]Other ways of expressing the truth are these:

A GREAT DANGER. There is a danger, a great danger, lurking here. Man, in trying to find identity with God, the inner Spirit of all, may

---

Man must neither any longer feel separate from fellow-creatures, nor feel any separateness between different component parts of his being; he must become a whole, a unity, consistent in all parts; there must be no in consistency between his thought, his word, his deed, between his intellectual, emotional, and active being-s; his religion must not be kept in a water-tight compartment, carefully preserved from contact with his daily life in the world; his religion must pervade his whole being, guide his houghts, as well as words, as well as actions; his week-days must be as his Sundays; he must be conscious in feeling as well as in intellect, i.e., he must not allow himself to be run away with, swept off his feet, by his feelings; he must deliberately choose, and feel, only the right and appropriate emotions; his personal life, as a separate-seeming individual, must become subordinate to his impersonal life as really one with the Universal; the centre of egoism, the hardness of heart, must be dissolved, by n i r-v é ḍ a, v i-s h ā ḍ a, v a i-r ā g y a, deep dispassion, *plus* m a h ā-k a r u ṇ ā, passionate compassion for all suffering. Truly 'the hard in heart cannot see God'; and 'the meek', the soft in heart, 'shall see God', and become sovereign ruler and king over their earthly bodies, and, some day, over the whole earth, literally, also, when the majority of human beings have learnt the great lesson of Evolution, have subordinated ego-ism to altruism and universalism, and have thereby brought the millennium the Golden Age, Saṭya-yuga, again—to the Earth. "Seek in the heart the source of evil, and expunge it...It is a plant that lives and increases throughout the ages...He who would deliberately identify himself with the Satan of the outer flesh of our body. This is illustrated by the story of Indra and Virochana in the *Upanishaṭs*, and of the fall of the archangel Azaziel into the state of Satan in the Christian and Muslim legend.[1] The consequences of

enter upon the Path...must tear this thing out of his heart. Then the heart will bleed and the whole life of the man seem utterly dissolved. This ordeal must be endured. Each man is to himself absolutely the Way, the Truth, and the Life. But he is so only when he grasps his whole individuality firmly, and, by the force of his awakened spiritual will, recognises this individuality as not himself, but that thing which he has with pain created for his own use, and by means of which he purposes, as his growth slowly developes, to reach to the life beyond individuality:" (*Light on the Path*, Theosophical Publishing House, Adyar, Madras.) This opening out of the Individual soul to and into the Universal Spirit, takes place, in each case, in its own good time. It cannot be forced. It begins from within. The soul grows as the flower grows, by its own vital force, and in accord with the cyclic laws of life. But the gardener can make the conditions which are most favorable to the growth. The older generation teaches the outlines of general geography to the younger generation. The actual visiting of any of the places of the earth has to be done by the grown-up. So has the message of Essential Religion to be given by the father to the child, and to remain in his mind as seed, to put forth root and shoot, branch, leaf, bud, blossom, and fruit, in its own good time. Then the 'heard' will become the 'seen'.

[1] A'zāz-i-El seems to mean "the Supreme Greatness

such subtle error are endlessly disastrous; as when the public *servant* commits the grievous mistake of regarding himself as the public

---

of God". The Majesty of Benevolence, inverted, becomes the Pride of Malevolence. *Demon est Deus inversus.* There is another, and fine, conception of Satan in Hebrew theology. God commands his highest angel to 'act' as his reverse and adverse, as Satan, deliberately to test and strengthen and advance souls to salvation, through sin and suffering. When they fail to stand his tests and temptations, Satan rejoices—outwardly; inwardly he weeps. Ultimately, when they spurn him, he gnashes his teeth—outwardly; inwardly he rejoices greatly. Nāra-ḍa (n ā r a m, m o k s h a m, ḍ a ḍ ā ṭ i, 'he who brings release, salvation') is a very different yet similar figure in Purāṇic mythology. He is a well-known devotee and favorite of Vishṇu, and his chief 'sport and pastime' is to cause wars between kings, by subtle praises of one to another, to arouse their jealous pride. Kḥwājā Khizr is yet another, different yet similar, figure in Islāmic legend. In Purāṇic mythology Inḍra, the king of the ḍ é v a s, gods or angels, also discharges the duty of tempting and trying ṛ ṣ h i s, y o g i s, aspirants for psychical and spiritual perfection and m o k s h a, through the agency of a p s a r ā - s, nymphs. In Buḍḍhism, Māra is the great tempter. Etymologically, the word means the 'slayer', but actually it is used as synonymous with Kāma, Eros, Love-Lust; because carnal love-lust leads to death. *Birth* of physical body necessarily means *death* of it, later. Also, Lust precedes and generates all the other evil passions, which 'slay' the good spiritual emotions and affections. This will be expounded, later on, more fully.

master; or the *trustee* makes himself the *proprietor;* or the basis of the social organization is shifted from *vocational temperament* and aptitude to *hereditary* caste, all duties are forgotten, and all rights are grabbed, as by divine *birthright*, without need of any *worth*. The most supernal blessing then becomes the most infernal curse. In earlier times, this sacred truth, of the identity, in essence, of Man and God, was not always preached publicly, lest it be not understood, but turned away from, and so put to shame, by those not interested in and not ready for it; or becoming cheap, be treated with levity and ridicule by the light-minded, in whom familiarity breeds contempt; or, worst of all, being disastrously misunderstood, breed arrogance instead of humility, hateful scorn instead of love. But the conditions are different to-day. The general level of intelligence is much higher. The opposite error, of sensual and proud egoism, is rampant. Corrective counsel is greatly needed and is perhaps more easily applicable. Argument has perhaps greater chance. Finally, there seems no other resource, no better alternative, for fighting the forces of darkness, whose chief weapon is viciously false propaganda, than to try to spread right knowledge. The very purpose of genuine religion is to guard man against such perversion, to lead him from the small self to the Great Self, from sinner to saint, from selfishness to selflessness, from Darkness to Light, from Untruth to Truth, from Evil to Good, from Satan to God, from *Khuḍī* to Khuḍā, from *Angra Mainyu to Spenṭa Mainyu*, from Matter to Spirit, from the Third person to the First, from Jīv-āṭmā to Param-āṭmā, from Egoism to Altruistic Universalism.

Mazaḍā Ahurā!...Ma-ibyo ḍāvoi ahvāo asṭavaṭ chā hyaṭ chā manangho āyapṭā.

Hyaṭ ṭā ūrvāṭā sashaṭhā yā Mazaḍāo ḍaḍāṭā...khīṭī chā anīṭī chā...aṭ aipī ṭāīsh anghahaṭī ūshṭā.

Yayāo spanyāo ūīṭi mravaṭa yéma angrém no-īṭ nā manāo, nō-īṭ séngha, nō-īṭ khraṭavo, na édā varanā, nō-īṭ ūkh-ḍhā, nō-īṭ shyaoṭhnā, no-īṭ ḍaé-nāo, no-īṭ ūrvāno sachanṭé. (*Z.*, Gāṭhā, 28. 2 ; 30. 11 ; 45. 2)

Lord Mazaḍā Ahurā !, grant unto us
To realise the difference between
Our two selves, the physical lower one,
And th' other, higher, of the better mind.
Of these two selves that Mazḍā gave to us,
The higher self points ever to the Right,
The lower one misleads towards the Wrong ;
Determined by these two are all our acts.
The Brighter Self unto the Darker says:
Neither our minds, nor well-cognised beliefs,
Nor duties, manners, words, nor our deeds,
Nor our religions, nor our souls agree.)

Ḍvā suparṇā sayujā sakhāyā
Ekam vṛksham pari-shasvajāṭé ;
Ṭayor-ékah pippalam svāḍu aṭṭi,
An-ashnan Anyo-abhi-chākashīṭi. (*U.*)

(Two birds do nest upon the self-same tree ;
One tastes the fruits—now bitter, and now sweet ;
The other looketh on eternally.)

Manas ṭu ḍvi-viḍham prokṭam

Shuḍḍham ch-āshuḍḍham éva cha ;
Ashuḍḍham kāma-sankalpam,
Shuḍḍham kāma-vivarjiṭam. (U.)

(The mind is of two kinds, one good, one bad ;
Motived by selfish egoist desire,
Is the bad mind ; inspired by altruism,
Free from all foul desires, is the good mind.)

Ashā and Ḍruj (Love and Hate, Ichchhā or Rāga and Ḍroha or Ḍvésha); Ārmaiṭī and Ṭārmaiṭī (righteous activity and wrongful activity); Spenta-Mainyu and Angra Mainyu, good or bright Spirit or Mind and bad or dark one; Vohu or Vahishto Mano and Achishto Mano, pure mind and impure mind; such are other words, in the Zoroastrian Books, for the same pair of opposites, the two *ūrvāṭā*[1], given to us by Ahurā Mazaḍā, the One 'Great Wise all-ideating all-creating' Principle of Consciousness.

Very great is the need to be ever alertly and watchfully on guard against the awful danger of deliberately identifying ourselves with the lower, selfish, Evil mind, the baser nature, instead of with the higher, un-self-ish Good mind, the nobler nature, and the Universal Self. Thls asmi-ṭā, aham-kāra, *khuḍi*, ego-ism, the lower self, is indeed the element of Satan in man. *It* is the

[1]The Qurān mentions two angels, Hārūṭ and Mārūṭ. Shri J. M. Chatterji, *The Ethical Conceptions of the Gāṭhā*, suggests that these are the same as those known to the Jews and the pre-Christian Armenians as Horot and Morot ; to the Zoroastrians as Haurvāṭā and Amereṭā ; to the Vaiḍikas as Ṛṭam and Amṛtam.

root of all lust and hate, all greed and pride of 'martial glory' and 'land-hunger', all adultery and robbery, all rape and murder, all sadism and masochism, all aggression, all self-assertion and and other-suppression, all the most monstrous tyranny and oppression, all political and religious bigotry, fanaticism, persecution and cruellest torturing of dissentients and innocents. "Thy will, O Lord!, Thou Universal Self of All!, not mine!" —says the servant of God and Humanity, the servant of God in Man. "My will, O fool!, thou slave of mine!, not thine!" says the unwitting, or, far worse, the witting slave of the Satan in Man. Be ever on guard, vigilantly, against that Satan! God and Satan are both *within* us!

THE MANY NAMES OF THE ALL-PERVADING ONE SELF. Science no longer denies this first and most important truth, of the Universal Self, the all-pervading Principle of Consciousness; as we have seen before. Scientific materialism is dead. It is generally recognized that Consciousness is indefeasible. It proves the existence of matter and of the senses which perceive matter. It cannot be proved by the senses or by matter. It illuminates itself as well as all other things.

Brahma sarvam āvṛṭya ṭishthaṭi.
Ṭasya bhāsā sarvam iḍam vibhāṭī. (*U.*)
(Brahma abides, enveloping all things;
All things appear, illumined by Its light.)
Allāho be kulle shayīn muhīṭ.
Allāho nūr us-samāvāṭi wal arḍ. (*Q.*)
(Allāh surroundeth and encloseth all;

His light illumineth all heaven and earth.)

In Him all things live and move and have their being...Do not I fill heaven and earth? saith the Lord...The Spirit of God filleth all the earth, and that (space or heaven) which contains all things. (*B.*)

He is the light that lighteth every man and everything (*B.*)

Great Heaven is intelligent, clear-seeing, and is with you in all your doings. (*C.*, *Shi King.*)

Obviously, Consciousness, God's Consciousness, Man's Consciousness, the Self's Consciousness, includes, encompasses, illumines all things. 'To be' is 'to be known'; to know is to recognize and thereby impart existence. *Esse est percipi. Viḍyaṭé* (is known) is *viḍyaṭé* (exists.)

This Consciousness, this I, is behind every name and form and act.

Kéchiṭ Karma vaḍanṭy-énam,
    Sva-bhāvam aparé janāh,
Éké Kālam, paré Ḍaivam,
    Pumsah Kāmam uṭ-āparé,
Éṭam éké vaḍanṭy-Agnim,
    Manum anyé, Prajā-paṭim,
Inḍram éké, paré Prāṇam,
    Aparé Brahma Shāshvaṭam.
Brahma-iva sarvāṇi nāmāni, sarvāṇi rūpāṇi,
    sarvāṇi karmāṇi bibharṭi. (*Bh.*, *M.*, *U.*)

(Some call It Karma, some Self-Nature name It,
Some call It Time, and others call It Fate,
Some say It is th' eternal Urge and Surge
Of Prime Desire, some name It Agni too,
The Luminous Fire which leadeth all to Self.

Some name it Manu, Universal Mind,
Some Prajā-paṭi, Lord of Progeny,
Some Inḍra, Chief of all great Nature-Forces,
Some Brahma, Vast, Eternal, Infinite,
Which as the 'I', the Universal Self,
Hidden, yet Manifest too, everywhere
Wears, bears, and does, all forms and names and acts.)[1]

---

[1]The following Skt. quotations give many more names, used by different schools of thinkers or devotees, and at the same time prove widespread recognition of the fact that the *Same* Mystery is meant by all the different names:

Yam Shaivāh sam-up-āsaté Shiva iṭi,
Brahm-éṭi Veḍānṭinah,
Bauḍḍhā Buḍḍha iṭi, pramāṇa-patavah
Karṭ-éṭi Naiyāyikāh,
Arhan-iṭy-aṭha Jaina-shāsana-raṭāh,
Karm(a)-éṭi Mīmāmsakāh,
So-(A)yam vo viḍaḍhāṭu vānchhiṭa-phalam
Ṭrailokya-nāṭho Harih.
Ké-chiṭ ṭām Ṭapa iṭy-āhus,
Ṭamah ké-chiṭ, Jadam paré,
Jñānam, Māyām, Praḍhānam cha,
Prakṛṭim Shakṭim-apy-Ajām,
Vimarsha iṭi vā Shaivāh,
Aviḍyām iṭaré janah. (*Ḍevi Bhāgavaṭa*).

Ésha éva Vimarshash, Chiṭih, Chaiṭanyam, Āṭmā,
Sva-rasā, Uḍiṭā, Parā-varā, Svā-ṭanṭryam,
Param-Āṭmā, Aun-mukhyam, Aishvaryam,
Saṭ, Ṭaṭṭvam, Saṭṭā, Sphuraṭā, Sārah, Māṭrikā,
Mālinī, Hṛḍayā, Mūrṭih, Sva-samviṭ, Spanḍa-iṭy-āḍi-shabḍaih Āgamaih uḍ-ghushyaṭé.

In the Zoroastrian scriptures it is called Vahma, the same as Brahma of the Veda-Upanishaṭs, in its all-comprehensive transcendent aspect; and Ahurā Mazaḍā in its active and immanent aspect, as Universal mind, Brahmā. Another name for Vahma, in the Zoroastrian scriptures, seems to be Zerouane Akerane, (Skt. Sarvam or Sāram Akāraṇam?) 'the Uncaused Cause of all causes', or 'the Causeless Essence of all'. Some Sūfis make a similar distinction between Ahaḍ and Allāh-ar-Rahmān-ar-Rahīm.

(*Gupṭa-vaṭī Ṭīkā* on *Ḍurgā-Sapṭa-shaṭī*, 'Up-oḍghāṭa' or Introduction.)

(Shiva, Brahma, Buḍḍha, Karṭā, Arhaṭ, Karma, Thought, All-holding Consciousness, Universal Memory, Self, Self-taster, Awake, Before-and-After, High-and-Low, Self-dependence, Supreme Self, Eagerness, Urge, Lordliness, Being, Essence, Thatness, Existence, Vibration, Core, Measuring Mother, Matter, Cycling Wreath, Heart-Image, Self-awareness, Motion, Breath, Ṭapas, Ṭamas, Unconsciousness, Objectivity, Knowledge, Māyā (Illusion), Praḍhāna (Root, Source), Prakṛṭi (Nature), Shakṭi (Energy), Aviḍyā (Error)—all these are only Its names.)

The following is an attempt by an ancient Roman poet along the same lines:

"Ogugia calls Me Bachchus; Egypt thinks Me Osiris; The Musians name Me Ph'anax; the Indi consider Me Dionysus (Ḍivā-nisham, Day-Night); the Roman Mysteries call me Liber; the Arabian Race, Adonis (same as Dionysus)!" (Ausonias, quoted by H. P. Blavatsky, *Isis Unveiled*, ii. 302.)

The distinction between Impersonal Absolute Brahma, the Motionless Spectator, and personalised Brahmā, the Active Creator, is the same.

Spenṭā Mainyū sraoṭū Mazaḍāo Ahuro yéhyā *Vahmé* vohū frashī manangha ahyā khraṭu fro mā sāsṭū vahishṭā...Aṭ hoī *Vahmém* ḍémāné garo niḍāma. (*Z.*, Gāṭhā, 45. 6, 8).

(Lord of benignant Spirit, Mazaḍā !,
Listen to this my prayer, and teach me well
What he should do who would with a pure mind
Seek earnestly to find the Peace of Brahm' !
...May we find Brahma in the House of Songs.)

Yé jī aḍāīsh ashā ḍrujém venghaīṭī,
hyaṭ asamshuṭā, yā ḍaībīṭānā fraokhṭā,
amérétāīṭī ḍaévāīsh chā mashyāīsh chā,
aṭ ṭoī savāīsh *Vahmém* vakshaṭ Ahurā.
(*Z.*, Gāṭhā, 48. 1).

(May Ahurā give us the truth of Brahm',
May He unite us with that Absolute,
When we have undergone successfully
The disciplines whereby the Vice in us
Is overthrown by Virtue, which make man
Divinely meritorious, and which bring
Salvation unto men and gods alike.)

...Vésṭā *Vahmeng* Séraoshā rāḍhangho...
(*Z.*, Gāṭhā, 46. 17)

(By worship and devotion know ye Brahm'.)

Ṭaḍ viḍḍhi pra-ṇı-pāṭéna pari-prashnéna sévayā. (*G.*)

(Know it by earnest quest, and questioning,
With due submission and with humble heart
And service, of the old and wise who know).

In the Buddhist scriptures too the name Brahma is given to the Supreme;

(Brahma am I, Great Brahma, the Supreme,

The Unsurpassed, Perceiver of All Things,
Controller, Maker, Fashioner, Lord of All,
Chief, Victor, Ruler, Father of All Beings
That ever have been, are, and are to be.)
(*Kévaḍḍha-Suṭṭa, Ḍīgha-Nikāya* ; *BB.*, 115).

Yehovah (Jehovah, Yahveh) is the Hebrew word; Hayy and Yahyā are the Arabic words for the same; O-hau, O-hau-hau, are the Sāma-Veḍa's names for it; J(I)āo is the Phoenician. All these names are formed of the vowel sounds aspirated; the breathings of man, in short; each of which breathings 'names' and invokes God. 'So-(a)ham,' '(a)ham-Sah', 'That am I', 'I am That', is the a-japā Gāyaṭrī, the 'unspoken perpetual prayer', of each and every living being. It is un-uttered, yet is uttered in and by every ingoing and outgoing breath; for none can live at all without perpetual support from Him, the *Anima Mundi*, the Soul of the World, the Life-breath of the Universe.[1]

[1] It is noteworthy that there are some 'natural' sound-names of the Supreme. First, there is the inner sound of the AUM (pronounced Om), like the humming of the bee, or the sound heard when the ears are tightly closed. With a little practice, this sound can be heard, within the head, between the ears as it were, even without closing the ears. It is the an-āhaṭa nāḍa, 'un-struck or un-uttered sound', mentioned in connection with yoga-ways. Graduations of it are mentioned in the Upanishaṭs and Yoga books. "The Word was with God and the word was God," says the English Bible.

In the Chinese religions It is called Yi (the Changeless Principle of Change), T'ien (Heaven,

---

Probably the original Hebrew word means 'sound', rather than 'word'. Ákāsha, (which means Space, as well as the primal 'element' filling Space), whose 'attribute' or 'quality' is 'sound', (as 'touch' of 'air', 'taste' of 'water'), is the *first* manifestation; therefore it may well be said that 'the word', i.e., sound, was with God, and was God.

Next after this natural primal name, which seems to be the Hidden, Inner, Name, sometimes spoken of in mystical works as 'the lost (i e., hidden) word or name', there comes the first uttered name. This is some form or other, in the older languages, of a collocation of the primary vowels, combined with the aspirate, and sometimes the nasal also; e.g, O-hau-hau in the Sāma-véḍa, also Huvā-hāyi, Huvā-hoyi, Hāyi-Hāyi, (cf. 'Ā-hāi! Ā-hai', of some boatmen's songs); Iao, among the Phoenicians and the Egyptians; Y(od)-H(é)-V(au)-H(é), in Hebrew; Hayy in Arabic, also Yahyā; T (Ch) ao, in Chinese; Heu-Heu, among some African Negro tribes. And so on. The sound of 'breathing', wherein and whereby the (non-yogī) living human being realises his Self-existence, continuously, incessantly, 'I am', 'a s m i', 'ahmi', is imitated in its various shades by these names. A person in great pain, groaning, utters but a form of this primal sound, and thereby calls upon the Supreme for help, unconsciously. All sorts of 'moods of mind', 'states of being', of grief, wonder, fear, anger, enquiring curiosity, sorrow, joy, may be, and are, expressed by such exclamations, interjections, interrogations, as Àh!, Hā!, Oho!, Oh!, Hūṁ! Hūṅ!, Aiṅ! Hāy!, Ahā!, Wāh!, Ūṅ?, Ai-hai!; and so forth.

Heavenly Destiny, Divine Ordainment, Fate), T'ai Chi (the Great Ultimate or Origin), Ch'i (Universal Energy), Tao (the Unnameable and Indescribable Principle of All Activity; the Way, the Reason, of the Universe), Hun Tun or Hun Lun (Chaos), Ming (Destiny), Shen (Spirit), Hsuen (the Mysterious). Jainism, like Buḍḍhism, gives ultimately the same name, i. e., 'the Supreme Self', to the Ultimate Mystery as Vaiḍika Dharma does. Thus, in a fine prayer-hymn, which is in common use among Jainas, we read:

> Yo ḍarshana-jñāna-sukha-sva-bhāvah,
> Samasṭa-samsāra-vikāra-bāhyah,
> Samāḍhi-gamyah *Param-Āṭma*-sanjñah,
> Sa Ḍéva-dévo hrḍayé mam-āsṭām.
> Sarvam nirā-krṭya vi-kalpa-jālam,
> Samsāra-kānṭāra-nipāṭa-héṭum,

The name Aham, given to the I, the Self, (Universal as well as Individual), in Samskrṭ, (the word etymologically means the deliberately 'well-constructed and refined language') embodies all the above significance and more. In the Samskrṭ alphabet, A is the first and H is the last letter-sound. The Self, A-h(am), is the First and the Last, and comprehends all; the first and last letters of the alphabet include between them all the other letters and all knowledge of all things, which can be expressed by means of letters and collocations of them. The special natural significance of each letter of the alphabet is mentioned in the *Tanṭra*-books. (See *Isis Unveiled*, ré Hewa, Eva, Iao, etc., with the help of the Index).

Viviktam-Ātmānam av-ékshya-māṇo,
Ni-līyasé ṭvam *Param-Āṭma*-ṭaṭṭvé.
Yaih *Param-Āṭmā*-(A)miṭa-gaṭi-vanḍyah,
Sarva-vi-vikṭo, bhṛsham an-avaḍyah,
Shashvaḍ-dhyāṭo manasi, labhanṭé
Mukṭi-nikéṭam vi-bhava-varam ṭé.
(*J.*, AMIṬA-GAṬI, *Sāmāyika-pātha.*)

(May He abide always within my heart,
'The Supreme Self', the One God of all gods,
Transcending all 'this-world's' ephemera,
By deepest meditation reachable!
They who have passed beyond all arguments
And doubts and false attachments of this world,
They only can behold in purity
'The Supreme Self', and in It merge themselves.
Who take their refuge in that 'Supreme-Self',
Stainless, beyond particularities,
And fix their minds on It devotedly,
Unfailingly they gain Its Blessedness.)

Says Kwan-yin-tse :

Find the Tao in *Your-Self* and you know every thing else...The holy man recognises Unity in Multiplicity and Multiplicity in Unity...The One is eternally unchangeable.[1]

A western poet has written:

Some call It Will, and some call It God ;
Some call It Fate, and some call It God ;
Some call It Evolution, and some call It God ;
Some call It Chance, and some call It God ;
Some call It Force, and some call it God.
Some call It th' Unknowable, some call it God.

---

[1] See Suzuki, *History of Chinese Philosophy*, pp. 42-'3.

Whatever the name each person who has attained to the stage of 'thinking' may give to It, the Ultimate Mystery has to be recognised.

But its nearest, dearest, fullest, greatest, and withal most intelligible and intimately familiar name is 'I', the Self in Me and in All alike.

So-(A)ham asm-īṭy-agré vyāharaṭi ; ṭaṭo-
(A)ham-namā-bhavaṭ ; ṭasmāḍ-apy-éṭarhy-
āmanṭriṭo-(A)ham ayam iṭy-év-āgré ukṭvā
ṭaḍ-ānyan-nama brūṭé, yaḍ asya bhavaṭi. (*U.*)
('I Am' is what He uttered first of all,
Therefore his principal, best, and most true
Name is the 'I' ; and so we see that when
A person is thus questioned : 'Who are you ?',
He first of all says : 'I am', then he adds
Whate'er his special name is—'So-and-so'.)
Āṭmanas-ṭu kāmāya sarvam vai priyam bhavaṭi. (*U.*)
(All things that may be dear to us are dear
For the sweet sake of our-Self alone.)
Aṭachā ahmāi vīspānām vahishṭém,
Khaṭhroyā nā Khāṭhrém ḍaidīṭā. (*Z.*, *Gāṭhā*, 43. 2).
(Give me the gift that is the best of all,
Give me the Inmost Self of all the Selves.)
Yoi Moi Ahmāi séraoshém ḍāna chayas chā.
ūpājimén haūrvāṭā amérétāṭā. (*Z.*, *Gāṭhā*, 45. 5).
(Who fix their love and choice on Me alone,
Me who reside in them, they do attain
Self-knowledge and Eternal Deathlessness
The Higher Self and Immortality.)
Yam labḍhvā ch-āparam lābham
manyaṭé n-āḍhikam ṭaṭah,
Yasmin sṭhiṭo na ḍuhkhéna
guruṇ-āpi vi-chālyaṭé. (*G.*)

(Than gain of Whom there is no greater gain;
When fixed in Whom, sorrows shake one no more.)

God is the Universal Self; the individual self is 'heaven in us'. The immaterial divine essence, Ryochi, is 'God in us', and dwells in each individual. It is the *true* Self. The false self is an acquired personality arising from perverted beliefs; it is 'persona', i.e., that general idea of our nature which we have built up from experiencing our effect upon the world around and its effect upon us. Ryochi is 'al-one being' or 'al-one knowing', as the summum bonum, 'bliss'; it is the light which pervades the world; it is immortal all-knowing Good. It is the mediator and reconciler of 'the pair of opposites', namely, Ri and Ki, world-soul and world-matter respectively, attributes, both, of God, who is their union. Similarly the human soul embraces both Ri and Ki. As the essence of the world, God enfoldeth the world, but at the same time, He is also in our midst and even in our own bodies. (NAKAE TAJU).[1]

[1] Nakae Taju, the 'Sage of Omi' is a "distinguished Japanese philosopher of the seventeenth century. He belonged to the Chu-Hi school of philosophy which had migrated from China". The above account of his view is abridged from C. G. Jung. *Psychological Types*, pp. 268-269, whose description is based upon Tetsujiro Inouye, *Japanese Philosophy*, (1913). The 'bliss' of Ryochi is the same as the ānanḍa of Brahma, *lazzaṭ-ul-ilāhiyah*, beatitude; 'persona', 'personality', is the same as the individualised purusha, jīv-āṭmā, *shakẖs*; the *Yoga-sūṭra* explains how this 'persona' is con-creted, conglomerated, upon the basis of asmiṭā, egoism, by the growths of rāga. ḍvésha, abhinivésha, likes, dislikes, and stubborn complexes.

Sūfis say:

Kufr o ḍīñ har do ḍar raha-ṭ poyāñ,
Wahḍahu lā sharīk-ilah goyāñ. (*S.*)
(Belief and misbelief are galloping,
Both, on the road to Thee, both calling loud
For what is the One Only Ultimate!)
Momin o Ṭarsā, Yahūḍ o nék o baḍ,
Jumlagāñ rā hasṭ rū sūyé Abaḍ. (*S.*)
(Muslim, Christian, or Jew, or good or bad,
All turn their eyes to the Eternal One.)

The prophet Muhammad said:

Aṭ-ṭurqu il-Allahi kan nufūsu banī Āḍama. (*H.*)
(There are as many ways to God as souls;
As many as the breaths of Adam's sons.)

A profound truth. Each individualised soul manifests an infinitesimally different aspect of the One Infinite. Therefore its involution, its return-journey to God, must also be, in the same degree, infinitesimally different from that of all others. Christian theology has a saying to the same effect: "As many as are the breaths in the nostrils, so many are the ways to God". But the Goal is ever the Self-same.

Ruchīnām vai-chiṭryāḍ
ṛju-kuṭila-nānā-paṭha-jushām
Nṛṇām Éko gamyas-
Ṭvam asi payasām arṇava iva.
(*Shiva-Mahima-sṭuṭi.*)

(Thou the One Goal of all the many paths
Some easy, straight, some winding, difficult,
Men follow as they variously incline—
As of the countless streams the one vast sea!)

Yé-py-anya-ḍévaṭā-bhakṭā
yajanṭé shraḍḍhay-ānviṭāh,
Ṭé-pi Mām éva, Kaunṭéya !,
yajanṭy-aviḍhi-pūrvakam. (*G.*)

(Who worship other gods with heart of faith,
They too adore but Me behind those forms,
Unknowing yet of the one direct way.)

Indeed all names belong to It alone.
The Qurān says :

Lillāhul asmā ul husnā. (*Q.*)

(All beauteous names are His—the Book declares.)

It tenderly adds the adjective "beautiful", lest younger souls be disturbed. Elsewhere Muhammad has explained :

Ṭo kallimun annāso alā qaḍre uqūlahum. (*H.*)
(Speak unto men according as may be
Capacity of their intelligence.)

So Kṛshṇa has said the same :

Yaḍ yaḍ vibhūṭi-maṭ saṭṭvam
Shrī-maḍ ūrjiṭam éva vā,
Ṭaḍ Ṭaḍ év-āva-gachchha ṭvam
Mama téj-omsha-sambhavam.[1] (*G.*)

(Whatever shows forth glory, splendour, might—
Know from My ṭéjas-aspect is it born.)

---

[1]Souls not yet sufficiently experienced and advanced, are apt to be repelled, even greatly angered, on hearing such statements as are quoted on preceding pages, of the identity, in essence, of man, nay, of all living things, with God. Such scriptural declarations ***must not*** be pressed upon them. For them, the Third Person, 'He', is enough ; later on, they will turn to the First Person, 'I'.

Ṭān akṛṭsna-viḍo manḍān
krṭsna-vin-na vīchālayéṭ;
Na buḍḍhi-bhéḍam janayéḍ
ajñānām karma-sanginām. (*G.*)

(Let not the man, who knoweth all, disturb
The slower minds of those who know not all;
Do not confuse child-minds with abstract thoughts;
They must continue for some more time yet
To learn from pious rituals and works.)

Speaking out too much and too freely about things which they cannot yet comprehend will

---

In the meanwhile, for the purposes of creedal and communal peace, they should be entreated to ponder the question: "Has the *same* God created *all* the races of men, past and present, or have different Gods done so? If the same, then must not the same truths about Himself, and the same commands for mutual goodwill and peace among men, be embodied in all the religions of the past and the present; with only as much surface-difference as there is between the complexions and clothings and languages of these different races, and the climatic and other natural conditions of different countries?"

It is true, there are some sects, in *all* religions, which are firmly convinced that God deliberately creates some souls (belonging to those sects) to enjoy heaven eternally, and other souls (belonging to all the other sects) to suffer hell perpetually. Unhappily this stage of extreme self-righteousness has to be passed through, it seems, by every soul, at some time or other, in the course of its eonic evolution. One can only very gently and humbly invite such to reflect whether the All-Merciful God can possibly be so cruel.

only perplex child-minds. As the English proverb wisely advises, 'give milk to the babes and meat to the strong.' But the elders have to take care that they diligently coax the babes on towards the stronger food in due time, and do not try to keep them on milk all their life, as priestcraft does but too extensively.

A Sūfī supplies the needed comment on the Qurānic adjective "beautiful".

Ba nāmé āṅ ké Ū nāmé na ḍāraḍ,
Ba har nāmé ke kḥwānī sar bar āraḍ.
(He hath no name, and yet whatever name
Ye may call out, He lifts an answering head.)

Another says plainly:

Ḍar mazhabé ā'shiqāne Yak-rang,
Iblīs o Isrāfīl asṭ ham-sang. (*S.*)
(In the religion of the souls that love
The Changeless One, Satan weighs just the same,
And is hewn out from the same block of stone,
As Purity's Archangel Isrāfīl.)

Yet another says,

Chūn nék o baḍ as Kḥuḍā-e ḍīḍanḍ,
Rū az hama ḵhalq ḍar kashīḍanḍ. (*S.*)
(The wise saw Good and Evil both as God's;
And so they drew their hearts away from both,
And fixed them on the Master of the Two.)

Finally, the Qurān itself emphatically declares the whole truth:

Al kḥairo wa-s-sharro min Allāhi-ṭā'lā. (*Q.*)
(Both Good and Evil come from the High God.)

One of the Qurānic names of God is Al-Muzil, the Misleader and Tempter and Tester; as Māyī, the 'Illusion-maker,' in Veḍa-Upanishats.

And the full significance of the *Giṭā*-verse, quoted above, is that while the radiant and magnificent forms of life and existence manifest the Ṭéjas or *Jalālī* aspect of the Supreme Self, other forms express others of His infinite aspects.

Vishtabhy-Āham Iḍam kṛṭṣnam
Ék-ámshéna sṭhiṭo jagaṭ. (*G.*)

(The whole of all this restless moving world
Is but a little part of Me; the rest
Of Me is ever in eternal rest.)

For, indeed, He, the I, is the One in which all the Many is ever included; the One, of which the Many are but as the attributes.

Wahḍaṭ ḍar *Zāṭ*, Kasraṭ ḍar Sifāṭ. (*S.*)
(In Essence, Unity; Attributes, Multitude).

Guṇānām Āshrayas-ṭv-Éko,
Nirguṇah Kévalah saḍā;
Guṇ-opa-guṇakānām ṭu
Samkhyā n-aiv-éha viḍyaṭé.
Éko Ḍharmī ḍharma-shūnyah,
Ḍharmās ṭu sakalam jagaṭ;
Praṭyaksham Khé Mahā-Shūnyé
(A)sankhy-āndāni bhramanṭi hi.
(*Yoga-Vāsishtha*).

(Substratum of all Attributes is One,
Al-one, Eternal, Void of Attributes;
Of these, major and minor, count is not.
The One Possessor of all Attributes
Is yet devoid of all these Attributes·
This may we see e'en with the eyes of flesh.
Does not this Infinite expanse of Heaven,
Vast Emptiness of Space, (Plenum of Self),
Hold all these countless ever-whirling orbs,
'Eggs of the Infinite', untouched by them?).

While warning the wise man not to disturb the simple mind, to the advanced and thoughtful soul capable of hearing and holding wisdom, Kṛṣhṇa says clearly :

Maṭ-ṭah para-ṭaram n-ānyaṭ
kin-chiḍ-asṭi, Ḍhanan-jaya !
Mayi sarvam iḍam pr-oṭam
sūṭré maṇi-gaṇā iva.
Yé cha-iva sāṭṭvikāh bhāvāh,
rājasāh, ṭāmasāsh-cha yé,
Maṭ-ṭah év-éṭi ṭān viḍḍhi,
na ṭv-Aham ṭéshu, té Mayi.
Sukham, ḍuhkham, bhavo, bhāvo,
Bhayam, ch-ābhayam éva cha,
Yasho-ayasho, ṭapo, ḍānam
Maṭ-ṭah sarvam pra-varṭaṭé.
Maṭ-ṭah smṛṭir-jñānam ap-ohanam cha. (*G.*)

(Nought is outside of Me ; all This is strung
On Me, as beads upon a thread ; all moods,
All acts, good, bad, mixed, all are Mine alone ;
Yet am I not in them ; they are in Me.
Joy, sorrow, life, death, fear, and fearlessness,
Fame, infamy, gifts, acts of sacrifice,
All these arise from Me and Me Al-one ;
From Me, in Me, forgetfulness of Self
And folly's utmost limit ; from Me too
The Wisdom of remembrance of the Self.)

Puṇyam cha pāpam cha pāpé.
(SHANKAR-ĀCHĀRYA, *Shārīraka Bhāshya.*)

(Sin, merit, both are sin, for both do bind
The Soul—with chain of iron, or of gold.)

From the transcendental standpoint, each term of every pair of opposites is necessary to throw it into relief, to bring it into existence, by contrast, and also to neutralise it, ultimately. Good cannot possibly ex-ist without contrasting evil. Hence to abolish evil, we must abolish good also ; neither love nor hate are to be assigned to the Absolute Self, which includes both *equally*.

Pari-ṇaṭi saba jīvana kī
    ṭīna bhānṭi baranī ;
Éka pāpa, éka puṇya,
    éka rāga-haranī.
Jā méṅ shubha ashubha anḍha,
    ḍoū kara karma-banḍha,
Vīṭa-rāga-pari-ṇaṭi hī
    bhava-samuḍra ṭaranī.
Ṭyāgu shubha-kriyā-kalāpa,
    karu maṭa kaḍā cha pāpa,
Shubha méṅ na magna hoi
    Shuḍḍha-ṭā bisaranī.
Yāvaṭa shuḍḍh-opa-yoga
    pāvaṭa nāhīṅ mano-ga,
Ṭāvaṭa hī karana yoga
    kahī puṇya-karanī.
Ūṅcha nīcha ḍashā ḍhār,
    chiṭa-pramāḍa ko biḍār,
Ūṅchalī ḍashā ṭé giro
    maṭa aḍho ḍharanī.
Bhāga Chanḍra !, yā prakāra
    Jīvana hai sukha apāra,
Yāhī ké aḍhāra syāḍ—
    Vāḍa kī ucharaṇī.

(*J.*, BHĀGA CHANDRA)

(Three-staged the Path of souls inherently ;
Each soul must pass through all successively ;
First is the stage of vicious selfishness ;
To it succeeds the time of virtuousness ;

Last comes the stage free from all loves and hates,
All personal desires. This last, the path
Lighted by Duty only, helps the soul
To break the bonds of sin and merit, too,
Forged by the passions which imprison it;
And takes it safe across life's stormy sea.
Give up the wish to earn merit for heaven;
But do not therefore cease from purity,
Nor dream of ever doing deed of sin.
Observe the rules prescribed for piety,
Till the mind merges in the fount and source
Of Purity. Bear patiently the states,
Now high, now low, which fortune brings to thee;
Guard watchfully 'gainst errings of the mind;
See it falls not from noble to base mood.
Such is the only way to fill with Peace
Of mind and heart the life upon this earth;
Such is the essence of what Jina taught.)

The Bible of Judaism and Christianity also clearly indicates that all pairs of opposites, including the pair of Good and Evil, are in the One:

Shall evil befall a city, and the Lord hath not done it? (*B.*, Amos.)

I form the light and create darkness; I make peace and create evil; I am the Lord that doeth all these things...I have created the smith that bloweth the fire of coals, and bringeth forth a weapon for his work; and I have created the waster to destroy. (*B.*, Isaiah.)

We have seen before, that in Vaiḍika Ḍharma (now, in its corrupted form, in current practice, known as 'Hinduism'—and which living religion today is free from unfortunate degenerations, caused by the evil ingrained in human nature together with the good ?), God is the Destroyer as Rudra, Tempter and Tester as M ā y ā-v ī, Punisher and Corrector as Yama, and so on; that Islam recognises Him, as Al-Qahhār, Al-Jabbār, Al-Muzil, Al-Mumīṭ, i. e., the Wrathful, the Oppressor, the Misleader and Tester, the Slayer of the sinful ; and so forth.

The mystery, the perplexity, the anguish of the heart torn between faith and doubt, faith in the ultimate Beneficence of the Supreme, doubt created by the glaring fact of endless misery of all degrees, within each self and all around—this conflict vanishes as soon as we realise that 'I' is *the* 'I' ; that 'I am' means '*the* I *is*'; that God, Lord, Allah, Īshvara, all ultimately mean the Universal, all-pervading, Self ; that all Good and all Evil, the seeds of all the noblest virtues and all the basest vices, are all in *Me*, in every 'individual self', *because* they all are in the Universal Self ; that all life, all the World-process, is incessantly, and inevitably, the Interplay of Opposites, of endless pains, sorrows, miseries, and corresponding endless pleasures, joys, delights ; all which balance and neutralise each other in the Absolute Self, the Self ab-solv-ed from all relative 'opposites', *zaujain*, *ziḍḍain*, ḍ v a m-ḍ v a m. But the 'child-mind' cannot, and must not be expected to, see the whole Truth. It has to evolve and grow to the stage of the 'parent-mind', and become able to stand on its own feet, and develope the power of self-conscious intro-spection, a n ṭ a r-ḍ ṛ s h t i *chashm-i-basīraṭ*, 'mental eye', 'inner eye', before it will be able to reduce the Third Person into the First Person, the 'He' into the 'I'. Then it will recognise it-self, and every self, as a piece of the Self, and as the maker of its own destiny; which destiny, in the 'infinite' view, is the same for all; endless Play, Pas-time, Drama, of equal Tragedy and Comedy. Till then, i.e., so long as it remains a 'child-mind', it must rest in the arms, or be helped along by the hands, of a 'parent', an 'elder'.

Without the Self, without the Principle of Consciousness, the Universe disappears, and science vanishes. All things else may be doubted, the Self cannot be. The doubter cannot doubt himself. Scientists have therefore grown wiser and have receded from the gush and rush of materialistic turbulence natural to the first flush of the growth of science. The faith of the great scientists of the day has been already mentioned, that this world is a world governed by Spirit and not by Matter; unless, indeed, we endow Matter with all the qualities of Spirit; and then it means only that we have ex-changed the connotations of the two words. And this Supreme Spirit is in Me, is I.

As Christ says:

Believe Me that I am in the Father and the Father is in Me...He that has seen Me has seen the Father... If ye had known Me ye should have known my Father also. (*B.*)

And as Muhammad says also:

Anā Ahmaḍ bilā mīm. (*H.*)
Man rā-anı rā al Haqqa. (*H.*)
Man a'rafa nafsahū faqad a'rafa Rabbahu. (*H.*)
Nas-ullāhā fa'ansāhum anfusahum. (*Q.*)
Ahmaḍ am I, minus the letter 'm',
Which means, 'I am Ahad, the One alone.'
He who hath seen Me surely hath seen God.
He who hath known him-Self hath known his God.
He who forgetteth God forgets him-Self.)

Confucius says:

What the undeveloped man seeks is others; what the advanced man seeks is him-Self. (Quoted in *Ency. Brit.*, 14th edn., Art. Confucius.)

Hayashi-Razan, an eminent scholar of Chinese classics, of the seventeenth century, says:

The human mind, partaking of Divinity, is an abode of the Deity, which is the Spiritual Essence. There exists no highest Deity outside the human mind.

(*Shinto-Dinju*, quoted in *Ency. Brit.*, *Ibid.*)

The heavens are still; no sound.
Where then shall God be found?
Search not in distant skies;
In man's own heart He lies.

(*Shao Yung*, translated and quoted by H.D. Gibbs, *The Religions of Ancient China*, 1011—1077).

Shinṭoists...consistently upheld the theanthropic doctrine of *Kan-nagara*, of man being essentially divine; *Kan-nagara*, *kan* from *kanu*, and *nagara*,...'man himself divine'...The divine and the human are one in quality; Only, the latter is temporary, the former enduring. The everlasting divinity is called human dụring the time it resides on this planet. (Inazo Nitobe, *Japan*, pp. 309-321).

This, in Veḍānṭa, is the distinction between Param-āṭmā and Jīv-āṭmā; in Sūfism, between *Rūh-ul-arwāh* and *Rūh*; in Gnostic Mysticism, between God and Son of God.

As the Christ says:

I and my Father are one...Yet is my Father greater than I...I am in my Father, and ye in me, and I in you. (*B.*)

In the words of Shankar-āchārya,

Saṭy-api bhéḍ-āpa-gamé,
Nāṭha ! Ṭav-āham, na māma-kīnas-Ṭvam !
Sāmuḍro hi ṭarangah
Kva-chana samuḍro na ṭārangah ! (*Shat-paḍī.*)
(Though all false sense of separateness be past,
Yet am I Thine, My Lord !, and not Thou mine !
The wave unto the ocean doth belong ;
Never the ocean to the tiny wave !)

I have said, ye are gods ; and all of you are children of the Most High. (*B.*, Psalms, 82. 6.)

It is with reference to this that Jesus says,

Is it not written in your laws, 'I said, ye are gods?...Say ye (to me)...'Thou blasphemest, because, I said, 'I am the son of God'? (*B.*, John.)

The Truth of the Infinite is indeed not easy to put into words which are finite, and so easily and so frequently misunderstood. What wonder that Buḍḍha and other great Teachers became silent, when questioned on ultimate mysteries, by persons not ready and not able to under-stand the thought behind the veil of words.

Man a'rafa Rabba-hū kal-lā lesānuhū. (*H.*)
(The man who findeth God loseth his speech.)
Gurōs-ṭu maunam vyākhyānam,

Shishyās-ṭ-ūchchhinna-samshayāh. (*Guru-Gīṭā.*)
(The speaker doth discourse quite speechlessly,
Yet are the pupils' doubts wholly re-solved.)
Mahramé īn hosh juz bé-hosh n-īsṭ;
Mar zabān rā mushṭarī juz gosh n-īsṭ. (*S.*)
(Only th' Unconscious knows this Consciousness;
The tongue's sense but the speechless ear can guess.)
Girā a-naina, naina binu bānī,
Kehi biḍhi an-upama jāi bakhānī!
Sūna bhīṭi para bibiḍha ranga ké
ṭanu bina likhé Chiṭéré!

(ṬULASI ḌĀS, *Rāmāyaṇa* and *Vinaya Paṭrikā.*)

(Sightless the tongue is, voiceless are the eyes;
How then describe that Vision, all unique!)
Wall—Emptiness; the Painter—Bodiless;
Yet pictures infinite in forms and hues!)

I am in the Father, and the Father in me... I am in my Father and ye in me, and I in you...Abide in Me, and I in you...without Me you cannot do anything. (*B.*, John, xiv.)

Yé bhajanṭi ṭu mām bhakṭyā,
Mayi ṭé, téshu ch-āpy-Aham. (*G.*)
(They who love Me with love sincere, they are
In Me, and I also am e'er in them.)
Ū ḍar ḍile man asṭ, wa ḍile man ba-ḍasṭe Ū;
Chūn āyīnah ba-ḍasṭe man, wa man ḍar āyīnah. (*S.*)
(He's in my heart, my heart is in His hands;
This mirror's in my hand, and I in it.)

All things are Himself, and Himself is concealed on every side; *Iḍrā Rabbā*, X. 117; Adam Kadmon, (Āḍam-i-Qaḍīm) the Eternal Man or Self of the Kabalists, contains in Him-Self all the souls of the Israelities, and He is Him-Self in every soul. (*Sohar*, or *Zohar*, Introduction, pp. 305, 312; quoted by H. P. Blavatsky, in *Isis Unveiled*, II, 342.)

Yasṭu sarvāṇi bhuṭāni Āṭmany-év-ānu-pashyaṭi,
Sarva-bhūṭéshu ch-Āṭmānam ṭaṭo na vi-jugupsaṭé,
ṭaṭo na vi-chikitsaṭé. (*U.*)
(Who seeth all in Self and Self in all,
Doubteth no more, nor hateth any more).

We have noted elsewhere that the ability of a person to put off any one particular religion, and put on any other, proves that the soul of the human being is superior to all particular religions, and can judge between them all at will.

The case for the supremacy of the I has been still more conclusively put in some Sūfī verses:

Zāṅ ki usṭā rā Shināsā ham ṭu ī,
Jumla usṭā rā khuḍ Usṭā ham ṭu ī.
Chūṅ Haqīqaṭ rā Muhaqqiq khuḍ ṭu ī,
Ain haq īn-asṭ ain-ul-Haq ṭu ī.
Hasṭiyé Rab rā Mujawwiz chūṅ ṭu ī,
Bil-yaqīn Allāh-e-Akbar khuḍ ṭu ī. (*S.*)
(Since thou decidest who is fit to take
Or not to take for Teacher, thou thy-Self
Must surely than all teachers greater be.
Since thou dost judge that this is True, this Not,
Maker of Truth, most True, thy-Self must be.
Since thou determinest whether God is
Or is not, surely thine own Self must be
The inmost being of Godhead, Greatest God.)

2. Evolution, Phylogenesis, Rebirth

So far, we have endeavoured to expound the fundamental Truth of truths, viz: There is an Ultimate Mystery behind all Life, behind all the World-process, behind the whole 'Uni-verse,' (from Lat. *unus*, one, and *vertere*, to turn; 'that which revolves round the One'); It is the Creator, Preserver, Destroyer, of all objects; It can be best and most nearly understood and recognised in terms of Spirit and Mind; It is All-pervading Spirit and Universal Mind; It is the Principle of all Life and Consciousness; It is the Spirit, Soul, Life, Mind of the whole World; It's nearest, dearest, best, most common, indeed universal, name is 'I'; It, as 'I', bears every name, wears every form, knows, desires, does, everything that is known, every desire that is felt, every act that is done—'I am so-and-so; I know, wish, do, this and that'; thus, every living thing, which regards itself as 'I', especially Man, who self-consciously regards and speaks of him-self as 'I', is, in essence, one with It; It, that Ultimate Mystery, is our very Self—*so all religions declare*; though *all* names belong to It, still, every religion, every language, has given It one or two names which are most frequently used in it, e.g., Param-Āṭmā, Āṭmā, Brahma, in Vaiḍika Dharma (or Hinḍuism) and Samskṛṭ; Allāh, Rab, Mālik, Maulā, in Islām (or Mohammedanism) and Arabic; Khuḍā, in Persian; God, (perhaps another form of Khuḍā) in Christianity and English; Ahurā-Mazaḍā, in Zoroastrianism; Jehovah, in Judaism (Hebraism, the Jewish religion); Saṭ Srī Akāl, (the Timeless), in Sikhism; Āṭmā, Brahma, Shūnya, Amiṭ-ābha, in Buḍḍhism; Āṭmā, Param-āṭmā, Nir-anjana, in Jainism; Ṭāo in Ṭaoism; Shangṭi (the One

Supreme Being), Tien (Heaven), Tai-Chi (the Great Ultimate) in Confucianism; Ame-no-mi-naka-nushi (Heaven-centre-ruling Deity, the Absolute Universal Self), in Shintoism. We have also seen that the World-process is one unending Drama of infinite inextricably mingled Tragedy-and-Comedy, 'Pairs of Opposites', wherein God is perpetually forgetting himself into Man, and Man is perpetually remembering himself back into God again.

Out of this arises the next important truth, viz., that of samsāra-chakra, *charkh-i-gardūn*, 'cyclical wheeling', 'revolution' of involution (of Spirit in Matter) and re-evolution (of Spirit out of Matter), of regress and progress, a v-ā-r o h a and ā-r o h a, *izāl* and *irtiqā*. This corresponds to, and links up with, the scientific view of Evolution and Phylogenesis. Some religions speak of Re-births of the same soul in several physical bodies, one after another. Others interpret 'progress' differently. Other English words for re-birth are re-incarnation and metempsychosis; Skt., p u n a r - j a n m a; Arab-Per., *tanāsukh*. The Vaidika doctrine is well known, that the soul comes to the stage of man after passing through many lower forms, and takes numerous rebirths in the human form. In fact, Hinduism, Buddhism, Jainism, Sikhism, are so full of it that it is not needed to quote texts in proof. It does not appear that the Bible and the Qurān contain any explicit affirmation of rebirth. *But they nowhere deny it either*. And Christ said that the prophet Elijah had come again as John the Baptist.

Behold, I will send you Elijah the prophet before the coming of the great and dreadful day of the Lord. (*B.*, Malachi.)

Jesus began to say unto the mutlitudes concerning John the Baptist...For all the prophets and the law prophesied until John. And if ye will receive it, this is Elias (Elijah) which was for to come. (*B.*, Matthew.)

King Herod the tetrarch...beheaded John in the prison. (*Ibid.*)

And his disciples asked him...and Jesus answered...that Elias is come already, and they knew him not, but have done unto him whatsoever they listed. ...Then the disciples understood that he spake unto them of John the Baptist. (*Ibid.*)

The Prophet Muhammaḍ also has said:

Yā ayyohal insāno innakā kāḍihun elā Rabbekā kāḍihan fa mulāqihe,...laṭarkabun-na ṭabaqan an ṭabaq. (*Q.*)

(O Man! thou hast to go back unto God,
Thy God, thy Self, with labour and with pain,
Ascending stage by stage, plane after plane.)

Kṛshṇa says:

Anéka-janma-samsiḍḍhas
ṭaṭo yāṭi parām gaṭim.
Bahūnām janmanām anṭé
jñāna-vān Mām prapaḍyaṭé. (*G.*)

(Many the births that man has to pass through,
Before the Supreme Knowledge comes to him,
And he accomplishes his destiny,
Reaches the Final Goal, and findeth Me.)

And there are texts in the Qurān which may be interpreted as meaning that man lives and dies repeatedly, even as worlds are created and destroyed repeatedly.

Man-vanṭarāṇy-a-sankhyāni,
sargah, samhāra éva cha,
Krīdan-niv-aiṭaṭ kuruṭé
Paraméshthī punah punah. (*M.*)

(Cycles and cycling worlds, all numberless,
Creations and destructions, doth He make
Over and over, as in playful sport—
The Lord of all, standing beyond them all.)

Innahū yabḍa-ul-khalqa summa yoīḍoh ; le yajze-yallazīna āmanu wa a'melus-saulehāṭe b-il qisṭe... Kama baḍa-anā awwala kḥalqin noīḍah...Yakḥloqo-kum fī buṭūni-ummuhāṭi-kum khalqam-minā bā'ḍe khalqin zulumāṭin salas.. (*Q.*)

(He makes a world-creation ; then again
He reproduces it, so that He may
With justice recompense those who believe
In God's Word and do good to fellow-beings.
God sayeth—As We did originate
The first creation, so we reproduce...
He in your mother's wombs createth you,
Creation on creation yet again.)

Minhā kḥalaqnā-kum, wa fī hā noīḍu-kum,
wa minhā nukḥruju-kum elā ṭa'āraṭīn-ukḥrā. (*Q.*)

(From out the earth have I now given birth
To you, and I will send you into it
Again, and bring you forth from it again,
Again, repeatedly, until the End.)

Summā ba'asmā-kum min bā'de mauṭe-kum la'alla-kum ṭushkurūn. (*Q.*)

(I gave you birth again after you died,
That you may think of Me with gratitude.)

Ahyānā bā'ḍe amāṭanā...Kul yohyi hallazī anshā-ahā awwalamarra. (*Q.*)

Yukḥrijul hayya minal mayyaṭi, wa yukḥrijul mayyaṭa minal hayyī. (*Q.*)

(He made us live again after our death.
He made you live before, and can again.
He makes the living dead, the dead alive.)

Kaifā ṭakfurūnā billāhé wa kunṭum amvāṭan fā ahyakum summā yumīṭokum summā yohyikum summā ilaihe ṭarja'ūn. (*Q.*)

(How can you make denial of your God
Who made you live again when you had died,
Will make you dead again, again alive,
Until you go back finally to Him ?)

The well-known lines of Maulānā Rūm[1] may be regarded as explicit comment on these texts, fixing the right interpretation.

Ham cho sabzā bārahā royīḍah am,
Hafṭ saḍ hafṭāḍ qālib ḍīḍah am ;
Az jamāḍī murḍam o nāmī shuḍam ;
Waz numā murḍam ba haiwāṅ sar zaḍam ;
Murḍam az haiwāni o āḍam shuḍam ;
Pas che ṭarsam kai ze murḍan gum shuḍam ?
Hamlaé ḍīgar bi-mīram az bashar,
Ṭā bar āram az malāyak bāl o par ;
Az malak ham bāyaḍam jusṭan ze jū,
Kulle shayīn hālikun illā Wujh-Ū.
Pas a'ḍam garḍam a'ḍam chūṅ arghanūṅ
Goyaḍ am 'Innā ilaihā rāje'ūn'.
Bāre ḍīgar az malak parrāṅ shawam,
Āṅ che anḍar wahm n-āyaḍ āṅ shawam. (*S.*)

---

[1] *Masnawī*, Book III, p. 334, (Cawnpore edition).

(Like grass have I grown o'er and o'er again;
Seven hundred seventy bodies have I seen.
From out the form of mineral I passed
And as a vegetable lived again;
From out the vegetable form I died
And lifted up a head as animal;
The form of animal I put away
And took the human shape of Adam-Eve;
Why shall I fear that if I die once more
I shall be lost? Nay, I shall surely gain,
At the next onset, dying out of man,
The flowing locks and shining wings of angels.
And finally, when next I take my flight
From e'en that world, I surely shall become
That which beyond all comprehension rests!
For all things pass except the Primal Cause,
The Cause of Causes, the Face of the Self,
Which is Non-being of Aught-Else than Self,
(For Self is the Negation of Not-Self).
And when I am in such Non-Being, then
My Being in Non-Being shall resound
In organ-tones, 'Thou hast returned to Me'.)

Elsewhere, in the same *Masnawī*, Rūmī repeats:

Āmaḍah awwal ba iqlīmé jamāḍ;
Az jamāḍī ḍar nabāṭī ofṭāḍ;
Sālahā anḍar nabāṭī umr karḍ,
Waz jamāḍī yāḍ n-āwarḍ az na burḍ;
Waz nabāṭī chūṅ ba haiwānī fuṭāḍ,
N-āmaḍ-ash hāl-é nabāṭī héch yāḍ;
Ham-chun-īn iqlīm ṭā iqlīm rafṭ,
Ṭā shuḍ aknūṅ āqil-o ḍānā wa zafṭ;
Aqlahāé awwalīn-ash yāḍ n-īsṭ,
Ham azīṅ a'ql-ash ṭahawwal karḍanī-sṭ,

Ṭā riyaḍ z-īn a'ql pur-hirs o ṭalab,
Saḍ hazārān a'ql bīnaḍ bu-l-'ajab.
Gar-ché khufṭa gashṭ o shuḍ nāsī ze pésh
Kai guzāranḍ-ash ḍar-an nisiyān-e-khwésh.
Bāz az ān khwāb-ash ba béḍārī kashanḍ,
Ṭā kunaḍ bar hālaṭé khuḍ rīsh-khand. (*S.*)
(First into state of mineral he came;
And then, as vegetable, ages spent,
Forgetting all he felt as mineral;
Then into state of animal he passed,
Oblivious of the vegetable state;
Ascending thus, stage after stage, he now
Is man, intelligent, knowing and strong,
Yet all forgetful of his previous states.
From this stage of intelligence also
He has to rise, since it is full of greeds
And clingings to small things and jealousies.
When he has done so, then a myriad paths
Of knowledge, wonder, and great mysteries,
Will open out before him endlessly.
He will not be allowed to lose him-Self;
He will be dragged out of his Night of Sleep,
Into the Day of Wakefulness again,
Till he laughs at him-Self in ecstasy.)

The same succession of mineral, vegetable, animal, human, and higher kingdoms of nature is to be found in the ancient Samskṛṭ books, and also in modern science.

Uḍbhijjāh, svéḍa-jāsh-ch-aiva,
 anda-jāsh-cha jarāyu-jāh;
Iṭy-évam varṇiṭāh shāsṭré
 bhūṭa-grāmāsh-chaṭur-viḍhāh. (*Purāṇas.*)
(Four are the orders of the living things
That dwell on this our earth—the mineral,

The vegetable, animal, and man;
First fissiparous, then gemmation-born,
Then oviparous, viviparous last.)
Sṛshtvā purāṇi vividhāny-ajay-Āṭma-Shakṭyā,
Vṛkshān, sarīsṛpa-pashūn, khaga-ḍamsha-maṭsyān,
Ṭais-ṭair-aṭushta-hṛḍayo manujam viḍhāya
Brahm-āva-boḍha-ḍhishaṇam muḍam āpa Dévah.
(*Bh.*)

(House after house did God make for Himself—
Mineral and plant, insect, fish, reptile, bird,
And mammal too. But yet was He not pleased.
At last He made Himself the shape of Man,
Wherein He knew Him-Self the Vast Immense,
The final greatest Greatness limitless,
The all-including Universal Self,
Pervading all, Eternal, Infinite—
And then the Lord of All was satisfied.)

Khalaq-al-insāna alā sūraṭ-ir-Rahmān.* (*H.*)

God created man in His own image...And God saw everything that He had made, and behold it was very good. (*B.*)

The Jewish (Hebrew) *Qabbālā* has an axiom:

A stone becomes a plant; a plant, a beast; a beast, a man; a man, a spirit; and the spirit, a god.

The Hebrew (Jewish) *Zohar* says:

All souls are subject to the trials of transmigration; and men...do not know how many mysterious trials and transformations they must undergo...The souls must re-enter the Absolute Substance whence they have emerged. But to accomplish this they must develope all the perfections, the germ of which is planted in them; and if they have not fulfilled this condition during one life, they must commence another, a third, and so forth, until they have acquired the condition which fits them for re-union with God.[1]

The Purāṇic legend is that living forms may be dichotomised (i.e., dually classified) into the unmoving and the moving, which are sub-divided into the four main kingdoms of nature, which include eight million four hundred thousand species. The last figure may or may not be of the same sort as the many modern 'scientific speculations' regarding the age of the earth, the distances and the numbers of the visible and invisible stars, the size of the universe (or rather our sidereal system, an infinitesimal atom of the Infinite Universe), the numbers of radiations from metals, the velocities of electrons, the time it would take for one element to 'break down' into another because of radiations, the number of millions of eggs laid by one cod-fish at one laying, the number of atoms contained in the earth, the number of miles from the sun or our earth to the nearest star, etc.—speculations based on mathematical calculations. But the succession of the various orders of life is very much the same as that sponsored by modern science. Thus:

Sṭhāvaram vimshaṭér-laksham,
jala-jam nava-lakshakam,
Kūrmāsh-cha nava-laksham syur-
ḍasha-laksham cha pakshiṇah,
Ṭrimshal-laksham pashūnām cha,
chaṭur-laksham ṭu vānarāh,

[1] *The Universal Text Book of Religion and Morals* by Annie Besant.

Ṭaṭo manushyaṭām prāpya
ṭaṭah karmāṇi sāḍhayeṭ.
(*Bṛhaḍ-Vishṇu-Purāṇa.*)

(The mineral and the vegetable worlds,
Unmoving, count 'tween them two million forms ;
Nine hundred thousand, the aquatics then ;
Reptiles, as many ; birds, a million ;
Then comes the mammal world, three millions ;
Four hundred thousand kinds of anthropoids ;
Two hundred thousand human species, last.)

It is explained that all these are not to be supposed as co-existing to-day or at any other given time in the past or the future. The majority of them 'have had their day' and disappeared, like the monster-saurians, the twelve-legged horse, the aurochs, the sabre-tooth tiger, the pterodactyl, the dinornis, many amphibia, and innumerable forms representing the critical junction-points between the kingdoms ; and many will appear and disappear in the future.

Bhūṭéshu vīruḍbhya uḍ-uṭṭamā yé
Saṛī-sṛpās ; ṭéshu sa-boḍha-nishthāh ;
Taṭo manushyāh ; pramaṭhās ṭaṭo-pi,
Ganḍharva-siḍḍhā vibuḍhā-nu-gā yé ;
Dev-āsurébhyo Maghavaṭ-praḍhānā
Ḍaksh-āḍayo Brahma-suṭās ṭu ; ṭéshām
Bhavah parah ; so-ṭha Virinchi-vīryah ;
Sa Maṭ-paro ; Aham ḍvija-ḍéva-Ḍévah. (*Bh.*)

('Mongst living growing things, than minerals
Are vegetables higher ; and than these
The forms that freely move about ; than these
The animals that have intelligence ;
Then human beings ; and then the several grades

Of spirits, angels, and perfected men;
Then the high gods born from the Primal Mind,
First Ideator, First Intelligence;
And finally the Self in which all Rests.)

Zoroaster says;

Yé vahyo vanghéūs ḍazaḍé yas chā hōī vārāī rāḍaṭ
Ahuro kshaṭhrā Mazaḍāo aṭ ahmāī akāṭ ashyoyéhoī,
no īṭ vīḍāīṭē apémé anghéūs ūrvayésé.
(*Z.*, Gāthā, 51-6).

(In each succeeding birth the Great God gives
To him who seeks His favour by good deeds,
Greater Self-knowledge, greater self-control;
But unto him who acts not well but ill,
He gives a worse fate in each following life.)

Ṭān Aham ḍvishaṭah krūrān
samsāréshu narā-ḍhamān
Kshipāmy-ajasram ashubhān
āsurīshv-éva yonishu. (*G.*)

(Those evil ones, the hateful, cruel, mean,
Fall into evil wombs, birth after birth,
Till by reaction consequent, in pain,
They learn to turn into the ways of good.)

Man is the 'crown of creation', *ashraf-ul-makhlūqāṭ*.

Sanāṭanam guhyam iḍam bravīmi,
Na mānushyāṭ shréshtha-ṭaram hi kin-chiṭ. (*Mbh.*)
(This ancient secret is disclosed to thee:
There is naught nobler than 'humanity'.)

This is so only because in the human form God becomes able to recognise Him-Self, and to realise that He is All and Every-thing, again, after millions of years of forgetfulness of the Self's Glory.

Sūfis generally believe in rebirth, *rija'ṭ*, and *irṭiqā*, ascent; and have more technical distinctions than even the Vaiḍikas on this point. Thus, reincarnation as man is *naskḥ*; as animal is *maskḥ*; as vegetable is *faskḥ*; as mineral is *raskḥ*.[1] Such degradation, as in schools, from higher to lower stage, class, is very rare, though detention is not so infrequent. Because the Self runs through and wears all forms, therefore the thread of evolution runs through them all continuously, and man has in him the seeds and potencies of all the kingdoms of Nature. All is indeed everywhere and always, because God is everywhere and always; and all is in God, the Self.

---

[1] "Ahmaḍ ibni Sābiṭ, Ahmaḍ ibni Yabūs, Abū Muslim of Kḥurāsān, Shaikḥ-ul-Ishrāq, and the famous Omar Kḥayyām, were exponents of the doctrine of transmigration and re-incarnation, basing their arguments on (the Qurān) Sūraṭ-ul-Bāqarā, verses 61-92, Sūraṭ-ul-Māiḍah, v. 55, etc.": Kḥāja Kḥān, ***Studies in Ṭasawwuf***, p. 132. Translations of some of these verses, as made by Maulvī Muhammaḍ Alī, M. A., LL. B., President Ahmaḍiyya Anjuman-i-ishāaṭ-i-Islām, Lahore, are reproduced below:

"And certainly you have known those among you who exceeded the limits of the Sabbath; so We said to them: Be (as) apes, despised and hated": (65). "...What then is the reward of such among you as to this, but disgrace in the life of this world, and on the day of resurrection they shall be sent back to the most grievous chastisement; and Allah is not at all heedless of what you do"; (85). "And most certainly

3. Karma.

The third important truth is that of reward and punishment. Virtue and merit are rewarded; vice and sin punished; some day, somewhere, sooner or later, here or hereafter. All religions equally proclaim this great truth. As we sow, so must we reap. This Law of Karma is only the scientific law of cause and effect, or, better, of action and reaction, working on the psychical and spiritual plane. Karma works from within. Because the Self is in all, therefore pain given, means, later, pain suffered; and pleasure given, becomes pleasure received. Sins as well

---

We gave Moses the book, and We sent apostles after him, one after another; and We gave Jesus, the son of Mary, clear arguments, and strengthened him with the holy revelation. What !, whenever then an apostle came to you with that which your souls did not desire, you were insolent, so you called some liars, and some you slay": (87). "Evil is that for which they have sold their souls;...so they have made themselves deserving of wrath upon wrath, and there is a disgraceful chastisement for the unbelievers": (90). Al Bāqarā.

"....(Worse is he) whom Allah has cursed and brought His wrath upon, and of whom He made apes and swine, and he who served the devil; these are worse in place and more erring from the straight path": Al-Māiḍah. Maulānā Muhammad Ali, in his comments, says that the words 'apes' and 'swine' are not to be taken literally. The learned Sūfis, whom Khạja Khạn mentions, as above, seem to have thought otherwise. More on this point will be said in a later foot-note.

as merits come home to roost, without fail. Failure would be possible if souls were really wholly separate. They are not. The One Self, *Rūh-ul-rūh*, *Rūh-i-ā'zam*, *Rūh-i-ālam*, Param-Aṭmā, Jagad-Āṭmā, Sūṭr-Āṭmā, Vishv-Āṭmā, Oversoul, Anima Mundi, the Collective Unconscious, the Supra-conscious, Universal Spirit, binds them all together. Therefore escape from consequence is impossible. If my hand hurt my foot, shall not the hand also feel the pain? Vaiḍika Dharma and its off-shoots and reforms, Buḍḍhism, Jainism, Sikhism, current 'Hinduism', are so permeated with the idea of Karma, and this fact is so well-known, that no texts need be quoted; yet, a few may be. The very word Karma has now become part of many languages.

Bani Āḍam ā'zāi yak ḍīgar anḍ,
Ke ḍar āfrīnish ze yak jauhar anḍ.
Chu uzwé ba-ḍarḍ āwaraḍ rozgār,
Ḍigar uzwa-hā rā na mānaḍ qarār. (*S.*, SĀ'ḌĪ).
(The progeny of Adam, all are parts
And limbs of one and the same organism,
Risen from the Same Essence, every one;
And can it be, while one limb is in pain,
That other limbs should feel at restful ease?.)

Sahasra-shīrshā Purushah
sahasr-ākshah sahasra-pāṭ. (*V.*)
(The countless heads, eyes, ears, and hands and feet
Of living beings are all parts of One Man.)

When one member (of the body) suffers, all the members suffer with it; or one member be honored, all the members rejoice with it. (*B.*, Paul.)

Sukhasya ḍuhkhasya na ko-pi ḍāṭā,
Paro ḍaḍāṭ-īṭi ku-buḍḍhir-éshā ;
Svayam kṛṭam svéna phaléna yujyaṭé ;
Sharīra, hé !, nisṭara yaṭ ṭvayā kṛṭam.

(*Garuda Purāṇa.*)

(Sorrow or joy none other gives to us;
False is the thought that others give us these;
Our own deeds bring us their own just fruit—
Body of mine ! repay by suffering !)

Woe unto them that call evil good, and good evil... Be not deceived; God is not mocked; whatsoever a man soweth, that shall he also reap...They that sow iniquity and sow wickedness, reap the same...To him that soweth righteousness shall be a sure reward. ...Men do not gather grapes of thorns or figs of thistles...The wages of sin is death...He shall reward every man according to his works...Give and it shall be given unto you...With the same measure that ye mete withal, it shall be measured to you again...God will render to everyone according to his deeds...Unto Thee, O Lord !, belongeth mercy; for thou renderest to every man according to his work. (*B.*, Job; Psalms; Proverbs; Matthew; Luke; Romans; etc.)

Wa mā asawbakum min-mosībaṭin fa bemā
kasabaṭ ayḍīkum...wa mañya'mal misqāla
zarraṭin kḫairuñ-yarah ; wa mañya'mal misqāla
zarraṭin sharrañ-yarah...F-al yauma lā
ṭuzlamo nafsun shai-añwa lā ṭuzzauna illā mā
kunṭum ta'malūn. (*Q.*)

(Whatever of misfortune falls on one,
Of one's own doings it is the result.
The atom's weight of good that you have done,
That you shall see come back to you again;
The atom's weight of evil you have wrought,

That also must you meet unfailingly.
Be sure, no soul shall be dealt with, this day,
Unjustly, in the least; and you shall not
Requited be with aught but what you did.
Jazā-un be mā kānu yā'malūn. (*Q.*)
(Thou shalt receive requital and reward
In just return for whatsoe'er thou dost.)
Hṛḍi sṭhitah Karma-Sākshī...
svasy-aiv-Ānṭara-Pūrushah...
Yamo Vaivasvaṭo Ḍévo
yas-ṭav-aisha hṛḍi sṭhiṭah,
Ṭéna cheḍ-avivāḍas-ṭé
mā Gangām mā Kurūn gamah.[1] (*M.*, *Mbh.*)
(This Ruler-Yama who dwells in thy heart,
Watchful, awake, as thine own Āṭmā-Self,
Unfailing witness of thy smallest deeds—
If He no quarrel has with thee, then thou
Needst not make pilgrimage to holy shrines,
To Kuru-kshéṭra or to Gangā's stream.)
Har che bar mā-sṭ, az mā-sṭ. (*S.*)
(Whate'er befalleth us, cometh from us.)
(These deeds of yours shall verily be brought
Back unto you, as if you were yourself
The author of your own just punishment. (*H.*)
Yāo īshuḍyo ḍaḍénṭé ḍāṭhrānām ha chā
ashā-ūno Yāoschā, Mazaḍā !, ḍrégvoḍévyo;

[1] A western poet has put the truth of the Law of Karma more softly and soothingly:
All Nature is His Art unknown to thee;
All Chance, His Order which thou caust not see;
All Discord, His Concord not understood;
All partial Evil, His all-reaching Good.
Take heart, beloved !, in erring reason's spite;
Whatever wrong there is, will be set right.

Yā frashā āvishyā, yā vā, Mazaḍā !, pérésaīṭé
ṭayā,...ṭā chashménéng ṭhvisrā hāro aībi
ashā aībi vaénahī vispā. (*Z.*, Gāthā, 31. 13, 14)
(Great Mazaḍā !, Thou doest requite all deeds
Unto the pious and the impious ;
For thou dost see with Thy All-seeing eyes
The secret and the openly expressed
Desires of human beings, or good, or bad.)
Yaṭhā āīsh iṭhā varéshaīṭé
...Raṭūsh shyaoṭhanā rajishṭā
ḍrégvaṭa-échā hyaṭ chā ashāūṇé...
...Hyaṭ Ṭhvā anghéūsh jāṅṭhoī ḍarésém
pao-ūrvīm, hyaṭ ḍāo shyaōṭhanā mīzhḍavāṅ
yā chā ūkhghā, akém akāī vaṅghūhīm ashīsh
vanghaové Ṭhvā hunarā ḍāmoīsh ūrva-ésé
apémè. (*Z.*, Gāthā, 33. 1 ; 43. 5).
(Great Raṭush !, Thou does give unto each one
Just retribution, even as he is,
Vicious or virtuous, or false or true.
Thou, Mazaḍā !, that art both First and Last,
At the beginning and the end of life,
According to Thy fixed eternal Laws,
Thou dost award to each his just desert,
Reward or punishment, in word and deed,
Ill unto ill and good unto the good.)

O men ! learn ye these laws of happiness and misery which Ahura Mazaḍā has ordained. They are, the suffering of pain for a long time for the wicked, and blessings for the righteous, by which they attain happiness. (*Z.*, Ahūnavaḍ Gāṭhā, xxx. 11.)

Good and evil do not wrongly befall men ; but Heaven sends down misery or happiness according to their conduct. From the loving example of one family a whole state may become loving ; and from its courtesies, courteous. From the ambition and perverseness of one man, the whole state may be thrown into rebellious disorder. Such is the nature of the influence. (*C.*, *Liki*, 39. 18.)

Those who do evil in the open light of day—men will punish them. Those who do evil in secret—God will punish them. Who fears both man and God—he is fit to walk alone. (*T.*, Kwang Tze, 23. 8.)

Whoso casteth a stone on high, casteth it on his own head; and a deceitful stroke shall make wounds. Whoso diggeth a pit shall fall therein; and he that setteth a trap shall be taken therein. He that worketh mischief, it shall fall upon him, and he shall not know whence it cometh. (*Bible Apocrypha*, Ecelesiasticus).

The Way of Heaven is to bless the good and to punish the bad; the end of punishment is to promote virtue and make an end of punishing. (*C.*, *Shu King.*)

The recompense of good and evil follows as the shadow follows the figure.

(*Ṭa Ṭai-shang Kan Ying Pien.*)

(If a man speak or act with evil thought,
Pain surely follows him, e'en as the wheel
Follows the ox that drags the cart along.)

(*Bu.*, *Mahā-vagga*, 6. 31. 7.)

Yo apy-aḍutthasya narasya ḍussaṭi,
Suḍḍhassa posassa an-angaṇassa,
Ṭam éva bālam pachchéṭi pāpam,
Sukhmo rajo pati-vāṭam va khiṭṭo. (*Ḍh.*)
(The man who hurts the sinless innocent,
Unto that thoughtless man returns that hurt,
Unfailing, as fine dust flung 'gainst the wind).

Aṭṭā hi Aṭṭano nāṭho,
ko hi nāṭho paro siyā;

Aṭṭanā 'va su-ḍanṭéna,
nāṭham labhaṭi dullabham.
Aṭṭā hī Aṭṭano nāṭho,
Aṭṭā hi Aṭṭano gaṭi ;
Ṭasmā saññamay-Aṭṭānam,
assam bhaḍram 'va vāṇijo.
Aṭṭanā 'va kaṭam pāpam
aṭṭa-jam aṭṭa-sambhavam
Abhi-manṭhaṭi ḍum-méḍham
vajiram 'va 'sma-mayam maṇim.[1] (*Dh.*)

(Self is the Self's protector, master, lord.
Who other can be such? If ye control
And discipline your-Self, ye gain a Friend
Such as ye cannot have outside your-Self.
Self only is Self's final refuge, goal ;
Then train it well, so it will swiftly take
To whatsoever righteous goal ye seek.
The sin arising from within one-self,
Churns up that evil mind within it-self,

[1] The Samskṛṭ form of these Pālī verses, uttered by the Buḍḍha, would be:

Āṭmā hi Āṭmano nāṭhah ;
ko hi nāṭhah parah syāṭ ?
Āṭman-aiva su-ḍānṭéna
nātham labhaṭi dur-labham.
Āṭmā hi Āṭmano nāṭhah,
Āṭmā hi Āṭmano gaṭih ;
Ṭasmāṭ samyamay-Āṭmānam,
ashvam bhaḍram iva vāṇijah.
Āṭman-aiva kṛṭam pāpam,
Āṭma-jam, Āṭma-sambhavam,
Abhi-maṭhnāṭi ḍur-méḍhasam,
vajram iva ashma-mayam maṇim.

E'en as the diamond-grinder's grinding stone
Grinds down the jewel-stone till it shape true.)

Uḍḍharéḍ-Āṭman-Āṭmānam
n-Āṭmānam ava-sāḍayéṭ;
Āṭm-aiva hy-Āṭmano banḍhur-
Āṭm-aiva ripur-Āṭmanah;
Banḍhur-Āṭm-Āṭmanas-ṭasya,
Yén-Aṭm-aiv-Āṭmanā jiṭah;
An-Āṭmanas-ṭu shaṭruṭvé
varṭéṭ-Āṭm-aiva shaṭru-vaṭ. (*G.*)

Paraspara-bhayāṭ kéchiṭ pāpāh pāpam na kurvaṭé;
Rāja-ḍanda-bhayāṭ kéchiṭ, Yama-ḍanda-bhayāṭ paré;
Sarvéshām api ch-aiṭéshām Āṭmā yamayaṭām Yamah;
Āṭmā samyamiṭo yéna, Yamas-ṭasya karoṭi kim.
Na Yamam Yama iṭy-āhur,-Āṭmā vai Yama uchyaṭé.
(*Mbh.*, *M.*)

(Save and uplift your-Self by your own Self;
Degrade it not; your-Self is your best Friend,
If your High Self but masters your low self;
But if your low self rears rebellious head,
Then your High Self is sharpest Enemy.
For fear of one another, some refrain
From sin; others for fear of the king's rod;
Some, fearing Yama's judgment after death;
But Judge of Judges is the Inner Self;
In whom this Inner Judge is satisfied,
He hath no fear of any other Judge.)

Yaḍi n-āṭmani puṭréshu;
Na chéṭ puṭréshu, napṭṛshu;
Na ṭv-éva ṭu kṛṭ-oḍharmah
karṭur bhavaṭi nishphalah;
Shanair-ā-varṭamānas-ṭu
Karṭur mūlāni kṛnṭaṭi. (*M.*)

Aṭy-ugra puṇya-pāpānām
iha-iva phalam ashnuṭé.
Hṛḍayé sarva-bhūṭānām
Anṭar-yāmī Yamah sṭhiṭah. (*Mbh.*)

(Sin doth not always bear its painful fruit
Unto the sinner, here on earth, at once;
But, circling, it reacts unfailingly,
And cuts the sinner's very roots of being;
And often it inflicts the consequence
Upon the children and grandchildren too,
[As patently the sins of venery];
Never goes sin without its due return;
And deeds of noble goodness, or dire sin,
Bear their just fruit, here, in this very life.
Never is there escape from consequence,
Because the Great Judge dwells within each heart).

In the last line is the secret of the perpetual Day of infallible Judgment. No one can escape him-Self, his own heart and memory and conscience, and avoid reward or expiation.

Doubts, disputes, problems, have arisen, in this connection, regarding Free-Will and Destiny (ḍishta), Liberty and Necessity, Vitalism and mechanism, purusha-kāra and ḍaiva, uḍyoga and niyaṭi, *qaḍr* and *jabr*, *mukh-ṭār* and *majbūr*, sva-ṭanṭra and para-ṭanṭra, Self-Choice and Determinism; the same thing being meant by many names. Also, problems have arisen regarding conflict between God's Mercifulness and Forgiveness of sins, on the one hand, and His Justice and Restraint of Wickedness on the other.

All such doubts are reduced, controversies allayed, problems solved, views reconciled, if we bear in mind duly that the Great, Infallible, Subtle, all-seeing Judge is ever *within* us; we are compelled, ultimately, by our own heart, our own conscience, our own Self, to expiate our sinful karma and to receive reward of our meritorious karma. What we do from pure sense of Duty, is neither sin nor merit, and has no such 'binding' consequence. If any one feel that he is helpless to commit sin, he shall be equally helpless to endure punishment. If the most innocent child drink poisonous liquid by sheerest mistake, it will, by that same mistake, suffer painful resultant illness, even death. If anyone deliberately commits sin, he will equally knowingly suffer the penalty. The Justice which arises within our-Self, and compels us to make voluntary restitution, is also the greatest Mercy, since it *purifies* the soul. To feel 'compelled' to commit sin, and 'free' to avoid punishment, is not reasonable.

Mā-ém ba luṭf-e-Haq ṭavallā karḍah,
V-az ṭāa'ṭ o māsiyaṭ ṭabarrā karḍah,
Har-jā ke i'nāyaṭé Ṭo bāshaḍ,
Nā-karḍah cho karḍah, karḍah chūṅ nā-karḍah !
Ai ! nék na karḍah, va baḍī-hā karḍah !
W-angāh ba luṭfe-Haq ṭavallā karḍah !
Bar u'fwu ma-kun ṭakiyah, ke hargiz na buwaḍ
Nā-karḍah cho karḍah, karḍah chūṅ nā-karḍah !

(OMAR KHAYYĀM)

(Some say: In God's great Mercy we have faith,

And take no thought of good or evil deed ;
On whomsoe'er His eye of Favour rests,
His 'not-done' deeds of good become all 'done',
And his 'done' deeds of evil all 'un-done' !
O thou ! that didst not do one deed of good,
But hast been doing many deeds of ill !
Do not deceive thyself, that if thou throw
Thyself upon the Mercy of High God,
Thy sins will be forgiven in such wise
That the 'done' deed shall be as if 'not-done',
And the 'not-done' become as if 'twere done.)
[All the great sages with one voice declare—
Whom the Lord loveth, him He chasteneth,
With trials sore and penalties severe,
Which cleanse him of his sins and make him pure,
And worthy of His love and love of all.]

It is an outstanding characteristic of our baser, lower, nature, that we are always trying to fasten on *others*, all the blame for *our own* faults, vices, sins, crimes. 'God made me do this ; He created me like this ; He must forgive me ; I am not to blame' ; 'Fate, Chance, Nature, compelled me' ; 'the other person started the quarrel' ; 'the other nation began the war ; we are completely innocent' ; and so on, and so forth. A glaring, ridiculous, conclusive every-day illustration is—a child runs carelessly, stumbles, falls, hurts itself, begins to cry ; the mother runs up, picks up the child, beats the floor, and the child is completely satisfied, ceases to cry : 'the floor was to blame, not I.' In the earlier 'child-mind' stages, a personal God outside is to praise or to blame ; in the later 'sage-mind' stage, the Impersonal all-pervading God *within* more than without, is to praise or to blame.

The Qurān puts it more strongly :

Mā asābekā min hasanaṭin fa min Allāhī, wa mā asābekā fa min sayāṭin fa min nafasak. (*Q.*)

(Whatever good ye have, is all from God ;
Whatever evil, all is from your-self.)

What is meant is, of course, that all that is good comes from the element of the Higher Self in us, the essence of which is God ; while all that is evil, comes from the lower element, viz., the self-ish self in us.

The Sūfis have made it clear :

Har che az zain o shain-i shumā-sṭ,
Sar ba sar muqṭazā-i a'in-i shumā-sṭ.
Har che a'in-i shumā ṭaqāzā karḍ,
Jauḍ-i-faiz-i-Man huwaiḍā kard.

(Good, evil, both are all your own demand ;
Whate'er *your* heart desired, My bounty gave.)

Nature is a Continuity. Life, The Ever-living Self, *whose* Nature it is, is not only a Continuity but also a Unity. Because Life is a Unity, therefore is Nature a Continuity; therefore are all the constituents of the universe inter-dependent, smallest or largest. The One Life runs through all forms ; an unbreakable thread, Sūṭr-Āṭmā, Thread-Soul ; strings, threads, nets, weaves them all together inseparably ; and makes of them a Continuity. Every atom is constantly sending out, and receiving, infinite vibrations to and from all other atoms. The same particles of gaseous, liquid, solid substances are circulating through all sorts of living bodies.

and things; the same thoughts, feelings, desires, volitions, through all minds. All living things are influencing each other, sharing in each other's pains and pleasures, willy-nilly. Any change, any disturbance, in any department of Nature, has reverberations and repercussions in all other departments. 'The fool hath said in his heart, there is no God," and thinks he will evade the consequences of his evil ways; but God is hiding all the time in that same heart, as much as in the wise heart; and He will impel him, from within, to put himself in a position where he will have to eat the bitter fruit of the tree of evil that he has planted; thus will

[1] Western scientists are coming to see this Continuum of Life and Consciousness more and more: Thus, "When we view ourselves in space and time, we are obviously distinct individuals; when we pass beyond space and time, we may, perhaps, form ingredients of a *continuous* stream of Life": Sir James Jeans, Address at annual meeting of the British Association for the Advancement of Science, quoted in ***The Modern Review*** (of Calcutta) for February, 1935, p. 227. It may be added that it is not neccssary to pass beyond space and time to feel this continuity. Indeed, ***continuity*** necessarily ***involves*** space and time, and is possible only in them. Beyond them there is Eternity, Motionlessness, Unity; or indeed the Absence of both Unity and Multiplicity; instead of Continuity; for Continuity means Unity running through Multiplicity, Self through not-selves. Mr. Whately Carington, in his books, ***Three Essays in Consciousness***, and ***The Quantitative Study of Trance Personalities***, reviewed in ***The Theosophist*** for February,

the erring one learn wisdom by sad experience. As nothing can pass out of the Whole, sin and merit are always being balanced up by their respective consequences. The Whole as such is ever in a state of perfect equi-librium, s a m a-ṭ ā, *w a h ḍ a t.*

Sukhasy-ānanṭaram ḍuhkham,
ḍuhkhasy-ānanṭaram sukham ;
Chakra-vaṭ pari-varṭéṭé
Sukha-Ḍuhkhé ḍivā-nisham. (*Mbh.*)
(After joy, sorrow ; after sorrow, joy ;
After day, night ; and after night, the day ;
Ceaseless rotate they on the wheel of Life ;
O'er and between the two, broods Peace alway.)
Inna ma'l usra yusrin fa inna ma'l usré yusra. (*Q.*)

1935, argues to the effect that: "Physiologists and biologists, chemists and physicists, are showing with increasing success that there is no kind of discontinuity to be observed between conscious and non-conscious matter; hence the universality of Consciousness....This Consciousness is fundamentally *one*...Apparently distinct consciousnesses are united by a Common Sub-Consciousness...(There is) a Universal substratum of Consciousness animating all structural forms...(It is possible) to envisage (national panics, enthusiams, etc., are proof) a process of expansion or enlargements of consciousness without loss of individuality, until in the limit each will be co-extensive with Universal Consciousness". This is all good sound Yoga-Véḍānṭa and Ṭasawwuf and Gnostic-Mysticism. Only the word 'comparatively' has to be added before 'Universal', for the 'non-comparative' Universal is—'non-comparative'; there is no expansion or gradation in or for or to It.

(After pain, pleasure cometh, verily;
So too comes sorrow surely after joy.)

The scientific laws of causation, of action and reaction, of conservation of energy and indestructibility of matter amidst perpetual transformations of form, all arise out of this same fact, viz., that the Self is ever-complete and contains all, once for all, and all actions, vibrations, movements, arise within It, and end within It, issue from It, and return to It.

Pūrṇam aḍah, pūrṇam iḍam,
pūrṇāṭ pūrṇam uḍachyaṭé,
Pūrṇasya pūrṇam āḍāya
pūrṇam év-āvashishyaṭé.

(That Spirit-world is Full. This Matter-world
Is Full also. If from the Full the Whole
Is taken out, the Whole remains the Full.)

As the Sūfīs say:

Huwal āna kamā kāna.
(He is as He was.)
I am that I am. (*B.*)

There is nothing new under the sun; That which is, is That which was. (*B.*, *Eccles.*)

Jīrṇāni vāsāmsi yaṭhā vihāya,
Navāni gṛhṇāṭi naro-parāṇi,
Taṭhā sharīrāṇi vihāya jīrṇāni,
Anyāni samyāṭi navāni ḍéhī. (*G.*)
Praṭi-kshaṇa-pari-ṇāminī Prakṛṭih;
Chiṭi-shakṭir-a-pari-ṇāminī. (*Sānkhya-Yoga.*)
(E'en as a man puts off his worn-out clothes
And puts on new ones, even so the Self
Casts off old bodies and takes up new ones.

God's Garment, Nature, changes hues and forms,
Moment to moment, tireless, ceaselessly;
His Consciousness continues e'er the same.)
Kullu yaumin huā fishāṅ. (*Q.*)
Ḍam-ba-ḍam gar shawaḍ libās baḍal
Marḍ-i Sahib-i-libās rā che kẖalal. (*S.*)
Ṭa'iyun būḍ kaz hasṭī juḍā shuḍ,
Na Haq banḍa, na banḍa bā Kẖuḍā shuḍ.
(*S., Gulshan-i-Rāz.*)
(Each moment is He in a diff'rent state.
But how may it affect the One who wears
These Many garbs, if these change ceaselessly?
A Limitation, Definition, *seems*
To shape out in the sea of Boundless Being;
Nor God grows Servant, Nor the Servant God.)

Dream-worlds, world-dreams, world-dramas, arise and disappear endlessly; the 'substance-quality-quantity' of Infinite Consciousness in, for, from, by, out of, which they are made and come and go, remains the same. Multiply the endless infinite circle of the zero by any finite number; it remains zero.[1]

---

[1] NOTE: *On Karma, Rebirths, and Evolution.*

The following is abridged from the art. 'Metempsychosis', *Enc. Brit.*, 14th. edn.:

"The theory of the transmigration of souls is usually associated with the ancient Egyptians; with the teaching of Pythagoras and the Buddha; and was also held by a sect of early Christian heretics. The idea is much older than these creeds, and *exists throughout the world.* It is often bound up with the idea of a plurality of souls, in a single individual, one of which is separable. Thus the Poso-Alfures of Celebes believe in three

4. Other Worlds and Planes of Being.
The fourth great truth, common to all religions,

---

souls, (a) the *inoso* or vital principle, (b) the *angga*, or intellectual, and (c) the *tanoana* or divine element which leaves during sleep. The Orphic religion of Greece, and the Eleusinian Mysteries, included faith in metem-psychosis. Pythagoras was its first famous exponent in Greece. Plato accepted it and enhanced its importance. In Jewish literature, there are traces of it in Philo Judeus, and it is definitely adopted in the Kabbala. Within the Christian Church, it was held in the first centuries by Gnostic sects; by the Manicheans in the 4th and 5th centuries; in the Middle ages, by the numerous sects collectively known as Cathari. Giordano Bruno, van Helmont, Swedenborg, Goethe, Lessing, Charles Bonnet, Herder, Hume, Schopenhauer, and other notable thinkers held it or respected it. Modern Theosophy, which draws its inspiration from India, has taken it as a cardinal tenet; it is, says a recent theosophical writer, 'the master-key to modern problems, among them the problem of heredity'."

As regards the Jews and the early Christians, Origen, one of the most learned Fathers of the Christian Church, taught, in the 2nd century, A. C., that "forth from God come all spirits that exist, all being dowered with free-will. Some refused to turn aside from the path of righteousness...and took the place of Angels. Others, in the exercise of their free-will, turned aside from the path of duty, and passed into the human race, to recover, by righteous and noble living, the angel condition...Others, still in the exercise of their free-will, descend yet deeper into evil and become devils...All were originally good—by innocence, not knowledge...Angels may become men, men angels; and even the evil ones

is that as there is the physical world corresponding to man's five outer senses and the waking state,

---

may climb upwards once more, and become men and angels again" : (De Principii, *passim* ; quoted in the *The Universal Text Book of Religion and Morals*, by Annie Besant). But Origen's form of the doctrine was condemned at a Church Council, A. D. 533.

Josephus, *De Bello Judaico*, says: "They say that all souls are incorruptible ; but that the souls of good men are only removed into other bodies, and that the souls of bad men are subject to eternal punishment;" and again: "...all pure spirits...live on in...heavenly places, and in course of time they are again sent down to inhabit sinless bodies ; but the souls of those who have committed self-destruction are doomed to a region in the darkness of the under-world." This last sentence is an almost exact equivalent of a verse of the *Isha-Upanishaṭ*,

Anḍham ṭamah pra-vishanṭi
yé ké ch-Āṭma-haṇo janāh.
(Into deep darkness do they fall who turn
Away from their true Self and slay It thus.)

"Origen, Clemens Alexandrinus, Synesius, Chalcidius, all believed in metem-psychosis ; so did the Gnostics, who are unhesitatingly proclaimed by history as a body of the most refined learned and enlightened men" ; H. P. Blavatsky, *Isis Unveiled*, I, 12.

Gibbon, (*Decline and Fall of the Roman Empire*, ch. 47, text and notes), says: "The disciples of Jesus were persuaded that a man might have sinned before he was born (John, ix, 2), and the Pharisees held the transmigration of virtuous souls, (Josephus, de Bello Judaico). Since the introduction of the Greek or

so there are other worlds corresponding to subtler senses and other states of his consciousness; that

---

Chaldean philosophy, the Jews were persuaded of the pre-existence, transmigration, and immortality of souls."

The Hebrew word for metempsychosis is *gilgūlim.* The *Enc. Brit.*, 14th edn., art. 'Kabbalah', says, "The doctrine was adopted by the Kabbalists in defiance of the Jewish philosophers." The main doctrines of the Kabbala, outlined there, are the very same as those of Vēḍānṭa and Ṭasawwuf. "The *Zohar* states that 'all souls must undergo transmigration';...the Jewish literature of this subject of transmigration is an exceedingly rich one": J. Abelson, *Jewish Mysticism*, 164, 165.

The following is an abstract of a very remarkable article, 'The Ancient Wisdom in Africa', by Patrick Bowen, in the *Theosophist* (Adyar, Madras) for August, 1927: "As a boy, ten or twelve years of age, following my father's wagon through the wild Bushlands of the Northern Transvaal, I gained the friendship of many *Isanusi* (Wise Men) of the Zulus. One of these, Mankanyezi ('the Starry One') said to me, 'Within the body is a soul; within the soul is a spark of the *Itongo*, the Universal Spirit. After the death of the body, *Idhlozi* (the soul) hovers for a while near the body, and then departs to *Esil-weni*, the Place of Beasts. This is very different from entering the body of a beast. In *Esilweni*, the soul assumes a shape, part beast and part human. This is its true shape, for man's nature is very like that of the beast, save for that spark of something higher. After a period, long or short, according to the strength of the animal nature, the soul throws aside its beast-like shape, and moves onward to—a place of rest. There

through these the soul of man passes between death and rebirth in this world, even as he passes

---

it sleeps, till a time comes when it *dreams* that something to do and learn awaits it on earth; then it awakes, and returns, through the Place of Beasts, to the earth, and is born again as a child. Again and again does the soul travel thus, till at last the man becomes true Man, and his soul, when the body dies, becomes one with the *Itongo*, whence it came. The common man cannot understand more than that the *Itongo* is the Sipirit of his Tribe; but the Wise Ones know that It is the Spirit within and above all men, even all things; and that at the end, all men being one in Spirit, are brothers in the flesh.' Mankanyezi, a year or two later, predicted to me that I would meet one of his 'Elder brothers', an Elder in the Family (Society) to which he belonged, 'whose members are the guardians of the *Wisdom-which-comes-from-of-old*; they are of many ranks, from learner to Master, and Higher Ones whose names may not be spoken; and there is one member at least in every tribe and nation throughout this great land' (Africa). This prediction came true, and I did meet other members of the Fraternity, and also saw proofs of clairvoyance and telepathy and will-force, and received teachings. Mandhlalanga ('Strength of the Sun'), chief of a very small community of Berbers, or rather Khabyles, Kha-beel-ya, [? Arab. *Qabīlā-s*] who, for reasons unexplained, had come away, five thousand miles, from their home in North Africa, and had identified themselves with the Zulus, taught me in the secret Bantu tongue: '*Itongo* is all Substance, all Power, all Wisdom; but it is also above and beyond them, eternally Unmanifest. There are but two manifestations, Universal Mind and Universal Matter. Force is simply that portion of Mind

through dreams in the night between day and day; that there are sub-human, super-human, and

---

which endows Matter with Form. At first both Mind and Matter were un-individualised; a vast amorphous mass; growing denser and denser; ether, gas, liquid, solid. When, how, why, Individuality began—only the *Itongo* can know. It was like the starting of myriads of whirlpools on the surface of the ocean. In matter the Soul has reached the aphelion of its cycle; now it begins its long slow return journey. It climbs slowly from mineral to plant, animal, man; up through the lower mind to the higher, till, at last, its cycle complete, it merges into its source, the *Itongo*, ceases to be Individual, becomes one with the All. On his journey, from and back to the *Itongo*, man is born again and again. His physical body dies, as also his lower mental principles; only his higher mental principles survive from age to age, retaining, throughout the Cosmic Cycle, the individuality bestowed upon them at its opening. The Principles are: (1) the physical body (*umzimba*); (2) the etheric body (*isitunzi*); (3) the lower mind (*amandhla*); (4) the animal mind (*utivesilo*); (5) the human mind (*utivomuntu*); (6) the spiritual mind (*utivetongo*); (7) *Itongo*.' "

In terms of Yoga and Veḍānṭa, these are (1) **anna-maya-kosha**, (2) **prāṇa-maya-kosha**, (3), (4) and part of (5) **mano-maya-kosha**, rest of (5) and (6) **vijñāna-maya-kosha**, (7) **ānanḍa-maya-kosha**, and **Āṭmā**. In terms of Theosophical literature, they are, (1) the physical body, or **sṭhūla-sharīra**, (2) **prāṇa**, or the etheric double, (3) **linga sharīra**, (4) **kāma-rūpa**, (5) **manas**, (6) **buḍḍhi**, (7) **Āṭmā**. In another Véḍānṭic and

co-human kingdoms of beings which inhabit them; and that man, by special efforts and processes of training can develop the inner senses

---

Rāja-yoga scheme, the main 'bodies' or s h a r ī r a s, are (1) s ṭ h ū l a, gross, dense, physical, which includes the first three, (2) s ū k s h m a, subtle, astral, which includes the next two, (3) k ā r a ṇ a, causal, equivalent to the sixth; Āṭmā being the wearer of the three bodies.

Mr. Bowen continues: "The Brotherhood is called, in the ancient Bantu speech, *Bonabakulu abase-Khemu*, i.e., *The Brotherhood of the Higher Ones of Egypt*. (Khem, whence 'Chem-istry'. was an ancient name of Egypt). It was founded by a Priest of Isis in the reign of the Pharaoh Cheops, to spread *The Wisdom which comes from of Old*, among all races and tribes of Africa, and the study and practice, among its members, of *Ukwazi-kwasi-thabango*, which means, *The Science which depends on the Power of Thought* (Yoga). The grades of the Brotherhood are: (1) the Pupil, (2) the Disciple, (3) the Brother, (4) the Elder, (5) the Master, (6) Those who Know (*Isangoma*), (7) *Abakulu-bantu*, i. e., Perfect Men, for whom rebirth has ceased, who dwell on earth in physical form by their own will, and can retain or relinquish that form as they choose. By getting full control of the vibrations of his higher planes, a developed Man may despatch through the Cosmic Ocean of which he is a part, ripples of various kinds and intensities, which will produce effects, according to their nature and strength, on all strata, most of course on the most sensitive highest strata, of the other 'whirlpools' or 'individualities'...".

and the latent powers which can open these worlds to him.

The above long, and yet all too condensed and short, account of the belief of Africa, has been incorporated here, in pursuance of the method of this compilation: to show how numerous, how widespread in space, persistently continuous in time, are the votes cast by Demos in favor of the immortality, evolution, or revolution, and rebirths, of souls. The article, 'Transmigration', in the *Ency. of Rel. and Ethics*, occupies sixteen double-column large quarto pages of minute print, equal to some eighty pages of this book. It shows that the belief has been, and is, spread all over the world, in all known history and anthropology, in one form and another, among primitive peoples of all the continents, and has also been held by the Indian, Persian (Irānian, Zoroastrian), Egyptian, Jewish, Greek, Roman, Celtic, and Teutonic nations. In the Christian world, the belief, suppressed for a time, seems to be reviving among the educated and thoughtful, as a necessary complement and corollary of the fact of evolution.

The Encyclopedia of Islam, art. '*Tanasukh*', says, in effect, that "the belief in metempsychosis is widespread in India and among several sects of the Muslim world. Shahrasṭāni takes the word *ṭanāsukḥ* in a wide sense, viz., the successive lives and rebirths of the world, in cycles of revolution, of varying durations, 30000, 70000, 360000 years, and so on. (Cf: Vedic y u g a s, k a l p a s, m a h ā-y u g a s, etc.) In another sense, it means the diffusion and distribution of the Divine Spirit among the beings of our world. Extreme Shīās believe in the descent or incarnation (*hulūl*) of all or part of the Divine Principle in certain

Modern science indicates this possibility by the expression, 'extension of faculty'; and

---

men. (Cf., Vedic a v a-ṭ ā r a s, a m s h-ā v a-ṭ ā r a s, etc.). In the popular sense, of passing from one body to another, the belief is held by several Shīā sects. Among the Mo'ṭazilas, the disciples of Ahmad b. Hā'iṭ taught that God first created beings in a kind of paradise [Saṭya-Yuga, Golden Age, Arcadia, Eden]; then those who were guilty of disobedience were sent by him into our world in the form of men or animals, according to the gravity of their sins; they then migrate from form to form until the effects of their sins have ceased. The Ismāīlīs did not admit the passage of the soul into the bodies of animals; but they did admit successive (human) lives until it recognised the Imām; then it rose to the world of Light. The Nusāirīs believe that sinners of their religion will be reborn into other religions; outright infidels will become camels, mules, asses, dogs, etc.; there are seven degrees of metempsychosis according to them. The Druses believe that the souls of the enemies of their religion will enter the bodies of dogs, monkeys, and swine. The Kurds and the Yazidis believe in transmigration into the bodies of men and also animals, and in successive existences separated by an interval of 72 years. According to Saiyad Sharīf Djurdjānī, *ṭanāsukḥ* is the passing of the soul to a new body without intervals on account of the inclination of the spirit for the body".

All sorts of beliefs, as to the kinds of transmigration, similar to those of these Muslim sects are to be found among the different sects of other religions also. The belief in the continuous existence of the

clairvoyance and telepathy have been proved by psychical research, conducted by recognised scientists. Y o g a-s i ḍ ḍ h i s, ḍ i v y a-s h a k ṭ i s, *kamāl*, *mo'jizah*, *karāmāṭ*, *raushan-zamīrī*, 'divine powers', 'the luminous heart', 'perfections', 'miraculous powers', 'magical powers', have been believed in, everywhere, always. They are only *extensions* of such powers as we daily exercise, and not, in the least, more surprising than these. S v a r g a s, n a r a k a s, l o k a s, b h u v a n a s ; *jannaṭs* and *jahannums, bahishṭs* and *ḍozakhs*, *arsh-es* and *arḍ-s*, *lauhas* and *ṭabaqas* ; paradises and purgatories, heavens and hells of higher and lower levels, and subtler and grosser planes of matter ; are affirmed by all religions. They are subjective as well as objective ; *in* us, and also *outside*; as joy and woe in us, parks and jails outside us.

Ḍ é v a s and u p a-ḍ é v a s, g a ṇ a s and p ā r s h a ḍ a s, s i ḍ ḍ h a s and v i ḍ y ā-ḍ h a r a s, a p s a r ā s and g a n ḍ h a r v a s, y a k s h a s and r a k s h a s ; *farishṭās* and *malāyak*, *parīs* and *jinnāṭ* ; *frāvarshis*, *farshārs*, *amesha-spenṭas*, *yazḍs*; *ḍévs* and *ḍarvanḍs*; *iblīsas* and *shaiṭāns*; d a i ṭ y a s and a s u r a s ; angels and devils,

soul, and its births and rebirths into physical bodies, is common to almost all. Of course, there are also sects, in all religions, which deny such transmigration ; very few in Hinduism ; many in Islam ; many in Christianity. Also, some texts of the Quran, and of venerated Muslim writers, which some commentators interpret as favouring belief in re-incarnation, others interpret otherwise.

good and evil spirits of earth, water, fire, air, woods, hills, etc., fairies, gnomes, sylphs, nymphs, undines, dryads, salamanders, brownies, banshees, elves, imps, fiends, demons, devils, etc., are common to all religions and all peoples. As human bodies are made of certain forms of matter, so the bodies of these are said to be composed of other forms of matter, which are not ordinarily perceptible to our senses (as human bodies are not, to theirs); except in special conditions; as air becomes 'visible', when, as whirlwind, it 'puts on' a column of dust, sand, or water. To think that no other forms of life are possible than such as are cognisable by human senses, is surely to depart very greatly from due modesty. Scores of species of these, high and low, gentle and fierce, as of herbivorous and carnivorous animals, and of savage and civilised human beings, are named in the scriptural books.[1]

[1] Jewish and Christian theology distinguishes nine kinds of angels grouped in three great classes: (1) Seraphim, Cherubim, Thrones, (2) Dominions, Virtues, Powers, (3) Principalities, Archangels, Angels. The Jewish Kabbala adds Eons, Sephiroṭh, Dignities; Izeds (Yazds), Shadim, Sephiroth, Malakim, Teraphim, Elohim, are also spoken of. In Islam, five kinds of Jinns, related to the five elements, are recognised; and it gives special prominence to four great archangels, Jibra-īl, Mikā-īl, Azrā-īl, Isrāf-īl; somewhat like the four Loka-pālas and eight Ḍik-pālas of the Vaidika Purāṇas. In Judaism, "Rahmiel is the angel of Mercy; Tahriel, of Purity; Pedaiel, of Deliverance; Tsadkiel,

Different from these are certain disembodied human spirits, floating midway, so to say, between 'this-world' and the 'other-world' proper, of heaven-and-hell, in an abnormal way, like lunatics and maniacs in a community. They are kept tied to the earth, for varying periods, before passing on to the 'other-world,' by various strong unfulfilled desires. Some of these spirits are good but feeble and foolish, others powerful and malignant, according to the quality and strength of their manias. They are known as prétas, pishāchas, etc., of many kinds, in Vaiḍika Ḍharma; *g̣hools*, *āsébs*, etc., in Islam; ghosts, vampires, incubi, sucubbi, etc., in Christianity.

There is no sufficient cause to deny these non-human 'spirits', 'sprites', 'nature-spirits,' nor to

---

of Justice; Raziel, of the Divine Secrets": J. Abelson, *Jewish Mysticism*, 127. In the Arabic language also, which is a cousin of the Hebrew, (since Arabs and Jews are descendants of the two sons of Abraham respectively, by tradition), Rahm means mercy; Ṭahar, Purity; Feḍā, Deliverance, Submission; Siḍq, Justice, Honesty; Rāz, secret; and so on. These words indicate great outstanding attributes of the Universal Self or Consciousness; and also embodiments of them, as 'characteristic ruling passions', in personalities.

H. P. Blavatsky, *The Secret Doctrine*, III. 402, says: "Sephir is Aḍiṭi, Mystic Space. The Sephiroṭh are identical with the Hindu Prajā-paṭis (Āḍiṭyas), the Ḍhyān Chohāns of Esoteric Buddhism, the Zoroastrian Amsha-spents, and the Elohim, the 'seven angels of the presence', of the Roman Catholic Church."

worship them. But the better sort, friendly to man, and willing to help, as inferiors or as superiors, may be utilized by special processes, in the same way as domestic animals, or as superior human friends possessed of power and authority. If, on the contrary, the evil sort are evoked, (particularly the disembodied human spirits), by ṭ ā n ṭ r i k a processes of black magic, j ā d ū, (Skt. y ā ṭ u, whence the name y ā ṭ u-ḍ h ā n a for the Atlantean race, called also Rākshasas), physical and moral ruin ensue without fail. Prayer for the release of such earth-bound souls, and for the upward progress of spirits of all kinds, and, indeed, of all living things and beings, is the duty of men, prescribed by all religions. Various rituals and ceremonies, (the *essential* elements in all of which are the benevolent sympathetic all-loving *will-force* of the officiant, and his *mental and moral purity*), are also prescribed and practised in all religions; for purifying the mental, moral, psychical, superphysical, spiritual atmosphere, as fragrant incense purifies the physical; and for attracting and facilitating the operations of the good spirits; and driving off, and hindering or sterilising and counteracting the work of, the evil 'nature-forces', or the evil disembodied human ghosts; as perfumes vivify healthy, and disinfectants kill unhealthy, microbes.

In connection with the science and art of Yoga or Sulūk, and its stages, *maqāmāṭ*, b h ū m i-s, the inner side of all religions recognizes three principal layers, bodies, vehicles, sheaths, 'principles,' in the make-up of man, which are in touch, respectively, with corresponding worlds or planes as well as with one another. Vedānṭa names them sṭhūla, sūkshma, and kāraṇa, *i. e.*, physical, subtle, and causal. The Jainas know them as auḍārika, ṭaijasa, and kārmāṇa sharīras. The Buḍḍhists' nirmāṇa-kāya, sambhoga-kāya, ḍharma-kāya correspond. Christian mysticism calls them body, soul, and spirit.[1] Jewish mystics designate them as *nefesh*, *ruah*, and *neshāmāh* (*nūsmā*). Ṭasawwuf uses the Ar. words *nafs*. *rūh*, and *nafs-i-nāṭiqā*, or *nafs*, *ḍil*, *rūh*. These three, in the individual, the microcosm, the pindānḍa or kshuḍra-virāt, the *ālam-i-saghīr*, have their correspondents in the Universal, the Macrocosm, the Brahm-ānda or Mahā-Virāt, the *Ālam-i-kabīr*. These are called in Samskṛṭ, Vaishvā-nara (or simply Virāt), Sūṭr-āṭmā (or Hiraṇya-garbha or Prāṇa), and Sarva-jña (or Īsha, Anṭaryāmi, etc.); in Sūfī terms, *Jism-i-kul* or *Shakl-i-kul*, *Rūh-i-kul* or *Ṭabīyaṭ-i-kul* or *Nafs-i-kul*,

[1] "Your whole Spirit and Soul and Body": (*B.*, Thessalonians). In the Egyptian *Book of the Dead*, these same three seem to be indicated by *Khā*, the body, Kā or Rā, the soul, Bā, the higher soul or Spirit. In the Greeco-Roman religion we have *carnis*, *umbra* (or *manes*), and *anima*. Some early Christian Fathers, like Ireneus, speak of "carne, anima, spiritu". The Zulu terms for these have been mentioned before, at p. 195, *supra*.

and *Aql-i-kul*; the collective total material Body, the collective total Vitality, the collective total Intelligence. The correspondence to Action, Desire, Knowledge, is obvious.

Many kinds of *nafs* and *rūh* are also distinguished, corresponding to the kinds of s h a r ī r a s, k o s h a s, etc. The corresponding states, planes, worlds, are j ā g r a ṭ, s v a p n a, s u s h u p ṭ i (*i. e.* waking, dreaming, and slumbering) states; or b h ū h, b h u v a h, and s v a h l o k a s; *ālam-i-shahāḍa* (or *-mulk* or *-nāsuṭ*), *ālam-i-misāl* (or *-malakūṭ*), *ālam-i-jabrūṭ*, etc.[1] Subdivisions are also distinguished. The Sūfis speak of *nafs-i-ammārā*, *nafs-i-lawwāmā*, *nafs-i-muṭmainna*, *nafs-i-mulhima*, *nafs-i-Rahmānī*, etc. These are lower and higher states of the soul, from one standpoint; from another, they may be said broadly to correspond with the five k o s h a s of Vedānṭa and s k a n ḍ h a s of Buddhism. Another distinction is the one between *nafs-i-jārī* and *nafs-i-muqīm*, 'the wandering body' and 'the stationary body'. *Jism-i-laṭīf* and *jism-i-kasīf*

[1] Mention has been made of the seven *arḍ-s* ('earths') and the seven *arsh-es* ('heavens') recognised in Islam. They are the same as the fourteen b h u v a n a-s or l o k a-s, seven below, p ā ṭ ā l a-s, and seven above, b h ū h, b h u v a h, s v a h, m a h a h, j a n a h, ṭ a p a h, s a ṭ y a m. *Ālam-i-mā'nī*, (the world or plane of 'ideas'), *ālam-i-lāhūṭ*, *ālam-i-hāhūt*, etc., are mentioned in Sūfī books as beyond *jabrūṭ*; so ṭ u r ī y a, ṭ u r y-ā ṭ ī ṭ a, etc., in Véḍānṭa. See R. A. Nicholson, ***Studies in Islamic Mysticism***, pp. 122-125.

mean the same, *i.e.*, the fine or subtle body and the dense or gross body. This is the same pair as the ā ṭ i-v ā h i k a and the ā ḍ h i-b h a u ṭ i k a s h a r ī r a s of the Véḍānṭa, or the k h é-c h a r a c h i ṭ ṭ a or s ū k s h m a-s h a r ī r a and the s ṭ h ū l a-ḍ e h a of the Yoga. The Sūfi Jāmī has hinted this living separation of the subtle from the gross body thus :

Ḍāḍ ū ḍil bā har kasé,
Man *ze* ghairaṭ be-murḍam basé !
Yak bār bi-mīraḍ har kasé,
Béchāra Jāmī bārahā ! (*S.*)

(The Loved One gave him-Self to every one,
And of that shame of Other-ness I die !
All other human beings die but once,
This helpless Jāmī dies repeatedly !)

Elsewhere he tells,

Aṅ Yahūḍ-o Mōmin-o Ṭarsā magar
Ham-rahī karḍanḍ bāham ḍar safar.
Pas Yahūḍ āwarḍ un-che ḍīḍa būḍ,
Ṭā kujā shab rūh-e ū garḍīḍa būḍ ;
"Ḍar pay-é Mūsā shuḍam ṭā Kōh-i-Ṭūr,
Har ḍo gum gashṭém w-az ishrāq-i-Nūr".
Bāḍ-az-āṅ Ṭarsā ḍar-āmaḍ ḍar kalām,
Ke "Masīh-am rū namūḍ anḍar maqām."
Pas Musalmāṅ gufṭ, "Ai yārān-i-man,
Pésh-am āmaḍ Musṭafā Sulṭān-i-man." (*S.*)

(A Jew, a Muslim, and a Christian too,
Happened to come together on the road.
Walking and talking, first the Jew described
Whereto his soul had wandered in the night ;
"I followed Moses to the Mount of Ṭūr,
Where both of us were lost in Blaze of Light."

The Christian said, "My Christ appeared to me."
Lastly the Muslim said, "Beloved friends,
To me my king and Prophet showed himself.")

In these lines, Jāmī not only speaks of the soul wandering away from the body during sleep, but also shows that there are many mediators, helpers, guides ; and that each earnest soul is helped, in dreams, visions, and super-physical states, by the great personage in whom it may have placed its whole-hearted faith and trust. Incidentally, he provides a beautiful instance of the brotherliness of the wise and pious of all religions.

Muhammaḍ gave, to the select, the counsel :
Muṭo qabl un ṭamūṭo. (*H.*)
(Die before you die.)

The Ṛṣhi of the Upanishaṭs gives the same advice, to the promising disciple worthy of receiving it :

Ṭam svāṭ sharīrāṭ pra-bṛhén-munjāḍ-
ishīkām iva ḍhairyéṇa. (*U.*)
(As from the thatching-grass the core is drawn,
So from the body should be drawn the soul
With patience, perseverance, fortitude.)

I knew a certain man—whether in body or outside of body, I know not, God knoweth—who was rapt into Paradise and heard things ineffable, which it is not lawful for a man to repeat...I knew a man...caught up to the third heaven.

(*B.*, Paul, 2 Corinthians.)

"The children of *this* world marry and are given in marriage ; but they which shall be accounted worthy to obtain *that* world and the resurrection from the dead, neither marry nor are given in marriage. Neither can they die any more; for they are equal unto the angels, and are the children of God, being the children of the resurrection. (*B.*, Luke.)

The Jaina prays:

Sharīraṭah karṭum ananṭa-shakṭim,
Vibhinnam Āṭmānam apāsṭa-ḍosham,
Jinénḍra !, koshāḍ-iva khadga-yashtim,
Ṭava prasāḍéna mam-āsṭu shakṭih.
(*J., Amitagaṭi, Sāmāyika Pātha.*)
(E'en as a sword is drawn out from its sheath,
So to draw out my pure ethereal soul
From this gross body, do thou teach me, Lord !)
Bahir-a-kalpiṭā vṛṭṭir-mahā-viḍéhā.
(*Yoga-Sūṭra*, iii. 43.)
(The pow'r to pass out from this case of flesh,
In subtle sheath, and roam about at will—
Mahā-vi-ḍéhā is this power named.)

The soul, the āṭi-vāhika ḍéha, sūkshma-sharīra, jnāna-ḍéha, nirmāṇa-kāya, *nafs-i-jārī, jism-i-laṭīf, jism-i-misāl,* subtle body, 'astral' body, has to be loosened from the physical body, the sṭhūla-sharīra, bhauṭika-ḍéha, jada-ḍéha, *jism-i-kasīf, jism-i-shahāḍa, nafs-i-muqīm,* the gross or dense body, the body of flesh, by regulated fasts and vigils, physical and psychical disciplines, and various subtle introspective processes, of yoga-*sulūk*, under the guidance of a wise guru-*murshid, pīr-i-mughān,* yogī, ṛshi, who has himself passed through the experience and achieved the 'freedom' of the subtle body from the gross-body. After the successful achievement of this great experience, the 'subtle' wears the 'dense', as a person wears a suit of clothes, and can pass into and out of it at will. Then only may the person be said to be 'free' of the bonds of Karma on the earth-plane, the bonds which cause his unconscious and involuntary births and deaths here; then he is m u k ṭ a, has gained *najāt*, freedom, so far as this plane is concerned[1]. This, in the technical 'superphysical' sense; in the 'metaphysical' sense, unshakeable and permanent *conviction* of Self-dependence and Immortality and Universality is 'freedom' from all fear and doubt.

5. THE LAW OF ANALOGY OR CORRESPONDENCES.

Another important truth is the truth of s a m a-ḍ a r s h i ṭ ā, 'same-sightedness', the Law of Correspondences, or the Law of Analogy, as it may be called in modern terms. This Law of Analogy, indeed, is the basis of that method of induction which is the foundation of all science. As the 'microcosm', the *ālam-i-saghīr*, the

---

[1] 'The Art of Dying', 'The Craft of Dying', 'The Science of Death', is dealt with in various books of many dead and living religions. See *The Tibetan Book of the Dead*, by Evans-Wentz (with Foreword by Sir John Woodroffe); *The Secret of the Golden Flower, a Chinese Book of Life*, by R. Wilhelm and C. G. Jung; and, of course, the *Yoga-Sūṭra*, and the literature of Yoga generally. *Eu-thanasia* is the Greek word for 'good dying'.

kshudra-virāṭ, so the 'macrocosm', the *ālam-i-kabīr*, the mahā-virāṭ; as the terrene man so the heavenly man—this is the way the Hebrew, Christian, Islāmic, and Véḍic mystics put it. As one, so all, in short; because individual and universal are the same.[1] As the atom so the solar system—as the scientists put it.

Yāvān ayam vai purushah,
Yāvaṭyā samsṭhayā miṭah,
Ṭāvān asāv-api Mahā-
Purusho loka-samsṭhayā. (*Bh.*)
Viḍyā-vinaya-sampanné
Brāhmaṇé gavi hasṭini,
Shuni cha-iva shva-pākē cha
Panḍiṭāh sama-ḍarshinah. (*G.*)
(As are the components, organs, and parts
Of single human beings—such are those
Of the Vast Macro-Cosmic Man also.
The learned cultured brāhmaṇa, endowed
With the humility which is the crown
Of virtues, as also the elephant,
The cow, the dog, and eater of the dog
—Spirit of the same Spirit are all these,
And Matter of the same Root-Matter too,
Only arranged in ever-varying forms;
And the same Laws of Nature work in all—
Thus the same-sighted Wise do understand.)

A Sūfī almost translates this:

Muhaqqiq hamīn bīnaḍ anḍar ebil
Ke ḍar khūb-rūyān-e Chīn o Chagil. (S.)
(The wise see in the camel's frame,
The same laws manifest

[1] See *The Science of the Self*, p. 110-115.

As in the beauteous Chinese dame
Or Chagil's belle, the best.)[1]

[1]Khājā Khān, at p. 89 of his excellent work, *The Philosophy of Islam,* says: "Referring to Sūraṭu Hā Mīm, 41. 53, (of the Qurān) it may be gathered that God has referred to certain signs in the heavens and in the individualities of men. From this, Sūfis have constructed a theory of micro-cosm and macro-cosm, e.g., the twelve zodiacs are the twelve holes in the human body; the seven planets are the five senses plus the senses (organs) of talking and understanding. The body is the earth; the bones, the mountains; space, the sea;...This, as well as the theory of the five elements and twenty-five g u ṇ a s, qualities, possess a distinctive Hindu stamp. The Muslim philosophy in Southern India is so much mixed up with that of the Hindus, that it is difficult to distinguish it." But the difficulty should be welcomed very heartily. Is there any need to distinguish, to see difference, instead of agreement? Is not 'mixing up', assimilation, very desirable, very helpful? The correspondences between the 'large' and the 'small', the Infinite and the Infinitesimal, have been described, in various ways, in the *Purāṇas,* the *Upanishaṭs,* the *Smṛṭis,* the *Véḍa* itself, repeatedly. And now, as said in the text above, western Science is discerning them. Some scientists have even put forth the view that the orbs of heaven are living beings. For a brief statement of the reason 'why' of the Law of Analogy, working in all departments of Nature, the reader may see the present writer's *The Science of Peace,* 2nd edn., p. 333. Detailed and astonishing illustrations of it are to be found in those marvellous mines of 'occult' knowledge, H. P. Blavatsky's *Isis Unveiled* and *The Secret Doctrine.* The ancient

The mystery of the earthly man is after the mystery of the heavenly man...The wise can read the mysteries in the human face. (*Ju.*, *Zohar*, II, 76 a).

As above, so below. (*Ju.*, Kabbalist axiom.)

Just as the soul fills the body, so God fills the world; as the soul bears the body, so God endures the

---

Samskṛṭ work, *Nirukṭa*, explains how and why certain Véḍa-texts have to be explained in three ways, metaphysical or āḍhy-āṭmika, scientific or yājñika (or āḍhi-ḍaivika), and historical or aiṭi-hāsika (or āḍhi-bhauṭika); each interpretation being true. Madame Blavatsky's works explain how these and other interpretations, in terms of other sciences, are all correct. She speaks of the 'seven-fold' key to the Scriptures. Khājā Khān, at p. 13 of his book above mentioned, gives a diagram showing twenty-eight 'potencies', inherent attributes or principles, *Asmāi-Ilāhi*, and twenty-eight *corresponding* 'manifestations,' *Asmāi-Kiyānī*, in the Universe at large. If he had only pursued the same 'principles' in their manifestations in the human being in particular, he would have seen that the view was not peculiarly 'Hindu', but natural and universal. Iu the Purāṇa-Mythos, Brahmā, the Creative Cosmic Mind (of our Solar Cosmos or System) first creates seven (or ten) mānasa-puṭra-s, 'mental sons'. These are called the primal, primeval, prajā-paṭis, patriarchs, progenitors, of all types of living beings. They correspond to, or are the same as, the Sephiroth, Angels, Elohim, etc., of the other religions; see f. n., p. 201, *supra*. They are also the 'presiding deities', the 'vitalising souls', of the seven (or ten) planets of our solar system. Each planet has its own types of life; they all exchange their jīvas, also, in accord with 'occult' laws; as the

world ; as the soul sees but is not seen, so God sees but is not seen. (*Ju.*, Talmūḍ, quoted by J. Abelson, *Jewish Mysticism*, pp. 155-56).

> Yaṭhā pindé ṭaṭhā Brahm-āndé. (Véḍānṭa axiom.)
> (As is the small man, such the Cosmic Man ;
> As the 'small egg', such the vast 'orbs of Space'.)

This s a m a-ṭ ā, this uniformity, in the working of the laws of Nature, can be due to nothing else than the Unity of Nature's God ; as one so all, as once so always, as here so everywhere ; because the Same One Self is in all, is ever present, is everywhere present. It is also the *basis* of that *Equality* which the democratic heart craves after, and rightly within due limits. The Véḍānṭa states the metaphysical fact on which the Law of Analogy, s a m a ṭ ā, is based, as S a r v a m S a r v a ṭ r a S a r v a ḍ ā, 'All is everywhere and always'. *Ṭasawwuf* describes

---

various countries and continents of this earth exchange 'colonists', 'immigrants' and 'emigrants' ; which is only another illustration of the working of the Law of Analogy, on the minutest as well as the vastest scales. The reader who may be interested in this line of thought, or 'science', or 'speculation', may consult H. P. Blavatsky's great books, and some of the later 'theosophical' literature. The famous American philosopher, William James, in his book, *A Pluralistic Universe*, descants magnificently on the idea entertained by a German thinker, Fechner, that the Earth is a living being, a great cosmic Individual. In Indian mythos, of course, she is Pṛṭhvī-Ḍévī, the great 'goddess' Earth.

it as *Indirāj-i-Kul-f-il-Kul*, 'the Immanence of the All in all, in each and everything'. The Bible speaks of it as "the fulness of Him that filleth all in all." The Jewish sacred book, *Ṭalmūḍ*, honored next after the *Old Testament* of the Bible, says: "No atom of matter, in the whole vastness of the universe is lost; how then can man's soul, which comprises the whole world in one idea, be lost?"[1]

The whole of the sun is imaged in every the most microscopic dew-drop reflection, and every such reflection comes from, is present and included in, the vast light-sphere of the sun.

Viḍyaté sa cha sarvasmin,
sarvam ṭasminsh-cha viḍyaṭé,
Ṭasmāḍ Samviḍ iṭi prokṭah
Param-Âṭmā mah-āṭmabhih.
(*Vāyu-Purāṇa.*)

(Since Everything exists in Consciousness,
And Consciousness exists in Everything,
Hence Samviṭ, 'Principle of Consciousness',
Is one of the great names by which they know,
The great-souled ones, the Supreme Self of All.)

Science speaks of the potency of infinite multiplication present in each seed, germ, microbe; of infinite vibrations of each atom perpetually affecting all other infinite atoms; of infinite photographs being conveyed to each point of space eternally by infinite rays of light from all directions from the most distant stars and

[1] Riley, *Bible of Bibles*, p. 148.

planets; of infinite sights, sounds, etc., filling all space constantly, and needing only appropriate apparatus to be caught; and so forth.[1] Obviously, to know *all* about the least little atom, is to know all about the Universe, for each part of a Whole is inseparably connected with all the other parts of the Whole.

6. THH LONG LINE OF THE SPIRITUAL HIERARCHY.

Another thought, which all religions hold unitedly, is that, as the chain of evolution extends below man, so it extends above him also; and that advanced souls, forming a Spiritual Hierarchy, take care of the Human Race, and guard and guide it on its upward path, as parents and teachers do their children and pupils. Famous western scientists also have openly expressed their belief that this must be so. All the religions mention these hierarchs. Vaiḍika Ḍharma calls them Avaṭāras, Amshas, Kalās, Vibhūṭis, Kumāras, Manus, Ṛṣhis, Munis, of many degrees. Buddhism names them as Buḍḍhas, Praṭyéka-buḍḍhas, Boḍhi-saṭṭvas. Jainism knows them as Tīrṭhan-karas and Arhaṭs.

[1] "There is no material point that does not act on every other material point. When we observe that a thing really *is* where it *acts*, we shall be led to say, as Faraday was, that all the atoms interpenetrate, and that each of them fills the world": Bergson, *Creative Evolution*, p. 214.

Islām knows them as Quṭubs, Ghauses, Waṭaḍs, Abrār, Baḍals, Akhyār, Walis, Nabis, Rasūls. Christianity calls them Sons of God, Messiahs, Thrones, Principalities, Powers, Prophets, Saints. Judaism calls them Patriarchs, Prophets, Sages. Zoroastrianism knows them as Soshyants, 'Renovators, whose task is to re-interpret the Eternal Truth from time to time', 'Lovers of mankind', also *Naroish-naro*, i.e. 'Men of men', Supermen.[1]

Ṭao-ism says:

> The High Emperor of the Sombre Heavens descends to earth...hundreds...(upon) hundreds (of) times, to become the companion of the common people and teach them the truth,...to heal the sick,...to endure suffering patiently and give his life again and again, that his pain may be a spring of joy and righteousness to many hearts[2].

Kṛshṇa and Ḍévi-Shakṭi say:

> Yaḍā yaḍā hi ḍharmasya
> glānir-bhavaṭi, Bhāraṭa !,
> Abhy-uṭ-ṭhānam a-ḍharmasya
> ṭaḍ-Āṭmānam sṛjāmy-Aham.

---

[1]The word Soshyanṭa, it seems, etymologically means 'lovers' of mankind, also 'renovators' of Humanity as well as of Truth, 'givers of a new, a second, birth to mankind', by giving birth afresh to the Eternal Truths, for their instruction, purification, and advancement. Zoroastrians believe in "three prophets... Oshedar-Cami, Oshedar-mah, and Sosiosh, preceded by Zarathustra" : H. P. Blavatsky, *Isis Unveiled*, II, 467.

[2]Quoted by J. Estlin Carpenter, *The Place of Christianity in the Religions of the World*, p. 60.

Pariṭrāṇāya sāḍhūnām
vināshāya cha ḍushkṛṭām,
Ḍharma-samsthāpan-ārṭhāya,
sambhavāmi yugé yugé. (*G.*)
Iṭṭham yaḍā yaḍā bāḍhā
dānav-oṭṭhā bhavishyaṭi,
Taḍā ṭaḍ-āva-ṭīry-Āham
karishyāmy-ari-sankshayam.
(*Ḍurgā-sapṭa-shaṭī.*)

(To guard the good and slay the wicked men,
And re-establish on firm base My Law,
I manifest My-Self age after age.
When law and righteousness decline and fade,
And vicious sin uplifts a fearless head,
Then I incarnate to redress the world.[1]
Whene'er the evil ones oppress the good,
I will take birth, and slay them without fail.

Éṭan-nān-Āvaṭārāṇām
niḍhānam bījam Avyayam,
Yasy-āmsh-āmshéna jāyanṭé
ḍéva-ṭiryang-nar-āḍayah. (*Bh.*)

(My Universal Mind is the One Fount,
Exhaustless, the One ever-fruitful Seed,
Of all the Sparks infinitesimal,
Atomic, countless, that ensoul all forms
High, low, of gods, men, animals;
While rarer Sparks of greater Light and Might
Appear as Avaṭār's to guide them right.)

---

[1]Faizī has translated this famous verse into Persian thus,

Chu bunyāḍ-i-Ḍīn susṭ garḍaḍ basé,
Numāyém Khuḍ rā ba shaklé Kasé.

Another reading of the first line is,

Cho ahwāl-i-ḍunyā bi-garḍaḍ khasé.

Muhammad says:

Le kullé qaumin hāḍ...In min ummaṭin' illā ḳhalā fīhā nazīr...Wa la qaḍ ba asna fi kulli ummaṭin Rasūlan. (*Q.*)

(To every race great Teachers have been sent.
God hath not left any community
Without a prophet, warner, and true guide.
He sendeth Prophets to the ignorant
And those misguided into evil ways,
Raising these prophets up from 'mongst themselves
To purify them, and to teach to them
His signs and wisdom and philosophy.)

Inn-Allāhā yaba'so lihāzehil ummaṭé a'lā rasé kullé méyaṭé sanaṭin maṅ-yujaḍḍaḍ lahā ḍīna-hā.

(*H.*, recorded by Abū Dāūḍ).

(At the beginning of each 'hundred years',
God sends, for every race, a teacher who
Revives Religion freshly for the world.)

Kāna fī Hinḍé nabī-yun aswaḍ-ul-laune isma-hū Kahinan.[1] (*H.*, recorded by Ḍailamī, in Ṭārīḳh-i-Hamḍan, Bāb-ul-Kāf.)

(A Nabī-Prophet lived and taught in Hinḍ,
Dark of complexion, Kahin was his name.)

Zālekā fazl-Ullāhé yoṭīhé maṅ-yashāo, w-Allāho zul-fazl-il. Allāho yā'lamo haiso yaja'lo rasālaṭahu. (*Q.*)

(Such prophetship is a great gift from God.
And God is very generous. He also knows
Who worthy is to be His messenger.)

The Zoroastrian Gāṭhā says:

Anghéūsh ḍaréthrāya fro ashahyā frārénṭé véré-jaḍāīsh senghāīsh Saoshyanṭām khraṭavo...

---

[1] *I.e.*, Kṛshṇa, which means 'the Dark One'.

Aṭ ṭoī anghém Saoshyanṭo ḍakhyūnām yōī kshanūm vohu manangha hachāonṭé...

...Yé ḍāṭhaébyo érésh Raṭum kshyāmsa ashivāo chisṭā. (*Z.*, Gāthā, 46. 3; 48. 12; 51. 5)

(Take up the disciplines enjoined by them,
The Saoshyanṭas, Lovers of Mankind,
Masters of Yoga, for thy soul's welfare;
In thought, in word, in deed, yea, take them up!
In every land, of e'en barbarians,
Are there Saoshyanṭas who have attained
The Great Peace of the Universal Self.
This Sovereign of the World, the Self of All,
Hath sent down righteous Prophets unto us,
Saoshyanṭas, to show us the Right Path.)

The theurgists and Platonists of the earlier centuries of the Christian era seem to have distinguished between Theo-pneusty (inspiration or the mysterious power to hear orally the teachings of a god), Theo-pathy (assimilation of divine nature), and Theo-phany (actual appearance of a god in man), as grades of spiritual progress.

The Buḍḍha says:

In due time another Buḍḍha will arise. He will be known as Maiṭréya (which means 'he whose name is kindness').

Jesus says:

I will come again and receive you unto myself, that where I am, ye may be also. (*B.*)

Behold, I will send you Elijah the prophet before the coming of the great and dreadful day of the Lord. (*B.*, *Malachi.*)

And elsewhere we read in the Bible:

Out of thee (Bethlehem) shall He come forth unto Me that is to be ruler in Israel; whose goings forth have been from of old, from everlasting. (*B., Micah.*)

The last words are especially significant.

God hath not left himself without witness in any land. (*B.*)

Isaiah says:

The Spirit of the Lord God is upon me. (*B.*)

The Spirit of the Lord shall rest upon him (i. e. Jesus). (*B.*)

And Jeremiah:

And the Lord said unto me—Behold, I have put My words in thy mouth." (*B.*)

In the Qurān, the fact is emphasised over and over again that it is Allāh who is speaking through the lips of Muhammad.

Even simply to bear these great souls in mind, as loving helpers, as examples, as standards, as proofs of the possibility for all of high achievement; and, much more, to get into touch with them, by developing spiritual and moral merit, and opening up the subtler senses, 'extending' the faculties into the superphysical, the finer and more ethereal, planes; this helps our own progress as members of the vast *Fraternity* of Man, nay, of all living beings.

The Fundamental Truths and Teachings remain ever the same, but the frame-works in which they manifest, decay and lose vitality, over and over again, in race after race, age after age, clime after clime, tongue after tongue. The words, the forms, become hackneyed, with the lapse of centuries; and human hearts respond to them no longer, vividly and actively. The new spiritual impulse, the new descent of the divine fire of life, that is needed to vivify afresh those Truths and Teachings, and give them a new birth in the living frame of a new language and new forms, in a new generation, or a new race, new place, new epoch—such divine afflatus can be given only by such Supermen. They incarnate as Founders of Religions; and, by the fire and fervour of their *ishq-i-haqiqī*, *karam-bā-khalq*,[1] Love divine and universal, Brahma-nishthā, vishva-préma, loka-hiṭ-éhā, the ardent flame of their compassion for mankind, fed constantly by the fuel of their deeds of self-sacrifice—by such ṭapas-fire in their own hearts, they set aflame the hearts of other human beings, all around, with similar love of God and of mankind. Thus they give a new life-time, of a whole great era, to the Eternal Truths, and so give birth to a new civilisation. This is their supreme work—of bringing into the world afresh, a great influx of spiritual, moral, emotional force. The intellectual work, also indispensable, of re-proclaiming the basic eternal truths is also done by them; but that of

[1] Bā khalq karam kun ke Khuḍā bā ṭo karam kard: (Sā'ḍī); 'Since God loves thee, thou too shouldst love all beings.'

expounding and reconciling their teachings, is done afterwards by studious followers, lesser persons. While these latter remain true servants of the Spirit, and well-wishers of mankind, the religion flourishes. When they become false, selfish, aggressive, proud, malevolent, then they begin to divide instead of reconciling and uniting; sects arise and multiply; decay begins.[1]

[1] The creators of a movement, who give it its origin, its life, its energy, its emotional impulse, and its actional impetus, are, usually, other than those who give it its detailed philosophy, and do its teaching, and guiding, its right direction; even as the parents of a child are usually other than its teachers. This does not mean that the teacher and the teaching begin to exist, are born, after the parents and the child; but only that the work of education, the clear exposition of the philosophy, begins after the child, the movement, has been born. As history has gone, so far, usually philosophy and movement have acted and re-acted on, and helped to define, each other. If parents and teachers have been in consultation with each other before the child is conceived and gestated and born, or if parents are also teachers—then the conditions for successful growth are most favorable. Only in rare cases, of some avaṭāras, *insān-ul-kāmil*, *mazhar-i-atamm*, have the aspects of Al-Bādī and Al-Alīm, Brahmā and Vishṇu, Creator and Teacher, been combined; and then also, the two aspects have scarcely been equally manifested. Either the aspect of Knowledge as Teacher, or of Action as History-maker and Warrior, or of Desire as Inspirer of Love and Devotion and Purifier of soul, prevails, and manifests more than the other two; but,

It should also be noted that the Evolutionary Chain or Spiral of living beings, high and low, stretches infinitely, above as well as below, according to the Scriptures of the nations; and modern science also vouches for it. Thus:

Looking at the matter from the most rigidly scientific point of view, the assumption that amidst the myriads of worlds scattered through endless space, there can be no intelligence as much greater than man's, as his is greater than a black beetle's; no Being endowed with powers of influencing the course of Nature as much greater than his, as his is greater than a snail's; seems to me not merely baseless but impertinent. Without stepping beyond the analogy of what is known, it is easy to people the cosmos with entities in the ascending scale until we reach something practically indistinguishable from omnipotence, omnipresence, and omniscience.[1]

---

of course, never exclusively; for all three aspects are inseparable, though distinguishable.

The reader who cares to pursue the subject further, may look into the present writer's *Kṛṣhṇa, A Study in the Theory of Avaṭāras*.

[1] Prof. T. H. Huxley, *Essays on Some Controverted Questions*, p. 36 (edn. of 1892). Prof. Huxley was one of the most renowned scientists of Britain, in the last quarter of the last century. More recently, the late more famous A. R. Wallace, and also the living very old Sir Oliver Lodge have publicly professed adherence to the same belief. The latter has written: "Two things I am impressed with—the first, the reality and activity of powerful, but not almighty, helpers, to whom,

7. The Goal Of Life—To Feel the Self in All.

The great truth which may be mentioned last here, is only another aspect of the first. The Self comes back to It-Self, remembers its forgotten Infinitude. The Wanderer returns Home. In symbol, the Serpent of Wisdom and of world-cycles swallows its own tail. A circling of the soul is completed. Extremes meet. The Infinitesimal is seen to be the Infinite. The Individual and the Universal become One.

The 'end' 'aim', 'purpose', 'goal', 'object', 'fundamental value' of life is dual. The preliminary purpose is a b h y-u ḍ-a y a, *ne'maṭ-i-ḍunya-vī, iqbāl-manḍī*, prosperity, success, in the life of this world, enjoyment of the good things of the earth, through the sensor and motor organs; it is threefold, (1) ḍ h a r m a, (2) a r ṭ h a, (3) k ā m a, (1) *ḍayānaṭ*, (2) *ḍaulaṭ*, (3) *lazzaṭ-uḍ-ḍunyā*, or (3) Sense-joy, refined by (2) Wealth, regulated by (1) Law; in other words, happy (3) Family-life, beautified by (2) Property and artistic possessions, restrained, controlled, regulated by (1) Religion-inspired Law of Right-and-Duty. This first triple end of life is to be pursued in the first half of life. The second half of life is to be

---

in some direct and proximate sense, we owe guidance and management and reasonable control; and next, with the fearful majesty of still higher aspects of the universe, culminating in an Immanent Unity which transcends our utmost possibility of thought."

devoted to the achievement of the final goal, m o k s h a, *najāṯ*, 'salvation', freedom from all sorrow, *Summum Bonum*, Nis-shrēyas, *Hazz-i-ā'lā*, Greatest Good, Joy than which there is no greater joy, 'to be like God', 'to become merged into God', 'to become God'.[1]

The final purpose of life, inherently cherished by every human heart, is Return to the Original State from which we have erred away; is the Assurance, the Realisation, that the whole World-process is the Play of one-Self, without restraint by an-Other, *Liberty* from all compulsion by another, Recollection of our-Self as Supreme Maker, Mender, and Ender of all, *Freedom* of the Spirit from the bonds of fear, doubt, sorrow, *Salvation* from sin, *Deliverance* from error, *Emancipation* from superstition, *Ab-solu-tion*, ab-solved-ness, Ab-solute-ness, from all limitation and its consequences. Some time, sooner or later this Freedom comes to each and every soul, after experience of all kinds of joys and sorrows, sins and merits, deeps and heights of life, *because* all souls *are* parts of the One Supreme Self; and it comes by the realisation that there *is no Other*, than the Self, which can restrain or compel. Vaiḍika Ḍharma, Buḍḍhism, and Jainism know this state as M u k ṭ i; also as N i r-v ā ṇ a,

---

[1] The reader who cares to pursue the subject of the 'Goal of Life' further, may look into the present writer's *The Science of the Self*, and *The Science of Social Organisation*.

annihilation or extinction *of the sense of separateness and egoism*, and blossoming of the sense, and tasting of the Bliss, of Oneness with the Universal Self, which constitutes the 'return' of the soul to its Source. Islām knows it by words which are exact equivalents of M u k ṭ i and N i r-v ā ṇ a, *viz.*, *Najāṭ* and *Fanā-f-Illāh*. The last word means extinction or annihilation *into* God, with its accompanying ecstasy of joy, *Lazzaṭ-ul-Ilāhiya*, B r a h m-ā n a n ḍ a, Spiritual Blessedness, dissolving into the 'Bliss of God', the opposite of v i s h a y a-ā n a n ḍ a, or *lazzaṭ-uḍ-ḍunyā*, worldly 'joy of sense-objects'. The Jewish Kabbalists call it 'the Palace of Love'; the Gnostics, 'the Pleroma of the Eternal Light'; the Christians, 'the Kingdom of Heaven'. Christianity calls it also the Beatitude of Salvation accomplished, Supreme Blessedness and Divine Bliss; the soul feels 'salved', 'saved', from 'death'; i. e., that death of the 'soul' which is 'the wages of sin'; the break-up of the 'subtile body', s ū k s h m a - s h a r ī r a, which results from persistent gross sin; death of the physical body is, of course, inevitable. St. Paul speaks of "the Glorious Liberty of the Sons of God". And again, he says:

Stand fast therefore in the *Liberty* wherewith Christ hath made us *Free*, and be not entangled again with the yoke of *Bondage*. (*B.*, Paul.)

The Truth (of the identity of the Individual with the Universal) will set you free. (*B.*)

There is no 'other-ness,' no *ghair-iyat*, no iṭara-ṭā, left in this state of Bliss. All is I. "The Universe grows I". Purusha becomes Brahma; Jiv-āṭmā becomes Param-Aṭmā; Amsha becomes Pūrṇa; the Part, the Whole; *Anāniyaṭ-i-aḍnā, Shakhsiyaṭ-i-aḍnā*, the Individual, becomes *Anāniyaṭ-i-ā'lā, Shakshiyaṭ-i-ā'lā*, the Universal; Chiṭṭa becomes Chiṭ; Vi-shishta-Chaiṭanya, limited, particularised, individualised consciousness, Vi-shishta-Saṭṭā, speci-fic existence, becomes Chaiṭanya-sāmānya, Universal Consciousness, Saṭṭā-sāmānya, gener-al, Universal Being; *Khuḍ* or *Khuḍī* becomes *Khuḍā*; the Drop becomes the Ocean; the Infinitesimal, the Infinite; Man becomes God.

As described by those who have experienced the realisation, there is, in it, the 'intellectual conviction' of identity of one-self with the Universal Self; there is also the 'affective' or 'emotional feeling' of that union, a very great exaltation, a sense of utter security and certainty; as the first romance of perfectly reciprocated human love raised to a very high degree, even to infinite degree, for here we have love of all, instead of only two; and there is also the 'actional' or 'volitional' aspect of the 'will', the 'resolve', to become, or, indeed, of having become, a 'missionary of God', a 'son of God'; of one's (triple) body being now an 'instrument', an 'organ', of the Universal Will-Life-Intelligence.

Bhakṭih, Par-ésh-ānu-bhavo vi-rakṭih
Anyaṭra cha-isha ṭrika éka-kālah. (*Bh.*)
(Love Universal, sense of Dei-ty,
Surcease of selfish act—all three in one.)
All are but parts of One stupendous Whole,
Whose body Nature is and God the Soul. (POPE.)
Yaḍ, Agné !, syām Aham Ṭvam,
Ṭvam vā ḍhā syā Aham. (*Ṛg-Véḍa*, 8. 44, 23)
(Lord Agni ![1] Fire and Light and Guide Within !
Ordain that I be Thou, and Thou be I !)

Man ṭū shūḍam, ṭū man shuḍī,
Man ṭan shuḍam, ṭū jāṅ shuḍī,
Ṭā kas na goyaḍ bāḍ az īṅ,
Man ḍīgaram, ṭū ḍīgarī. (*S.*)

(I am none else than Thou, and Thou than I ;
I am Thy body and Thou art My Soul.
Let no one say hereafter that I am
Other than Thee, or Thou other than I.)
Yaṭhā saṭah purushāṭ késha-lomāni,
Ṭaṭh-Āksharāṭ sambhavaṭ-īha Vishvam. (*U.*)
(As to the human being, hairs and nails,
So is this Cosmos to th' Eternal Self.)
Haq jān-i-jahān asṭ, wa jahāṅ jumla baḍan ;
Tauhīḍ hamīn asṭ ; ḍigar shéwa o fan. (*S.*)
(One single Body—this Whole Universe ;
God—its One Soul ; spirits, souls, angels all—
Its organs and its senses ; th' elements,
And all the Natural Kingdoms are its limbs—
Such the significance of Unity.)
Ṭaṭ sṛshtvā ṭaḍ-év-ānu-prā-vishaṭ...
Esha vai Vishva-rūpa Āṭmā Vaishvā-narah...

---

[1] 'Agré nayaṭi,' 'That which leads forward', is 'Ag-ni', the Divine Fire Within.

Ṭaṭra ko mohah kah shokah Ékaṭvam
anu-pashyaṭah. (*U.*)
(The Self creates this world and enters in,
As soul in body, to the very nails.
The Total of All Bodies and All Souls
Is His One Single Body and One Soul.
For him who sees him-Self in every self,
In everything, there is no longer left
Any perplexity, doubt, sorrow, fear.)

Other names for this Bliss are *surūr-i-jāwéḍānī*, the 'permanent intoxication', *isṭighṛāq*, 'mergence' into the One, Brahma-līnaṭā, 'disappearance in Brahma', Āṭma-lābha, the 'finding of the Self', *wisāl*, 'union', sāyujya, 'identification' with God, *wahḍaṭ*, éki-bhāva, kaivalya, 'on(e)li-ness', sol-itude, soli-tariness, Āṭm-ānanḍa, Āṭma-raṭi, Āṭma-ṭṛpṭi, 'Self-bliss', 'joy in Self', 'Self-content', bhakṭi-rasa, 'bliss-bath of love', mahā-bhāva, the 'great emotion', bhūmā, the state of being 'the greatest', 'the most', Infinitude.

Willy-nilly, consciously or sub-consciously, all living beings, all things, are all the time trying to reach this Eternal Fount of Peace which is *within themselves*, this Self of all, this Universal Love. All genuine earnest Philosophical and Religious Questing is but Home-sickness; yearning for the Heaven from which we have erred and fallen away; pining for the Garden of Eden from which we have been exiled, through the serpent-wiles of false Māyā-Desire, Ṭṛshṇā, *Hirs*,

Ṭama'; longing to regain our own forgotten and lost Self.

Mama varṭm-ānu-varṭanṭé
manushyāh, Pārṭha !, sarvashah.
Yé yaṭhá mām pra-paḍyanṭé
ṭāns-ṭaṭha-iva bhajāmy-Aham.
Ṭé-pi Mām-éva, Kaunṭéya !
yajanṭy-a-viḍhi-pūrvakam. (*G.*)
(Mankind are everywhere marching to Me.
Whatever road they take, I meet them on it.
In every form each soul seeks Me, the Self.)

Self-consciousness, All-Self-consciousness, is the one purpose and goal of all evolution, the one ever very near and yet seemingly "far-off divine event to which the whole creation moves," as western modern poet and philosopher also see and say, more or less gropingly; while the scriptures of the nations say and show the Great Truth in full blaze of light.

Manyé-ush hachā ṭhvā é-é-āonghā
Yā-ishā anghush po-uruyo khavaṭa.
(*Z.*, Gāṭhā, 28. 11)
(By force of knowledge and expanding thought
Shall we return to Thee, unto that state
Which was at the beginning of our life.)
Kaṭ vé kshaṭhrém, Mazaḍā !, yaṭhā vāo hakhmī ...paré vaskhémā...yaṭhā...ūrvāīḍ-yās...ayénī paīṭī.
(*Z.*, Gāṭhā, 34. 5, 6.)
(Thou art beyond all this we see, Supreme !
Teach us what resignation, fortitude,
And what detached aloofness from the world,
May join us unto Thee, Lord Mazaḍā !
And make us thus to realise our-Self.)

Ṭach-chhruṭam ṭach-cha vijñanam,
Ṭaḍ-ḍhyānam, ṭaṭ param ṭapah,
Ayam Āṭmā yaḍ-āsāḍya
Sva-svarūpē layam vrajēṭ.
(*J.*, SHUBHA CHANDRA, *Jñān-ārṇava.*)
(The deepest learning and the highest science
And meditation and asceticism
Are that the Self should re-cognise It-Self
And lose Itself in Self eternally.)

The Jewish Mystic Books say :

All things of which this world consists, spirits as well as bodies, will return to their principal, the root from which they proceeded. (*Ju.*, *Zohar*, II. 218b, quoted in H. P. Blavatsky's *Isis Unveiled*, ii, 271).

Bahūnām janmanām anṭé
jñānavān mām pra-paḍyaṭé. (*G.*)
(After the soul has passed through many births,
It knows, and comes back to Me, in the end.)
Life is a going forth, death is a returning home.
(*T.*, *Tao Teh King.*)

Gar che ḍīwār afganaḍ sāyah ḍarāz
Bāz garḍaḍ sūye ū āṅ sāyah bāz. (*S.*)
(Long is the shadow that the wall casts forth,
When the Sun falls upon the earth at dawn ;
Yet it turns back again, as the Sun climbs,
Till it is lost in the wall's base at noon.)
Innā l-Illāhī wa innā Ilaihi rāje'-ūn. (*Q*)
(From Allah do we come, for Him we are,
And to Him verily is our return.)

The beautiful poem of Sā'di, *Mā-muqīmān*, is an extended comment on this verse of the Qurān. Only the first and the last lines are given below :

Mā muqīmān-e-kū-e-Ḍilḍār ém ;

Rukh ba ḍunyā wa ḍīṅ na mī ārém ;
Bulbulān-ém, ke az qazā wa qaḍar,
Ofṭāḍah juḍā ze gulzār ém.
...Man na ḍānam ke anḍar īṅ|hairaṭ,
Ba wisālé ke ḍāḍ paighāmé,
Ke ba chashmān-i-ḍil ma-bīṅ juz Ḍosṭ,
Har che bīnī be-ḍāṅ ke mazhar-i-Ū-sṭ. (*S.*, Sā'ḍī.)
(In the Beloved's Garden did we dwell!
His Will, as Destiny, did cast us out,
To wander, seeking, in this labyrinth.
But now we've done with this world and its creeds.
After long yearnings and far wanderings
The wonder comes! He filleth all our being,
With His own Self—Yea, 'tis the Beloved!—
And a vast music in our Soul resounds,
"Ye are united with Me once again,
With the heart's eye see now naught but the Friend;
For whatsoever ye behold, ye know
Is but the glory of the Beloved!")

Miṭṭrasya chakshushā pashyema. (*V.*)
(See we the whole world with the One Friend's eye.)

Gauharé juz Khuḍ-shināsī
n-īsṭ ḍar bahr-é wujūḍ ;
Mā ba girḍé Khwēsh mī
garḍém chūṅ girḍābhā. (*S.*)
(Self-knowledge is the only pearl
In the sea of life;
Like whirlpools round our-Self we whirl
In incessant strife.)

Na vā...paṭyuh, jāyāyāh, puṭrasya, viṭṭasya,...
—Aṭmanas-ṭu kāmāya sarvam vai priyam bhavaṭi. (*U.*)

(Not for its own sake is aught dear to us ;
Whatever thing or being, high or low,
Parents, spouse, child, friend, house, or gold, or god,
Is dear to us—is so for sake of Self.)
Kufr o ḍīn har ḍo ḍar raha-ṭ poyāṅ,
Waḥḍahū lā sharīk-ilah goyāṅ.
Har kas ṭālib-i-Yār anḍ, che hushyār o che masṭ ;
Hama jā kḥānai ishq asṭ, che masjiḍ che kanishṭ.
Ṭu-hī Maqsūḍ hai, Ka'bā
wa Buṭ-kḥānā bahānā hai. (*S.*)
(Sceptic or faithful, both run after Thee,
Seeking the One Great Ultimate of all.
Sober, inebriate, sane or insane,
Each one for the Beloved One doth seek ;
Musalmān's mosque or Magian's fire-place,
Each is the sacred shrine of Love Divine.
Thou art the Goal for which all are asearch ;
Temple and Kā'bā, both, but roads to Thee !)

A comparatively recent Indian Sūfi poet bursts into song, as below, with the first joy of the Great Discovery :

Jis simṭ nazar kar ḍékhé hai,
us Ḍil-bar kī phulwārī hai,
Kahiṅ sabzī kī hariyālī hai,
Kahiṅ phūloṅ kī gulkāri hai ;
Ḍin rāṭ magan kḥush baithé haiṅ,
aur ās Usī kī bhārī hai ;
Bas āp hī Wah dāṭārī hai,
aur āp hī Wah bhandārī hai.
Har ān haṅsī, har ān kḥushī,
har waqṭ amīrī hai, bābā !,
Jab āshiq masṭ faqīr hué,
phir kyā ḍil-gīrī hai, bābā ! (*S.*, NAZIR.)

(Whichever way the eye is turned, it sees
The Garden of the Loved One burgeoning,
Blooming and bloss'ming with life upwelling
From the One Fount, which gives and takes
back too;
He is the Giver, He the Gatherer;
He is the one main stay of all our hopes;
All days are one long laugh, all nights one joy,
All life one opulence and affluence—
When once the heart all worldly things disowns,
And owns again its Own-Self's ecstasy.)

And again:

Āshiqé zār hūṅ maiṅ, tālib-é-ārām nahīṅ,
Nang-o-nāmūs-e-ḍuniyā sé mujhé kām nahīṅ.
Bé-sar-o-pāyī kā usshāq ko khaṭrā kyā hai,
Asar-e-Ishq hai yah, garḍish-e-ayyām nahīṅ.
Ālam-e-Īshq kī ḍuniyā hī nirālī ḍékhī,
Sahr-o-shām wahāṅ yé sahr-o-shām nahīṅ.
Bé nihāyaṭ, jiskā pāyā hai nahīṅ pāyāṅ,
Jis jagah ham pahuṅché haiṅ, āghāz hai,
anjām nahīṅ.
Fikr ḍuniyā kī malāmaṭ kī ṭujhé kyā hai, Nazīr !,
Ashiqoṅ méṅ ṭo akélā tū hī baḍ-nām nahīṅ.
(*S.*, NAZIR).

(I am a Lover dire, no seeker of delights!
What have I got to do with this world's
praise or blame?
What care the reckless Lovers that their
words lack sense?
This is th' effect of Love, and not of
Fortune's wrath.
The world of Love is very different from
this world;

Sun-dawn and eve-light *there* are not *this*
morn and eve.
Love's Ocean, boundless, fathomless—
where'er ye are
Ever only beginnings in it, ne'r an end !
What fear hast thou, my heart !, of the
world's idle talk ?
Thou art not th' only censured Lover
in the world !).

Rūmī sings the same great lesson in another mood :

Bar Shāh-e khụb-rūyāṅ
wājib wafā na bāshaḍ,
Ai zarḍ-rūye āshiq !
ṭū sabr kun, wafā kun ! (*S.*)
(The King of Beauty owes no duty,
Of fidelity to a *single* one !
Thou pale-faced lover ! do thou cover
Thy love with resignati-on !
Be faithful ever, and forget never,
His constancy is to *every* one;
As to every dew-drop, of the Sun !
He loveth all; do *thou* love all;
So thy smallness shall be all undone,
His Greatness shall by *thee* be won,
And thou shalt gain *All* of the One !)

"Make the Great Discovery for yourself, freshly, each of you, all of you, brothers and sisters !, sons and daughters !"—this is the one teaching of all the Great Teachers, of all the Great Scriptures, of all the Great Religions.

Spénṭém at Ṭhvā, Mazaḍa !, ménghī, Ahura !, hyaṭ mā vohū pairé jasaṭ manangha pérésaṭ chā mā chish ahī, kahyā ahi, kaṭhā ayāré ḍakshārā férasayāī ḍīshā aibī ṭhvāhū gaéṭhāhū ṭanushī chā. (*Z.*, Gāṭhā, 13. 7).

(Conscience, the higher mind, awoke in me,
Shook me and questioned me : "Think ! careless one !,
Who art thou ? Whose art thou ? I ask thee, say !
Why art thou here ? What for ? And doing what?
When wilt thou learn the purpose of thy life ?
When understand thy body and thy mind ?
And in that moment did I realise,
Thou art the only Holy One, the Whole,—
Mazḍā !, Mahā-Ḍéva !, Mahā-Ḍhāṭā !,
Creator Great, Most wise, the Soul of All,
From Whom, for Whom, and unto Whom alone
Are all souls, 'asu-s', Great Lord 'Ahu'-ra !)
Āṭmānam vijāniyāṭ...Āṭmā vi-jñéyah...
Āṭmānam an-vichchhāmah, yam Āṭmānam
an-vishya sarvāmsh-cha lokān av-āpnoṭī...
Āṭmā vā aré ḍrashtavyah shroṭavyo
manṭavyo niḍiḍhyāsiṭavyah...(*U.*)
(Deep hid in the heart cave, seek thine own Self...
The Self is the one thing to seek and find...
Yea, let us seek the Self, for finding It
We find within It all the countless worlds...
There is Naught-Else than the One Self Alone,
In very truth, to be sought, thought, seen, known.)
Know thy-Self. (SOLON, the Greek Sage.)

Hearken unto Me (the Supreme Self), my son; blessed are they who keep My ways...Blessed is the man that heareth Me, watching daily at My gates... For whoso findeth Me, findeth life, and shall obtain favour of the Lord....But he that sinneth against Me wrongeth his own soul...and loves death. (*B.*, ***Proverbs.*** vii, 1—36.)

Nas-Ullāhā fa'ansāhum anfusehum. (*Q.*)
(He who forgetteth God forgets him-Self.)
Ko-(A)ham, kas-ṭvam, kuṭa-āyāṭah,
Ṭaṭ-tvam chinṭaya, Taḍ-iḍam, bhrāṭah!
(SHANKAR-ĀCHĀRYA.)

(What is I and what is Thou?
(Whence is each, what for, and how?
What the truth of all this show?
Ponder this, my brother! now!)

Kim ṭé ḍhanéna, kim-u banḍhubhir-éva vā ṭé,
Kim ṭé ḍāraih, puṭraka!, yo marishyasi;
Aṭmānam an-vichchha, guhām pravishtam,
Piṭāmahās-ṭé kva gaṭāh, piṭā cha. (*Mbh.*)
(What hast thou got tc do with riches; what
With kinsfolk; what with loved and loving spouse?
Of these none shall bestand thee, O my child!,
When the dread Messenger of Death shall come!
Where are thy parents and their parents gone!
Seek then th' Immortal Self, Master of Death,
Eternal Refuge, hiding in the cave,
The Cave profound of thine own living heart!)

"My father sent me...I go the Father," says Jesus, i. e., 'to My own Universal and Supreme Self'; and every soul has to say it, and thus triumph over Death.

Jā ké ghar sukh kā bhandārā
So kyoṅ bharmai ḍar ḍar mārā!
(In thine own home, the Treasury of all joy!
And thou a-begging thus from door to door!)
Ho ke Sulṭān-i-Haqīqaṭ isī āb-o-gil méṅ,
Ḍar ba ḍar misl-i-gaḍā ṭhā, mujhe mā'lūm na thā.
(*S.*)
(Though King of all the World, in mud and mire,
I begged from door to door—I knew Me not!)

Ṭvam ṭu bhūmi-paṭéh puṭro!
na jāngalika-sanṭaṭih! (*Yoga Vāsishtha.*)
(Though art the King's Son, Sir!, no jungle-child,
Though lost in infancy in this vast wild,
And reared by forest-folk, from Truth beguiled!)
Shréshtham vāṇijyam ṛṭam amṛṭam mama-iṭan-
Marṭyén-Āham krīṭa-vānasmy-A-marṭyam. (*U.*)
Éshā buḍḍhi-maṭām buḍḍhir-,
Manīshā cha manīshiṇām,
Yaṭ Saṭyam an-ṛṭén-éha
Martyén-āpnoṭi Māmṛṭam. (*Bh.*, xi. 29. 22.)
Iha chéḍ-avéḍīḍ-aṭha Saṭyam asṭi,
Na chéḍ-ih-āvéḍīn-mahaṭī vi-nashtih. (*U.*)
Iha-iva sanṭo aṭha viḍmas Ṭaḍ vayam,
Na chéḍ-avéḍīr mahaṭī vi-nashtih;
Yé Ṭaḍ viḍur-amṛṭās-ṭé bhavanṭi;
Aṭh-éṭaré ḍuhkham ev-āpi-yanṭi. (*Bṛhad U.*)
(Best of all trades is mine—that I have sold
My mortal things and bought Immortal Soul!
This is true Wisdom; this, best Enterprise;
That we should part with Lie and lay in Truth,
And with the mortal buy th' Immortal Self!
Great is our loss if we fail to buy back
Our 'birthright' with this 'pottage-mess' and gain
Our Deathless Self while still in mortal sheath;
Let us make sure to see Him while still here;
If we do not, then very great our loss,
And we pass o'er and o'er from pain to pain;
But if we do, then Deathless Bliss our gain!)

Great is the yearning of the Elders of the Race, the Sages, Saints, Seers, Prophets, that the youngers should make this Great Discovery and so be freed from all sorrows; even as is the yearning of the mother and the father that their little ones may attain majority and become able to stand on their own feet.

Samsāriṇām karuṇay-āha Purāṇa-guhyam. (*Bh.*)
(Of pity for mankind, Shuka did teach
The Ancient Sacred Secret unto all.)
Ḍarḍ-e-ḍil ké wāsṭé insān ko paiḍā kiyā;
Var-na ṭāa'ṭ ké liyé kuchh kam na ṭhīṅ Karrobiyāṅ.
(*S.*)

(God entered into human shape, to feel
Ache of the Heart, commixt of Woe and Bliss.
To hymn His Glory there were Cherubim
In hosts; but He grew tired of hearing them,
And wished to feel the feel of human woe.)
Kufr Kāfir rā, wa ḍīṅ ḍīn-dār rā,
Qaṭra-é ḍarḍé-ḍilé Aṭṭār rā. (*S.*)
(Let sceptics in their disbelief rejoice;
And in their faith the faithful ones take joy;
One drop of the Divine Heartache for Me.)

My little children, of whom I travail in birth again until Christ be formed in you; (*B.*, Galatians.)

Until we all come in the unity of faith, and of the knowledge of the Son of God, into a perfect man, unto the measure of the stature of the fulness of Christ. (B., *Ephesians.*)

Work out your own Salvation, for it is God which worketh in you. (*B.*, *Philippians.*)

The law of the Spirit of Life in Christ Jesus hath made me *free* from the law of life and death. (*B.*, Paul.)

Some may interpret 'the law of life and death', as 'the law of involuntary re-births':

The thing that hath been, it is that which shall be; and that which is done is that which shall be done...The wind goeth toward the south, and turneth about unto the north; it whirleth about continually, and the wind returneth again according to his circuits... All the rivers run into the sea; yet the sea is not full; unto the place from whence the rivers come, thither they return again. (*B.*, Eccles.)

This Law of Cyclicity is true of things physical as well as things spiritual or psychical.

For as many as are led by the Spirit of God, are the sons of God. (*B.*, *Romans.*)

By the help of the Best Purity, by the help of the Supreme Purity, O Ahura Mazaḍa, may we see Thee, may we draw near Thee, may we become one with Thee for Eternity. (*Z.*, *Yasna*, ix. 12.)

"We become One with Thee", by realising that the individual is, in essence, identical with the Universal.

The pure in heart shall see God. (*B.*)

Such souls no longer need the prohibitions and the injunctions, the negative 'don'ts' and the positive 'do's', the nishéḍhas and viḍhis, the *mana's* and the *kun's*, of Religions Ethics. They have risen from 'don'ts' and 'do's' into '*be*' (perfect). They are themselves the embodiments of Law, Ḍharm-āṭmā, *Salīm.*

Nis-ṭrai-guṇyé paṭhi vicharaṭo
ko viḍhih ko nisheḍhah.

(SHANKAR-ĀCHĀRYA.)

(Since they have mastered 'the three attributes';
Of knowing, wishing, and performing acts;
Of light, and darkness, and vast restlessness;
Which, manifesting in 'th' opposéd pairs',
Create the world and keep it ever going;
And are no longer mastered by those three;
And since the Law of Universal Love

Reigns ever-wakeful now within their hearts,
No other laws of 'do's' and 'don'ts' they need.).

The souls which have achieved this realization of the Oneness of all Life, this non-separateness from all others, this inseparable connection and unbreakable relationship with all other living beings—they are called Pūrṇa-purushas, Ḍivya-purushas, Jīvan-Mukṭas, Avaṭāras, Perfect Persons, Divine Persons, the 'Living-Free', 'Deity descended (into human form)', in Veḍānṭa; Buḍḍhas, Boḍhi-saṭṭvas, the 'Enlightened,' the 'Wisdom-souled', in Buḍḍhism; Arhaṭs, the 'worthy,' Ṭīrṭhan-karas, 'the helpers-across, the ferrymen, of others,' in Jainism; Sons of God, Messiahs, Christs, ('Christos' means the 'anointed' with Divine Wisdom) in Christianity; *Insān-ul-kāmil*, *Marḍ-i-ṭamām*, *Mazhar-i-aṭamm*, Perfected Men, Completed Men, Divine Men, Incarnations or Manifestations of Divinity, in Islām.

Be ye perfect, as your Father in heaven is perfect... And ye shall know the Truth (of the essential identity of the individual with the Universal Self), and the Truth shall make you free (of all fear)......Ye are gods...(*B.*)

(God says : But follow thou My laws, O man !,
And thou shalt sure become like unto Me ;
Then if thou say, 'Let there be this', it *is* !) (*H.*)
Mayi ḍhārayaṭash-chéṭah
upa-ṭishthanṭi siḍḍhayah. (*Bh.*)
(If any one will fix his heart on Me,
All secret sacred Powers shall wait on him !)

Such perfected, completed, souls, having achieved at-one-ment with the All-Self and therefore with all selves, can and do try to make atonement for all; to make all realise at-one-ment.

Labhanṭé Brahma-nirvāṇam
 ṛshayah kshīṇa-kalmashāh,
Chhinna-ḍvaiḍhā yaṭ-Āṭmānah
 sarva-bhūṭa-hiṭé raṭāh.
San-ni-yamy-énḍṛiya-grāmam
 sarvaṭra sama-buḍḍhayah,
Té prāpnuvanṭi Mām éva
 sarva-bhūṭa-hiṭé raṭāh. (*G.*)

(The pure souls that have washed away their sins,
And cast off doubt and sense of separateness,
And all duality of 'I' and 'thou',
That see with Love the Same Law everywhere,
And always are intent on good of all—
They have found Me, and found My deathless Peace.)

Kasé marḍé-ṭamām asṭ az ṭamāmī
Kunāḍ bā kẖwājagī kāré gẖulāmī. (*S.*)

(They are the perfect men who, being such,
Out of the greatness of their loving hearts,
Make themselves small to slave continuously
To make th' imperfect ones perfect also.)

Degrees and kinds of rapport between the individual and the Universal (or, mostly, a higher individual, a personal god, a great angel), between the part and the (mostly comparative) Whole, the small and the Great, are distinguished as s ā l o k y a, s ā m ī p y a, s ā r ū p y a, s ā y u-j y a, ā v é s h a, k a l-ā v a ṭ ā r a, a m s h-ā v aṭāra, pūrṇ-āvaṭāra, etc., in Vedānṭa and Yoga; and as *wajḍ, jazba, wasl, qurb-i-farāyaz, qurb-i-nawāfil, burūz, hulūl, mazhar-i-aṭamm*, etc., in Ṭasawwuf; i.e., nearness of several degrees, assimilation of many degrees, and identification of various degrees.

In the ascent, *urūj*, āroha, to this perfect realization of the identity of individual and Universal, the soul passes through three main inner stages. In terms of knowledge, they constitute the three main 'views,' ḍarshanas: (1) Dualistic Theism or Deism, (2) Pantheism, (3) Monism; (1) Ḍvaiṭa, (2) Vishishṭ-āḍvaiṭa, (3) A-ḍvaiṭa; (1) *Ījāḍiyah*, (2) *Shuhūḍiyah*, (3) *Wujūḍiyah*[1]; (1) the popular view of Causation, *i.e.*, an extra-cosmical personal God has created the cosmos, (2) the Scientific view of Causation, *i.e.*, that Force and

---

[1] *Ījāḍ*, from the root *wajḍ*, means '*giving* existence (to what was non-existent)', 'invention', 'creation'. *Wujūḍ*, from the same root, means 'existence', 'being'. *Shuhūḍ* means 'witnessing', 'seeing'. As usual, there is much hair-splitting and drawing of 'nice' distinctions, as to what exactly the *shuhūḍiyah* doctrine is. As usual, also, there is, there must be, an element, a piece, of truth, in each view. Broadly and comprehensively speaking, the doctrine is that God, Spirit-Force, 'witnesses' the 'manifestation' of the infinite Mater-ial attributes that are inherent in Him-Self; and this manifestation-and-witnessing is the World-Process plus God, the Interplay of Spirit or Mind or Energy or Force, and of Matter; of Thought and Extension; of Purusha

Matter, or Thought and Extension, are inseparable aspects of the same thing, and are undergoing transformations constantly, (3) the Metaphysical view of Causation, *i.e.*, that the cosmos is the Dream-Illusion of the One Spirit or Self or Principle of Consciousness; (1) the Ārambha-vāḍa of Nyāya-Vaisheshika, (2) the Pariṇāma-vāḍa of Sānkhya-Yoga, (3) the Vi-varṭa (or Ā-bhāsa or Aḍh-yāsa)-vāḍa of Mīmāmsā-Veḍānṭa.

The Sūfis put the three stages in three logia, mahā-vākyas, *kalemā-s*; (1) *Hama az Ū-sṭ* 'all is (made) *by* Him,' (2) *Hama anḍar* (or *ba*) *Ū-sṭ*, 'all is *in* Him'; (3) *Hama Ū-sṭ*, 'all *is* He'. Other forms of the logia are (1) *Lā ma'būḍah* (or *maqsūḍah*) *illā Hū*, 'none is to be adored but He,' (2) *Lā mashahūḍah illā Hū*, 'none is to be witnessed, sensed, felt, experienced but He,' (or 'none is the Witness but He'), (3) *Lā maujūḍah illā Hū*, 'Naught is but He'.

A Samskṛṭ verse sums up all these three and their sub-varieties in terms of the Prepositions which signify the Relations between Nouns through Verbs; here, the Relations between God and the World through al-Mighti-ness, to which the grammatical trinity broadly corresponds.

Yasmin, Yasya, Yaṭo, Yasmāṭ,
Yéna, Yam, Ya Iḍam Svayam,

---

and Prakṛṭi. For fuller exposition of the different views that have arisen under the *shuhūḍiyah* view, the reader may consult the excellent books of Khājā Khān, viz., *Studies in Ṭasawwuf* and *the Philosophy of Islam*.

Yo-smāṭ parasmāṭ cha Parah,
Ṭam prapaḍyé Svayam-bhuvam ![1]
(I take my refuge in th' Eternal Self,
Subject of all, Self-born, Self-evident,
In, Of, From, For, and By, and Unto Whom
All 'This' innumerous Object-world exists;
Who *is* This all too; and Who, being This,
Yet shines transcendently beyond This all !)

Out of Him (the Self), through Him (the Self), in Him (the Self), all things are. (In the original Greek: *Ex auton, kai di auton, kai eis auton ta panta*). (*B*., Paul.)

The three views correspond broadly to the temperaments of (1) Active Energism, (2) Devotional Pietist Mysticism, (3) Enlightened Gnosticism. They are not inconsistent at all with each other, much less antagonistic; except when each is emphasised to the exclusion of the others, in the false spirit of extremism. When the final stage is reached, all views are seen to be complementary and supplementary aspects of one another. Perfect evolution requires perfect equipoise of all, (1) Active Service of Mankind, because of (2) Philanthropy, due to the (3) Knowledge that all are One-Self ; the knowledge

---

[1] In the *Bhāgavaṭa*, the verse occurs in the following form :

Yasmin Iḍam, Yaṭash-ch-Éḍam,
Yén-Éḍam, Ya Iḍam Svayam,
Yo-smāṭ Parasmāch-cha Paras-
Ṭam prapadyé svayam-bhuvam.
(*Bh.*, Gajendra-Sṭuṭi.)

that (*a*) the One Self, (*b*) dreams the Interplay of Self (Force) and Not-Self (Matter), of Soul and Body, and (*c*) manifests also in 'personal i. e., individualised, gods', as Rulers of endlessly graded larger and smaller worlds, orbs, solar and sidereal world-systems.

We have referred before to the three main functions or aspects of the mind. They correspond to the three Primal Guṇas of the Nirguṇa, the *Sifāṭ* of the *Zāṭ-i-lā-sifāṭ*, the Attributes of the Attributeless, the *Zāṭ-i-sāḍij*, Shuḍḍha-Saṭ, Ṭaṭṭva-māṭra, Pure Being, Pure Essence, Mere That-ness ; the *Munqaṭa'-ul-ishāraṭ*, *Lā-ṭa'iyun*, *Lā-ba-sharṭ-i-shay*, *Majhūl-un-nās*, Nir-anjana, Nir-vishésha, Nirmala, Shuḍḍha, the Unconditioned, Undefin-able, 'No'-thing, Attributeless, Ab-solute, ab-solv-ed from all limitations, Devoid of all marks, stains, particularities, specialities ; Param-Āvyakṭa, *Ghaib-ul-ghuyūb*, the Utterly Hidden ; Āṭyanṭ-Āṭīṭa, *Ghaib-i-Muṭlaq*, the absolutely Transcendant ; Saṭṭā-māṭra, *Wajūḍ-i-bahaṭ*, Being-in-itself ; Whose Infinite all-enclosing Generality and Universality can be described only by apa-vāḍa of all aḍhy-āropa, by *ṭanzīh* of all *ṭashbīh*, by negation of all particular affirmations, rejection of all de-fini-tions, repudiation of all narrowing characterisations, of all names and forms ; na-iṭi, nāma-rūp-āpalāpa, ākāra-nirākaraṇa, vishéshaṇ-āpavāraṇa, *isqāṭ-ul-ishāraṭ*, *inqiṭa'-ul-ashkāl*, *ṭarḍīd-ul-hayākal*, 'I am this,

—No,' 'I am that,—No,' 'I am that other,—No,' 'I am I al-One,' 'I am that I am'.[1] The careful reader will see that these, mostly negative, adjectives and descriptions, can belong to 'No-Thing' but the Universal Self in and of all.

It is well-known that the view of Buḍḍhism and Jainism as to the indescribability of the Ultimate Fact otherwise than by negatives, is exactly the same. So too is that of the Jewish mystics. The Hebrew book, *Zohar*, says:

God, *En-sof*, 'No-End,' Infinite [Skṭ., A n-a n ṭ a, Arab.-Per. *Lā-inṭihā*] is above all creatures and all attributes.[2] When these things have been removed,

[1] The reader, if he desires a more detailed exposition of the subject, may refer to the present writer's *The Science of Peace* and *The Science of the Self*.

[2] Arabic scholars usually derive the word *Sūfī*, whence *Ṭasawwuf*, from the *Sūf* (spelt with a *swāḍ*), which means 'woollen cloth', and not from the *Sūf* (spelt with a *sīn*), which means 'wisdom'. They say that, in the earlier days, it was customary for Sūfī-s, ascetic-mystic-gnostic-devotee-philosophers, who had retired from the world, to wear a woollen blanket or gaberdine; as the s a n n y ā s ī-s of India still wear ochre-colored cloth, and as some sects of Christian monks used to wear sack-cloth. Others think that the word is connected with *safā* (spelt with a *swāḍ*), which means 'purity'. Yet others connect it with the Greek *sophia*, 'wisdom', whence the Arabic *fal-safā* (a transformation of 'philo-sophy'), and *sūfisṭā* (i.e. 'sophist', the man of pseudo-wisdom, the specious reasoner). Hebrew and Arabic scholars might consider whether the Hebrew *En-Sof* can be translated as Arabic A'yn-Sūf (with *sīn*) or A'yn-

there is left neither attribute, nor shape, nor form. He can be postulated only negatively. We cannot tell what God is; we can tell only 'what He is not.' For the creation of the world, which is an emanation of the Divine, the Infinite became, as it were, contracted, *Ṭsimṭsum*, and took on certain attributes of the finite. To this finite, belongs 'darkness,' evil, [Skṭ., ṭ a m a s]. The finite, the world, opposite extreme of the Infinite, is evil. Evil, sin, are *Kelifoth*, 'coverings', screens which hide the Truth; [S k ṭ., k l é s h a s, ā v a r a ṇ a s, u p ā ḍ h i s.] Whatever in the world is evil, and not of the Divine, cannot be real. Hence evil is that which has no being [a-s a ṭ]; it is a sort of illusion [m ā y ā]; it is a state of absence, negation; it is a thing which merely appears to be, but is not. It is man's duty to strive after re-union with the Infinite; his pursuit of the finite, the false, constitutes evil. He can attain the real only when he seeks the Real, Who is his fount, his home.[1]

Sāf (with *swāḍ*), which would mean 'mere pure Intelligence or Consciousness, i.e., 'no-thing-ness', or 'Sheer Purity', i. e., 'no-thing-ness', 'no-mixture', again.

[1]This quotation is abridged from pp. 128-132 of Dr. J. Abelson, *Jewish Mysticism*, (The Quest Series), in his own words. Another western writer says: "In Egypt they have a popular rhyme which is thus rendered by Canon Gairdner,

> Whatever idea your mind comes at,
> I tell you flat, God is not that."

The original is perhaps,

> Kulla mā haṭarā bi bālik,
> F-Allāhu siwā zālik.

Thus popular instinct and religio-metaphysical meditation come to the same conclusion. Extremes meet.

We have seen before that the compassionate teachers "temper the wind to the shorn lamb". They tell the earnestly seeking soul that evil is 'no-thing.'[1] They add the explanation that this is so because all 'limitation' is the mark of 'nothingness.' What passes, vanishes, must be nothing. Sorrow and evil pass; they must be nothing, like dreams. Bye and bye, the earnest seeker after true religious consolation will realise, that what he knows as joy and good also passes, is limited in time, space, condition; and so must be nothing too. Finally, he realises, that the Everlasting Peace of the Eternal and Infinite Self transcends the make-believe, the drama, of both good and evil, both joy and sorrow; that good is good and joy is joy by contrast with evil and with sorrow; that, in the World-drama, his part is to be consciously on the side of the good; that the souls that are as yet unconscious of their identity with All, are indeed intensely conscious of only separateness, and 'know no better,' will be on the side of evil, which is 'error', erring *away from* the Supreme and *into* the body of flesh with its inherent selfishness; and that as he himself has erred but returned, so all these others

---

[1]Spinoza, a philosopher famous in Europe, is a very earnest expounder of this view, in philosophical language; but he, like Hegel, leaves behind perplexity and confusion in the mind, instead of lucid convictions, because he speaks of the Ultimate Fact, the Primal Substance, the Absolute, in terms of the third person, as 'It', instead of the first person, 'I', 'Self', Ego.

also will, each in his own proper time and without fail, come back to the Right Path and reach Home. Soon or late, each 'erring' soul tires of its 'wanderings'; the mood of v a i-r ā g y a, 'world-weariness' and 'passionate compassion' for all the 'wanderers in the dark' comes upon it; and it begins the 'Homeward Journey'.

There is One Alone [*i.e.*, the Uni-versal Self], and there is Not-a-Second: Yea, He hath neither child nor brother; Yet is there no end of all His labor [*i.e.*, this endless World-Process]; neither is His eye satisfied with riches [for all the Universe is His always]; neither saith He, For whom do I labor, and bereave My soul of good [i.e., forget My infinity and fall into limitation]. This is also Vanity (M ā y ā, L ī l ā). Yea, it is a sore travail [k l é s h a, in the *Yoga-Sūṭra*, 'misery-breeding original sin or error of Self-forgetting']. (*B.*, Eccles. 4.)

This sore travail hath God given to the sons of man to be exercised therewith...to seek and search out by wisdom concerning all things that are done under heaven...I gave my heart to know wisdom and to know madness and folly...In much wisdom is much grief, and he that increaseth knowledge increaseth sorrow...I have seen all the works that are done under the sun; and behold, all is vanity and vexation of spirit...There I saw that wisdom excelleth folly, as far as light excelleth darkness...This also is vanity. (*B.*, Eccles.)

I know that there is no good in them, but for a man to rejoice and to do good in his life. (*B.*, Eccles.)

> Ḍuhkham éva sarvam vivékinah. (*Yoga-bhāshya*).
> Anḍham ṭamah pravishanṭi yé Aviḍyām upāsaṭé;
> Ṭaṭo bhūya-iva ṭé ṭamo ya-u Viḍyāyām raṭāh. (*U.*)

Viḍyām ch-āviḍyām cha,
yas ṭaḍ véḍ-obhayam saha
Aviḍyayā mṛṭyum ṭīrṭvā
Viḍyayā amṛṭam ashnuṭé. (*U.*)
Na sukham na cha vā ḍuhkham,
na moksho n-āpī banḍhanam,
Na puṇyam na cha vā pāpam,
iṭy-ésha Param-ārṭhaṭā. (*U.*)

(To him who sees the difference between
The Staying and the Fleeting, all this Show
Of Shadows, pleasant-painful, all is pain.
Who worship Error, pass into the Dark;
And they who worship Truth-ful Wisdom—they
Into a deeper Darkness *seem* to pass,
In which all long-loved finites disappear;
But soon the Glory of the Self shines forth,
In which all finites are, eternally.
To know the Truth, we must first Error know;
By Error, we pass through the gates of Death;
And then, by Truth, to Deathlessness we go.)

Good is good, evil is evil, wisdom is wisdom, folly is folly; though both are parts of the one Drama. The soul has to pass from evil to good, from folly to wisdom, to become Son of God, Jīvan-mukṭa, *Insān-ul-kāmil*, and win back the lost, i.e., merely forgotten, Immortality.

'Descent' along the *Qaus-i-nazūl*, Avāroha-mārga, and its attendant *isbāṭ-ul-ishāraṭ*, aḍhyā-ropa, 'putting on, assumption, of particularising marks and limitations', and selfish *ṭashbīh*, nāma-rūpa, 'donning of name-and-form'; and then reascent along the *Qaus-i-urūj*, Ārohamārga, and its appertenant *isqāṭ-ul-ishārat*, a p a - v ā d a, 'putting off, repudiation, of all de-finition', and unselfish *tanzih*, n i r-ā k a r a ṇ a, 'negation of limitations,'—are both part of *lahv*, l ī l ā. Yet the latter is better.

The pair, of good as well as evil, virtue and vice, merit and sin, is also part of the World-Illusion in this wise, together with all other countless pairs.

Since this ever-changing, 'ever-whirled-and-whirling' 'world', j a g a ṭ, the 'ever-going', *jahān*, the 'ever-leaping,' is made up of *nothing-else* than all the paired and opposed particularities which are negated, denied all existence, by each other ; which indeed neutralise, nullify, abolish each other; therefore, all religions hold that this world, with all its weal and woe, is indeed, in essence, a s a ṭ, *a'ḍam*, non-being, no-thing ;[1] "vanity of vanities" (*B.*); M ā y ā,

[1] It does seem very hard to believe, to 'realise', that all the *solid* things, our bodies, these houses, trees, towns, mountains, the whole earth—are 'un-real', are 'no-thing.' Yet it is certain that they are *always changing*, even *vanishing*. But what changes, is not permanent ; and what is not permanent, *cannot* be *real*. Only That Which sees that 'all these things' of 'This' Object-World are changing, unreal ; and distinguishes the changing from the Changeless ; That is and must be It-Self Changeless, Real, Eternal Mind, Infinite Consciousness, Omnipotent Energy of Will-and-Imagination. From It does all 'This' manifestation *appear*, Dream-like, Illusory, (Solids, Liquids, Gases, Ethers, Atoms, Electrons, Protons, Neutrons, Plutons, all) ; by That it is

illusion, Līlā, play, Krīdā, (creat-ion), sport, pastime, Svapna, dream, Nashvara, perishing, Bhrama, 'circling' hallucination, Maru-marīchikā, desert-mirage, (*U.*); *Lahwun wa la'ibun*, idle sport and play,[1] *Ṭasalluf*, delusion, *Fisāna*, story, *Sar-āb*, mirage, *Fiṭna*, deception, *Ja'l* of the *Jā'el* (Māyā of the Māyī), magic-forgery, false snare of illusion, *Kḥayāl* or *Kḥwāb-i-Kḥuḍā*, the thought or the dream of God (*S.*); *Hāḍisun*, *Hālikun*, *Bāṭila*, fleeting, perishing, nullity. (*Q.*)

In this Infinite and Eternal Miracle of Imagination are to be found all possible experiences —of the 'sub'-conscious 'under-worlds', and the 'supra'-conscious 'upper-worlds'; of hells and heavens; of the most horrible nightmares and the most beautiful paradises; of the most simple and the most complex, the most childlike and artless and the most sagelike and profound, the most frivolous and frolicsome and the most serious,

---

maintained for a while (for a Moment, eye-wink or millions and billions of human years); into It does it vanish—again and again, periodically, in minutest to vastest Cycles of alternate Waking and Sleeping, Restlessness and Rest, Outbreathing and Inbreathing, Cosmos and Chaos, Power and Peace.

[1]Some say the name Al-Lah is connected with or derived from *lahv*, and means the Great Player, Playwright, corresponding with the Veḍic Kavi, the Ancient Poet and Dramatist, Author of the World-Drama; others derive it from *walhum*, love; still others from the Hebrew El, (Arab. Al, That), God.

solemn, earnest, and grand, types and characters; the most empty show and the Fullest Reality.

Haqāyaq-ul-ashiyā sābiṭun,
w-al ālamu hāḍisun. (*H.*)
Kullu shayīn hālikun illā Wajh. (*Q.*)
Kullu shayīn mā-siwā-Allāhu bāṭila. (*H.*)
(The Essence bides; the world's a passing dream.
The Cause, the Face of God, God's very Self,
Alone persists; effects all pass and die.
All-Else-than-God is wholly null and voiḍ.)
Annāsu niyamin, fa ezā māṭu inṭabahu. (*H.*)
Innamul kaunu kḫayālun, wa huā
Haqqun fi-l haqīqaṭé. (*H.*)
(Men who are living here are in a dream,
And when they die then shall they be awake;
For all this world is a mere thought—the thought
Of Him who is the True, whose thought is Truth.)

Some others of the many names of this Omnipotence of the Supreme Self, this Magic-Power of Desire, this all-compelling Force of Will-and-Imagination, which is the motive-force behind all this Dreaming are Ṭ r s h ṇ ā, V ā s a - n ā, K ā m a - S a ṇ k a l p a, A v i ḍ y ā, *Hirs*, *Ṭamannā*, *Havas*, *Arzū*, *Kḫayāl*.

Jumla iṅ ḍām asṭ o ḍān-ash ārzū,
Ḍar guréz az ḍām-hāyé āz zū. (S.) (āz, hirs; zū, zūḍ)
(Know all this is the snare spread by Desire;
Flee from those snares as soon as e'er thou canst.)

'After life's fitful fever sleep ye well'; 'After tasting all things, hold fast by the Good; which is God Al-one'. After exhausting the world's experiences of joy and sorrow, good and evil, realise that they are all 'vanity of vanities', all dreams-of your own mind's creating, that you your-Self are (is) the only True, Good, Beautiful, Free, Infinite, Eternal, Changeless Reality; that God Al-one is; 'I Al-one am'; and all This Else-is-Naught, is Dream, is My Will-and-Imagination, and 'I' can create, maintain, destroy, anything, as 'I' please, by sufficiently intense and strong Will-and-Imagination.

> Ḍhyānikam sarvam év-aiṭaḍ-
> yaḍ-Éṭaḍ-abhi-shabḍiṭam ;
> Na hy-an-aḍhy-āṭma-viṭ kash-chiṭ
> kriyā-phalam up-āshnuṭé. (*M.*)

(All this, the Object-world that we call 'This',
It is made up of Thought; he who knows not
This truth, his actions bear not wholesome fruit.)

> Mahramé īn hosh juz bé-hosh n-īsṭ,
> Mar zabāṅ rā mushṭarī juz gosh n-īsṭ.
> Har ke béḍār asṭ ū ḍar kḥwāb-ṭar ;
> Hasṭ béḍārī-sh az kḥwāb-ash baṭar,
> Har ke ḍar kḥwāb-asṭ béḍārī-sh beh ;
> Hasṭ gḥaflaṭ a'yn hushyārī-sh beh. (*S.*)
> (None but th' Unconscious knows this
> consciousness ;
> The tongue's speech but the speechless
> ear can guess.

He who seems now awake is in deep dream;
His wakefulness is false and worse than sleep.
And he who seems asleep doth truly wake;
The true sleep's better than false wakefulness.)

> Yā nishā sarva-bhuṭānām
> ṭasyām jāgarṭi samyamī,
> Yasyām jagraṭi bhuṭāni
> sā nishā pashyaṭo munéh. (*G.*)

(That which is night for others, therein wake
The Careful ; while that which is day for all
Is night for him who sees the inner world.)
Na ṭaṭra chakshur gachchaṭi, na vāg gachchhati,
no manah...Vijñāṭāram aré kéna vijānīyāṭ. (*U.*)

(The eye can reach It not, nor speech, nor mind ;
By means of what can ye the Knower know ?
It-Self doth know It-Self and All-Else too.)
Ai bar-ṭar az kḥayāl o qayās o gumān o wahm
W-az har-che gufṭa-ém o shanīḍ-ém wa
kḥwānḍa-ém ! (*S.*)

A'yān aisā ke har shai méṅ nihāṅ hai,
Nihāṅ aisā ke har shai méṅ a'yān hai. (*S.*)

(O Thou ! that dost transcend our highest thought,
Imagination, guess, conjecture—all,
And all that has been spoken, heard, or read !
Thou that art hidden so in everything
As to be plainly visible everywhere,
And manifest in all things in such wise
As to be hid in utmost mystery !)
Maghribī ! āṅ-che ṭu ash mī ṭalabī ḍar kḥalwaṭ,
Man a'yān bar sar-i-har kūcha wa kū mī bīnam.
(Man of the West !, what thou wouldst fain
Seek in far space's dark retreat,
That I behold spread out full plain
Here, now, in every lane and street.) (*S.*)

Yasya sarvāṇi bhūṭāni
Āṭma-iv-ābhūḍ-vijānaṭah
Ṭaṭra ko mohah kah shokah
Éka-ṭwam anu-pashyaṭah. (*U.*)

Iḍānīm asmākam patu-ṭara-vivék-añjana-jushām
Samī-bhūṭā ḍrshtis-ṭribhuvanam api Brahma
manuṭé. (BHARṬṚ-HARI.)
(For whom all things have now become him-Self,

Who knows that I al-One exist in all,
For him there is no more sadness or hate.
With new eye-lotion dropped into our eyes,
Of the same-sighted knowledge, all the worlds
And their contents are seen by us as Brahm'.)

Questioning arises, again and again, in the sensitive heart of the earnest seeker, (whatever the formal religion he professes). It arises even after he has arrived at the stage of thought and feeling which has been described before as A ḍ v a i ṭ a - v ā ḍ a or A ḍ hy ā s a - v ā ḍ a, or the *Wujūḍiyah* view, or the 'meta-physical or illusionary or will-and-imagination theory of causation'. The questioning can be finally set at rest only by long-continued meditation on that view. In the meanwhile, some more citations may be made, of the 'poetical' answer, of the mystic-gnostics of all religions, to that questioning. These are helpful in preparing for and then clarifying and strengthening the 'metaphysical' answer and Vision.

Jo mazā inṭizār méṅ ḍékhā
Wo nahīṅ wasl-e-Yār méṅ ḍékhā. (*S.*)
(The ache of yearning for the Belovéd
Is sweeter far than joy of clasping Him.)

The English poet Tennyson wrote:

'Tis better to have loved and lost
Than never to have loved at all.

It would give a deeper, more consoling and comprehensive, if less emotionally poignant, meaning, if we say:

'Tis better to have lost and found
Than never to have lost at all.

Ḍarḍ-e-ḍil ké wāsṭé insān ko paiḍā kiyā,
Warna ṭā'aṭ ké liyé kāfī na ṭhīṅ karrobiyān ? (*S.*)
Kufr kāfir rā, wa ḍīṅ ḍīṅ-ḍār rā,
Qaṭra-é ḍarḍ-é-ḍilé Aṭṭar rā ! (*S.*)
(To know the joys of Heartache, God made man;
For service He had made angels enough !
Doubters, let doubt ; believers, let believe ;
Drop of Divine Heartache, let me receive !)

If I held Truth in my hand, I should let it go, for the joy of pursuing it is greater than that of finding it.

(Sir W. Hamilton, *Metaphysics*, I. lec. 1.)

The love-chase is more exciting, more pleasurable, than the love-capture.

N-Āham ṭu, sakhyo !, bhajaṭo-pi janṭūn
Bhajāmy-amīshām anu-vṛṭṭi-vṛṭṭayé;
Yaṭh-āḍhano, labḍha-ḍhané vinashṭé,
Ṭach-chinṭay-ānyan nibhṛṭo na véḍa. (*Bh.*)
(Friends ! if I seem to run away from you,
My lovers and My loved ones !, I do so
In order that ye may run after Me,
The more distraught, the more whole-heartedly
As a man who has found a precious gem,
Then lost it, can now think of nothing else,
So, having glimpsed and lost Me, ye will search
With all your heart and mind until ye find.)

An old Chinese proverb says :

To journey hopefully is better than to arrive.

Illusion, Dream, Romance, Imagination, is more sweet than Dis-illusioning 'Reality'— unless the Reality is that of the Infinite Spirit which includes all unrealities, all the most glorious, and blissful, (as also inevitably the most horrid and agonyful), Dreams.

Another western writer says:

It is the *trying* to find out that is the real prize; the race, not the winning; the battle, not the victory.

The soul is always experiencing and enjoying the swing between losing and regaining.

[God gave all gifts to Man, but kept back Rest ;]
For "If I should," said He,
"Bestow this Jewel also on my Creature,
He would adore My gifts instead of Me,
And rest in Nature, not the God of Nature ;
So both should losers be.
Yet let him keep the rest,
But keep them with repining Restlessness ;
Let him be rich and weary, that, at least,
If Goodness lead him not, then Weariness
May toss him to My Breast" !

(GEORGE HERBERT.)

God forgets Himself in order, first, to feel the Divine Heartache of longing for Him-Self; and then to feel the Divine Bliss of re-collecting, re-membering, re-cognising, re-covering Him-Self. This is one way of putting the Truth. But the full way of putting it is,

Purṇam Aḍah, purṇam Iḍam,
Purṇāṭ purṇam uḍachyaṭé,
Pūrṇasya purṇam āḍāya
Purṇam évā-va-shishyaṭé. (*U.*)

(This endless universe is all derived
From Spirit Infinite; yet, taking out
The Endless Whole from the Whole Infinite,
The fullness of the pseudo-infinite,
Th' illusion of this ever-fleeting dream,

From the True Infinite, the One who Dreams
Yet changes never—E'er the Full remains.)[1]
Gar kẖurī juzā-e ze sāgẖar gẖam,
Jām-e-Jamshéḍ rā zanī bar-ham!
Mulk-e-shāḍī hamīṅ ḍihanḍ ba bāḍ
Mālikān-é balā wa gẖam ḍar ḍam.
Ḍarḍ-manḍān-e zakẖm-e-ṭégẖ-e-furāq
Mī na kẖwāhanḍ az kasé marham.
Ba jahāṅ ḍar hamésh paiḍā-ī,
Lék ḍar chashm-i-man na mī āyī!
Ai! ke ḍar héch jā na ḍārī jā,
Būl-a'jab māṅḍah am ke har jā-ī!
Anḍarūn o burūṅ, wa az pas o pésh,
Ḍar chap o rāsṭ, wa zér o bālā-ī!
Ḍar libās-é ḍuī na mī gunjī
Z-āṅ-ke mashhūr-ṭar ba yak-ṭā-ī!
Ḍosh goyiṅḍa-é aḍā mī karḍ,
Az ḍil-é-zār sauṭ-e-shaiḍāī,
Ai! ba-chashmān-i-ḍil ma bīṅ juz Ḍosṭ!
Har che bīnī bi-ḍāṅ ke mazhar-i-Ūsṭ!

(SĀ'ḌI, *Mā Muqīmān.*)

(If thy lips taste one sip of that Heartache,
Thou wouldst dash down Jamshéḍ's Bowl of
Delights!
They who have been sore wounded by the Sword
Of Separation from the Belovéd,
Seek from None-Else for any salve or balm!
The wealth of worldly pleasures, to the winds,
Instant, they cast, who own the wealth Divine
Of yearning for the Vision of His Face,
And ever breathe the sad sweet sighs of Love!

[1]For reconciliation of Changeless and Changeful, see *The Science of Peace*, and *The Science of the Self*, bv the present writer.

O my Beloved !, how wonderful art Thou,
That, being everywhere, nowhere art Thou !
That wearest all the forms that there can be,
Yet canst not be encompassed by mine eyes !
To left, to right, above, and down below,
Within, without, before, also behind,
There is no time, no place, where Thou art Not !
So famously Uni-que, Al-One, art Thou,
Garb of An-Other never can fit Thee !
Last night a devotee in ecstasy
Whispered "Whate'er thou seest, it is He" !)

God, tired of sole-ness, K a i v a l y a, *Wahdat*, Al(l)-oneness, L-one-liness, Soli-tude, went 'forth', went 'out' of Him-Self, and 'multiplied', burst forth into an infinity of forms, and held high revel of emotions, most solemn and most cheerful, most heavy-laden and most light-hearted, most terrible tragedy and most frivolous comedy. Tiring of that mad Riot of Shiva-Rudra, Rahmān-Qahhār, Double-Faced Janus of Peace and War, Gaurī-Kālī, Ghaffār-Ghazzāb, He decides that it is all Vanity of Vanities, Māyā, Fisāna, Dream and Imagination, Khwāb and Khayāl, and withdraws into Him-Self and goes into the Deep Sleep of Chaos; till Desire to Wake and Play surges again within Him.

Ze ḍariyā mauj-e-gūnā-gūn ḍar-āmaḍ,
Ze Bérangī ba rangé chūn bar-āmaḍ. (*S.*)
Aparé Brahmaṇī Brahmā
Sva-bhāva-vashaṭah Svayam,
Jāṭah Spanḍa-mayō niṭyam
Ūrmir-ambu-niḍhāv-iva. (*Yoga Vāsishtha.*)

(The peaceful Ocean heaves with mighty waves,
And, from the Formless, countless forms break forth;
The Colourless sparkles and coruscates
With countless colours, 'this', 'this', 'thus' and 'thus'.)
(In the Vast Ocean boundless, fathomless,
A giant billow surges; in th' Immense
Sleep of the Infinite Eternal Space
There is a Stirring, and a Central Point
Of Whirling Vibrant Restlessness doth rise;
From Restful Brahm', restless Brahmā is born.)

---

[1] Brahma is the Universal Impersonal Self, Param-Āṭmā, Allāh, Ahaḍ; Brahmā is *a* personal creator, ruler, preserver, destroyer, of a particular world-system, ilāh, el. One final question, one last doubt, remains. Why should God feel the need to play and sleep? Pari-pūrṇasya kā spṛhā; *al āna kamā kāna.* The Ever-full should not suffer such 'lack', such 'want', such 'need'? Deep meditation on the logia, 'One-without-a-Second', 'lā mā-siwā-Allah', 'lā-maujūḍah illā Hū', 'Aham éva Na maṭṭo Anyaṭ', 'I-Not-Another'—will loosen this last knot. The present writer's *The Science of Peace* and *The Science of the Sacred Word*, and the more recent work, *The Science of the Self*, (in English), also the last chapter of *Samanvaya* (in Hinḍī), may perhaps help the enquirer in this work of reconciling 'Change' with 'Changelessness,' if he happens to be interested in the great problem, and cares to pursue it.

Briefly: God having forgotten Him-Self into an Outer World, recognises the No-thing-ness of any such outer, any such other; withdraws it all into, and remembers, Him-Self; and also beholds that the

Ékākī na ramaṭé...Ékākī kāmayaṭé, jāyā Mé syāṭ... Paṭish-cha paṭnī ch-ābhavaṭ...So-kāmayaṭa bahu syām pra-jāyéya...ḍviṭīyo Ma āṭmā jāyéṭa. Āpayaṭo vai ṭāvany-onyasya kāmān sarvān...Ḍviṭīyāḍ vai bhayam bhavaṭi...Ḍviṭīyo vai sa-paṭnah. (*U.*)

Manv-anṭarāṇy-asankhyāni
Sargah samhāra éva cha,
Krīdan-niv-aiṭaṭ kuruṭé
Paraméshthī punah punah. (*M.*)

(The Solitary feels un-satisfied ;
A nameless restlessness surges within ;
He wishes: May I have a Mate who may
Play with Me. He becomes Nature and God,
Husband and Wife. And then He wished again:
May I be Many and have second 'selves';
And there were Many Progeny to Both.
Countless desires arise between the Two
Of every sort, of most opposéd sorts ;
And find expression, first ; and then surcease ;
For, with a Second, is born rivalry,
Fear of An-Other, souring of the sweet ;
And then the One goes back to Soli-tude.
Thus, ceaselessly, the Overlord of All,
Transcending every limit, 'sits on high',
And makes, unmakes, remakes worlds, o'er and o'er
In cycles, smallest, largest, as in Play.)
Allāhu jamīlun wa yohibb-uj-jamāl. (*H.*)
Kunṭu kanzam makhfiyun fa ahbabṭu
An ā'rifa fa khalaq al khalqa li ā'rifa. (*H.*)

Affirmation and the Negation of the 'Other', the 'This', the 'outer World', are *simultaneous*, not successive ; hence there has been, there is, there will be, No Change, and He is and will be ever as He was, 'I am that I am', 'Full, Free from all Limitation'.

(I was a hidden treasure; I desired
To see My-Self; I therefore did create
This World of forms and lives beyond all count,
That I may realise My-Self therein.
Beauty must ever love to be admired
And to be loved, eagerly, passionately;
God is most Beautiful; shall He not love
That Many may behold that Loveliness
In Him, and that He may Him-Self also
Behold His own Self's Beauty in them all?)
Yā ayyohal nafs-ul-muṭmainna,
Arjé'al elā Rabbeka rāziyaṭun marziya,
Fa ḍukhḥuli fi u'bbāḍi wa ḍukhḥūli jannaṭi. (*H.*)
Al-arwāhun junūḍun mujanniḍa,
fa mā tā'rafu minha ilṭafa,
wa mā ṭankara minha akhṭalifu. (*H.*)
(O Soul! that hath found rest in God! Turn back
Unto thy Lord; for He takes joy in Thee,
And thou too dost rejoice in Him. Mix then
With these My servants. Enter Paradise!
The souls that do not recognise the One
Ensouling all—they differ 'mongst themselves;
The souls that, in each other, Me behold,
They bathe in Love, and Love is Paradise!

All the great religions describe this Ultimate Principle, either as Tri-Une, Trinity-in-Unity, Unity-in-Trinity, or as possessing three principal Attributes, g u ṇ a-s, *sifāṭ*. They are the Principles of (1) Be-ing, Ex-ist-ence, 'outer' manifestation, which is possible only by Action, movement, Motion, (2) Joy, Bliss, which is possible only by fulfilment of Desire, and (3) Awareness, Knowledge, Wisdom, through Cognition. These are named in Vedānta as Sat, Ananda, Chit, summed up in Chaitanyam, Infinite Principle of Life and Consciousness; in Christianity as the Way, the Life, the Truth; or, as Omni-presence, Omni-potence, Omni-science; in Tasawwuf they are called *Wujūd*, *Shuhūd*, *Ilm*, summed up in *Nūr*, the supernal Light of Consciousness, *Nūr-i-Qāhir*, primal over-powering Light; Param Jyotih, the final Light, the (Jewish) *Or En-sof*, the Infinite Light, by which and in which Light all the Universe is illumined. In Chinese Taoism or Laotsism, they are called Hsing, Chih, and Ch'i (Form, Substance, Pneuma), the three potentialities of Hun Tun (Primal Chaos).[1] Personifications of, or broadly corresponding to, the three Principles are, Brahmā—Shiva—Vishnu; Lakshmī—Gaurī—Saraswatī; Son—Holy-Ghost—Father; Al-Mālik—Ar-Razzāq—Al-A'līm. In the Jewish religion, Kabalistic Judaism or Hebraism, the Three are Chochmah—Kether—Binah, or Hakama—Jāh—Binah, or Hakam—Hasad—Jasad, or Sephira—Kether-Adam-Kadmon, as the primary emanations of the Unknowable En-Sof. The scientific triad may be said to be Matter—Force—Mind. In a Craft Lodge of Masonry, they are indicated by the Pillars of Strength—Beauty—Wisdom.

Manju-shrī—Amit-ābha—Avalokit-éshvara, the three aspects of the Incorporeal Buddha, in Buddhism; Ahura-Mazda—Spento-mainyush—

[1]Suzuki, *History of Chinese Philosophy*, p. 30.

Ārmaiṭi, (or Ahura-Mazḍā—Vohu-mano—Ashā; or Ahura the Self-existent, Maza the Great, and Ḍā the Knower), the three aspects of Zerouane Akerané, the Unmanifest, in Zoroastrianism; indicate the same Tri-Unity. Ahura Mazḍa says: "I am Protector, Life-giver and Nourisher, Knower, and the most spiritual Evolver.....I am of the name Ahura, Bestower of Life, and the name Maza-ḍa, Greatest and most Wise"; (*Z.*, *Yashṭ*, i. 12). In Plato's mysticism, they are the principles of Goodness (the Object of Action, realised by Power of Action for all as for Self, the Way of realising the Common Self of all in and by Action); of Beauty (the Object of all Desire, the One Self being the Supremely Beautiful Object of such Heart's Desire of all, being the Joy, the Life, of the Heart); and of Truth, (or Reality, the Object of Cognition, the Self being the One and Only Ever-True, Ever-Real).

Vaiḍika theology has many hymns, each singing a 'thousand names' of the Supreme as Vishṇu, or as Shiva, or as Shakṭi-Ḍévī. Islām has a 'hundred holy names' of Allah. The Hebrew religion has Sefiroth, Eloh-im, like Gabri-el, of Might, Rafi-el, of Healing, Mikai-el of Strength, Seraphi-el of Harmony, and so on. In Islam, Jibrā-īl[1] is the angel of Earth, Knowledge, and Revelation, Mikā-īl of Water, Existence, and Protection, Azrā-īl of

[1] Khājā Khān, *Phil. of Islām*, p. 45, says these correspond to Véḍic "Kshiṭi, Varuṇa, Agni, Inḍra." See p. 200, *supra*.

Fire, Power, Death and Destruction, Isrāf-īl of Air, Intention, and Resurrection, etc. All these are the vyaktis, *kāyanāt*, manifestations, of the shaktis, *shuyūnāt*, powers, potentialities, of the Self; they are the personifications of the Māḍhurya and Aishvarya vibhūṭis, the *Jamālī* and *Jalālī sifāṭ*, the sweetly beautiful and the blazingly compelling and awful powers and glories, of the Supreme—which all living things manifest, each in infinitesimal degree, and which shine forth strongly in the higher spirits, cherub-im, seraph-im, angels, ḍévas, *farishṭas*, as in suns, moons, cataclysms; in flowers, butterflies, babies; as in cyclones, simooms, blizzards, avalanches, volcanic eruptions, earthquakes, continent-sinking-and-upheaving cataclysms.

Infinite, like Him-Self, must be, are, the masques, which the Eternal Masquerader is ever, everywhere, everyway, putting on and off, fatiguelessly! Why? Because it is pleasant 'pass-time' to be 'all-ways' forgetting One-Self in order to remember One-Self 'all-ways'; to be 'all-ways' losing, seeking, finding, re-losing, pursuing, re-finding One-Self. Time, it has been remarked by a humorist, is the greatest enemy of man; he is always trying to kill it, and never succeeding. The jest is true in the profoundest sense; and it is true not only of Time, but of Space, and of Motion, too, all three; and all three are indestructible, un-kill-able, because the would-be Destroyer Him-Self deliberately gives to them

His own Ever-lasting-ness, by bearing them in His Universal Mind, His Eternal and Infinite Will-and-Imagination.

The soul which has merged itself into God, consciously endeavours to realize the 'sweeter' attributes, and show them forth by a life of serenely wise, devotedly philanthropic, and actively beneficent service of fellow-beings. Very highly advanced souls may sometimes have to manifest consciously the 'compelling' attributes also, like the avaṭāras, messiahs, prophets.

Bhéḍa-buḍḍhi-vi-nir-mukṭah
sarva-bhūṭa-hiṭé raṭah. (*U.*)
(Freed from the sense of separateness, the soul
Engageth in the service of the Whole.)
Kasé marḍé-ṭamām asṭ, az ṭamāmī
Kunaḍ bā kẖwājagī kār-é-gẖulāmī. (*S.*)
(Being perfected, freed, the Master braves
The noble task of slaving for the slaves.)

As Kṛshṇa says:

Ḍāsyam aishvarya-vāḍéna
jñāṭīnām ṭu karomy-Aham. (*Mbh.*)
Pari-ṭrāṇāya sāḍhūnām,
vi-nāshāya cha ḍush-kṛṭām,
Ḍharma-sam-sṭhāpan-ārṭhāya
sam-bhavāmi yugé yugé. (G.)
(Under the designation of the Lord
I do the work of slave for all the world.
To save the virtuous, destroy the vicious,
And to establish Law Divine anew,
I manifest My-Self age after age.)
Évam pra-varṭiṭam chakram
n-ānu-varṭayaṭ-īhā yah,

Agh-āyur-inḍriy-ārāmo
mogham, Pārṭha !, sa jīvaṭi. (*G.*)
(He who thus helpeth not to keep the Wheel
Of Life and Love and Law revolving aye,
His life is selfish, sinful, lived in vain.)
Saiyaḍ-ul-qaum kẖāḍima-hum. (*H.*)
(The leader is chief servant of the tribe.)
Āñ ke kẖiḍmaṭ karḍ, ū makẖḍūm shuḍ;
Āñ ke kẖuḍ rā ḍīḍ, ū mahrūm shuḍ. (*S.*)
(He who served others was by others served,
Who looked but to himself was thrust aside.)
He that is greatest among you shall be your
servant. (B.)

He who has seen, known, realised most fully the Truth of the identity of all selves in the One Self, he is the greatest and most free and willing servant.

Ye shall know the Truth, and the Truth shall
make you free. (*B.*, John.)
Ṛṭé jñānān na Mukṭih. (U.)
Jñanān Mokshah. (*U.*)
(Freedom there's none unless ye know the Self.
But if ye know the Truth, then are ye free.)
Ke bé-ilm na ṭawān Kẖuḍā rā shinākẖṭ. (*S.*)
(Ye cannot realise God till ye *know*.)

Mā'rifaṭ, *irfān*, p r a - j ñ ā n a, the higher subtler j ñ ā n a, the 'spiritual knowledge', is essential one-third part of the triple, tri-part-ite, threefold, means to *najāṭ*, Deliverance from all ills.

Such then is the *final* purpose of life in all religions—to find God, *i. e.*, know and realise the Self as God; after having fulfilled its *preli-*

minary purpose, of tasting the things of the world, in accordance with Law and Religion and Science, i. e. Religio-Scientific Law[1]; and, by toiling consciously on the side of the forces of Good, to help others to do the same. This is what the Way of Knowledge leads unto.

---

[1] On this point, something more will be said later, in the chapters on 'The Way of Devotion' and 'The Way of Works'.

CHAPTER III

The Way of Devotion, or The Emotional Constituent of Religion

THE WAY OF DEVOTION.

The Way of Devotion is not a separate path at all; but is so-called only for certain special purposes. In the life of the human being, cognition, desire, and action are inseparable. The Way of Devotion is only one of the three inseparable departments. It is the department of Right Desire, Good Feelings, Deep and High Emotions, Noble Ethics.

If Right Knowledge is the head, Right Love is the heart, and Right Action is the limbs, of organic, psycho-physical, bodily-mental Life. Love, Devotion, even genuine love human, infinitely more Love Divine, is the Joy of Life. *Ishq-i-majāzī*, Vishay-ānanḍa, Mānava-préma, is but the reflection, in the limited, of *Ishq-i-Haqīqī*, Brahm-ānanḍa, limitless Bhagavaḍ-bhakṭi. Without rich emotion, encyclopedic science is as a desert without a stream, as bare bald mountains without vegetation, as the most beautiful human body without a living soul in it, is as a corpse. Knowledge is ful-filled, completed from half into whole, when love is married to it, and the children of noble acts are born to the two. Science plus Philanthropy, Bene-volence, is Bene-science, is Wisdom; Wisdom plus Helpful Activity, Bene-ficence, is Righteousness. Let us achieve Righteousness and all things else shall be added unto us.

> Ḍharmāḍ-arṭhash-ch kāmash-cha,
> Sa kim-arṭham na sévyaṭé ? (*Mbh.*)
> (Pleasure and Wealth both flow from
> Righteousness,
> Why not pursue it, then, whole-heartedly ?)

The commandments of all the great religions, on the subject of Ethics, are identical, for all practical purposes.

1. The Five Principal Virtues, Disciplines.

Sāmāsika Dharma, 'The duty of Man in brief,' enjoined by Manu, who is regarded by the followers of Vaiḍika Ḍharma (Hinḍuism) as the Primal Law-giver, is the same as the five Yamas of Yoga and the Pancha-shīla of Buḍḍha. It is also five of the ten Commandments of Moses, which are re-uttered and confirmed by Christ too. They are to be found in the *Qurān* also, though not all in one place. Thus Manu says:

> Ahimsā, Saṭyam, Asṭéyam,
> Shaucham, Inḍriya-nigrahah,
> Éṭam Sāmāsikam Ḍharmam
> Chāṭur-varṇyé-bravīn Manuh. (*M.*)
> (Harmlessness, Truth, Honesty, Cleanliness,
> Restraint of senses from all erring ways,
> —This is the 'Whole Duty of Man in Brief,'
> For every one in every walk of life—
> Thus Manu, Father of the Race, declares.)

Buḍḍha's "Five Virtues" are:

Pāṇ-āṭipāṭā-véramaṇī, musā-vāḍā-véramaṇī, aḍinn-āḍānā-véramaṇī, surā-méraya-majja-pamāḍa-tthānā-véramaṇī, kāmesu-michchhā-chārā-véramaṇī.

Sir Edwin Arnold's sweet version of these must be borrowed from his wonderful and immortal poem, a veritable scripture of Buḍḍhism, *The Light of Asia*, and be given a place here reverently.

Kill not—for Pity's sake—and lest ye stay
The meanest thing upon its upward way.
Bear not false witness, slander not, nor lie;
Truth is the speech of inward purity.
Give freely and receive, but take from none
By greed or force or fraud, what is his own.
Shun drugs and drinks which work the wit abuse;
Clear minds, clean bodies, need no *soma* juice.
Touch not thy neighbour's wife, neither commit
Sins of the flesh unlawful and unfit.

The Jaina religion says the same:

(Sṭhūla-) prāṇ-āṭi-pāṭa-viramaṇa-vraṭa; (sṭhūla-) mṛshā-vāḍa-viramaṇa-vraṭa; (sṭhūla-) a-ḍaṭṭ-āḍāna-viramaṇa-vraṭa; (sṭhūla-)maiṭhuna-viramaṇa-vraṭa; (sṭhūla-) parigraha-parimāṇa-viramaṇa-vraṭa. (Jaina Scriptures.)

(The five Resolves are, broadly: to refrain
From taking life; from speaking untrue word;
From taking what is not willingly given;
From all unlawful love; from ownership
Of goods beyond the limits of strict needs.)

Maḍya-māmsa-maḍhu-ṭyāgaih
sah-āṇu-vraṭa-panchakam,
Ashtau mūla-guṇān-āhur-
gṛhiṇām Shramaṇ-oṭṭamāh.

(*J.*, SAMANṬA-BHAḌRA.)

Maḍya-māmsa-maḍhu-ṭyāgaih
sah-oḍumbara-panchakam,
Ashṭā-véṭé gṛha-sṭhānām
ukṭā mūla-guṇāh shruṭau.
(*J.*, SOMA-ḌÉVA.)

Himsā-asaṭya-sṭéyāḍ
a-brahma-parigrahāch-cha vāḍara-bhéḍaṭ,
Ghṛṭān-māmsān-maḍyāḍ-
viraṭir-gṛhiṇo-shta-mūla-guṇāh.
(*J.*, *Mahā-purāṇa.*)

(Besides the five, three others: to refrain
From flesh-foods, butter, and from 'maddening' drinks—
Eight are root-virtues for the family-man.)

Himsāyām, anṛṭé, sṭéyé,
maiṭhuné cha, parigrahé,
Viraṭir-vraṭam—iṭy-ukṭam
sarva-saṭṭv-ānu-kampakaih.
(*J.*, SHUBHA CHANḌRA, *Jñān-ārṇava.*)

(Slaying, false speaking, theft, lust, greed to hold
Aught as one's own exclusive property—
To give up these, and wish well unto all,
This is the essence of all virtuous vow.)

Moses' Commandments are:

Thou shalt not kill,...not bear false witness,...not steal,...not commit adultery,...not covet anything that is thy neighbour's. (*B.*)

Fear God and keep his commandments—this is the whole duty of man. (*B.*, Ecclesiastes.)

Christ repeats these commandments of Moses and adds others.

Specific condemnation of intoxicating liquor, supplementing the commandments of Moses and

Jesus, may be found elsewhere in the Bible; thus:

Woe unto them that rise up early in the morning, that they may follow strong drink; that continue until night, till wine inflame them. (*B.*, Isaiah.)

Muhammad commands:

Wa lā yaqṭulūn-an-nafs-allāṭi harram Allāho illā bil haqqī.
Wajṭanebū qaul-az-zūré.
W-as-sareqo w-as-sareqaṭo faqṭa'u aiḍeyahoma.
Al khamro amalish-Shaiṭānī.
W-allazīna-hum le furūjehim hāfizūn. (*Q.*)
(Slay none; God has forbidden it, except
Justice require it...And avoid false words...
Woman and man who steal shall lose their hands ...
Intoxicants are Satan's own device...
They who avoid unlawfulness in sex,
And watchfully and resolutely control
Their senses, they alone achieve success.)

ADDITIONAL AND FARTHER-REACHING VIRTUES. These five duties or virtues, prescribed by Manu, Buddha, and the other great Teachers, are for the laity, the householders. For him who has renounced the worldly life, the s a n n y ā s ī, b h i k s h u, *faqīr*, hermit, the y o g ī or *sālik*; who, not that he may enjoy superhuman status, but that he may serve his fellow-creatures better, aspires after spiritual and psychical mysteries and powers and the Great Peace;—for him stricter y a m a s and n i-y a m a s, *zohḍ* and *ṭaqashshuf*, *ibāḍaṭ* and *riyāzaṭ*, abstinences and performances, devotions and disciplines, are ordained. These take the five duties to their extreme culmination.

The Buddhist bhikshu or shramaṇa has to cultivate five more shīlas or virtues, viz., avoidance (1) of eating except at the fixed time, (2) of seeing and hearing dance, song, instrumental music, theatrical shows, (3) of flower-garlands, perfumes, unguents, and all self-decoration, (4) of high seats, luxurious couches, (5) of gold and silver. These make the ten qualifications, ḍasha-shīla. At yet higher stages these have to reach a climax in the ten pāramiṭās, 'extreme perfections':

Ḍāna, Sīla, Nekkhamma, Paññā, Viriya, Saṭya, Kshānṭi, Aḍhitthāna, Méṭṭī, Upékkhā. (*Bu.*)

(Such Charity as gives away e'en life
To whosoe'er may ask for it; adherence
To rule of Noble Conduct in despite
Of even torture; Absence of Desire
For things of sense of e'en the mildest sort;
The Luminous Intelligence that sees
The heart of everything; Tireless Endeavour
For good of all; Patient Forgivingness
Of the worst torments even; Truthfulness
In face of death itself; and Fortitude
Of Will-to-right, dauntless 'fore obstacles;
Immense Compassion for all living things,
Blind souls, that wander helpless in the dark;
The seeing of the Process of the World
With Perfect Equanimity of Soul.)

The purpose of these negative and positive disciplines, forbearances and observances, is to turn inwards, the currents of vitality and consciousness, which flow outwards, into the physical organs, in the normal man. By such ascetic inward direction of them, gradually the subtler superphysical organs are re-awakened; and the journey made easier, on the Upward Path of Renunciation of the things of this world and all selfishness; the Path of Re-ascent to the Spiritual state of Universality. The annals of every religion show us examples of highly advanced souls which have achieved various degrees of these 'extreme perfections.'

The yamas and ni-yamas, as given by Paṭanjali, are:

Ahimsā-saṭy-āsṭéya-brahma-chary-ā-pari-grahāh yamāh.

Shaucha-sanṭosha-ṭapah-svādhyāy-Éshvara-praṇi-ḍhānāni niyamāh. (*Yoga-Sūṭra.*)

(Avoidance of all slaying, nay, of hurt
To mind or body, of a living thing;
Of falsehood in all speech, and e'en in thought;
Of all unlawful gain or coveting;
Of sex-indulgence, or in body or mind;
Of all sense of possessive ownership;
Such are the *yamas*. Then, the *niyama-s*:
Observance of the utmost purity
That may be possible for body of flesh;
Contentment with whatever may befall;
Study of Sacred Science of the Self;
Restraint of body by determined will;
And, last, complete surrender of one's will
To God's, replacement of one's own small self
By the Great Self, by utmost trust in Him.)

When his questioner persistently asks, "What more good thing shall I do, that I may have eternal life," Christ also adds the Yoga-injunction of renunciation of all property, in which the sense of mine-ness, egoistic separatism, is centred, "If thou wilt be perfect, give what thou hast to the poor and follow Me." (*B.*) He also adds, as do the other great Teachers, for the sake of such high aspirants, ready for Yoga, *Sulūk,* 'communion' with God and God's Nature, ready for ascetic disciplines and ever-greater abandonment of carnal pleasures—for such he adds a b h a y a-ḍ ā n a , complete non-resistence and radical abstinences from sin ; not only by deed, but by speech and thought also, thereby 'not destroying but fulfilling the prophets' ; completing, for the renunciant anchorite, what Moses prescribed for the ordinary householder. For such high aspirants, mere ordinary goodness and virtuousness are not enough ; they must achieve greater and greater 'saintliness'.

For such more earnest whole-hearted seekers, Muhammad too enjoins *fuqr* and *sukn*, complete renunciation of property and cultivation of uttermost contentment, a - p a r i - g r a h a and s a n-ṭ o s h a, etc., like the other teachers.

Al-fuqro fakḥri. (*H.*)
(Pride do I take in utmost poverty.)

The Véḍic law commands that s a n n y ā s ī - s, persons in the fourth stage of life, retired from the household life, anchorites, must not defile their hands by the contact of money. The apostles of Christ provided "neither gold, nor silver, nor brass in their purses," and "the Son of Man (Jesus) had not where to lay his head". Peter spurned an offer of money for imparting his spiritual powers, saying :

Thy money perish with thee, because thou hast thought that the gift of God may be purchased with money. (*B.*)

In the Jaina 'commandments', of the five virtues for the laity, the word s ṭ h u l a, 'broadly', 'generally', occurs as a qualifying adjective; for the 'ascetics', the limitation or modification is dropped.

It should be noted that any one of the five y a m a s or s h ī l a s, carried to its logical *extreme,* involves the annihilation of the separating individualising physical and material sheath or body, the complete renunciation of individualised existence. It should also be carefully borne in mind that the duties of the household life are very different, in degree, from those of the life of renunciation and asceticism.

So single-mindedly should the ascetic, all-renouncing, *sālik*, y o g ī, 'mystic-gnostic', concentrate on the Supreme Self, contemplate his own identity with the All, that he must not allow himself to covet, or be tempted by offers of, even 'god'-like powers and enjoyments.

Ḍar āṅ manzil buwaḍ kashf o karāmāṭ ;
Walé bāyaḍ guzashṭan z-āṅ maqāmāṭ.
Agar ḍunyā wa uqbā pésh āyaḍ,

Nazar karḍan ḍar āṅ hargiz na shāyaḍ.
Agar garḍī ṭu ḍar Ṭauhīḍ fānī,
Ba Haq yābī baqāé zinḍaganī. (*S.*)
(Unselfishness, all-lovingness—as these
Grow in the aspirant for uni-on
With God, with All, illuminations come,
And extra-ordinary happenings too;
Let him not dwell on these things, but pass by
All things of this world and the other worlds.
Let him pursue with single mind the One,
And merge himself in One-ness with the All;
Thus, losing his small life, he gains All-Life,
Losing a 'time', he gains Eternity.)

Ṭé samāḍhā-vupa-sargāh, vyuṭṭhāné siḍḍhayah...
Sṭhāny-upa-nimanṭraṇé sanga-smay-ā-karaṇam,
punar-an-ishta-prasangāṭ. (*Yoga-Sūṭra*).
Ih-āmuṭra-phala-bhoga-virāgah.
(SHANKAR-ĀCHĀRYA, *Shārīraka-Bhāshya.*)

Na yoga-siḍḍhīr-a-punar-bhavam vā
May-yarpiṭ-āṭm-échchaṭi Maḍ-vin-ānyaṭ.
Mayi ḍhārayaṭash-chéṭah upa-ṭishthanṭi siḍḍhayah..
Anṭarāyān vaḍanṭy-éṭān yunjaṭo yogam-uṭṭamam...
Nahi ṭaṭ kushal-āḍrṭyam ṭaḍ-āyāso hy-ap-ārṭhakah.
(*Bh.*, xi, ch. 15.)

(These super-physical experiences
And powers will, as bye-products, appear,
Epi-phenomena, when mind is rapt
In contemplation of the One-in-All;
They are distractions from the End and Aim;
The yogī should be-ware, and studiously
Avoid all such temptations; for they bind
To things of subtle sense, new selfishness,
And greater, more intense, more evil; since

Far greater powers may now be misused.
Therefore, renunciation of all wish
For selfish pleasure, power, privilege,
Must be the one sole beacon-light for Him
Who seeks the Deathless Life of All for all.)

Let no one deceive himself by thinking and *hoping*, and subtly *wishing:* 'I will *desire* nothing for myself; *then* all powers will and should come to *me*'. This is a plain self-contradiction. Of course, persons without *any* spirit of renunciation also snatch powers from Nature by strength of will and intellect, developed in the course of evolution; as western scientists have done, before our eyes. But we all see also that they have *not* won thereby any peace of mind, any real happiness, any sense and certainty of Immortal Life, for any one; instead, the very opposite. Of course, that opposite too has its own acute 'pleasure' of intensely active, restless, rushing, 'fast life' of intoxicated excitement and frantic passions and emotions; palaces of luxury beyond dreams, on the one side, asphyxiating gases and millions writhing in death-agony, on battle-fields and in war-trenches, on the other. To the souls that are at that stage of cyclic life and evolution, at which such fever and frenzy of excitement and rush-lust is preferred to the happiness of repose of soul and peace of body—for such, 'religious platitudes and sermons' have no use. They must go their own way, till their hour strikes, and the call comes from within themselves, after experience of terrible consequences, to turn from the Arc of Descent, A v-ā-r o h a-p a ṭ h a, A ḍ h o-m ā r g a, *Qaus-i-nazūl*, to the Arc of Re-Ascent, Ā-r o h a-p a ṭ h a, Ū r ḍ h v a-m ā r g a, in the Cycle of Life. On the path of Ascent, stage by stage, subtle *super-physical* experiences and powers unfold and enfold of themselves, in accord with laws embodied in that cyclic life; as *physical* experiences and powers, teething, crawling, standing, toddling, running, learning, adolescence, puberty, progenition, decay, appear and disappear, of themselves. But on this upward path towards Union with the All, and the ever-growing abandonment of separate individuality, the soul holds all such superphysical powers, with anxious care, with reluctance, as heavy burden of sacred trust for the use of others, in constant fear and trembling lest it be tempted to misappropriate them for its own personal uses.[1]

CONTROL OF TONGUE, THE SECRET OF ALL CONTROL. Among the sense-organs again, the tongue is the most radical, most dangerous, most necessary yet most difficult to control, in respect both of what goes in by it, and of what goes out from it.

Christ says:

Not that which goeth in at the mouth defileth a man; but that which cometh out of the mouth, this defileth him...Those things which proceed out of

[1] See *Light on the Path*, (T. P. H., Adyar, Madras).

the mouth come from the heart; and they defile the man. For out of the heart proceed evil thoughts, murders, adulteries, fornications, thefts, blasphemies. These are the things which defile a man. (*B.*)

Elsewhere the Bible says:

If thou sit at a bountiful table, be not greedy upon it...Eat, as it becometh a man...and devour not, lest thou be hated...Be not insatiable, lest thou offend... A very little is sufficient for a man well nurtured... Sound sleep cometh of moderate eating; he riseth early and his wits are with him...Show not thy valiantness in wine, for wine hath destroyed many...Many have fallen by the edge of the sword; yet not so many as they that have fallen because of the tongue. (*B.*, Apocrypha, Ecclesiasticus.) Every kind of beasts, birds, serpents, things in the sea, is tamed, and hath been tamed, of mankind; but the tongue can no man tame; it is an unruly evil, full of deadly poison. (*B.*, St. James.)

Kṛshṇa says:

Vishayā vi-ni-varṭanṭé
    nir-āhārasya ḍéhinah,
Rasa-varjam; raso-py-asya
    Param ḍṛshtvā ni-varṭaṭé. (*G.*)
Inḍriyāṇi jayanṭy-āshu
    nir-āhārā manīshiṇah,
Varjayiṭvā ṭu rasanam;
    ṭan-nir-annasya varḍhaṭé.
Ṭāvaj-jiṭ-énḍriyo na syāḍ-
    vijiṭ-āny-énḍriyah pumān,
Na jayéḍ-rasanam yāvaj—
    jiṭam sarvam jiṭé rasé. (*Bh.*)

(Lusts of the senses leave the man who fasts—
For food supports and strengthens all desires—
Excepting taste for food and feel of self.
Indeed it waxes with the want of food;
But leaves him when the Supreme hath been seen.
Over no organ is control secure
Until the tongue has been placed under curb.
When that is conquered, all else are subdued.)

Asked by a follower to mention the one all-pervading principle which runs through and upholds all virtues, Muhammad explained thus:

Fa akhaza be lesānihī wa qāla kuffa a'laika hāza......Wa halyakubb-unnāsa fin nāri alā wujūhehim illā hasāiḍo al-sīnaṭehim. (*H*).

(The Prophet touched his tongue and said: Control
The reign of this sense-organ o'er yourself...
Men are hurled headlong into fires of hell
By loads of evil that their tongues have reaped.)

Zoroaster says:

Gūsṭā yé manṭā ashém ahūm-vish vīḍvāo,
Ahura!, érézukhḍhāī vachanghām kshayamno
hijvo-vaso Thvā āṭhrā sukhrā, Mazaḍā!,
vanghāū vīḍāṭā rānnayāo. (*Z.*, *Gāṭhā*, 31-19.)
(Illumination and all that is Good,
Lord Mazaḍā!, Thou givest unto him,
The hero, valiant in righteous war,
Who ever thinks, hears, speaks of Rectitude,
Who knows the Self, is wise, controls his tongue,
And tells the truth in soft convincing words.)
Yoī ḍush-khraṭhvā aéshémém varéḍém rāmém
chā, khāīs hijūbīs fakhuyas ū afasuyanṭo...
ṭoī ḍaévém ḍān yā drégvaṭo ḍaénā. (*Z.*, *Gāṭhā*, 49-4.)
(They who, seeing yet blind, spread, all around,

Intolerance and insolence and hate,
By th'evil words of their unbridled tongues,
Know them to be the devils on this earth,
Disseminators of the Creed of Hate.)

Manu says:

An-ārogyam, an-āyushyam,
a-svargyam ch-āṭi-bhojanam,
A-puṇyam, loka-vi-ḍvishtam,
ṭasmāṭ ṭaṭ pari-varjayéṭ.
Vāchy-arṭhā nihiṭāh sarvé
vāṅg-mūlā vāg-vi-nis-sṛṭāh;
Ṭasmāḍ yah sṭénayéḍ vācham,
sa sarva-sṭéya-kṛn-narah.
Ahimsay-aiva bhūṭānām
kāryam shréyo-nu-shāsanam,
Vāk ch-aiva maḍhurā shlakshṇā
pra-yojyā ḍharmam ichchhaṭā.
Yasya vāṇg-manasī shuḍḍhé,
samyag-gupṭé cha sarvaḍā,
Sa vai sarvam av-āpnoṭi
Véḍānṭo-pa-gaṭam phalam.
N-ārun-ṭuḍah syāḍ ārṭo-pi,
na para-ḍroha-karma-ḍhīh;
Yayā-sy-oḍ-vijaṭé vāchā
n-ālokyām ṭām uḍīrayéṭ. (*M.*)

(Ill-health, ill-mind, thence many sins, short life,
Loss of good name, and loss of paradise—
All these follow excessive and ill meals;
Let the wise man avoid such carefully.
And since all thoughts and feelings are enwrapt
In words, and are conveyed by them to others,
He who misuses words empoisons all;
Let the wise man then guard well all his speech.
If ye have to instruct, direct, command,

Use speech that may be smooth and soft and sweet.
Whose mind and speech are pure and well-controlled,
Only he finds the fruit of Final Truth.
Touch not another to the quick, though you
Yourself are hurt; let malice sway you not;
And carefully eschew the speech of pride,
Unsocial, which perturbs all and repels.)

Saṭyam brūyāṭ, priyam brūyāṭ,
na brūyāṭ saṭyam apriyam,
Priyam cha n-ānṛṭam brūyāṭ,
Ésha ḍharmah sanā-ṭanah. (*M.*)

(Speak but the Truth, but speak it sweetly too;
So it may gratefully pervade and soothe
And influence the mind of him who hears.
Tell it not harshly so as to annoy,
Repel, and be rejected wastefully.
Nor ever tell an untruth, sweet or harsh.
Such is the ancient way trod by the wise.

Luqmān-i-zamāṅ ṭu kḥuḍ hai, gar bhūkh se yak luqma kam khā. (Hinḍusṭānī Proverb).

(Luqmān, the wisest of the world, art thou
Thyself, if thou but eat one morsel less
Than hungry tongue clamours to thee to eat.)

God is Ar-Razzāq, the giver of *rizq*, livelihood, the daily bread. Christ prayed: "Give us this day, O Lord! our daily bread"; Bread Spiritual as well as Bread Material. The Veda-Ṛshi prayed: Anna-paṭé, annasya no ḍhéhi, an-amīvasya shushmiṇah, "Lord of Food, give us the food that will bring health and strength, not disease"; and proclaimed, Annam Brahma, "Food is Brahma, the Principle of Life, the Life-Supporter, Nourisher." The 'daily bread' is not to be treated with levity, much less to be despised, or abused and misused, by over-eating or wrong-eating. Eating, Mating, Speaking, the most elemental functions of life, are also the most sacred, to be performed most carefully. Never can too much care be taken over them. Ill-discharged, they lead to every misery. Well-performed, they lead to every happiness.

The successful issue of diplomatic negotiations, upon which depend the peace and welfare of vast nations, often hangs upon the finding of just the *right formula, in words*, which will smooth down the ruffled feathers and bristling hair, and draw back into their sheaths the outflung claws, talons, beaks, fangs, of all the 'human' eagles, bears, and lions concerned.

The metaphysic and psychology of the solemn religious injunctions are plain. It is matter of common knowledge that "Sex and Hunger rule the world". Abuse of these two appetites is the cause of 90 per cent of the physical and mental diseases, wars, and all other ills, of humanity. Lawful use of them is the source, directly or indirectly, of all its joys. But Hunger is clearly deeper and more elemental than Sex. It extends literally and manifestly from birth to death; Sex does not. It means self-preservation, continued existence, life itself; Sex means only self-multiplication; as Acquisitiveness, whence Property, means self-expansion, self-aggrandisement. And speech means self-existence either as friend or as enemy of all around. To indulge too much or wrongly in food, or speech, or sex, is to accentuate one's own egoism, to antagonise and provoke other's egoisms, and to make oneself and others physically and mentally sick.

All earthly joy and woe may well depend upon right-use and mis-use of Bread, ultimately; and not only mundane, but also supra-mundane. Out of such right-use and mis-use, respectively, arise, clear intellect and darkened mind, virtues and vices, merits and sins, wisdom and criminal error, and their corresponding supra-mundane consequences, in the future life, after death. Only when deprived of the daily bread, man realises the tremendous greatness, value, sacredness of it; for as vitality is almost greater than intelligence, even thus is Bread-power almost greater than even Mind-power, Science-power, and far greater than Arms-power, Military-power, steam-power, powder-and-gas-power, electricity-power, etc., which are its bye-products, and than Labor-power which it makes possible.

Āhāra-shuḍḍhau saṭṭva-shuḍḍhih,
Saṭṭva-shuḍḍhau ḍhruvā smṛṭih,
Smṛṭi-lambhé sarva-granṭhīnām
vi-pra-mokshah. (*Chhānḍogya U.*)

(When Food is pure, Mind too is pure and bright;
Thence Memory clear and sure, of cause-effect;
Thence Solving of all Knots and Complexes;
Thence Freedom from all Misery of Soul,
And crossing from the Dark to realms of Light.)

2. REVERENCE FOR PARENTS, TEACHERS, ELDERS.

Commandments to honour the teacher, the father, and the mother above all others, are also to be found in the forefront of the scriptures of all religions. Injunctions to love children are ont needed ; the mere fact that the younger generatino lives and grows, is ample proof that Nature herself inevitably and successfully compels the older generation to foster it.

Parental affection, like water, necessarily flows down the slopes of time, from older to younger generation. Of course, there are exceptions, in the shape of monsters who devour their own offspring. They only prove the rule. Even wolf and tiger and serpent *mothers* always foster their young, though the fathers sometimes kill and even eat them. Filial affection, on the other hand, being, by law of nature, unavoidably selfish in the beginning, requires some persuasion and labour to ascend upwards. Hence the injunctions, specially laid upon the younger, to honor the elder. Parental, particularly maternal, affection is naturally so strong that it does not need to be strengthened by the scriptures. Even so, Vaiḍika Ḍharma makes it a Duty to rear up progeny virtuously. How the parental feeling, which makes even animal mothers fight with sublimely reckless heroism in defence of their young, makes even the gentle Christ indignant, may be seen in this :

Whosoever shall offend one of these little ones that believe in Me, it is better for him that a mill-stone were hanged about his neck and he were cast into the sea. (*B.*)

Shankar-āchārya sings:

Ku-puṭro jayéṭa, kva-chiḍ-api ku-māṭā na bhavaṭi.

(Many the sons unfilial; never was,
And never is, a mother that was not
And is not, tender mother to her sons.)

Yam māṭā-piṭarau klésham
sahéṭé sambhavé nṛṇām,
Na ṭasy-āpachiṭih shakyā
karṭum varsha-shaṭair-api. (*M.*)

(The travail that the parents undergo,
To make life for their children possible—
Hundreds of years of service may not make
Adequate recompense for it at all.)

Filial devotion and respect for elders are the very foundation of an unselfish life. (*C.*, Analects.)

Moses and Christ say:

Honor thy father and thy mother. (*B.*)

Muhammad says:

Bil wāliḍaini ihsāna. (*Q.*)
Al jannaṭo ṭahaṭa qaḍamil umm. (*H.*)
Ana ashkurūli w-al-wāliḍaik. (*Q.*)

(Serve and revere the parents. Heaven is spread
Beneath the feet of mothers everywhere.
God sayeth: Be ye grateful unto Me,
And to your parents e'en as unto Me.
Remember with what pain and fainting-fits
Your mother bore you nine months in her womb,
And then with dire travail did bring you forth,
And nourished you with her own milk for years.)

Very truly, very wisely, does the Prophet declare thus. The sweetest, most holy, most benignant names of Allah, God, are Ar-Rahmān, the Beneficent, Ar-Razzāq, the Nourisher, Al-Ghaffār, the Forgiving. Who more *rahmān*, *razzāq*, *ghaffār* to the child than the mother? Where the mother-heart is, there is Godhead; where Godhead is, there is heaven. Therefore:

(Where'er the mother's foot doth tread,
There surely heaven lies outspread.)

The Veda says:

Āchārya-ḍévo bhava, piṭṛ-ḍévo bhava, māṭṛ-ḍévo bhava. Prajā-ṭanṭum mā vy-ava-chchhéṭsīh. (*U.*)

(Let thy preceptor and thy father be,
And let thy mother be, above them all,
Thy gods and guardian angels in thine heart;
So keep unbroken thou, from age to age,
The line of life in noble progeny.)

The image of the mother, enshrined in the heart of the son and the daughter, will effectively prevent that heart from erring into the ways of vice and sin, and will guard it from many dangers due to weaknesses and temptations. The generation that does not cherish, in its heart, honor and gratitude towards its older generation, is not likely to make itself worthy of being honored by its own younger generation; and the whole nation will thus lose continuity between past and present and future, and degenerate and decay rapidly. Saṭ-sanga, vṛḍḍha-sévā, keeping near to the virtuous, the experienced, the aged, and pondering carefully and reverently over their conversations and their ways, is more livingly educative and useful than the study of many books.

Jawāṅ rā sohbaṭé pīrāṅ hisāré ā'fiyaṭ bāshaḍ. (*S.*)
(The company of wise, experienced,
Virtuous and loving elders is, indeed,
A rampart of protection for the young.)
Sohbaṭé sāleh ṭo-rā sāleh kunaḍ. (*S.*)
(Wise company will make thee also wise;
From vicious friends thou canst but gather vice.)

Intelligent, reasonable, 'ancestor-worship and hero-worship' means the maintenance of high family-traditions. Therefore Manu and Vyāsa, translating the Veḍa, say:

Māṭā-piṭroh priyam kuryāḍ, āchāryasya cha sarvadā;
Ṭésh-véva ṭṛshu ṭushṭéshu ṭapah sarvam samāpyaṭé.
Ṭa éva hi ṭrayo lokās-ṭa éva ṭraya āshramāh,
Ṭa éva hi ṭrayo Veḍās-ṭa év-ōkṭās-ṭrayo-gnayah;
Upāḍhyāyān ḍash-āchāryah,
shaṭ-āchāryāns-ṭaṭhā piṭā,
Sahasram ṭu piṭṛīn māṭā
gauraveṇ-āṭi-richyaṭé. (*M.*)

(Serve mother, father, teacher studiously;
If ye succeed in winning the applause
Of these three, ye have done all there's to do,
And gained all that can be worthy to gain.
They the three worlds, the three life stages they,
They the three Veḍas, the three Sacred Fires.
Than teacher, yea, the father hath more weight;
Yet in the educator-quality
And right to reverence, the mother doth
Exceed the father by a thousand times.)

N-āsṭi maṭṛ-samā chhāyā, n-āsṭi māṭṛ-samā gaṭih,
N-āsṭi māṭṛ-samam ṭrāṇam, n-āsṭi maṭṛ-samā priyā.

Kukshau san-ḍhāraṇaḍ-ḍhāṭrī, jananāḍ jananī smṛṭā,
Angānām varḍhanāḍ ambā, vīra-sū-ṭvéna vīra-sūh,
Shishoh shushrūshaṇāṭ shushrūh,
māṭā ḍéham an-anṭaram. (*Mbh.*)

(No cooler and more grateful shade is there,
From all the scorching heat and glare of life,
No refuge, no protection, yea, no love,
Greater than is found in that one word, 'Mother.'
Because she 'bears' the child within her womb,
She's named the ḍhāṭrī; jananī, because
She 'giveth birth' to him; and ambā too,
Because she fondly 'fostereth his limbs'
And makes them grow; and vīra-sūh also
Because she trains him so that he may grow
To be a 'hero'; shushrū, too, her name,
Because she ever sweetly 'cares' for him.
'Mother' and 'child'—two bodies, yet the same!)

The sweetest and most famili-ar names, in every religion, for God are, Father in Heaven, Saviṭā, *Bāḍī*, *Khāliq, Abbā*; for His Omnipotence, Mother-Nature, Loka-māṭā, Holy-Ghost, *Immā* (Hebrew). In the mythology of the dead Egyptian religion, the trinity was Kneph or Ammon, the Father, Neith or Muth, the Mother, and Phtah or Khons, the Son; also Osiris, Isis, Horus. The Trinity-in-Unity of every religion is the Primal Family of Purusha-Prakṛṭi-Jīva, Brahma-Māyā-Manushya, or Ishvara-Jagaṭ-Jīva, (*V.*); Vahme-Gayeṭhā-Ḍaeva, (*Z.*); Father-Mother-Son, (*B.*); God-Nature-Man (Science). The noblest sermon that the Buḍḍha preached, the Mahā-Mangala-Suṭṭa, 'The Song of the Greatest Blessing,' is a hymn to the happy family.

...A-sévanā cha bālānam,
Paṇḍiṭānam cha sevanā,
Pūjā cha pūjaneyyānam,
Éṭam Mangalam uṭṭamam...
Māṭā-piṭu-upatthānam,
Puṭṭa-ḍārassa sangaho,
Anavajjāni kammāni,
Éṭam Mangalam uṭṭamam...
Ṭapo cha, brahma-chariyam cha,
Ariya sachchāna ḍassanam,
Nibbāna-sachchhi-kiriyā cha,
Éṭam mangalam uṭṭamam.
(*Bu.*, *Mahā-Mangala-Suṭṭa*)

(To shun the erring vicious ; serve the wise ;
Honor the worthy ; and do blameless deeds ;
To wait on father-mother reverently ;
And care all tenderly for wife and child ;
Deny one-self ; observe due continence ;
See clear the truth of the Four Noble Truths—
Woe, Cause, Surcease, the Way to gain Surcease ;
To govern daily life by all these truths,
And realise Nirvāṇa at the end—
Such is the Blessed Life, the Blessed Life.)

Piṭā-(A)ham asya jagaṭo,
Māṭā, Ḍhāṭā, Piṭā-mahah,
Gaṭir, Bharṭā, Prabhuh, Sākshī,
Ni-vāsah, Sharaṇam, Suhṛṭ,
Pra-bhavah, Pra-layah, Sṭhānam,
Ni-ḍhānam, Bījam, A-vyayam. (*G.*)

(I am the Father-Mother of this world,
Spouse, Master, Ruler, Judge, Witness, Nurse, Friend,
Lover, Beloved, Abode, the only Goal
And Final Refuge, Place of Birth and Death,
I am (is) the Deathless Seed of All the World.)

Yā fédhrōī vidāṭ paiṭhyayé, chā
vāsṭraébyo, aṭ chā khaéṭaové,
ashāūni ashavabyō. (*Z.*, Gāṭhā, 53.4.)
(He is the Father, Husband, Servant, Lord,
He is the Comrade—He is all to me.)
Brahmaṇā pūrva-sṛshtam hi
Sarvam Brāhmam iḍam jagat. (*Mbh.*)
(Since Brahmā did create all moving things,
They are all Brāhma, Brahmā's progeny.)
Al-khalqo a'yāl-Allāhi, fa ahabbul-khalqi il-Allāhi
man ihsāna ilā a'yālihī. (*H.*)
(All creatures are the family of God;
And he the most beloved is of God
Who does most good unto His family.)

The duty of loving fidelity between husband and wife, implicit in the relationship of Father-Mother; and the avoidance of adultery and all unlawful sex-relations; these are also expressly enjoined by all scriptures. The Bible says that husband and wife "are no more twain, but one flesh; what therefore God hath joined together let no man put asunder."

Manu ordains that "they shall perform all the duties of life together, side by side, s a h a - ḍ h a r m a - c h ā r a, and be faithful to each other unto death and beyond". The Quran commands that if a husband has more wives than one, he shall love all equally; "if thou canst not deal equitably and justly with each and all, thou shouldst take only one". The Véḍānṭa and Sānkhya tell us that the Primal relationship is indeed the Conjugal Marital Relationship of God and His Nature, Purusha and Prakṛṭi, Brahma and Māyā, *Zāṭ* and *Sifāṭ*; (another aspect of which appears as *Abā-i-Ulavī* and *Ummuhāṭ-i-Siflī*, the Celestial Fathers and the Terrene Mothers); and that all other relationships, of paternity, maternity, filiety, fraternity, etc., and all spiritual affections and unselfishness, are born from and subsequent to it.

Yāḍṛg-guṇéna bharṭrā sṭrī
sam-yujyéṭa yaṭhā-viḍhi,
Ṭāḍṛg-guṇā sā bhavaṭi,
samuḍréṇ-éva nimna-gā.
Uṭkarsham yoshiṭah prāpṭāh
svaih svair-bharṭṛ-guṇaih shubhaih. (*M.*)
Vyāla-grāhī yaṭhā vyālam
balāḍ-udḍ-haraṭé bilāḍ;
Ṭaṭhā paṭi-vraṭā nārī
paṭim niraya-gāminam. (*Smṛṭi.*)
Prajan-ārṭham sṭriyah sṛshtāh,
sanṭān-ārṭham cha mānavāh. (*M.*)

(As is the husband's quality of soul,
As, too, the nature and the circumstance
Of man's and woman's mating, such becomes
The wife's soul-quality also. The rivers run
Into the sea, and make their waters salt;
Sea-waters rise and clasp the sunny air,
And from their brackishness turn into sweet.
As the strong serpent-charmer drags the snake,
Resisting, all-unwilling, from its hole
Into the light and air, so doth the wife,
Loving, devoted, clinging to her spouse,
Drag back the fallen man from hell itself.
One righteous aim of marriage is, no doubt,
To take joy in each other's beauteousness;

But greater, higher, nobler far is this—
To know divine heartache and anxious joy
Of fatherhood and of sweet motherhood.
That they be fathers—were men fashioned men ;
That they be mothers—women were made women.)

Mohsinin, gḥaira musāfihīn,
wa ṭā muṭṭakhizi akhḍan. (*H.*)

(Marriage has been enjoined because it helps
To save the pair from immoralities,
To shun the waste of vital healthful power,
And to save woman from degradedness.)

(Where there is happy union between
Husband and wife, there shall be harmony
Between the parents and the children all ;
And sweet and generous affection too
Twixt brothers, sisters ; all the family
Will be in happy state perpetually.
Loving example of one family
Will make the neighbourhood, nay, the whole state,
Loving ; and courteous, from its courtesies.)

(*C.*, *THR.*, 263.)

The Chinese word for 'culture' or religion is *chiao.* It is derived from the word for 'filial piety', *hsiao.* Confucius says, in the *Hsiao-king* (*Classic of Filial Piety*):

"The gentle-man teaches filial piety in order that man may respect all those who are fathers in the world. He teaches brotherliness in the younger brother, in order that man may respect all those who are elder brothers in the world...Those who love and respect their parents dare not show hatred and rudeness to others...Filial piety is the basis of virtue, and the origin of culture. To do the right thing and walk according to the right morals, thus leaving a good name in posterity, in order to glorify one's ancestors, is the culmination of filial piety." (LIN YUTANG, *My Country and My People*, p. 171; pub: 1938.)

Recent western poets have also recognised that wise parenthood is the spiritual culmination and sweetest fruit of weddedness; though a horrible flood of brazen, screaming, shameless, naked, animal sexuality, and very unregulated contraception, and wish to avoid all parental responsibility while snatching all sorts of lawless sexual excitements and pleasures, seems to have burst in an overwhelming flood on the world, after the Great War of 1914-1918.

> Womanliness means only Motherhood;
> All love begins and ends there—roams enough,
> But, having run the circle, rests at 'Home'.
>
> (BROWNING.)

3. THE GOLDEN RULE OF CHRIST.

"Whatsoever ye would that men should do to you, do ye even so to them."

This is stated repeatedly in the positive as well as the negative form, in the Vedic scriptures. It is also contained in one of the sayings of the Prophet Muhammaḍ. It is to be found in the Scriptures of all religions.

The negative aspect of the Golden Rule, it may be noted, is the source of all the 'preventive' or 'constituent,' 'shānṭika,' 'nigraha,' 'kshéma,' *insiḍāḍī*, functions of the state; and the positive aspect, of the 'promotive,' 'ministrant,' 'paushtika,' san-graha, anu-graha, 'yoga,' *imḍāḍi*, functions.

Vyāsa says:

Shrūyaṭām Ḍharma-sarvasvam,
shruṭvā cha-iv-āva-ḍhāryaṭām,
Āṭmanah praṭi-kūlāni
parésham na sam-ā-charéṭ;
Na ṭaṭ parasya kurvīṭa
syāḍ an-ishtam yaḍ Āṭmanah,
Yaḍ yaḍ Āṭmani ch-échchhéṭa
ṭaṭ parasy-āpi chinṭayéṭ. (*Mbh.*)

(Do not to others what ye do not wish
Done to yourself; and wish for others too
What ye desire and long for, for yourself
—This is the whole of Ḍharma, heed it well.)

Muhammad says:

Afzal-ul-īmāni-unṭohibba linnāsé mā ṭohibbo
le-nafseka, wa ṭakraho lahum mā ṭakraho
le-nafseka. (*H.*)

(Noblest religion this—that thou shouldst like
For others what thou likest for thyself;
And what thou feelest painful for thyself,
Hold that as painful for all others too.)

A verse of the *Bhāgavaṭa* says the same, in slightly varied form:

Éṭāvān avyayī ḍharmah saḍbhir-niṭyam anu-shthiṭah,
Yal-loka-shoka-harshābhyām Āṭmā shochaṭi hṛshyaṭi.
(This Ḍharma stands unchallenged changelessly,
That I should sorrow when my fellow-beings
May sorrow, and rejoice when they rejoice.)

Stating the golden rule, Muhammad says, "This is the noblest religion"; Christ describes it as

"This is the law and the prophets" ; Vyāsa, in the *Mahā-bhāraṭa*, laying it down, says, "This is the whole of Ḍharma." A disciple asked the Chinese Master, "Is there one word which may serve as a rule of practice for all one's life ?", and Confucius answered :

> Ṭzu-kung wen yueh : 'you yi yen, er ko yi
> Chung sheng hsing chih choh hu ?' Ṭzu yueh :
> 'Chī Shu hu ! Chi so pu yu, wu Shih yu jen.'[1]
>
> (*C.*, Analects, 15. 23 ; also 12. 2.)

> (Is 'Reciprocity' not such a word ?
> Do not to others what you do not want
> Done to yourself—this is what the word means.
> If you act thus, your public life will not,
> Nor will your private life, arouse ill-will.)

The Buḍḍha's single word is samān-āṭmaṭā. The Buḍḍha appealed specially to those souls which were ready to enter the Path of Renunciation, San-nyāsa or Naishthika-brahma-charya, *Fuqr* and *Ṭark-i-ḍuniyā.* Perhaps his chief purpose (as perhaps also Christ's) was to create a great band of Spiritual Volunteer-Helpers of mankind, able to practise extreme self-denial ; and Shankar-āchārya's idea seems to have been similar ; though the vihāras, maṭhas, abbeys, monasteries, nunneries, con-

[1] This transliteration of the original Chinese words was very kindly supplied to me by Prof. Tan Yun Shan, then residing in Shri Rabindranath Tagore's famous institution, Shanṭi-nikéṭana, by letter dated 16-7-1937.

vents, Sūfi *kḥāneqāhs,* that grew up later, came, by degeneration, to embody the very opposite of that idea. For the ordinary householders as such, the Buddha enjoined the pañcha-shīla abstinences and the four positive observances, *viz.*, (1) ḍāna, charity, (2) priya-vachana, gentle speech, (3) arṭha-charyā, earning of livelihood, but governed by the purpose of social service, by philanthropic intention in all the activities of life, trade, etc., and, finally, the secret of all goodness and virtue, (4) samān-āṭmaṭā, 'equal-souledness,' 'equality,' 'similarity,' nay, 'sameness,' of all souls; whence same-sightedness, feeling of, sense of, non-separateness; and the possibility and necessity of observing the Golden Rule. This samān-āṭmaṭā is the same as the Upanishaḍic and Qurānic Spiritual Democracy of Equality or indeed Identity of Souls.

Some other statements of the Golden Rule, in the several scriptures, in varying forms, are:

Āṭm-aupamyéna sarvaṭra
  samam pashyaṭi yo-(A)rjuna!,
Sukham vā yaḍi vā ḍuhkham,
  sa yogī paramo maṭah.
Sarva-bhūṭa-sṭham Āṭmānam
  sarva-bhūṭāni ch-Āṭmani,
Īkshaṭé yoga-yukṭ-Āṭmā
  sarvaṭra sama-ḍarshanah.
Yo Mām pashyaṭi sarvaṭra
  sarvam cha mayi pashyaṭi,
Ṭasy-Āham na pra-ṇashyāmi,
  sa cha Mé na pra-ṇashyaṭi.

Sarva-bhūṭa-sthiṭam yo Mām
bhajaṭy-ékaṭvam āsṭhiṭah,
Sarvaṭhā varṭamāno-pi
sa yogī Mayi varṭaṭé. (*G.*)

Sarva-bhūṭeshu ch-Āṭmānam,
sarva-bhūṭāni ch-Āṭmani,
Samam pashyan Āṭma-yājī,
Svā-rājyam aḍhi-gachchhaṭi.
...Svasya cha priyam Āṭmanah
...sākshāḍ Ḍharmasya lakshaṇam. (*M.*)

Māṭṛ-vaṭ para-ḍāréshu,
para-ḍravyéshu loshta-vaṭ,
Āṭma-vaṭ sarva-bhūṭéshu
yah pashyaṭi sa panḍiṭah.
(*Hiṭo-paḍésha.*)

(*By self-analogy* who feels for all
In gladness or in sorrow, everywhere,
The highest yogī is he to be deemed.
He who hath joined his self to the Great Self,
And seeth all in Me and Me in all,
Same-sightedness he gaineth everywhere.
Who sees Me everywhere and all in Me,
He never loses Me, nor I lose him.
Who, having gained the Great Identity,
Loves Me in all—wherever he may be,
And howsoever, he abides in Me.
Who sees Me in all beings, and all in Me,
He sacrifices unto Me in all;
His life is all one constant 'sacri-fice',
'Good-act'; he only gains the true S v ā - r ā j y a,
'Reign of the Higher Self,' Kingdom of Heaven.
Who looks on other's wives as on his mother,
Who looks at other's gold as so much dross,

Who feels for others *as he feels for self*,
He is true p a n d i ṭ, he is true wise man.
The final mark of Duty, Righteousness,
Legal and moral Lawfulness, is this—
That what ye hold *as dear and good for self*
And which your inner higher self approves,
Ye hold as dear and good for others too;
And what ye may not like for your own self,
For others like it not, in the same way.
Who *feeleth as his own* the joys and sorrows
Of others, he is the true yogī, he
Hath truly 'joined' his own soul with all souls.)

Pity the misfortunes of others; rejoice in the well-being of others; help those who are in want; save men in danger; rejoice at the success of others; and sympathise with their reverses, *even as though you were in their place.*

(*T.*, Ṭai-Shang-Kan-Ying-Pien, *THR.*, 223.)

When abroad, behave to everyone as if interviewing an honored guest; in directing the people, act as if you were assisting at a great sacrifice; do not do to others as you would not *like done to yourself*; so there will be no murmuring against you in the country, and none in the family; your public life will arouse no ill-will nor your private life any resentment.

(*C.*, Analects, xii. 2.)

Har che bar khuḍ na pasanḍī
bar ḍīgarān ma pasanḍ. (*S.*)
(Whate'er thou likest not *for thine own self*,
For any person else, too, like it not.)
Sabbé ṭasanṭi ḍandassa,
sabbésām jīviṭam priyam;
Āṭṭānam upamam kaṭṭvā,
na haneyya na ghāṭayéṭ. (*Dh.*)

(All shrink from suffering, and all love life;
Remember that thou too art like to them;
Make thine own self the measure of the others,
And so abstain from causing hurt to them.)

Love thy neighbour *as thy-self.* (*B.*)

Note that the Golden Rule does not attempt the futile and impossible task of abolishing and annihilating egoism. On the contrary, it makes Egoism the *measure* of Altruism. 'Do not foster the *Ego* more than the *alter*; care for the *alter* *as much as* for the *ego.*' To abolish egoism is to abolish altruism also; and *vice versa.* This is the injunction for the normal man, the ordinary householder. It is varied in special circumstances.

What a man hates to receive on the right, let him not bestow on the left; what he hates to receive on the left, let him not bestow on the right; this is what is called the Principle, with which, as with a measuring square, to regulate one's conduct.

(*C.*, Great Learning, *THR.*, 222.)

What I do not wish others to do to me,
that also I wish not to do to them.

(*C.*, Analects, 5. 11.)

Ushṭā ahmāi yahmāi ushṭā kahmāi chīṭ...

(*Z.*, Gaṭhā, 43. 1.)

(Skṭ: Ishtam asmai yasmai ishtam kasmai chiṭ.)
(That which is good for all and any one,
For whomsoever—that is good for me...
What I hold good for self, I should for all.[1]
Only Law Universal is true Law.)

---

[1] To some, this may seem to be a perhaps simpler and more easily intelligible statement of what the

Corollaries of the Golden Rule are:

Yaḍ anyair viḍiṭam n-échchéḍ
  āṭmanah karma pūrushah,
Apa-ṭrapéṭa vā yasmān,
  na ṭaṭ kuryāṭ kaḍā-chana. (*Mbh.*)

Yaṭ sarvéṇ-échchhaṭi jñāṭam,
  yan-na lajjaṭi ch-ācharan,
Yéna ṭushyaṭi ch-āṭm-āsya,
  ṭaṭ saṭṭva-guṇa-lakshaṇam. (*M.*)

(What he would hide from others; would not like
Others to know; what his own heart feels shame
To do—let him not ever do such act.

What he is willing may be known by all;
What his heart feels no shame at all to do;
What satisfies his 'con-science', his best Self,[1]
—That has on it the mark of Righteousness.)

Ko nu sa syāḍ upāy-oṭra,
  yén-āham ḍuhkhiṭ-āṭmanām,
Anṭah pravishya bhūṭānām,
  bhavéyam ḍuhkha-bhāk saḍā.
  (*Mbh.*, Anu-shāsana parva, ch. 50-51.)

(O! who would tell me of the sacred way
Whereby I might enter into all hearts
That suffer, and take all their suffering
Upon myself for ever and for aye.).

German philosopher Kant formulated as 'the categorical imperative', twenty-five centuries later.

[1]For nature and meaning of 'con-science,' as 'joint-science' of the Common Self of a 'community,' see *The Science of the Self*, pp. 186-193, by the writer.

I was anhungered and athirst, naked and sick, in prison....Inasmuch as ye have done it unto one of the least of these My brethren, ye have done it unto Me. (*B.*).

Another corollary of the Golden Rule is: Refrain from fault-finding, carping, cavilling, back-biting, ill-natured criticism, scandal-mongering, malicious libelling, defaming, slandering—all only too common and too destructive of friendliness and human happiness.

The disease of men is this that they neglect their own field, and go to weed the fields of others, and that what they require from others is great, while what they lay upon themselves is light. (*C.*, MENCIUS, *THR.*, 113.)

To attempt to correct others while one's own virtue is clouded, is to set one's own virtue a task for which it is inadequate. (*T.*, KWANG-TZE.)

He who smites will be smitten; he who shows rancour, will find rancour; from reviling comes reviling, and to him who is angered comes anger.

(*Bu.*, Uḍāna-varga, xiv. 3.)

Therefore,

Na hi véréna vérāni sammanṭ-īha kaḍā-chana;
A-véréna cha sammanṭi, ésa ḍhammo sanāṭano.

(*Dh.*)

(Never by hates are hates extinguishéd,
Only by love may hate be changed to love
And cease as hate—such is th' Eternal Law.)

Rājan! sarshapa-māṭrāṇi
para-chhidrāṇi pashyasi,
Āṭmano bilva-māṭrāṇi
pashyan api na pashyasi. (*Mbh.*)

(Faults, mustard-small, of others, ye see well;
Your own, as large as bél-fruit, ye see not.)

And why beholdest thou the mote that is in thy brother's eye, but considerest not the beam that is in thine own? (*B.*)

Suḍassam vajjam aññésam,
attano pana ḍuḍḍasam;
Parésam hi so vajjāni
opuṇāṭi yaṭhā bhusam;
Aṭṭano pana chhāḍéṭi
kalim 'va kiṭavā satho.
Na parésam vi-lomāni,
na parésam kaṭā-kaṭam,
Aṭṭano 'va avékkhéyya,
kaṭāni a-kaṭāni cha. (*Dh.*)

(The faults of others we see easily;
Our own are very difficult to see.
Our neighbour's faults we winnow eagerly,
As chaff from grain; our own we hide away
As cheating gamblers hide their loaded dice.
Omissions and commissions and ill-deeds
Of others do not try to pry into,
[Unless your duty 'tis as public judge],
But scrutinise your own most carefully.)

THE REASON FOR THE GOLDEN RULE. The Golden Rule is the direct outcome, or complementary aspect, of the Ultimate Spiritual Truth of truths. Why should I do unto others as I would be done by? Because 'I' and 'others' are all One I, One Universal Self; because, therefore, what I do to others I do to myself, in and through those 'others'; and 'sins, as well as good deeds, come home to roost'; so that, soon or late, 'As I do unto others, so it *shall* be done unto me.'

Yas-ṭu sarvāṇi bhuṭāny-
Āṭmany-év-ānu-pashyaṭi,
Sarva-bhūṭéshu ch-Āṭmānam
ṭaṭo na vi-jugupsaṭé. (*U.*)

(He who sees all in Self and Self in all,
He hates, fears, scorns not any, any more.)

Yéna kéna prakāréṇa
yasya kasy-āpi janṭunah,
Sanṭosham janayéḍ-dhīmāns-
ṭaḍ-év-Éshvara-pūjanam.
Prāyasho loka-ṭāpena
ṭapyanṭé sāḍhavo janāh;
Param-ārāḍhanam ṭaḍ-hi
Purushasy-ākhil-Āṭmanah.
Bhūṭa-priya-hiṭ-éhā cha
ḍharmo-yam sārva-varṇikah;
Jyoṭir-Āṭmani n-ānyaṭra
sarva-janṭushu ṭaṭ samam. (*Bh.*)

(The Light of Consciousness is in the Self,
And in all living things It shines the Same,
Therefore to give joy to some living thing,
And feel the pain of others as one's own,
Is the best worship of Divinity,
Most pleasing unto Him who lives in All.)

Difficulties ré the Golden Rule. The Golden Rule is not always easy to interpret and apply for the purposes of daily life. Yet it is intended for nothing else than daily practice. It can be followed fully and wisely only by those who have risen beyond personality, have 'let out ego and let in God.' The Teachers have said seemingly different things, at different times. But the inconsistency is only apparent. The all-reconciling principle always is : *Difference of circumstance makes difference of duty.* But the heart should always be bene-volent ; sincerely, not by profession only, like that of the horrible Inquisitors of the Medieval Ages, and of the cruel hypocrites in all religions ; though the duty may, at times, require the giving of pain to another ; like that of a surgeon operating on his own child.

Jesus says :

Resist not evil ; if any smite thee on the right cheek, turn the left to him as well...Bless them that curse you ; love your enemies and pray for those who persecute you.

Buḍḍha says :

Conquer hatred with love.

Muhammad says :

Iḍfa' b-illaṭi he-ya ahsan. (*Q.*)

(Recompense evil, conquer it, with good.)

Manu says :

Kruḍhyanṭam na praṭi-kruḍhyéḍ-
ākrushtah kushalam vaḍéṭ. (*M.*)

(Wroth be not with those who are wroth with you ;
To those who speak harsh words, reply with sweet.)

Vyāsa says :

A-kroḍhéna jayéṭ kroḍham,
a-sāḍhum sāḍhunā jayéṭ,
Jayéṭ kaḍaryam ḍānéna,
jayéṭ saṭyéna ch-ānṛtam.

(*Mbh.*, Viḍura-nīṭi.)

(With kindness conquer rage ; with goodness malice ;
With generosity defeat all meanness ;
With the straight truth defeat lies and deceit.)

Buḍḍha repeats the words of Vyāsa :

Akkodhéna jiné koḍham,
asāḍhum sāḍhunā jiné,
Jiné kaḍariyam ḍānéna,
Sachchén-ālika-vāḍinam. (*Dh.*)

Jainism says :

Conquer your wrath by sweet forgivingness ;
And by humility check vanity ;
By truth straightforward stay all crooked fraud ;
And by contentment peaceful, vanquish greed.
(*J.*, Dasa-veyaliya, *THR.*, 228.)

They rejoice not if revered, nor be angry if insulted ; but they only are capable of this who have passed into the eternal harmony of God.
(*T.*, KWANG TZE.)

Tulya-ninḍā-sṭuṭir-maunī,
san-ṭushto yéna-kéna-chiṭ,
A-ḍvéshtā sarva-bhūṭānām,
maiṭrah, karuṇa éva cha,
Harsh-ā-marsha-bhay-oḍ-végaih
mukṭo yah sa cha mé priyah. (*G.*)

(To censure or to praise—always the same ;
Content ; bearing in silence everything ;
Angry with none ; helpful and kind to all ;
Free from all gusts of pride and fear and rage ;
Such are the wise souls that are dear to Me.)

If thine enemy be hungry, give him bread ; if he thirsty, give him water ; so shalt thou heap coals of fire upon his head ; and so the Lord shall award thee ; [for thy enemy will feel ashamed of his hostile feeling, and his head, his face, will 'burn' with shame, and he will give up enmity and become thy friend, and that will be thy great reward]. (*B.*, Prov.) He that is slow to anger is better than the mighty; and he that ruleth his spirit, than he that taketh a city...Hatred stirreth up strife; but love covereth all sins...A soft answer turneth away wrath; but grievous words stir up anger. (*B.*, Proverbs.) Perfect love casteth out fear. (*B.*)

Yo vé uppaṭiṭam koḍham
    raṭham bhanṭam 'va ḍhārayé,
Ṭam aham sāraṭhim brūmi,
    rasmi-ggaho iṭaro jano. (*Ḍh.*)
Yah sam-uṭ-paṭiṭam kroḍham
    a-kroḍhena ni-yachchhaṭi,
Sa éva shūro vi-jñéyah,
    na yoddhā-pi mahā-raṭhah. (*Mbh.*)
(He who restrains his rage from bolting with him,
He is true warrior and true charioteer,
Not he that slays in battle many foes.)
Séṭūns-ṭara dusṭarān, a-kroḍhéna
    kroḍham, saṭyén-ānṛṭam. (*Sāma-V.*)
(Cross carefully the bridges hard to cross;
Cross Hate with help of Love; Untruth, of Truth.)

Mā vo ghnanṭam mā shapanṭam praṭi-voché ḍévayanṭam; sumnair-iḍ-va āvivāsé. Chaṭurash-chiḍ ḍaḍamānāḍ vi-bhīyāḍ ā-ni-ḍhāṭoh; na ḍur-ukṭāya spṛhayéṭa. (*Ṛg-V.*, I-41.9.)

(Repay not blow by blow, nor curse by curse,
Nor by base trick the meanest craftiness;
But shower blessings in return for blows
And curses and mean craftinesses, all.)
Vi-muchya...kroḍham...Brahma-bhūyāya
    kalpaṭé. (*G.*)
(Who gives up anger, he attains to God.)

But Kṛshṇa also says: "Therefore fight (against the wrong-doer and oppressor)"; and himself fought against and destroyed such, throughout his long life. And Muhammad too says: "Fight in the way of God, for the weak among men, women, and children"; and was a great leader of battles himself. And Manu says: "There is no quicker and surer road to heaven than to give up life fighting for the protection of women and children". Christ also, when he "found in the temple those that sold oxen and sheep and doves, and the changers of money sitting....he....made a scourge of small cords....drove them out of the temple...and poured out the changers' money and overthrew the tables"; he also pronounced heavy curse against the scribes and the pharisees and against those who offend against children; and also said: "I came not to send peace but a sword". Socrates, famed the wisest man of Greece, said:

We ought not to retaliate or render evil to any one, whatever evil we may have suffered from him". (Plato, *Crito.*)

His famous dictum is: "It is better to suffer wrong than to do wrong". Yet he fought in three wars against the enemies of Athens.

Lao-tse said: "Recompense injury with kindness". Confucius asked: "What then will you return for good?"; and added as his own view: "Recompense injury with justice, and return good for good". Lao-tse's disciple, Chuang-tse, two hundred years later, answered Confucius: "To the good I would be good; and to the not-good I would also be good, in order to make them good. To those who are sincere, I am sincere; and to those also who are not sincere, I am sincere; thus all grow to be sincere".

Christ says the same thing:

Love your enemies, bless them that curse you, do good to them that hate you, and pray for them which despitefully use you and persecute you;...for if you love them which love you, what reward have ye? Do not even the publicans the same? (*B.*)

Mencius, the great expounder of Confucius, is regarded, with Lao-ṭse and Kung-fu-ṭse (Confucius), as the third of "the three blessed, pure, and holy ones of China, Loshi, Koshi, Moshi"[1]. He too has said:

---

[1] The nuances of pronunciation of one language are, as is well-known, difficult to reproduce in transliteration by the alphabet of another language. Ṭsu, Ṭse, Tzu, Tze, means 'philosopher' or 'wise man' in the Chinese language. 'Lao' remains uniform. Confucius was named 'Ch'iu' by his mother "because of the noble proportions of his forehead. In the *Analects*, he refers to himself several times as Ch'iu; and again as Chung Ni, his other cognomen. But he is mostly spoken of by his family surname of K'ung...K'ung-fu-tzū or Confucius, meaning K'ung the Philosopher"; (Biography, prefixed to *The Analects*, The World's Classics Series). Mencius is Meng-tse; he was the most famous exponent of the views of Confucius. Kwang Tze, (Chuang Tzu, Kouang Tsu, Chwang Tse, etc.) was, similarly, the most famous expounder of Taoism, i.e., Lao-tse's philosophy. Y. L. Fung, *History of Chinese Philosophy*,

If another treat him perversely, the man of superior quality will turn round upon himself and say, 'I must have been wanting in propriety; how else should this have happened unto me?'; and will be especially observant of propriety. If the perversity of the other, and unreasonableness, are still the same, the superior man will again turn round upon himself and say, 'I must have failed to do my utmost', and will proceed to do his utmost. (*C.*, *THR.*, 226.)

Reconciliation of all views will be found in the following principles and illustrations:

Aḍhikāri-bhéḍāḍ ḍharma-bhéḍah; sāḍhya-bhéḍāṭ sāḍhana-bhéḍah; prasṭhāna-bhéḍāḍ ḍarshana-bhéḍah.

A-ḍandyān ḍandayan rājā
ḍandyānsh-cha-iv-āpy-a-ḍandayan,
A-yasho mahaḍ-āpnoṭi
narakam ch-āḍhi-gachchhaṭi. (*M.*)

(Duty differs with different-functioned men;
So means do vary with varying ends;
And outlooks upon Life, Views of the World,
Aspects of Truth, do vary with view-point.
The king who fails to punish criminals;
Or punishes, instead, the innocent;
He is hurled into infamy and hell.)

"The cloak of charity covers a multitude of sins" is a Biblical proverb; and Manu also says:

(pub. 1937) tells us (p. 408) that Confucius was born in 551 B.C. and died in 479 B.C.; Mencius (372-289 B.C.); Chuang Tzu (369-286 B.C.). Confucius, as a young man, visited at least once, Lao-tse, then very old. Soon after, Lao-tse went into and disappeared in the mountains, in the ancient way, common in India, of yogi-s and sannyāsīs.

Ḍānam ékam Kalau Yugé. (*M.*)
(While other virtues reign in other ages,
In th' Age of Discord, Charity prevails.)

But "Charity begins at home" is another western proverb; and Manu also says:

Shakṭah, para-jané ḍāṭā
Sva-jané ḍuhkha-jīvini,
Maḍhv-āpāṭo vish-āsvāḍah
Sa ḍharma-praṭi-rūpakah. (*M.*)

(The man who, being able, helpeth not
His kinsfolk living in distress and want,
But giveth unto others, thinketh ill
And acteth ill. His thought and act are like
The burning venom that is honey-hued;
Of real duty it is copy false;
It is not charity but self-display.)

So does wise Paul say:

If any provideth not for his own, and specially for his own household, he hath denied the faith and is worse than an unbeliever. (*B.*).

This supplies commentary on Christ's saying:

Take no thought, what shall we eat? What shall we drink?...But seek *first* His kingdom and His righteousness; and all these things shall be added unto you. (*B.*)

The two sayings are in perfect accord and supplement each other. The word *first* in the Christ's saying is the key. So the *Upanishaḍ* says:

Éṭaḍ-év-Āksharam Brahma,
Éṭaḍ-év-Āksharaṁ Param,
Éṭaḍ-éva viḍiṭvā ṭu
Yo yaḍ-ichchaṭi ṭasya ṭaṭ. (*U.*)

(He who hath seen the Infinite, the Self,
Unperishing, Eternal, Brahma, All—
Whatever he desireth, that is his.)

Such are illustrations of the truth that Duty varies with circumstance; and that achievement of God, of His kingdom, of His righteousness, is the highest and Ultimate Duty of man, on the fulfilment of which, all others are fulfilled automatically, without failure or mistake. A-h i m s ā, 'non-violence', 'non-hurting', 'harmlessness', 'thou shalt not murder', is the very first of all scriptural ethical commandments, as we have seen above. Yet also the right, nay, the duty, of 'defence' of self, and of dependents even more, has been recognised, even enjoined, by scriptures, and laws, in all times and climes; with special exceptions for special reasons. H i m s ā, 'harming', 'slaying', of the *innocent*, must be distinguished from ḍ a n ḍ a, 'punishment', of the *guilty*, the criminal, the aggressor, the brutal invader. As to who is to be held guilty and aggressor, in which circumstances—this has to be decided by 'divine law' and 'human law', in the manner, mentioned before, at p. 81, in which the 'Divine Will' can be ascertained.

The governing principle, which illuminates the whole problem, and makes possible the correct solution of each particular case, is:

Ḍésha-kāla-nimiṭṭānām
bheḍair-ḍharmo vi-bhiḍyaṭé. (*Mbh.*)
(Diff'rence of time and place and circumstance
Makes difference of duty and of right.)

The general rule is: Return good for evil; forgive; suffer, rather than cause suffering. This is so, less reservedly, for the teacher, the priest, the man of God; with still less exception, when the injury is done to himself; without any reservation, when the injured person is a *faqīr*, s a n-n y ā s ī, hermit. The special rule is: Fight against and resist evil; with physical force, passively or actively, negatively or positively, as conditions may permit and require; this is so, specially, for the householder, the man of and in the world; particularly when those dependent on him for protection are threatened; yet more particularly for the 'public servant'; unreservedly and without exception for the policeman, the soldier, the magistrate, whose express duty it is to protect the people from miscreants. In short, h i m s ā, 'hurting the *innocent*,' is clearly distinguished in the Vḗdic Scriptures, and in all others also, explicitly or implicitly, from ḍ a n ḍ a, 'punishing the *guilty*'. And the right of private defence of person and property has been recognised, always, everywhere, as said above.

Gurum vā bāla-vṛḍḍhau vā
    brāhmaṇam vā bahu-shruṭam,
Āṭaṭāyinam āyānṭam
    hanyāḍ ḗv-ā-vichārayan. (*M.*)

(The poisoner, the incendiary,
The robber, and whoso commits assault
With lethal weapon, and the ravisher,
And one who tries by force to oust from land
—These should be slain unhesitatingly.)

This is for the ordinary person, the householder, the public servant. The renunciant hermit follows another law. He has given a b h a-y a-ḍ ā n a, 'freedom from fear,' to all and every one.

Detailed treatment of this subject is exceedingly important for the *practical* purposes of manifold and very various and complicated daily individual and collective social life. It has been attempted elsewhere[1]. A brief outline will be included in the next chapter, on 'The Way of Works' Here, it is enough to say that the *Golden Rule* cannot but remain a *mere pious wish, unless and until* it is provided with a full technique; i. e., a complete *Social Organisation*. This would make clear what the main stages and situations are in each individual life; what the main occupations and positions are in the total social life; and what the duties and corresponding rights are that attach to each such stage and occupation. Then every one would know *what he should wish for himself and therefore for others*, in any given time-place-circumstance.

4. The Immortal Virtues and the Deadly Sins.

The 'Seven Immortal Virtues' of Christianity, *viz.*, Faith, Hope, Charity, Justice, Prudence,

---

[1]In the present writer's *The Science of Social Organisation, or The Laws of Manu*; *Ancient vs. Modern Scientific Socialism*; *The Science of the Self*; and various pamphlets.

Temperance, and Fortitude, generally correspond with the Shat-sāḍhanas, 'the Six Helpful Means' of upward progress, of the Véḍānṭa, *viz.*, Shama, Ḍama, Upa-raṭi, Ṭiṭikshā, Shraḍḍhā, Sam-ā-ḍhāna, *i.e.*, charitable Tranquillity, self-'restraining' Prudent Temperance, Resignation, all-enduring Fortitude, Hopeful Faith and Faithful Hope, just and all-reconciling Single-mindedness and Collectedness of mind. The 'Seven Deadly Sins,' Pride, Covetousness, Lust, Anger, Gluttony, Envy, and Sloth, are the same as the Shad-ripus, 'the Six Internal Enemies,' Kāma, Kroḍha, Lobha, Moha, Maḍa, Maṭsara, *i. e.*, Lust, Hate, Greed, Infatuation, Arrogance, and Jealousy ; Infatuation covers Gluttony and Sloth, also Fear.

THE TWO MAIN SINS. The sins have been reduced to two, in almost the same terms, by Kṛshṇa some five thousand years ago, and by Maulānā Rūm, about seven hundred.

Inḍriyasy-énḍriyasy-ārṭhé
Rāga-Ḍvéshau vyavasṭhiṭau ;
Ṭayor-na vasham-ā-gachchhéṭ,
ṭau hy-asya pari-panṭhinau. (*G.*)

(Lust, ape of Love, and Hate, Anger, Dislike—
To every object of each sense attach.
Be thou on guard, pass not into their power ;
They block thy passage on the upward path.)

Kāma esha, Kroḍha esha...
viḍḍhy-ēnam iha vairiṇam. (*G.*)

Khashm o Shahwaṭ marḍ rā ahwal kunaḍ,
Z-isṭiqāmaṭ rūh rā mubḍal kunaḍ. (*S.*)
(Hatred and lust are the two inner foes.)
(They twist man's eyes and make his vision false,
And from the straight path lead his soul astray.)

5. The Single Seed of the Two Root-Sins.

The Yoga tells us that Asmiṭā, Aham-kāra, 'I-am-ness' (of the separatist individualised 'I') *Khuḍī*, Egoism, is the yet more subtle root, from which both lust and hate sprout forth as obverse and reverse ; and that the final seed, from which this egoistic selfishness too proceeds, is A-viḍyā, *Wahm*, the Un-truth, Falsehood, Error, Nescience, self-deceit, that 'I am not the Infinite One; but am this one particular infinitesimal body of flesh and blood and bone, among many such bodies; am therefore something quite separate from my fellow-beings; and that each one of these is utterly separate from all others and from the One Self'. This self-ish Un-truth, *Nā-Haq*, A-saṭ, is the ultimate source of all wrong feeling, wrong desire wrong conduct. This a-viḍyā is the real *kufr*, *Kufr* means, literally, 'hiding the truth,' *lā-haq*. non-truth, *i.e.*, considering *mā-siwā-Allah*, 'any, other-than-God', as actor. In affirming separate 'I-ness', (as contra-distinguished from the universal 'I AM'),the *nafs*, the ego, commits *shirk*,[1]

[1]For these definitions of *kufr* and *shirk*, see Khaja Khan's *The Secret of Anal-Haq*, pp. 68, 83, 123, 151. *Shirk* means 'joining', joining something to God, placing

ḍvaiṭa, bhéḍa, sankara; it 'adds' the 'impurity', mala, *kasf*, of the Finite, to the 'purity', shuḍḍhi, *luṭf*, of the Infinite. Khuḍā, overpowered by Khuḍī, becomes an indvidual or particular Khuḍ, a separate self; Brahma, enveloped by Māyā, becomes Jīva; Uṭṭama Purusha, Purush-oṭṭama, Param-Āṭmā, surrendering to (Ḍaivī and Mūla-)

---

beside God something other-than-God, and believing it to have real existence also; whereas true Islam regards God as the Only Being, and all other-than-God as non-Existent; just the same as Véḍ-ānṭa. Gradually, *kufr* has come to mean disbelief in the Islamic religion generally. Thus the *Gulshan-i-Rāz* says:

> Ke rā kufr-é-haqīqī shuḍ piḍīḍār,
> Ze Islām-é-majāzī gashṭ bé-zār. (*S.*)
> (Whoever glimpsed the real Disbelief,
> From outward Islam he did turn away.)

"Apparent Islam consists in the observance of ordinances, and real Islam consists in the extinction of self [*disbelief* in the false self, the lower self, egoism]... *Kufr* is covering up the Oneness of Existence under the screen of Multiplicity. *Shirk* is considering the One Real Existence as two. *Kufr* and *shirk* of *Sharīaṭ* are pollutions, from sins; those of *Ṭarīqaṭ*, are love of the (sensuous) world; and those of *Haqīqaṭ*, are the establishment of *ghair* ['other,' iṭara, ḍviṭīya, a 'second'], and not seeing the Oneness underlying Multiplicity"; *The Secret of An-al-Haq*, pp. 114, 213. The difference between Véḍic Karma-kānda and Véḍ-ānṭa, and between 'Churchianity' and real Christianity is the same.

Prakṛṭi, A-viḍyā (Mūlā, and Ṭūlā) becomes Jīv-āṭmā; mukṭa becomes baḍḍha; *āzāḍ* becomes *asīr*. Thus it is that God plus Satan, angel plus devil, is man. In very truth, quite visibly, is there an angel as well as a devil in everyone of us. See the same face now in smiles, and again in frowns.

Az bahāyam hissa ḍārī, waz malāyak nīz ham,
Bu-g'zar az haḍḍ-é-bahāyam, k-az malāyak bug'zarī.
(*S.*)

(A piece of beast, a piece of angel, thou!
If thou wilt only rise above the beast,
Then wilt thou pass beyond the angel too!)

Yea, we can rise on stepping-stones
Of our dead selves to higher things.
(TENNYSON.)

Thus it comes about that:

Pra-kṛṭéh kriyamāṇāni guṇaih karmāṇi sarvashah,
Aham-kāra-vi-mūdh-āṭmā karṭ-āham-iṭi manyaṭé. (*G.*)

(This Nature of the Universal Self,
This Universal Nature, doeth all;
Yet man, deluded by false egoism,
Believes '*I* am the actor,' not *that* Self.)

This *Aham-kāra*, Ego-ism, *Khuḍī*, feel of separate self, appears as a triple Desire, (1) syām, 'may I always be,' (2) bahu syām, 'may I be more,' (3) bahu-ḍhā syām, 'may I be many'; in other words, *hirs*,' *ṭama*', cravings, urges, for (1) self-preservation, (2) self-expansion, (3) self-multiplication. In Véḍ-ānṭa they are called the three éshaṇā-s, (1) loka-ishaṇā, (2) viṭṭa-ishaṇā, (3) ḍāra-suṭa-ishaṇā.

In Buḍḍhism, (1) bhava-ṭṛshṇā, (2) vi-bhava-ṭṛshṇā, (3) kāma-ṭṛshṇā. Jainism knows them as (1) āhāra-sanjñā, (2) parigraha-sanjñā, (3) maiṭhuna-sanjñā. Sūfis call them the primal desires for (1) *zamīn*, (land, whence food and self-preservation), (2) *zar*, (wealth), (3) *zan*, (wife). In Christian lands the popular names for these are (1) 'wine', (in place of food), (2) 'wealth,' (3) 'woman'. Western psycho-physiology knows them as the primal instincts, cravings, impulses, appetites of (1) Hunger, (2) Acquisitiveness, (though this is not yet clearly recognised as an elemental radical factor, equally with the other two, which completes, with them, the primal triad of the root Egoistic-Desire), and (3) Sex; āhār-échchhā, ḍhan-échchhā, raṭ-īchchhā. The new psycho-analytic science, or, rather, branch of psychology, would perhaps name them as, (1) the ego-complex, (2) the property-complex, (3) the sex-complex. Hṛḍaya-granṭhi, 'heart-knot,' kāma-jaṭā, 'tangled desire-roots', are the expressions, corresponding to 'complex,' found in the old books, (*Upanishaṭs* and the *Bhāgavaṭa.*)

These three primary desires or appetites, vāsanās, āshayas, impulses, instincts, are, indeed 'simplexes' rather than 'complexes' But since all the emotions accrete and conglomerate 'complicatedly' around and on them, they appear as 'complexes'. In connection with 'food', the emotions appear in their most direct and elemental or simple forms; with 'possessions', they become more indirect and complicated; with 'sex', most so. Secretiveness appears in relation to all three, but least to food, most to sex, in man. Out of these three elemental appetites, in order that they may be satisfied in due measure, with 'alliance for existence,' and without internecine 'struggle for existence', arise the three fundamental institutions of Society, (1) Law-Religion, (2) Property, (3) Marriage and Family.

The sublimated forms of these innate primal appetites are: (i) the Wish-*to-be-always*, the Religious Instinct, of attaching one-Self to, identifying once Self with, the Eternal; also the Wish for 'lasting name and fame', 'a niche in history', yashah, kīrṭi, *ṭār'if*, *shuhraṭ*, *nām-warī*; (ii) the Wish-*to-be-more*, the Wish for rich artistic possessions, the proprietary and aesthetic instinct, to have ḍhanam, *ḍaulaṭ*; (iii) the Wish-*to-be-many*, the *power*-instinct, the Wish to *rule* over others and be depended upon by them. The correspondents are Ḍharma, Arṭha, Kāma, *ḍīn*, *ḍaulaṭ*, *ḍunyā*; the elemental lower forms are, wish for (1) food, (2) growth of body (especially muscle) and goods, (3) spouse and progeny. Wisdom—Wealth—Health, (the wish to be 'healthy, wealthy, and wise'), this triad is another aspect of the same.

The altruistic three instincts, corresponding, and opposite, to the three egoistic ones, are to be seen in the verse:

Bhunkṭé bhojayaṭé cha-iva,
guhyam vakṭi shṛṇoṭi cha,

Ḍaḍāṭi praṭi-gṛhṇāṭi,
shad-viḍham miṭṭra-lakshaṇam.
(Not only eats, but feeds, also ; not only
Receives confidings but gives such, in turn ;
Not only takes, but makes, gifts—the true friend.)

The Self, which *is* Immortal and Omniscient ; knows all past, present, future, all succession of events, which are Its own imagined creations ; knows all senses, all 'tastes' of all 'foods'[1]; this Self has, *as it were*, 'forgotten' that fact, 'hidden the truth,' fallen into a-viḍyā and *kufr* of Its own Free-will, for *lahw o la'ib*, līlā, 'idle sport and play,' and has *made* itself mortal and little-knowing ; It now tries to *make* itself pseudo-immortal and all-knowing, and *maintain itself* in unbroken continuity, by taking physical and mental *food.* The Self, which *is* Omnipresent ; because all things are already, always, present *in* It, has, *as if*, veiled Its eyes to that fact, and *made* itself small ; It now tries to *make* itself all-encompassing, in counterfeit, by growing bigger and bigger in body, and securing *more and more wealth* and possessions. The Self, which *is* Omni-

[1]The Samskṛṭ word for Self, viz., Āṭman, Āṭmā, etymologically means, that which sa-ṭaṭaṁ aṭaṭi, aṭṭi, aṭy-éṭi méyān, mā iṭi nishéḍhaṭi sarvān pari-miṭān, i.e. 'that which moves in, into, pervades, everything, always ; which eats, (a ṭ, to eat), tastes, everything ; which transcends all limitation ; which negates, repudiates, all limited things, all particularisations'. The Greek words *etymon*, 'original root,' *etymos*, 'true', also *atmos*, 'air', seem to be connected.

potent; which already contains all potencies, all powers, all forms, within Itself; has, *so to say*, blinded Itself to that fact, *made* Itself weak and confined Itself to one form; It now tries, vainly, erroneously, futilely, to regain its all-mightiness, by reproducing itself, pro-generating itself, in a series of *many* forms, all subject to its will and power, through a *spouse*, a counterpart, a reversed image and reflection of itself. Thus does Egoism work, giving rise to endless errors, wrongs, ill-wishes, through the branching of each of these three into endless derivative forms of like and dislike, love and hate, kāma and krodha, *shahwaṭ* and *kḥashm*.

The counteractives of the three down-dragging appetites, the correspondingly opposed attruistic instincts, Desires, Deliberate Resolves, are those of (1) a-himsā, (2) a-pari-graha, (3) brahma-charya; (*1*) *ṭark-i-īzā-rasāni*, *ṭark-i-siṭam*, (*2*) *ṭark-i-ḍaulaṭ*, *fuqr*, (3) *ṭark-i-shahwaṭ*, *ṭajrīḍ*, *husūr*, *zabṭ-i-nafs*, *a'smaṭ*; (1) harmlessness, non-violence, (2) non-possessiveness, non-proprietorship, voluntary poverty, (3) continence. The other shīla-s, *kḥūbī-s*, *kamāl-s*, virtues, perfections, yama-s and ni-yama-s, will all come under these; while Saṭya, *Haq*, in the highest sense, of the One Truth of the Unity of all, stands above and gives birth to all the three and their subordinates.[1]

[1]For fuller exposition of the whole subject of Desires, Emotions, Egoistic and Altruistic impulses, their

6. The One Seed of all the Virtues.

As wrong desires all take their rise from the Falsehood of selfish and separative Egoism; from the stubborn feeling that individual selves are really separate and different from one another and from the One Universal Self; so all right desires, good feelings, virtues, flow from, or are but aspects of, selflessness, unselfishness, self-sacrifice, nir-aham-kāriṭā, *bé-khuḍī*, which is the corollary of the Great Truth of the One Self in all. "Love God with all thy heart," said Christ, and also, "Love thy neighbour as thy-Self"—because God is thy inmost Self, and thy neighbour is the same.

As Lust-Hate are the dual shoots that sprout from the seed of selfish Egoism, so bhakti and karuṇā, *ishq-i-haqīqī* and *rahm*, pure spiritual love and compassion, spring from selfless Altruistic Universalism. The Véḍānṭa tells us that Primal Desire, Māyā-illusion, Aviḍyā-Nescience, has two chief shakṭi-s, *quḍraṭ-s* or *shuyūnāṭ*, *viz.*, āvaraṇa and vikshépa; one 'veils,' blinds, the eyes to the Reality; the other 'flings', 'distracts', drives, the soul towards the things of the Unreal. The Sūfis would perhaps call them *hejāb* and *īzāl*. From the standpoint of the Infinite Self, Desire is the deliberate Desire

genetics, classification, and how the baser can be subjugated to the nobler, the reader may, if he cares to pursue the subject, see the present writer's *The Science of the Self*, ch. vi, and *The Science of the Emotions*.

for L ī l ā, Play, Pas-time; for the World-Drama of S ṛ s h ṭ i, *Kḥalq*, Creation-Preservation-Destruction, by means of the powers of *Irāḍah* (*Éṭabār*, *Ikḥṭiyār*, *Kḥwāhish*) and *Ṭaswwur*, K ā m a and S a n-k a l p a, Will and Imagination. From the standpoint of the individual self, it is the instinctive 'desire' of 'lust-hate', which 'blinds' first, then 'drives' into wrong action. Self-knowledge, V i ḍ y ā, *Irfān*, Truth, counteracts and conquers these two, respectively; with the help of ṭ y ā g a and v y-a v a-s ā y a, *ṭark* and *mujāhiḍa*, renunciation and perseverent practice of self-control, v a i-r ā g y a and a b h y-ā s a, *mujānibaṭ* and *munāzilaṭ*, surfeited and dis-gust-ed turning away from the world, and resolute self-direction towards the Spirit; so it strengthens and perfects the virtues of spiritual love and compassion, of charity and altruistic service, s a r v a-b h ū ṭ a-h i ṭ a (*G.*) or *kḥiḍmaṭe-kḥalq* (*S.*).

Sarvam Āṭmani sampashyéṭ
sat ch-āsaṭ cha samāhiṭah ;
Sarvam Āṭmani sampashyan
n-āḍharmé kuruṭé manah. (*M.*)
(See all in Self, truth, untruth, right and wrong ;
Whoever sees all in the Self, him-Self,
He cannot turn his mind to sin again.)

Love...God with all thy heart...soul...mind :... Love thy neighbour as thy-Self (God). On these two commandments hang all the law and the prophets. (*B.*, Matthew.)

St. Paul repeats the teachings of the Véḍaṣ, of the Old Testament (Proverbs), of Jesus ; and indirectly indicates that the working of the Golden Rule must be governed by a complete system of publicly proclaimed and recognised rights-and-duties; that, indeed, without a complete Social Organisation, with well-defined rights-and-duties, it is entirely unworkable:

Bless them which persecute you, and curse not. Rejoice with them that do rejoice, and weep with them that weep. Be of the same mind with one another. As much as lieth in you, live peacably with all men. Dearly beloved, avenge not yourselves. If thine enemy hunger, feed him; if he thirst, give him drink; for in so doing thou shalt heap coals of fire on his head. Be not overcome of evil, but overcome evil with good. ...Rulers are not [i.e., *ought not to be*, though they unhappily but too often are] a terror to good works, but to the evil...Render therefore to all, their *dues*: tribute to whom tribute is *due*; custom to whom custom; fear to whom fear; honour to whom honour. Owe to no man anything, but to love one another.

He that loveth another hath fulfilled the law. For this, thou shalt not commit adultery, not kill, not steal, not bear false witness, not covet; and if there be any other commandment; it is [all] briefly comprehended in this saying, namely: Thou shalt love thy neighbour as thy-Self.[1] Love worketh no ill to his neighbour. Love is the fulfilling of the law." (*B*., Romans.) "...The Truth [of the Unity of the Self] shall make you free [of all vice, sin, doubt, fear, sorrow]. (*B*., John).

A-samshayam, mahā-bāho!,
mano ḍur-ni-graham chalam;

[1]See pp. 312, 298, 64, 309, *supra*.

Abhyāséna ṭu, Kaunṭéya !,
vai-rāgyéṇa cha gṛhyaṭé.
Yaṭo Yaṭo nish-charaṭi
manash-chanchalam a-sṭhiram,
Ṭaṭas-ṭaṭo niyamy-aiṭaḍ-
Āṭmany-éva vasham nayéṭ. (G.)

(Hard to control, no doubt, this restless mind;
Yet by 'distaste', 'dis-gust', for things of sense,
'Turning away from' fleeting worldly things,
And by 'persistent turning to' the Self
Of this most fickle mind, dragging it back
Again and yet again with resolute will,
Whenever it escapes to wayward ways,
It can, no doubt, be brought under control.)

Parānchi khāni vy-aṭṛṇaṭ Svayam-bhūh;
Ṭasmāṭ parāṅg-pashyaṭi, n-ānṭar-Āṭman;
Kash-chiḍ-ḍhīrah Praṭyag-Āṭmānam aikshaḍ
Āvṛṭṭa-chakshur-amṛtaṭṭvam ichchhan. (U.)

(The Self-born pierced all senses outwards; hence
All human be-ings look Without them-Self;
One here, one there, desiring Deathlessness,
Directs his mind aright, and looks Within.)

Chashm banḍ o gosh banḍ o lab bi-banḍ;
Gar na bīnī rūy-e Haq, bar mā bi khand. (S.)
(Shut off thy eyes, ears, lips, and senses all,
From outward things; surely thou wilt see God.)

Ḍar nazar kun jumla ṭan rā, ḍar nazar,
Ḍar nazar rau, ḍar nazar rau, ḍar nazar.
Haq ba jāṅ anḍar nihān o jāṅ ba ḍil anḍar nihāṅ,
Ai nihāṅ, anḍar nihāṅ, anḍar nihāṅ, anḍar nihāṅ!
Īṅ chunīṅ ramz-asṭ ayāṅ, khuḍ bé-nishān o bé bayāṅ,
Ai jahāṅ anḍar jahāṅ, anḍar jahāṅ, anḍar jahāṅ! (S.)

(Look within; yea, look within; yea, look within!
See the make of thy body from within!

Life in the heart, Self in the life, behold !
World within world, world within world, sans end !
Such is the Secret, speechless, yet all plain ;
Without or mark or word, yet everywhere !)

Puṇyam cha pāpam cha pāpé. (Véḍānṭa maxim.)
(Sin, merit, both are sins ; for both do bind
The soul unto the whirling wheel of change.)

Chūṅ nék o baḍ az Khuḍāe ḍīḍanḍ,
Rūy-az hama ḍo ḍar kashīḍanḍ. (*S.*)

(The Wise saw Good and Evil both from God,
Therefore from both they drew their heart aside.)

Jānāmi ḍharmam na cha mé pra-vṛṭṭih,
Jānāmy-a-ḍharmam na cha mé ni-vṛṭṭih ;
Kén-āpi ḍévéna hṛḍi sṭhiṭéna
Yaṭha niyukṭ-osmi ṭaṭh-ācharāmi. (*Mbh.*)

The good that I would do, that I do not ;
The evil which I would not, that I do. (*B.*, Paul.)

Lā ṭaharraka zarraṭin illā ba a'zm-Illāh. (*H.*)
(No atom stirs except by God's command.)

As a western proverb says : "To understand all is to forgive all." And to understand all is possible only by understanding one's own heart, one's own Self, fully. The only way for each one of us to become really charitable towards all who may seem to be erring, or to be causing hurt to us, is to see, by introspection, a n ṭ a r-ḍ ṛ s h t i, p r a ṭ y a k-c h e ṭ a n ā, *sair-i-nafasi*, how full of all possible weaknesses, wicked wishes, grievous mistakes, our own heart and life are.

I am the Truth, the Life, the Way. (*B.*)
Saṭyam saṭsu saḍā ḍharmah...
saṭy-ākārās-ṭrayo-ḍasha ;

Ṭrayo-ḍash-aiṭé-ṭi-balā...
a-saṭyāṭ shaṭravah smṛṭāh.
(*Mbh.*, Shānṭi-parva, chs. 160 and 161.)

(Thirteen chief virtues are but forms of Truth;
Thirteen chief vices too rise from Untruth.)

Aṭ ṭoī, Mazaḍā!, ṭém maīnyūm asha-okshayanṭāya sarédyayāo khāṭhrā maéṭhā mayā vahishṭā varéṭū manangha ayāo aroī hākurénéṃ yayāo hachinṭé ūrvāno. (*Z.*, Gāṭhā, 33. 9)

(May this my Conscience, Mazaḍā!, show to me
The Truth, Thy Inmost Spirit, Greatest Good,
Ideal of Ideals, to guide me
Aright in ways of Righteousness alway.
Having achieved that goal, I will have gained
All lesser things to which my soul inclines.)

Saṭyān-n-āsṭi paro ḍharmah. (*Mbh.*, Shānṭi, ch. 160.)
(Religion there is none higher than Truth.)

As-Sūfī lā mazhabu lahū illā mazhab-ul-Haq. (*S.*)
(Religion else than Truth Sūfis know not.)

The Truth of the real Identity of separate-seeming selves appears as Love in the aspect of Emotion. Love for elders, superiors, becomes Reverence, Adoration, Worship; for youngers, inferiors, Tenderness, Compassion, Pity; for equals, Friendship, Affection, Esteem. These words, expressive of feelings, indicate the corresponding virtues and duties also. Where the Truth of the Uniting Higher Self reigns, there, inevitably, 'joy becomes duty, and love becomes law', and all virtues wait attendant. Even so, the Untruth of Separateness becomes Hate, which sub-divides into, Fear of the stronger, Anger against equals, Scorn of the weaker, with numerous degrees and modifications.[1]

The imperial Rescript of Japan issued in 1890, which is the foundation of the moral education of the growing generations in all the schools of that great nation, and has been a vital factor in its marvellous rejuvenation, paraphrases these same eternal and perennial teachings.[2] Loyalty, filial piety, family affection, conjugal harmony, truth, friendship; modesty, moderation, benevolence, learning, arts, public good, common

[1]For details on this point, the reader may see *The Advanced Text Book of Hinduism*, Pt. III; *The Universal Text Book of Religion and Morals, Pt. II*, edited by Dr. Annie Besant; and *The Science of the Emotions*, chs. 4, 5, 7, 8, by the present writer.

[2]The above, ré the Imperial Rescript of Japan, was written in 1930. Internal psychological causes, and external political causes and world-causes, have, between that year and the present (1939), driven Japan also within the ambit of the awful Cyclone of War-Mentality; which has been raging, latterly, between rival Imperialist-Militarist-Capitalist-Nationalist Powers, on the one hand, and, on the other, between the antagonistic Ideologists of Socialism-Communism and of Facism-Nazism, respectively; all which only illustrates the difficulty of following the just middle course that Confucius taught equally to both China and Japan; (despite which teaching, China has been torn by internal wars all along, and has now been invaded fiercely by Japan, to forestal others, practically since 1931); and emphasises the need for distributing very extensively and intensively the *Spiritual Bread* that has been rained

interests, respect for just laws, courage, faithfulness, reverence—these are the virtues the Rescript emphasizes, and, as shown above, they all are the sweet and healthy fruits of the tree of non-separateness. The sense of non-separateness, the opposite of separatism, is the source of righteousness, right dealing with one another, whence trust, 'solidarity', 'fraternity', strength, 'alliance for existence'. "Righteousness exalteth a nation ;" (*B.*). *Per contra*, imperialistic, selfish, ruthless, unrighteous aggressiveness and exploitation abases the nation which practises them, and overthrows it sooner or later by breeding distrust and 'struggle for existence' inside and outside it.

Only he who is wise with the wisdom of the Higher Self can steer safely the difficult course of virtue between vices :

Be straightforward, yet mild ; gentle, yet dignified; strong, but untyrannical ; energetic, but not arrogant ; tolerant, yet stern ; mild, yet firm ; complacent, but reverent ; incisive, yet considerate ; docile, yet daring ; magnanimous, but discerning ; resolute, yet sincere ; courageous, but just. (*C.*, *Shu King.*)[1]

7. God in Man.

All religions therefore pre-eminently proclaim the Recognition of the Universal Self, as

---

like manna from Heaven, by all the the Lovers of Mankind, and which only can allay all heart-burnings, assuage all heart-hungers, and create Love in place of Hate, if anything can, at all.

[1]See p. 38, *supra*.

the one sure guide in all situations, the one certain means of effectively subordinating man's lower nature to his higher nature, his lower self to the Higher Self, *khuḍī* to *Khuḍā*, the *nafs-i-ammārā* (the sense-ward-driving desire) to the *nafs-i-Rahmāni* (the Divine Element in man), a h a m - k ā r a (egoism) to B r a h m a - b h ū y a (Universalism, the state of all-including infinite Brahma or God), a-s h u b h ā v ā s a n ā (impure desire) to s h u b h ā v ā s a n ā (pure desire), a n - é k a ṭ ā, b h é ḍ a - b u ḍ ḍ h i, *ṭaf-raqā, infisāl, ghairiyaṭ,* (sense of separateness), to é k a - ṭ ā, a-b h e ḍ a-b u ḍ ḍ h i, *wahḍaṭ, iṭṭisāl, a'iniaṭ,* (sense of unity), s v-ā r ṭ h a to p a r - ā r ṭ h a and p a r a m - ā r ṭ h a, *khuḍ-gharazī* to *bé-gharazī*, ḍ o s h a s to g u ṇ a s, *razāel* to *fazāel,* egoism to altruism and universalism, selfishness to unselfishness, vices to virtues, competitiveness to co-operativeness, individualism to socialism and communism in the finest and only true sense ; viz., in the sense of *spiritual* equality, or rather, *identity,* and *material equitability* (not an impossible material equalitarianism).[1]

[1]The reader may see *Ancient vs. Modern Scientific Socialism,* by the present writer, for fuller considerations.

A doubt may arise here. It is said above that the recognition of the Universal Self enables us to subdue our lower Self. But on the other hand, it is also true that unless change of heart takes place, the vision of the One does not arise. Apparently there is a vicious circle. What is the solution ? This: Both

In the system of Confucius:

Jen is the fundamental virtue. It is sympathy, *fellow-feeling*. This fellow-feeling is the reason of the Golden Rule. It is the Tao; it is the road which must be travelled by every human being. The Tao is the feeling of fellowship, and the feeling of fellowship is the Tao. Without it, one will not be kept from doing to others what one would not have done by others to him. All virtues spring from *Jen*,

---

the high and the low are ever-present, ever bound together, in every one of us, in all Nature, God's Nature, our nature. They are always turning round and round each other. Now the one is uppermost; again the other prevails. The going down of either, coincides naturally with the rising up of the other. This phenomenon *appears* in the human mind as the *wish* and *effort* to put one down and lift up the other. A friend once asked: "I have acquired an *intellectual* understanding of the Vēḍānṭa—the doctrine of the One Life; but how can I *realise* it?" I asked: "What distinction do you make between *intellectual* understanding and *realisation*?" He said: "Keeping the truth *always* in mind, and acting it out in *all* deeds." "Very good; now, what is the difference between *some times* and *always*, *some deeds* and *all deeds*? Is it not one of degree only?" "Yes." "The same is the difference between intellectual understanding and realisation, p a r o k s h a and a-p a r o k s h a, *shanīḍah* and *ḍīḍah*, 'the heard' and 'the seen'. There can be no intellectual understanding without *some* degree of realisation, at least in imagination. Continuous understanding and corresponding constant action—is only a higher degree, much higher, let us grant, of intellectual understanding".

loyalty, filial piety, courage, wisdom, propriety, faithfulness, righteousness, long-suffering, humaneness, benevolence. There are only two moral principles, fellow-feeling or Altruism, and its opposite, Egoism. *Jen*, fellow-feeling, is *man himself*. Jen is the reason of love. Only different shades of meaning of *Jen* are, prosperity, kindheartedness, charity, sincere sympathy, and *unselfishness*. When a man behaves as his heart desires, yet never transgresses the mean, he has reached perfect adjustment between natural impulses and moral discipline. He is now *Jen* itself. He is *Seng Jen*, a holy man. He behaves as freely and innocently as a child fresh from the bosom of nature, and all that he does never deviates from the Middle Way, Chung Tao.[1]

We have only to read *Jen* and *Tao* as the Higher Self to see that the above is nothing else than Véḍānṭa and Ṭasawwuf. *Jen* as fellow-feeling flows from non-Egoism, un-self-ishness, the suppression and denial of the lower self; which in turn, is the result of the conscious or sub-conscious predominance of *Jen* as the Higher Self; on identification with which, the sage is known as *Seng Jen*, Brahma-bhūṭa, Jīvan-mukṭa, *Insān-i-kāmil*.

N-īsṭ anḍar jubba-am ghair az Khuḍā. (*S.*)
(There's naught within my robe but God Him-Self.)
Lisā fī jnbbaṭin siwā Allah. (*S.*)
(What else-than-God is there within my cloak ?)
Brahm-aiva san Brahm-āpyéṭi.

---

[1] Abridged from Suzuki, *History of Chinese Philosophy* pp. 51-56, in his own words.

Brahma véda, Brahm-aiva bhavaṭi.
Ṭaḍ Brahm-āsmy-aham A-ḍvayam. (*U.*)
Brahma sam-paḍyaṭé ṭaḍā. (*U.*,*G.*)
(He knoweth Brahm' who is already Brahm';
'Brahma am I, other-less, secondless.'
Cleansed of all sins, holy in body-mind,
Knowing the cyclic process of the world,
His being, all and whole, becometh Brahm'.)
Ā'rif o mā'rūf ba mā'ni yak asṭ;
Āṅ ke Kḥuḍā rā be-shināsaḍ Kḥuḍā-sṭ. (*S.*)
(The Knower and the Known are but the same
Who knoweth God is God; God knows Him-Self.)
Uṭṭamā sahajā-vasṭhā...;
Brahma-bhūyā-ya kalpaṭé.
Kantakam kantakén-éva,
yéna ṭyajasi ṭam ṭyaja.
(*Purāṇa*, *G.*, *U.*)
(The nat'ral state is best...the state of Brahm'.
As when a thorn has pierced into the foot
Men with another thorn do draw it out,
And then cast both the thorns away from them,
So, now that worldly things have been renounced,
Renounce renunciation, and be Free.)
Sar-barahna n-īsṭam, ḍāram kulāhé chār ṭark,
Ṭark-e-ḍunyā, ṭark-e-uqbā, ṭark-e-Maulā,
ṭark-e-ṭark. (*S.*)
(Upon my head I bear a four-fold helm;
Of four renunciations is it made;
Renunciation of (1) this world, (2) the next,
(3) God personal, (4) renunciation too.)
Ṭyaja ḍharmam a-sankalpāḍ,
a-ḍharmam chāpy-alipsayā,
Ubhé saṭy-ānṛṭé buḍḍhyā,
buḍḍhim param-nishchayāṭ.

Ṭyaja ḍharmam a-ḍharmam cha,
ṭaṭhā saṭy-ānṛṭé ṭyaja,
Ubhé saṭy-ānṛṭé ṭyakṭvā
Yéna ṭyajasi ṭan ṭyaja.
(*Mbh.*, Shānṭi, 329-344.)

Vāsanās-ṭvam pari-ṭyajya
Moksh-ārṭhiṭvam api ṭyaja. (*Mukṭika U.*)
Na pāpam na cha vā puṇyam,
na banḍho n-āpi mokshaṇam,
Na sukham na cha vā ḍuhkham
iṭy-éshā param-ārṭhaṭā. (*U.*)

(Cease to initiate new acts, so shalt thou cease
To make new bonds of 'merit' ; cease from greed
Of any gain, so shalt thou cease from 'sin' ;
Pass from the relatively true and false—
By judging well the nature of the two ;
Then quitting *that* for which thou givest up,
Renouncing 'worldly false' and 'worldly true',
Rise above both, fast holding to the One.
Give up desire for e'en Deliverance.
Nor sin nor merit ; neither bond nor free ;
Nor joy nor sorrow—this, the Verity.)

Mam-éṭi baḍhyaṭé janṭur-,
na mam-éṭi vi-muchyaṭé,
Aham-ṭā-mama-ṭé ṭyakṭvā,
mukṭo bhava, mahā-maṭé ! (*U.*)

(Bondage is—"mine" ; Freedom—to say
"not mine" ;
Give up I-ness and mine-ness and be free !)

Qalam anḍar ba sūraṭ kḥwésh bar zan,
Hisāré-nafs rā az békḥ bar kan.
Tā na garḍaḍ nafs ṭaba' rūh rā,
Kai ḍawā yābī ḍilé majrūh rā. (*S.*)

(Thy pen strike through the writing of thy 'self' ;
Dig up this fortress of thy lower self !
Until this lower self (*nafs*) submits itself
Unto the higher Self (*rūh*), till then thy heart,
Thy wounded heart, will know no rest from pain.)

A western poet has put the same idea in other words :

Love took up the harp of life,
And smote on all the chords with might ;
Smote the chord of 'self,' which, trembling,
Passed in music out of sight. (TENNYSON.)

Christian mystics have put the idea more powerfully and nobly than this poet :

Though Christ a thousand times
in Bethlehem be born
But not within thyself,
thy soul will be forlorn ;
The Cross of Golgotha thou lookest to in vain,
Unless within thyself it be set up again.
(SCHEFFLER.)

The Sūfīs have said, similarly :

Nūh guft, 'Ai sar-kashāṅ ! man man na-yam,
Man zi jāṅ murḍam, zi Jānāṅ mī ziyam.
Chūṅ bi-murḍam az hawās-é-bul-bashar,
Haq ma-rā shuḍ samm o iḍrāk o basar.
Chūṅ ki man man n-īsṭam, īn ḍam zi-Ūsṭ,
Pésh-e īṅ ḍam har ke ḍam zaḍ kāfir ūsṭ. (*S.*)
(Said Noāh to his disobedients :
Ye faithless ones !, have faith !, I am not I ;
Believe that my small self died long ago ;
The One Life of all life now lives in Me !
When all the senses died within my being,
Of sep'rate individuality,

Then Truth, God, came and dwelt within my heart,
And was my understanding, ear, eye, speech.
Yea, only since my death I truly live;
Whate'er lived in me ere that was my foe.)

And the Buḍḍha too :

(They call me Gauṭama who have no faith
In what I say; but they who do believe—
As the Enlightened One, the Buḍḍha, they
Call Me, the Teacher, and the Blessed One.
And this is right; for even in this life,
Have I passed to Nirvāṇa, and the being
Of Gauṭama has been extinguished.)

And Enoch walked with God; and he was not; for God took him. (*B.*)

He that findeth his life shall lose it; and he that loseth his life for My sake shall find it. [And again] Whosoever will save his life shall lose it; and whosoever will lose his life for My sake shall find it. [And again] He that loveth his life shall lose it; and he that hateth his life in this world shall keep it unto life eternal. (*B.*)

Sira rākhé sira jāṭa hai,
sira kāté sira hoe;
Jaisé bāṭī dīpa kī,
kati ujiyārā hoe.
Sīsa uṭārai, bhuiṅ ḍharai,
ṭā para rākhai pāo,
Ḍāsa Kabīrā yoṅ kahai,
aisā ho ṭo āo. (KABIR.)

(Wilt keep thy head? Then it will be cut off!
But cut it off thyself, thou'lt grow a better!
Snip the burnt wick, a brighter flame will glow!

Cut off thy head, thy smaller selfish self,
And place thy foot upon it fixedly!
If thou canst do so, then come unto Me!)

Jesus says:

Believest thou not that I am in the Father and the Father in me? The words that I speak unto you, I speak not of myself; but the Father that dwelleth in me, he doeth the works. (*B.*)

And St. Paul:

I live, and yet not I, but Christ liveth in me. (*B.*)

So the Qurān, though uttered by the Prophet Muhammad, was spoken by God:

Gar che Qur-āṅ az labé Paighambar asṭ,
Har ke goyaḍ Haq na gufṭa Kāfir asṭ. (*S.*)
(The Qurān through the Prophet's lips did come,
But whoso says God spoke it not, speaks false.)

Ishvarah sarva-bhūṭānām
hṛḍ-ḍéshé-(A)rjuna! ṭisthhaṭi,
Bhrāmayan sarva-bhūṭāni
yanṭr-ārūdhāni māyayā. (*G.*)

(God dwelleth in all hearts and turneth them
Around, as by machinery, at will.)

Sarv-ājīvé sarva-samsṭhé bṛhanṭé
Asmin Ham-so bhrāmyaṭé Brahma-chakré,
Pṛṭhag-Āṭmānam Préríṭāram cha maṭvā;
Jushtas-ṭaṭas-Ṭén-āmṛṭaṭvam éṭi. (*U.*)
(This Whirling Wheel of Brahma, vast, immense,
This 'Planetarium', 'Asterarium',
In which all souls are whirling without rest,
And being born and dying o'er and o'er,
So long as they believe they are the 'whirled',
Fixed on the spokes and tyres, all separate
From the Fixed Whirler at the Central Nave—

Whoever glimpses his Identity
With It, at once gains Immortality
And finds himself at Rest in Heart of Peace.)
Shréshtham vāṇijyam ṛṭam amṛṭam cha mé-sṭi!
Marṭyén-āham krīṭa-vān asmy-Amarṭyam.
Jānāmy-aham shevaḍhir-iṭy-aniṭyam,
Na hy-a-ḍhruvaih pr-āpyaṭé hi Ḍhruvam Ṭaṭ;
Ṭaṭo mayā, Nachi-kéṭash!, chiṭo-(Agnih);
A-niṭyair-ḍravyaih pr-āpṭa-vān-asmi Niṭyam!
(Behold! My trafficking is truest, best,
And profitable most! For I have sold
My mortal 'pottage' all, and bought with it
My 'birthright' of Immortal Affluence!
I know all store of worldly goods doth pass,
And the un-sure can never win the Sure;
Therefore have I invoked the Fire Divine
And burnt up in It all these transiencies,
And by that sacrifice of mortal things
Have I obtained th' Immortal Self of All!

God (the Sense of Oneness with all, and all that that means) descends into and fills wholly, He blooms and blossoms in, the soul that opens itself out to Him by Love Universal. God loves His lover and identifies Himself with him, so that whatever the latter does, he does in the Great King's name, and by His Royal Warrant.[1]

---

[1] As has been said by a great teacher, "*Personality* is the synonymn for *limitation*; the more selfish, the more contracted, the person's ideas, the closer will be cling to the lower spheres of being, the longer loiter on the plane of selfish social intercourse." Yet this experience of even intense personality, of existence as an individual separate from other individuals, is

Yé bhajanṭi ṭu Mām bhakṭyā,
Mayi té ṭéshu ch-āpy-Aham. (*G.*)
(Who love Me are in Me, and I in them.)
Ḍāsānām anu ḍāso-(A)ham. (*Bh.*)
(I am the servant of My servants ever.)
(Whoso advanceth but a span to Me,
I go a cubit unto him—saith God.) (*H.*)

No man can come to Me except the Father...draw him...Abide in Me and I in you......I am in my Father, and ye in Me, and I in you. We know that we dwell in Him, and He in us, because He hath given us of His Spirit. (*B.*)

F-azkurūni azkarakum w-ashkurūli
wa lā takfurūn. (*Q.*)
(Avoiding gratefully all sense of separateness,
Think of Me e'er, and I will think of you.)
Yo Mām pashyaṭi sarvaṭra,
sarvam cha Mayi pashyaṭi,
Ṭasy-Āham na pra-ṇashyāmi,
sa cha Mé na pra-ṇashyati. (*G.*)
(Who seeth Me in all, and all in Me,
I ne'er lose hold of him, nor he of Me.)

Obviously, the purpose of Love-Devotion is Union; Marriage, in the case of physical bodies; Identification, in the case of jiva and Ishvara,

---

necessary, unavoidable, on the arc of descent. The craving for immortality begins as a conscious craving for personal immortality, at the junction point, where Descent ends and Ascent begins; it ends with the realisation that Immortality belongs to the Impersonal, and that personalities are not separate from each other, but are all, always, ever, everywhere, identified in and with the Impersonal and Universal.

rūh and *Rūh-ul-arwāh*, individual soul-spirit and Universal Spirit. The Samskṛṭ word n a- m a h, 'salutation', interpreted according to the methods of the *Nirukṭa*, means n a, not, m a h, 'I', i.e., 'not I but Thou'; 'Thy will, not mine'; not the individual ego, but the Universal Ego. In some Véḍic prayers, the closing words are, more expressly, n a m a m a, 'not mine'. This is the inner significance of 'I *bow* to thee', i.e., 'I bow to Thy Will', 'I submit to and will carry out Thy command.'

Whatsoever thou lovest
That become thou must;
God if thou love God,
Dust if thou love dust.

If thou dwellest on the lowest
Then the lowest must thou be;
Fix thy thought upon the Highest,
And the Highest shalt thou be.
(ENGLISH POETS.)

Har āṅ chīzé ke mā'būḍé ṭo āmaḍ,
Hamāṅ Maulā-e-mā'būḍé ṭo āmaḍ;
Har āṅ chīzé ke ḍāyam ḍar ḍilé ṭ-usṭ,
Hamāṅ, hush ḍār, ākhir hāsilé ṭ-ūsṭ.
Gar gul guzaraḍ ba khāṭir-aṭ, gul bāshī;
Wa-r bulbule bé-qarār, bulbul bāshī;
Ṭu juzw-ī, wa Haq Kul asṭ; gar rozé chanḍ,
Anḍésha-i Kul pésha kunī, Kul bāshī. (*S.*).
(Whatever with thy heart thou dost desire,
That is thy God adored, undoubtedly;
Whatever thing is in thy heart alway,
That, be thou sure, thou shalt attain, at last.
If rose be in thy heart, thou'lt be a rose;

of the last thoughts of the departing soul; *after* which, the inward and upward retirement should not be disturbed even by whispered Véḍa-hymn or Qurān-verse or other scripture-reading, however sacred.[1] And, since the law of analogy

[1] "At the last moment the whole life is reflected in our memory, and emerges from all the forgotten nooks and corners, picture after picture, one event after the other. The dying brain dislodges memory with a strong supreme impulse, and memory restores faithfully every impression entrusted to it during the period of the brain's activity. That impression and thought which was the strongest, naturally becomes the most vivid, and survives, so to say, all the rest...No man dies insane or unconscious....Even a madman, or one in a fit of *delirium tremens*, will have his instant of perfect lucidity, at the moment of death, though unable to say so to those present. The man may often appear dead. Yet from the last pulsation, from and between the last throbbing of his heart and the moment when the last spark of animal heat leaves the body—the brain *thinks*, and the Ego lives, in those few brief seconds, his whole life over again. Speak in whispers, ye, who assist at a death-bed, and find yourselves in the solemn presence of Death. Especially have you to keep quiet just after Death has laid her clammy hand upon the body. Speak in whispers, lest you disturb the quiet ripple of thought, and hinder the busy work of the Past casting on its reflections upon the veil of the future....It is a wide-spread belief among all the Hindus that a person's future pre-natal state and birth are moulded by the last desire he may have at the time of death. But this last desire, they say, neces-

prevails throughout, since the small is as the great, and deep sleep is similar to death; therefore, little children should be tenderly and reverently taught, and all grown-up men and women should make it a rule, to recite some beautiful, holy, soul-elevating, heart-refining verses of earnest prayer, before they go to sleep each night; so, their dreams will be beautiful, their minds will make sub-and-supra-conscious progress, and their subtler inner bodies will develope rightly.

Where the identification between the individual and the Universal Soul has been really and genuinely made; when the individual body, by purity, self-denial, wisdom, has become 'fit temple for God'; then only may 'miraculous powers' be entrusted to, and be exercised by, it, without danger:

> Whatsoever ye ask in My name,
> that shall be done. (*B.*)
> Kḥāsān-i-Kḥuḍā Kḥuḍā na bāshanḍ,
> Lékin ze Kḥuḍā juḍā na bāshanḍ. (*S.*).

---

sarily hinges on to the shape which the person may have given to his desires, passions, etc., during his past life. It is for this very reason, viz.—that our last desire may not be unfavorable to our favorable progress—that we have to watch our actions, and control our passions and desires throughout our whole earthly career;" *The Mahatma Letters*, pp. 170-171. This is for the ordinary human being; the daily prayers and worships and ethical injunctions of all religions help towards such happy ending. The conditions of Y o g a-s i ḍ ḍ h a-s are, of course, different.

(The favorites of God may not be God,
But neither are they separate from God.)

Mayi ḍhārayaṭash-chéṭah,
Upa-ṭishthanṭi siḍḍhayah. (*Bh.*)

(He who hath fixed his heart, his soul, in Me,
My Powers and Perfections wait on him.).

The Yoga and Véḍānṭa mention the grades of Siḍḍhas and Ṛṣhis; Sūfīs speak of such as *Kāmil*, *Akmal*, *Mokammal*, etc.; Buddhism mentions Chohans, Ḍhyān Chohans, Boḍhisaṭṭvas, Buḍḍhas; Jainism, Arhaṭs, Siḍḍhas, Muni-s, Tīrṭhan-karas, etc.; Christianity also mentions hierarchies of Saints and Angels, etc.[1]

Angels...principalities...powers;...gods, whether in heaven or in earth,...goḍs many and lords many;... principality, and power,...and dominion;...principalities and powers in heavenly places...(*B.*, Romans, Corinthians, Ephesians, etc.)

A Great Danger. As on the Path of Knowledge there is the great danger of mistaking the lower self for the Great Self; so, on the Path of Devotion, there is that of supposing love of some one person or personal deity to be the whole of true Universal Love; mistaking *ishq-i-majāzī* (selfish love) for *ishq-i-haqīqī* (selfless divine love); imagining kāma and rāga to be bhakṭi and préma. *Kḥuḍā* must be very carefully distinguished from *kḥuḍī*; the *nafs-i-lāwwāmā*, (the soul that warns, the warning voice), the *nafs-i-muṭmainna*, (the soul of peace), the *nafs-i-mulhima*, (the soul that receives divine

[1]See pp., 200-201, *sup* .

inspirations), and the *nafs-i-rahmāni*, (the soul of divine compassion), from the *nafs-i-ammārā*, (the earth-ward soul of worldly sensuousness);[1] the *shuḍḍham manas*, the pure mind, from the *a-shuḍḍham manas*, the impure mind; the higher Sva from the lower sva; otherwise, indeed, Sva-rāj, Self-government will become devil-government.

> Ḍvā Suparṇā sayujā sakhāyā
> Samānam vṛksham pari-shasvajāṭé;
> Ṭayor-ékah pippalam svāḍu aṭṭi,
> An-ashnan anyo abhi-chākashīṭi. (*U.*)
> (Two birds of wondrous plumage rest awhile
> On this most curious tree of bodied life;
> One eats the sweet-sour fruits with eager greed,
> And suffers many ills in consequence;
> The other looketh on compassionately.)

Very subtle is this dangerous Error of egoism. A hair's-breadth divides heaven from hell. Both are ever-present in us. Now the one prevails; now the other. The wish to save, is heavenly; the wish to become a saviour, may lead to purgatory.

> Innahū jasro jahannum wa inna alaihe mamarro jamī-il-khalq, aḍaqqo minn-as-shair wa ahaḍḍo minn-as-saif. (*Q.*)

---

[1] *Nafs-i-ammarā* may be regarded as the equivalent of ṭṛshṇā-chiṭṭam or vyuṭṭhāna-chiṭṭam; *nafsi-lawwāmā*, of ni-shéḍha- or ni-roḍha-chiṭṭam; *nafsi-muṭmainna*, of prashama-chiṭṭam; *nafsi-rahmānī*, of mahā-karuṇā-chiṭṭam; *nafsi-mulhima*, of praṭi-bhā-chiṭṭam or yoga-chiṭṭam. See p. 204, *supra*.

(Over Avernus runs, thin as a hair,
Sharp as a sword, a bridge o'er which must pass
All souls—only the good can safely cross it.)

Kshurasya ḍhārā nishiṭā ḍur-aṭyayā
Ḍurgam paṭhas-ṭaṭ kavayo vaḍanṭi. (*U.*)
(Sharp as the razor's edge is th' ancient path,
Most difficult to tread—the wise ones say.)

Ashīma ashāī vohu kshaṭhrém mananghā...fro ṭāīsh vīspāīsh Chinvaṭo frafro péréṭum ..yéng khé ūrvā khaéchā khraoḍaṭa ḍaénā hyaṭ aībī-gémén yaṭhrā Chinvaṭo pérétush, yavoī vīspaī ḍrujo démānāī asṭayo...Yā isho sṭāonghaṭ ā paiṭhi ākāo arédréng ḍémāné garo séraoshāné. (*Z.*, Gaṭha, 46. 10, 11 ; 50. 4.)

(With Conscience, Rectitude, and self-control
As Guides, enable us to cross the Bridge,
C h i n v a ṭ, 'Discriminating' right and wrong,
And 'separating' good from evil souls.
'Th' unhappy souls whose Self condemns themselves,
When they come to the Bridge that 'separates',
Are thrust away into the House of Lies,
And have to suffer there long lengths of time.
I worship Thee, O Lord !, that on the way
Unto the house of Beatific Song,
The Song of Deep Devotion unto Thee,
I may pass safely, e'er adoring Thee.)
(The soul of man, in joy of holiness,
Of perfect holiness, walks o'er the bridge,
Far-known, well-kept, the mighty Chinvaṭ Bridge,
Safely and steadily by virtue's aid.)

(*Z.*, Vishtasp, vi, 42.)

Strait is the gate and narrow is the way which leadeth unto life, and few there be that find it; [yet also] the kingdom of God is ***within*** you. (*B.*)

The meaning is that the higher Self is within us, and the lower self is also within us; to pass from the one to the other is very, very, difficult; and yet also very easy. A geometrical line runs between our higher nature and our lower nature; each is always trying to pull the soul over this line to its own side.[1]

---

[1] In the Vḗḍic and Purāṇic mythos, one of the Creator Brahmā's m ā n a s a-p u ṭ r a-s, 'mind-born sons', Kashyapa (an anagram of Pashyaka, the 'Seer', Sūri, Sūrya, the Sun) marries A-ḍiṭi and Ḍiṭi (the spiritual and the material aspects or natures of the Earth); by the former, he procreates the ā ḍ i ṭ y a-s, ḍ ḗ v a-s, gods; by the latter, the ḍ a i ṭ y a-s, titans. The 'step-brothers' are ever at war, and prevail by turns.

Ḍḗvāsh-cha Asurāsh-cha prakṛṭayah.
(SHANKAR-ĀCHARYA, *Bhāshya* on *Chhānḍogya U.*)
(Gods, titans—the two Nature-qualities,
Good, evil; altruism and egoism;
Both are inherent in each living thing.)

In the Hebrew, Christian, and Islamic legend, God creates angels; and the highest of them, Azaziel, promptly developes pride, a h a m-k ā r a, *khuḍī*, rebels, and becomes Satan, the prince of d'evils. God then creates the Garden of Eden (the far past Saṭya-yuga, the Golden Age); puts Adam, sexless, there; then takes a 'rib' out of Adam and makes Eve; which signifies that man gradually became herm-apbrodite, andro-gyne, and then separated into two different sexes. God forbade the two to eat of the fruit of the Tree of Knowledge. But Satan entered the Garden and beguiled them into eating it; i. e., into knowing each other carnally; and they 'fell' out of the Garden, and

THE ONE SAFEGUARD. All souls that would

---

clothed themselves in skins; i. e., they sank deeper and deeper into matter, and were born into denser and denser bodies; and the Human Race knew the joys and woes of involution and evolution. Such was the 'original sin', 'a-viḍyā', 'error'. Bye and bye, when Christos, the 'anointed with Spiritual Wisdom', arises within man, he attains the 'second childhood' of pure and perfected 'Nocence', in place of the 'in-nocence', 'ignorance', of first childhood; and then he re-enters Heaven.

A witty English writer has remarked: "Adam was the first cad; he peached against his wife; when questioned by God, he said, 'She tempted me'." He has done injustice to his primal progenitor. What Adam meant was obviously what a child would mean if he said: "The mango tempted me and I did eat", i.e., the mango was tempting. Even so, those first human children of God were tempting to each other, and 'in-nocently' committed 'the original sin'. With this sin are connected all possible emotions, 'sense of shame and guilt' of selfish sexuality, as well as 'sense of fulfilment, satisfaction, (honest and righteous 'pride', the opposite of 'shame'), and virtue of unselfish parenthood—which is the redemption of that sin.

In the wider and deeper sense, 'the original sin' is the putting on at all of a body of matter, however ethereal at first. This 'error' of identification of the Infinite with a 'finite' is the prime cause of all 'misery', **klésha**, (as well as corresponding pleasures). In terms of the Yoga, from this original **a-viḍyā**, arise successively, **asmiṭā**, **rāga**, **ḍvésha**, **abhi-ni-vésha**, i.e., egoism, like, dislike, 'stubbornness', (clinging infatuation, confirmed sentiment, 'complex' personality

walk on this sword-edge bridge-path and pass through this strait gate safely, must cultivate

---

made up of loves and hates and all sorts of derivative emotions. 'Pleasures' as well as 'pains', inseparable, are both included under k l é s h a, 'misery', by Védānṭa and Yoga, from the standpoint of the v i v é k ī, 'the sensitive and discriminating thinker'; not from that of the ordinary person, immersed in the world.

We look before and after,
And pine for what is not;
Our sincerest laughter
With some pain is fraught;
Our sweetest songs are those
That tell of saddest thought.

(SHELLEY).

In the *Zoroastrian* Scheme, Spenṭa Mainyu and Angra Mainyu, 'the bright mind' and 'the dark mind', are the ever-working ever-opposed forces. (One is tempted to think that the English word 'anger' is connected with this *Zend* word 'angra', and the Skt. 'angha', to blame, and 'agha', sin). Popularly, but not correctly, Ormuzd (Hormuzd, Ahura-Mazada) has been substituted for Spenṭa, (Skt. s h v é ṭ a, white), and Angra-mainyu has been transformed into Ahriman. Philosophically, Ahura-Mazaḍa is the source of both Spenṭa and Angra.

Thus, always, everywhere, has the human mind recognised the inevitable ineffaceable 'antagonism' of the Dual Principles; an 'antagonism' which is also a 'protagonism'; for, without both, the World-process were impossible.

Yaḍ ḍévā akurvams-ṭaḍ-ḍaiṭyā
abhi-ḍruṭya pāpmanā aviḍhyan. (*U.*)

Love Universal selflessly, by constantly meditating on the presence of the Self in all.

(What the gods made, the titans ran behind
And stained with sin; hence nothing in the world
Is free of either virtue or of vice.)
N-āṭy-anṭam guṇa-vaṭ kin-chin-
N-āṭy-anṭam ḍosha-vaṭ ṭaṭhā. (*Mbh.*)
(Nothing is wholly good or wholly ill.)

The Indian maker of famous hymns, Sūr Ḍās, sings,

Ḍayā-niḍhi! Ṭérī gaṭi lakhi na parai!
Akarama karama, karama ṭéṅ a-karama,
A-ḍharama ḍharama karai! (SŪR ḌĀS.)
(Lord of Pity! We know not thy way!
Out of sin Thou drawest virtue; from it, sin in play!)

The renowned Scotch novelist, Sir Walter Scott, has included a song to Ahriman, in his story, *The Talisman*, which is a commentary on the text quoted above from the *Upanishaḍs*.

Dark Ahriman! whom Irak still
Holds origin of woe and ill!...
Sure art thou mixed in Nature's sourc
An ever-operating force,
Converting good to ill;
An evil principle innate,
Contending with our better fate,
And, Oh! victorious still!
Where'er a sunny gleam appears,
To brighten up our vale of tears,
Thou art not distant far;
'Mid such brief solace of our lives,
Thou whett'st our very banquet-knives
To tools of death and war.

Miṭṭrasya chakshushā sarvāṇi bhūṭāṇi pashyéyam. (*V.*)
(May I behold all beings with the friend's eye.)

Evam ṭu pandiṭair jñāṭvā
sarva-bhūṭa-mayam Harim
Kriyaṭé sarva-bhūṭéshu
bhakṭir-a-vyabhi-chāriṇī.
(*Vishṇu-Purāṇa.*)

Yasṭu sarvāṇi bhūṭāni
Āṭmany-év-ānu-pashyaṭi,
Sarva-bhūṭéshu ch-Āṭmānam,
ṭaṭo na vi-jugupsaṭé. (*U.*)

(The wise, who see the Lord enshrined in all,
Give service unto all in consequence.
Who seeth in all beings the Self, him-Self,
And all in the same Self, he hates no more.)

Ai ba chashmān-i-ḍil ma-bīṅ juz ḍosṭ,
Har che bīnī bi-ḍāṅ ke mazhar-i-Ū-sṭ. (*S.*)
(Friend! with the loving vision of the heart
Naught else than friend canst thou see anywhere.
Thou knowest now that all are but His forms.)

Ab hauṅ kāsoṅ baira karauṅ,
Phiraṭa pukāraṭa Prabhu nija mukha ṭéṅ
Ghata ghata Hauṅ biharauṅ. (SŪR ḌĀS.)
(How may I bear hate now to any one,
When my own Lord goes round proclaiming loud

[Lurking and working ever, thou,
The human heart within,
All wish, most virtuous-seeming now,]
Thou goadest into Sin !
But also, on the other hand,
An ever greater glory springs
From ruins of the broken past ;
And sin its own repentance brings,
Till Man stands Perfected at last.

With his own blessed lips : "I am at play
Hidden behind the beating of all hearts.")
Jo ghair kū āp kar pichāné,
Phir kyūṅ karé ḍushmanī, ḍīwāné !

(*S.*, BAHRI, *Man-lagan.*)

(O lunatic !, if thou dost recognise
That others are thy-Self, whom canst thou hate ?)

Hama ḍosṭ, 'all are friends', is the necessary consequence of *Hama Ū-sṭ*, 'all is He.'

Such is the Way of Devotion, the way of *ṭasfīya-i-ḍil*, (from *safā*, clean, pure, whence also *Sūfī* and *Ṭasawwuf*[1]), or chiṭṭa-parikarma or chiṭṭa-prasāḍanam, (as the Yoga-shāstra calls it), 'the cleansing of the heart,' 'the toilette of the mind,' 'the purification of the soul'—with its disciplines and practices, its vows and observances, negative and positive, its storing and perfecting of the five virtues and the further virtues, its casting off of sins, its gradually complete self-effacement, its extinction of the lower smaller worse egoistic self. It is but another and inherent aspect of the Way of Knowledge, for the realization of the identity of all selves in the Universal Self.

THE CROWNING VIRTUE OF HUMILITY. A very important teaching of all religions is that we should welcome the strokes of fortune as coming from God, our own Inmost Self, for our soul's chastening and refinement and further progress on the Path of Ascension, Ūrḍhva-gaṭi, Āroha,

[1] See p. 246, *supra*.

Qaus-i-Urūj, the Arc of Ascent, the opposite of the Path of Declension, Aḍho-gaṭi, Av-āroha *Qaus-i-nazūl*, the Arc of Descent.

Whom the Lord loveth, He chasteneth. (*B.*)

Yasy-ānu-graham ichchhāmi
ṭasya sarvam harāmy-Aham. (*Bh.*)
Ārṭo, jijñāsur-arṭh-ārṭhī,
jñānī cha, Bharaṭ-arshabha!
Chaṭur-viḍhā bhajanṭé Mām,
janāh sukṛṭino-(A)rjuna! (*G.*)

(Whom I wish well unto, I rob of all
That he holds dearest and most near his heart;
Thus stricken from the world, he comes to seek
With deadly earnestness to know the Truth
Of how the wealth of Happiness is found;
And then he learns the Supreme Final Truth
That Happiness is Self and in the Self—
Such the four states of him who loveth Me.)

Ezā ahabb Allāho a'bḍan
aghṭammahū b-il-balāé. (*H.*)

(When God doth love a servant, then he sends
Sorrows to try him, and embraces him
Around the neck with arm of adverse fate.)

Wa la nablowannakum be shai-im min al-khaufe w-al-jū-e wa naqsim min al-amwāli w-al-anfusi w-as-samarāṭ; wa bashshiris sābirīn allazīna ezā asabaṭa-hum musībaṭun qālu, inna l-illāhi wa inna ilaihi rāje-ūn, ulā-ika alaihim salawāṭum miṅrrabehim wa rahmah; wa ulāika humul mohṭaḍūn. (*Q.*)

(Ye will be tried in many ways, indeed;
With fears and hungers, yea, with loss of fruit,
And loss of property and life itself.
But unto those who, when afflictions fall
Upon them, say, calmly and patiently,

'We all are God's, to Him shall we return,'
Unto them give this good news that ye are
The foll'wers of the right course on which rest
The Mercy and the Blessings of the Lord.)

Fuqr bhī hai Haq kī bakhshāyish kā ganj
Jis sé khush ho ḍé usī banḍé ko ranj. (*S.*)
Fahm o khāṭir ṭéz karḍan n-īsṭ rāh
Juz shikasṭa mī na gīraḍ fazl-i-Shāh. (*S.*)
(Want is a blessing in disguise from Him;
Who pleases Him, to him He sendeth pain;
To sharpen th' intellect is not the Way;
The Royal Gift is for the broken heart.)

Kshuḍhā-ṭṛsh-ārṭā jananīm smaranṭi.
(SHANKAR-ĀCHĀRYA.)
(Children forget the mother, in their play,
Until they feel a-hungered and a-thirst.)

Heaven makes hard demands on faith.
(*C.*, *Shi King*, *THR.*, 38.)

Humility is the root of honour, lowliness the foundation of loftiness; the world's weakest overcomes the world's hardest.
(*T.*, *Tao Teh King*, *THR.*, 102.)

Pride goeth before destruction, and a haughty spirit before a fall.... The fear of the Lord is the beginning of knowledge. (*B. Prov.*)

Blessed is the man that endureth temptation; for when he is tried, he shall receive the crown of life which the Lord hath promised to them that love Him. (*B.*, James.)

Té aṭi-mānén-aiva parā-babhūviré; ṭasmān n-āṭi-manyéṭa; parā-bhavasya h-aiṭan mukham, yaḍ aṭi-mānah. (*V.*, *Shaṭapaṭha Brāhmaṇa.*)

(The titans took great pride; therefore they fell.
Let no one therefore overween himself.
Pride is the very gateway to defeat.)

Pérésā chā nāo yā hōī;...
Rafédhrāya voūru-chashānė dōīshī mōī
yā vé avifrā. (*Z.*, Gāṭhā, 43. 10; 33. 13.)
(Put tests and questions on me, Mazaḍā!
Whate'er afflictions Thou mayst put on me,
As blissful favours will I take them all.)

Blessed are the poor in Spirit, for theirs is the kingdom of heaven...Blessed are the meek, for they shall inherit the earth...Blessed are the pure in heart, for they shall see God. Blessed are ye when men shall revile you and persecute you...for great is your reward in heaven. (*B.*)

The Kingdom of God cometh not with observation; neither shall they say, lo here!, or lo there!; for behold, the kingdom of God is within you. (*B.*, Luke.)

It is better to hear the rebuke of the wise, than... the song (of praise) of fools. (*B.*, Eccles.)

Yam pra-shamsanṭi kiṭavāh,
Yam pra-shamsanṭi chāraṇāh,
Yam pra-shamsanṭi banḍhakyah,
Na sa jīvaṭi mānushah. (*Mbh.*)
Sulabhāh purushāh, Rājan!,
Saṭaṭam priya-vāḍinah;
A-priyasya cha paṭhyasya
Vakṭā shroṭā cha ḍur-labhah.

(VĀLMĪKI, *Rāmāyaṇa.*)

(The man who fills with joy and swells with pride,
When he is praised by gamblers and paid bards
And vicious women—he is dead though living.
Easy to find are men who always speak
Soft, pleasing, honeyed words of flattery;

Rare—who speak fearless, and who humbly hear,
Words that are harsh to hear but good to heed.)

Even if we brothers over the whole earth give good examples of holiness and edification—in that is not the perfect happiness; even if we spoke all tongues and knew all wisdom and the whole of the scriptures, and were able to reveal the future and the secrets of the heart; even if we spoke with the tongues of angels and knew the courses of the stars and the powers of herbs, and all the treasures of the earth were revealed to us, and all virtues and powers of birds and beasts and fishes and also the properties of mankind and of trees and stones and roots and water—even in that there is not perfect happiness. When we endure abuse of words and wickedness of treatment, without becoming angry, when we instead think in humility that we are really deserving of it all—that is perfect happiness. If we endure patiently hunger and cold and blows, and all sorts of suffering, injustice, contempt, and harshness, and regard them as trials and crosses, and think how much more we ought to suffer—that is perfect happiness. (ST: FRANCIS of Assissi.)

Sorrow is better than laughter; for by sadness... the heart is made better. The heart of the wise is in the house of mourning; but the heart of fools is in the house of mirth. (*B.*, Eccles.)

The hurt child is clasped closest to the mother's breast.

Vai-rāgya, *mujānibaṭ*, a very storm of revolt from the world of the senses, and of passionate compassion for all who suffer, is indispensable for abhyāsa, *munāzilaṭ*, turning towards and finding the world of the Spirit.

Who can by searching find out God? The Kingdom of Heaven is taken by storm. (*B.*)

Later on, when the world of the Spirit has been found, the world of matter is assigned its proper place in subordination to it; and the great passionings and extreme efforts needed to achieve success, sink into tranquil routine of newly understood and freshly organised duties, after that success has been achieved.

N-āyam Āṭmā pra-vachanéna labhyah,
Na méḍhayā na bahunā shruṭéna,
Yam év-aisha vṛṇuṭé ṭéna labhyah,
Ṭasy-aisha Āṭmā vi-vṛṇuṭé ṭanūm svām.

N-āviraṭo ḍush-chariṭān,
n-āshānṭo, n-ā-sam-āhiṭah,
N-āshānṭa-mānaso v-āpi
prajñānen-ainam āpnuyāṭ. (*U.*)
Ḍhyāna-yoga-paro niṭyam,
vairāgyam sam-up-āshriṭah,
Vimuchya kāmam kroḍham cha,
Brahma-bhūyāya kalpaṭé. (*G.*)

(By eloquence this Self may not be found,
Nor by much learning, nor sharp intellect;
But if a soul loves It with its whole heart,
Then It too gives Its love unto that soul,
And unto it Its loveliness unveils.
Unless man turn away from evil ways,
Unless he cease from quivering restlessness,
Unless his greed for worldly things die out,
Unless his mind resign and quiet down,
Unless he long for It with all his strength,
He will not gain the Luminous Insight,
The Radiant Vision will not dawn on him.

Only by thinking of It constantly,
Only by casting off all lusts and hates
And all his clinging to the finite, may
He gain the glory of the Infinite,
And thus gain all the world, becoming Brahm'.)
Allāho yajṭabī ilaihe manyashāo. (*Q.*)
God draws unto Him-Self the soul He loves.)
Heaven when about to save one, will protect him
with compassion. (*T. Tao Teh King, THR.*, 58.)
(Heaven loves the people; therefore gives them aid;
But can there be true love which does not lead
To strict direction, [and correction too,
Of its own object on the Righteous Path,
The Path which leads to lasting Happiness ?]
It is not 'loyalty', not 'law-fulness',
Which unto right instruction does not lead,
Of its own object whom it wishes well.
[Hence Heaven, since It loveth, chasteneth].
There are few persons in the world who love
Yet also know the faults of those they love;
Few also those who hate, yet also know
The virtues, of the object of their hate;
[But Heav'n knows all and guides accordingly].)
(*C., THR.*, 238.)

As much as the Infinite is more than the Finite, so much must the love of God for His progeny be more than can ever be the children's love for God; but the love of God for His progeny is not blind, as that of so many human parents; it is very wise, and knows how to guide, very far-sightedly. The child may forget the mother when engaged in play; but the mother's heart is always fixed upon it, even when she seems most deeply engaged in other work; and she is always running up to it, whenever any mishap threatens. We have seen before, that the Higher Self is always watching, and wishing well to, and endeavouring to redeem the lower self Īshvara-prasāḍa, shubh-ānu-ḍhyāna anu-graha, *ṭawajjuh-i-Ilāhi*, *ṭawajjuh-i-Ilqāī*, the 'grace' of God, also guru-kṛpā, *mehr-i-shékḥ*, the compassion of the spiritual preceptor and guide, is always helping the worthy seeker, silently. It is true that the seeker must walk the way with his own legs, and must see the Face he seeks with his own eyes; yet is a true guide very helpful, nay, almost indispensable, to make the journey straight, short, safe, and to provide a lamp for illumining the deep darkness. But the guide cannot force himself on the pilgrim; he attracts and influences supra-consciously, always; but must be sought by the Pilgrim consciously, before he can help consciously.

Ham Khuḍā kḫwāhī wa ham ḍunyā-i-ḍūṅ,
Īṅ muhāl asṭ o khayāl asṭ o junūṅ.
Na gum shuḍ ke rūy-ash ze ḍunyā bi-ṭāfṭ
Ke gum-gashṭa-é khwésh rā bāz yāft. (*S.*)
(God thou desirest, and the world also—
Absurd thy thought, and insane thy desire!
If thou wouldst find thy God, turn thou away
Thy face from worldly things; and do not fear
Thou wilt be lost if so thou turn away;
Rather thy lost Self thou shalt gain again.)

Ye cannot serve God and Mammon both. (*B.*)

Vipaḍah sanṭu nah shashvaṭ
ṭaṭra ṭaṭra, Jagaḍ-Guro!,

Bhavaṭo ḍarshanam yaṭ syāḍ
a-punar-bhava-ḍarshanam. (*Bh.*)

(May ills befall us o'er and o'er again,
O Thou Benignant Teacher of the Worlds!
For so alone are we compelled to think
Of Thee, and pray to Thee, and turn to Thee
With our whole heart, whole being, and then see
Thy Face Divine—whereafter sorrow ends.)

Lau ya'lam-ul-momin niālahū min-al-a'jré f-il masā-
yab laṭamanna annahū quréza b-il-maqāriz. (*Q.*)

(The man of faith—if he but understood
What blessings would flow unto him from strokes
Of what men deem ill-fortune, he would crave
That he be cut with scissors piece by piece.)

Kā'ba Kā'ba hai, Sanam-kḥānā Sanam-kḥāna,
Lék tūtā ḍil hi aslī manzilé Jānāna hai. (*S.*)

(Kābā is sacred Kā'bā doubtlessly,
And Fane of worshipped Image sacred Fane
Also, for sure—but yet the Broken Heart
Is the true permanent abode of God.)

'Tis only through the broken heart
That Christ can enter in.
(ENGLISH POET)

The sacrifices of God are a broken spirit; a broken and a contrite heart, Thou wilt not despise. (*B.*)

Love not the World, neither the things that are in the world. If any man love the world, the love of the Father is not in him. For all that is in the world, the lust of the flesh, the lust of the eyes, and the pride of life, is not of the Father, but is of the world. And the world passeth away, and the lust thereof, but he that doth the will of God abideth for ever. (*B.*, John.)

Parīkshya lokān karma-chiṭān, brāhmaṇo
nirvéḍam āyān; n-āsṭī kṛṭam kṛṭéna;
Ṭaḍ-vijñān-ārṭham sa gurum év-ābhi-gachchhéṭ,
samiṭ-pāṇih, shroṭriyam Brahma-nishtham. (*U.*)
(Now hast thou tasted to the full, the sweets,
And even more, the bitters, of the worlds
Thy Karma earned; hast deeply tested them.
If thou hast had enough, wantest no more
Of those embittered sweets that burn the mouth,
Hast seen such cannot rest thy souls unrest,
Then, Child of Brahma! turn thee now to seek,
Thy long-forgotten Father; then, for help
In that Great Questing, go with humble mind,
To some true Teacher, wise, benevolent,
Who knows the Sacred Science, and is fixed,
Steadfast, in Brahma-Super-Consciousness.
Make fuel of thy heart, and offer it
Unto the Sage; and he will light therein
The Fire Divine that maketh all Life new,
And shows—thy Father and thy-Self are One.)

O men and women! when your passion, inherently rooted in you, will have exhausted its vitality and been torn out, when sinful thoughts have been abolished, then will you be rewarded for that great achievement; therefore gird up your loins for that high emprise; otherwise, in the end, you will have to exclaim, Alas! Alas! (*Z.*, *Yasna*, iii. 7.)

Foxes have holes and the birds of the air have nests, but the Son of Man hath not where to lay his head. (*B.*)

And therefore, because he gave up all p a r i-g r a h a, all sense of possession, sense of 'egoistic mine-ness', and embraced uttermost poverty, *fuqr*, *sukn*, n i s h-k i n-c h a n a-ṭ ā, therefore the

Son of Man became and was the Son of God. The soul which ties itself to nothing, no-thing-in-particular, necessarily includes everything, the All.

A recent western poet, whose path in life was very full of sadness and care, has illustrated the same ancient teaching of the great teachers and lovers of mankind, with such profound and genuine emotion of heart, that his words deserve to be reproduced here.

When so sad thou canst not sadder,
Cry—and upon thy so sore loss
Shall shine the traffic of Jacob's ladder
Pitched betwixt Heaven and Charing Cross.
Yea, in the night, my Soul, my daughter!
Cry, clinging Heaven by the hems,
And lo! Christ walking on the water,
Not of Gennesareth but Thames.

O World invisible! we view thee,
O World intangible!, we touch thee,
O World unknowable!, we know thee,
Inapprehensible! we clutch thee!
Does the fish soar to find the ocean,
The eagle plunge to find the air,
That we ask of the stars in motion
If they have rumour of Thee there?

Not where the wheeling systems darken
And our benumbed conceiving soars,
The drift of pinious, would we hearken,
Beats at our own clay-shuttered doors.
The angels keep their ancient places,
Turn but a stone and start a wing!

'Tis ye, tis your estranged faces
That miss the many-splendoured thing !
(FRANCIS THOMPSON.)

Nirbala kĕ bala Rāma. (Hinḍī proverb.)
(God is the srrength of the weak and the meek.)

Repentance, humility of spirit, utter faith in and self-surrender to God, (at first a Personal, ultimately the Impersonal and All-personal)—this is the only way to Salvation.

Alam Kalau vraṭais-ṭīrṭhair-
Yogaih shāsṭrair-alam makhaih,
Alam jñāna-kaṭhā-lāpair-
Bhakṭir-ĕk-aiva mukṭi-ḍā.
(*Bhāgavaṭa-Māhāṭmya.*)

(Enough of pilgrimages, vigils, vows,
Porings o'er books, and Yoga-practices,
Put by all sacrificial rituals,
Have done with philosophic arguments—
Give all thy heart, give all thy love, to God ;
So only from all fear wilt thou win free.)

Saḍ kiṭāb o saḍ waraq ḍar nār kun,
Jān o ḍil rā jānib-ĕ-ḍil-ḍār kun. (*S.*)
(Fling all thy piles of books into the fire ;
And turn thy heart unto the Hearts' Desire !)

In the ages of Kali, of perpetual warrings ; of ruthless riot and revel of egoism, lawlessness, disorder ; of tyrannical oppression of the weak by the strong ; of the torturing of innocents by wolves and tigers in human shape; in such periods, renunciation of the world, absolute surrender to God, and life in convents, monasteries, m a t h a-s, *khānegāhs*, or the forests—is the natural refuge of the weak and the sensitive. But horrors follow them there also.

When we happen to come across descriptions of the debaucheries, abortions, infanticides, in these 'houses of religion'; and of the doings of the Inquisitors in mediæval Europe; and of other religious fanatics elsewhere; of their burnings and buryings alive, their flayings, mutilatings, rackings, of men, women, and children—such horror grips the heart that it becomes difficult to read on, and the whole soul cries in agony: Why, why dost Thou permit such dire cruelties! The only, and sufficient, answer and consolation is that truly does God, the God *in* the victims, *suffer* it all *Him-Self*, for the extreme experience, (in the deepest sense 'en-joy-ment'), of the tragic side of the World-Drama; for the greater glory and bliss of the 'victims' in their after-life; for their exaltation in heaven and on earth as the martyrs whose blood is the seed of the tree of Virtue; for making enviable use of them as exemplars with which to infect the world with heroism; for expiating wholly all their possible past sins, making them reflect poignantly on the nature of the world-process and the meaning of life, teaching them to put their faith in the Self, and not in anything or person else; for taking them to His Infinite Heart the more closely; for creating the indefeasible desire for expiation in the souls of (the inversed God or Satan, the pseudo-God, *in*) the 'victimisers,' by inevitable reaction and revulsion of feeling, whereby they too will be compelled from within to expiate their grievous sins, will be regenerated in due course, and will regain the paradise they have now lost; and, finally, for the teaching to all, turn by turn, age after age, of the lesson of Saṭya, 'steadfastness in Truth,' A-himsā, 'non-violence,' Ṭyāga, 'self-sacrifice,' Brahma-charya, continence, self-control, and Nir-aham-kāriṭā, 'denial of and freedom from ego-ism, the lower and smaller self'; from which conquest of the lower self, 'self-effacement,' flow all the other virtues and perfections of the soul, especially 'the crowning virtue of Humility', *ṭawakkul*, Ishvara-pra-ṇi-ḍhāna, resignation, submission, surrender to and utter trust in God, the Universal Self. Truly is Humility, with its patience under suffering, the crown of virtues, since it means that the false separative ego, which asserts itself as 'other than others,' has been let out, and God, the Universal, all-pervading, all-including Ego, has been let in.

Humility is indeed only another name for non-egoism. That, in its fullness, results from Saṭya, Truth, not only the practice of truthfulness in speech, but the realisation of the Ultimate Truth of the Oneness of all selves in the Universal Self. From non-egoism arise naturally all the five principal, and the many derivative, virtues spoken of before, in ever greater perfection. Of the five principal virtues, three may be regarded as including the other two, and as being the counter-actives of the three 'appetites,' root-desires, mentioned earlier. Ahimsā, non-violence, is the opposite of Loka-ishaṇā, *Hirs-i-ḍunyā*, *hawas-i-zinḍagī*, Hunger of mind and body, wish for self-maintenance, (which cannot be fulfilled without hurting some one else, more or less), and consequent Kroḍha, *Khashm*, Hate of others; truthfulness of speech may be regarded as part of this, for untruthfulness is intended to hurt others, directly or indirectly. Brahma-charya, *Pāk-ḍāmanī*, *Par-héz*, Continence, purity, is the opponent of Ḍāra-suta-ishaṇā, *Ārzū-e-ṭawal-luḍ*, and Kāma, *Shahwaṭ*, Lust, sexuality, wish for self-multiplication. A-pari-graha, Ṭyāga, *Fuqr*, *Sukn*, renunciation of possessions and property, is the opposite of Viṭṭa-ishanā, *Ṭama'-i-zar*, and Lobha, *Ṭaw-illa'*, Greed, acquisitiveness, wish for self-aggrandisement; non-stealing is obviousiy included in it. Thus is Truth the fount of all virtues, and Humility the crown of them.

Be it remembered, here, that, for the Path of Descent of the soul and of Pursuit of Matter by it, the three appetites, in due degree, are the sources of the (1) religious and legal, (2) the property, and (3) the home and family instincts and institutions—all righteous, *in due degree.*

Another reminder must be given here also, again, in connection with the *practice* of the virtue of humility, viz., that 'Duty varies with Circumstance.' While everyone should *feel* humble in *heart*, and before the Supreme Self; it will not do always to *show* humility to every *vi-*

cious human being one may have to deal with. The task, the duty, of acting with discrimination, can never be shirked without grave danger. To reflect, to discriminate, is no doubt often more difficult than to act on the spur, the impulse, of the moment. Yet it is not safe. Advance in human evolution means clear thinking and wise discernment. The simple mind naturally wants to be given some very simple rule to go by. We have seen before, that a companion of Muhammad's asked him to name just one virtue which covers all; and that a similar request was made to Confucius by a disciple. Arjuna also said to Kṛshṇa:

> Vyā-mishréṇ-éva vākyéna
> buḍḍhim mohayas-īva mé;
> Ṭaḍ ékam vaḍa nish-chiṭya,
> Yéna shréyo-(a)ham āpnuyām. (*G.*)

> (Thy speech, commixt of many subtle thoughts,
> Confuses my poor mind. Therefore tell me
> Some *one* thing, sure and certain, beyond doubt,
> By following which I may attain to Good.)

So also does Shaunaka say to Ugra-shravā, the son of Roma-harshaṇa, the great reciter of ancient legends:

> Bhūrīṇi bhūri-karmāṇi
> Shroṭavyāni shruṭāni cha;
> Ṭasmāṭ sāḍho !-(a)ṭra yaṭ sāram,
> Ṭaḍ uḍ-ḍhṛṭya manīshayā,
> Brūhi nah shraḍ-ḍaḍhānānām,
> Yén-āṭmā sam-pra-sīḍaṭi. (*Bh.*)

(Many the pious acts, many the rites
And ceremonies that the books lay down ;
And more the ethics and philosophies ;
Impossible to compass, for weak men.
Good friend and benefactor ! if thou wouldst
Help us, then thou must teach to us, in brief,
The essence which thou hast extracted thence,
By thy superior intelligence,
So that our souls may rest in peace at last.)

The Great Teachers have, all of them, themselves felt the need of summing up all their injunctions and counsels in some simple formula; and have, accordingly, all enunciated the Golden Rule. But we have seen above that it is impossible to obey it satisfactorily in daily life, without the back-ground of a wisely thought out complete Social Organisation, fitted with a whole network of clearly defined duties and corresponding rights. The same considerations apply equally to the active exercise of the virtue of Humility.

The five virtues, placed in the forefront of their teaching, by Manu, Moses, Buddha, Christ, Muhammad, all alike, are not merely 'other-worldly' virtues. They are of the greatest and most immediate *practical* use in *this* world. They are the cement which enables human beings to cohere in an organised society. As soon as they fall below a minimum degree in any community, that community begins to decay and break up. Is it not plain that reckless 'violence' towards, and hurting of, others, for the satisfaction of one's own 'hunger' of body and 'ambition' of mind, and consequent widespread hatreds; deliberate 'falsehood' to cheat others of their dues, false propaganda and false advertisements on enormous scales, and consequent all-pervading mutual distrusts and fears; over-indulgence in 'impure foods and drinks', and excess of 'lust' and 'sensuality' in wedlock and in adultery, and consequent over-population, endless diseases, insanities; and excessive 'covetousness', 'greed for property and possessions,' and 'theft' of neighbour's goods, with frantic competition, and vast exploitation of the weaker—is it not plain that these, the vicious opposites of the five virtues, all aggravating each other, are the *root-causes* of civil wars, class wars, economic wars, national and racial military wars, and world-wars which threaten to destroy civilisation and fling man back into the beast? Very *practical*, very *real*, very *physical*, very *material*, then, is this aspect of Religion, though its only foundation is the *theoretical*, *ideal*, *Metaphysical*, *Spiritual* Fact of the Unity of all selves in the Universal Self.

Ḍharmāḍ-arṭhash-cha Kāmash-cha,
Sa kim-arṭham na sévyaṭé? (*Mbh.*)
Kḥuḍā ko pāyā ṭo kyā na pāyā
Kḥuḍā milā ṭo sabhī milā hai. (*S.*)

(All Riches and all Pleasures flow from Law—
The law of rights-and-duties that is shown
In final truth by Religion alone—
Men! Why do ye not then follow the Law!
If ye gain God, what can remain ungained?

Find God and ye shall surely find all else !)
Achieve righteousness and all things
else shall be added. (*B.*)

THE MUTUAL BALANCING OF PLEASURE AND PAIN. After all, Pain is the inseparable companion of Pleasure. The Metaphysical, Divine, Law of Polarity, Duality, Opposition, Ḍvam-ḍvam, 'Two-and-two,' *Ziḍḍain* and *Żaujain,* 'Opponents-Spouses', necessitates both. That man deliberately, sadistically, inflicts torture upon fellowman—excites the sense of horror to its utmost, no doubt. But willing submission to such torture, for a noble cause, in the name of the Universal Self, developes Heroic Humility to its utmost, also. And there is the consolation, that the unfailing Law of Action and Reaction makes ad-just-ment inevitable. The souls of all, victim and victimiser, have to pass through *all kinds* of experience, in the course of the vast eons of cyclic evolution.[1] The victim has been

[1]Some sects of Christianity, *e.g.*, the Calvinists, are said to hold that some souls are pre-destined to eternal Hell, and others to eternal Heaven. There are corresponding sects in Hinduism and Islam, which also believe in niṭya-nārakikas or *nāriyāṅ* and niṭya-svārgikas or *nūriyāṅ.* The element of truth in these beliefs is that 'heaven' and 'hell', love and hate, bliss and misery, are eternal facts; but the souls that dwell in those regions, and pass through those states, are always changing; like the inmates of the pleasure parks and the prisons of a great city. Each 'person has to taste all experiences, of all joys and all sorrows,

the victimiser. The victimiser *shall* be the victim. So far as the mere physical pain is concerned, Nature's winds, waters, fires, earthquakes, accidents of all kinds, predaceans, reptiles—are always inflicting awful tortures upon human beings as well as animals. Human beings have to learn to keep an equable mind in pain as well as pleasure. What right have we to take all the mass of pleasure (no whit less, by metaphysical calculus, than the total mass of pain, in the universe) which we derive from 'the world beautiful', as our *due*, and give no thanks for it, and not balance it against the pain, which we equally derive from 'the world horrid?' What right have we to only cry out and make complaint against the latter ?

Aṭr-aiva svargah, aṭr-aiva narakah. (*Bh.*)
(Heaven is here, in us, and so is Hell.)

Ghair-haq gufṭand ke bar ālam-e-bālā-sṭ Bahishṭ;
H ar jā ke waqṭe-khushé rū ḍihaḍ, āṅ jā-sṭ Bahishṭ.
(*S.*)

(They err who say that Heaven is on high ;
Wherever there is joy, there Heaven is nigh.)

Ḍuhkheshv-an-uḍ-vigna-manāh,
sukhéshu vi-gaṭa-spṛhah,
Vīṭa-rāga-bhaya-kroḍhah,
sṭhiṭa-ḍhīr-munir-uchyaṭé. (*G.*)

---

turn by turn, one after another. Indeed, Love *is* Heaven, and Hate *is* Hell ; and both may be found anywhere and everywhere, on this planet and plane, or on any other planet or star and plane, which is as far from this, as this is from that.

Ḍuhkhé ḍuhkh-āḍhikam pashyéṭ,
sukhé pashyéṭ sukh-āḍhikam ;
Sukha-ḍuhkha-mayam sarvam
jñāṭvā ṭāpéna muchyaṭé. (*Purāṇas.*)
(Not 'whelmed by sorrow, nor elate in joy,
Of others' greater pains and pleasures think,
To check despair and overweening pride.
Who thus sees weal and woe spread everywhere,
He casts off lust, hate, fear, and gains the Peace.)

Whoever shall humble himself as this little child, the same is the greatest in the kingdom of Heaven... Whoever shall exalt himself shall be abased, and he who shall humble himself, shall be exalted...God giveth grace to the humble. (*B.*)

(Pride bringeth loss ; humility, increase ;
This is the way of Heaven. He comes to ruin
Who says that others do not equal him.)
(*C.*, *Shu King*, *THR.*, 101.)

Inna Allah lā yohibbo kulle mukhṭālin fukhūrin. (*Q.*)
(God loveth not the self-conceited proud.)

Sukham shéṭé hy-ava-maṭah
sukham cha praṭi-buḍhyaṭé,
Sukham charaṭi lok-ésmin ;
ava-manṭā vi-nashyaṭi. (*M.*)
(The wise who bear slights humbly, sleep, wake, walk
With tranquil mind ; the slighter perisheth.)

Thus does God's Nature educate all into true Humility ultimately, and into the Duty of mergence of the individualistic into the Universal (and therefore social) Will, the true Spiritual Communism and Socialism.

DEVOTION TO DUTY. The ultimate lesson of it all, for purposes of practical action in daily life, is : Do your Duty devotedly. But to do our duty, *we must know precisely what our duty is.*

> Avarénāya vīchiṭhahyā narém
> narém svakhyāī ṭanūyé. (*Z.*, Gāṭhā, 30.2.)

> (Let each man ascertain with heed and care
> What he *ought*, what his duty *is*, in life,
> That which is good and right for him to do.)

Duty is what is 'due', 'debt', ḍ é y a (Skt.), *ḍāḍ* (Per.), ḍ ā ṭ h a (Z.), 'something to be given to another,' which 'ought' to be done, which is u c h i ṭ a (Skt.), u s h ṭ ā (Z.),[1] 'desirable', right and proper. Obviously, what is right and proper to do, 'Duty', differs with circumstances, as noted before[2], with position in life, profession, age, special situation, (normal or abnormal, fortunate or unfortunate, straitened or prosperous), of the person concerned. The child, the youth, the middle-aged, the old; the student, the householder, the retired publicist, the religieux; the educator, the ruler, the merchant, the workman; all have different duties. The same man in health, and in illness, has different duties. The duty of the Educator may be said, in terms of 'family feeling', to be Maternal Tenderness, Com-

---

[1] Shri J. M. Chatterji, *Gāṭhā*, (p. 148), connects the Zend word u s h ṭ ā with the Skt. root v a s h, to 'wish', the past participle of which is v a s h i ṭ a. The Skt. root i s h also means to 'wish'; its p. p. is i s h t a, the 'wished-for', the 'desirable'.

[2] See pp. 74, 307-317.

passion, nourishing of the mind and body of the younger generation; that of the Ruler-Protector, to be Paternal Justice, Regulation, Disciplining, Balancing; that of the Trades-man, Fraternal Helpfulness and Charity; that of the Workman, Filial Service, Obedience, *abḍiyaṭ*. But the general rule, for the mature of mind and body, is:

Do your Duty, your *Farz*, your *Kṛṭya*, to your fellow-beings; in the spirit of philanthropy, of Devotion to the forces of Good in the World-Drama; in good fortune and ill, without thought of gain for yourself; undeterred by indolence or doubt or fear of suffering; content with 'the remains of the sacrifice' if any, and without even them if there are none; full of utter faith in the Omniscient Wisdom of the Universal Supra-conscious, with complete submission and surrender of your small self to that Infinite Self. This is the ultimate practical lesson of all Religion.

Tao is near, and men seek it at a distance. Duty lies in what is easy, and men seek it in difficult tasks. Let each man love his parents, and respect his elders; there will then be tranquillity in all the land. (Mencius, quoted by Inazo Nitobe, *Japan*, p. 346.)

Uṭṭhānam ch-āpi ḍaivasya
hy-an-uṭṭhānam cha ḍaivaṭam;
Prājñāh purusha-kāré ṭu
varṭanṭé ḍaivam-āsṭhiṭāh. (*Mbh.*)

(Inactive indolence, active emprise—
Both equally are caused by Ḍaiva-Fate;
We know not what is fated, what is not;
Therefore the wise take action duteously
And strenuously, leaving result to Fate.)

Take no thought for the morrow...(Even) one sparrow shall not fall on the ground without your Father. The very hairs of your head are all numbered. ...(Yet) whatsoever (of duty) thy hand findeth to do, do it with all thy might. (*B.*)

Ishvarah sarva-bhūṭānām
  hṛḍ-ḍéshé-(A)rjuna ! ṭishthaṭi,
Bhrāmayan sarva-bhūṭāni
  yanṭrā-rūdhāni Māyayā.
Ṭasmāḍ a-sakṭah saṭaṭam
  kāryam karma sam-āchara ;
A-sakṭo hy-ācharan karma
  Param āpnoṭi pūrushah.
Karmaṇy-év-āḍhi-kāras-ṭé,
  mā phaléshu kaḍā-chana.
Mā karma-phala-héṭur-bhūr-
  mā ṭé sang-osṭv-a-karmaṇi.
Yajña-shisht-āshinah sanṭo
  muchyanṭé sarva-kilbishāṭ ;
Bhunjaṭé ṭé ṭv-agham pāpāh
  yé pachanṭy-āṭma-kāraṇāṭ. (*G.*)

(God bideth hidden in the hearts of all,
And turneth them around, as if they were
All mounted on an infinite machine.
Therefore the part assigned to thee do well,
Thy Duty, and cling not to thought of fruit.
So acting, with detachment from all thought
Of selfish gain, thou hast already gained
The Highest Gain there is to be attained.
Only the remnants of thy sacrifice
Are, by the Law, permitted unto thee.
Who makes and tastes all tasteful goods and foods
Himself, alone, he makes and tastes but sin.
To do thy duty is thy only Right—

Duty of Service of thy fellow-beings ;
No right hast thou to wish for other fruit.
Think not of gain, nor of inaction either,
And self-deluding slothful idleness.)

Qulūb-ul-khalāyak fī asābi-ir-Rahmān. (*Q.*)
Ramze "al-kāsib habīb Allah" shinau,
Az ṭawakkul ḍar sabab gḥāfil ma shau.
Rau, ṭawakkul kun ṭu bā kasb, ai umu !
Jehḍ mī kun, kasb mī kun, mū-ba-mū. (*S.*)
(Around the fingers of Almighty God
The hearts of all His creatures ever twirl.
Therefore, the secret of all righteous will
Is, not to shirk, but to do manfully
Thy Duty in accordance with God's Will.
The Prophet said, "The *worker* loveth God
And is beloved of God". O ! be not blind,
But see the true import of what he said.
Surrender thy whole being unto God,
But be not negligent of this great fact
That only duteous action proves thy faith,
And that effects are not produced sans cause.
Thy effort, as a cause, is in His Will.
Prove thy submission by thy righteous deeds ;
Thy duty, by a hair's-breadth e'en, shirk not.)[1]

---

[1]The ever-recurring question of Free-will *vs.* Destiny has been dealt with before, at pp. 183—186. No one believes in Destiny so completely and sincerely as to make no movement to lift the morsel from his plate to his mouth, and allow 'Destiny' to do so for him. Of course, in the metaphysical transcendental sense, from the standpoint of the Infinite, every movement of every atom, every experience, is predestined, ultimately ; but every human *effort* is included in this

Supreme is the Bliss of such Mergence of the small will into the Great Will, of such Dutiful surrender, such Humility.[1] When mutual mergence, and identification of life, being, interests, of spouse and spouse, in finite human marriage, are so blissful; infinitely greater must be, is, the Bliss of the mergence of the Finite and the Infinite; the Joy of the realisation that jīva is Brahma, *rūh* is *Rūh-ul-Rūh, Rūh-i-Ā'zam*, that Man is very God. The ecstatic joy of this realisation has been described in all religions. God is Love. Love is God. Mutual Devotion, Devotion of one to All, of All to each—this is the goal of the Path of Devotion.

Pūrṇ-ānanḍ-aika-rūpa-Rasa-boḍhah...
Raso vai sah...Sa ésha rasānām Rasa-ṭamah... kṛṭsno Rasa-ghana éva...
Āṭmanas-ṭu kāmāya sarvam vai priyam bhavaṭi.

'every movement'. From the empirical standpoint of the Limited, every human experience depends, immediately, upon, and is necessarily connected with, an *effort* of some sort, negative or positive; i.e., will-ful, or careless, or lazy *non*-exertion also is to be regarded as 'negative effort', as contra-exertion.

Purusha-kāra-pūrvakaṭvāṭ sarva-pravṛṭṭīnām, upāyah praṭyayah. (Vāṭsyāyana, *Kāma-sūṭra*, I. 1. 38.)

(All human movements and experiences are preceded by human effort; hence effortful means must be regarded as the cause of the results desired.)

[1] 'How ascertain the Great Will ?'—this question is dealt with at p. 81, *supra*.

Ānanḍam Brahmaṇo viḍvān
na bibhéṭi kuṭash-chana. (*U.*)
(One taste, sap, Savour of Life-Consciousness,
One relish, one full feel of Bliss compact—
He is the only Savour in the world,
He is the flavour-essence by which all
The savors of the world are flavoréd.
Whate'er is dear is Dear for sake of Self.
He who has known the Taste of that Great Bliss
Of gain of Self—he knoweth fear no more.)

Ye are the temple of God...Ye are the salt of the earth...If the salt lose its Savor, with what shall it be flavored ?...What shall it profit a man if he gain the whole world but lose his own soul ? (*B.*)

Rejoice in the Lord, always, and again I say,
Rejoice. (*B., Paul.*)

He saith: "I am the ground of thy beseeching." Wouldst thou learn thy Lord's meaning in this thing ? Learn it well: Love was His meaning. Who showed it thee ? Love. What showed He thee ? Love. Wherefore ? For love. (Mother JULIAN of Norwich, *Revelations of Divine Love.*)

Beloved, let us love one another; for love is
of God, and everyone that loveth is born of
God and knoweth God. He that loveth not,
knoweth not God. For God is Love. (*B.*)

Ma bāḍā héch ḍil bé ishq-bāzī,
Agar bāshaḍ haqīqī yā majāzī ;
Majāz āyīna-ḍār-é-rūy-e-mā'nī-sṭ,
Sar-é-īn jalwa ham ḍar kū-e-mānī-st. (*S.*)
(Be there no heart wholly devoid of love—
Be that love human or be it divine;
For human love too mirrors love divine;
The flame of this lights up the path to that.)

Better to have loved and lost
Than never to have loved at all.
Love wisely—that is best; for to do that
Is to love all the living things of God,
And to give each its due of loving justice;
But if thou canst not, then love foolishly;
'Tis better far than not to love at all.

A western writer has said well:

God is love in essence. Love is God in solution. In so much as we love we are in God and God is in us, and in so far as we do not love we are without God, in this world or any other. The Ideal Church of all religions and philosophies is the same. It is the union of all who love in the service of all who suffer.

The lower love, of the lower self, one's own little particular separative self, *khuḍī*, a h a m-k ā r a, desires to *take*; the higher love, of the larger Self, the Universal all-embracing Self of all, desires to *give*. "He wants my body; I want his soul." The conflict between Pleasure and Duty, P r é y a s and S h r é y a s, S v-ā r ṭ h a and P a r a m-ā r ṭ h a (*V.*), L ā b h a and N i b b ā n (*Bu.*), Ḍruj and Ashā (*Z.*), *Gḥarz* and *Farz* (*S.*), Heart and Head, selfishness and selflessness, Egoism and Altruism; this conflict is dissolved, and the antagonists are reconciled, only when *ego* and *alter* realise their identity, when every *alter*, 'other', becomes an *alter-ego*, the small self becomes the All-Self.[1] Then 'worthiness' and

[1] In western philosophy, Epicureanism is regarded, popularly, as the school of thought which holds that refined sensuous pleasure is the best aim of life; and Stoicism

'pleasurableness' become identical; Joy becomes Duty and Duty becomes Joy, Law becomes Love and Love becomes Law. The mother lives, in and for the baby; her altruistic tending of the baby, with utter disregard and sacrifice of her personal comfort, is the means of her own 'personal' comfort, of her very life. Such is the open paradox of love, Mother-love, God-love. The soul still lingering on the Path of Descent, P r a-v ṛ ṭ ṭ i, *Nazūl*, naturally clings to the smaller self; the soul which has turned the junction point, and crossed over to the Path of Ascent, *Urūj*, N i-v ṛ ṭ ṭ i, equally naturally clings to the Larger, the Infinite Self.

Ṭyāgén-aikén-āmṛṭaṭvam ānashuh. (*U.*)

---

as that which thinks that virtue alone brings happiness, and that the performance of duty, at the cost of whatever pain may be involved, is the highest end of life. The distinction commonly made between 'hedonism' and 'eudaimonism' is much the same. But, strictly, the difference between the views of Epicurus and Zeno, both Greeks, and contemporaries, (340-270 B.C.), was not at all so sharp. Thus Epicurus is reported as saying: "If thou wilt make a man happy, add not unto his riches, but take away from his desires", and "We cannot live a life of pleasure which is not also a life of prudence, honor, and justice; nor lead a life of prudence, honor, and justice, which is not also a life of pleasure": (Baldwin, *Dictionary of Philosophy*, art. 'Epicureanism'). This is sound Véḍānṭa and Vaiḍika Ḍharma also.

(They only can taste Immortality,
Who can eschew the taste of mortal joys.)
Ṭṛṣhṇā-kshaya-sukhasy-aiṭé
n-ārhaṭah shodashīm kalām. (*Bh.*)
(These earth's delights that thou hast listed out,
They weigh not e'en as much as one-sixteenth
Of the deep Joy of Ceasing of Desire.)
Na viṭṭéna ṭarpaṇīyo manushyo;
Lapsyāmahé viṭṭam aḍrākshma chét ṭvā;
Jīvishyāmo, yāvaḍ īshishyasi ṭvam;
Varas ṭu mé varaṇīyah sa éva. (*Katha U.*)
('Man lives not by material bread alone'.
No vastest wealth can satisfy the soul.
Death! while we see thee not, so long we live!
And, with the body, earthly goods all die.
The soul craves immortality, not wealth!)

But—the Ḍharma tells us, as the Bible does, that there is a time for everything, a time for duly regulated Desire, and a time for Desirelessness.[1]

Shréyash-cha Préyash-cha manushyam éṭah;
Ṭau sam-par-īṭya vi-vinakṭi ḍhīrah;
Shréyo hi ḍhīro abhi préyaso vṛṇīṭé,
Préyo manḍo yoga-kshémāḍ vṛṇīṭé. (*U.*)
(The Good comes unto Man; also the Pleasant.
Each asks to be accepted. The wise man,
Of steady and calm mind, compares the two,
Discerningly discriminates 'twixt them,
And chooses not the Pleasant but the Good.
The hapless child-mind chooses otherwise.)

Anyach-chhréyo anyaḍ-uṭ-aiva préyah...Āṭmā-yam jyéshthash-cha shréshthash-cha (préshthash-cha)..préyah puṭrāṭ, préyo viṭṭaḍ, préyo-(a)nyasmāṭ sarvasmāṭ. (*U.*)

---

[1]See p. 74, 75, *supra*.

(The Good is one ; the Pleasing is another...
But Self is both. It is the Greatest Good;
It is the Dearest and most Pleasing too;
And Ancient-most by far. It is more dear
Than riches, spouse, or child, or any thing.
Whate'er is dear is dear for sake of Self.)

Anyā hi lābh-opanishā,
Anyā nibbāna-gāminī. (*Dh.*)

(The way of worldly gain is one ; another,
The way that leadeth unto the Great Peace.)

It has been well said that "Every question of conduct, to be finally settled, must be carried up for decision to the court of the Supreme Mother". As the particular is to the Universal, the part to the Whole, so is each duty to Virtue in general. Each immediate end, purpose, aim of or in life, is more or less consciously subordinated to or connected with another beyond it; until, in the case of a consistent life, we finally trace them all up to the final aim. This aim, in all religions, is the finding of, and the merging into, the Supreme Self or God. In other words, each question is tied to some other question; that to another; until we come to the final question, 'Who am I, and What is This, and What is the Relation between I and This'. The answer to this answers all questions; including those relating to the reconciling of various particular duties with each other and with Virtue in general; and also those pertaining to the reconciling of the Pleasant in general and the Good in general.

The gain of one's own soul, recognition of

one's own and of all others' identity with the Universal Self, and the permanent *tasting* of that Divine Savour, is the goal of the Devotional aspect of the Tri-une Way called Religion.

Kulle shayīn hālikun juz wajh-i-Ū.
Gar ṭu-ī ḍar wajh-i-Ū, hasṭī ma jū,
Chūṅ na-ī ḍar wajh-i-Ū, hasṭī ma jū. (*S.*)
(All forms appear and pass. His Being lasts.
If thou art in that Being[1]—as thou art,
Since how else couldst thou say 'I am,' 'I am'—
Then thou art sure of deathless Being too,
And there is nothing more for thee to seek.
If part and parcel of Him thou be not,
Vain then thy search for Deathlessness would be.)

The joy of that Divine Union, the only and the final cure for all the world's sorrows, must be, and is, inevitably, unconsciously at first and consciously afterwards, striven for and achieved by all souls.

Bishkanaḍ ḍasṭé ke kḥam
ḍar garḍané yāré na shuḍ,
Kor beh chashmé ke lazzaṭ-gir ḍīḍāré na shuḍ. (*S.*)
(Be paralysed the arm that knows not Rest
In tender curve around the Loved One's waist;
Be blind the eyes that tasted ne'er the Bliss
Of the sweet Vision of the Loved One's face.)

---

[1] In theosophical phraseology, '*If* the fifth principle, Manas, has attached itself to the sixth, Buḍḍhi, which is inseparable from the seventh, Āṭmā'; in Véḍānṭa-language, 'If the individualised self, jīva, has attained the consciousness of being identical with the Universal Self, Brahma'.

Shakle-insāṅ meṅ chhipā Ṭū,
mujhe mā'lūm na ṭhā;
Chāṅḍ bāḍal meṅ chhipā thā,
mujhe mā'lum na ṭhā. (*S.*)
(I saw Thee not before—I see Thee now,
Belov'd! Thou peepest forth from every face!
I saw Thee not before—behind the clouds
Belovéd! Thou didst hide, I see Thee now!)

Ṭaḍ yaṭhā priyayā sṭriyā sam-pari-shvakṭah, na bāhyam kin-chana véḍa n-ānṭaram, taḍ vā asya éṭaḍ āpṭa-kāmam a-kāmam rūpam shok-ānṭaram. (*Bṛhaḍ U.*)

(As loving man and wife, when they embrace,
Are both dissolved in but one feel of Love,
One feel of Unity, and know naught else,
Outside their body or inside their mind;
E'en more, the Soul when it embraces God,
And feels its Unity with the All-Self,
Passes beyond all sorrow, all desire;
For all desire is now for e'er fulfilled.)
Yuvaṭīnām yaṭhā yūni,
Yūnām cha yuvaṭau yaṭhā,
Mano-(a)bhi-ramaṭé, ṭaḍ-van-
Mano mé ramaṭām Ṭvayi. (*Sṭoṭra.*)
(As maid delights in youth, and youth in maid,
So may my mind rejoice in Thee, my Lord!.)

If the soul is to go on to higher spiritual blessedness, it must become woman—yes, however manly you may be among men. (Cardinal NEWMAN.)

Let him kiss me with the kisses of his mouth. For Thy love is better than wine....Behold, Thou art fair, my Beloved, yea, pleasant...Also, our bed is green...His left hand is under my head, and His right hand doth embrace me. (*B.*, Song of Songs.)

Mīrā ké Prabhu gahira gambhīrā!
Ạḍhi-rāṭa Prabhu ḍarshana ḍéngé
Prema-naḍī ké ṭīrā!
Hirḍaya rākho ḍhīrā!
(Be patient, O my heart! for Mīra's Lord
Is very shy; He comes not till midnight;
Then will He show His Beauty unto Thee
On the steep bank of Love's deep-flowing stream!)

Upon an obscure night,
Fevered with Love's anxiety,
—O hapless happy plight!—
I went, none seeing me,
By night, secure from sight,
And by a secret stair, disguisedly.
Without a light to guide,
Save that which in my heart, burnt in my side.
That light did lead me on,
More surely than the shining of noon-tide,
Where, well I knew, that One
Did for my coming bide.
Upon my flowery breast,
Wholly for Him, and save Him-Self for none,
There did I give sweet rest
To my Belovéd One.
The fanning of the cedars breathed thereon,
All things I then forgot.
My cheek on His, who for my wooing came,
All ceased, and I was not,
Leaving my cares and shame
Among the lilies and forgetting them.

(ST. JOHN OF THE CROSS.)

A REMINDER. A reminder is needed here. Man's Duty is to obey God's Will, his own Inmost Self's Will. That Will is, (if the teachings of the

Scriptures, quoted before, and also of Science, be worthy of faith), that the soul should pass into Life Mortal, and then pass again through Death into the Life Immortal. Man can carry out this Will best, and attain to the *Summum Bonum*, the Greatest Good, Paramam Shréyas, *Khair-i-Mahz*, Nis-shreyasa, *Wājib-ul-Wujūḍ*, Supreme, Pure, Self-complete Being, *Surūr-i-Jāwéḍānī*, Immortal Happiness and Peace; by diligently and faithfully discharging the duties of the four successive natural stages of life, and by following some sub-variety of one of the four main classes of human professions, occupations, means of livelihood, during the second stage of life. Human beings pass through these stages everywhere, more or less, by inner compulsion as well as outer force of circumstances, but they have been deliberately systematised in Véḍism (i. e. Vaidika Dharma or Hinduism). Thus:

Ṛṇāni ṭrīṇy-apā-kṛṭya
    mano mokshé ni-véshayéṭ,
An-apā-kṛṭya ṭāny-éva
    moksham ichchhan vrajaṭy-aḍhah. (*M.*)
Āḍau vayasi n-āḍhīṭam,
    ḍviṭīyé n-ārjiṭam ḍhanam,
Ṭriṭīyé na ṭapas ṭapṭam,
    chaṭurṭhé kim karishyasi. (*Hiṭ-opaḍésha.*)

(The son of man, in being born, is born
With three great 'social debts' upon him; first,
The debt unto the ḍéva-angels, who
By God's command have made this Nature-World.
Of th' objects of the senses which he tastes;

The next to his Ancestors, who have given
His body to him wherewith he knows life;
The third is to the Sages who have stored
Knowledge, age after age, to light his mind.
By pious public works he pays the first;
By rearing virtuous progeny, the next;
By handing knowledge on, he pays the third;
He who, without repaying these great debts,
Strives to win Freedom
—stronger grow his bonds;
Instead of soaring height—deeper his fall.
If in the first part of thy life thou didst
Not gather precious knowledge virtuously;
Nor cherish spouse and child, nor earn fair means,
In the next quarter; nor perform good deeds
Of self-denial, charity, sacrifice,
In the third portion of thy mundane life;
How in the fourth, the age of feeble eld,
All unprepared, cans't find thy Self and God!)

Only the person who has honestly discharged these three congenital debts can be permitted to sell his body of earth, made thus into one of high worth, and buy therewith the Immortal Body of Ethereal Light.

Personal and Impersonal Devotion. The danger, of mistaking devotion to a person, for devotion to the Impersonal or All-personal, has been referred to before.[1] Yet the former is a

[1] See p. 348, *supra*. The language of prema, bhakṭi, *ishq-i-haqīqī*, love of and devotion to God, is so similar to the erotic utterances of kāma, *ishq-i-majāzī*, carnal love of and devotion to a person of the opposite sex, that the two become practically

necessary stage on the progress to the latter. The final perfection of devotion, as Love Universal, has to be preceded, in the evolution of the soul, by the love personal.

---

indistinguishable ; see, f.i., the passages quoted at pp. 39, 227, 231-234, 256-259, 262-263, 387-389, *supra.* In conduct also, since it is easier to roll down than to climb up, *facilis descensus averni*, in the case of even the most sincere and earnest cultivators of 'spiritual' love, it only too often runs into the 'carnal'. The past history, and the reports of the current doings, of many 'religious' orders and cults, (—and new ones keep cropping up all over the world—), especially of some of the b h a k ṭ i-cults and so-called *sūfī*-sects of India, are proof. Of course, besides the sincere aspirants who go astray, or are cruelly deceived, there are many groups composed of 'faith-giving fools' who *wish* to be gulled and fleeced and debauched, and of 'faith-demanding knaves' who pose as 'spiritual guides, preceptors, mentors', and *will* to dupe and rob and corrupt, under cover of 'religion'. Or, why go outside for warning knowledge ? Everyone can, indeed, find enough evidence of the danger, if he will only look into his own heart. We have noted (p. 321, *supra*) that the seeds of all the vices and all the virtues, all the angels and all the devils, are ever present in every human heart ; the set which *prevails*, makes the 'character' of the person, makes him good man or bad man, sinner or saint. There are only two poles to the human axis, the cerebro-spinal column ; the soul has only two courses open ; to travel laboriously towards the upper pole, the B r a h m a - r a n ḍ h r a the pituitary and the pineal glands, k a n ḍ a - s,

This personal love has many grades and degrees, according as it gives more and more of service, and takes less and less of return. The human being begins as a baby, with intensely

---

c h a k r a - s, and regain the lost Paradise ; or to slide easily down towards the lower pole and the sexual plexuses. Each half of the pole has its own 'branchings' and 'complexes', and the two sets often mix. When the soul makes an effort to ascend, but fails to gain assured foothold, and slips, it takes down with it a higher quality of mentality, a refinement, which makes sensuous enjoyments keener and more alluring. A western writer has observed well that there is no voluptuousness like to mystic voluptuousness. The 'religious' and 'mystical' experiences of many 'brides of Christ', 'milkmaids of Kṛshna', '*shaiḍās* of Muhammaḍ', and devoted disciples of g u r u - s, *pīr-s*, *murshiḍs*, *sheikhs*', etc. become but too often experiences of carnal voluptuousness ; some of the worst perversions take place under cover of Vāma-Shakṭi-pūjā, in the East and the Black Mass in the west. Love, attempted to be transferred from the physical to the superphysical, too frequently falls back to the physical plane with added momentum. What the psycho-analysts call 'transference', is partial illustration of the same fact. The emotions that should flow towards the physical spouse, or the superphysical ideal, begin to flow towards the physical psycho-analyser, or the physical g u r u, *pīr*, priestly 'mediator', 'father-confessor', 'spiritual guide'.

The finer superphysical love, so long as it does not become wholly (i. e., predominantly) transmuted from 'psychical' into 'Spiritual', experiences all the

selfish love for the mother, and ends as a parent, with selfless love for children. Especially selfless is the love of the mother, all-giving, all-for-

---

transports, agonies, ecstasies, elations, depressions, deadly jealousies, humble reconciliations, bitter wrongs, generous forgivings, shames, restorations of trust, in short, all the infinite shades of all sorts of passions and emotions that form the turbulent retinue of the common carnal love. Only, in the case of the 'psychical' love, they are all of correspondingly subtler quality; at least they ought to be; though they often are not; as witness the violent, even murderous feuds, caused by jealousy, between even the immediate disciples and followers of even every Founder or Reformer of Religion. In fact, Jealousy and Love are very closely connected; They are the two end-links of the chain of the six main passions, (see p. 318, *supra*). Jealousy is, in a sense, the very culmination of the 'miseries'. It includes all the other five. It is responsible for the greatest, most extensive, failures of humanity; failures with the most wide-reaching consequences, and on the largest scales; as in politics. The gates of besieged towns and forts have often been opened to the foe by jealousy. Battles, which have changed the course of history, have often been lost through treachery born of jealousy. Great causes have been betrayed by jealousy. The word 'envy' or 'jealousy', occurs on almost every page of Plutarchs' *Lives*; the name of no other human emotion occurs so often.

Kāma, in the broad general sense of Desire, is the very root-cause of the Universe; and we have seen that Sex-kāma is the climax of Desire, though it is not its fundamental form.

giving. The mother is nourishing Mercy incarnate; the father protective and instructive Justice. She represents the *jamāli* aspect, the m ā ḍ h u r y a, ḍ a y ā, k a r u ṇ ā, ḍ h ā ṭ ā, k a l y ā ṇ a attributes, the Beauty and Sweet Tenderness, of

---

Kāmas-ṭaḍ-agré sam-avarṭaṭ-āḍhi
Manaso réṭah praṭhamam yaḍ-āsīṭ;
Saṭo banḍhum asaṭi nir-avinḍan
Hṛḍi praṭishyā kavayo manīshā.
(*Ṛg-V.*, 10. 29. 4.)
Kāmah Sanāṭana-ṭamo-(a)bhavaṭ.
(*Mbh.*, Anu. ch. 131.)
Jyāyān samuḍrāḍ-asi Kāma Manyo.
(*Aṭharva-V.*, ix. 2. 2. 3.)
Samuḍra iva hi Kāmah.
(*Taiṭ. Brāh.*, II. 2. 5. 6.)
Kāma-banḍhanam-év-éḍam,
N-ānyaḍ-asṭ-īha banḍhanam. (*Ibid.*, 8. 9. 5.)
Kāma-maya év-āyam purushah.
(*Bṛ.-U.*, 4. 4. 5.)
Saṭyam pushpa-phalam viḍyāḍ
Añ-ṛtam mūlam Āṭmanah. (*Bh.*)
(Kāma arose the first, foremost of beings,
Preceding and presiding over all.
It was the germ of Mind. The wise ones saw,
Deep searching in the heart with all their mind,
Its Falsehood was half-brother unto Truth.
Kam'-Error is manure; Truth, flower and fruit.
Kāma is the most ancient of all ancients,
More deep, far-spread, than seas or Space itself.
The bonds of Kāma are the only bonds
That bind the Soul of man; indeed the soul
Is naught else than a vortex made of Kāma.)

When such is the very constitution of God's own

God; he, the *jalālī* aspect, the aishvarya, prabhu-ṭva, pra-ṭāpa, ni-yanṭā, vi-dhāṭā attributes, His Awe-inspiring and Compelling Order-liness. She embodies the ministrant

---

Nature, it is obviously not possible for any one to avoid all risks of falling back, even while treading most carefully and assiduously, the Path of Ascent. We have noted that each and every soul must, by metaphysical law, because it is identical with the All-Soul, pass through *all* experiences in Infinite Time and Space and Motion. Failure, falling back, striving again, and rising again, higher and higher, is part of such total of Experience; in fact, a very common part, in all departments and phases of life. But it is possible, and right and proper, for persons who have arrived at a certain stage of evolution, to be on guard, to the best of their ability, against slipping back from the upper half to the lower half of the pole. In such guarding, a thorough grasp of the nature and varieties of the emotions is of great help; for, obviously, the guarding is self-guarding, against the baser Emotions, and by means of perpetual self-examination, sva—chiṭṭa—parīkshā, *Khuḍ-hisābī*, constant awareness of what is going on within one's own mind.

In the Samskṛṭ literature of Vėḍism are included systematic expositions of *Bhakṭi-shāsṭra*, 'The Science and Art of Divine Love'. The ends of human life are, primarily, two, Kāma or Vishay-ānanḍa, Sense-Enjoyment, and Moksha or Brahm-ānanḍa, Spiritual Bliss. But refined Kāma, through Marriage and Family-life, is not possible without Arṭha, Property, and that is not possible without Ḍharma, Law-Religion. Hence the one end, Kāma, becomes triple,

and promotive functions of the State; he, the constituent and preventive. But human maternal devotion to children, though so sweetly selfless, is generally exclusive, limited to one's own children. It seldom extends to even the nearest neighbour's families. But God's Family is the Whole Universe.

As in the life of the family, so in the larger life, which includes the life beyond this life and also the life of the community, society, nation, humanity, and even the other kingdoms of nature,

---

Ḍharma—Arṭha—Kāma. So Moksha also becomes triple, Bhakṭi—Yoga—Moksha. Each of these becomes the subject of a Shāsṭra, a science; and has text-books devoted to it. The works on Bhakṭi-shāstra contain much helpful information on the subject of the emotions and their sublimation. A noteworthy feature is that they distinguish many forms which are expressed in language very different from the erotic: thus, the love of the servant devoted to his master, as of Hanumān for Rāma; of friend devoted to friend, as of Arjuna for Kṛshṇa; of parents devoted to child, as of Dasha-raṭha and Kausalyā for Rāma, of Mary for Jesus, of Fāṭimā for Hasan and Husain; and of children for parents. This last is the safest form, of Devotion to God, for human beings to cultivate. Nature prompts us to regard God and His Nature as our Father and Mother. All religions instruct us also to the same effect. In the cultivation of this Spiritual Emotion, there is least danger of going astray. Yet it too is not *wholly* safe! There *is* the danger of becoming *too* dependent, of wanting and begging too much, of shirking self-reliant exertion.

the soul passes through stages. The guru, āchārya, Brahma-viṭ, *murshiḍ, shéikḥ*, *pīr*, *ā'rif*, *Haq-shinās*, priest, saint, spiritual preceptor, godly counsellor, 'knower of God', is the father-mother here. If he or she is the physical parent also, the relationship is best and safest. But it is difficult for all parents to discharge the sacred and delicate function of spiritual guide too. Therefore all religions have evolved and differentiated out a class of such. But very evil consequences have arisen, after certain limits. Such is the way of Nature. She follows a Law of perpetual Swing, from Extreme to opposite Extreme, back and forth. Vaiḍika Ḍharma, by express provision in its Social Organisation, includes the vocation of priests as that of a sub-class under the general class of those following 'the learned professions'. This general class, it is enjoined, should be made up of persons who are by *temperament*, 'men of viḍyā and ṭapas, *irfān* and *zohḍ*, men of *knowledge and* of *philanthropic virtue* and *self-denial.*[1] But spiritual preceptorship of

[1] Véḍic 'priesthood' is not organised into a Church and a Hierarchy (—unless, perhaps, in a very loose sense, by simply *popular* recognition of greater or lesser learning or other merit—) as it is in the case of Buḍḍhism, western State-Churches, Roman Catholicism. Strict organisation of a priesthood, necessarily imparts to it, the faults (together with the merits) of 'bureaucracy' and 'mechanisation'. These faults are peculiarly incongruous with the intimate, personal, un-'official', confidential, loving, spiritual relations, which ought to

the children by the parent in each family is also encouraged. Buḍḍhism, Jainism, Christianity, Islām, beginning with missionary *bhikshus*, *shramaṇas*, *kshapaṇas*, *yaṭis*, apostles, disciples, *asahāb*, companions, *momins*, faithful ones, *imāms*, *kḥalīfās*, etc., have also (—even despite some efforts in some cases, especially in Islām, to avoid it—) inevitably developed very potent priesthoods. Such are very good, very self-denying, very helpful in the beginning; but they always degenerate (as do 'kinghoods'), pass over to the opposite extreme, and develope tendencies to demoniac treachery; so that the shepherd and the sheep-dog devour the sheep which they are set to guard from all harm. History may be said to be largely the history of the martyrdom of humanity at the hands of its trustees, its 'mother' and 'father', its priests and its rulers, its 'edu-

---

subsist between 'minister' and 'ministered', 'pastor' and 'flock'. Organised bodies, it is well-known, can do more good than individuals; but, if the spirit becomes perverted, can become far worse tyrants than individuals. In Véḍism, the practice has been for each family to choose its own priest or rather priest-family. That system has also its disadvantages as well as merits. It is always the old story of 'the mean between extremes'; *some* organisation and also *some* individual freedom; neither rigidity nor looseness, but elasticity. And, do what we may, we cannot escape evil, altogether, until we give up good also. Life is a perpetual choice between evils. Wisdom consists in choosing the lesser, in any given circumstances.

cators' and its 'protectors', its 'spiritual power' and its 'temporal power'.

Yasy-ānké shira-āḍhāya
janah svapiṭi nir-bhayah,
Sa éva ṭach-chhirash-chhinḍyāṭ,
taṭṭra kam pari-ḍévayéṭ. (*Mbh.*)

Sarvam ṭam par-āḍāḍ-yah Āṭmano-anyaṭra brahma...kshaṭṭram...lokān...ḍévān....bhuṭāni....sarvam véḍa. (*Br. U.*)

(The child goes trustfully to sleep, with head
Upon the parent's knee ; if that same parent
Cuts off the head, and murders his own child,
How and to whom may the slain child complain ?
Whoever placed his faith without reserve,
Not on him-Self, but some one Else-than-Self,
Brāhmaṇa, Kshaṭṭriya, Vaishya, or god,
Or other living or non-living thing,
Whate'er he made himself *dependent* on,
That thing or person did give him away,
And did betray that purblind trust, some day.)

If the spiritual guides and the temporal protectors of the people themselves betray their trust, and prey upon the people, who can redress that awful wrong ? The only answer is : The People themselves, under Divine impulsion from within, specially focussed in new great leaders.

Ai basā Iblīs Āḍam-rūy asṭ,
Pas ba har ḍasṭé na bāyaḍ ḍāḍ ḍasṭ. (*S.*)
(Many a fiend doth wear the human shape ;
Give not the hand of trust to every hand.)

Guravo bahavas-tāṭa !, shishya-viṭṭ-āpa-hārakāh ;
Viralā guravas-ṭé yé shishya-san-ṭāpa-hārakāh.
(*Guru Giṭā.*)

(Many the guides who take away full soon
The pupil's goods, but very few, alas!
Those that can take away his ache of heart.)

The Scriptures themselves warn us against false priests and false prophets. Manu says:

Pāshandino vi-karma-sṭhān
baidāla-vraṭikān shathān,
Haiṭukān baka-vṛṭṭīmsh-cha
vāng-māṭréṇ-āpi n-ārchayéṭ.
Na vāry-api pra-yachchéṭ ṭu
baidāla-vraṭiké ḍvi-jé,
Na baka-vraṭiké vipré
n-ā-véḍa-viḍi ḍharma-viṭ.
Yé baka-vraṭino vīprāh
yé cha mārjāra-linginah,
Ṭé paṭanṭy-anḍha-ṭāmisré,
(kṛṭvā) sṭrī-shuḍra-dambhanaṃ.
(*M*., iv. 30, 190-200.)

(Priest-hypocrites, immoral, evil-living,
That purr, and pry, and pounce on prey cat-like;
That argue much; or pose with downcast eyes,
Looking devout, calm, modest, like to herons,
But ever watchful snapping up like lightning,
Any unwary fish that may pass by—
Avoid such; do not even speak to them.
Not even water should be given to such
By him who Duty knows, and right from wrong.
Such vicious priests, who ever do deceive
The ignorant and simple men and women,
Will surely fall into the darkest hells,
Created by their own conscience for them,
And suffer there until they change their heart.)[1]

[1]There is a current notion that *Manu-smṛṭi*, the chief religious law-book of Véḍism, held in reverence

Muhammad warns his followers against impostors:

Yakṭobuna ba ayḍihim wa yakūluna hāzā min inḍ-Illāh, wa mā howā min inḍ-Illāh. (*Q.*)

(With their own hands they write, and yet pretend,
And tell you falsely—This is writ by God.
Indeed it is not writ by God at all.)

Believe not every spirit, but try the spirits, whether they are of God, because many false prophets are gone out into the world. (*B.*, John.)

Beware of false prophets, which come to you in

---

next only to the Vēḍas, has been written by brāhmaṇas for brāhmaṇas, and therefore praises them inordinately, and gives them supreme authority in every respect. Such a notion is based on insufficient and prejudiced study of the original, and on observation of the current absurd claims and evil behavior of priests. An impartial study of the whole book, (though it probably, almost certainly, has some spurious interpolations, as now available), shows that the ancient Law-giver has based his Scheme of Civilisation on the triple foundation of (1) the spiritual-hearted self-denying Educator (the true brāhmaṇa), (2) the chivalrous self-sacrificing Protector and Defender (the true kshaṭṭriya); and above all, (3) the selfless Mother (the true woman; see pp. 288-292, *supra*). These three, when they strenuously live up to the ideal he places before them, he praises to the skies, he ranks above all the gods. But when they fall from that ideal, and become corrupt, then he condemns them down to the deepest hells. Which careful student of human history is prepared to say that genuine civilisation, anywhere and anywhen, has flourished where these three have been corrupt; or has not flourished, where these three have done their duty?

sheep's clothing, but inwardly they are ravening wolves. Ye shall know them by their fruits. (*B.*)

...Take heed that no man deceive you: for many shall come in My name, saying, I am Christ; and shall deceive many ..Then if any man shall say unto you, Lo, here is Christ, or there, believe it not. For there shall arise false Christs, and false prophets, and... they shall deceive the very elect....The scribes and the Pharisees sit in Moses' seat...All their works they do for to be seen of men; they make broad their phylacteries, and enlarge the borders of their garments, and love...the chief seats...and greetings, in the markets, and to be called of men, Rabbi, Rabbi...But woe unto you, scribes and Pharisees, hypocrites! for ye devour widows' houses, and for a pretence make long prayer...ye are like whited sepulchres, which indeed appear beautiful outward, but are within full of dead men's bones and of all uncleanness. Even so ye also outwardly appear righteous unto men, but within ye are full of hypocrisy and iniquity.

(*B.*, Matthew, chs. 7, 23, 24).

Such evil priests and kings must be thrust away, and replaced by virtuous ones, by the people themselves[1], under the direction of trustworthy leaders of ascetic philanthropic quality,

---

[1] *Manu*, chs. 4, 7, and *Mbh.*, Shānṭi-parva, chs. 90, 91, 92, say: "The tears of the weak consume the deceiver and oppressor more surely, at last, than the hottest fires. Power, entrusted to the ruler, for the general good, if misused, turns against him, and destroys him root and branch. The priest-scientist, who takes gifts from such a vicious ruler, instead of restraining him, falls into many hells together with that ruler.

and eminent in knowledge. The scriptures enjoin upon the People to do so; and history shows how this has been done, over and over again.

Experience of such awful treacherousness has its own uses, necessarily, in the providence of God's Nature. The soul of the victim receives a terrible shock which transforms it. Its own latent selfishness is exposed to itself; it desired worldly advantages too much, and not spiritual gains also sufficiently, and had made itself small, mean, petty, pitiable, pitiful, k ṛ p a ṇ a; it is now thrown back upon its Higher Self, by a violent revulsion; it plumbs far depths and touches unknown heights, (which heights and depths are all within its own infinite consciousness in fact), at a bound; it gains the true humility; also the appurtenant courage and power, (for true humility becomes the same as true majesty, since it regards all selves as equal, spiritually, and not itself as smaller than all others); and then it attains freedom, sooner or later, from spiritual as well as all other enthralment to others, to an-Other, to any Other.

We have seen before[1] that every one is himself, ultimately, the sole judge over all religions and all preceptors, since he can accept or reject any he likes. After all, who is to decide between the 'true prophets' and the 'false prophets', the 'true Christs' and the 'false Christs',

[1] See pp. 56-59, 162, *supra*.

the 'true g u r u - s', and the 'false g u r u - s', the 'mediators to God' and the 'mediators to Satan'? Only he can decide, and ultimately *has* to decide—he, the man in the street, to whom these prophets and Christs and g u r u s and mediators say: 'Accept me', 'accept me'. He alone can judge, for him-Self, by him-Self, which of these is true, which false. The miseries brought by excessive faith in any, arouse this almighty, but till now sleeping, Self within him, and he realises vividly the truth of the scriptural declaration:

Yah Āṭmano-anyaṭra brahma vā, kshaṭṭram vā, lokān vā, ḍévān vā, bhūṭāni vā, sarvam va, véḍa, ṭam sarvam par-āḍāṭ; brahma, kshaṭṭram, lokāh, ḍévāh, bhūṭāni, iḍam sarvam yaḍ ayam Āṭmā. (*U.*)

(Whoever made himself dependent, blind,
Utter and slavish, upon anything,
Regarding it as *other* than him-Self—
Outside and independent of him-Self—
Priests, rulers, worlds, gods, living or dead things,
Any, or all;—that *other* will deceive,
Betray, and ruin him, until he learns,
That all these are *within* him-Self, the Self,
And knows him-Self as Master of them all.)

The conscience, the higher soul, of the betrayer also unavoidably awakens some day; he too undergoes revulsion of feeling, and helplessly makes expiation by equal suffering, and also learns the same humility.

Very cruel, as well as very beautiful, is this process; all this World-process. Faith, Trust, Love, is very beautiful; Deception, Betrayal, Murder of Innocents, is horribly cruel. But the

God within, has Him-Self chosen to pass through all experiences, before returning to the Primal Peace.

Anéka-janma-sam-siḍḍhas-
ṭaṭo yāṭī parām gaṭim. (*G.*)

(After the tasting of full many lives—
Of pleasures, pains, joys, utter miseries—
The Soul regains its Fullness, and returns
Unto the state of Perfect Wholeness, lost
By Its Self-willed wilful Obliviscence—
Transforméd into Reminiscence now.)

Inna Ilaihā rāje'ūn...laṭarkabunna ṭabaqan an ṭabaq. (*Q.*)

(Back unto God, ascending stage by stage,
Must ye return with labor and with pain.)

Ordinarily, the soul developes slowly the purer aspect of family relationships and affections, and the accompanying self-denial, *ishq-i-majāzī*, *muhabbaṭ*, *īsār*, préma, priṭi, anu-rāga, ṭyāga. It also cultivates, side by side with these, love of, faith in, and reliance for refuge upon, a living spiritual preceptor, and also a higher unseen *barzakḥ* or 'mediator', a messiah, a *nabī* or prophet, a *rasūl* or messenger of God, an avaṭāra, or incarnation of divine power, an *insān-ul-kāmil*, perfect man, an ishṭa-ḍéva or beloved form of deity represented by high ḍéva or angel, that manifests one *ism*, nāma, name, aspect, i. e., power or energy, of God—all which are facts in Nature. Through such mediator it seeks to reach God—whatever the highest conception, (generally that of a Personal God, separate from the devotee and from all creation), which the devotee concerned may be able to form.

And these mediators[1], in every religion, are indeed very near and dear to God:

> Khās-ān-e Khuḍā Khuḍā na bāshanḍ,
> Lékin ze Khuḍā juḍā na bāshanḍ. (*S.*)
> (The devotees of God may not be God,
> Yet neither are they separate from God.)
> Ḍāsānām anu-ḍāso-(A)ham. (*Bh.*)
> (I serve My servants—thus declareth God.)

He that believeth on Me, the works that I do shall he do also, and greater works than these shall he do; because I go unto my Father. And whatsoever ye shall ask in my name, that will I do, that the Father may be glorified in the Son. If ye ask anything in my name, I shall do it....This is my commandment, that ye love one another as I have loved you. Greater love hath no man than this that a man lay down his life for his friends....Ye are my friends if ye do whatsoever I command you. Henceforth I call you not servants; for the servant knoweth not what his lord doth; but I have called you friends. (*B.*)

---

[1] The distinction between mediators and mediums should be understood clearly. (See H. P. Blavatsky, *Isis Unveiled*, pp. 487—488). It is, possible for persons of each of the two types to be either beneficent or maleficent; but, usually, mediators are spiritual adepts, holy persons, pure in thought and deed, and strong of will, the superhuman morality and sanctity of whose lives (whatever their outer creed) attracts pure, beneficent, high, and powerful spiritual influences to them, for the helping of human beings. Mediums, on the contrary, are spiritual or rather psychical slaves, weak

So long as the soul is not able to get over the sense of personality, personal sin, weakness, danger; so long as it clings to a separate body of its own and desires to continue a separate individual existence; so long it must tie itself to some such highly advanced soul, embodiment of spirituality, in-carna-tion of the Spirit; even as children must seek the protecting help of parents, until they attain maturity; and it must evoke such help by its own loving reverence and earnest cry for it in the way of whole-souled prayer.

After the vision, the realisation in oneself, of the Impersonal has been reached, through such very help; after that, the love and reverence for the spiritual preceptor and the mediator, ought to, and do, become deeper than ever. and a profound gratitude is added to them, in every truly illumined soul; even as the right-minded son and daughter, nourished and fostered tenderly, by parents, until they have reached majority of body and mind, feel, if possible, greater love and reverence and gratitude than they did, or even could, for those parents, while they were little children.

Herein is large part of the satisfaction of the requirements of personal emotion, of the

---

of will, sickly of nervous system, unable to resist evil influences; more often than not they are taken possession of, obsessed, by evil spirits, either disembodied human spirits, or nature spirits, i. e. 'sprites', which normally belong to other planes and kinds of matter than humans do.

needs of the heart, that religion is expected to, and does, bring to all sincere souls. Clearly, there is no conflict here between head and heart; but much soothing, nay, very joyful, harmony instead.

If the followers of different religions quarrel with one another—one saying that Kṛshṇa is the *only* personage who should be followed and honored, another that Zoroaster is the *only* such, a third that Moses, a fourth that Buḍḍha, a fifth that Jina, a sixth that Christ, a seventh that Muhammad, is the *only* such, then the plain cause is that they are not sincere devotees but arrant egoists; that none of them really honors and follows the great Master whom he pretends to honor and follow; but that each really loves his own narrow and conceited *little* self; and wishes to impose that little self and its small-minded opinions upon all the world; for the satisfaction of his own vanity, and the tasting of a false greatness, under cover of the true greatness of the Master; which true greatness he only belittles and drags in the mire by his own false understanding of it. But they will all grow wiser, bye and bye, turn by turn, each in his own due time.[1]

On the other hnad, in the name, for the sake, by the example, of each great Master, have men, and women, and even little children, over and over again, throughout history, risen, and

[1]See pp. 68-73, *supra.*

are rising today, here and there, to great heights of self-denial and self-sacrifice, of uttermost suffering and death for love of fellow beings, of heroic martyrdom to bear witness to their faith; heights of heroism, dharma-shūraṭā, *shahā-ḍaṭ*, which may well evoke envy and shame, and greater sweetness than before, in the breasts of even the angels.

Because I naturally love and honor my own parents beyond the parents of others, is that a reason why I should insist that others should also love and honor my parents beyond, or instead of, their own? If I am at all right-minded, and not insane, I should be the first to say to my neighbour: Even as I revere my parents most, so should you yours; but, as I regard and love you as my cousin, so I shall, next after my parents, revere your parents as the cousins or brother and sister of my parents, and therefore as my uncle and aunt; and even so should you revere my parents as your uncle and aunt. Your parents have done for you what mine have done for me. They have washed you of soiling vices, fed you with the milk and bread of life, tended you day and night, guarded you from the dangers and illnesses of sin, taught you anxiously the same soul-wisdom, and brought you to majority of years and maturity of body and mind, so that you can now stand upon your own feet, and even help and care for others, even as you have been helped and cared for. Your first duty, therefore, is to your parents, even as mine is to mine.

Also, the Teachers themselves advise us, nay, command us, to think, not of them, but of the teachings:

Unzur elā mā qāla, wa lā ṭanzur elā man qāla.
(Hazraṭ ALI.)
(See *what* is said; do not see *who* says it.)
Khuz mā safā, ḍā mā kaḍar. (*H.*)
(Gather the good, and cast aside the bad.)

Yukṭi-yukṭam up-ā-ḍéyam
vachanam bālakāḍ-api;
Anyaṭ ṭṛṇam iva ṭyājyam
apy-ukṭam Paḍma-janmanā.
(*Yoga-Vāsishtha.*)
A-miṭrāḍ-api saḍ-vṛṭṭam
bālāḍ-api su-bhāshiṭam. (*M.*)

(What stands to reason, take it readily,
If uttered even by a little child;
That which offends the reason, put aside,
Though it be said to be part of God-spell.)

Jagaḍ-éva gurur-Jagaḍ-guruh. (Skt. proverb.)
Az zamāna moaḍḍibu. (*H.*)
(The one World-Teacher is the World itself.
Take needed lessons from the March of Time.)

If the followers of the several religions, (or rather of the re-proclaimers, of the same One Universal Religion, in different languages and times and climes), were only thus loving, simple, straight of heart, only a little reasonable; they would fill their own homes and all other homes of the whole world with loving paeans of joy, and with mutual service and the real blessings of religion; instead of filling them, as they have been doing, century after century, with the cruel cries of hate and war, bloodshed and torture, and turning religion from the greatest blessing into the worst curse of mankind.

The soul which has learnt the true humility, cannot behold these conflicts without the greatest agony of heart. Its only consolation is the faith that they also must serve the ultimate purpose of the World-Drama, planned and operated by the Divine Will-and-Imagination. The worst and most saddening feature of these terrible conflicts is that they are all about the merest words and names, utterly non-essential forms and superficial trivialities. If instead of hastily and excitedly 'misunderstanding', men would only endeavour quietly and leisurely to 'understand', each other, then they surely would, instead of hating, honor the founders of other religions, even though in a lesser degree than the founder of their own, and would *multiply* their joy, by giving and receiving sympathy and con-gratulations, on all appropriate occasions, of the holy-days of each religion, instead of *marring* it wholly, by mutual antipathy and obstructions, and even riots, looting, arson, bloodshed, murders.[1]

[1] A western clergyman, Dr Westcott, has well said: "It requires a serious effort to enter with a living sympathy into the character of another man, or of another class, or of another course of thought; to feel, not with a sense of gracious superiority, but of devout thankfulness, that, here and there, that is supplied which we could not have provided; to acknowledge how peculiar gifts or a peculiar environment, how long

To the soul which has seen the great Vision of Self-in-All and All-in-Self, *meum* and *tuum* are reduced to a minimum, if they cannot vanish altogether while fleshly tenement lasts. Religions, in the plural, disappear for him; only Religion, in the singular, remains.

Guft̤-o-gū-e Kufr o Ḍīn
ākḥir ba yak jā mī kashaḍ;
Kḥwāb yak kḥwābé-st̤, ammā
mukḥt̤alif tā'bīr-hā. (*S.*)

(Doubt. Faith, both turn around, and end in, One
Th' interpreters differ, the Dream's the same.).

Hama kas t̤ālib-e Yār anḍ
che hushyār o che mast̤,
Hama jā kḥāna-e ishq ast̤,
che masjiḍ che kanisht̤. (*S.*)

(Sane and insane, all are asearch, love-lorn,
For Him, in mosque, fire-temple, church, alike.
The only God is the One God of Love,
And Love calls from all these, each one *His* home.)

---

discipline or intense struggle, have conferred upon others the power of seeing that which we cannot see". If the ways of education were different, i. e better, there would be no serious effort required for this very desirable attitude. It would be the natural thing to appreciate the good points of others, instead of depreciating.

Right education, if any god at all, is

"The god which can the giftie give us
To see ourselves as others see us."

If we all were diligently taught, in our earliest years to see with other's eyes as well as our own, we would see much more, and our life would be so much the richer, with others' special and peculiar virtues and experiences and gifts as well as our own.

Yé-py-anya-ḍevaṭā-bhakṭāh
yajanṭé shraḍḍhay-ān-viṭāh,
Ṭé-pi Mām-éva Kaunṭéya !,
yajanṭy-a-viḍhi-pūrvakam.
Yé yaṭhā Mām pra-paḍyanṭé
ṭāns-ṭaṭh-aiva bhajāmy-Aham
Mama varṭm-ānu-varṭanṭé
manushyāh, Pārṭha ! sarvashah. (*G.*)

(They who do worship other gods with faith,
They also indirectly worship Me.
From all sides are men coming unto Me;
I meet them on whichever way they come.)

Ṭrai-guṇya-vishayā Véḍā,
nis-ṭrai-guṇyō bhav-Ārjuna ! (*G.*)
Nis-ṭrai-guṇyé paṭhi vicharato
ko viḍhih ko ni-shéḍhah.
Na varṇā na varṇ-āshram-āchāra-ḍharmā,
Na Mé ḍhāraṇā-ḍhyāna-yōg-āḍay-opi,
Na ḍuhkham sukham n-aiva banḍho na mokshas-
Ṭaḍ-éko-vashishtah Shivah kévalo-(A)ham.
(SHANKAR-ĀCHĀRYA).

(The Veḍic ritual deals with finite things,
Objects of finite thoughts, desires, and acts.
Pass on beyond these three unto the One.
He who has passed beyond the three and seen
The One, and steadfast moves upon Its Way,
He no more needs from others 'yeas' and 'nays';
He has become a law unto him-Self.
No caste, class, creed, or stage of life are Mine,
No concentration, meditation, yog',
No sorrow, joy, bonds or deliverance;
I am the Restful One and all is Mine!)

Gufṭam-Ash, "Ṭā chanḍ ḍar
parḍah nihāṅ kḥwāhī shuḍan,

Waqṭ āṅ āmaḍ ke ḍīgar rū na poshānī ze man!"
Gufṭ, "Man bé-parḍah am,
gar parḍah bīnī, āṅ ṭu-ī!
Ṭa ṭu hasṭī, ḍar hazārāṅ parḍah pinhān-ī ze Mā!"
(MUINUḌḌIN CHISHṬĪ).

("For how much longer", so I asked my Lord,
My Lover and Belovéd, My heart's God,
"For how much longer wilt Thou keep Thy Face
Close hid behind this screen? Sure, it is time
That Thou unveil Thyself to Thy slave's eyes!"
He said, "*I* ever *am, without* a *screen*!
Seest a screen? Then that screen is thy-self,
Thy separative and egoistic Self!
While *thou art*, fixed in sense of separateness,
Countless as living bodies are the veils
Thou flingest o'er Me, keeping Me unseen!
Thy separatist small self itself is screen!
My-Self is by the self-less ever seen!)

Che ṭaḍbīr, ai Musalmānāṅ!,
Ke man khuḍ rā na mīṅ ḍānam;
Na Ṭarsā na Yahūḍī am
Na Gabr am na Musalmān am.
(SHAMS ṬABREZ.)

Sūfī shuḍ n-īsṭ, n-īsṭ rā mazhab n-īsṭ;
Bā Yār rasīḍa rā ḍigar maṭlab n-īsṭ.

Rab-ras Rab shuḍ; ṭamām Rab rā Rab n-īsṭ.
Har jā khurshéḍ hasṭ āṅ jā shab n-īsṭ. (*S.*)
Shauq hai jab ṭak pasé parḍah jamālé Yār hai,
Hat gayā parḍa ṭo phir ḍīḍār hī ḍīḍār hai. (*S.*)

Haḍīse muṭrib o mai go,
Wa rāze ḍahr kam-ṭar jo,
Ke kas na kushūḍ o na kushāyaḍ
Ba hikmaṭ īṅ moammā rā. (*S.*)

Asrār-i-azal rā na ṭū ḍānī wa na man,
Īn harf-i-moammā na ṭū khwānī wa na man,
Hasṭ az pas-e parḍah gufṭ-o-gū-e man o ṭū,
Chūn parḍah bi-yufṭaḍ, na ṭū mānī wa na man.
(*S.*)

(What can I do, friends !, I know not myself,
I have forgot my-self, quite lost my-self !
I am not Christian, neither Jew am I,
Nor Zoroastrian, nor Musalmān;
I only know that I am only I !
The Sūfī is no more—his lower self
Is now no more—and that which is no more
Any religion can possess no more.
He, who has found his God, is God, is Self;
Who is all God can need no other God;
Where the sun shines night can no longer be.
So long as the Belovéd's Loveliness
Is hid behind a veil, love's longings last;
But when the veil uplifts, all longings go,
And only Vision face to face abides.
Strike on the harp of thine own inner being,
And drink to fill, the wine of Love Divine.[1]
No argument may ope the mystery
Which the deft touch of Love alone can ope.
While there remains the sense of 'I' and 'thou',
Nor 'thou' nor 'I' can probe this mystery

[1] Literally translated, the verse means: "Don't bother your head about unfathomable mysteries; enjoy yourself while you may, with wine and music". Esoterically interpreted, *muṭrib*, (a Persian stringed instrument) is s ā i y a m ḍ a i v ī v ī ṇ ā, 'this divine harp' of the nervous system, on which the Self plays, the Self whose Nature and ways are understood, not by arguing, but by insight, intuition; the song is the

Of the World's Dawning; neither 'I' nor 'thou,'
Can read this mystic rede illegible.
With screen between, is talk of 'me' and 'thee',
The screen of this gross flesh and blood and bone,
This curtain of dense selfish egoism ;
When the veil lifts, there's no more 'thou' *and* 'I,'
But all the Uni-verse grows *On* (*e*)-*ly* I.)

This chapter on the Way of Devotion may well close with a noble song by a great devotee, who bore witness splendidly to his faith, by the martyrdom to which he went, with compassion on his face for those who slew him, knowing no better, and with a verse on his lips, of reminder to all, of the Spiritual Race of the lovers and helpers of humanity :

Sarmaḍ ! gila-go na shuḍ,
niko shuḍ ke na shuḍ ;
Lab bé-huḍa-go na shuḍ,
niko shuḍ ke na shuḍ.
Minnaṭ-kash-e Charkh̤ na mī
shuḍī ākh̤ire-kār,
Kār-é ke niko na shuḍ,
niko shuḍ ke na shuḍ.

---

a n ā h a ṭ a n ā ḍ a, 'the voice of the silence', heard within the 'head' or the 'heart', when all the physical senses have been closed ; (some 'esoteric' schools teach concentration in the heart, some in the head); the wine is the wine of 'love divine', and also a superfine secretion, a - m a r a - v ā r u ṇ ī, 'the wine of the immortals', 'the elixir of life', which forms in the brain and the nervous system, when listening to that 'unuttered sound' is practised. Such is the indication of old books and wandering ascetics.

Sarmaḍ ! ba kū-e ishq baḍ-nām shuḍī !
Az ḍīn-e Yahūḍ sū-e Islām shuḍī !
Mālūm na shuḍ, kai az Khuḍā o Ahmaḍ
Bar-gashṭa, ba sū-e Lachhman o Rām shuḍī !
Sarmaḍ ! gḥam-e ishq bul-hawas rā na ḍihanḍ !
Sōz-e-ḍil-e parwāna magas rā na ḍihanḍ !
Umr bāyaḍ ke Yār āyaḍ ba kinār ;
Īṅ ḍaulaṭe-Sarmaḍ hama kas rā na ḍihanḍ !
(Sarmaḍ ! thou ne'er dids't cringe
and whine and pray,
Nor ever let thy lips abase thy-Self,
Even before the rolling vault of Heaven !
They say, 'Twas not well done' ; but Sarmaḍ says,
'It was well done that it was not well done' !
Sarmaḍ ! they scorned thee, treading lone the lane
Of Love, amidst the towns of Judah's creed,
And of the faithful followers of Islām,
Then also of the votaries of Rām.
Lovers of their small selves alone thou found
Mostly ; and *very few* of the *One* Self.
Sarmaḍ ! the blissful ache of Love Divine
To seekers of the senses is not given.
The flame of heart is for the moth alone ;
The fly upon the filth can know it not.
A whole lifetime of yearning, sad and mad—
Then only thy Loved One came to thy arms !
This Wealth Infinite that belongs to thee,
Sarmad ! alas ! to all may not be given !)[1]

[1] Sarmaḍ was a spiritual descendant of Mansūr who was martyred by the then Kḥalifā of Bagḥḍāḍ, in 920 A. C., for going about the streets exclaiming An-al-Haq, ('I am God', A h a m B r a h m a). After wandering about, in search of God, in the western countries of Asia, Sarmaḍ came to Delhi, in the days of

Aurangzeb, became a Sūfī-Véḍānṭī, and went about in the streets, God-intoxicate, careless whether there was any clothing on his person or none at all, shouting An-al-Haq, like Mansūr, from time to time. Aurangzeb ordered him to be killed. He went to his martyrdom, with sad smile of compassion on his face for those who 'knew no better', and song of triumph over Death, on his lips, for the instruction of the future generations:

Arsa būḍ, awāza-é Mansūr kuhan shuḍ,
Man jalwa ḍiham bār-e ḍigar ḍār o rasan rā !
(Long years have passed
since Mansūr gave the world
His message; and its holy influence
Grows faint; I must revive it now, and give
Fresh power to it with the help of these,
The headsman's binding ropes and block of wood!
Death gives a larger Life to Sons of God!)

CHAPTER IV

The Way of Works, or the Volitional Constituent of Religion

In life, cognition-desire-action, j ñ ā n a - i c h c h h ā-k r i y ā, *ilm-kẖwāhish-fa'l*, are always rotating. We perceive something; we feel a desire for or against it; we act to secure or remove it. New activity brings new knowledge; that engenders new desire; that causes new movement. Thus are the three life-functions always circling round and round; inseparable, though distinguishable. The same three factors are the distinguishable but inseparable components of Religion. We begin life, as infant, with desire (for nourishment) predominant; then pass on, as child, to (aimless-seeming) restless activity; then slowly develope intelligence and gather knowledge, connected, systematic, organised; then have larger desires, ambitions; more complicated activities, enterprises. So in Religion, the first stage is desire (more or less inchoate) for 'nourishment for the soul', for something more than this life offers; then comes activity, 'the way of works', *sharia'ṭ*, k a r m a-m ā r g a, rites and ceremonies; then a somewhat clearer notion of the other worlds, and of God; then more earnest desire for God, 'the way of devotion', b h a k ṭ i-m ā r g a, *ṭarīqaṭ*, yearnings, fervors, ardours, worships, internal prayers and beseechings, passionings and compassionings; then the 'action' of intense study, reflection, v i - c h ā r a, *ghaur*, *khauz*, 'mental exploration', 'intellectual diving, moving, searching all round', the 'internal' side of y o g a-practices; then 'the way of knowledge', 'illumination', 'the Finding of the Sought', j ñ ā n a-m ā r g a, *haqīqat* or *ma'ārifat*; after which, there is deliberate desire for the good of all, conscious philanthropy, (not only temperamental goodness as that of a good child), and deliberate appropriate dutiful activity, all three in one.[1]

Yogās-ṭrayo Mayā pr-okṭāh,
Nṛṇām shréyo-viḍhiṭsayā;
Jñānam, Karma cha, Bhakṭish-cha;
N-opāyo-ny-osṭi kuṭra-chiṭ.
Nir-viṇṇānām Jñāna-yogo
Nyāsinām iha karmasu;
Ṭéshv-a-nir-viṇṇa-chiṭṭānām
Karma-yogas-ṭu karmiṇām;
Yadṛchchhayā Maṭ-kaṭhā-ḍau
Jāṭa-shraḍḍhas-ṭu yah pumān,
Na nir-viṇṇo n-āṭi-sakṭo
Bhakṭi-yog-osya siḍḍhi-ḍah.
(*Bhāgavaṭa*, xi. ch. 20.)

(Three ways have I declared, for helping men,
Walking which, they may gain the Highest Good;
The Ways of knowledge, Love, and Pious Works.
For the child-mind that clings yet to the world,
There is the Way of Rites and Pious Works.
For those not clinging nor yet surfeited,
Who have heard rumours of Me, and have felt

---

[1]See p. 86, *supra*.

Vague longings and strong stirrings of the heart,
The Way of Worship is the helpful way.
For those who are world-weary, 'dis-illusioned ,
Seek but for rest from all this Vast Illusion
Of whirling purgat'ries and paradises,
And have no wish left to initiate
New enterprises, but only to pay
All unpaid 'debts', do 'duties' undischarged—
For them the Way of Knowledge is the Way.)

For the soul which has found the Final Object of all Seeking, the three Ways have merged into one. For the yet seeking and slowly and steadily progressing, the three are distinguishable. Since 'action' is most 'manifest'; desire and cognition are hidden; they manifest in and through action; therefore, differences, quarrels, also 'manifest' most in the 'actions' of 'children', 'child-minds'.

Accordingly, differences between religions are most apparent in the third department, viz., Karma-kāṇda, *Sharīyaṭ or Mā'milāṭ*, sacraments, rites, ceremonies and observances. Yet the differences are only apparent. There is very substantial similarity underneath the surface. The dresses of men seem to differ greatly; yet because the human shape enclothed by them is the same, all dresses have to shape themselves to it more or less closely.

1. The Vedic sanḍhyā-upāsanā, the Christian *prayer*, the Muslim *namāz*—are the same. The essential parts of all are almost exactly the same. Indeed they are almost like

translations of one another. They all pray to the Ultimate Source or Reservoir of all Cosmic Energy, Mental, Physical, Biotic, for Right Intelligence and Righteous Will, inner illumination and guidance, protection from evil temptations, and strength of mind to do the right duty. Obviously, if the intelligence is right and righteous, and the will strong and guided by that intelligence, everything will go right.[1]

---

[1] Psychologically, prayer is essentially prayer to the God *Within* All, the Collective Consciousness, the Principle of Consciousness, Omnipresent, Omnipotent, Omniscient. The latest 'scientific' name of this Ultimate is the 'Total Unconscious'. It is a new and significant variant of the old 'Unmanifest', **a-vyakta**, *bāṭin*, 'hidden'. 'Praying' is, mostly, an 'unconscious' i.e. unwitting, non-deliberate, (in a comparative few, a deliberate), wishing and willing that this 'Unconscious' may *become conscious*, in the person praying. A scientist, an inventor, 'concentrating' upon the solution of some problem, is thus *praying*, performing **yoga**, that the all-knowing Unconscious *within* him, may become conscious in his brain in respect of that part of All-Knowledge which he (the person praying) desires. Young souls can only gradually transfer their prayers from 'a god without' to 'the God within'. As children, we pray to our father, mother, elder, guardian, for everything. When grown up, we 'pray' to ourselves, we insist upon ourselves, we *will*, to stand upon our own feet, and avoid troubling others with requests for help, as much as possible. But this is not always possible. Then we, (even though grown-up, yet not grown sufficiently strong), *have* to seek the help of others, who are senior,

Aum ! Bhūh, Aum ! Bhuvah, Aum ! Svah.
Aum ! Ṭaṭ Saviṭur-varéṇyam bhargo Ḍévasya
ḍhīmahi, ḍhiyo yo nah prachoḍayāṭ. Aum !
(*V.*, *Gāyaṭrī.*)

---

stronger, superior. Always in the last resort, the final work has to be done by one-Self. The mother and the father may give food, the teacher information ; but the eating, masticating, digesting, absorbing, understanding, assimilating, must be done by one-Self. So are there prayers to the personal gods, i s h t a - ḍ é v a-s, *malāyak*, *auliyā*, ṛ s h i s, *pīr-s*, mediators, angels, saints ; and behind them all is the perpetual unavoidable 'prayer' to the Impersonal Omnipresent God. Of this 'perpetual prayer', the incessant act of breathing, 'praying to the god of air', *atmos*, is a primary simple manifestation. In its spiritual aspect, this 'breathing' is called, in Véḍism, the *a-japā gāyaṭrī*, 'the unuttered inaudible, prayer'; in which, every breath signifies, 'That am I', 'That am I', 'I am That', 'I am That', *So(A)ham*, *Sah Aham*, or, reversed, *Aham Sah*. Without the perpetual in-filling, in-coming, of that Great Pure I, and the out-going, out-casting, of the impurities of the small I, the small I cannot live at all.

Har nafasé ke furo mī rawaḍ,
Mumiḍḍ-e hayāṭ asṭ;
Wa chūn bar mī āyaḍ,
Mufarreh-e zāṭ;
Pas ḍar har nafasé ḍo némuṭ
Maujūḍ ast,
Wa bar har némaṭé shukré wājib. (*S.*, *Sā'ḍī.*)

(Each breath that goeth in strengthens the life ;
Each that comes out, the body purifies.

Aum ! Agné ! naya supaṭhā rāyé
Asmān, vishvāni, Ḍéva !, vayunāni viḍvān ;
Yuyoḍhy-asmaj-juhurāṇam éno
Bhūyishthām ṭé nama ukṭim viḍhéma.
Aum ! (*V.*)

Aum ! Vishvāni !, Ḍeva ! Saviṭar !, ḍuriṭāni parāsuva, yaḍ bhaḍram ṭan na āsuva ! Aum ! (*V.*)

Each breathing in-and-out two blessings brings ;
Then think of Him with each, with twofold thanks.)

Praying for *display* of piety, is obviously wrong ; and not only useless but harmful. Ordinarily, prayer in secrecy and solitude is sincerest and most full of deep emotion. In conditions of widespread, profound, national surge of feeling, in the presence of great danger or actual calamity, mass-prayer is obviously commanded by nature itself. Congregational prayer is right, useful, effective, in other circumstances also, if sincere and single-minded Solitary study has its own uses ; so has joint class-room study. It all depends upon the object in view, the temperaments and the requirements, of the persons concerned, and the general surrounding conditions.

"Prayer opens the spiritual sight of man, for prayer is desire, and desire developes into *will*. The magnetic emanations proceeding from the body at every effort—whether mental or physical—produce self-magnetisation and ecstasy...Jesus has given the advice : 'When thou prayest, thou shalt not be as the hypocrites are ; for they love to pray standing in the synagogues and in the corners of the streets, that they may be seen of men...But when thou prayest, enter into thy closet, and when thou hast shut thy door, pray to thy Father in secret'...." (H. P. Blavatsky, *Isis Unveiled*, I. 434.)

Aum !
Yaj-jāgraṭo ḍūram uḍaiṭi Ḍaivam,
Ṭaḍ-u supṭasya ṭaṭha-iv-aiṭi,
Ḍūraṅ-gamam jyoṭishām jyoṭir-Ékam
Ṭan-mé Manah shiva-sankalpam asṭu !
Yaṭ prajñānam, uṭa chéṭo, ḍhṛṭish cha,
Yaj-jyoṭir-anṭar-Amṛṭam prajāsu,
Yasmān na ṛṭé kinchana karma kriyaṭé,
Ṭan-mé Manah shiva-sankalpam asṭu !
Yén-éḍam bhūṭam bhuvanam bhavishyaṭ
Parigṛhīṭam Amṛṭéna sarvam,
Yasmiṅsh-chiṭṭam sarvam oṭam prajānām,
Ṭan-mé Manah shiva-sankalpam asṭu !
Aum ! (*V.*)

Aum !
Yo ḍévānām prabhavash-ch-oḍbhavash-cha,
Vishv-āḍhipo, Ruḍro, Maharshih,
Hiraṇya-garbham janayāmāsa pūrvam,
Sa no buḍḍhyā shubhayā samyunakṭu !
Aum ! (*U.*)

Aum !
In the three worlds, planes, states of consciousness
Waking, and Dreaming, and Deep Slumber too,
Father of all, may Thy Supernal Light
Inspire, illuminate, and guide our *minds* ;
We ope them to that Radiance Divine !
Aum !

Aum !
Supreme Director ! Lord of Warmth and Light,
Of Life and Consciousness, that knowest all !
Guide us by the *Right Path* to happiness !
And give us strength and will to war against
The sins that rage in us and lead astray !
We bow in reverence and prayer to thee !
Aum !

Aum!
Father Divine!, all sins ward off from us,
And all auspicious virtues grant to us.
Aum! (*V.*)

Aum!
This *Mind* Divine of mine, which wanders far
When I am waking, and comes back in sleep—
May this far-reaching light of lights *will* right!
This *Mind* of mine, which is intelligence
All-knowing; which is living consciousness,
And patient self-maintaining fortitude;
Which is the inner and immortal light
Without which we are naught—may it *will* right!
This *Mind* of mine, which in eternal grasp
Holds past and present and the future, all,
In which all other minds are interwoven
As warp and woof—may it *will* ever right!
Aum! (*V.*)

Aum!
Who did create and is the Lord of all,
Senses, sense-objects, souls, or high or low,
Ruḍra, the Seed of I-ness, and all-knower,
Maharshi, Who did generate at first
The Golden Egg wherein are interlinked
The wheeling globes by Prime Intelligence—
May He endow us with the *righteous Mind*.
Aum!

Bhaḍram karṇébhih shṛṇuyāma, Dévāh!
Bhaḍram pashyém-ākshabhir-yajaṭrāh;
Sṭhirair-angais-ṭushtuvāmsas-ṭanūbhir-
Vyashémahi ḍéva-hiṭam yaḍ-āyuh. (*V.*)
(May we hear words of sweetness with our ears;
May we see joyous sights with our eyes;
With firm and healthy limbs, may we live on
For so long as is good for our organs,

Sensor and motor, through which ye do live,
Ye gods ! ye Nature-forces ![1] Living thus
Shall we express and hymn your glories well !)

B-ism-Illāh-ir-Rahmān-ir-Rahīm.
Al-hamḍu lillāhi Rabb-il-ā'limīn.
Ar-Rahmān ir-Rahīm ! Mālik-i-yaum-iḍ-ḍīn.
Iyyāka na'buḍu, wa iyyāka nasṭa'īn ;
Ihḍin-as-sirāṭ-ul-musṭaqīm,
Sirāṭ-allazīna an amṭa a'laihim,
Ghair-il-maghzūb-i-a'laihim
wa lā-azzallīn. Āmīn ! (Q.)

Praise be unto the Lord of all the worlds !
O Lord of Mercy and Beneficence !
Master Supreme of the great Judgment Day !
Thee do we serve and Thee beseech for help ;
Show us the *Path* on which Thy blessings rest,
The *Straight Path* ; not of those who go astray,
On whom descends thy wrath and punishment !
Āmīn.)

Rabbana āṭina f-iḍ-ḍuniya hasanaṭan, wa f-il-
āḳhiraṭi hasanaṭan, wa qinā azāb-un-nār. (*Q.*)[2]

(O God of all !
Bestow on us all blessings in this world,
And also in the other future world ;
And save us from the fires of sin and hell.)

---

[1]The ḍ é v a - s, 'gods', are the nature-forces of the 'five elements, 'ākāsha-ether, air, fire, water, earth', with which the five sensor and five motor organs are connected, in Véḍist 'natural philosophy'.

[2]We have seen before, p. 285, *supra*, that the Véḍic 'Messiah' as well as the Biblical 'Nabī' have prayed for the 'daily bread'. In the above text, the Qurānic 'Ṛshi' does the same. The Véḍic verse, quoted just before, praying for long life of the physical

Our Father which art in heaven!
Hallowed be Thy name. Thy kingdom come.
Thy *will* be done in earth as it is in heaven.
Give us this day our daily bread.

And forgive us our debts, as we forgive our debtors. And lead us not into temptation; but deliver us from evil, for Thine is the kingdom, and the power, and the glory, for ever. Amen! (*B.*, N. T.)

Lead me, O Lord, in Thy righteousness. Make Thy *Way* straight before my face. Cleanse Thou me from secret faults. Keep back Thy servant from presumptuous sins; let them not have dominion over me. Wash me thoroughly from my iniquity, and cleanse me from my sin.

---

body and for auspicious sense-objects, has the same significance. The affairs of this world are by no means to be neglected and despised. Quite obviously, by the declarations of all religions, right conduct in this world is the necessary condition of welfare in the next. That there *is* a next world, all religions are agreed; and if the question were to be decided by the 'democratic' method, and were put to a universal plebiscite, the vast majority of the two thousand million human beings who inhabit this earth, including the 170 or so millions of even the Soviet Russia of today, would surely say 'Yes'! Therefore, it is right that we should pray for, and exert ourselves to win, well-being in both worlds. The Véḍic Ṛshi, indeed, declares expressly that "Religion is that which secures happiness here as well as hereafter".

Yaṭo Abhy-uḍaya-Nis-shréyasa-
siḍḍhih sa Ḍharmah. (*Vaishêshika-Sūṭra.*)

Search me, O God !, and know my heart, try me and know my thoughts, and see if there be any wicked way in me; and lead me in the *Way* Everlasting.

Show me Thy *Ways*, O Lord ! Teach me Thy *Paths*; and lead me in Thy Truth; Thou art the God of my Salvation. Open Thou mine eyes that I may behold wondrous things out of Thy law. Quicken thou me according to Thy Word. Remove from me the way of lying. (*B.*, O. T., Psalms.)

Shemaa Israel ! Aḍonai Elohenu, Aḍonai Eihad !

Yehi rason millefanekha, Aḍonai Elohenu velohe aboṭhenu, sheṭṭargilenu Beṭhoraṭheka veṭhaḍbikenu bemisswoṭheka, ve-al ṭebienu liḍe heṭ velo liḍe abera velo liḍe nissayon velo liḍe bizzayon veṭharhikenu miyesser haraa; veṭhadbikenu beyasser haṭṭob veṭh-nenu lehen velhesseḍ velrahmin be-énekha vebene kol roenu veghomlenu hasaḍim ṭobim. Barukḥ Aṭṭa Aḍonai gomel hasaḍim ṭobim leammo Israel. Amen.

(Hear, O Israel ! the Lord is our God, the Lord is One. May it be Thy will, O Lord our God, and God of our fathers, to cause us to walk in Thy law and cleave to Thy commandments; and lead us not into sin, transgression, temptation, and contempt. Remove from us every evil inclination and cause us to adhere to the good. Oh, grant us grace, favour and mercy in Thy sight, and in the sight of all that behold us, and bestow gracious favours on us. Blessed art Thou, O Lord, who bestowest gracious favours on Thy people Israel. Amen.)[1]

---

[1]The original Hebrew words of this prayer, in roman characters, and also the translation, included in the text above, are taken from the pamphlet, a book of prayers of all faiths, published by the Theosophical

The 'Honovar'-prayer, (so named because of the words 'ahu-vairaya' or 'ahuna-vairayo' which occur in it), is held as sacred in Zoroastrianism as the 'Gāyaṭri' prayer is in Vēḍism. It is:

Yaṭhā ahu vairayo, aṭhā Raṭush, ashāṭ chiṭ ha chā, vanghéush ḍazaḍā manangho, shyaoṭhananām anghéush Mazaḍā-i kshaṭhrém chā Ahurāi ā. Yim ḍreguvyo ḍaḍāṭ vāsṭārém.

(Fix we our minds in worship on the Lord,
Of Right and Might, of Wisdom and of Power,
Who gives us *Conscience* to do godly deeds,
And also gives Detachment from the World,
And patient Resignation whence we gain
Solace in time of weakness and of pain.)[1]

Publishing House, Adyar, Madras, in 1925, under the title of "Union of all Faiths in a Common Act of Worship". The word 'Israel' is said to be composed of 'Isr', 'righteousness' and 'El', 'omnipotent'; hence it means, 'those who walk righteously in the Law of omnipotent God'. The reader, if he happens to be curious in matters of philology *cum* philosophy, may consult those mines of occult lore, H. P. Blavatsky's *Isis Unveiled* and *The Secret Doctrine*, (with the help of the Indices) for the connections between Indian, Phoenician, Hebrew, and Greek Ḍyaur-nishā, Ḍivā-nisham, Dionysus, Adonai, Adonis, Adam-Adami, Adam, Āḍi-Manu, Āḍi-nāṭha, Eden, A-Ḍ-N-Y; and between Indian A-I-U-M, É-O-M, A-I-A-O, H-A-Y-A-V-A, and the western I A O, Jaho, Jah, Jahveh, Jehovah, Jove, Eve, Yahveh, Yahya, I-hi-we, Hawwā, J-H-V-H, Iachchus, Oe-Ao-Hoo, Oi-Ha-Hoo; Ḍyaus-piṭr, Jupiter; etc.

[1]This rendering is based on the interpretation made by Shri J. M. Chatterji, *Ethical Conceptions of*

...Apāno ḍarégo jyāīṭīm, ā kshaṭṭhrém vanghéush manangho; ashāṭ ā éréjūsh paṭho yaéshu Mazaḍāo Ahuro shaéṭī. (*Z*., Gāṭhā, 33. 5.)

...Ahmāṭ avā manangha yā véréjyé-īḍyāyī manṭā vāsṭrayā...(33. 6.)

...Ahuro Mazaḍāos chā ārmaīṭīsh chā ashém chā frāḍaṭ gaéṭhém manas chā vohu kshaṭṭhrém chā... āḍāī...(33. 11.)

---

the Gāṭhā, (2nd edn.), pp. 11,592 ; so also are all the other renderings of Gāṭhā-texts, given in this book, based on his. Scholars can check and correct by the original texts, reproduced here in roman letters. Another version of the Honovar is as below ; it is only a versified form of the words (slightly altered for purposes of metre) of the English translation by Dr. Irach J. S. Taraporewala (see p. 47, *supra*), which appeared in *The Bombay Theosophical Bulletin* for September, 1937.

(As the earth's sovereign ruleth o'er the earth,
E'en so the Spiritual Teacher rules
The Mind of all, because of the Great Power
Of Rectitude and all the other gifts
Of the Good Mind. The Strength of Ahura,
And all those other gifts that go with it,
Are given to him who worketh for the Lord
In service of his brethren to his best.
May the Good Mind inspire us so we may
Bring solace to the souls of all in need !)

Dr. Taraporewala says that, like all the other Saviours "after years of struggle with his lower self, Zarathusṭra gets Illumination", and begins the work of his mission with the utterance of "the Ahuna-vairya, 'the Holy Word of sacrifice'..."

Yā shyaoṭhanā yā vachanghā yā yasnā amérétāṭém ashém chā ṭaībyo ḍāonghā, Mazaḍā! kshaṭṭhrém chā haūrvāṭāṭo aéshām ṭoī, Ahurā!, éhyā poūruṭémāīsh ḍāsṭé (34. 1.)

Aṭ chā hoī sachanṭū manangha ukhḍhāīs shyaoṭhanāīs chā; kshnūm Mazaḍāo Vahmāi ā fraoréṭ yasnās chā...Ḍāongho éréjūsh paṭho yāṃ ḍaénām Ahuro Saoshyanṭo ḍaḍaṭ (53. 2.).

(Grant me long life, Lord Mazaḍa!, Fortitude,
And the right mind; and show me
the *Straight Path*,
O'er which Thou broodest, and which
leads to Thee.
Lord! give me such a Mind as makes men Wise
And dutiful...The wealth of Rectitude,
From which all other wealth flows of itself,
And Conscience Just, and Patient Fortitude,
And right Activity, bestow on me.
Come unto me, Great Mazaḍa! with Thy hands
Full of those duties, righteous words and deeds,
Which bring Spirituality, detached
Aloofness from the world, Salvation thence.
Right thoughts, right words, right
deeds—by these we gain
Knowledge of Mazaḍā, and thence of Brahm';
The *Straight Path* that the Loving
Lord Soshyanṭ
Gave us—may we not ever err from it.)

Aṭ ṭoī, Mazaḍā! ṭém mainyūm asha-okshanṭāya sarèḍyayāo khāṭhrā maéṭhā mayā vahishṭā varéṭū managhā ayāo aroī hākurénèm yayāo hachinṭé ūrvāno. (33. 9.).

(May this my mind, Lord Mazaḍa! show to me
The Truth, Thy inmost Spirit, Greatest Good,

28

Ideal of Ideals, to guide me
Aright in ways of Righteousness alway.
Having achieved that goal, I will have gained
All lesser things, to which my soul inclines.)
Sīshā nāo ashā paṭho vanghéūsh
khaéṭéng manangho. (34. 12.)
(Teach us the path of conscious Rectitude,
Great Lord ! wherein Conscience rests satisfied.)

Ashā, Rectitude, Right Desire, **Vahishṭam Manah**, Right mind, Right knowledge, **Ārmāīṭī**, Right will, Right action, **Kshaṭṭhram**, Patient and Steady Detachment, and **Managhā**, thoughts, **Vachanghā**, words, **Shyaoṭhanā**, deeds—these words are of very frequent occurrence in the *Gāṭhās*.

A brief, and very common, Véḍist prayer to be cleansed of sins, and be forgiven, is :

Pāp-oham, pāpa-karm-āham,
pāp-āṭmā pāpa-sambhavah,
Pāhi mām, Pundarīk-āksha !,
sarva-pāpa-haro bhava. (*Mbh.*)

(Sinful am I, sin-acting, and sin-born,
Sin-natured. Cleanse Thou me from all my sin !)

It may be noted that Aum (pronounced as Om), Āmīn, Amen, respectively used by Vaiḍika Ḍharma, Islām, and Christianity, are the same word, all meaning, "Be it so", besides other meanings.

A Jaina prayer-hymn is :

Arahanṭa namo ! Bhagavanṭa namo !
Param-éshvara Jina-rāja namo !

Prabhu pāran-gaṭa, parama mahoḍaya,
Avināshī, akalanka, namo!
Ajara, amara, aṭi-shaya aḍbhuṭa-niḍhi,
Pravachana-jalaḍhi-mayanka, namo!
Kévala-gyānā-ḍarshé ḍarshiṭa,
Lokā-loka-sva-bhāva, namo!
Nāshiṭa-sakala-kalanka-kalusha-gaṇa,
Duriṭa-upaḍrava-bhāva, namo!
Asharaṇa-sharaṇa, vi-rāga, nir-anjana,
Nir-upāḍhika, Jagaḍ-īsha, namo!
Boḍhi ḍīnu an-upama ḍān-éshvara,
Gyāna bimala, sūr-īsha, namo![1]
(Thou that deservest every praise!
The Lord of every glory, Thou!
Our God Supreme! We bow to Thee!
Stainless, decayless, wonderful,
Exhaustless fount of marvels all;
The One Sole object of all hymns,
Who can be glimpsed but in the glass
Of Soli-tary Consciousness,
That has negated all the taints
Of restless sins, disturbances,
Attachments to false fleeting things,
That stain Thy Purity of Peace!
Thou Refuge of the refugeless!
Thou Formless, Moveless, Passionless!
Lord of the Worlds! Thee we adore!
Most Generous of givers, Thou!
Give us that greatest gift of all—

---

[1] This prayer is also taken from the Theosophical publication mentioned before, pp. 430-431, *supra*. For some verses from another Jaina prayer, in Samskṛṭ, see pp. 145-146, *supra*.

The Luminous Intelligence
And Final Knowledge of Thy-Self!
Give us this gift! We bow to Thee!)

The Buddhist prayer, in most common use, is:

Buḍḍham sharaṇam gachchhāmi,
Ḍharmam sharaṇam gachchhāmi,
Sangham sharaṇam gachchhāmi.
Aum! maṇih padmé, Aum!

(Ah! Blessed Lord! O High Deliverer!
Ah! Lover! Brother! Guide! Lamp of the Law!
Source of all Wisdom, Fountain of all Light!
I take my refuge in Thy name and Thee!
I take my refuge in Thy Law of Good!
I take my refuge in Thy Order! Aum!
The gem-like drop of dew—my little soul—
Ah! may it pass into the Lotus-bloom
That floats upon the Sea
Of Thy Infinity!)

A few verses from Sikh prayers are:

Sarab Kāla hai Piṭī apārā,
Dévi Kalikā Māṭa hamārā,
Manuyā Guru mohi, Manasā Māyī,
Yin mo ko saṭ-krīyā parhāī.
Dévi Shivā! vara mohi yahai
Shubha karmoṅ ṭé kabahūṅ na turūṅ,
Na darūṅ ari sé jaba āi larai,
Nishchaya kari apanī jīṭa karūṅ.
Thādha bhayé kara jora kar,
Vachana kahā shira nāe,
Panṭha chalai Ṭava jagaṭa méṅ
Yav Ṭum karo sahāe.

(GURU GOVINDA SINHA, *Vichiṭra Nāṭaka* and *Chandī Chariṭra.*)

(Th' Eternal is my Father measureless,
My goddess-Mother is Eternity,
My Teacher is my Mind ; its Intuition
Is my good Nurse. They teach me to do right.
Thou blessed Consort-Nature of the Lord !
Grant me this boon that I may never turn
From the Right Path of Duty ; never fear
To war 'gainst evil ; and may always win !
I fold my hands in humble prayer to Thee !
I bend my head in lowly reverence !
Ordain that Thy Path may be trod by all !
Give me the strength to make it plain to men[1] !

Another great prayer, common to the several religions, common because it arises spontaneously from the unsophisticated human heart, which is the same all over the earth, for Darkness, outer as well as inner, is the great enemy of the good, and Light their great friend, may be noted :

Aum ! Ṭamasō mā Jyoṭir gamaya,
Asaṭo mā Saḍ gamaya,
Mṛṭyor Amṛtam ! Aum ! (*V.*)

(Lead me from Darkness unto Light; lead me
From the Unreal to the Real; lead
Me from the mortal to th' Immortal Self !)

Il allazīna āmanu yukhṛijahum
min az-Zulmāṭi il an-Nūr ! (*Q.*)

---

[1]These last three prayers, Jaina, Buḍḍhist, and Sikh, have some words in them, which make it possible, according to the mood of the devotee, to regard them as addressed to a 'personal' embodiment of the Supreme, viz., Mahāvīra Jina, or Buḍḍha, or the goddess Ḍurgā.

(Those who have found the faith are taken out
Of Darkness into Light, ye faithful ones !)
Nūrun alā nūrin yahḍillāhū
li nūrihī mañyashāo. (*Q.*)
(Light blazing upon Light, God guideth him,
To whom He gives His grace, unto His Light.)

(Ocean of mercy ! dwell within our heart
Ever, and give such Light unto our mind,
That we may love, serve, worship Thee, our God !
Ever Thy presence may we feel near us,
Thou art our Father, Mother, Master, all !)
(*Si.*, *THR.*, 31.)

Lead, kindly Light, amid th' encircling gloom,
Lead thou me on !
The night is dark, and I am far from home,
Lead thou me on !
(Christian Hymn, by NEWMAN.)

An old Greek hymn to Minerva, goddess of Wisdom, sprung from the *head* of Jupiter, (which implies that she is the personification of the aspect of *omni-science* of the Supreme), sings :

Great Goddess, hear !, and on my darkened mind,
Pour thy pure Light in measure unconfined ;
That Sacred Light, O all-preceding Queen,
Which beams eternal from thy face serene.
My soul, while wandering on the earth, inspire
With thine own blessed and impulsive Fire.
(PROCLUS, translated by Thomas Taylor.)

All the old 'dead' religions, and many of the living, but smaller and less known, religions of the less-developed, primitive or degenerate, peoples, have similar prayers for "illumination" of the mind and body, for guidance and inspiration, for being shown the right way and given the strength to tread it.

Let us note that most of these great elemental heart-prayers are prayers for the collective 'we', 'us', rather than the single 'me'; and even where the singular is used, the intention is plain, of righteous and loving relationship with all. Indeed, prayer without love, love of fellow-men as much as of God, (because the former is the beginning of the latter), is hollow, is mockery. The measure of the power of prayer to help is the measure of the love in the heart which prays.[1]

---

[1]Some other purposes and benefits of prayer may be noted. It is as the toilette of the mind, the soul. It is bathing in the pure waters of spiritual emotion; looking into the mirror of introspective self-examination; making sure that no unseemliness is left uncorrected, before presenting oneself before and to the Supreme, and then going forth to work among fellow-creatures, or retiring to rest for the night. Detailed considerations, in this regard, are offered in the writer's *The Science of Social Organisation*, I, 376-392. As to the times for prayer, obviously all times are good in which the soul feels the need for it. The significance and value of the a-japā-gāyaṭrī have been referred to, at p. 424, *supra*. The more advanced, the more pure, the more (wisely) 'child'-like the soul, the more it performs every act, 'keeping near' to the Parent, desirous to please the Parent, as if the Divine Father-mother is looking on and approving. Still, for the ordinary

2. But since men cannot always avoid temptation, and darkness falls upon their hearts and eyes, from time to time; nay, but too frequently; and they err into sin again and again;

---

person, and for regulation of the day's routine, the hours of sunrise and sunset are recommended by most religions. The glories of God's Nature are most manifest then. Three beautiful English hymns may be quoted, to illustrate:

An Hour with Thee.

An hour with Thee! when earliest day
Dapples with gold the eastern grey!
O what can frame the mind to bear
The toil and turmoil, cark and care,
New griefs which coming hours unfold,
And sad remembrance of the old?
One hour with Thee!
An hour with Thee! when sun is set!
O what can teach me to forget
The thankless labors of the day,
The hopes, the wishes, flung away,
Th' increasing wants, the lessening gains,
The master's pride who scorns my pains?
One hour with Thee!

Ave Maria.

Ave Maria! blessed be the hour,
The time, the clime, the spot, where I so oft
Have felt that moment in its fullest power
Sink o'er the earth, so beautiful and soft,
While swung the deep bell in the distant tower,
Or the faint dying-day-hymn stole aloft,
And not a breath crept through the rosy air,

therefore all religions prescribe expiation; and all in three steps: pashchāṭ-ṭāpa, prakhyāpana, prāyash-chiṭṭa; *nadm*, *éṭarāf*, *kaffārā*; repentance, confession, expiation.

Bāz ā, bāz ā, un-che hasṭī bāz ā,
Gar kāfir o gabr o buṭ-parasṭ-ī, bāz ā;
Iṅ ḍar-gahe Mā ḍar-gahe nā-umeḍī n-īsṭ;
Saḍ bār agar ṭauba shikasṭī, bāz ā! (*S.*)
(Come back, come back,
whate'er thou art, come back—

And yet the forest-leaves
seemed stirred with prayer.
Ave Maria! 'tis the hour of prayer!
Ave Maria! 'tis the hour of love!
Ave Maria! O that face so fair!
Those downcast eyes beneath th' Almighty Dove!
Ave Maria! may our spirits dare
Look up to thine and to thy son's above!

Earth has no sorrow that Heaven cannot heal!
Come, ye disconsolate!, where'ver ye languish,
Come to God's altar, fervently here kneel,
Here bring your wounded hearts,
here bring your anguish,
Earth has no sorrow that Heaven cannot heal
Joy of the desolate, Light of the straying
Hope, when all others die, fadeless and pure,
Here speaks the Comforter, in God's name saying,
"Earth has no sorrow that Heaven cannot heal!"
Go, ask the infidel, what boon he brings thee,
What charm for aching hearts can he reveal,
Sweet as the blessed promise that Hope sings us,
"Earth has no sorrow that Heaven cannot heal!".

Sceptic, or worshipper of stone or fire!
My House is not a house of hopelessness!
If thou hast broke thy vow a hundred times,
Yet still repent, and come again to Me!).

Api chéṭ su-ḍur-āchāro
bhajaṭé Mām ananya-bhāk,
Sāḍhur-éva sa manṭavyah
samyag-vy-ava-siṭo hi sah. (*G.*)

(However gross his sins, if he will turn
To Me and love Me with unswerving heart,
He is a saint, he has resolved aright.)

When in the wrong, do not hesitate to amend.
(*C.*, *THR.*, 47.)

(Be not ashamed of your mistakes, for you
Will thereby aggravate them into crimes...
Do not defend, and do not try to hide,
That which was wrong and sinful in your past.)
(*C.*, *Shu King*; *Liki*, *THR.*, 111.)

(If one has done bad deeds of wickedness,
But afterwards repents and mends his way,
Resolving not to do such any more,
But practise reverently all that is good—
He, in the long run, will be sure to gain
Good fortune, and will change calamity
Into sweet blessing through the lessons learnt.)
(*T.*, *Tai-Shang Kan-Ying Pien*, *THR.*, 50)

Khyāpanén-ānu-ṭāpéna,
ṭapasā-ḍhy-ayanéna cha,
Pāpa-kṛn-muchyaṭé pāpāṭ...
prāyash-chiṭṭaih pṛṭhag-viḍhaih.
Yaṭhā yaṭhā naro-(a-)ḍharmam
svayam kṛṭvā-nu-bhāshaṭé,
Ṭaṭhā ṭaṭhā, ṭvach-év-āhih,
ṭén-ā-ḍharméṇa muchyaṭé.

Yaṭhā yaṭhā manas ṭasya
dush-kṛṭam karma garhaṭi,
Ṭaṭhā ṭaṭhā sharīram ṭaṭ
ṭén-āḍharméṇa muchyaṭé.
Kṛṭvā pāpam ṭu san-ṭapya
ṭasmāṭ pāpāṭ pra-muchyaṭé,
N-aiva kuryām punar-iṭi
Ni-vṛṭṭyā pūyaṭé ṭu sah.
(*M.*, xi, 46, 227, 228, 230.)

(Burning remorse, confession, and amends
And expiation in the proper ways,
And sacred studies and ascetic life—
By such are sinners washed clean of their sins.
As he repents his evil acts committed,
As he confesses them with deep remorse,
As he resolves he will not sin again,
His sins peel off from him as snakes' dead skins,
And he feels clean again in body and soul.)

Except ye repent, ye shall all perish...Repent ye, and be converted, that your sins may be blotted out... If we confess our sins, He is faithful and just to forgive, and to cleanse us from all unrighteousness. (*B.*)

(They who, when they commit a crime or wrong,
Remember God and beg Him to forgive,
And do not persevere in what they did,
But turn their heart from sin, repent, amend—
They will gain pardon surely from the Lord.)
(*THR.*, 49 ; *Q* , 2. 155 ; 5. 43 ; 6. 54 ; 3. 129, 130 ; 16. 20 ; 4. 145.)

The 'new' science of psycho-analysis, with much groping and many mistakes and corrections, is slowly developing a modern form and technique, for this ancient method of the purging of the soul, from 'sin' and 'toxic' passion and emotion, which make both soul and body sick with 'psychoses' and 'neuroses'. The latest advance of this 'new' science is embodied in the word 're-education'; i. e., psycho-analytic treatment, to be safe and successful, must 're-educate' the patient. 'Re-education' is the new name for what was formerly called 're-generation', 're-birth' 'the second birth', 'conversion', 'change of heart'. The old words had become hackneyed and lost significance. The old priest-doctors had forgotten that significance and become quacks or worse. A change was necessary. Therefore, nature, collective human nature, is bringing it about. Religion is becoming scientific. Science is becoming religious. The new healer will have to be a healer of body and soul both, simultaneously; for both always fall ill together, though, usually, the one more and the other less. The future 'medicine-man' will have to be such, on the high level of 'spiritual scientist', 'scientific priest'. The new tendency towards 'prison reform' and 'prisoners' education' is working in the same direction; but it seems to be suffering from one serious and dangerous defect, viz., it *does not* guide the criminal to make *repentant expiation* to the victim; the consequence of which is likely to be that jail may come to be regarded as a desirable place of comforts, which can be easily secured by crime.

3. All religions equally enjoin discriminate 'charity' to the deserving, pāṭré ḍāna, *zakāṭ*, and the construction of "pious works,"

churches, mosques, temples, alms-houses, rest-houses, wells, tanks, hospitals, schools, roads, aqueducts, and plantations of groves and avenues of fruiting, flowering, and ornamental trees, etc.—all dedicated for public use in the name of God. The modern 'secular' way of satisfying this need of the individuo-social heart is, 'subscriptions' and 'donations' to public institutions or movements, educational concerns, schools, universities, libraries, scientific institutes, hospitals, charitable endowments of all sorts.

4. All call their Scriptures by names having the same significance, *viz.*, 'the Word of God': B r a h m a-v ā k y a, *Kalām-ullāh*, Go(d)-spel(l). All arrange them in the same way, a ḍ h y ā y a and m a n ṭ r a , 'chapter and verse', *sūrah* and *āyaṭ*. All have written immense and numerous b h ā s h y a s, commentaries, *ṭafsīrs* and *tashrīhs* on them. All have evolved a M ī m ā m s ā, Science of Theology and Exegesis, *Fiqah*. All interpret them in various ways, literal, allegorical, mystical, moral, anagogic, arithmetical, 'prophetic', etc. All believe their respective religions to have two aspects ; one, for the masses ; another, for the few advanced souls. As the Upanishaṭs are the r a h a s y a, 'secret', of the Vedas ; so the Qabbālah is that of the Old Testament or Hebrew part of the Bible; *Bāṭinī* Ṭasawwuf, that of the Quran ; the Gnosticism and Mysticism of St. John and St. Paul and the Book of Revelation, that of the New Testament, the Christian part of the Bible; and these 'hidden', 'esoteric', 'occult'

teachings of all the religions are almost exactly the same. All believe in a four-fold source of religious law: *Qurān—Hadis—Ijmā'—Qayās*; Revelation — Tradition — Canonical Regulation (i.e., Episcopal Legislation, Learned Opinion, Good Custom, also Example of the Wise and Godly)—Conscience; Shruṭi—Smṛṭi—Saḍ-āchāra—Aṭma-ṭushṭi (or Hṛḍay-ābhy-anujñā); which all correspond to the modern legal Statute—Custom—Precedent—Equity.[1]

5. Because man clings to form, being himself naught else than God incarnate in a form, and finds it difficult to turn at once to the Formless, therefore all religions try to take him, step by step, from outer worship to the Inner Worship. But religion becomes ruthless priestcraft, when, instead of leading the people on from step to higher step, endeavour is assiduously made to stultify their intelligence, and fill it with irrational and debasing superstitions and fears, and keep them fixed to the lowest step for ever, in order that they may be preyed upon the more easily.

---

[1]The 'cha' in Manu's verse: (1) Shruṭih, (2) Smṛṭih, (3) Saḍ-āchārah, (4) Svasya *cha* priyam Āṭmanah—indicates that all four are inter-dependent; all are needed to make good sound law-ḍharma acceptable to all. The first three represent Society and Socialism, the last, the Individual and Individualism. This last, since the 'Individual' is in essence the 'Universal', 'law unto him-Self', ultimately becomes Universalism, when the Individual is such as has consciously realised its identity with the Universal.

Apsu ḍévā manushyāṇām,
ḍivi ḍévā manīshiṇām,
Bālānām kāshtha-loshtéshu,
buḍhasy-Āṭmani ḍévaṭā. (*Agni Purāṇa.*)

(The child-soul's gods abide in wood and stone;
Of average man, in holy lakes and streams;
Of the intelligent, in heavenly orbs;
The wise man's God is his Immortal Self.)

The Christian Scriptures distinguish between "milk for babes" and "meat for the strong". We have recorded before, Kṛshṇa's counsel: "Those who know more should not shake the minds and the faiths of those who know less, too violently"; and Muhammad's advice: "People should be spoken to and taught according to the measure of their intelligence."[1]

A western poet makes a repentent sinner say:

I thought I could not breathe in that fine air
That pure severity of perfect light,
I wanted warmth and color......Now I know
Thou art the highest and most human too.
(TENNYSON)

Zoroastrianism eschewing all worship of forms, has yet established the *Agyāri*, the Āṭash-Bahrām, the visible fire, symbol of the Spiritual Fire of Life and Consciousness, the Fire round which all human beings should gather to derive therefrom Heat and Light, warm Vitality, and En-light-enment of Mind, common Consciousness

[1]See pp. 150-151, *supra*.

of Unity and Brotherhood, and common Purpose of General Welfare and United Effort to achieve that Purpose. This *Agyārī*, (Skṭ. Agni-agārā, the 'storing-place of fire') is the correspondent of the 'Agni-hoṭra' ceremony of Védism.

An Islamic legend says that Moses rebuked a simple-hearted cobbler for praying to God to appear to him, so that he might put a pair of fine shoes on His feet. But the Voice of God, from within him, rebuked Moses, in turn :

Ṭū barāyé wasl karḍan āmaḍī,
Nai barāyé fasl karḍan āmaḍī. (*S.*)
(Thou wast sent down to bring souls near to Me,
And not to thrust them thus away from Me.)

So, the chronicles of Roman Catholic Christianity record that, once upon a time, there was a juggler, who made his living by going about and showing his tricks to the village-folk and townsfolk, with balls and knives. He attained great skill, and therefore even fame, in his art; though he could not always earn enough for his meals. One day he went into a church, and saw monks praying before a beautiful image of the Madonna, the holy Virgin Mary. He had a very simple heart, and a great love for the Madonna suddenly entered into it. When the monks went away, he, wishing to show his devotion to the Virgin, and knowing no other way, began to perform his tricks, with his head on the floor and feet in the air. The monks returned, happened to peep in through the chinks of the closed door, and saw the clown. They felt angry, and wished to enter, and remove him by force. Suddenly a haze came upon their eyes. Through it they saw a 'vision': the Madonna descended from her pedestal, and with her mantle wiped the sweat that was streaming from his brows. They fell upon their knees, and bowed their heads to the floor, murmuring: "Blessed are the pure in heart, for they shall see God."

The Bhakṭi-legends of Hinduism are full of similar stories, of soul-purifying 'visions', won by simple heart and faith undoubting, the faith that can move mountains, through child-like works of worship, very acceptable to the All-pervading Spirit of Love.[1]

[1] Hari Ḍas, (from whom Akbar's famous musician Ṭān-sén acquired his art), was a great devotee of Kṛshṇa. The beautiful youthful dancing form of the deity was the object of his special adoration. When he used to play on the vīṇā and sing a dancing-song in ecstasy, he and his disciples often had the 'vision' of 'the azure image' descending from its pedestal and dancing before them. The legends say that the emperor went to Hari Ḍas' cottage in disguise, in company with Ṭān-sén, in the right mood; and the 'glorious vision of Beauty Incarnate' was vouch-safed to him also. Ṭulasī Ḍās is the author of the famous Hinḍī *Rāmāyaṇa*, which has been the Bible of the Hinḍū people for the last three hundred years. He was a contemporay of Hari Ḍās. He was devoted to the Rāma-incarnation. At first, he was a householder; and, devotee as he was, the times being troublous, his piety was tinged

Image-worship would serve its rightful purpose, if it is kept within strict limits; *not* positively encouraged; and if the elders and spiritual ministers keep constantly reminding the people that the image is only a symbol, a remembrancer, of the One God. Islāmic tradition says that, when Umar expressed doubts as to the utility of kissing the Black Stone, *Hajr-ul-aswaḍ*, fixed within the Kā'ba, (which ceremonial kissing Muhammad had ordained), Ali explained to him:

Al hajru Yamīn-ullāh f-il arḍ.

(The stone is as God's right hand on the earth.)

Accordingly, all religions have their specially sacred shrines, sacred bathing places, sacred

---

with anxiety for his goods. One night, he had occasion to come out of his house, soon after midnight. He 'saw' a magnificently handsome and mightily manly youth, armed with bow and arrows, pacing up and down, sentry-wise, in front of the house. He went up eagerly and asked: "Who are you, and why pacing up and down?" A sweet rich-toned voice answered: "A friend of mine lives in this house and is anxious for his household goods; so I am keeping guard." And, with a smile, the youth vanished. A great awe and a great joy and a great shame filled the soul of Ṭulasī Ḍas, and made tumult therein: "I have seen my Lord! But I have put Him to so much trouble by my sordid worry over some wretched pots and pans!" At once 'he gave them all away, and followed Him', and became the author of the Hindu's 'New Testament.' Such are the beautiful heart-purifying soul-uplifting legends, of the true devotees, of all races and religions.

towns, places of pilgrimage, etc. The purpose of all is to keep the mind fixed on higher and higher religious thoughts, spiritual ideas and virtues. To the soul not yet advanced to the stage of capacity for abstract contemplation, the attaching of progressively abstract, first super-physical, then meta-physical, concepts with concrete physical objects, acts, movements, of various kinds, is of very great help, nay necessary.

Hinḍuism has, from time immemorial, its well-known seven Paviṭra-puri-s, Sacred Towns of Pilgrimage. These are, from north to south, Māyā-purī (now Hara-ḍvāra, Hardwar), Maṭhurā (Muttra), Ayoḍhyā (Ajodhyā), Kāshī (Benares), Avanṭikā (Ujjayini, Ujjain), Kānchī (Conjeeveram), and Ḍvārakā. These were all great seats of learning, centres of education, brahma-purī-s, viḍyā-pīṭha-s, in the earlier days, like modern 'university' towns. Kāshī still is such, and has continued to be so, unbrokenly, for at least three thousand, and probably five thousand, years. Another set of four 'holy places' of pilgrimage, chaṭur-ḍhāma, consists of Baḍarī in the Himālayas, Jagan-nāṭha on the eastern sea-coast, Rām-éshvara on the southern sea-coast, Ḍvārakā on the western sea-coast. Hundreds of new temple-towns, (like the cathedral-towns of medieval Europe and mosque-towns of western Asia), have sprung up within the last two thousand years, of which a score or so now come only next after the above-mentioned seven and four, in public estimation.

The Buḍḍha, shortly before leaving this world, advised his followers to make centres of pilgrimage of four places, *viz.*, those of (1) his birth, Lumbinī-vana, (2) his enlightenment, Buḍḍha-Gayā, (3) his commencement of his work of mercy and preaching, Sār-nāṭh[1] in Benares, and (4) his passing into Para-nirvāṇa, *viz.*, Kushī-nagara. He did so, presumably, to satisfy the unconquerable human craving for something visible, something tangible, even in religion; and to create external means of binding human hearts together, by establishing common interests and meeting-places for persons from all parts of the world, in a religious atmosphere and a pure mood of spiritual exaltation and aspiration. Trade and commerce and ideas all travel along

---

[1] There seems to have been a great temple of Shiva, here, in the days of the Buddha; and the deity was imaged as 'the Lord and Protector of deer', of which, there seem to have been great herds here, then, specially protected and preserved *from* (not *for*) hunting, by local public religious feeling. As such Protector, the image of Shiva was named Sāranga-nāṭha, now shortened by non-literary popular usage into Sār-nāṭh; and the place was known as Sāranga-vana, 'Deer Park'. Compare the great saying of Christ: "Other sheep have I, which are not of this flock" (i.e. Jews). Christ is the 'shepherd'. Humane feeling towards animals, 'religious' in India, is beginning to express itself 'secularly' in the west, in such institutions as the Yellowstone Park of the U.S.A., in Zoos, and in laws for the protection of wild life, here and there.

such pilgrim-routes and help to spread common culture, common sympathy, humanism.

The Prophet Muhammad destroyed the three hundred and sixty idols of Macca, because he perceived the ill effects of excessive idolatry. Yet, realizing the needs of the human heart, he preserved one, *viz.*, the Temple built by Abraham, Kā'ba, the Cube, with its *Hajr-ul-Aswaḍ* and *Hajr-ul-Yamān*; and, with great foresight, made it the principal place of Islāmic worship, a uniting centre of an ordained pilgrimage, the *Hajj*. Muslims, offering prayers at the prescribed hours, always turn their faces in the direction of the Kā'ba, in whatever part of the world they may happen to be. But Muhammad ommited not to teach that, though enjoined for common practice, it was not spiritually essential. For, indeed:

Wa lillāh-il mashriqu w-al maghribu, fa aina mā ṭowallu fa summā Wajh-ullāhī; inn-Allāhā wāseūn alīm ...Laisal birra an ṭowallu wujūha-kum qibal-al-mashriqī w-al-maghribī, wa lakinnal birra man āmana b-illāhī w-al-yaum-il-ākhirī w-al-malāyakāṭi w-al-kiṭābi w-an-nabīyīna. (*Q.*)

(Since God is omni-present, all-pervading,
Since He is in the east as well as west,
Whichever way ye turn, God's Face is there;
His Presence doth pervade the Universe...
It is not righteousness to turn the face
To east or west, but to believe in God,
And in the Day of Judgment when you must
The consequence of your good deeds and ill
Meet with unfailingly, and to have faith

In angels, scriptures, and the prophets too.)
Lā inḍa Rabbi sabahun wa lā māsun. (*H.*)
Wa hua mākum aynama kunṭum. (*Q.*)
(For God there is no morning and no eve;
And He is with you wheresoe'er you are.)

The courtyard, the corridors around the central Cubical Temple, and the sacred Ẕam-Zam well near the centre of the courtyard of the Kāba, are very like the precincts of the great temples of South India. The method of worship too has many items quite similar to those which prevail in Indian temples. The pilgrims drink the water of the well and sprinkle it over their bodies, and put on two pieces of *ehrām* or unsewn cloth, like the Indian a v a s ī y a (ḍ h a u ṭ ī, ḍ h o ṭ ī) and u ṭ ṭ a r ī y a; make *ṭawāf,* p a r i - k r a m ā, circum-ambulation, of the temple; kiss the holy stones, the *Hajr-ul-Aswaḍ*, the Black Stone, and the *Hajr-ul-Yamān,* the Brown Stone, fixed inside the cubical room; and sit in meditation. These stones are said to be meteorites, left, as they fell from the heavens, unshaped by human hands, like the Shiva-lingas in some famous Indian temples.[1] Pilgrimages, *hajj*, y ā ṭ r ā, are made by Islāmic pilgrims to other sacred places also, especially Medina, and Najaf, Karbala, Meshed, etc. The Islamic tradition is that the Kā'ba

[1]The Bible also, (Exodus, 20) says: "If thou wilt make me an altar of stone, thou shalt not build it of hewn stone; for if thou lift up thy tool upon it, thou hast polluted it."

temple was originally erected by Abraham, also known as Khalil.

The holy place of the Hebrew religion is Jerusalem.

The Christian religion too, naturally and rightly holds in great veneration, and regards as places of pilgrimage, the places which have been sanctified by the birth of Christ, Bethlehem; by his upbringing in early years, Nazareth; his baptism, the river Jordan; his ministry, the sea of Galilee or Gennesareth, and the towns on its shores, Tiberias, Capernaum, also the town of Jerusalem; and finally, his crucifixion, Calvary. Besides these, it has its holy towns, like Rome, Kiev, Canterbury, Lourdes, etc., and its specially sacred shrines and churches, where the images of the Blessed Virgin and the Bambino are worshipped with incense, lighted candles, water-sprinklings, (by persons of the Roman Catholic persuasion), much in the Hindū way, and miracles are believed to be performed, especially of healing.

The worship of the ideal Mother and Babe is, indeed, not only common to all religions, but is their purest, sincerest, most natural, and most ennobling part. So necessary is it for the human heart, that Buddhism in China has found out a Kwanyin Buddha, a female Buddha with a divine babe, to worship; she is the 'Goddess of Mercy', the 'Hearer of the World's prayers'.[1] And

---

[1] F. W. S. O'Neill, *The Quest for God in China*, pp. 153-154.

Fāṭimā and Hasan-Husain are as prominent in Islām, as Madonna and the Babe in Christianity; or Yashoḍā and Kṛshṇa, and Kausalyā and Rāma, in Hinḍuism.

But here, as elsewhere, the human heart runs to excess, and converts good into evil. The followers of Islām, not content with the one central Temple, also worship tombs and mausolea which are as uselessly and mischievously numerous as the Hinḍū temples and images; though the wisest elders of Islam and Christianity and Vaiḍika Dharma say:

Ḍilā! ṭawāf-i-ḍilān kun, ke Kā'ba-é makhfī-sṭ,
Ke āṅ Khalīl binā karḍ, wa īṅ Khuḍā khuḍ sākhṭ.
Ṭā kai ziyāraṭ-i-maqābir, ai afsurḍah!
Yak gurba-i-zinḍa beh az hazār shér murḍah! (*S.*)
(Thy-Self, the Self in all hearts, O my heart!
Go, circum-ambulate, circle with love!
For every living heart is made by God
And is the inner mystic Kā'ba true;
While th' outer Kāba was built by Khalīl.
How long, what for, wilt thou make pilgrimage,
O luckless one! to dead tombs? One live cat
Is better than a thousand lions dead!)

Pūrṇasy-āvāhanam kuṭra,
Sarv-āḍhārasya ch-āsanam,
Pra-ḍakshiṇā hy-An-anṭasya,
Hy-A-ḍvayasya kuṭo naṭih. (*Parā-pūjā.*)

(How can the All-pervading, Who holds all,
Be brought into a temple and confined
To a small image on a pedestal?
How fix the Omnipresent to one spot!

How can the Infinite be circled round
By pigmy man! How may we bow to Him
Who has no Second that could bow to Him,
Who is our very Self, naught else than We!)

Na nāka-pṛshthé, na Mahéṇḍra-loké,
Na nāga-rājyé, na rasā-ṭalé vā,
Na parvaṭ-āgré, na samuḍra-garṭé,
Na ch-āshta-siḍḍhishv,-an-iḍam hi Mokshah.
Na pāṭālam na cha vivaram girīṇām
Na-iv-ānḍha-kārah kukshayo n-oḍaḍhīnām,
Guhā yasyām nihiṭam Brahma shāshvaṭam,
Buḍḍhi-vṛṭṭim avishishtām kavayo véḍayanṭé.
(*Yoga-bhāshya.*)
(Not in the heavens, nor the underworlds,
Not in the hollow caves of trackless mountains,
Nor in black darkness of the ocean's deeps—
The cave where Brahma shines is the heart-cave
Of Mind which is filled with the Consciousness
"*I* am *not* any finite passing *This*.")

Bā-wujūḍé ke muzhḍa-e Ṭérā,
nahn-o-aqrab,
Safahe Masahaf pai likhā ṭhā,
mujhé mā'lūm na ṭhā. (*S.*)
(Though it is writ plain in the Holy Writ,
God sayeth, 'I am nearer unto thee,
O purblind man! than thine own jugular vein!'
Yet, being blind, I could not read that writ.)

It is not hidden from thee, neither is it far off. It is not in heaven, that thou shouldst say, "Who shall go up for us to heaven, and bring it unto us that we may hear it and do it?" Neither is it beyond the sea, that thou shouldst say, "Who shall go over the sea for us, and bring it unto us that we may hear it and do it?"

But the Word is very nigh unto thee, in thy mouth, and in thy heart, that thou mayst do it.

(*B.*, Deuteronomy, 30, 13-14,)

That which thou art thou dreamest not; so vast
That lo! time present, time to be, time past,
Are but the sepals of thy opening soul
Whose flower shall fill the universe at last.
Thou ponderest on the moon, the stars, the sky,
When the winds gather, how the waters run,
But all too lightly deemest of thy-Self
Who are a thousand miracles in One!

(JAMES RHODES.)

So, too, have the followers of the Buḍḍha taken to image-worship in excess. Philologists tell us that the very name, invented by the neighbouring Persian-speaking peoples, for "idol," *viz.*, *buṭ*, is but a corruption of the word 'Buḍḍha'; because the countless images, which they saw scattered all over the tracts now called Afgḥānisṭān, Ṭurkisṭān, etc., were all described to them, by the worshippers, as 'Buḍḍha'-images. Yet none has declared more emphatically than the Buḍḍha, that "Within our-Self deliverance must be found," and not from images.[1] His very last words were:

[1] Prof. B. K. Sarkar, in his paper on 'Religious Categories', (pp. 191-217 of *The Religions of the World*, vol. I, pub. by the Rāma-Kṛshṇa Mission, Calcutta, 1938), describes how Confucius, who died a disappointed and un-appreciated reformer, was, some two hundred years later, described by Mencius as "the embodiment of highest perfection'; "three hundred years after his death

Āṭṭa-ḍīpā viharaṭha,
Aṭṭā-saranā, an-añña-saraṇā,
Vaya-ḍhammā sankhārā,
appamāḍéna sampāḍéṭha. (*Bu.*)
(Be lamps unto your-Self, and refuge too.
Seek not for refuge from aught else than Self.
Desires, and tendencies made by them, pass.
The Self abides. Achieve It heedfully.)

---

he was made Duke and Earl"; another two hundred years later, Sze Ma-chien described him as "divinest of men"; by the end of the first century A. C., "his birthplace became a goal for pilgrims," emperors included; "in A. C. 178, a likeness of his was placed in his shrine, instead of the commemorative wooden tablet"; "in 267, an imperial decree ordered the sacrifice of a pig, a sheep, and an ox, to Confucius, at each of the four seasons; the first complete Confucian temple was built and dedicated in 505 A.C.; about 555, it was exacted that a Confucian temple should be built in every prefectural city". Prof: Sarkar also says that "Muhammad's death...surprised even Caliph Omar as something impossible or inconceivable...Subsequent generations enriched his life-story with details of his miracles. In the third century after his death, Ibn Habban of Andalusia went so far as to say that Muhammad was not a human being subject to hunger and thirst." These instances are typical of how extravagant beliefs gradually grow up round the memories of great persons. The child-mind cannot see the miraculousness of the 'familiar'. It invents romances. They are its nourishment; and should not be wholly forbidden; otherwise, the child-mind will languish. But, also, when the stage of adolescence and youth has been reached, they must be replaced more and more

It is well-known that the teaching of Mahāvīra Jina is not different from that of the Vedānta, even in words, so far as the most important of them are concerned.

Nayaṭy-Āṭmānam Āṭma-iva,
Janma, Nirvānam éva, vā,
Gurur-Āṭmā-(Ā)ṭmanas,-ṭasmāṭ,
N-āny-osṭi param-ārṭhaṭah.
(*J., Samāḍhi-shaṭaka.*)

(The Self doth lead it-Self to a new birth ;
Or to Nirvāṇa's freedom from such birth.
No other Master has the Self than Self.)

These are almost the very words of Véḍism:

Āṭma-iva dévaṭāh sarvāh,
sarvam Āṭmany-ava-sṭhiṭam,

---

by the miracles of the familiar, the so-called 'real'. Similar myths have grown up around the names of Kṛshṇa and Christ. Those connected with Kṛshṇa are specially imaginative; because they have had many more centuries to grow. The Quran (13. 38 ; 21. 7, 8 ; 25. 20) itself expressly declares that prophets are mortal, and eat food, and go about in the markets, and have wives and children, like other human beings. No prophet has claimed immortality for his physical body. Nevertheless, extravagant, fantastic, superstitious beliefs grow up about them. There are sects of excessively 'faithful' ones, which believe that the bodies of Kṛshṇa and Jesus Christ were made, not of ordinary, but some peculiar ethereal, matter. In the past, the *odium theologicum* of utterly senseless, yet very bitter, controversies between rival sects, over such subtleties and hair-splittings, has caused much bloodshed.

Āṭmā hi janayaṭy-éshām
karma-yogam sharīriṇām. (*M.*, xii. 119.)
(The Self is all the gods; all's in the Self;
The Self it-Self puts on the bonds of Karma;
And then it frees it-Self from them, again.)

Yet there is a great deal of worship of images of the Ṭīrṭhan-karas, among the Jainas to-day; though less so, and perhaps in a more refined form, than among the Hinḍūs; and there are a considerable number of Jaina temples, some exceedingly beautiful, scattered all over India, and located on admirably selected sites. Competent judges have recorded their opinion, that from the viewpoint of art, the Ḍīlwārā Jain temples on Mount Abu rank immediately after the Tāj Mahal of Agra.

The Founder of the Sikh reform of Hinḍuism, Guru Nānak, has also taught the very same essentials of Veḍānṭa.

Kāhe re, mana!, bana khojana jāī!
Sarab-nivāsī, saḍā alékhā, ṭo saṅg rahaṭ saḍāī.
Puhupa māṅhi jasa bāsa basaṭu hai,
Mukura māṅhi jasa chhāyī,
Ṭaisé hī Hari basaṭa niranṭara
Ghatahi méṅ, khojahu, bhāī!
Bhīṭara bāhara Ékahi jānau,
Yaha Guru gyāna baṭāī.
Kahe Nānaka, binu Āpā chīnhé,
Mitai na Bhrama kī kāī!

(Why wilt thou go into the jungles, Why!
What hopest thou to find there, O my mind!
E'en as the scent within the flowers dwells,

And as thy image in the glass is held,
So God within thine own heart ever bides ;
Seek Him with earnestness—and find Him there !
Also in everything and everywhere !
Outer and Inner, know, are but the same—
So does the Teacher teach thee finally.
Until thou know thy-Self, so Nānak says,
From the World-Mirage thou canst not get free.)

Another hermit of the Punjab has sung in his own mother-tongue :

Dhūndné-hār nū dhūndh khāṅ ṭū,
Pāyā paraṭ ḍé ghar ḍā ras ṭaiṅ nū,
Kahīṅ ṭū ḥī na howai Yār sab ḍā,
Phirai dhūndhaṭā jangalāṅ bichcha jin nū.
(But seek the Seeker for a while, O friend !
He whom thou seekest in all *others*' homes,
And in thick jungles, getting lost thy-Self,
Haply He is thy-*Self*, the Friend of all !)

Yet is there much reversion to image-worship among Sikhs too ; much merely formal repetition, without realization of the meaning of their sacred book, the *Granṭha Sāhab*, (a collection of the noble and elevating hymns and writings of the Gurus) ; and even ritualistic worship of copies of it, wrapped in costly cloths, placed on ornamental stands, with whisks made of expensive kinds of animal hair waved over them by devotees, in the great and beautiful central Golden Temple at Amriṭsar, and in subordinate *sanghaṭs* in many towns.

As said before, such formal worship is unavoidably craved by the child-mind. Within due limits, it is desirable and indeed indispensable. As apparatus, exercises, games, social work, of various kinds, are needed in kindergarten, school, college, university, for physical, intellectual, and one important part of moral, education and character-formation ; even so, such worships are needed, in the beginning, for the spiritual, and the rest of the moral, and emotional, education of the growing soul. But, obviously, such apparatus ought not to be clung to, after its work is done, its utility exhausted. The means should not be allowed to overpower and destroy the end.

Excessive clinging to external things is weakness and not wisdom. It should be diligently discouraged. Multiplication of images, eikons, idols, tombs, mausolea, etc., and of temples, pagodas, churches, mosques, etc., beyond a due proportion to the population, should be diligently discouraged, and not encouraged, by the wise and the learned of each religion. As a fact, Islām teaches that a new mosque should not be built within reach of the voice of the *mua'zzin* (the caller to prayer) of an existing mosque; and, similarly, Hinḍū scriptures say that it is much greater piety to maintain an existing old temple in good repair than to build a new one[1].

[1]The real purpose of pilgrimage is excellently illustrated in a conversation which a Musalman saint, Junaiḍ, held with a person just returned from Mecca : "From the hour you began journeying away from your

6. All have pageants, eikon and bambino processions, *Maulūḍ* and Kaṭhā and Kālakshépa, *Ḍulḍul* and *Tāziā*, Rāma-līlā and Kṛshṇa-līlā, *Muharram* and Piṭṛ-

---

home, have you been journeying away from your sins also ?" "No." "Then you have made no journey. At every stage where you halted, had you advanced a stage towards God ?" "No." "Then you have covered no stages. When you changed your ordinary clothing for pilgrim's garb, did you discard your vices and put on virtues ?" "No." "Then you have not put on the pilgrim's garb. When you stood at the mount Arafaṭ, did you stand in contemplation of God ?" "No." "Then you have not stood at Arafaṭ. When you went round the Kā'ba, did you behold all aspects of the immaterial Spirit ?" "No." "Then you have not gone round the Kā'ba. When you ran between Safā and Marwā, did you achieve Purity (Safā) and Considerateness (Murawwaṭ) ?" "No." "Then you have not done any real running. When you reached the place of sacrifice, did you sacrifice your worldly desires ?" "No." "Then you have not made sacrifice. When you threw the pebbles, did you throw away whatever sensual ideas were in your mind ?" "No." "Then you have not thrown the pebbles, and have not performed the pilgrimage."

All religions have similar rites and ceremonies, all of which are "outward symbols of inward graces", some more refined, some less. If done in the right spirit, under right guidance, they are as 'initiations', and leave behind permanent impressions of great value. The Eleusinian mysteries have been referred to before, at p. 77, *supra*.

p a k s h a, holy-days of fasts, festivals, lamentations, É k ā ḍ a s h ī and *Ramzān* and *Lent*; though few of these are in accord with the injunctions of the basic scriptures. All have a sabbath-day; Vḗḍism on the first, eighth, and eleventh days of each lunar fortnight; Judaism on Saturday; Islām on Friday; Christianity on Sunday; and so forth; for rest and recuperation.

Incidentally it may be noted that all the finest products of the fine arts, and some also of the useful arts, poetry, drama, dancing, music, painting, sculpture, architecture, clothing, metal-work, town-planning, gardening, tree-planting, road-making, etc., have found their greatest patron in, and drawn their most splendid inspiration from, religion, in all ages, and in all countries. This is but natural; for true religion ministers to, and further sublimates, the most elevated emotions, whose conscious expression is 'fine art'; and, if philanthropy be the noblest of all emotions and the active essence of religion, as it surely is, then all 'useful art' also. Religion has thus secured some of the purest joy to humanity, even in the life of the senses. Correspondingly, when religion has degenerated, by excess, by hypocrisy, by lack of intelligence, by low and evil nature, of custodian and of follower, or has been strangled, suffocated, buried, cremated, by overbearing and overpowering materialism, then art has also degenerated into coarse, vulgar, sensual, or even outright barbarous, savage, brutal, horrible forms.

If the religious leaders of the various communities had only sufficiently large heart and wise head; if they would sit down together and consult with each other benevolently; if they would make a good selection from all these very varied forms of manifestation of religious or religion-colored emotion, especially from the festivals; and would advise their respective followers to join with the others in all those selected forms and festivals; then they would double and treble the joy of each community; instead of marring it all, by promoting separateness, antagonism, riots and fatal fights, and ever-rankling revengefulness; as throughout the medieval ages in east and west alike, and as even at present in India. Such mutual consultation and co-operation, between religious leaders, is as necessary today as between politico-economic leaders; for rapid earth-encircling transport and communication have mixed up all nations, races, religions; and the only alternative to 'organising for war', and the destruction of civilisation, is systematic 'organisation for peace', over the one double problem, 'adequate and equitable distribution of (a) Spiritual and (b) Material Bread'.

7. All religions have sacraments, samskāras, *sunnaṭs*, initiations, solemn ceremonies, originally intended to refine and improve mind and body, and to bring about 're-generation', 'the second birth', 'becoming as little children

again', 'consecration', *ṭaqḍīs*, upa-nayana, ḍviṭīya-janma, *nava-joṭ* (*Z.*)[1].

All insist on cleanliness by frequent bathings and washings, snāna, shaucha, *wuzū*. Zoroastianism emphasises it more than almost any other virtue; indeed, it includes all virtues under 'purity' in the broad sense.

Purity is for man, next to life, the greatest good; that purity which is procured by the law of Mazaḍa for him who cleanses himself with good thoughts, words, and deeds." (*Venḍiḍāḍ*, Fargard, x. 18, 20.)

The Christian saying is well-known, that "Cleanliness is next to godliness."[2]

8. All use physical appliances to help concentration of the mind during devotions, like the *tasbīh*, the *mālā*, the rosary; and enjoin special postures and movements of body and limbs, during prayers.

---

[1] Some of the finer sacraments are such that if they were duly performed by wise and spiritual-minded 'scientist-priests', much of the nervous and mental disease, that is now dealt with by psycho-analysts and psychiatrists, would be avoided.

[2] An anecdote is related of a young candidate for ordination as Christian priest, who was asked by a senior, during examination, to expound "next—on which side of godliness?" (i. e., next before or next after). He promptly and rightly said, "on both sides." In current Hinduism, this vitally important scientific principle of cleanliness has been reduced to the absurdity of senseless 'don't-touchism', as between thousands of mutually exclusive 'castes' and 'sub-castes'.

9. All have j a p a, *azkār*, litanies; u p a-
v ā s a, *roza*, fast; j ā g a r a ṇ a, *shab-bédāri*,
vigil ; to fix heart on God and God in heart.

10. Vaiḍika Ḍharma, Islām, Judaism, all,
unhappily, as currently practiced, believe that the
Great God (and not only evil sprites) can be
propitiated by ceremonial bloodshed ; and all
therefore practise animal-sacrifice; but all, happily,
believe that *ṭark-i-haiwānāṭ*, m ā m s a - v a r -
j a n a , avoidance of flesh-meats, and *nafs-kushī*,
ṭ ṛ s h ṇ ā - ṭ y ā g a , i n ḍ r i y a - n i g r a h a , a s-
m i ṭ ā - n i r o ḍ h a , self-sacrifice, are the higher
and better way of life and worship, and refrain
from animal food on 'holy' days. The real and
profound meaning of animal-sacrifice is that the
animal-*in*-man, the beast-*in*-man, the lower base
selfish nature *of* man, his lust, anger, pride, timidity, egoism, symbolised by the goat, the buffalo,
the horse, the camel or the cow, and lastly man,
should be slain.[1]   But that same selfishness,

---

[1]Another, and very good, explanation also is suggested in Gaṅgā Prasāḍa's *The Fountain-head of
Religion*, (pp. 140-143), on the basis of Haug's *Essays*.
The ceremony of *go-méza* is described in the Zend
Avesta. The word is obviously nothing else than the
Zend form of the Skt. g o - m é ḍ h a. Dr. Haug says :
"*Géush-ūrvā* means the universal soul of Earth, the
cause of all life and growth. The literal meaning of
the word, soul of the cow, implies a simile, for the earth
is compared to a cow. By its cutting and dividing,
ploughing is to be understood. The meaning of that
decree...is that *the soil is to be tilled*...as a religious

instead of allowing itself to be slain, twists the scriptural metaphor into literal service of itself; slaughters innocent animals and feeds itself with their flesh, while professing that it is feeding God

---

duty." Gangā Prasāḍa adds that "G o - m é ḍ h a means (1) exoterically, in its ā ḍ h i-b h a u ṭ i k a sense, the ploughing of land for agriculture, and (2) esoterically, in its ā ḍ h y-ā ṭ m i k a sense, the control of one's senses". In Skt., g o or g a u h, from the root g a m, to go, means 'whatever goes'; hence, the earth, which goes round the sun; the senses, which go after their objects; the rays of the sun; cattle; arrows; speech; etc. Along this line of interpretation, each sacrifice may be regarded as intending the fostering, in special ways, of the kind of domestic animal after which it is named. But it must be admitted that the detailed descriptions of the ceremonies, mean, by the *letter*, much slaughter of animals, revel and carousal, hail and wassail.

In *Mbh.* Shanṭi-parva, ch. 345, (Kumbhakonam edn.) is described a great dispute between the ṛ s h i - s, 'sages, saints, seers', and the ḍ é v a s, 'gods' ('those who play through the senses'), as to whether sacrifices should be bloodless or bloody. The ṛ s h i s decided in favour of the bloodless.

Bījair-yajñéshu yashtavyam
  iṭi vai Vaiḍikī Shruṭih,
Aja-sanjñāni bījāni,
  Chhāgam no hanṭum arhaṭha.
N-aisha ḍharmah saṭām, devāh !,
  Yaṭra baḍhyéṭa vai pashuh,
Iḍam Kṛṭa-yugam shréshtham,
  kaṭham baḍhyéta vai pashuh. (*Mbh.*)

therewith. No sacrifice can be acceptable to God, the Rahmān, the Shiva-Shankara, the Benign, Auspicious, Merciful, the Universal Life, except the sacrifice of one's own lower self and selfishness.

Go ye and learn what that meaneth, I will have mercy and not sacrifice. (*B.*, Matthew.)

I desired mercy and not sacrifice; and the knowledge of God more than burnt offerings." (*B.*, Hosea.)

To obey is better than sacrifice, and to hearken than the fat of rams." (*B.*, I Sam.)

(God sayeth :) If I were hungry, I would not tell thee, for the world is mine, and the fullness thereof. Will I eat the flesh of goats, or drink the blood of bulls? Offer unto God thanks-giving, and pay thy vows unto the Most High. (*B.*, Psalms.)

(The Vedas say ye shall make sacrifice
With vegetable seeds and grains of corn.
A j a, the word which ye would say means 'goat',
Means grains unsprouted, and not goats at all.
Ye must not slay these harmless animals;
Must not create blood-guilt and cruel sin
In this the Age of virtuous Innocence,
And change it into th' Age of murderous War.)

Buḍḍha's most manifest reform has been the practical abolition of such formal blood-*sacrifices* in India; and though he did not succeed in abolishing animal food, he has, no doubt, reduced it among large sections of the people. His interruption of king Bimbisāra's sacrifice has been made famous by that unique poem, *The Light of Asia*, of Sir Edwin Arnold. The Jainas are well-known for their extreme avoidance of killing.

I delight not in the blood of bullocks, or of lambs, or of he-goats...Bring no more vain oblations...When ye make many prayers I will not hear; your hands are full of blood. (*B.*, Isaiah.)

The sacrifices of God are a broken spirit. A broken and contrite heart, O God, thou wilt not despise. (*B.*, Psalms.)

Shall I come before God with burnt offerings; with calves a year old? Will the Lord be pleased with thousands of rams, or with ten thousands of rivers of oil?...He hath showed thee, O man, what is good; and what does the Lord require of thee, but to do justly, and love mercy, and to walk humbly with thy God? (*B.*, Micah.)

"He that killeth an ox is as if he slew a man.

(*B.*, Isaiah.)

Sacrifice and offering thou dids't not desire; mine ears hath thou opened; burnt offering and sin offering hast thou not required....I will praise the name of God with a song and will magnify him with thanksgiving. This shall please the Lord better than an ox or bullock that hath horns and hoofs. (*B.*, Psalms, chs. 40 and 69.)

He that findeth his life (egoism) shall lose it; and he that loseth his life for My sake (the sake of the Self, Universalism) shall find it (as the Immortal Universal Life). (*B.*)

Jehḍ kun ḍar bé-kḥuḍī, kḥuḍ rā bi-yāb,
Zūḍ-ṭar, w-Allāhu-ālam b-is-sawāb.
Chanḍ ḍar banḍé kḥuḍī ? Az kḥuḍ bar ā !
Ekḥl in nālain f-anzur māṭ-rā ! (*S.*)
(Plunge into selflessness to find thy Self
At once, most certainly—God knows 'tis true.
How long wilt thou be bond-slave of thy self ?
Come out of thy small self into the Great !

Put off those dirty shoes of outer forms,
Enter the Temple, and its marvels see !)

Jab maiṅ ṭhā ṭab Hari nahīṅ
Ab Hari hai maiṅ nāṅhi ;
Préma-galī aṭi sāṅkarī,
Wā méṅ ḍo na samāṅhi. (KABĪR.)

(When I was, God was not; now that God is,
I am no more; yea, very strait the lane
Of Love Divine, it has no room for two !)
Ham moṭaqiḍ ḍā'wa-i-bāṭil nahīṅ hoṭé ;
Sīnéṅ meṅ kisī shakẖs ké ḍo ḍil nahīṅ hoṭé. (*S.*)
(How can we e'er accept the claim absurd
That there can be two hearts in the same breast.
God fills me—and for 'me' no space is left.)

Lisā fī jubbaṭin siwā-Allah. (*S* .)
Lisā fiḍ-ḍārain gẖairi. (*S.*)

N-īsṭ anḍar jubba-am gẖair az Kẖuḍā. (*S.*)
(Who is there in my cloak but God Him-Self ?
Who is there in both worlds except My-Self ?
There is naught-else-than-God within my clothes.)
Laṅyan al-Allāhā lohumohā wa lā ḍemāohā, wa lākin yan al-ohuṭṭaqwā min-kum. (*Q.*, ch. 22.)
(Neither the flesh nor yet the blood of these—
The sacrificial victims—reaches Him.
Keep your-self pure—that is what reaches Him.)

For the higher progress of the Soul, abstinence from blood-meats of all kinds is regarded as indispensable by Yoga and Sulūk. Alī, nephew and son-in-law of Muhammad, and said to be the first Sūfī in Islām after the Prophet himself, is reported as having advised the higher aspirants :

Lā taja'lu buṭūnakum maqābir-ul-haiwānāṭ. (ALI.)
(Make not your stomachs graves for animals.)

In Vaidika Ḍharma, apart from the higher metaphorical meaning of animal-sacrifice, the cumbrous ceremonial prescribed for the sacrifice of each animal is said to have been intended to restrict killing and drinking, and, at the same time, to give regulated and minimised vent to the sadistic and orgic tendencies of human beings when uncontrollable.[1] But though the formal 'sacrifice' may have diminished among some peoples (e.g., Christians have none), flesh-foods and spirituous drinks are but too common all over the world, particularly among the well-to-do.

Loké vyavāy-āmisha-maḍya-sévāh
Niṭyās-ṭu janṭor, nahi ṭaṭra choḍanā ;
Vyavasṭhiṭis-ṭāsu vivāha-yajña-
Surā-grahair, āsu nivṛṭṭir-ishtā. (*Bhāgavaṭa.*)
(The urge of sex, flesh-hunger, and wine-thirst,
Are ever there and need no stimulus.
The institutions of the marriage-bond
And ceremonial sacrifice were made
To limit them ; better is abstinence.)

If they cannot contain, let them marry ; for
It is better to marry than to burn. (*B.*, Cor.)

---

[1]There are periodic carnivals, Saturnalia, Bachchanalia, and festivals of unrestrained indulgence and riotous license, unfortunately, within the pale of every religion, even as there are intestines full of faecal filth within even the most beautiful human body. The inexorable indefeasible Law of Duality necessitates it.

11. The followers of all religions wear outer marks of one kind or another. Some wear tufts of hair on their heads, some on their chins, some practise tonsure. Some wear a yajnopaviṭa, 'sacrificial or sacred thread', across the chest over the left shoulder, and paint marks on their foreheads, some wear the *zunnār* round the waist, some wear *helāl* and *siṭāra*, crescent and star, on their caps, some carry a cross by a chain round their necks. All believe in the mysterious potency of special objects, and wear on their persons, *ṭāwīz*, yanṭra, amulets, phylacteries.[1] All have special forms of dress, often national, but sometimes religious also. If these distinctive marks and dresses were worn with an eye to artistic effect and mutual appreciation as well as to devoutness, it would all make for variegated beauty, interesting novelty, and greater total richness of social life. Instead of this, at present they often serve only as 'red rags to the bull,' mutually; because religious *mis*-leaders cultivate ferocity in their followings more than humaneness and rationality, and teach them assiduously that those who do not wear their hair in the same way (on the top of the head, or on the jaws and chin), or dress differently, or eat and drink other things, or speak and pray in another language, are strangers to be avoided, even enemies to be suppressed.

---

[1] And the potency is a fact; *subjectively*, because *strong faith* in something-else-than-self, however ima-

12. All call their places of worship by names which have the *same* meaning, *viz.*, 'House of God' (*church*), *Ḍév-ālaya* (mandira), *Baiṭ-Ullāh* (*masjiḍ*). All build them with heavenward-aspiring shikhara, kalasha, gopura; *munārā*, *ṭa'arum*, *gumbaḍ*; tower, dome, cupola, spire, steeple.

13. All have calls to prayer, *a'zāṅ*, ghantā, bell.

14. All offer prayers, masses, *fāṭihā* at *chehlum*, shrāḍḍha, for the dead; and have ceremonial funeral feasts, bhoja-s, *kanḍūri-s*.

15. All believe in special spiritual relationships of guru—shishya, *pīr-murīḍ*, saint—disciple.

16. All have rites and ceremonies, and ways of sitting up and down, or bending and kneeling and prostrating, or turning round and round, or carrying the hands to various parts of the body, and uttering special words, during sandhy-opāsanā, *namāz*, prayer. If one

---

ginary, as a helper (or a hinderer), *actually* produces mental concentration, mind-force, will-force, energy, and efficiency, (or the opposite), in the believer him-self; as 'the new psychology of the unconscious' illustrates freshly; and also *objectively*, for as we have seen before, pp. 191-202, and 214-222, *supra*, religion and science, both, justify belief in the existence of benign as well as malign *living* forces, of other sorts and types, than those cognisable by our physical senses, which *can* be attracted by the strong belief and emotion of human beings.

has an āsana, another has a corresponding *sajjāḍa*, or a pew.

17. All have priests: sexton, sacristan, beadle, verger, almoner, churchwarden, deacon, curate, chaplain, parson, vicar, rector, canon, prebendary, archdeacon, dean, suffragan, diocesan, prelate, bishop, Protestant archbishop and primate, Romish curé, abbé, cardinal, pope, Greek archimandrite, metropolitan, patriarch; pandās, pujāris, puro-hiṭa-s, yājakas, pandiṭs, ḍharm-āḍhikaris, sampraḍāy-āchāryas, temple-attendants of many degrees and names; *mua'zzins*, *mujāwirs*, *muṭawallis*, *mullās*, *mufṭis*, *ulemā*, *mujṭahiḍs*, *imāms*, *khalifās*; ḍasṭūrs, mobeḍs (Pārsis); scribes, pharisees, levites, rabbis (Hebrews); bonzes, phoongyes, talapoins, lamas (Buddhists); etc.—far too many of them.

18. All have sannyāsis, yaṭis, mandal-īshas, sāḍhus, bairāgis, uḍāsis, maṭh-āḍhīshās, sanṭs, mahanṭs; *faqīrs*, *miskīns*, *ḍarveshas*, *auliyās*, *sajjāḍa-nashīns*, *sheikhs*, *pīrs*, *murshiḍs*, *ṭakiya-ḍārs*; bhikshus, sṭhānaka-vāsis, shramaṇas, kshapaṇas, ṭhéras, mahā-ṭhéras, *lāmās*; anchorites, cenobites, monks, nuns, friars of scores of sect-or-order-names, abbots, priors, prioresses, abbesses, canonesses, novices—in excessive numbers, and very few genuine ascetics.

All have maṭhas, akhārās, ḍharma-shālās; monasteries, nunneries, almshouses; *vihāras*, *lāmāseris*; *ḍargāhs*, *ṭakiyās*, *khāniqāhs*

—mostly very badly mismanaged and only too often put to very sinful uses.[1]

19. All have subdivided into much too numerous sects, sam-pra-ḍāyas, panṭhs, *firqāhs*; literally hundreds, in Hinduism; also hundreds in Christianity, which is not generally known; and scores in Islam.[2]

---

[1] Max Muller writes in *Chips from a German Workshop*, I, 187: "The late Abbé Huc pointed out the similarities between the Buddhist and Roman Catholic ceremonials with such a *naiveté*, that, to his surprise, he found his delightful *Travels in Thibet* placed on the *Index* (*Expurgatorius*), 'One cannot fail being struck,' he writes, 'with their great resemblance with Catholicism. The bishop's crozier, the mitre, the dalmatic, the round hat that the great lamas wear in travel...the mass, the double-choir, the psalmody, the exorcisms, the censer with five chains to it, opening and shutting at will, the blessings of the lamas, who extend their right hands over the heads of the faithful ones, the rosary, the celibacy of the clergy, the penances and retreats, the cultus of the saints, the fastings, the processions, the litanies, the holy water; such are the similarities of the Buddhists with ourselves.' He might have added tonsure, relics, and the confessional."

[2] Very troublesome and disturbing to peace, this, no doubt. Yet, 'the darkest cloud has a silver lining', and 'the worst wind blows somebody good'. The patent fact that men interpret and modify and reshape the 'religion' of the Founder into any shape of any sect as they please, is proof patent that *they* are the masters of religion; not religion, their master. That they can

20. Vaiḍika Ḍharma is supposed to have one feature, *viz.*, the "caste-system," which is peculiar to it, and not to be found in any other religious scheme. The supposition is not quite correct, nor wholly incorrect. In every civilised society—and every civilisation is connected with a religion—the seeds, marks, outlines, of such a 'caste'-system are discernible; because they are inherent in human psycho-physical individuo-social nature. The seeds are sprouted, the outlines filled in, most fully, in Vaiḍika Ḍharma. All religions, directly or indirectly, sanction some laws and social institutions for the regulation of property, of the family-life, the administration of justice, the defence of the people, the wielding of executive authority; and so on. Vaiḍika Ḍharma enjoins a social structure, dealing with all aspects of human life, directly, comprehensively, systematically.

Let us recapitulate a little; for the subject has exceeding great importance.

The one craving of Humanity is for Bread; (*a*) Bread Spiritual, and (*b*) Bread Material. The one problem of problems is, How provide an adequate and equitable supply of the two to all. All religions seek to minister to both needs. Degenerations set in, in the practice of the religions, because of the growth of excessive selfishness in the custodians and trustees. Everything that is

and do change from any religion wholly into any other, is conclusively strong proof.

born, and grows, must also decay, and pass away, yielding place to new. Re-generations, new births, necessarily follow. Everything that dies, must be born again, in a new form. The soul, the idea, the ideal, the principle, remains the same. The em-bodi-ment, the expression, the vehicle, changes. In the Life of the Human Race, the present times, with their characteristic civilisation, of predominantly physical science and machinist intellectuality, require a 'democratic and socialist' Religion, which will include a 'democratic and socialist' Polity, i. e., a complete Social Organisation.

We have repeatedly noted before, that it is not enough to *pray*, however sincerely, that God's Will be done on earth; it is necessary also to *know* what that Will is; if we are to subserve it, to act in obedience to it. It is not enough to be *willing* to do one's Duty without greed for reward; it is necessary also to *know* what exactly that Duty is; if we are to discharge it actively and efficiently. It is not enough to be *ready*, even eager, to obey the Golden Rule of Conduct; we must also *know* what, in any given situation, we *ought* to wish, or not wish, for self and therefore for others; if we are to act according to that Rule *usefully*, without creating confusion all round.

Spirituo-Material Science, as taught in the great utterances and writings, the 'scriptures', of highly evolved members of the Human Race;

(a) a v a ṭ ā r a - s, ṛ s h i - s, *nabi-s*, *rasul-s*, messiahs, prophets, religious 'supermen', possessed of the 'divine fire', and of superhuman faculties of subtler sensation, perception, (clairvoyance, telepathy, clair-audience, 'prophetic vision', 'real dreams', etc.), and of finer intellection and intuition, and (b) scientific 'supermen', endowed with ab-normal, extra-ordinary, powers of observation, intellection, intuition, and tireless application and research; such spirituo-material science gives us the needed knowledge. It tells us, in the first place, (I-a) in broad outlines, what God's Will is, on the infinite-and-infinitesimal scale, what the Nature of the World-Process, and the Meaning of Life, are, and (I-b) what Man's General Duty is; and, in the second place, (II) how *Human Society* should be *organised*, and *Individual Life planned*, with clear specification and partition of all particular rights and corresponding duties, so that each one of us may be able to ascertain readily what his duty and corresponding right is, in any given situation, and both our needs, spiritual and material, may be duly satisfied, in accordance with that Nature and Meaning.

The normal human being is not a solitary. He is born in a family which lives amidst a community of families. He lives, grows, decays, dies, in a family amidst a community. His joys and sorrows are unavoidably and inseparably bound up with those of others. It is impossible for any individual to carry out the Divine Will, observe the Golden Rule, perform his Duty, and achieve any reasonable amount of Happiness here and hereafter, (i. e., secure Material and Spiritual Bread); (i) *if* the community, the society, amidst which he is born, lives, and dies, is not systematically *organised for peace* and prosperity, (which includes, as a subsidiary, organisation for *defence*); and (ii) *if* the life of the individual is not correctly mapped out and planned, and fitted into that social organisation, in such a way, that each person, in accord with his special temperament and vocational aptitude, (a) receives appropriate education, (b) readily secures, or is provided with, a suitable occupation for his and family's livelihood, with regard to that aptitude as ascertained and developed by his educators, (c) retires from bread-winning work in right time, to take up some one or more out of numerous kinds of honorary unremunerated public duties, in keeping with his special capacities, and, finally, (d) spends the last years of his physical life in ever greater absorption in spiritual exercises, meditations, well-wishing to the world at large, and promoting the general welfare by pouring into the moral atmosphere, a continuous stream of benevolence, 'good-will', and the powerful influence of high example of life well-lived in the past, and now incarnating God's blessings of renunciant selflessness, contented repose of soul, and all resignedness and spiritual peace.

Because Religion, to justify itself as the helper of mankind, has to secure for them, happiness here as well as hereafter; therefore it will not be out of place to give some account, briefly, of how Vẹdism endeavours to secure the former; in other words, of what its conception is, of the kingdom of God and His Righteousness on earth, *in practice*, for man as now constituted.

The Vẹdic Scheme of Individuo-Social Organisation.

The main great declarations of all Religions and of Science, on (I) the nature of the World-Process and the Meaning of Life, have been sketched in chapter ii above; and those on the General Duties of the human being, in ch. iii. In the briefest terms:

(I-a) The Infinite Spirit descends into denser and denser finite forms of matter, and then re-ascends back out of them, on all possible scales of Time, Space, and Motion, from minutest atom and microscopic animalcule to vastest star-system; and (I-b) at the stage of the human form, on the return journey, 'We should do unto others as we would be done by'.

As regards (II), Vaiḍika Ḍharma prescribes a Scheme of Individuo-Social Organisation, applicable to the whole Human Race, which makes an equitable partition, between the several human 'types', according to temperament, of different kinds of 'work-and-wages', 'labour-and-leisure', 'hardship-and-pleasure', 'rights-and-duties'; makes it possible to ensure 'necessaries' for every one; gives opportunity to each person to win additional, temperamentally suitable and desired, 'comforts' and 'luxuries', by special good work; provides appropriate incentives to such good work, for all; secures regulated and just play for all human instincts, egoistic as well as altruistic; reconciles individualism and socialism, imperialist capitalism and communist proletarianism, by vigilantly guarding against the one Sin, '*Excess*', through the sedulous cultivation and practice of the one Virtue, 'the Golden Mean'; and, by doing all this, it enables every one to know precisely what his particular duty, and corresponding right, is, in any particular situation; and gives, to every one, just opportunity as well as instruction for securing happiness, here and hereafter, as far as is humanly possible.

The details of this Scheme have been dealt with elsewhere.[1] They cannot be expounded here. But the main principles may be summed up in a few tetrads.

There are:

1. Four main types of human beings, by temperament and vocational aptitude; *not* by mere 'heredity', *but* by individual 'mutation' or 'spontaneous variation': (a) men (and women) of knowledge; (b) of action; (c) of acquisitive desire; (d) of undeveloped undifferentiated mentality and capacity, of general labor, of unspecialised work.

2. Four main classes of vocations, occupations, professions, with numerous sub-divisions under each: (a) the learned; (b) the executive; (c) the commercial; (d) the industrial or laboring.

3. Four main kinds of livelihood,: regulated (a) honoraria, fees, presents; (b) taxes, tributes, public salaries; (c) profits; (d) wages.

---

[1]In the present writer's *Ancient vs. Modern Scientific Socialism*; more briefly, in *The Science of the Self*, ch. vii; in much greater detail, in *The Science of Social Organisation*, Vols. I and II, a third being in preparation.

4. Four main stages of life: (a) student; (b) householder; (c) honorary unremunerated public worker, retired from competitive bread-winning; (d) renunciant ascetic, hermit, anchoret, recluse.

5. Four main physical appetites, urges, of: (a) hunger; (b) acquisitiveness; (c) sex; (d) rest, recreation, amusement, play, health, sense of physical well-being.

There are subordinate quartettes under each of these four. (5-i) Four kinds of food: (a) bloodless, light, easily-digested, but non-volatile, bland, mostly fruit-and-milk diets, for the spiritual scientist, who needs lucid mind and long calm steady thinking; (b) strong, stimulating, energy-producing foods, for the administrator, the executive officer, who has to decide and act quickly and meet emergencies; for soldiers, even flesh-foods and strong drinks, in moderation, (allowable, not desirable); preferably the flesh of wild animals that damage crops and multiply fast; not of animals to be reared for slaughter and eating; (3) 'staying' cereals, milk-foods, (also the flesh of crop-destroyers as above), for the tradesman and the agriculturist; (4) heavy foods, (nitrogenous), producing capacity for long-continued bodily exertion, for the workman and laborer.

(5-ii) Four kinds of special possessions, suited for the four temperaments, and for the carrying on of their professions, respectively, e.g., (a) books, and objects and means of observation and investigation; (b) weapons and subsidiaries; (c) machinery and other means of production and distribution; (d) implements of work.

(5-iii) Four kinds of marriages: (a) settled by wise elders; (b) by mutual self-choice, or by love-chase, and 'capture'; (c) for monetary consideration; (d) by blind passion.

(5-iv) Four kinds of recreation: (a) communion with Nature, contemplation of her beauties; (b) sports of various kinds, involving quickness of mind as well as body, hunting, racing, fencing, animal taming and training; (c) trials of luck with money-stakes, supervision of charitable works, home-athletics; (d) gymnastics, fairs, shows, simple games. The pleasure of 'pilgrimage' is appreciated by, and is open to all types; and pilgrimages may be and are performed during any of the four stages of life; but they are recommended for the last two. To the practical worldly benefits of pilgrimage, indicated on pp. 452-453 *supra*, may be added the liberalising education and aesthetic enjoyment that are derived from wide travel, and the seeing of other towns, cities, peoples, ways and manners, monuments of human art, and Nature's grand and ever-varied scenery, woods, waters, mountains, deserts, snows, and seas, which make Her poetry of the sublime, awful, beautiful, ever and everywhere the wonderful.

It must be borne in mind, always, that there is nothing exhaustive or exclusive about the lists given or distinctions drawn in any of the quartettes mentioned here; but only an indication of the predominant feature or quality. Patently, all organs and all functions are present in every living human Mind-Body; equally clearly, some are more strong and prominent in one, some in another; wherefore we call one person a professor, another a captain, another a banker, and a fourth a shepherd or mill hand; though all are men.

6. Four main psychical appetites, incentives, 'luxuries', cravings, for: (a) honor (public esteem); (b) power (official authority); (c) wealth (artistic possessions); (d) en-joy-ment (of one-self; compare the common phrase, 'we enjoyed our-selves thoroughly').

7. Four main 'ends' of life: (a) (observance of) lawfulness-and-morality, (which regulate) (b) wealth, riches, (which refine) (c) (psycho-physical) pleasure; (d) (spiritual) happiness, (en-joy-ment of the Great Self).

8. Four main social institutions: (a) Religion; (b) Property; (c) Family; (d) Government-Church-State.

9. Four main 'powers' of the State: (a) science power; (b) valour (military) power; (c) finance (bread-and-money) power; (d) labor power.

10. Four main sets of rights-and-duties, for the four main temperaments and professions: (a) duty to gather and to spread true and useful knowledge of all sorts; right to receive honour; (b) duty to develope the needed ability, and give protection to all who need and deserve it, and to maintain law and order and peace in the land; right to be entrusted with official authority and power of command; (c) duty to arrange for the production and distribution of all necessaries and comforts, in accord with the laws of the state; right to receive price (which will yield reasonable profits, within the limits permitted by the laws); (d) duty to give help and service to the others; right to receive adequate wages and be provided with amusements, (*panem et circenses*). Besides the special rights above mentioned, the general right belongs to all, to receive necessaries of life, and suitable means, in accord with their capacities, of discharging their duties properly, (a) e. g., libraries, laboratories, facilities for travel and research, (b) weapons, munitions, office apparatus, (c) machinery and all requisites for production, distribution, transport, (d) implements of work; and also the right to be provided with the respective livelihoods (and none other) which have been mentioned in section 3 above.

11. Four main duties of the older generation towards the younger, and of the state towards the people, viz., to: (a) educate, (b) protect, (c) nourish and cherish, (d) help in all other ways as needed. Briefly, to (a) teach, (b) guard, (c) feed, (d) serve. The constituent or preventive functions of the state are covered by (b); the ministrant or promotive, by the other three.

12. Four main interlinked subordinate organisations, which together make up the total Individuo-Social Organisation of the State or People as a whole: (a) educational; (b) protectional, (political, administrative, executive, military); (c) economic; (d) industrial. Only such a 'totally' complete organisation of the 'total' People makes the true 'totalitarian' State.

The (a) educational organisation is made up of the learned 'class' or professions and the student order or 'stage', i. e., of educator and educand in the broad sense; the (b) protectional, of the executive professions and the order of honorary publicists to guide and supervise them; the (c) economic, of the commercial professions as producers and distributors and of the order of householders as consumers; the (d) industrial, of the workman class, the laboring professions, of many grades, as the physical helpers of the community, and the order of renunciant ascetics as the spiritual servants.

13. Four main congenital social 'debts', laden with which, every human being is born: (a) to the 'gods' i. e., the forces of Nature, which spread out the universe of objects on which our life and senses feed, and all our experience is based; (b) to the 'ancestors', who have given to us our body, in and through which our life is lived; (c) to the 'sages, seers, scientists' of the past, who have left to us the stores of knowledge which

differentiate us from the lower kingdoms and refine and ennoble our life; (d) to the Supreme Self, which has given us the spark of life, our soul.

14. Four main ways of repayment of those debts and winning final Release, Spiritual Freedom, M o k s h a, *Najāṭ*, Salvation: (a) performing 'pious works', (such as plantation of trees, re-afforestation of denuded tracts; construction of water-works, wells, tanks, reservoirs, lakes, canals; protection and promotion of useful and beautiful animal life; purifying of the psychical and physical atmosphere by burning incense, chanting holy hymns and reciting scriptures and noble epics, lighting sacred fires and lights with special substances; whereby the stores of Nature, 'ether', air, fire, water, earth, which we use up or pollute, and also our depleted and struggle-and-passion-soiled mental powers, are replenished and sanitated; (in modern conditions, devising and carrying out measures for abating the 'smoke-nuisance', the 'noise-nuisance', for preventing the contamination of water and the growth of disease-germs, for converting sewage into manure and food for the soil, and such other 'public works', represent what in the earlier times were called 'pious works'); (b) rearing worthy progeny, *neither too many, nor too few*, (to preserve *balance* between produce and consumers), of the best quality possible; (c) giving knowledge, or helping the learned class to give it, to the new generation; also adding to the existing stores of knowledge, or enabling others to do so; (d) retirement from competition, renunciation, spiritual meditation, realisation of the identity of the individual with the Universal, and earnestly and constantly wishing well to all.

In the first two quarters or stages of each person's life, the individualist or egoistic instincts are given regulated play; in the last two, the socialist or altruistic instincts are brought to culmination. In this way are all 'isms' duly balanced and reconciled; the State exists for the Individual and the Individual lives for the State; each is for all, all are for each; to each is given according to his need, from each is taken according to his capacity.

We have noted before that all the factors of all these tetrads are inter-dependent, like the head, arms, trunk, and legs; or like the nervous, muscular, glandulo-vascular, and skeletal systems; of a single living human organism; also that only the main factors, groups, classes, can be broadly distinguished; while the sub-divisions intermingle, pass into, permeate and pervade each other, so subtly and inextricably, that attempt at any precise demarcation is bound to fail. As said in the *Gīṭā*: 'definition is a passing from the indefinite to the indefinite'. The arrangement by tetrads is also a matter of convenience only. The facts and factors may be, and elsewhere have been, grouped in duads and trinities as well as quartettes. The variety in the presentation of the ideas should, to the scrutinising mind, bring out the basic truths only the more clearly. Also, in detailed working, subordinate tetrads may be distinguished and formulated usefully, under each of the others, as under (5), above.

Such is a brief sketch of the ancient Vedic Individuo-Social Organisation. It is an essential part of Vḗḍism, one of the names of which is Varṇ-āshrama Ḍharma, 'the Duty of Social Vocational Classes and Individual Life-Stages.'

Some elucidative comments, and correspondences in the other religions, may be added.

A tree or animal, in its fullest development, shows only that which was latent in the seed or zygote. A 'civilisation' is only an explication of what is implicit in human nature. That nature is three-fold, cognitive-desiderative-active; or, if we wish to pursue the scheme of tetrads, also 'rest-ive', 'wishing to rest', 'to sleep in the unconscious', 'unwilling to keep awake and go forward'. Every civilisation has three corresponding aspects; the fourth being that of reactive weakening, fatigue, decay, after attaining zenith. The three are: (a) its stores of peculiar kinds of knowledge; and its special language, which embodies one out of the infinite shades of the All-Spirit; (b) its characteristic arts, recreations, ideals, aspirations, buildings, towns, worships, religion generally; (c) its ways of living, forms of government, enterprises, colonisations, conquests, commercial and mechanical activities of all sorts.

Each civilisation shows some differences from others, in respect of all these; but the general facts are the same in all.[1] Every human face and figure is different from every other; but the general features of all human bodies are the same. The more advanced and complex the civilisation, the more specialised and differentiated the three types (and many sub-types) of persons who carry on the three main (and many

[1] "We see the elaborate drainage-system of Knossos" (of the ancient times of king Minos in Crete) "and at once feel at home; the cosmetics found in an ancient grave strike us as pathetically up to date; the surprise which a visitor to a Museum expresses at the age of a given object is in exact proportion to his recognition of the object's essential modernity"; Sir Leonard Woolley, *Digging up the Past*, (Pelican Books, 1937), p. 14.

subordinate) functions of the three main aspects. But the three main types, with the fourth residual plasmic type, are to be found in all grades of communities of human beings; primitive, barbarous, 'semi-civilised'; as well as those which regard themselves as 'very advanced' and 'very highly civilised; even though, unhappily, these commit the most extensive and intensive mass-crimes of exploitation and butchery; as is shown by all known history; side by side with some humane and beneficent deeds of true greatness and glory, and many magnificent achievements, to-day, of science and valour combined; outracing the eagle and the wind itself high in the heavens, the giant fish in the depths of the ocean, leaving the fastest racer far behind on the land, capturing voices and music from all parts of the earth at once in any home they please; all which achievements, however, subserve only the very same fundamental 'appetites', though with 'longer circuiting.'

The Vḍic Samskṛṭ names for the four types are, (a) b r ā h m a ṇ a, (b) k s h a ṭ ṭ r i y a, (c) v a i s h y a, (d) s h ū ḍ r a. The Islāmic Arabic-Persian names are, (a) *ul-ul-ilm*, also *ul-ul-albāb*, (b) *ul-ul-amr*, (c) *zurrā*, (d) *muzḍ-war*; the three first occur in the Quran; simpler and more commonly used forms are, (a) *ā'lim*, (b) *ā'mil*, or *amīr* or *āmir* (from *amr*, to command), (c) *ṭājir*, (d) *mazḍūr*. The Zoroastrian names are, (a) airyamnā, (b) véréjen, (c) khaéṭush, (d) go-vāsṭrā.[1]

[1] These are possibly connected with the Skt. words, aryamā (which means the sun, also a friend, for the sun is the 'friend' and benefactor of all the world); vīrya-vān, (the virile, the mighty), or rājanya, (which is a synonym for kshaṭṭriya); kshiṭīsha or kshéṭrī, the owner or tiller of the soil, the field; the go-vāsī or go-véshi,

Akhyā chā khaéṭush yāsaṭ; ahyā
véréjéném maṭ airyamnā. (Z., Gāṭhā, 32. 1.)
Khaéṭéūsh chā ṭarémaīṭīm, véréjanakhyā
chā najaḍishṭām ḍrujém, airyamanas
chā naḍénṭo, géūsh chā vāsṭrāṭ
achishṭém manṭūm. (33. 4.)
Ké airyamnā, ké khaéṭus, dāṭa is amhaṭ
yé véṛéjenāi vam-ūhīm frasasṭīm. (49.7.)
(The khaéṭus, the airyamnā, also
The véréjen, runs seeking after this,
[The easy lazy pleasures of this world].
Be not our khaéṭus renunciant,
Do-nothing, indolent; our véréjen
Be not too violent; our airyamnā,
Be he not ignorant, lacking in knowledge;
Nor our gé-vāsṭrā, who serves all the world,
Be e'er downcast in spirit...In bad times,
When foes attack, what can th' airyamnā do?
And what the khaéṭus? The véréjen
Alone, with God's keep, can defend us then!).[1]

---

the dweller among the cattle, the keeper of the domestic animals.

[1] Ganga Prasada, M.A., M.R.A.S., in his excellent work, *The Fountain-head of Religion*, at pp. 91-93, quotes from Dr. Haug's and Prof. Darmestetter's and others' writings on Zoroastrianism and translations of its books, and says that the Zend names for the four castes were: "*Aṭhrava*, priest; *Raṭhaesṭao*, warrior; *Vāsṭriyofshyas*, cultivator; *Huiṭes*, workman"; also that "in the later scriptures of the Parsi religion", the names were changed to "*Horisṭaran*, *Nūrisṭaran*, *Rozisṭaran*, *Sorisṭaran*;...in Pahlavi, *Raṭhornan* (priests, Skt. Aṭharvan); *Raṭheshṭaram* (car-warrior, Skt. Raṭha-sṭha;

In Britain they used to speak of 'the three estates of the realm', (a) clergy, (b) nobility, (c) commons, to which a fourth has to be added now, (d) proletariat, (labor, workmen, industrialists). The other countries and languages of Europe have corresponding classes and words. Japan has, (or until recently had), (a), *kuge* (court nobles, kinsmen of the emperor), (b), *bushi*, or *buki*, or *sāmurai* (warriors), (c), *heimin*, (the common people), (d) *eta*, *hinin* (like 'outcastes').[1] China has (or until recently had), (a) scholars (literati, including officials, mandarins), (b) farmers, (c) artisans, (d) traders, merchants.[2] Very fortunately, it has never insisted on 'heredity'.

Compare the following verses from the Vḗḍas:

Mukham kim asy-āsīṭ, kim bāhū,
kim ūrū pāḍā uchyḗṭḗ?
Brāhmaṇ-osya mukham āsīḍ,
bāhū rājanyah kṛṭah,
Ūrū ṭaḍ-asya yaḍ vaishyah,
paḍbhyām shūḍro ajāyaṭa.
Purusha ḗv-ḗḍam sarvam,
yad bhūṭam yach-cha bhavyam;

Hoṭkshan (agriculturists, etc.); and *Basṭaryoshan* (who render all kinds of service)."

[1] *Ency Brit.*, 14th. edn., xii, 940, art. 'Japan'.

[2] *Ibid.*, v. 514, art. 'China'; Lin Yutang, *My Country and My People*, p. 182. It is remarkable that 'soldiers' are not included in this grouping; they have been regarded practically as 'out-castes' in China all along; hence, "the Chinese are the world's worst fighters", Lin Yutang, *ibid.*, 56; but the long-continued war between Japan and China is changing all this; see, e. g. *Mowrer in China* (Penguin Series), pub. 1938.

Sa bhūmim sarvaṭah spṛṭṭvā
aṭy-aṭishthaṭ ḍash-āngulam.
(*Ṛg-Véḍa*, 10. 90. 10, 11, 12.)
Rucham no ḍhéhi brāhmaṇéshu,
rucham rājasu nas-kṛḍhi,
Rucham vishyéshu shūḍréshu,
mayi ḍhéhi ruchā rucham.
Yaṭh-émām vācham kalyāṇīm
āvaḍāni janébhyah,
Brahma-rājanyābhyām, shūḍrāya
ch-āryāya svāya ch-āraṇāya cha.
(*Yajur-Véḍa*, 18. 48; 26. 2.)
Priyam mām, Ḍarbha! kṛṇu, brahma-
rājanyābhyām, shūḍrāya ch-āryāya cha;
Yasmai cha kāmayāmahé
sarvasmai cha vipashyaṭé.
(*Aṭharva-Véḍa*, 19. 32. 8.)

(What was the head of this Great Cosmic Man,
Humanity? What were its arms, its trunk
And thighs, and what did constitute its legs?
The man who had Brahm'-Wisdom was its head;
Who shone with guarding valour was its arms;
The settler and food-grower was the trunk;
Who ran at bidding, docilely, was legs.[1]
This Cosmic Man, the whole vast Human Race,
Embodied Principle of Consciousness,
Is everything that was, is, is to be;
Its universal mind includeth all.
With its ten organs, sensor, motor too,
It overspreads the earth, all-compassing.

---

[1] The interpretation in those four lines, of the four familiar, and now much misused, names is in strict accord with the etymology of the four words, brāhmaṇa, rājanya (kshaṭṭriya), vaishya, shūḍra.

O Lord of All! give mutual pleasantness
And love to all of us, our brāhmaṇas,
Our kshaṭṭriyas, our vaishyas, shūḍras, all.
May we speak pleasing words unto each other,
Always, we brāhmaṇas and rājanyas,
We gentle shudras, and we Ārya-vaishyas
Who are the refuge of us all for food.
Thou who articulatest all the parts
Of all this world, and organisest them!
Bind us in the strong bonds of love with all,
Our brāhmaṇas, rājanyas, shuḍras, āryas,
And all we like; and make our foes, our friends.)

The different countries, peoples, civilisations, have varied in the ranking of the classes; in the attaching of greater importance to one or another; in the forbidding or allowing of transfer of persons from one to another. The competition for higher rank, status, power, has generally lain between the 'medicine-man' of the tribe and its 'chief'; the 'magic-lord' and the 'war-lord'; the 'priest'-pope and the 'soldier'-king; the 'civil (temporal, military) power' and the 'spiritual power'; the 'scientific knowledge', and the 'valorous fighting prowess'. But, in modern times, finance power seems to have reduced both to service of itself; and, in turn, is now threatened with subversion and submersion by 'labor-power'. All which means only lack of just balance between the four powers. Also, in India, for many hundreds of years now, the principle of 'mutation' has been thrust aside by 'vested interests', and the four types, or 'castes', have been made rigidly 'hereditary', as nowhere else. A peculiar result has followed. Human nature being what it is, 'mesalliances' have been always occurring; and new sub-castes have been always forming, in ever increasing numbers. This has created a social agglomeration of a unique kind, an incoherent jumble of castes, sub-castes, and sub-sub-sub-castes; each 'hereditary', all mutually exclusive in respect of dining and marrying, and consequently, of fellow-feeling; which, still, are all, though very loosely and more and more ineffectively, tied together by the name 'Hindū', (i.e., 'Hind-ian', 'Ind-ian') and by something which may be called the remnants of a common culture.[1]

[1] The Indian Census Report, for 1891, stated the total number of 'castes' as 2378. The Census Report for 1931 says that the work of making a new and complete list was abandoned, and the population-figures of only the more important ones given, because there was constant fluctuation going on in the thousands of the minor sub-castes (especially among the so-called 'untouchables'), by fissions, on the one hand, and co-alescences of small groups, on the other. The *Enc. Brit.*, (14th. edn., 1929), iv. 979, says: Caste "has resulted in the creation of some three or four thousand social units, many of which are, however, not altogether homo-geneous, so that these figures do not represent all its ramifications." But the disastrous absurdity of this insanely endless and utterly irrational fissiparousness, its destructive effect on social cohesion, co-operation, solidarity, is being realised more and more, by the at all thoughtful and public-spirited members of the community; new forces, ideas, ideals, are working in the 'collective Hindu mind;' a movement is growing stronger, every day, for a reversion to the original four main 'caste-classes', in the first place, and, secondly, for placing them on the basis of personal temporament and actual profession, instead of mere birth; and bills for validating inter-caste marriages are being repeatedly introduced in the legislature, with success in part.

'Caste', or rather 'sub-sub-sub-caste', means today nothing more than a group of families, whose members dine and marry among themselves, and not with the members of any other group; who will not take food which has been 'touched' by persons of other castes. Whatever may have been the causes, in past times, (many speculations have been advanced as to these, fear of poisoning among others), there is no sense left in the practice, now.

The very sound scientific reason for avoidance of indiscriminate interdining and intermarrying is, of course, obvious. If we are to preserve and promote individual and racial health, we must eat pure food, drink pure drink, in company with clean-living sympathetic friendly persons of similar habits; and marry with persons of parity of temperament and compatibility of tastes, interests, likes and dislikes. But what is obvious to dispassionate reason, is made very obscure by perverse passion. "Time makes ancient good uncouth"; time meaning, here, the growth of cunning vested interests and tyrannical selfishness, wishful to grab all powers and avoid all responsibilities, on the one hand, and of weakness and superstition, or the other. 'Good customs by excess corrupt themselves'; excess, here, being, excess of effort to specialise, differentiate, fix, under the impulsion, not of reasonable far sight, but of very interested short sight. Other countries evolved only 'the divine right by birth of kings and patricians'. India evolved 'the divine *right* of *superiority*, of whole classes of priests, as well as of fighters, by *birth*'; and 'the God-ordained *duty* of *inferiority*, by *birth*', of other

---

A somewhat radical one was introduced by the present writer, in the Indian Central Legislature, of which he was then a member, in 1936; but could not be carried through.

whole classes of traders, agriculturists, 'untouchables', (like that of negro--slaves in America until the Civil War between North and South). Insurmountable barriers were created by forbiddal of interdining and inter-marriage. The remarkable fact is that, instead of fulfilling the scientific laws of healthy dietetics and eugenics (not only physical, but even more, psychical), the present practice, in regard to these matters, only too often causes gross violation of those fundamental laws. Unclean food, cooked by dirty and diseased persons, is often eaten, because the cook bears the same caste-*name* as the eaters. Disastrous mismatings are often perpetrated, because the parties bear the same caste-*name*. Such marriages are called s a-v a r ṇ a i. e., 'of persons of the same v a r ṇ a'. In reality they are extremely *a*-s a-v a r ṇ a, i.e., are marriages of persons of *not* the same v a r ṇ a. The word v a r ṇ a, by etymology, means (1) 'that which describes' (the position of a person in Society, viz., his *occupation*, his means of living), (2) 'that which he chooses' for himself, (again, his profession), (3) 'that which envelopes and covers him', (his color, his complexion). In no way does it mean what it is at present made to mean, i.e., a separate 'birth-caste'. That it continues to show, even in its perversion, the impress of its original and etymological sense, is proved by the fact that a very large number of the *caste*-names are names of *occupations*. The followers of each little limited 'occupation' became converted into rigidly hereditary 'castes'. Probably, they served the purposes of 'close' trade-guilds, at one time. But, before long, it seems, the purpose became confined to inter-dining and inter-marrying. Persons whose caste-*name* indicated a certain occupation, began to follow quite other occupations. At present, all sorts of 'castes' are following all sorts of 'occupations', excepting the 'priestly'. This last continues to be a jealous monopoly, but is beginning to be encroached upon.

All this gross perversion and de-rationalisation of 'caste' is coming to be seen more and more clearly by the new generation, under the tremendous stress of the times and world-movements; and they are breaking through the trammels in increasing numbers. But, as usual, there is the danger of going to the opposite extreme, of 'license' and 'licentiousness'.

What has been said above does not necessarily mean that 'hunger' and 'sex' are much worse mismanaged in the east than in the west. Competent eastern as well as western observant travellers have recorded that family life, *on the whole*, is not more unhappy in the east than in the west. Sex-slave traffic, prostitution, adultery, assault, violation, rape, group-rape, the horrors of life in brothels managed by brothel-keepers who trade in woman's flesh more ruthlessly than butchers in animal flesh, are to be found in every country, in varying forms. If one aspect is worse in any country, another is better. There are 'nature's compensations'. The safe conclusion is that there is much need and room for improvement in both these respects in every country. Such improvement is possible in these, as in all other respects, only by careful wise testing and training of temperaments and vocational aptitudes, by competent educators; and the providing of suitable occupations and livelihoods to all; within the setting of a comprehensive 'Planning', a systematic Social Organisation. Hunger and Sex are at the very roots of life. We cannot be too careful in regulating and refining their satisfaction. The subject has been referred to before (pp. 271-297, *supra*). Sinning against the laws of food and marriage, laws of religious science and scientific religion, the observance of which laws alone fully 'sanctifies' both—such sinning is the parent of all sins and crimes, is the cause of all the manias, wars, perishings of great civilisations. The Manu's solemn warning, of how such sins are visited upon generation after generation, has been quoted before (pp. 182-183, *supra*). Indeed, they tend to become aggravated with each succeeding generation, unless strong checks and remedies are applied from outside, until the end in disaster. It is certain that the community which allows that holy of holies, the mother-heart and the mother-body, to be polluted, corrupted, perverted, tortured, murdered, "that community is blasted by the thunder-bolts of God," (so Manu declares expressly, iii. 58). These thunder-bolts take the plainly visible shapes of 'rot' of body and mind, epidemics of infectious and contagious virulent diseases, and the mutual butcheries of war-madness; not to speak of floods, famines, plagues of many sorts (animals as well as epidemics), volcanic eruptions, earthquakes, and even more gigantic cotaclysms of Nature. The direct connection of these last with human sin is not plainly visible, but 'religious beliefs' (and 'occult science') assert it; and it need not be brushed aside too brusquely, for the chain of causation is very subtle, and all-pervading.[1]

---

[1] Annāḍ bhavanṭi bhūṭāni,
parjanyāḍ anna-sam-bhavah,
Yajñāḍ bhavaṭi parjanyah,
yajñah karma-sam-uḍbhavah.
...Sankaro narakāy-aiva,
kula-ghnānām kulasya cha. (*G.*)

The stern warning in the Bible to the same effect, is well-known, and may be reproduced here, with some comment.

"Thou shalt have no other gods before Me. Thou shalt not make unto thee any graven image, or any likeness of any thing that is in heaven above, or the earth beneath, or the water under the earth. Thou shalt not bow down thyself to them, nor serve them: for I, the Lord thy God, am a jealous God, *visiting the iniquity of the fathers upon the children unto the third and fourth generation* of them that hate Me; and showing mercy unto thousands of them that love Me, and keep my commandments". (*B.*, Exodus, 20.)

The results (in stultification of intelligence, weakening of Self-reliant will, growth of irrational superstition) of excessive image-worship, and some nature-facts connected therewith, we have noted before (pp. 474-475, 446-463, and 191-208, *supra.*); also how the intense faith of a devotee may 'vitalise' the 'image', created by his 'imagi'-nation (as a statue by a sculptor), make of it a focus, attract into it a ray of the all-pervading Life, or, perhaps, an already individualised denizen of another plane of matter (as a person enters into an actor's dress or a soldier's accoutrements); and convert it into a (for the time being) real angel (or devil, according to the quality and desire of the devotee). But 'graven images and likenesses' do not exhaust the list of 'other

---

(Good conduct and self-sacrifice bring rain;
Thence food; thence nourishment of living things.
...Adultery leads all concerned to hell.)
Abr n-āyaḍ az payé mana'é zakāṭ,
W-az zinā ufṭaḍ balā anḍar jehāṭ. (*S.*, Rūmī.)
(Clouds do not come where charity has ceased;
Misfortunes crowd all round on lawless lust.)

gods', mentioned in the first, and separate, verse quoted above. Nor are the commandments, alluded to in the last, only these, viz., against images and likenesses. Far worse than any other gods are Bacchus and Priapus, the gods, rather the devils, of 'evil eating' and 'evil mating'. The terrible consequences of the sins which are involved in the worship of these two, are much more glaringly patent, not only 'unto the third or fourth generation', but very many more, in the shape of awful hereditary venereal diseases, and alcoholism, piles, asthma, phthisis, insanity; strictly speaking, all possible diseases that are due to congenital defects and weaknesses of bodily organs and of mind, but some more glaringly manifest and painful, some less. Therefore, God has given commandments in respect of these two appetites in all religions; and the full commentary upon those commandments, which, if what has been said above be correct, are perhaps the most far-reaching and important, is supplied by spiritual, psychological, physiological, medical, science. We may rightly regard every well-proven Law of Nature, (and Nature is God's Nature), as one of God's Commandments. Such of these laws as are more directly and intimately concerned with the healthy conducting of human life, are regarded as God's Commandments more particularly; and have been prominently embodied in the several scriptures of the race. To love, or hate, 'Me', is to love, or hate, to obey, or break, the Commandments of the Supreme Self, "in Whom all things live and move and have their being".

Philosophy and psycho-physical science, *applied* to the administration of human affairs, give us the complete Scheme of Social Organisation sketched above. Each of the quartettes is important and inseparably related to all the others. But the most prominently important is that of the Four Types of human beings. The birth of these is governed by the two laws, of (1) Heredity, and (2) Spontaneous Variation or Mutation. The former arises from the Oneness of the Self, Spirit; the latter, from the Manyness of the Not-Self, Matter. Metaphysically, mutation is included in heredity; since the Many is included in, indeed created by, the Ideation, the Will-and-Imagination, of the One. All possible sorts of children are included in the parent; because each parent is the child of an infinite number of ancestors. There can be no effect which is not pre-existent, in seed-form, in the cause. "All is everywhere and always", because the One which contains all, is omni-present.[1]

In the latest terms of biology, we may say that all sorts of 'genes', 'potencies', are present in every germ. The idea of 'id-s' (biophor-id-s, 'determinants', composing the 'bio-phore', the unit of life) put forward by Weismann, some decades ago, seems to have been somewhat similar. Western scientists say they do not yet know *why* there is any *mutation*; (Julian Huxley, *We Europeans*, ch. iii). The philosophical and psycho-physical chapters of the old Indian works on Āyur-Vēḍa, medicine, suggest that the psycho-physical *moods* and conditions of the *parents* and the surrounding circumstances, the 'environment', stimulate some of these 'potencies' more than the others, *at every conception*; whence the peculiar character of each child. These potencies are countless, because of the countlessness of the possible 'combinations' of the countless possible 'quantities', 'amounts', 'degrees' of the three guṇa-s, 'attributes' of God's Nature, saṭṭva-rajas-tamas; (see pp. 87, 264, *supra*).

[1]See pp. 212-214, *supra*; *The Science of the Self*, pp. 21, 49-50, 54, 95; *The Science of Peace*, generally.

If the circumstances are similar, and similar 'potencies' (or 'gene-s') are stimulated, at a number of conceptions, the resulting children, of the same pair of parents, will be similar in face, figure, mentality, character. Therefore, twins are the climax of similarity, and illustrate best what is commonly understood by 'heredity'. If differing circumstances stimulate differing 'genes', the resulting children, of the same pair, will be dissimilar; these illustrate 'spontaneous variation'. The old Indian 'Science' of Jyoṭisha, Astrological Astronomy, fully supports and supplements the statements of Āyur-Véḍa, and states what conditions, times, etc., of conception will produce what kind of progeny.

Thus, then, from the transcendental stand-point, all 'mutations' also are covered by 'heredity' in the 'infinite' sense, for all possible potencies are pre-existent in the One Universal Parent; or, in the infinite multitude of particular parents from whom each germ is derived, each child is born; since each child has two parents; each of these parents, two; and so on, *ad infinitum*; and there is nothing really *new*, in any birth; but only a greater developement of some potencies in some cases, and of others in others. The atavisms, regressions, dominants, recessives, mutations, modifications, of present-day biology, and indeed the origin and evolution of all possible species, seem to be possible to explain only in this way. Only, for the practical purposes of every-day usage, from the empirical standpoint, it is best to regard the two laws, of heredity and of spontaneous variation as distinct, and even competitive; now the one prevailing over the other, in one case; and again, the other prevailing over the one, in another case.

All civilisations have instinctively endeavoured to organise their societies in accordance with the natural fact of these four types and the two laws of their manifestation. They have succeeded and prospered in proportion to the degree of their assimilation, though unconscious, of these principles. The old Indian civilization seems to have recognised, enunciated, and essayed to apply, the principles, consciously, clearly, deliberately. It has had, perhaps, a longer life than any other civilisation (except, perhaps, the Chinese). But ever since its classes of Educators and Protectors, or Spiritual Scientists and Benevolent Rulers, began to degenerate, to develope excessive selfishness, to push specialisation and differentiation beyond the bounds of human nature, for their own purposes; began to call themselves 'higher' and the others 'lower'; to exaggerate the principle of 'heredity' in favor of the 'higher' castes and against the 'lower' castes, and to ignore and suppress the principle of 'mutation'; since then, Indian civilisation began to decay. That it has not died out altogether, is due, probably,. to the continued presence therein, of some remnants and memories of 'Spiritual Science', 'Essential Religion'.

It should be added here that, though the element of 'heredity' has been grossly exaggerated and made rigid in India, it has not been possible to suppress the working of spontaneous variation altogether. Changes of caste, even from 'lower' to 'higher', have been going on, all the time; surreptitiously, of individuals; and, openly, now and then, of whole groups, which have decided to *give themselves* the name of a 'higher' caste, (brāhmaṇa or kshaṭṭriya), which name cannot be snatched away from them, particularly in the present conditions. Yet the solidarising articulating *virtue* of the truly scientific socialism of the old scheme has disappeared completely, and, instead, the vicious consequences of endless separatism and exclusiveness are rampant.

While in the Indian practice, 'heredity' has swamped 'variation', in the western systems of social 'structure' (not yet 'organisation') 'variation' and blind competition are too much to the fore; though heredity is necessarily at work also, all the time, and large numbers of persons naturally follow the family occupation, generation after generation. It is a very hopeful sign that in the more advanced western countries, educationists are making efforts to ascertain, in good time, the vocational aptitudes of their pupils; and some countries have begun to even appoint 'career-masters' in their schools. In a proper Social Organisation, based on psychological and physiological science, both the laws, of heredity and mutation, would be taken into account duly; but the latter would be made the deciding factor, whenever unmistakeable, for the purpose of assignment to a vocation. The one law reflects the Unity, *Waḥdaṭ*, É k a - ṭ ā, of the Self; the other, the Diversity, *Kasraṭ*, A n - é k a - ṭ ā, of the Self's Nature, i. e., Matter, the Not-Self which is the garment of the Self or Spirit.

As in the politico-economical life of nations, 'trustees' are always making themselves 'beneficiaries'; leaders are always becoming mis-leaders; protectors, oppressors; feeders, devourers; public servants, public masters; and are, thereby, perennially, causing rebellions and revolutions, and the appointment of new 'trustees' by the real 'beneficiaries', i.e., the People at large; so, in the socio-religious life, the 'spiritual power' is always trying to absorb the 'temporal power' (and *vice-versa*); the 'presbyter', 'priest', 'elder' is ever degenerating into the deceiver; the confessor is ever becoming the seducer and blackmailer; the saint, the sinner; the ascetic, the debauched and debauching voluptuary, even orgiast, and sadist; and is causing repeated secessions, revolts, re-forma-tions. In fact, every religious re-form is, in origin and in issue, a social, economic, and political revolution also; and, therefore, invariably gives rise to a new civilisation. When a man's body falls sick, a physician is needed to cure it; when the oversoul of a whole people falls sick, it requires, as history shows, a fresh influx of the Divine Spirit, a new advent of a new Son of God, an A v a ṭ ā r a, a Messiah, a *Rasūl*, to cure it, and give it a fresh birth in a new body, of 're-established Law' and 're-constructed society'; (p. 216, *supra*). Without right social structure, the noblest religio-ethical principles and exhortations have no chance; neither in a theo-cracy (ecclesiasticism, sacerdotalism), nor a timo-cracy (feudalism, militarism), nor a pluto-cracy (capitalism), nor a mobo-(or 'demo-') cracy (proletarianism). The four 'powers', the 'four estates of the realm', must be duly balanced for ethical teachings to have a chance.

Buḍḍha, and his contemporary, Mahā-vīra Jina (the founder of the Jaina religion), endeavoured to shift, and largely succeeded in shifting back, the basis of the Indian Social Organisation, from crass artificialised 'heredity', to elastic, rational, natural 'spontaneous variation' in respect of vocational temperament; thereby gave, to the Indian People and their civilisation, a new period of re-generation, a new lease of life, for about twelve centuries; and gave rise to an astonishing efflorescence of varied science and noble literature, (due to generous emulation between the Vaiḍikas and the Bauḍḍhas), and to great empires rivalling the contemporary Roman, Macedonian, Persian, and Chinese empires. Unhappily, the evil in human nature, the forces of a-v i ḍ y ā, selfish erring, de-generation, again succeeded in resuming their sway.

A whole chapter of the Buddhist *Ḍhamma-paḍa*, named 'Brāhmaṇa-vaggo', is devoted to the exposition of the nature of the *true* b r ā h m a ṇ a.

Na jatāhi, na goṭṭé hi,
na jachchā hoṭi brāhmaṇo;
Yamhi sachchan cha, ḍhammo cha,
So suchī, so cha brāhmaṇo.
Yassa kāyéna, vāchāya,
manasā, naṭṭhi ḍukkaṭam,
Samvuṭam ṭīhi thānéhi,
ṭam aham brūmi brāhmaṇam.
Na ch-āham brāhmaṇam brūmi
Yoni-jam maṭṭi-sambhavam;
A-kinchanam an-āḍānam
ṭam aham brūmi brāhmaṇam.
Divā ṭapaṭi āḍichcho,
raṭṭim ābhāṭi chanḍīmā,
Sannaḍḍho khaṭṭiyo ṭapaṭi,
Jhāyī ṭapaṭi brāhmaṇo.
Akkosan, baḍha-bandham cha,
a-ḍuṭṭho, yo ṭiṭikkhaṭi,
Khanṭi-balam bal-ānīkam,
ṭam aham brūmi brāhmaṇam. (*Dh.*)
Na jachchā vusalo hoṭi,
na jachchā hoṭi brāhmaṇo,
Kammanā vusalo hoṭi
Kammaṇā hoṭi brāhmaṇo.
(*Bu.*, *Vusala-suṭṭa* of the *Suṭṭa-nipāṭa*).

(Not matted locks, nor birth in any clan,
Or family, or from some mother's womb,
Can make a man a real brāhmaṇa.
He who is true, pure, dutiful; sins not

In deed, word, thought; gathers not worldly goods;
Bears patiently hard words, bonds, beatings too,
And lets not anger rise within his mind,
Strong with the strength of all forgivingness;
Him do I call a real brāhmaṇa.
Mere birth makes not a real brāhmaṇa;
Nor makes a shūḍra; deeds and ways of living,
Appropriate, make either one or th' other.
The sun doth make the day; the night the moon;
Courageous chivalry, the kshaṭṭriya;
Wisdom and thoughtfulness, the brāhmaṇa.)

Buḍḍha not only clearly recognises and supports the four types or classes, but is full of praise of the true b r ā h m a ṇ a, in many of the other verses of the chapter. But he does *not* believe in 'caste by *birth*'. Instead, he very strongly condenms it, and all pretensions based on it. He recommends vocational classes by *worth*, i. e., by suitable character, mental and moral constitution, and occupational disposition.

Jainism is, if possible, even more explicit.

Manushya-jāṭir-ék-aiva,
jāṭi-nām-oḍay-oḍbhavā;
Vṛṭṭi-bhéḍāḍ hi ṭaḍ-bhéḍāch-
chāṭur-viḍhyam ih-āshnuṭé.
Brāhmaṇāh vraṭa-samskārāṭ,
Kshaṭṭriyāh shasṭra-ḍhāraṇāṭ,
Vaṇij-orṭh-ārjanān nyāyāṭ,
shūḍrā nyag-vṛṭṭi-samshrayāt.
(Quoted in *Jaina Ḍharma kā Mahaṭṭva*,
a work in Hinḍī.)
Kammuṇā bambhaṇo hoi,
kammuṇā hoi khaṭṭiyo,
Kammuṇā vaisō hoi,
Suḍḍo hawai kammuṇā.

Sakkham khu ḍīsai tavo-viséso,
Na ḍīsaī jāi visésa kōī.
(*J.*, *Uṭṭar-āḍhyayana Sūṭra.*)

(The Human Race is one, though 'tis made up
Of many tribes with many names. But four
Broad classes may be plainly seen therein,
Caused by the differences of ways of living.
The men of studious vows are brāhmaṇas;
Who practise use of arms are kshaṭṭriyas;
Who gather wealth by lawful merchantry
Are vaishyas; those who live by service-wage
Are shūḍras. By their occupations only
Are the four thus marked off; no otherwise.
The 'birth' of any one cannot be seen
Upon his face; his actions can be seen.)

Only one or two well-known verses of Véḍist scripture need be quoted here. Many others have been gathered in Gangā Prasāḍa's work above referred to, and in the present writer's *The Principles of Sanāṭana Vaiḍika Ḍharma.*

Na vishesh-osṭi varṇānām
Sarvam brāhmam iḍam jagaṭ,
Brahmaṇā pūrva-sṛshtam hi,
karmabhir varṇaṭām gaṭam.
(*Mbh.*, Shānṭi-parva, ch. 186.)

Éka-varṇam iḍam sarvam
pūrvam āsīḍ, Yuḍhishthira !,
Kriyā-karma-vibhāgéna
chāṭur-varṇyam vy-ava-sṭhiṭam.
(*Ibid.*, Anushāsana-parva.)

Chāṭur-varṇyam Mayā sṛshtam
guṇa-karma-vibhāgashah;
Karmāṇi pra-vibhakṭāni
sva-bhāva-prabhavair-guṇaih. (*G.*)

prosper exceedingly, and will be in no danger from others; because it will automatically include a strong defensive military organisation. Also, and far better, it will set a beneficent example to other less advanced communities, and will help to organise them all for peace, in the same way. By creating a just balance of 'the four powers' within each nation, such an organisation automatically creates a balance of all kinds of powers between all nations. By making each people self-supporting and self-complete, it minimises cause for aggression by one on another; and instead, maximises inducements for intelligent, active, sympathetic co-operation of all the four classes of all nations, for the deliberate promotion of the good of all.

It should be re-iterated here that, for the sucessful balancing of the powers aforesaid, an indispensable requisite is the balancing of the production of consumable goods, especially 'the necessaries of life', and the consumption, i. e., the number of consumers. If there is disproportion here, if the former is small and the latter large, no other balancing will be possible peacefully. Fish multiply too fast; they cannot but devour one another. If men multiply beyond the power of the land (even where wisely and scientifically cultivated) to support them, they will not be able to help looting and murdering one another; or being destroyed wholesale by epidemics, famines, etc. Inordinate lust will inevitably breed inordinate hate; (see pp. 372-373, *supra*). Self-control, and thence birth-control, is the foundation of all other control. To control death, we must control birth. B r a h m a - c h a r y a, 'continence', (within scientific limits), is the way to strengthen and prolong the individual as well as the racial life. Kāma-Eros unbridled, is our worst enemy. To war against and subdue it, (not destroy, until the third and fourth stages of life), is the best and most truly '*moral* equivalent of war'. Battling against the 'forces of nature', to utilise them as far as possible, and against predaceans, is the rest of the moral equivalent. To the extent that the 'moral war' succeeds, 'physical wars and crimes' will diminish. Of course, complete abolition of all evil is obviously impossible; only a reduction is possible. Social Organisation and the 'Moral War' help each other, in a virtuous circle. The former promotes balancing of production and consumption and inducement for self-control and birth control, and these, in turn, strengthen and stabilise the former.

Such a Social Organisation achieves the Golden Mean in all respects. It gives duly regulated opportunity for the venting and purging of the egoistic instincts, the six (or seven) 'deadly sins' and 'manias' (see pp. 317-318, *supra*); because it provides them with appropriate objects and occasions; and thus transmutes and sublimates them from wrongful into righteous; e. g., lust into conjugal passion of love between spouses, 'sanctified' by parity of temper and compatibility of temperament between them, and therefore by public recognition and law and religion; hate into just indignation against wrong-doers; jealousy into laudable zeal in the guarding of public rights against private encroachments. We have seen before (pp. 74, 308, 317, 377, *supra*) that "to everything there is a season." Anything and everything is right, if placed or done in the right time, the right place, the right manner; wrong, in the wrong. The Scheme provides a solidarising mould into which can be poured, into appropriate parts and places, harmoniously, all the individuals of all the countless tribes, clans, families, 'castes', races, nations, dialects, religions, of the whole Human Family. Its tetrads are not in conflict with any particular creed

33

or science. Instead, it is based upon and utilises all the best established principles of all such sciences as psychology, physiology, biology, anthropology, sociology, eugenics, politics, eco-nomics, pedagogics. The Scheme tells us the right times, places, manners, for anything and everything, in great broad principles and outlines. By ordaining the retirement of the older generation from competitive bread-winning or money-making into honorary public service, after the second quarter of life, it abates all conflict between it and the younger generation; and at the same time ensures a constant supply of experienced, disinterested, benevolent, advisers and public workers. It fulfils all that is reasonable in the requirements of the Marxian and other Socialists and the Freudian and other Psycho-analysts. It makes unnecessary the premature tragic retirement of the very young into the refuge of ascetic 'orders', monasteries, etc.; which is, only too often, no refuge at all, but, instead, a falling from the frying pan into the fire. It secures active, unrepressed, but regulated, self-expression for youth; and also honorable and desirable repose for age. It tells us the Meaning of Life, reconciles heart and head, harmonises emotion and intellect, heat and light, and makes it possible for us all to fulfil all Life's purposes and realise all its aims and ends.[1]

---

[1] Dr. Lin Yutang, "combining immense learning with a shrewd eye and lively humanity", also a brilliant and at times exceedingly witty style, has produced "the truest, profoundest, most complete, most important book yet written about China," (as Nobel laureate Pearl Buck and others say), in the shape of *My Country and My People* (pub. 1938). He writes (pp. 93-102, 119):

"Still the question comes back eternally, like the sea-waves lapping upon the shore: What is the Meaning of

If representative, large-hearted, broad-minded Elders of the Nations would only sit together in a genuine League of All Nations and Religions, and

---

Life...The question has perplexed western philosophers, and it has never been solved...There are moments in our lives...when a sense of death and futility overcomes us, when we live more than the life of the senses and look over the visible world to the Great Beyond... Confucius was a realist, positivist, humanist. (Asked about death) he said: "Don't know life, how know death?" Confucianism, strictly speaking, was not a religion. It really never quite satisfied the Chinese... That deficiency was made up for by a Taoist or Buddhist supernaturalism...In times of national disorder, as during the change of dynasties, a great number of scholars shaved their heads and took monastic orders, as much for personal protection as out of feeling for the helpless chaos of the world... Many beautiful and talented girls at the end of the Ming dynasty took the monastic vow through disappointment in love caused by these catastrophic changes..." ; (see pp 71-72 *supra*).

Asceticism has been practised in all known times and climes, but, "Throughout the first and second centuries A. D., there was an almost world-wide resort to such repudiations of life, a universal search for 'salvation' from the distresses of the time...Amidst the prevailing slavery, cruelty, fear, anxiety, waste, display and hectic self-indulgence, went this epidemic of self-disgust and mental insecurity, this agonised search for peace even at the price of renunciation and voluntary suffering:" H. G. Wells, *A Short History of the World*, ch. xxxvi; (pub 1938).

C. G. Jung, leading psycho-analyst, writes: "Among my patients from many countries, all of them educated

seriously consider the principles and outlines of the Vedic Scheme of Organisation of the Whole Human Race; and *either* realise and endorse its virtue, and take steps to saturate the minds of the younger generation with those principles and outlines, and thus effectively commence bringing it into universal practice at once; *or* think out a better one, if they can; *if* they would only do so, and not otherwise, Humanity would win Peace and Happiness and establish heaven on earth.

21. Finally, we may note one more point of similarity between the living religions, which is matter for sad reflection upon the human weakness of egoism which insists on venting itself in religion also. All have split up into scores, ome into hundreds, of sects and sub-sects, because of opinionatedness and personal quarrels. This is bad enough; but there is worse. Every shine must have a deep shadow also somewhere. Within the pale of every religion there have grown up secret sects of 'black magic', *jāḍū*, yāṭu, vāma-mārga, the dreadful 'left-hand path' of fiend-worship, wherein the foulest rites and practices are indulged in, down to murderous human sacrifices of innocent children. Such sects and practices have to be constantly watched and warred against; even as the foul excretions

---

persons, there is a considerable number who came to see me, not because they were suffering from a neurosis, but because they could find no *Meaning in Life* or were torturing themselves with questions which neither present-day philosophy nor religion could answer....I too had no answer to give": *Modern Man in Search of a Soul*, pp. 266-267.

produced by the fairest living organisms, or the ashes, refuse, dirt, thrown up by the best machinery, have to be continuously wiped and washed away. Again, the agreement of all religions, fallen from their high estate into the evil hands of false priests and cruelly selfish mis-leaders, is so great that the mis-guided followers of the several religions all agree in the disastrous error also of saying: "My religion is the only true and wholly original one, or, at least, is far better than all others, and all others are heathen, pagan, *kāfir*, m l é c h c h h a, and must be suppressed!"; though it is patent that all beings are matter of the same Matter and spirit of the same Spirit'.

FORMALISM AND CATCHWORDS. Yet underneath this so disastrous error is the profoundest Truth hidden immediately. Interpret "*my* religion" as "the Religion of Me, the I, the Universal Self," and you pass at once from the most violent turmoil into the most blissful peace.[1]

[1] Also another truth which too is important, though less so, may be discerned beneath the excessively worded claim. Each religion, besides the general value, has a special value, i. e., emphasises some one aspect of the truth, some one virtue, sọme one kind of pious work, more than the other aspects, virtues, works, though all are needed. It does so, because of the special conditions, the peculiar time, place, and circumstance, in which it arises. Thus, it may be said, Vaiḍika Ḍharma emphasises the All-Pervading Self, Duty, all-comprehending Ọrder, and Balancing of all Duties; the Hebrew religion, the strict Justice of God, and His special Protection of those who place their faith in Him;

"*My* religion is the only true religion, what *I* believe is the only right belief, what *I* do is the only correct practice"—this amazing self-conceit, this outrageous self-importance, this enormous megalomania, this infatuation, this madness, of the false, illusory, most petty and paltry, individual egoistic self, is only the reversed reflection of the wondrous conception, the infinite import, the boundless greatness, the infallible beneficence and Saviourship, of the perfect Truth, Beauty, Goodness and Guidance of the eternal, immortal all-embracing *Universal Self*. The Religion of *that* Me is indeed the One and on(e)ly Religion, but it runs through all religions, and gives to each, whatever value of helpfulness to men it has; it makes peace between them all, when otherwise they would destroy each other. Who is greater than the Universal I which contains the whole universe? What is smaller than the individual I which is contained within a few

---

Zoroastrianism, Rectitude and Purity; Buḍḍhism, Renunciation and Compassion; Christianity, Non-Resistance of evil, Resignation, submission to God's will, self-sacrifice for others; Islam, Brotherly Equality and Resistance of Wrong: and so on. But, in the later developments of the civilisation belonging to each religion, the original ideas generally become so transformed as to be almost unrecognisable; the mediatorship, between God and man, of the particular founder of that religion, is especially regarded as indispensable for all human beings; and no other person is allowed to be such mediator or guide at all.

pounds of flesh and blood and bone and is perpetual slave to their caprices of birth, youth, age. death, their incessant swings between health and disease ? Yet this so small self apes the measureless greatness of the Great Self ! It does so *because* it *is* that Self in essence ;[1] it does so in grievously and ludicrously wrong fashion, because it has imposed upon itself the Error of imagining it-self *to be limited* to that same handful of flesh and blood and bone. Having made the Limitless limited, it tries to make the limited Unlimited ! *Demon est Deus inversus.* Satan is God inverted. Kḥuḍī is the imaged reversal of Khuḍā. Jīva is the denial of Brahma. Untruth is the tinsel imitation of Truth. The finite is negation, *inkār*, n ā s ṭ i k a-ṭ ā, 'a-theism', 'nihil-ism' of the Infinite.[2]

---

[1]As observed before, this is proven, if by nothing else, then by this single simple indubitable fact that any individual can change his particular creed for any other creed at will, can transfer his faith from any one religion to any other, thereby proving that there is *Something* in him which is superior to all particular religious, and which can assert itself at will ; even if the mind, through which it so asserts itself, be not educated, be even illiterate.

[2]It has been said by a western writer, that "the unique character of a religion is to be judged, not by the material it possesses in common with others, but by the special stamp it impresses upon it." This is very true, indeed obvious. If we want to see whatever 'uniqueness' there may be in any religion, we must, of course, 'differentiate', separate, must stress the 'differen-

A Great Danger. We have seen the danger on the Path of Knowlege, of the great error of taking one's own particular, individual, small self, for the Universal Self immanent in all living

---

tial', not the common, elements. But do we, should we, want to ? Is it useful, desirable ? Will it help the world ? *Every* individual *differs* from every other, in appearance, tricks of manner, etc., and in mind also ; so does every family, every clan, every tribe, every race, every nation, from every other, in *some* respects. But is it useful or necessary to *accentuate* these 'distinguishing' features ? Is it not enough simply to recognise and allow their existence ? Every human being has a 'unique' voice, by which he can be recognised in the dark ; therefore, when two persons utter the same words, shall we refuse to recognise that they *mean the same thing*, simply because they have uttered them in their *different voices ?* Is it not desirable, in the present condition of the world, to *soften* all differences as much as possible ; without trying or even wishing and hoping to *abolish* them—which would be to abolish Nature's Law of Diversity (amidst Unity) ? Have not Individualism, Familism, Clanism, Tribalism, Nationalism, Racialism, gone too far, much too far, already ? Is it not desirable to emphasise now Humanism, the common features, the Law of Unity (amidst Diversity), which alone makes society, socialised existence, genuine socialism, and Brotherhood possible ? (see pp. 70-71, *supra.*)

Ke rā kufr-é Haqīqī shuḍ piḍīḍār,
Ze Islām-é Majāzī gashṭ bézār. (*S.*)
(He who True Infidelity hath seen—
The Disbelief in the small lower self—
Disgusted with the Outer faith hath been.)

beings; also the similar error on the Path of Devotion, of regarding any one personal, separate, limited deity, as the whole of that same All-pervading, Impersonal, All-personal, Infinite, Eternal Self.[1] The corresponding error on the Path of Works, of ritual, of observances, is to cling tooth and nail to any one particular set of formalities as the only good and right set, in all times, in all places, in all circumstances, for all persons; and to insist upon their being observed by all, always, everywhere. It will be seen that all the three errors are only aspects of one another, all are manifestations of egoism, the one prince of all d'evils. Forced conversion, fanatical *tablīgh*, bigoted s h u ḍ ḍ h i, murderous persecutions of heretics, the horrors of inquisitions, religious wars, (wars and religious!), the utter corruption of the moral atmosphere of whole countries, and the debasement and enslavement of the mind and body of whole nations, are the consequence.[2] Solemn ritual, intended to draw the minds of all to God, becomes the cause of the drawing of swords against one another and of mutual butchery; even though the use of force

---

[1] Pp. 132, 348, 391.

[2] "According to the calculation of Voltaire, no less than ten million 'heretics' were burned to death 'at the request of the Church'...": Henry Thomas, *The Story of the Human Race*, p. 246, (pub: 1935). This is the work done in the name of one religion; no similar calculations seem to be available for similar work done, no doubt, in the names of other religions.

in matters of religion is expressly forbidden by the religion supposed to be the most energetic and successful in proselytising.

Thus, the Qurān says:

Lā ekrāhā f-iḍ-ḍīn......La-kum ḍīnu-kum walé yaḍīm......Uḍu' elā sabīli Rabbekā b-il-hikmaṭé w-al mauezzaṭil hasanaṭé. (Q.)

(There must be no compulsion exercised
In matters of religion......Unto you
Your faith be welcome; so my faith to me...
Let those who know not God be led to Him,
By those who know, with words of gentleness
And wholesome and wise counsel, in kind ways.)

And again:

Li kullin ja'lna min-kum shira'tan wa minhāja, wa lau sha-Allāho la ja'alakum ummaṭaṅ-wāhiḍah ......wa lākin leyabul-lowakum fī mā āṭa-kuṃ fā-sṭabequ-l-kḥairaṭo ... Yā ayyoh-allazīna āmanu lā yaskḥar qaumun min qaumin. A'sa aṅyakupū kḥairam minhum. (Q.)

(To every people have we given a law
And a way whereby they may reach to God.
If God had wished it so, He would have made
You all one people. He has not done so.
Wherefore let every people, on the way
Prescribed for it, press forward to good deeds.
And let none laugh at any other men;
Perchance they may be better than themselves.)

Great is the Māyā of words, their power for good or for evil. Riots, pogroms, serious and widespread social disturbances, wars, the misleading of whole nations for generations, in all departments of life, may be, have been, caused by the excessive prevalence of false catch-words and catch-phrases; or by the use of different words by different persons, who all mean the same thing, but do not properly understand one another's words. Almost all disputes and wrangles are due to the unwillingness or the inability to look behind and through the word to the meaning; and, as said before, almost all benevolent diplomacy and successful composition of differences and peace-making means only industrious explaining of the meaning of the parties concerned to one another. Not to understand is to misunderstand; to misunderstand is to be hostile; every stranger, whose language is at all strange, must be an enemy.

Thus, e.g., in the physician's science and art of physical healing, which ought to be as philanthropic and beneficent to the body as the priests' science and art of spiritual ministration ought to be to the mind, medical practitioners of different schools hold each other in contempt, and disagree, firstly, because they have more *amour propre* of various kinds than earnest wish to cure the patient, and, secondly, because each uses a special set of technical words, of the sounds of which he becomes so enamoured that he has no inclination and no power left to see that other sets mean very much the same thing. But while the doctors know and choose their respective words and drugs, the layman knows and chooses his doctors, knows who cures most and who kills most, and he can sense the common ideas behind the different sets of technicalities. He feels that the vaidya's three prakṛti-s, (corresponding to the three functions of the mind mentioned before), the *hakīm's mizāj-s*, the homeopath's 'temperaments', and the up-to-date modern 'scientific doctor's' (as yet inchoate and unclassified) 'personal idiosyncracies' (under cover of which comparatively recently invented expression he now accepts what he tried long to reject, *viz.*, peculiarities of psycho-physical temperament or constitution, which result in the fact, proverbially known to common sense, but not always recognized by 'scientific' practitioners, that what is food for one is poison for another)—the layman feels that these all at bottom mean the same thing; and he knows, in a general way, which system or method of treatment most suits a particular kind of constitution or disease, and is able to utilise all. The layman is, after all, the parent of the expert, and rears and feeds and clothes him and keeps him going. Even so in matters religious, while word-blinded paṇḍiṭs and *maulavis* and clerics may dispute endlessly, in exclusive praise of their own respective 'unique' books, rites, ceremonies, and masters, the impress and the power of the One Supreme Spirit are so strong in the heart of even the most unlearned, that he decides and chooses at will which outer religion to doff and which to don, even as clothes.

Seeing the potency for mischief in the excessive clinging to words and outer forms, the great Teachers of all religions have warned us again and again not to attach undue importance to them. The Protestant revolt against Roman Catholicism may, in one way, be regarded as at least partly a revolt against the misuse of religious terminology and the degradation of ritual into mummery by self-seeking or ignorant priests. Similar movements for reform within the folds of Vaiḍika Ḍharma (such as Buḍḍhism; Jainism; Shankara's Aḍvaiṭism; Rāmānanḍa's, Chaiṭanya's, Ṭulasī-ḍāsa's Bhakṭism; Kabīr's irenean Mysticism, Nānak's Sikhism; and latest, Ḍayānanḍa's Aryanism); and within Islām (e.g., Sūfism of many schools and shades of view and methods of yogic practice; Sunnism, Shīa-ism, Ahl-i-Haḍisism or Wahābism, Bābism, Bahāism, Agḥā-kḥānism, and, latest, Qāḍiyāni Ahmaḍism); which have been started from time to time, may also be regarded in the same light.

The Yoga makes it even an important part of the soul's discipline to discriminate between the s h a b ḍ a, the 'word,' the a r ṭ h a, the 'thing meant,' and the j ñ ā n a, the 'cognition or perception' of it, involving the element of the personal factor which requires adjustment and equation.[1]

The whole, and most valuable, work and wisdom of Socrates consisted in this discipline, viz., that he compelled persons, by close cross-examination, to make their own minds clear as to what exactly they meant by the words which they so glibly used, but which, in the mouths of

[1] *Yoga-sūṭra*, 1, 42.

most of them were, and are, only catch-words, without any precise, or sometimes even any, meaning.

Scriptural writings counsel us: "Do not cling to the letter which killeth, but to the spirit which giveth life eternal." "Look at the things of the flesh with the eyes of the Spirit, not at the things of the Spirit with the eyes of the flesh." Following this counsel, we will avoid hate and cultivate and promote love universal, which is the whole and sole object of religion.[1]

"In the glass of things temporal,
See the image of things spiritual."

LIVE AND DIE IN AND FOR THE UNIVERSAL LIFE. As preliminary preparation for that final renunciation of all egoism, the Teachers advise us to begin by offering up all our actions to God. Pray for light, for guidance, and then do everything in the name, for the sake, as if by command, of God. So, the mood, the prayer, "Thy will be done, not mine," will gradually become a permanent part, and then the very

[1] One very effective and useful way to get behind the sound to the sense, to distinguish between the word and the thought, to overcome letter-worship, to transcend Vệdo-latry, Qurāno-latry, Biblo-latry (more subtle fetters upon the soul than idolatry), is to study many languages, and compare parallel passages; and so to learn to recognise, with resolute and unbaffled intelligence, the same thought, the same familiar friendly face, behind many masks of many languages. (see pp. 68-70, *supra*).

essence, of our life and being; and thus the identification of our-self with the Supreme Self, of *ṭu*, ṭ v a m, thou, with *Haq*, Ṭ a ṭ, That, will become realized by and in Works, through and in Devotion, up to and in Illumination.

Wa yuṭemūn aṭ-ṭa'ma alā hubbehī miskīnau wa yaṭīmau wa asīrā. Innama nuṭa'ma-kum le wajh-Illāhi lā nurīḍo min-kum jaza-an wa lā shukūra. (*Q*.)

(The poor, the orphan, and the captive—feed
Them for the love, the sake, of God alone,
Desiring no reward, nor even thanks.)

Qul inna salāṭi wa nosoki wa mahyāya wa mamāṭe l-Illāhi Rabb-il-ālamīna. (*Q*)

(My prayer, my sacrifice, my life, my death,
Are all for God, the Lord of all the worlds.)
Alaihi ṭawakkalṭo wa hua ne'm al-Wakīl. (*Q*.)
(On Him do we rely with our whole heart,
He is our only refuge, safest, best.)

Man-manā bhava, Maḍ-bhakṭo,
Maḍ-yājī, Mām namas-kuru;
Aham ṭvām sarva-pāpébhyo
mokshayishyāmi mā shuchah.
Kaunṭéya! praṭi-jānīhi,
na Mé bhakṭah pra-ṇashyaṭi. (*G*.)

(Turn mind to Me, love Me with all thy heart,
Do acts of sacrifice for My sole sake,
Bend thy whole soul to Me, the Self of all,
And I shall wash thee clean of all thy sins.
Listen and know and trust, I promise thee,
No votary of Mine can e'er be lost.)

Yaṭ karoshi, yaḍ ashnāsi,
yaj-juhoshi, ḍaḍāsi yaṭ,
Yaṭ ṭapasyasi, Kaunṭéya!,
ṭaṭ kurushva Maḍarpaṇam. (*G*.)

(Whate'er thou dost, eating, or giving alms,
Ascetic discipline, or sacrifice,
Do it for My sake, offer it to Me.)

Come unto Me, all ye that are weary and heavy-laden and I will give you rest (*B.*)...Love God with all your heart...Whether we live, we live unto the Lord; and whether we die, we die unto the Lord; whether we live, therefore, or die, we are the Lord's...Whether, then, you are eating or drinking, or whatever you are doing, let everything be done to the glory of God. (*B.*)

"Come, ye blessed of my Father, inherit the kingdom...For I was anhungered, and ye gave me meat; I was thirsty and ye gave me drink...naked and ye clothed me." (*B.*, Mat. xxv.).

Lāo-tse, the great Teacher of China, says:

It is the way of Tao not to act from any personal motive, to conduct affairs without worrying about results, to taste without being aware of the flavor, to account the small as great and the great as small, to recompense injury with kindness. (*T.*, *Ṭao-Ṭe-King.*)

...*Z*araṭhusṭro ṭanvas chīṭ khakhyāo ūshṭaném ḍaḍā-īṭī paūrvaṭāṭém mananghas chā wanghéūsh Mazaḍāī...Aroījī huḍā-onghaho wīspāīsh Mazaḍā kshmāvasū savo. (Gaṭha, 33. 14; 34. 3.)

(Yea! *Z*araṭhushṭra dedicates to Thee,
Lord Mazaḍā!, his body and his soul...
In everything the righteous worker doth,
He sacrificeth unto thee, O Lord!)

(Each step that my feet take is but a part
Of circumambulation of the All;
Each act of service, at His bidding done;
Each lying down, for sleep, is at His feet
Prostration worshipful, and utter mergence
Of my small self in Him; each utterance

Voices His praise and Him ; each meal, each drink,
Is offering of food and drink to Him ;
He eats, drinks, sleeps, speaks, walks, acts,
lives in me.)[1] (KABIR).

Let the Osiris go ;[2] ye see he is without fault... He lived on truth, he fed on truth...The God has welcomed him as he desired...He has given food to My hungry, drink to My thirsty ones, clothes to My naked. (Egyptian *Book of the Dead*, quoted in H. P. Blavatsky's *Isis Unveiled*, II. 548.)

Pāṭré ḍānam; anna-ḍānam; viḍyā-ḍānam, the giving of physical food and of mental food, i. e., knowledge, to the *deserving*, is eulogised and enjoined in the Indian scriptures over and over again. 'Sacrifice', study, charity, ijyā, aḍhy-ayana, ḍāna, are the three permanent duties of the 're-generate' classes. (*M.*, *G.*).

KNOWLEDGE AND DEVOTION STERILE WITHOUT WORKS. We have to bear in mind that the emotional enjoyment of self-surrender and devotion to the Supreme, wholly legitimate as it is, is not enough. The 'freed' man has to slave for the 'slaves' who are yet bound by the fetters of doubts and fears and worldly desires. He has to realise, in his *actions*, that all mankind, nay,

---

[1] Unfortunately, the note of the original of this was lost and could not be traced while the pages were being taken through the press.

[2] The *soul*, found blameless, after death, by Osiris, the Egyptian Lord of Truth, (same as Véḍic Yama, and Islāmic Al-Qābiz and Al-Muhsiy, Lord of Death and Judgment), is given by the Deity the same status and name as His own, because blameless.

all living things, are one Infinite Brotherhood. Right knowledge and devotion, wedded to one another, are both sterile if they give not birth to good works. Faith and reason without works are worse than useless. Works witness the faith. The man's innermost heart-conviction is that according to which he acts. Deeds, not words, prove the real faith. The blood of the martyrs is the proof, and therefore the seed, of the faith.

By their fruits shall ye know them. (*B.*)

Sṭhāṇur-ayam bhāra-hāraḥ kil-ābhūḍ-
Aḍhīṭya Véḍam na vijānāṭi yo-(a)rṭham ;
Arṭha-jña-iṭ sakalam bhaḍram ashnuṭé,
Nākam éṭi Jñāna-viḍhūṭa-pāpmā. (*Nirukṭa.*)
Āchāra-hīnam na punanṭi Véḍāh
Yaḍy-apy-adhīṭāh saha shadbhir-angaih ;
Chhanḍāmsy-énam mṛṭyu-kālé ṭyajanṭi
Nīdam shakunṭā iva jāṭa-pakshāh. (*Vasishtha-Smṛṭi*)
Évam pravarṭiṭam chakram
n-ānu-varṭayaṭī-ha yah
Agh-āyur-inḍriy-ārāmo
mogham, Pārtha !, sa jīvaṭi. (*G.*)

(But block of wood, supporting a dead weight,
Is he who knows the Véḍa all by heart,
And yet knows not its sacred secret sense.
He who knows that, and also does good works
In keeping with that knowledge, he avoids
Down-dragging binding sins and gaineth heaven.
The Véḍas cannot help, however hard
They have been studied, and with all their six
Subservient sciences, the man of vice ;
They leave him at the moment of his death,
As fledglings leave a nest that has been fouled.

This Wheel of Life that I have set a-whirl—
He who helps not to keep it cycling on,
In the fixed ways of virtue, he does fail
In duty, living sinful life in vain.)

Bahum pi ché samhiṭam bhāsa-māno,
Na ṭakkaro hoṭi naro pamaṭṭo,
Gopo va gāvo gaṇayam parésam,
Na bhāgavā sāmaṅyassa hoṭi. (*Dh.*)

(Who talks much, learnedly, but acts not right
That senseless man is like one who should count
The cows of others o'er and o'er again,
But cannot have a sip of milk from them.)

Āchārah paramo ḍharmah,
shruṭy-ukṭah, smārṭa éva cha ;
Ṭasmāḍ asmin saḍā yukṭo
niṭyam syāḍ Āṭma-vān ḍvi-jah.
Āchārāḍ vichyuṭo vipro
na Véḍa-phalam ashnuṭé ;
Āchāréṇa ṭu sam-yukṭah
sam-purṇa-phala-bhāg-bhavéṭ. (*M.*)

(Right conduct and good deed—this is the highest
Ḍharma ; so all the Véḍas, Smṛṭis, teach.
The wise man, therefore, having seen the Self,
Acts gently and performs good works amain.
Who fails in conduct, Véḍas help him not ;
Who does not fail, all life's just ends he gains.)

Pathakāh, pāthakāsh-cha-iva,
yé ch-ānyé shāsṭra-chinṭakāh,
Sarvé vyasanino mūrkhāh,
yah kriyāvān sa pandiṭah.
(*Mbh.*, Vana-parva, ch. 314.)

(Students and teachers, and all others, who
Read the mere words of ponderous books,
know naught,

But only waste their time in vain pursuit
Of words; who *acteth* righteously is Wise.)

Ilm chanḍāṅ ke béshṭar kẖwānī,
Gar a'mal ḍar ṭū n-īst, nāḍān-ī,
Chār-pāy-é bar-ū kiṭāb-é chanḍ,
Na muhaqqiq buwaḍ na ḍānish-manḍ. (*S*).

(However great thy knowledge, if good deed
Is not thine also, then thou knowest naught;
But beast of burden thou, loaded with books,
Strutting along, and knowing not their sense,
Lacking all wisdom, ignorant of truth.)

Sayyaḍ-ul-quam kẖāḍim-ul-qaum. (*H.*)
(The leader of the tribe—who serves it most.)

Those who aspire to greatness must humble themselves. (*T.*, *Tao Teh King.*)

The meek shall inherit the earth, and theirs is the kingdom of heaven...Whosoever will be a chief among you, let him be your servant; whosoever will be great among you, let him be your minister...Whosoever shall exalt himself, shall be abased; and he who shall humble himself, shall be exalted...(*B.*) He that is greatest among you shall be your servant. (*B.*) He that is greatest among you, let him be as the youngest; and he that is chief, as he that doth serve. (*B.*, Luke).

Inna akramakum inḍ Allāhé atqākum. (*Q.*)
(Nearest to God and greatest in His eyes
Is he who is most good amongst you all.)

Sam-mānāḍ brāhmaṇo niṭyam uḍ-vijéṭa vishāḍ-iva,
Ava-mānasya ch-ākānkshéḍ amṛṭasy-éva sarvaḍā. (*M.*)

(The man of God doth ever shrink and flee
From marks of honour, as from poison-sting,
And welcometh indignity and task
Of lowliness as if 'twere nectar-draught.)

Ba ehsān āsūḍa karḍan ḍilé
Beh az alf raka'ṭ ba har manzilé. (*S.*)
Ḍil ba ḍasṭ āwar ke hajjé-akbar asṭ;
Az hazārāṅ K'āba yak ḍil behṭar asṭ.
Ḍil guzar-gāhé Jalīlé Akbar asṭ,
Kā'ba bun-gāhē Khalīlé āzir asṭ. (*S.*)

(To bring joy to one heart, by loving help,
Is better than a thousand litanies.
To reach and clasp a human heart with love—
This is the Greater Pilgrimage; the other,
To the stone K'āba, is the smaller one.
Better far is one living human heart
Than a whole thousand Kā'bas built of stone;
Within the former lives the Life of God,
The other's the dead work of Abra'm's hands.)

Ṭapas ṭīrṭham, kshamā ṭīrṭham,
ṭīrṭham inḍriya-nigrahah,
Sarva-bhūṭa-ḍayā ṭīrṭham,
Ḍhyānam ṭīrṭham an-uṭṭamam,
Éṭāni pancha ṭīrṭhāni,
saṭyam shashtham pra-kīrṭiṭam,
Ḍéhé ṭishthanṭi sarvasya;
ṭéshu snānam sam-ācharét.
Ḍānam ṭīrṭham, ḍamas-ṭīrṭham,
sanṭoshas-ṭirṭham uchyaṭé,
Brahma-charyam param ṭīrṭham
ṭīrṭham cha priya-vāḍiṭā,
Jñānam ṭīrṭham, ḍhṛṭis-tīrṭham
Ṭapas ṭīrṭham uḍ-āhṛṭam
Ṭīrṭhānām api ṭaṭ ṭīrṭham
Vi-shuḍḍhir-manasah parā. (*Mbh.*)

The glow of self-denial, sense-control,
Forgivingness, and gentleness to all,
Dwelling on God in mind, and truthfulness,
Contentment, charity, and chastity,

Soft words of friendliness, and fortitude,
Enlightenment, and purity of heart,
And knowledge that the Self is All in All
—Most blessed shrines, holiest of waters, these;
And all within your being, ever near;
Bathe in these sacred waters, worship here!)

Na nagga-chariyā, na jatā, na pankā,
N-ānāsakā, ṭhandila-sāyikā vā,
Rajo-vajallam, ukkutika-ppaḍhānam,
Soḍhénṭi machcham aviṭiṇṇa-kankham.
Kin ṭé jatāhi, ḍum-méḍha! kin ṭé ajina-sātiyā?
Abbhanṭaram ṭé gahanam, bāhiram pari-majjasi!
(*Dh.*)

(Nude endurance of sun, rain, heat and cold,
Long tangled hair, smearing with earth and ashes,
Fasting, sleeping on stone, tormenting postures,
And self-inflicted pains of every sort,
Can purify thee not, friend!, until thou
Wash clean thy heart of all unclean desire.
What is the use of matted hair, and what
Of raiment made out of the wild goat's skin?
Within thee there is ravening and sin,
Only the outside dost thou try to clean.
Different the way, from sin the heart to wean.

Now do ye Pharisees make clean the outside of the cup and the platter, but your inward part is full of ravening and wickedness. (*B.*)

Véḍās, ṭyāgash cha, yajñāsh cha,
niyamāsh cha, ṭapāmsi cha,
Na vi-pra-ḍushta-bhāvasya
siḍḍhim gachchhanṭi karhi-chiṭ, (*M.*)
(Study of scripture and ascetic life,
Ritual and sacrificial offerings,
Observances of rules and practices

Of orthodox religion, even gifts—
Avail him not at all whose heart is bad.)

Blessed is the man that endureth temptation; for when he is tried, he shall receive the crown of life, which the Lord hath promised to them that love Him...Pure religion and undefiled before God and the Father is this: To visit the fatherless and the widows in their affliction, and to keep himself unspotted from the world...What doth it profit, my brethren, though he say he hath faith, and have not works? Can faith save him?...By works was faith made perfect?... For as the body without the spirit is dead, so faith without works is dead also. (*B.*, James.)

Circumcision is nothing, and uncircumcision is nothing; but the keeping of the commandments of God (is everything). (*B.*, Corinthians.)

The good that I would, I do not; but the evil which I would not, that I do. (*B.*, Rom.)

Jānāmy-aḍharmam na cha mé ni-vṛṭṭih;
Jānāmi ḍharmam na cha mé pra-vṛṭṭih;
Kén-āpi ḍévéna hṛḍi sṭhiṭéna
Yaṭhā ni-yukṭ-osmi tathā-charāmi. (*Mbh.*)

(I know the right, yet cannot do the right;
I know the wrong, and yet I do the wrong.
It is as if some force dwells in my heart,
And drives me, and I helplessly obey.)

Have we not all one Father? Hath not one God created us? Why do we deal treacherously every man against his brother? (*B.*, Malachi.) One is your Master, even Christ, and all ye are brethren. (*B.*)

There is one Body and one Spirit. (*B.*, Ephesians.)

As the body is one and hath many members, and all the members of that one body, being many, are one body, so also is Christ. For, by one spirit are we all baptised into one body, whether we be Jews or Gentiles, whether we be bond or free...We have many members in one body, and all members have not the same office...There are diversities of gifts,...of administrations,...of operations, but it is the same God, the same Spirit, the same Lord, which worketh all in all... And whether one member suffer, all the members suffer with it; or one member be honored, all the members rejoice with it. (*B.*, Corinthians, viii; Romans, xii.) And this commandment have we from Him: That he who loveth God love his brother also. (*B.*, John.)

(He who permitteth his left-hand to be
Defiled with dirt and doth not wipe it clean
With his right hand, will make his body soon
Unclean in all its parts. What makes the whole
But parts? And what the human bodies? Limbs.
Let each limb care for every other, then.) (*Bu.*)[1]

In life we should be of use to others. (*C.*, *Liki.*)

In seeking a foothold for self, love finds a foothold for others; seeking light for itself, it enlightens others also. (*C.*, *Analects.*)

Brāhmaṇo-(A)sya mukham āsīṭ,
bāhū rājanyah kriṭah,
Ūrū ṭaḍ Asya yaḍ vaishyah,
paḍbhyām shūḍro ajāyaṭa. (*V.*)

(The men of knowledge constitute the head,
Of macrocosmic Man, the Oversoul;
The men of action are His mighty arms;
Men of desire, His chest and abdomen,
And men of labor, all-supporting legs;
Thus are all human beings parts of One Whole.)

[1] The note of the original Buddhist text was lost, unfortunately, and could not be traced while the pages were in the press.

Banī Āḍam ā'zāe yak ḍīgar anḍ,
Ke ḍar āfrīnish ze yak jauhar anḍ.
Chu uzwė ba ḍarḍ āwaraḍ rozgār,
Ḍigar uzwa-hā rā na mānaḍ qarār.
Ṭu k-az mihnaṭé ḍīgar-āṅ bé-ghạm-ī,
Na shāyaḍ ke nām-aṭ nihanḍ āḍamī. (*S.*)

(The progeny of Adam are all limbs
Of but one body, since in origin
And essence they are all identical.
If one limb of the body suffer pain
Can th' others ever rest in painless ease ?
If thou art careless of thy brother's pains
The name of man thou oughtest not to wear.)

Sāhab-ḍilé ba maḍrasah āmaḍ ze khạneqāh,
Ba shikasṭe a'hḍe suhbaṭé ahl-é-ṭarīq rā.
Gufṭam : Miyāne ā'lim wa ā'biḍ che farq būḍ,
Ṭā ikhṭiyār karḍī az-āṅ īṅ farīq rā ?
Gufṭ : Ū gilīm-e khẉésh ba ḍar mī baraḍ ze mauj,
W-īṅ jehaḍ mī kunaḍ ke bi-gīraḍ ghạrīq rā. (*S.*)

(A hermit broke his vow of hermitage,
And joined a school of teachers, good and wise.
Asked why he chose the latter's company
Above that of 'the men of practices,'
He said : The hermits think to save their own
Rag-blanket from the inundating waves,
The teachers try to save the drowning men.)

As-sayyo minni wa iṭmāmo min Allah. (*H.*)

(Effort is mine, to grant success is God's.
Man should propose, God only can dispose.)

Ṭarīqaṭ ba-juz khịḍmaṭé-khạlq n-īsṭ,
Ba ṭasbīh o sajjāḍa o ḍalq n-īsṭ. (*S.*)

(None other Path to God is anywhere
Than the whole-hearted service of His world.

Repeating God's names, turning o'er and o'er
The rosary of beads, the prayer-mat,
The wrap of rags—these do not make the Path.)

...Fravarḗṭā wāsṭrīm... no īṭ, Mazaḍā !, a-wāsṭrayo ḍa vāṅschīnā hūmḗrḗṭoīsh bakshṭā...(*Z.*, Gāṭhā, 31.10.)

(Choose ye the path of Action Dutiful...
For the deluded one who giveth up
All action—he forfeiteth welfare too.)

...Ashḗma dḗrḗḍyāī ṭaṭ mōī ḍāo Armaīṭī rāyo ashīsh wanghḗush gaḗm manangho. (43. 1).

(Give me, Lord Mazaḍā !, the Activism,
Of Duty on the path of Conscience straight,
Which only can uphold the Rectitude
Through which alone come blessings to the world.)

Not learning but doing is the chief thing.
(*Ju.*, *Mishna*, *Aboth*, ii. 17.)

He that turneth away his ear from the law, even his prayer shall be abomination. (*B.*, Proverbs.)

When ye spread forth your hands, I will hide mine eyes from you; yea, when ye make many prayers, I will not hear; your hands are full of blood. (*B.*, Isaiah).

Ruḍrāksham, ṭulasī-kāshṭham,
ṭri-pundram, bhasma-ḍhāraṇam,
Yāṭrāh, snānāni, homāsh-cha,
japā, vā ḍḗva-ḍarshanam,
Na-iṭḗ punanṭī manujam
yaṭhā bhūṭa-hiṭḗ raṭih. (*Purāṇa.*)

(Bead-necklaces and many rosaries,
And triple paint on forehead, ash on skin,
Wand'rings to shrines and off'rings into fire,
Mechanical recital of God's names,
Looking at eikons—all these help not man,
As does work for the service of the world.)

Sva-ḍharma-karma-vi-mukhāh,
Kṛshṇa-Kṛshṇ-éṭi rāviṇah,
Ṭé Harér-ḍvéshiṇo mūḍhāh,
Ḍharm-ārṭham janma yaḍ-Haréh.
(*Purāṇa.*)

(Who shirk their duty, and, for all to hear,
Cry loudly, Kṛshṇa ! Kṛshṇa !, they are cheats ;
They are not devotees but foes of God ;
For God sends incarnations of high souls
To make men do their duties, not cry words.)

Not every one that sayeth, Lord, Lord, shall enter into the kingdom of heaven ; but he that doeth the will of my Father which is in heaven...I will profess unto them, I never knew you ; depart from Me, ye that work iniquity. (*B.*, Mat. vii.)

Na mīṅ goyam ke az ḍunyā juḍā bāsh,
Ba har kāré ke bāshī bā Khuḍā bāsh. (*S.*)
Cho mīṅ bīnam ke nā-bīnā ba chāh asṭ,
W-agar khāmosh mī bāsham gunāh ast. (*S.*)

(I do not say : Go and give up the world.
I say : Be near God in whate'er thou dost.
If I should see a blind man with his stick
Wending towards a well, and warn him not,
Then I am surely guilty of his death.)

To share one's wisdom with others is called true wisdom ; to share one's wealth with others is reckoned meritorious. (*T.*, Kwang Tzu.)

Brāhmaṇah sama-ḍṛk, shānṭo,
ḍīnānām an-apékshakah,
Sravaṭé Brahma ṭasy-āpi,
bhinna-bhānḍāṭ payo yaṭhā. (*Bh.*)

(Even a saintly and impartial man,
Free from all selfish loves and hates—if even
Such should stand by, and see the poor oppressed,

And do naught to befriend them any way,
Then from them shall depart unfailingly
All learning and all virtue, as milk flows
Away from vessel leaking through a crack.)

Prāyasho munayo loké
svārṭh-aik-ānṭ-oḍyamā hi ṭé ;
Ḍvaipāyanas-ṭu bhagavān
sarva-bhūṭa-hiṭé raṭah. (*Bh.*)
Na karmaṇām an-ārambhān
naish-karmyam purusho-shnuṭé,
Na cha san-nyasanāḍ-éva
siḍḍhim sam-aḍhi-gachchhaṭi.
Labhanṭé Brahma-nirvāṇam
sarva-bhūṭa-hiṭé raṭāh. (*G.*)

(Most anchorets strive only for themselves,
And therefore fail ; but those who truly know,
Engage themselves in service of the world.
Not by avoidance of activity,
Nor by renunciation either, may
Freedom of soul be gained, or perfectness ;
Only by constant service of the world
May the great peace of Brahma be attained.)

Uṭṭamā sahaj-āvasṭhā, ḍviṭīyā ḍhyāna-ḍhāraṇā,
Ṭriṭīyā praṭimā-pūjā, homa-yāṭrā vidambanā.
(*Agni Purāṇa.*)

(The natural state is best, the feel of self
At one with the Eternal Self of all,
In tune with the Immortal Infinite ;
The labored contemplation of the One
Is next ; lower, is fixing of the mind
On some material image ; ritualism,
Offerings and sacrifices, pilgrimage,
And movings up and down of hands and feet,
Are self-deception, mummery, or pastime.)

Karmaṇy-év-āḍhi-kāras ṭé,
  mā phaléshu kaḍā-chana.
Ṭasmāḍ asakṭah saṭaṭam
  kāryam karma sam-āchara.
Ṭena ṭyakṭéna bhunjīṭhāh,
  mā gṛḍhah kasya-sviḍ ḍhanam.
Brāhmané...cha...shva-pāké cha
  pandiṭāh sama-ḍarshinah. (*G.*, *U.*)

(To do thy duty is thy only right;
Thou hast no right to crave reward or fruit.
Do all thy work with a detachèd mind.
Enjoy the joys thy fortune may bring thee,
But with aloofness, ready to give up.
Behold all, great and small, same-sightedly.)

If I have committed any sin against the law of brotherhood in relation to my father, mother, sister, brother, mate, or children; in relation to my leader, my next-of-kin and acquaintances; my co-citizens, partners, neighbours, my own townsmen, and my servants—then I repent and pray for pardon.

(*Z.*, *Paṭeṭ Pashémānī.*)

The beautiful poem, *Abu bin Aḍham*, must be brought in here with loving hands:

Abu bin Aḍham—may his tribe increase—
Awoke one night from a deep dream of peace,
And saw within the moonlight in his room,
Making it rich, like lily in full bloom,
An Angel writing in a book of gold.
Exceeding peace had made bin Aḍham bold,
And to the Presence in the room he said,
"What writest thou?" The Vision raised its head,
And with a look made all of sweet accord,
Answered, "The names of those who love the Lord."
"And is mine there?" asked Abu. "Nay, not so,"

Replied the Angel. Abu spoke more low,
But cheerily still, and said, "I pray thee, then,
Write me as one who loves his fellow-men."
The Angel wrote and vanished. The next night,
He came again with a great wakening light,
And showed the names which love of God had blest.
And, lo!, bin Aḍham's name led all the rest!.

FOLLOW THE SPIRIT, NOT THE LETTER. Warnings against false interpretations of scripture-texts by selfish, interested, or ignorant persons, desirous of increasing ritualism and formalism, are also given by all Teachers:

Yām imām pushpiṭām vācham
pra-vaḍanṭy-a-vipashchiṭah,
Véḍa-vāḍa-raṭāh, Pārṭha!,
n-ānyaḍ-asṭ-īṭi vāḍinah. (*G.*)

(They lack all sense who prate perpetually
About the Véḍa's ritual, and assert,
'There is naught else'; they verily know naught.)

Ṭam-éva ḍhīrō vijñāya
prajñām kurvīṭa brāhmaṇah,
Nā-nu-ḍhyāyéḍ bahūn shabḍān,
vācho viglāpanam hi ṭaṭ, (*U.*)

(The One Truth which bestoweth wisdom seek,
And think not many words, tis waste of Speech.)

Shāsṭrāṇy-abhyasya, méḍhāvī,
jñāna-vijñāna-ṭaṭ-parah,
Palālam iva dhāny-ārṭhī,
ṭyajéḍ granṭhān a-shésha-ṭah. (*U.*)

(Study the linkèd words, no doubt, but look
Behind them to the thought they indicate,
And having found it, throw the words away
As chaff when you have sifted out the grain.

Study the sciences; master their heart;
Having done so, cling not to many books.)
Gar ze sirré mā'rifaṭ āgah shawī ·
Lafz bu-guzārî suyé mā'nī rawī. (*S.*)
(If thou wouldst learn the secret of the True,
Let pass the word, the thought, the thought, pursue.)

Paḍa-jñair n-āṭi-nir-banḍhah
kartavyo muni-bhāshiṭé,
Arṭha-smaraṇa-ṭāṭparyān
n-āḍryanṭé hi lakshaṇam.
(Let not grammarians scrutinise
Too close the language of the wise;
The seers think more of the thought
Than of the words in which 'tis caught.)

Iṭihāsa-Purāṇābhyām
Véḍam sam-upa-bṛmhayéṭ,
Bibhéṭy-alpa-shruṭāḍ Véḍo
mām ayam pra-ṭarishyaṭi. (*M.*)
(Read Véḍa in the light of History,
The History of the Universe and Man;
The Véḍa fears the man who knows not much:
"He will deprive me of my rightful sense.")

Ṭū Qurāṅ gar bar īṅ nawa' kẖwānī,
Be-burī raunaqé Musalmānī. (*S.*)
(If thou interpretest the Qurān thus,
Thou murderest the beauty of Islām.)

And we are told that the real source of all true knowledge is within our-Self. Only he who has found that source will be able to understand the scriptures rightly. P r a ṭ i - b h ā, ḍ i v y a - ḍ ṛ s h ṭ i, y o g a - j a - j ñ ā n a, intuition, i s h r ā q, *ilm-i-huzūrī*, *kashf*, is recognised by all religions, as distinguished from ṭ a r k a, a n u - m ā n, *mashīyaṭ, ilm-i-husūlī*, intellectual argument, inference, reasoning. Various states, and degrees, of 'inner illumination', 'divine revelation', a n ṭ a h - p r a k ā s h a, ḍ i v y a - ḍ ṛ s h t i, m a n ṭ r a - ḍ a r s h a n a, *raushan-zamīrī, chashm-i-bāṭinī, ilhām*, are distinguished.

Ḍar ramz o kanāya na ṭawāṅ yāfṭ Khuḍā rā,
Masahaf-i-ḍil bīṅ, ke kiṭābé beh az īṅ n-īsṭ. (*S.*)

(In books and signs thou never wilt find God !
Read thine own heart with reverence and heed,
No holier writ is owned by any creed.)

Saḍ kiṭāb-o saḍ waraq ḍar nār kun,
Jān o ḍil rā jānib-é-Ḍilḍār kun. (*S.*)
(Give thousand-paged tomes unto the fire,
Give life and heart to the One Heart's Desire.)

Jo ilm-o-hikmaṭ kā Wo hai ḍānā,
ṭo ilm-o-hikmāṭ ke ham haiṅ mūjiḍ.
Hai apne sīné meṅ us sé zāyaḍ
jo bāṭ wā'ez kiṭāb méṅ hai. (*S.*)
(Since He knows all art and science,
we too can invent and know ;
In the human heart is hidden
more than all the Scriptures show.)

Ḍar haqīqaṭ kḥuḍ ṭu-ī Umm-ul-kiṭāb,
Kḥuḍ ze kḥuḍ āyāṭ-e kḥuḍ rā bāz yāb.
Lauh-e Mahfūz asṭ ḍar mā'nī ḍil-aṭ,
Har che mī kḥwāhī shawaḍ z-ū hāsil-aṭ.

(Thy-self the parent of all God-spell thou ;
All scriptures thine own heart will give enow.
The Sacred Guarded Tablet—thine own heart ;
Whate'er thou wishest, ask ; it will impart.)

Sarvam Āṭmani sam-pashyéṭ
sat ch-āsaṭ cha sam-āhiṭah.
Sarvam Āṭmani sam-pashyan
n-āḍharmé kuruṭé manah.
Āṭm-aiva ḍévaṭāh sarvāh,
Sarvam Aṭmany-ava-sṭhiṭam. (*M.*)
Sarvāsām viḍyānām hṛḍayam ék-āyanam. (*U.*)

(Behold all truth, all error, in thy-Self;
The Self is all the gods; all's in the Self.
Who thus beholds the Great Self in him-Self,
He cannot set his heart again on sin.
The one storehouse of all the sciences,
Known and unknown, is our own living heart.)

By such realisation of the unity of All life in and through Action, by service of fellow-creatures, is completed the triple realisation of the Secondless and Other-less Oneness, Shuḍḍh-āḍvaiṭam, *Ṭauhīḍ-i-zāṭī*, Bhāv-āḍvaiṭam, *Ṭauhīḍ-i-sifāṭī*, Kriy-āḍvaiṭam, *Ṭauhīḍ-i-afā'lī*.

Lauh-i-Mahfūz, the Guarded or Preserved Tablet, is the *hāfizā*, the Omniscient Memory, of God, in which all past, present, and future is eternally contained and preserved. The corresponding Samskṛṭ word is Chiṭra-gupṭa, the Hidden and Preserved Picture, or Ākāshic Record. God as Yama, Anṭar-yāmī, the Judge, the Inner Ruler, the As-Shakur and Al-Qābiz, the Giver of rewards and punishments, the Al-Muhsiy, the Recorder, has for Recording Angel, Chiṭra-gupṭa, Gupṭa-Chiṭra, the Secret Wonderful Picturer, Photographer; and the Record is His own

Memory, *Hāfizā, Lauh-i-Mahfūz*, Smṛṭi. One of the names of Brahmā, Mahaṭ-Buḍḍhi, *Aql-i-kul*, 'Total Universal Mind', is Smṛṭi, the Divine Memory, the *Nous-Demiurgos* of the Greeks; also Chiṭ, 'in which everything is stored up, collected', (chi, to gather); also Sam-viṭ, 'that all-pervading Consciousness, Awareness,' (viḍ, to know) which is the changeless eternal witness, knower of all past, present, future. Human knowledge is only the successive manifestation of what is ever-present in the Eternal Now of Omniscience. We can know and invent only because all art and science is already ever-present in our Self. We borrow and bring to light infinitesimal portions of it in succession.

The source of all true knowledge being such, the quintessence of the religion of Works, which is the inseparable consequence of the religion of Devotion and of Illumination, is:

Ashraf-ul-īmāni un yamanak an-naso, wa ashraf-ul-Islāmi un yaslam an-naso mil-lessaneka wa yaḍeka. (*Q.*)

(Noblest religion this—That others may
Feel safe from thee; the loftiest Islām
—That all may feel safe from thy tongue and hands.)

Perfect love casteth out fear. (*B.*)

Yasmān n-oḍ-vijaṭé loko,
lokān-n-oḍ-vijaṭé cha yah,[1]

---

[1] "Who giveth up the world, taking the vow, that he will cause no fear to any one, nothing can cause fear to him any more; all glorious worlds stand open unto him": *Manu*, vi, 39-40.

Harsh-āmarsha-bhay-oḍ-vēgair-
mukṭo yah sa cha Mé priyah. (*G.*)
(Who causes no disquiet to the world,
Nor is himself perturbèd by the world,
Who has won real Freedom, by being free
Of the excitements and disturbances
Of proud elations, fears, intolerances,
—Yea, such an one is ever dear to Me!)[1]

Namāzé zāhiḍān qaḍḍ o sujūḍ-asṭ,
Namāzé āshiqān ṭark-é-wujūḍ asṭ. (*S.*)

(The formal prayer is—sitting up and down;
The real—our own egoism to drown.)

And when thou prayest, thou shalt not be as the hypocrites are; for they love to pray standing in the synagogues and in the corners of the streets, that they may be seen of men...When ye pray, use not vain repetitions, as the heathens do, for they think that they shall be heard for their much speaking...Enter into thy closet, and when thou hast shut thy door, pray to thy Father which is in secret..." (*B.*)

Circumcision is nothing, and uncircumcision is nothing; but the keeping of the commandments of God (is everything). (*B.*)

---

[1] *The Book of the Dead*, the chief available sacred writing of the dead religion of ancient Egypt, contains directions for the soul, when it appears before the Judge of the Dead. It should be able to say: "I have made no one weep". Of course, the words, 'by any wrong action of mine', are understood. Otherwise no judge could ever punish a criminal, particularly one who has relatives.

Ḍilā ! ṭawāf-i-ḍilāṅ kun, ke Kā'ba·é-makhḥfī-sṭ,
Ke ān Khḥalīl binā karḍ, wa īn Khḥuḍā khḥuḍ
sākhṭ ! (*S.*)

(O ! circumambulate thy-Self, my heart !
Thou art the secret Kā'ba ! yea, thou art !
That outer Kā'ba Abraham designed,
Thou wast created by High God's own mind !)

Hajj che bāshaḍ ? *Ze* khḥuḍ safar karḍan.
Bā kujā ? Jānibé Hiḍāyaṭ-kār. (*S.*)

(What is the Pilgrimage ? To run away
From the small self. And travel whitherward ?
To the Great Self, whence all true guidance comes.)

Na hy-am-mayāni ṭīrṭhāni
na ḍévā mṛch-chhilā-mayāh ;
Ṭé punanṭy-uru-kāléna
ḍarshanāḍ-éva sāḍhavaḥ. (*B.*)

(Sanctums are not made of waters,
Nor gods of wood, clay, or stone ;
Very long they take to cleanse thee ;
Saintly heart is God's own throne.)

Aṭṭā hi Aṭṭano nāṭho, ko hi nāṭho paro siyā.
Aṭṭanā hi su-ḍanténa nāṭham labhaṭi ḍullabham. (*Dh.*)

(The Self is the protector of the self,
Who else than Self can be the Lord of self.
Who has encompassed and achieved him-Self,
Has gained That than which there's no higher gain.)

Ava-jānanṭi Mām mūdhā
mānushīm ṭanum āshriṭam,
Param bhāvam ajānanṭo
Mama bhūṭa-Mah-éshvaram. (*G.*)

(Men slight Me, hidden in the human frame,
Thinking, benighted, I must be far off,
Unwitting of Me as the Lord *in* all.)

Uḍḍharéḍ Āṭman-āṭmānam
n-āṭmānam ava-sāḍayéḍ ;
Āṭma-iva ḍévaṭāh sarvāh,
sarvam Āṭmany-ava-sṭhiṭam. (*G.* and *M.*)

(Uplift thy smaller self by the Great Self,
And do not drag the High down to the low.
The Self is all the gods, all 's in the Self.)

Āṭṭa-ḍīpā vi-haraṭha,
Āṭṭa-saraṇā, an-añña-saraṇā,
Vaya-ḍhammā sankhārā,
Ap-pamāḍéna sampāḍéṭha.
(Buḍḍha's last words.)

(Be to your-Self the one and only Light ;
Be to your-Self the one and only Refuge ;
Seek not for help from other-than-your-Self ;
All composites, all made-up things, are transient ;
Remembering this, find watchfully th' Immortal.)

Yā nishā sarva-bhūṭānām
ṭasyām jāgarṭi sam-yamī,
Yasyām jāgraṭi bhūṭāni
sā nishā pashyaṭo munéh. (*G.*)

(That which is night for others, therein wake
The careful ; while that which is day for all
Is night for him who sees the Inner world.)

Har ke béḍār-āsṭ ū ḍar kḥwāb-ṭar,
Hasṭ béḍārī-sh az kḥwāb-ash baṭar ;
Har ke ḍar kḥwāb-asṭ béḍārī-sh beh,
Hasṭ gḥaflaṭ ain hushyārī-sh beh,
Mahramé īṅ hosh juz bé-hosh n-īsṭ,
Mar zabāṅ rā mushṭarī juz gosh n-īsṭ. (*S.*)

(He who seems now awake is in deep dream,
And he who seems asleep doth truly wake.
The true sleep 's better than such wakefulness.

Only th' Unconscious knows this Consciousness;
The tongue's speech but the speechless ear can guess.)
Sālahā ḍil ṭalabé jām-i-Jam az mā mī karḍ,
Un-che kḥuḍ ḍāshṭ ze bégānah ṭamannā mī karḍ. (*S.*)
(Long years my heart for Jamshéḍ's wondrous Grail,
That mirrors all, begged others—all in vain;
And then at last it found that what it hoped
To gain from others, it-Self did contain!)
Bhūṭānām prāṇinah shréshthāh
prāṇinām buḍḍhi-jīvinah,
Kṛṭa-buḍḍhishu karṭārah
karṭṛshu Brahma-véḍinah. (*M.*)
Na Mé, Pārṭh!-āsṭi karṭavyam
ṭrishu lokéshu kinchana,
N-ān-av-āpṭam av-āpṭavyam,
varṭa-éva cha karmaṇi. (*G.*)
(Breathers of air are higher 'mongst living things;
'Mongst them, they that live by intelligence;
'Mongst them, again, they who have seen the Self;
Highest are they who *act* accordingly.
Naught have I left to do in all the worlds,
Nor is there aught which I have not attained,
Yet am I working for the world alway.)
Kasé marḍé ṭamām asṭ az ṭamāmī
Kunaḍ bā khwājagī kāré gḥulāmī. (*S.*)
(He is the perfect man who, being lord,
Can still to serve the lowliest afford.)
Afzal-ul-ashghāl khiḍmaṭ-ul-unnās. (*H.*)
(Finest of orisons—Service of Man.)

All religions put us on our guard against deceiving ourselves into indolence or carelessness or self-indulgence in vice, under cover of a false self-surrender to God, and of the pretence that whatever we do, even obviously immoral or evil, is done under impulsion from God, that we are helpless puppets, and 'therefore' cannot be held to punishment. In this 'therefore' is the great fallacy. The true 'therefore' runs thus: Since you regard yourself as helpless to avoid the doing of evil, 'therefore' you must regard yourself as helpless also to avoid the receiving of punishment. Causes and effects must be equated. Since we *feel* our-self able to act either the one way or the other, at will, therefore we should feel will-ing to bear the consequences also, of either.

Take no thought for the morrow (but) whatsoever (duty) thy hand findeth to do, do it with all thy might. (*B.*)

Īshvarah sarva-bhūṭānām
hṛḍ-ḍéshé-(A)rjuna ! ṭishthaṭi,
Bhrāmayan sarva-bhūṭāni
yanṭr-ārūṛhāni māyayā.
Mā karma-phala-héṭur-bhūr-
mā ṭé sango-sṭ-va-karmaṇi. (*G.*)

(God sits within the heart of every one,
Twirling all by His Magic, round and round,
As if bound firmly to a vast machine;
Yet thou must not avoid a single duty;
Only the wish for fruit must thou avoid.)

The Qurān holds the same language:

Qulūb-ul-kḥalāyaq fī asābe ir-Rahmān. (*Q.*)
(The hearts of living creatures are all fixed
Upon the fingers of Almighty God.)

Yet the ordained duties must not be neglected.

All sayyo minni w-al iṭmāmo min Allah. (*H.*)
(Effort is mine, to grant success is God's.)
Ḍaryā ba wujūḍ-e kḥwésh maujé ḍāraḍ,

Kẖas pinḍāraḍ ke kashā-kash bā ū-sṭ. (*S.*)
(The ocean heaves in surges of its being,
And the vast billows toss the straw about—
The straw thinks it is struggling with the waves.)

Prakṛṭéh kriya-māṇāni
gunaih karmāṇī sarvashah,
Aham-kāra-vimūdh-āṭmā
karṭā-ham-iṭi manyaṭé. (*G.*)

(Nature is operating everywhere,
Her forces cause all motions of the world,
But man, deluded by false ego-ism,
Imagines, 'I am doing all these things.')

Kār-kun ḍar kār-gah bāshaḍ nihāṅ,
Ṭū bi-rau ḍar kārgah bīṇ-ash ayāṅ,
Kār-sāz-é mā ḍurūn-é kār-e mā,
Fikr-i mā ḍar kār-e mā āzār-e mā. (*S.*)
(The Moving Force is hid in the machine,
Yet canst thou see Him working plain to view;
Thou the machine and He the moving force.
He is the guiding motive of 'my' work,
'My' *worry* o'er 'my' work is 'my' disease.)

Nahi kash-chiṭ kshaṇam api
jāṭū ṭishthaṭy-a-karma-kṛṭ.
Kāryaṭé hy-avashah karma
sarvah Prakṛṭi-jair-guṇaih.
Niyaṭam kuru karma ṭvam,...
mukṭa-sangah sam-āchara,
Nimiṭṭa-māṭram (bhūṭvā cha)...
Param āpnoṭi pūrushah. (*G.*)

(None can stay still a moment actionless;
Nature drives all resistlessly to act;
Thy fixèd duty do unfailingly,
But with detachment, knowing that thou art

But instrument ; and so shalt thou attain
The One and Only Doer of all deeds.)

All religions tell us that God, the Universal Self, is the one True, Beautiful, Good. We *know* the True, the Real, that which is ; we *desire* the Beautiful, the Lovely ; we *do* the Good, the Right. The Self al-One *is*, is known to be the Real, utter True ; the Self al-One is the most desired, the best Be-lov-ed, the Supremely Beautiful ; the Self al-One, all-pervading, all-uniting, is the final cause, motive, source, of all and any doing, any activity, that is benevolent, beneficent, wholly Good. The Self is Saṭyam, *lā maujūḍah illā Hū*, 'nothing else than It *Is*' ; the Self is Priyam, *lā maqsūḍah illā hū*, 'nothing else than It is *Be-lov-ed*' ; the Self is Hiṭam, *lā mā'būḍah illā Hū*, 'nothing else than It is Good and to-be-Served'.

Mystic, Gnostic, Yoga or Sulūk, disciplines. Thus may we see that all religions are in essence exactly the same ; and that that essence comes from God, and is intended in all to lead back to God by the same processes of *Yoga* or *Sulūk*. The seeds of such 'mystic, spiritual and psychical, exercise and discipline,' are sown in sanḍhy-opāsanā, *namāz*, prayer, and its accompaniments. These are : yama, niyama, (ṭapas, chiṭṭa-pra-sāḍana, chiṭṭa-pari-karma), āsana, prāṇ-ā-yāma, praṭy-āhāra, ḍhyāna, ḍhāraṇā, (nir-vikalpa, etc.), sam-ā-ḍhi; or *ṭahzīb-un-nafs, ṭasfīya-i-ḍil*, (*nafs-kushī, parhéz, pārsāī, riyā-*

zaṭ, *ṭanqīya-i-qalb*), *zikr*, *fikr*, *mujāhiḍā*, *ashgḥāl*, *habs-i-ḍam*, *murāqibā*, *mukāshifā*, (*kḥāli-uz-zehn etc.*) *mushāhiḍā* (*hāl*, *ḍiḍār*, *wajḍ*, *muā-yinā*); *i. e.*, vows, restraint of limbs and breath, abstraction of the mind from the senses, concentration, contemplation, absorption, rapt trance, ecstasy, beatific vision.[1]

All religions finally declare that He is all, *Hama Ū-sṭ*, Sarvam khal-viḍam Brahma, 'All is God, the Universe is I'; from which it follows, in all religions, that since Man is in essence God, the service of fellow-men is the service of God.

In as much as ye have done it unto the least of these, ye have done it unto Me. (*B.*)

Prāyasho loka-ṭāpéna
ṭapyanṭé sāḍhavo janāh ;

---

[1]*Ch'an* and *Zen* are respectively the names for *ḍhyāna*, meditation, in Chinese and Japanese Buddhism. They are probably the same word, (or also *jñāna*), with the pronunciation modified.

To each name of God, *ism*, nāma, corresponds a bhāva, *kḥaṭrā*, emotion, mood, force. Dwelling on a name, by means of japa, *zikr*, litany, opens up a whole world wherein that particular form of His Energy or aspect of His Nature, which is indicated by that name, is predominant.

Ṭaj-japas ṭaḍ-arṭha-bhāvanam...Yaṭas-ṭaḍ-vishayā maṭih....Yaḍ ichchaṭi ṭaḍ bhavaṭi. (*Yoga Suṭra, Bh., U.*)

(To dwell upon a name is but to dwell
Upon the meaning; and a man becomes
What he dwells on and wishes; mind is man.)

Param-ārāḍhanam ṭaḍ hi
Purushasy-ākhil-Āṭmanah. (*Bh.*)
(The good feel all the distress of the world
To be their own distress ; this is best service
Of Him who is the Soul of all the world.)

Yéna kéna prakāréṇa
yasya kasy-āpi janṭunah,
Sanṭosham janayéḍ ḍhīmāns-
ṭaḍ-év-Ēshvara-pūjanam. (*Bh.*)
(Give joy to any living thing—ye give
Service and worship to the Life of God.)

Gar ṭajallī kḥās kḥwāhī sūraṭé insāṅ bi bīṅ,
*Z*āṭ-ī-Haq rā āshkārā anḍarūn kḥanḍāṅ bi bīṅ.
(*S.*)
(Wouldst thou behold God wholly manifest ?
Look at thy brother's kindly face awhile !
Wouldst see Divinity at its sweet best ?
Then call forth on that brother's face a smile !)

Shakle-Insāṅ meṅ Kḥuḍā ṭhā,
mujhe mālūm na ṭhā ;
Chānḍ bāḍal meṅ chhipā ṭhā,
mujhe mālūm na ṭhā. (*S.*)
(Behind the mask of every human face
He hid, God, very God—I knew it not !
The Glory of the perfect moon was screened
Behind the fleeting clouds—I saw it not.)

Sṛshtvā purāṇi viviḍhāny-ajay-Āṭma-shakṭyā,
Vṛkshān, sarīsṛpa-pashūn, khaga-ḍamsha-maṭsyān,
Ṭais-ṭair-aṭushta-hṛḍayo, manujam viḍhāya,
Brahm-āvaboḍha-ḍhishaṇam, muḍam āpa Ḍévah.
(*Bh.*)
(House after house did God make for Himself,
Mineral, plant, insect, fish, reptile, and bird,
And mammal too. But yet was He not pleased.

At last he made Himself the form of Man,
Wherein He knew Himself, the Self of all.
And then the Lord of All was satisfied.)

Gauhar-é juz kẖuḍ-shināsī
n-īsṭ ḍar bahr-é wujūḍ ;
Mā ba girḍ-é kẖwésh mī
garḍém chūṅ girḍāb-hā. (*S.*)

(Like whirlpools round ourselves we whirl
In incessant strife ;
Self-knowledge is the only pearl
In the see of life.)

Ḍaryā ṭan asṭ, wa ḍil saḍaf,
wa Haq ḍar ū ḍur asṭ ;
Zīṅ bahr har ke ḍur baḍar
ārad bahāḍur asṭ. (*S.*)

(This body is the sea, the heart therein
The pearl-containing shell, the priceless pearl
Is God Him-Self ; he who can dive down deep
And find that pearl—the hero true is he.)

Lab bi banḍ o chashm banḍ o gosh banḍ,
Gar na bīnī rūy-e-Haq bar mā bi kẖanḍ. (*S.*)
(Shut lips and eyes and ears completely ; then
If thou see not the face of Truth, of God,
The secret Mystery of thine own Self,
Then tell me that I said what was not true.
Shut off the noises of the outer world,
And seek Him in the silence of your hearts,
And you will find Him and commune with Him.)

Sva-vishay-ā-sam-pra-yogé chiṭṭasya Sva-rūp-ānu-**kāra** iv-énḍriyāṇām praṭy-āhārah...Kaivalyam sva-rūpa-praṭishṭhā vā Chiṭi-shakṭih...Yogash-chiṭṭa-vṛṭṭi-niro-dhah....Ṭaḍā Ḍrashṭuh Sva-rūpé-(a)va-sṭhānam.

(*Yoga-Sūṭra.*)

(When all the senses are withdrawn away

From all their outer objects, then the mind
Behind them all doth turn upon if-Self,
And takes the form of Self. Or, rather, say,
The Self itself, when movements of the mind
Are hushed, stilled utterly, beholds It-Self,
Feels Its own Sole and On(e)ly Being, wherein
Nor space, nor time, nor any motion is,
And in at-one-ment with If-Self It rests.)

CHAPTER V

The One Way To Peace on Earth and Good Will among Men

The one purpose of Religion is to bind the hearts of human beings to each other and to God; and the realisation of the Self in all as the God in all, and the consequent service of all as the service of God, is the perfection and completion of Religion.

Love God (thy Self) with all thy heart and love thy neighbour as thy-Self. (*B.*)

But the laws of duality, polarity, ambivalence, and of cyclic swing between the two opposite extremes, inherently condition the manifestation of the One in the Many, *Éka* in *An-éka*, *Wahḍaṭ* in *Kasraṭ.*[1] Perversity becomes inseparable from Diversity; Egoism and Error become necessary to throw into relief Universalism and Truth; Sorrow, Joy; Hate, Love; proud Satan, the meek Son of God; Ahrimān, Spiṭama; Ḍaiṭyas, Ḍévas; Asuras, Suras; Sinners, Saints; Titans, Gods; Iblīs, Malāyak; Māra, Buḍḍha; Death, Life; Other-than-Self (Iṭara, *Ġḥair*, Not-Self), the Self

---

[1]*Wahḍaṭ dar ẕāṭ, Kasraṭ-ḍar-sifāṭ*; Éka-ṭā in the Parama-Ṭaṭṭva, the supreme Saṭ, the One Vishéshya, Ḍharmī; An-éka-ṭā, Nānā-ṭva, Ḅahu-ṭva, in the Guṇa-s, Vishéshaṇa-s, Ḍharma-s; Unity in Essence, Multiplicity in Attributes.

(Āṭmā, Sva, *Anā*). Therefore, Religion also falls from its high estate, becomes utterly perverted away from the essentials into non-essentials, and then into gross and cruel superstitions; separates the hearts of men instead of uniting them; and instigates mutual torture and murder instead of peace on earth and good-will among men. It does so, for a time, to rise again, by re-action, re-pentance, re-generation, re-formation, to a higher station. Paradise is lost, in order that it may be regained with fuller and firmer appreciation. Adam falls into sin, *asīrī*, bandha, the prison-house of fleshly matter, the sin and fetters of limiting satanic ego-ism, carnal lust, pride, *khuḍī*; aham-kāra, in order to rise again, through self-crucifixion, to salvation, *najāṭ*, *moksha*, deliverance, restoration, sol-ution and dis-sol-ution into the Ab-sol-ute God, ab-solv-ed from all limitations, *Fanā-f-Illāh*, Brahma-nirvāṇa, annihilation *into* God, limitless divine universalism and loving tenderness, and the Peace beyond all loves and hates.

Within the purview of available history, the medieval ages, in east and west alike, have been full of religious conflicts. The wars between Christians and Muslims during and after the Crusades, and the doings of the triple Inquisition have been particularly horrible. Europe has now, for some time, freed itself from the entanglements of Catholic-Protestant religious strife. But scarcely quite yet; and mostly nominally. The breaking away of the Irish Free State from

Britain, in 1921, was largely due to the same religious conflict. And in the whole of Europe the evil spirit has changed its form from communal to even worse politico-economic strife. The fires of hate burning underneath this are still the same as of old. The outer manifestation has taken on the shape of a conflict between excessively avaricious, ruthless, and sensuous individualism masquerading as patriotic nationalism, on the one hand; and, on the other, a communism or socialism which, wishing to share-and-share-alike, is truly spiritual and religious at bottom, but is so very sub-consciously, and is groping in the dark, and making many experiments and mistakes; because it is looking in the wrong direction and not finding the secret of true social organisation; because it does not realise that politics is rooted in economics, economics in 'domestics,' 'domestics' in psycho-physics, and that in metaphysics, which, in its fullness, is nothing else than Spiritual Religion, Spiritual Science of the Infinite, which includes, as parts, all sciences of all finites.

But in India, the religious and the secular, the communal and the politico-economic, conflicts and problems continue to be inseparably interwoven. It is perhaps India's destiny to perish or to provide one solution for both at once. Asia has given birth to all the great living religions. East and West, ancient and modern, have met here in a special way. The first All-Asia Education Conference took place in Benares, in India, in December-January, 1930-1931. India is situated in the middle of Asia; it stretches out one arm to embrace Buḍḍhist (and Shintoist, Taoist, and Confucian) Burma, China, Japan; another to embrace Islamic Afghanistan, Persia, Turkey, Arabia, Egypt, Africa, and also Hebrew and Christian Palestine and Europe; and it bears Buḍḍhist Thibet and Islamic Turkestan on her two shoulders. The bulk of the now very small Parsi population of the world, following the Zoroastrian faith, has had its home in the south-west of this country for nearly thirteen centuries; also, it is undisputed that the Gāthās of Zoroaster are a branch of the Véḍa, written in what may be regarded as another form of Véḍic Samskṛt. There is a very remarkable colony of Indian Jews too, numbering some thousands of souls, in the south. Tradition says that St. Thomas, one of the twelve apostles, came and planted the seed of Christianity on the south-east coast, shortly after the ascension of Christ; and the Christian community of India numbers over six millions today. Hindus, Jainas, Sikhs, barring a comparative handful of emigrants, have no other home than India; which is Motherland to over seventy *million* Muslims also; besides being the birthplace of Buḍḍhism and containing all the first sacred places of that religion. Confucianism, Laotsism, and Shintoism have practically all merged into an amalgam with Buḍḍhism.[1] Thus are all the

[1] At Sār-nāth, where Buḍḍha preached his first sermon,

living religions of the world gathered in this land. Therefore India's mission may perhaps be to inaugurate a new Re-form, a Re-incarnation, of the Eternal Universal Religion, in the shape of Scientific Religion. In that Religion, Consciousness, Self-Consciousness, the Principle of the Conscious and the Unconscious (as two aspects of the Self), is the common meeting-ground, nay, the one loved and loving parent, of both Science and Religion. These can be nothing else than the two halves, or, better, only two aspects, of the same One Whole Truth.

This is an elemental fact which has to be taken to heart, especially by Hindus and Muslims in India. Kṛshṇa has said :

Mama varṭm-ānu-varṭanṭé
manushyāḥ, Pārṭha ! sarvashah. (*G.*)
(The roads men follow—they all lead to Me,
At last ; though some are thorny and some fair.)

2500 years ago, in Benares, the centre of Véḍism, a great new temple of Buḍḍha has been built, within the last few years, close to the old Ashokan *sṭūpa* and ruins. It has been adorned with mural paintings by Japanese painters. Another great temple is being built by a Chinese benefactor. *Ḍharma-shālā-s*, free rest-houses and guest-houses, have been and are being built by Hindu and Burmese donors. And a colony of Buddhist *bhikshus* and students is growing up. Also, in Benares, besides the old Hindu temples, there are many Muslim mosques, a number of Jaina temples, Christian churches, and Sikh *sanghaṭs*.

Muhammad has said:

At-ṭurqu il Allāhi kan nufūsu bani Ādama. (*H.*)
(There are as many roads to God as souls.)

There is neither Jew nor Greek, there is neither bond nor free, neither male nor female, for ye are all one in Christ Jesus. (*B.*, Paul.)

Na varṇā na varṇ-āshram-āchāra-ḍharmāh
...Ṭaḍ Éko-va-shishtah Shivah Kévalo-(A)ham,
(SHANKAR-ĀCHĀRYA.)
(The soul hath no caste, neither any creed;
It is one with the Universal Life.)

N-aiva sṭrī na pumān ésha
na ch-aiv-āyam na-pumsakah;
Yaḍ-yaḍ-chharīram ā-ḍaṭṭé
ṭéna ṭéna sa yujyaṭé. (*Shvéṭa U.*)
(Not female, male, or neuter is the soul;
Whate'er the body that it putteth on,
For the time be-ing it becometh that.)

Hakīm Sanāī says:

Rūh bā a'ql o ilm ḍānaḍ zīsṭ,
Rūh rā Pārsī wa Ṭāzī n-īst. (*S.*)

Maulānā Rūm paraphrases him:[1]

Rūh bā a'ql asṭ o bā ilm asṭ yār,
Rūh rā bā Ṭāzi o Ṭurkī che kār. (*S.*)

---

[1]The revereuce in which Maulānā Jalāl-uḍ-ḍīn Rūmī is held among Muslims, has been mentioned before, (p. 75, *supra*). Another well-known saying about him is:

Masnawī-é Maulavī-é-Mā'nawī
Hasṭ Qur-āñ ḍar zabāné Pahlavī,
(The Masnawī of the great Maulavī,
Full of profoundest truths, of greatest value,
Is the Qurān itself in Pahlavī.)

By a slight further paraphrase, we may read:

Rūh rā bā Hinḍu o Muslim che kār.
(Persian or Turk or Arab are not known,
Or Hinḍū, Christian, Muslim, to the soul;
Wisdom and virtuous deed make the soul's life,
Not racial names and not communal strife.)

Religion should be worn as a winning smile, as a beautiful ornament, out of the gladness of one's own heart, to gladden the hearts of all others who behold it; not as a repelling frown, or as menacing weapons, out of fear and cruelty, and stimulating fear and cruelty all round. It should be worn principally in the heart, as philanthropic love and piety; not flaunted like signboards and labels, upon the face and forehead, in separative ways of wearing hair on head or lip or chin, or as differentiating paints or badges or clothes, for self-display and religion-advertisement, with purpose to emphasise separateness. Humanity, *insāniyaṭ*, m a n u s h y a-ṭ ā,—nay, divinity—is stamped by Nature, God's Nature, on the face of every human new-born infant; *not* any mark to show that it is Hindu or Muslim, Parsī, Christian, or Jew. Such distinctive marks

---

Masnawī is the name of the Maulānā's chief work. Pahlavī is the older name of the Persian language, now called Fārsī, in India. A famous Indian poet, (in Urdu and Persian). the late Sir Muhammad Iqbāl, has also written of the Maulānā:

Ke ū ba harf-e Pahlavī, Qurān nawisht.
(He wrote the Qurān in the Persian tongue.)

are artificially created by men themselves afterwards. They may have had their uses in special times and places and circumstances. To continue to insist upon them today, seems to be but disastrous short-sightedness.

Muhammad says:

Kulla mauḍin yulaḍu alā fiṭraṭ-ul-Islām. (*H.*)
(Yea, every child is born acknowledging,
Making submission unto, the One God.)

Vyāsa says:

Brahmaṇā pūrva-sṛshtam hi
sarvam Brāhmam iḍam jagaṭ. (*Mbh.*)
(Since Brahmā has created all this world,
All beings are His children obviously.)
Inn-Allāha khalaqa Āḍama alā sūraṭihī.
Fa innahu alā sūraṭihī.
Khalaq al insāna alā sūraṭ-ir-Rahmān. (*H.*)

These three sentences of the *Haḍis* are almost literal translations of the Biblical saying,

God created man in His own image. (*B.*)

Jīvo Brahm-aiva n-āparah. (*U.*)
(The individual soul is nothing else
In essence than the Universal Soul.)

Fiṭraṭ Allah illaṭi faṭar annāsa alaiha. (*Q.*)
(On God's own nature has been moulded man's.)

A nobly worded remonstrance, in Hinḍusṭānī verse, embodying some deep truths common to all religions, has been addressed by a Musalmān poet and lover of humanity, to all concerned, with special reference to the communal riots that have been breaking out every now and then between Hindus and Musalmans in India, during the last few decades, and, latterly, much too frequently, because of special wholly artificial economico-political misleadings. It should be given a place of honor here, as it should be given in the courses of every Indian School and College. The chief cure for *Politico-economic conflict* is to teach to all, and to carry out in practice, the principles of *Scientific Social Organisation.* The chief remedy for *Communal strife* is to teach the new generation that *All Religions are One in Essentials*, as the poem indicates in a few pregnant words:

Yā Rām kaho, yā Rahīm kaho,
 ḍonoṅ kī gẖaraz Allāh se hai;
Yā Ishq kaho, yā Préma kaho,
 maṭlab ṭo Usī kī chāh se hai;
Yā Ḍharma kaho, yā Ḍīn kaho,
 maqsūḍ Usī kī rāh se hai;
Yā Sālik ho, yā Yogī ho,
 manshā ṭo ḍilé āgāh se hai.
Kyoṅ laṛṭā hai, mūrakh banḍé!,
 yah ṭérī kẖām-kẖayāli hai,
Hai péṛ kī jaṛ to Ék Wahī,
 har mazhab ėk ėk dālī hai.
Banwāo Shivālā yā Masjiḍ,
 hai īṅt wahī, chūnā hai wahī,
Me'mār wahī, mazḍūr wahī,
 mittī hai wahī, gārā hai wahī;
Ṭakbīr kā jo kuchh maṭlab hai,
 nāqūs kā bhī manshā hai wahī;
Yah jinko namāzaiṅ kahṭé haiṅ,
 hai unke liyé pūjā hi wahī.
Phir larṇé sé kyā hāsil hai!
 Zī-fahm ho ṭum, nāḍān nahīṅ!

Jo bhāi pe ḍauṛéṅ ghurrā kar
 wah ho sakṭé insān nahīṅ !
Kyā qaṭl wa ghāraṭ, khūṅ-rézī—
 ṭarīf yahī īmān ki hai ?
Kyā āpas méṅ laṛ kar marnā—
 ṭā'līm yahī Qur-ān ki hai ?
Insāf karo, ṭafsīr yahī
 kyā Véḍoṅ ké farmān ki hai ?
Kyā sach-much yah khūṅ-khwārī hī
 ā'lā khaslaṭ insān ki hai ?
Ṭum aisé buré ā'māl pe apné
 kuchh to Khuḍā sé sharm karo !
Paṭṭhar jo baná rakkhā ṭum néṅ,
 is ḍil ko zarā ṭo narm karo !

(Say Rām, or say Rahīm, both mean but Him ;
Say Prém, or Ishq, both mean the Love of Him ;
Say Ḍharm, or Ḍīn, both mean the Way to Him ;
Yogī, or Sālik, both are pure Heart filled with Him.
God—the One Root ; religions—each a shoot !
Why will ye fight, then, like the mindless brute !)
Build mosque or temple—stone, brick, lime—the same ;
Workmen and master-builder—all the same ;
The *a'zāṅ* and the conch both call to Prayer,
Name it ***Namāz*** or p ū j ā as you please.
Why will ye fight ! Has not God given you mind !
Scarce e'en the animals are so purblind !
Murder and rapine—is this meant by Faith !
The Qurān—does it teach to loot and slay ;
Or does the Véḍ' command you to do this !
Is this the noblest conduct in a man !
Brothers ! soften your stony hearts, take shame
 A little, and foul not His holy name !

CHAPTER VI

Education and the Educationist

Such is a brief, and very feeble and imperfect survey, of the vast subject of the Essential Unity of All Religions. Endeavour has been made here to place before the reader only what seemed to be the core of the whole subject. It is desirable that something should be said, at the close, about its bearing on Education; as has been said at the beginning.[1]

Education is the seed and root, civilization is the flower and fruit. If the cultivator sows good and wholesome seed, his community will reap sweet and wholesome fruit; if bitter and poisonous, then bitter and poisonous. Our cultivator, our culture-maker, is the teacher. That he may cultivate well and wisely, he should be a 'Man of God,' Brāhmaṇa, Maulavī, 'Divine,' Rabbi. These characteristic words of four religions, all mean exactly the same, 'Man of God, Brahma, Maulā, Deus, Rabb'. He should be a *missionary* of God, and not a *mercenary* of Satan, the opposite, opponent, Enemy, of God.

If the educationists, the priests, the scientists of Europe, its brāhmaṇas, *maulavīs, rabb-īs*, divines, the men of all the learned professions, whose clear duty it was, had brought up the

[1] Pp. 30-32, *supra*.

younger generations along right and righteous lines, occasion would never have arisen for the World-War of 1914 -'18. If, after it had arisen, they had resolutely refused to surrender their souls and prostitute their learning, religion, science, law, to the Satan-driven militarist-kshaṭṭriyas and mammonist-vaishyas of those countries; if they had acted as true brāhmaṇas; if they had concerted together and risen as one man, in their might of Spirit and of Science, against those false kshaṭṭriyas and false vaishyas; if they had proclaimed and led conscientious objection in all the belligerent countries[1]; then Satan would surely have been defeated, the tremendous mischief would have been nipped in the bud, and the earth saved from the vast, sordid, senseless butchery, agony, and devastation; which originated in the wholesale despiritualisation and demoralisation, by false educationists and false education, of great nations; and entailed world-wide misery, pauperisation, and yet further demoralisation.[2]

[1] There were honorable exceptions, f.i., Mr. Bertrand Russell, the scientist philosopher. He became a conscientious objector and suffered the penalty of imprisonment for a while.

[2] The conscience and the higher mind and the better judgment of the scientist-brāhmaṇas of Europe is beginning to awake, too late. The famous Dr. Einstein took steps (in 1932), to start an anti-war association. (He is now, in 1939, a fugitive and exile from home, because of the anti-Jew drive in Germany

High ethical quality, the fatherly heart, is far more needed in the educator, as also in the legislator, the administrator, the head of every

---

and Austria). Prof. H. E. Armstrong wrote in *Nature*, with the purpose of awakening scientists to a sense of their duty: "A century of science seems to have brought us to a wonderful understanding of things that do not matter, while telling us little that will help to fill our bellies and suffer one another with equanimity, let alone gladly and with Christian amity... In future, the *scientific worker*, to be worthy of the name, *must justify himself through social service*, in the first instance." In other words, he must be a true b r ā h m a ṇ a, not only an intellectual and scientific guide, but also a spiritual, moral, domestic, civic, political, and economic guide, philosopher, and friend, or indeed, as a benevolent parent, to his people, counselling them wisely for their good in all departments of their life. Prof. Crew of Edinburgh, in an address on "Science and Society," (in Dec., 1931) said: "Science has been prostituted through man's greed... to serve his lusts... The greatest problems of the day relate to *spiritual* as opposed to material adjustment... In this world there is the knowledge and there is the power to refashion society. But there is not the *will* to do so, and we have *no ideal toward which to aim.* We know a little of the methods of supporting life... *but not how to live, nor what to live for*... Science has become the servant of man's lust for power and is now the tool of the tyrant. We need to discover *what is good for mankind*, and then see to it that the power that knowledge gives is used for that end. Knowledge without affection... has set the world alight in a blaze of hatred and misery... A new moral outlook

family, firm, business, industry, concern, department, institution, where many are subordinate to one, than any amount of intellectual clever-

is demanded. *Whence will it come?*" Prof. Crew does not say. It can come only from that One Scientific Universal Religion which is the essence of all religions; which tells us 'what is good for mankind' 'what to live for', what is the 'ideal toward which to aim', what is the Meaning, Purpose, End and Aim, of Life, and also tells us 'how to live', *how* the scientific worker can 'justify himself through social service'. It does all this by means of its Scheme of Social Organisation. Why is the *righteous will* absent? Because the new generations are being born in lustful sensual materialistic carnal passion, not in loving spiritual affection because they are being grievously *mis-educated*; because the sources of life are poisoned. The 'moral equivalent of war' is war against inner lower nature first, and outer nature-forces next; Right Education would saturate the collective mind of the Human Race with this exceedingly *Practical Truth.*

The above text and foot-note were written in 1932. Since then, many peace-movements have been set afoot. A prominent one is the World-Fellowship of Faiths, which started work in Chicago, in 1933. "People of All Faiths, Races, and Countries (attended)...seeking spiritual solutions for man's Present Problems—such as War, Persecution, Prejudice, Poverty-amidst-Plenty, (Un-employment), Antagonistic Nationalisms, Ignorance, Hatred, Fear." The Theosophical Society was founded very much earlier, in 1875, in New York; with three unquestionably laudable objects: (1) "To form a nucleus of the Universal Brotherhood of Humanity,

ness. A good heart will take itself and also others very far on the right road, even without the help of a very clever head. A clever head,

---

without distinction of race, creed, sex, caste, or colour; (2) to encourage the study of Comparative Religion, Philosophy, and Science; (3) to investigate unexplained laws of nature, and the powers latent in man." These objects work towards the same end, World-Peace and World-prosperity. The T. S. has its head-quarters now at Adyar, Madras, in India; and branches in more than fifty countries. Parliaments of Religions have been held in important towns of several countries, since 1893, when the first was held in Chicago; also to promote Peace. The League of Nations was instituted in 1920, "to promote International Co-operation and achieve International Peace". Associations of scientists have been formed in several countries, which are now beginning to give attention directly to the 'human' aspect of science, to the bearing of science on corporate human life. 'Science has far outrun morals', is an idea which is frequently expressed in public writings. 'The International Council of Scientific Unions', which has a special 'Committee on Science and its Social Relations', has its head-quarters in Delft, Holland.

All in vain. The scientists' awakening has come too late. More: it seems that even yet they do not realise that the greatest and most wonderful discoveries of physical science, merely, will not avail to stem the tide of evil, will only worsen its rush and violence, unless they first think out *a technique for the working of the Golden Rule, a comprehensive Scheme of Social Organisation*, which would not only make it possible to apply, but would offer effective psychic inducement to every one to help in applying, those discoveries, for

directed by a bad heart, will mislead itself and others very soon into the pit; the cleverer, the sooner. It is much more important that education

---

the promotion of the general welfare of all mankind, instead of the welfare of any one nation, or any one class or group of persons in that nation.

Every 'Great Power' has been increasing its armaments desperately, madly, during the last few months, and also talking of peace all the time. Over *fifty-five million men* are, at present, (in 1939), under arms, as standing armies and reserves, in the 'human' world. The expenditure on them, in 1938, is reported to have been just over *thirty-five hundred million pounds*. Out of this, the share of the seven Great Powers, viz., (in the order of amounts), Russia, Germany, Japan, Britain, France, U. S. A., Japan, Italy, came to just under thirty-two hundred million pounds. Huge new loans have been taken by the Governments of all, in the current year. Every day brings the Great Horror, the Doom of Armageddon, nearer. Spain has just finished its terrible civil war, and begun executions of those suspected to be against the new régime. Japan and China have been already engaged in a deadly struggle for more than two years now. 'Clashes' and 'incidents', on frontiers, in other countries, are of daily occurrence. This week's papers (second week of August, 1939) report that "Events are moving fast in Europe", the "Powers are busy testing their fighting forces in mock battles", "Army, navy, and air force maneuvres are taking place on a stupendous scale", in the several countries. The general conflagration may burst forth any day, and reduce 'modern' civilisation to ashes, in Europe; out of which that wondrous Phœnix, Humanity, may take hundreds of years perhaps, to rise again, there.

should build up *a strong and good character* in the educand, than impart lots of information and develop mere intellectual cleverness or even

---

It is all so utterly senseless. Everyone feels and says so. Yet, some inexorable Fate, Nemesis, clutches the necks of all the leaders of all the countries(—and *none* is fee from mortal crime, though some may be more guilty—) in its overpowering paralysing grip, and is dragging them all, together with their hypnotised and helpless peoples, towards the mouth of Purgatory.

If only this vast human energy of fifty-five million men, prepared for slaughter of combatants and butchery of non-combatants, and the energy of the many millions more, engaged in manufacturing munitions and small and huge implements for carrying on war by land, sea, and air; if all the vast human labor represented by thirty-five hundred million pounds a year; if all this were spent on promoting general human welfare scientifically, instead of general massacre; the whole surface of the earth could be made to bloom and blossom and fruit, like one vast corn-field and orchard, garden and park. The madness of 'original sin', Māyā, a-viḍyā, glamour, *takabbur*, *hirs*, blind greed and pride, lust and hate, prevents. Each 'Great Power' is trying to increase its 'man-power', by offering inducements to its people to 'increase and multiply'. What for? That there may be more 'fodder for cannon'! What more horrible blindness and Satan-worship can there be!

The great teachers and lovers of mankind cry in vain: 'Love one another', 'Do unto each other as ye would be done unto.' The forces of Darkness are again steadily gaining on the forces of Light. All these vast armies cannot be supported by the nations much longer. The earth is groaning in agony under the

talent. And this can be done much better by *example* than by precept; indeed, only by example. The words of those who do not themselves follow their own advice are not believed, because it is felt that they do not believe them themselves. The true educationist, brāhmaṇa, *maulavī*, 'divine,' is he who possesses both vidyā and tapas, *ilm* and *zohd*, knowledge and self-denial. Wisdom is science plus philanthropy.

Consoling, ennobling, all-uniting, spiritual religion has everywhere degenerated into selfish, superstition-breeding, deceiving, dividing priestcraft; protective and promotive administration has become grabbing and tyrannising statecraft; benevolent adjudication has turned into rapacious lawyercraft; healing medication behaves as avaricious leechcraft; all-nourishing trade and commerce has been metamorphosed into all-ruining 'frenzied finance,' stock-jobbing, share-gambling, currency-juggling, 'demonetising' and 'devaluating' of current coin at governmental will, utterly artificial forced inflating and deflating of prices, 'combines,' 'corners,' 'associations' and 'companies' for wholesale swindling, brazenly false 'puffing' and 'booming,' reckless pennywise

---

intolerable burden, moral and material, of Hate-Fear and Economic Drain. The great Disarmament must come before long, either by *mutual slaughter* or by *mutual agreement.* Only a Divine Miracle of the most gigantic proportions, a psychic cataclysm, can now bring about disarmament by mutual agreement. May that Miracle happen!

pound-foolish speculation-craft; and life-sweetening, life-creating, life-fostering conjugal domesticity has been converted into lust-craft; all because all-guiding Education has itself become greatly mis-guided; because the Educator has forgotten his true mission, gone astray, lost the compelling moral force and spiritual power of ascetic self-denial; has begun to submit to the militarist and the capitalist, instead of directing and correcting them; has degraded his great function into herd-teaching, mechanical, bureaucratic, indirectly and not unoften directly cruel pedagogue-craft. A vicious circle has been set up. From bad seed, bad fruit; thence worse seed, worse fruit; until the end in Armageddon.

The whole life of the most civilised human communities is pervaded by excess of egoism, appurtenant individualistic desire for high and fast living, indulgence of lusts, and the unavoidably consequent hates.[1] Modern Civilization has indeed become a veritable and most reckless "Rake's Progress" in every department of life, individual, social, national, domestic, financial, economic, political. States have been piling up national debts and armaments, with an extravagant thriftlessness and utter disregard of consequences,

---

[1]See pp. 147-150, *supra*. The 'six internal enemies,' when they go beyond all bounds, turn into the six main kinds of mania, respectively, eroto-, cido-, avaritio- (or klepto-), phobo-, megalo-, and zelo-mania. In mass-form, they become sensualism, militarism, capitalism, (mutual) terrorism, imperialism, nationalist diplomatism,

which would be considered stark suicidal and homicidal madness in an individual. A more and more excessively large proportion of the available human energy and labor is being forced into occupations which produce and distribute, not the primal necessaries and comforts of life for all, but (1) luxuries, things of sport, pastime, amusement (often obscene), and sensuous enjoyment for the few, or even for many; and, far worse, (2) vast quantities of implements of war by land, sea, and air, whose one insane object is the destruction of human life, labor, and property; while, no one can gainsay, the only sane purpose of government is the promotion of these same for general human welfare. Such is the awful waste, turmoil, agony, caused by the statesmen of to-day, who think themselves so clever and so practical.[1]

---

[1] 'PRACTICALITY.' Of the many false ideals, mischievous catchwords, and ruinous ways of living, which, together with many great and good things also, undoubtedly, (especially such applications of physical science as are really benevolent), have been created by western civilisation, few are more deceptive and dangerous than the catchwords 'practical' and 'practicality'.

Most of us are enamoured of these words and use them frequently, especially when it *suits* us, in order to describe ourselves as 'practical' and the opponent as 'unpractical'. Formerly, when Religion was in power, it used to be: 'My doxy is orthodoxy, your doxy is heterodoxy.' To-day, when Politics is all-absorbing, all-

And the educationist-scientist, careless of his duty, does nothing to check it. Instead,

---

devouring, it is: 'My view, my opinion, my suggestion, my scheme, is practical, yours is unpractical.' In other words, 'What suits *me* is practical, what suits *you* is unpractical'. Though we see daily that what was wholly unpractical, chimerical, yesterday, is very practical, nay, utterly familiar, to-day: steam, gas, electricity, radio, aeroplane, submarine, Soviet Russia, Fascist Italy, Nazist Germany, Saṭyāgraha, etc. But 'by their fruits shall they be judged'. Behold the results of the great 'practicality' of the very clever and very 'practical' statesmen and politicians of the west, in all the main concerns of life, Religion, Education, Domesticity, Economics, Politics. *Will* makes practicality.

Religion, of which Good Morals are the fruit, has been 'practically' abolished from the life of the 'advanced' nations, and 'Morals have been revolutionised,' in various ways; and licensed Sensualism and Free Love, on the one side, and Self-control and Family Life, on the other, are at death-grips.

In Politics, the 'practical' Legislatures, where not abolished, have become the homes of rapacious personal and sectional selfishness, bitter quarrels, endless intrigues, smart self-display, clap-trap orations, instead of earnest philanthropic consultation for the good of all. The seeds of class war and civil war within each nation are being sown and nourished by vicious, haphazard, short-sighted, hand-to-mouth legislation. The armies of the Powers, which totalled about *twenty* million men, costing about five hundred million pounds annually, before the World-War, 'the war to end war,' to-day, after that Butchery of eight to thirteen million men and destruction of some fifty thousand million pounds he truckles to Satan and his agents. 'Eat, drink, and be merry to-day—those few who

---

worth of human labor mis-spent on the production of devilish war-material, and the consequent mortgaging and enslaving, for long generations, of the labor of whole nations of the weaker and the poorer peoples—to-day, these armies are three times as large in number and six times as heavy in cost. Fangs, claws, beaks, talons, and sharks' teeth, for fighting and murdering on land, in air, in water, and the hates, greeds, lusts, prides, fears, and distrusts, which are the motive power behind these weapons, are sharper and fiercer than ever.

In Economics, these 'practical' wise persons have brought about World-Bankruptcy after the World-War, and have raised the armies of the *Un*-employed to a total of some thirty millions in the west, (those in the east, uncounted, being probably five times as many), side by side with the above-mentioned army of those ***Mis***-employed in preparing for the Devil's own infernal work of world-wide butchery—all because they find that the old maxims, 'Honesty is the best Policy' and 'No trading on Credit unbacked by equal Cash Deposit,' are no longer 'practical'; that 'Trading on reputation only, on Credit *without* Cash or Kind', is much more 'practical'; and that such ideas as that of the best and wisest and genuinely philanthropic representatives of the nations, oonsulting together and co-operating, to spend a half or even a fourth of the vast sums now being spent annually on the *Mis*-employed and the *Un*-employed, on settling these millions of the two kinds, gradually, year by year, on the immense unoccupied reclaimable and cultivable areas of Canada, Australia, South America, Africa, and thereby solving

can; tomorrow will take care of itself; why should the present generation stint itself for the

---

the problems of Disarmament and Unemployment both, at once, are 'unpractical' and 'impossibly idealistic'.

In 'Domestics', western 'practicality' has so arranged matters that the number of divorces has, in some of the big towns of the west, come to be quite half that of the marriages, annually, and the period between marriage and divorce is shortening down from years to months and even weeks. 'Morals have been revolutionised' by contraceptives, and yet the population is multiplying unmanageably, embittering the struggle for bread, and making wars inevitable in the absence of systematic colonisation. The percentage of births outside of wedlock is increasing immensely also. And so too is increasing the percentage of the insane and the venereally diseased. We have noted before, the insane rivalry, between the national governments of the west, for the increase of 'man-power'. All the while, that very uncommon commodity, 'common sense', keeps crying, in vain, 'Cut your coat according to your cloth', 'Balance your family budget', 'Live within your means', 'All the Heads of the Great Families called Nations—conspire and concert together rationally, to make your populations self-sufficient for necessaries, to keep them within the capacity of your respective lands, (or, of the total surface of the earth, co-operatively and scientifically managed), to feed and clothe and house'.

In Education, 'High and Fast Living', 'the Thrills of perpetual Rushing,' 'Civilisation is the multiplication of wants and of means to satisfy them', is the ideal inculcated; in place of the 'unpractical' old 'goody-goody' 'Plain Living, High Thinking,' and 'the peaceful Joys of Repose'. Science has outrun Philanthropy by far; is

sake of the next? Let us leave them debts instead of assets.' Such seem to be the current

---

being prostituted to personal and national vices and hatreds; and is perfecting gases which, rained by aeroplanes, will asphyxiate in a few hours the whole of the vast populations of huge capitals like London, New York, Paris, Berlin. Vivisectional experiments on human infants and adults are now and then reported in the papers. The press has become the extensive and intensive means, on a vast scale, of false propaganda, lying advertisements, and public deception, instead of enlightenment. The view of life, *viz.*, that it is, and ought to be, an incessant *struggle* for existence, holds the field, and the opposite view, *viz.*, that life is made possible only by *alliance* for existence, and the perpetual self-sacrifice of the older generation for the younger, (instead of leaving them vast national debts to repay or repudiate as they can), is vainly struggling to make itself seen and heard. The results are visible in all the other departments of life.

In Art and Recreation, 'meals, movies, motors,' the 'night-side' of the huge capital towns, 'wine, women, wealth', have become, and are becoming more and more, the sole ends of life; and the finer and more delicate ethereal spiritual forms of enjoyment, and 'communion with Nature', are being forgotten.

Such are the consequences, in its own home, of the cleverness of the modern west, whose greatest 'practicality' is the endeavour to maintain its 'glorious civilisation' by the ruthless economic and political exploitation of weaker classes and peoples.

It may be that the condition of mankind was, on the whole, no better in the past, at any time; has indeed, been much worse, very often, almost

philosophy of life and the moral atmosphere, which govern and pervade the politics, economics, and

---

certainly; during the four or five thousand years of 'civilisation' of which the history is now known. It may be that the present times are the best, at least in some important respects, that Humanity has known so far. But that is all the more reason why greater effort should be made, to combat and eradicate the great evils that are patent, with the help of Universal Scientific (1) Religion, and (2) Social Organisation.

The duty of publicists to-day is to be, not only nationalist, but also humanist, and to think out and place before the public, diligently, such balanced ideals, outlooks, 'long' views, comprehensive and consistent schemes, *based on human psychology*, for social reorganisation and reconstruction, dealing with all the main concerns of human life, individual and collective, as will enable the Peoples of the World to avoid deceptive catch-words, blind imitation, short-viewed temporising patchwork and opportunism; will help them to find the virtuous golden mean between the two vicious excesses and extremes of eastern degeneracy and western non-re-generacy; will show them how to avoid the evil and secure the good in each of the two, ancient east and modern west, to the utmost extent possible; and will thereby prove that the action of Providence in bringing East and West together was not wholly a mistake, not a devil's work but an angel's. The only true Practicality is that which is based on a sound, far-sighted, comprehensive Theory, and constantly bears in mind, and strives to approximate, a high Ideal. All other patch-work and snatch-work 'practicality' is supremely unpractical.

'domestics' of this vast Rake's Progress called Western Civilisation—or, at least, of that class

---

Rail, steam-ship, aeroplane having abolished all artificial political boundaries, the best minds of all the nations, see, and say, that a *World-organisation* is the only way of escape from the present imminent disaster, and is, indeed, inevitable. Thus: "Separate sovereignty has become impossible": (H. G. Wells, *A Short History of the World*, p. 309). Yet the men in power seem determined to have a bout of universal war, first.

To illustrate how the human world is increasingly recognising the need for the True Practicality of a World-wide Organisation, under the new name of 'Planning', the following extracts are taken from the address of Dean Curtis W. Reese, D. D., given to the assemblage of the World Fellowship of Faiths, at Chicago, in 1933. The address is titled "Introduction to a Planned Society", and is printed on pp. 97—102 of *World Fellowship*, edited by Charles F. Weller, (pub. 1935). The volume is a full report of the Proceedings of the Sessions (extending over 83 meetings) of the Fellowship, and includes "242 addresses, significant statements, by 199 leading spokesmen of practically All Faiths, Races, and Countries." Dean Reese says:

"The idea of planning on a nation-wide and long-run basis has made great headway alike in the theory of monarchical, democratic, and communistic countries." Then the speaker goes on to illustrate how it has been working in Japan, Germany, France, Russia, England, Italy, Spain, America. "Russia, of course, is the outstanding example of national planning—The plan involves—*what to produce, how much, when, where,* and *at what price*...It is not surprising that Russia is making great headway, for with a philosophy of social control,

in it which has power in its hands, the powers of the purse and the sword. Signs of reaction are, no doubt, appearing, here, there, everywhere. A vast unrest is shaking the whole human world. In Russia, a tremendous revolution has been effected ; whether wholly for good, or wholly for bad, or partly for both, it is not yet possible to say. The psychological defects of it have been mentioned before. Excess naturally defeats itself. But the reaction seems likely to involve a worse Armageddon before it completes itself. And more. There is the danger that when it has successfully asserted itself, humanity may swing round from one extreme to another; from autocratic and tyrannous despotism, through aristocratic feudalism and militarism, and plutocratic capitalism and mammonism, and misconceived

---

...a general plan,...and detailed planning,...success...is practically assured. It is not too much to say that in Russia *national planning* takes on *religious significance.*" The speaker, expressing his own view, says, towards the close, "The social goal is a classless society...The goal of a classless world is far more powerful than the bitterness of class struggle."

We may add : 'Classless' yes, if you are thinking of only the two classes, 'Rich and Poor', or of 'rigid birth-castes' ; and not of the four natural Types, which *cannot* be abolished ; the non-recognition of which, and of corollaries, is the serious flaw in the Russian Experiment, and is inevitably causing mistakes, disturbances, bloody 'purges', and, fortunately, also great *modifications* in the whole policy.

and mishandled socialism and communism, back to mobocratic anarchism and the law of the jungle; and thence, over again to the autocratic, 'monarchic', despotic rule of the strongest jaw and maw, the sharpest fang and claw, the cunningest and most ruthless dictator-brain—the old, old, vicious circle of past history.

Obviously this is not desirable. And it is possible to avoid, only if the *Educationist* will do his duty resolutely, combining scientist and priest in himself. From the long past instinctive group-life and primitive communism of 'uncivilised' tribes, through the present phase of intensely competitive, separative, egoist individualism, back to deliberate, conscious, scientifically planned co-operative socialism on a higher level; not the unnatural, mechanical or 'machinist', equalitarian', 'authoritarian', and therefore necessarily unstable, 'communism', now being experimented with in the west; but a natural 'socialism', based on psychological laws and facts, *a 'socialism' of individuo-social organization by temperamental aptitudes and vocations and equitable partition of the means of livelihood and of the prizes of life*, as outlined before; such seems to be the desirable course of human progress.[1] The

[1] "It is the goal of commerce to organise all the resources of the earth for the supply of the wants of mankind; it is the goal of science to diffuse one system of knowledge; it is the goal of politics to combine all countries in one harmony of justice, peace,

artificial, ineffective, or rather positively harmful, and very expensive current system of education; which inculcates wrong ideals and views and aims of life; swamps the end under the means; suffocates the vital principles under loads of showy but essentially paltry details; requires costly buildings, heavy salaries, great quantities of furniture and apparatus of many kinds, all utterly disproportionate to the resources of the (at least eastern) people; which, withal, neglects nature, and artificialises even so-called nature-study; prepares mostly only for the learned pro-

---

and progress. Similarly it is the goal of religion to inspire one faith:" J. Estlin Carpenter, *The Place of Christianity among the Religions of the World, p. 113.*

If we add to the above: "It is the goal of labor to give the help indispensably needed for the achievement of the other goals"; and that "These goals can be respectively achieved by the organised co-operation of the vaishyas, *ṭājirs*, men of acquisitive desire and wealth-management, of the brāhmaṇas, *ā'lims*, men of knowledge, of the kshaṭṭriyas, *ā'mils*, men of action, and of the shūḍras, *mazḍūrs*, men of labor, of *all* countries, races, nations"; also that "Faith and Knowledge go together, being but aspects of one another, unshakeably founded on the One Science of the Infinite which includes and supports and synthesises all the sciences of the Finite"—if we add this, then we would see that that which Mr. J. E. Carpenter visualises, is just what the *Varṇa-Āshrama-Ḍharma* of Manu endeavours to realise. Be it noted that that scheme *does not* conflict with the right and reasonable use of machinery; instead, it will help greatly to make *such*, and only such, use possible.

fessions, and does not test, ascertain, develope, and train the various vocational aptitudes and temperaments—such education needs, cryingly, to be replaced by a more natural, useful, and comparatively inexpensive system, which would educate each person for an appropriate specific occupation[1]; would inculcate right ideals; and would thereby change the whole moral and spiritual atmosphere of all civilisation before long.

A great modern educationist, Edouard Seguin, after a whole lifetime of work, came to the conclusion that "The *common things* of daily life have even *greater educational value* when the hands can use them....In such matters, the means and instruments are more easily remembered than the philosophy of their application; *whilst that philosophy is the very thing which is above all not to be forgotten*".[2] This non-comprehension or forgetting of the philosophy, the principles, is the consequence either of self-seeking or of intellectual incapacity, and leads to the prevalence of catchwords and the degenerations into the "crafts" mentioned above.

The same educationist says, again,[3] that "*The great agency for socialising all pupils is love.* To develop their sense of affection, as were developed their senses of sight, of hearing, and others, does not demand new instruments or

---

[1] Western educationists have begun to give attention to this, now. [2] See Fynne, ***Montessori and her Inspirers***, pp. 162, 169, (pub. 1924). [3] ***Ibid.***, p. 208.

new teachers, but the extension of the same action upon their feelings. To make the child feel that he is loved, and to make him eager *to love* in his turn, *is the end of our teaching as it has been its beginning* . . . For our pupils, science, literature, medicine, philosophy, each may do something; but *love alone can truly socialise them*; those who love them are their true rescuers". Such love, together with certain psychological principles, constitutes the only basis of true socialism. And therefore the greatest educationists are those greatest lovers of mankind, *the Founders of the Religions which bind the hearts* of human beings into One and give birth to new civilizations.

Trust all to love, it is a God
That knows the outlets of the sky. (EMERSON.)

Civilization is justified of its name only when it is permeated by good-will, nay, loving active sympathy, self-restraint, moderation, courage, forbearance, strong sense of duty ; when these preponderate definitely over sensuality, arrogance, hate, greed, jealousy, selfish fear. Only the former qualities of heart can establish the longed-for millennium of true socialism, as distinguished from artificial and forced communism, on the one hand; and, on the other, from the oppressive individualism, manifesting as heartless capitalism and ruthless militarism, which the vast masses of men are now suffering from, because of the permeation of society by the latter evil qualities. No mere cleverness of metallic machinery or official machinery, no 'technocracy' or any other 'cracy', no administrative 'efficiency' or diplomatic skill in coining oily or pompous phrases with shifty meaning, will avail. The heart must be filled with the 'religious' emotion of 'benevolence', 'sympathy', first. True Socialism can be founded only upon the sense of the Oneness of all Life, which means the realization of the Supreme Self. To be able to help humanity to such civilization, the teacher should obviously have realized that Oneness in himself; should have assimilated all the body of right thought and right feeling which flows from it; and should diligently give education accordingly, 'leading the younger generation to the same realization.'[1] Then only will the educationist be able to justly and truly socialise civilization. Such is the great significance and value of Religious Education; or, let us say, Spiritual Instruction; since the word religion repels many, to-day, because of its associations of priestcraft. Rightly understood, the R' of Religion is, indeed, the greatest and most important of the four R's of Education.

The Scriptures speak of the kingdom of heaven on earth. This kingdom is obviously a Self-government wherein the Higher Self reigns

---

[1]This is the etymological and the philosophical significance of u p a-n a y a n a, the Vẹ́dic ceremony corresponding to the modern 'taking of a child to, and his admission in, a school.'

and legislates. The Higher Self lives in the souls which have realized their oneness with all other selves, and are therefore (lower-) self-denying and wise, philanthropic as well as experienced. In this simple fact is to be found the only key to all human problems. If the Higher Self brood over the family, the domestic life will be happy; for then joy will be duty and love will be law. If it govern the field of economics, the distribution of necessaries and comforts will be equitable, for there will be no accumulation of wealth for greedy selfish purposes, but only for the promotion of public welfare, through proprietors who will regard themselves as trustees, and will find their heart-nourishment and ample recompense and satisfaction in the mere fact of being the channels of public good and the recipients of public appreciation. If it regulate politics, none will be for the 'party', and all will be for the State; because the administration of all affairs will be just, upright, benevolent, promotive and protective of all right interests; and therefore no 'parties' will be needed or formed at all, on lines of conflicting religious creeds or clashing economic interests. If it reign in shop, market-place, factory, business-concern, police-station, army-organisation, law-court, town council, hospital, ship, railway train, wherever human beings have to deal with each other, there all duties will be discharged honestly, promptly, courteously, sympathetically, ministering to the happiness of all concerned. If it inspire legislation, the laws will be good and wise, far-sighted and beneficent to all sections of the people, of all temperaments and vocations, and the just interests of all will be duly secured and promoted. If it guide education, all the affairs of the people will be righted through the rightly-educated new generation. Wherever the Higher Self, as embodied and manifest in the wise, selfless, philanthropic man and woman, trusted and honored, select and 'elect', of the people, 'representative' of all that is best in the people, reigns, rules, legislates, directs, guides, advises—*there* is the kingdom of heaven, for there is the reign and rule and influence of righteousness. Most of all is it necessary that the Higher Self should reign in the Home of Education and the Hall of Legislation. To inculcate this noble meaning of Sva-rāj, Self-government, (i.e., the Rāj of the *Higher* Sva, government by the *Higher* Self, of the people), in the collective and the individual intelligence of mankind, to fill the hearts of all, men and women, young and old, with this great truth, is the only way to achieve, and then to maintain, true Self-government. Such inculcation can be most effectively done in the 'Home of Education', which should be the noblest 'House of God.' In the next degree, it can be done by an enlightened, spiritual, genuinely 'religious' Press.

The person to be entrusted with the very responsible task of education, (of the young in a school or a college, and of the general public by means of a journal) should therefore be a 'man of God',[1] by apt temperament, and not by birth; he should be full of ṭ a p a s, *zohḍ*, *pietas*, self-denial, and of v i ḍ y ā, p r a ̣- j ñ a n a, *irfān*, *gnosis*, the all-including, 'spiritual' knowledge, as well as of v i - j ñ ā n a, *ilm*, the detailed 'material' knowledge. Himself having realized true 'spiritual' *equality*, *fraternity*, and *liberty*, he will be able to give the education which will necessarily give rise to the civilization of true (and not false, forced, unstable) 'material' equality, i.e., equitability; of loving fraternity, and paternity and filiety also; and ordered liberty. This is not the place to enter into the details thereof; they have been dealt with elsewhere.[2]

[1] See p. 568, *supra*.

[2] "The Supreme produces all things. Its virtue nourishes them. Its nature gives them form. Its force perfects them. The Supreme, engendering all things, nourishes, developes, fosters, perfects, ripens, tends, and protects them. Production without possession, action without self-assertion, developement without domination—this is Its mysterious operation. It loves and nourishes all things, but does not act as master." (*Tao Teh King*.)

In this brief extract from the writing of the sage, Laoṭse, may be found the quintessence of the spirit of the expression of the Higher Self in all types of *dutiful* men. 'Production without possession' is for the wealth-making 'man of desire'; 'action without self-assertion' is for the 'man of action'; 'developement without domination' is for the benevolent man of wisdom, the patriarchal educator.

Briefly, the educationist must be a self-dependent, independent, yet humble.hearted and all-loving missionary, whose example and whose moral force, soul-force, may daunt and deter wrong-doers however high-placed, and whose very presence may spread benevolence. He must not take any help, even honoraria, from the evil-minded. The scriptures utter strong warning against this.

Arṭhasya purusho ḍāsah,
n-ārṭho ḍāsas-ṭu kasya-chiṭ. (*Mbh.*)
Sarvéshām éva shauchānām
arṭha-shaucham vishishyaṭé.
Y-orṭhé shuchih sa hi shuchih,
na mṛḍ-vāri-shuchih shuchih. (*M.*)
(Slave of his economic interest
Is man ; and not his interest his slave.
Of all the purities, the purity
Of means of livelihood is the most high.
Whose gains are gotten without taint of sin,
He only is pure truly—not the man
Who washes hands with earth and water oft.)

Chūṅ gharaz āmaḍ hunar poshīḍah shuḍ,
Chūṅ khuḍī āmaḍ Khuḍā poshīḍah shuḍ,
Saḍ hijāb az ḍil ba sū-é ḍīḍah shuḍ. (*S.*)

(Where greed comes forth, there probity retires ;
When the small self unveils, the Great Self veils ;
And hundred veils the heart flings o'er the eye.)

In terms of the Véḍānṭa, Māyā-Desire has two principal powers or functions ; (1) ā v a r a ṇ a, which 'veils' the eye of reason, 'blinds' it to all but the immediate object of the particular desire, shuts it off from all sense of proportion, of balance, of 'the truth in the mean'; (2) vikshépa, which 'flings', 'drives', 'pushes', the whole soul in pursuit of the desired object, to the neglect of all duties. The counteracting, neutralising, opponents of these two forces are, respectively, the force of vai-rāgya, 'dis-illusion-ment', 'dis-passionate desirelessness', 'dis-taste', dis-gust' with the world, *mujānibaṭ*, born of sensitive experience of one's own and, much more, of other's miseries; and abhy-āsa, 'perseverent pursuit,' *munāzilaṭ*, of the Truth.[1]

Therefore let the revered and loved 'preceptor' 'teacher', 'master', the guru, āchārya, upādhyāya, the *pīr-i-murshiḍ*, *mua'llim*, *aṭāliq*, diligently preserve his disinterested benevolence, his dispassionate yet compassionate desirelessness, his perseverent and 'independent' gaze upon the Truth, at all costs. The economic bias is all-vitiating. A person cannot but side with, and wish well and give support to, what nourishes him, however evil it may be. The quality of the intellectual fruit is determined by the quality of the economic root.[2] Therefore:

Yo rājñah praṭi-gṛhṇāṭi
lubḍhasy-och-chhāṣṭra-varṭinah,

---

[1] See pp. 326-327, *supra*.

[2] The Educational System of a State should never be fed with revenues from any such sinful sources as Excise Duties on intoxicating drugs and drinks. Manu condemns very strongly the rulers who draw any revenue from any such vicious and sinful trades.

Sa paryāyeṇa yāṭ-īmān
narakān éka-vimshaṭim. (*M.*)

Chūṅ dihaḍ qāzī ba ḍil rishwaṭ qarār,
Kai shināsaḍ zālim az mazlūm-ī-zār. (*S.*)

(The educationist who doth accept
Money from evil, greedy, lawless kings,
Can no more reprimand and chastise them,
But will support them in their evil deeds;
And must pass with them through hell after hell.)
(The judge who findeth room within his heart
For bribes, no longer can discriminate
The tyrant from the victim of his crime.)

By promotion of such evil-doing, he vitiates the education of the whole younger generation, and thereby ruins the whole civilisation and the whole State. Let him do nothing which will lead insidiously to the selling of his independence, his conscience, his soul. His responsibility is the greatest in the whole of the body politic. He is in charge of the new generation. He makes or mars the whole State, the whole civilisation, the whole people, by the way in which he brings up the new generation.

Ezā fasaḍ al-ā'lim, fasaḍ al-ālam. (*H.*)
Zallaṭ al-ā'lim, zallaṭ al-ālam. (*Q.*)
(Yea, when the learned and intelligent
Err from the right path, all the world goes wrong.)

Yad yaḍ ācharaṭi shréshthas
ṭaṭ-ṭaḍ-év-éṭaro janah.
Sa yaṭ pramāṇam kuruṭé,
lokas-ṭaḍ anu-varṭaṭe. (*G.*)

(As doth conduct himself the honored man
So will behave the others, copying him.)

Can the blind lead the blind? Shall they not both fall into the ditch? (*B.*)

Aviḍyāyām anṭaré varṭa-mānāh,
Svayam-ḍhīrāh panḍiṭam-manya-mānāh,
Janghanya-mānāh pari-yanṭi mūdhāh,
anḍhén-aiva nīya-mānā yaṭh-ānḍhāh. (*U.*)
(Wise in their own conceit, sunk deep in error,
Stumbling into pit after pit, they go,
The luckless ones, blind followers of the blind.)

Annāso a'lā ḍīn-e-mulūkehim. (*H.*)
(Men imitate the faith and ways of kings.)

Yaṭhā rājā ṭaṭhā prajāh. (Skt. proverb.)
(As the king is, such are the people too.)

'Knowledge is power.' The educationist has knowledge. He has power to influence the soul, the mind, for good or for evil. The soldier, who has only the sword, can at most compel only the body. The priest is more powerful than the king. Priestcraft is more disastrous than kingcraft. Without its help, more or less, direct or indirect, kingcraft is not possible. Church and State in alliance for human welfare, can make a heaven of earth; in alliance for human enslavement and exploitation, they make a hell of it. And spiritual power can control and curb temporal power.

Viḍyā ha vai brāhmaṇam ājagāma:
Gopāya mām; shévaḍhis-ṭé-(a)ham asmi;
Asūyakāy-ān-ṛjavé-(a)yaṭāya,
Mām mā ḍāh; vīrya-vaṭī ṭaṭhā syām! (*V.*)
(Science came to the 'Man of Knowledge'; said:
Take me and guard me as a sacred trust;
And give me not unto the crooked ones,

Impure, evil of mind, un-Self-controlled,
Jealous, proud, cruel, full of greed and lust.
Impart me only to the good and pure,
The gentle-minded and benevolent;
Then shall I grow in power to help the world.)

Nā-brahma kshaṭṭram ṛdhnoṭi,
nā-kshaṭṭram brahma varḍhaṭé;
Kshaṭṭrasy-āṭi-pra-vṛḍḍhasya
Brāhmaṇān praṭi sarvashah,
Brahm-aiva san-niyanṭṛ syāṭ;
kshaṭṭram hi Brahma-sambhavam. (*M.*)

(The spiritual and the temporal powers,
Both need each other; neither can maintain
Itself and prosper, if not helped by th' other.
But should the Militarist grow perverse,
And try to overbear the Scientist,
It is the latter's duty to restrain
And curb the former; and he *can* do so;
For Science is the parent of the Sword;
Knowledge, which makes, can break the things of war.)

Brāhmaṇam ṭu sva-ḍharma-sṭham
ḍṛshtvā bibhyaṭi ch-éṭaré,
N-ānyaṭhā kshaṭṭriy-āḍyās-ṭu,
vipras-ṭasmāṭ ṭapash-charéṭ. (*Shukra-nīṭi.*)

(When kshaṭṭriyas, entrusted with the sword,
Behold the brāhmaṇa deviating not
From virtuous duty, then are they afraid,
Not otherwise, and stray not from their own.
The man of God should, then, deny himself,
To keep the balance of the human world.)

A western poet has described such a person:

And prophet-like the lone one stood
With dauntless words and high.

That shook the sere leaves from the wood
As if a storm passed by.

Western history tells us that the Church, when manned by good and genuine priests, has often checked the tyranny of despots and saved the people from cruel oppression. On the other hand, when manned by devils incarnate in human shape, like the Inquisitors, it has allied itself with cruel despots and made the earth groan, and the cry of agony of whole nations has risen to Heaven to bring down the avenging sword of God upon the heads of the tyrant priests and kings. In ancient Indian tradition, *ṛshis* have directly punished and blasted wicked kings. In the history of Islām also, saintly and learned men have often checked the oppression of rulers, *sulṭāns* and *pādishāhs*. Christianity also has had many heroic reformers and martyrs who faced the wrath of the mighty. Judaism has nourished great prophets like Jeremiah who strongly reproved the iniquitous of their day.

Let the educationist rise then to the height of his mission. Let him not hanker after money and sense-enjoyments. The price of benevolent wisdom, of philanthropic learning, is not money, but loving honor, reverence. Are parents to be paid with cash for cherishing their children and making perpetual sacrifices for them ?

Inna akrama-kum inḍ-Allāhā aṭqā-kum. (*Q.*)
(Give highest place of reverence unto those
Who are God-fearing and God-loving men ;
For the most good are nearest unto God.)

Let him be content with the bare necessaries of life. Let him live in voluntary poverty. So the fire of his *ṭapas*, *zohḍ*, soul-force, will grow ever greater, brighter, mightier. All good men will love and revere him. All evil men will stand in awe of him, and, seeing him stand steadfast in virtue, will gradually turn to good ways. Greedy sense-seekers will be shamed into self-restraint, beholding him so reverend, so talented, so able to seize, yet refraining. All will request him to make good and wise laws, which others will execute under his guidance. The good and wise alone can make good and wise laws; and good and wise laws alone can promote the general welfare. Indeed, when men of God are abroad, men of law need be but few. Moral laws, implanted in the heart, make legal laws, imposed from without, unnecessary. Impulsion from within is far better, far more effective, than compulsion from without. As prevention is better than cure, so education is better than legislation. Thus high is the value and the purpose of Education. Thus high is the mission of the Educationist. Only the man of Brahma, of Maulā, of Rabb, of God, (not by birth, but by worth, by high qualification), the man who has realized that the Great Self lives in all selves, should be entrusted with the high task of Education, and of Legislation.

The people are happy who produce amidst themselves a fair number of such brāhmaṇas, *maulavis*, 'divines,' rabbis, true educators of the people in the best and largest sense, by precept and by *example*; not professional religion-mongers, sowers of hatreds and dissensions, or pedagogues, pedants, spreaders of false and vicious ideals and useless and misleading knowledge. Such a people will be sure to possess a justly socialized civilization, where the golden mean will reign, and which will give the greatest happiness to the greatest number. Realising that "No man liveth unto himself . . . . we are all parts of one another," that God "hath made of one blood all nations that dwell upon the face of the earth," (*B.*), that "Human beings (of different types and classes) are as head, arms, trunk, and legs unto one another," (*V.*), that "All creatures are members of the one family of God" (*Q.*), that "The children of Adam are members and limbs of one another," (Sā'ḍi), they will reconcile Individualism and Socialism, (known to the ancient philosophers of China as the principles of Yang Chu, "each for him-self," and Mih Teih, "loving all equally,") in a rational Social Organisation. They will build the strongest and surest, nay the only, foundations for *World-Peace* on earth, by, and because of, *Good-Will* among men. Their 'men of God' will be able to create such *Good-Will* among men, by (1) establishing *Peace* between the *Creeds*, through the exposition of the *Unity*, as well as the philosophical and scientific rationality, of them all in *Essence*, and by (2) explaining to them, as part of that Essence, the *principles* of a complete Social Organisation which will fulfil the just, reasonable, and natural requirements of each and all; which will provide every person with suitable work-and-'wage,' and every work-and-'wage' with the right person; and will ensure that 'machinery', metallic as well as official, is so used that, while human drudgery is steadily reduced more and more, human starvation is not increased, and that there is a real and wide spread of general welfare.

SCIENTISTS OF THE WORLD! THE HEAVIEST RESPONSIBILITY RESTS UPON YOU! FOR YOU DISCOVER AND SPREAD THE KNOWLEDGE, WHICH OUGHT TO BE USED FOR GOOD, BUT IS BEING USED FOR EVIL! THEREFORE, ILLUMINATE MATERIAL SCIENCE WITH SPIRITUAL SCIENCE! ADD DETERMINED PHILANTHROPY TO YOUR SCIENCE! AND UNITE! AND SHOW TO MANKIND THE RIGHT WAY OF ORGANISATION. FOR HUMANITY HAS EVERYTHING TO LOSE, IT PERISHES, IF YOU DON'T! WHEREAS, IF YOU DO, IT IS SAVED, IT LIVES, IT FINDS PEACE AND HAPPINESS FOR ALL!

CHAPTER VII

Conclusion

Let us conclude with two very small but very beautiful stories, illustrative of the Essential Unity of all Religions; one from Véḍic, one from Islāmic, writings.

Once upon a time, six blind men happened to come near a standing elephant. They felt, with their hands, different parts of the huge animal, and began disputing about its nature. One caught the end of the tail, and said it was a broom or brush. Another felt the trunk, and declared it was a huge python. A third found an ear, and affirmed that it was a large winnowing-fan. A fourth found the abdomen, and maintained it was a vast drum. A fifth stroked a leg, and asserted it was a thick column. A sixth grasped a tusk, and was sure it was a very large pestle. A seventh person happened to pass, and saw them disputing. He had eyes, was a man of vision, a man of wisdom. He explained to them what it was; a compound of all their 'opinions'; and not a mechanical but a living compound; and owner and user of them all. Each one of the different material sciences, views one facet of the Universe of Matter; each one of the several religions emphasises one aspect of the Spirit; the Science of Religion, the Religion of Science, Meta-physic, *Ṭasawwuf*, Gnosis, V é ḍ ā n ṭ a, synthesises them all.

Once upon another time, a Rūmi, an Arab, a Persian, and a Turk, happened to become fellow-travellers on the road of Life. Long trudging on the dusty, sandy, stony, thorny, now ice-cold, now burning-hot, tracks, made them hungry and thirsty for the nourishment that brings Strength and Peace. They did not know one another's mother-tongues. By signs they communicated, and brought out all the coins they had, to purchase food. What should they buy ? The Arab said, *Enab* ; the Turk growled, *Uzam* ; the Persian shouted, *Angūr* ; the Rūmī roared, *Asṭāfīl*. Faces frowned ; eyes reddened ; fists clenched ; blows began. An itinerant Fruit-Vendor passed along. Such Vendors of Vital Nourishment generally know the few all-important life-preserving words of many tongues. They have to deal with many customers of many sorts. He rushed in between, and placed before them his basket full of the Fruit of Life. Fists unclenched, voices sweetened, eyes softened, faces smiled. Each one found the Self-Same object of his Heart's Desire in that basket. Arabic *enab*, Turkish *uzam*, Irānī *angūr*, Rūmī *asṭāfīl*, Pahlavī *ḍākḥ*, Samskṛṭ *ḍrākshā*, English *grape*, all mean one and the same fruit, and very sweet fruit.

Each drew a circle to shut others out,
As heretics, rebels, things to flout ;

But Loving Wisdom knew the way to win,
It drew a Circle that took all in !

Faqaṭ ṭafāwaṭ hai nāma hī kā,
  Ḍar asl sab éka hī haiṅ, yāro !
Jo āb-i-sāfī ke mauj méṅ hai,
  Usī kā jalwā habāb méṅ hai ! (*S.*)

(Only names differ, Beloved !
  All forsooth are but the same.
Both the ocean and the dew-drop
  But one living liquid frame !)

Dear brothers and sisters ! we have met here on the Road of Life, coming from far and near, and all are hungry and thirsty for the Bread and the Water of Life, which is Love born of the sense of the all-Pervading Unity of the Supreme Spirit. We have begged, from the abounding vineyards, of the large-hearted, most generous, most charitable, growers of the Fruit of Life, the great authors of the Sacred Scriptures, who brood anxiously and lovingly over mankind, as mothers over their little children, a little of their Fruit, that we may share it equally here ; and that, when we wander out to other places, or back to our respective homes, we may bear its sweet taste in our mouths, and carry its good seeds of Unity and Love, for planting there and everywhere.

So many castes, so many creeds,
So many paths that wind and wind,
When just the art of being kind,
Is all the sad world needs ! (ELLA W. WILCOX.)

And the one and only sure art of being kind, is to bear diligently in mind the Great Truth of the Unity of our-self with the One Eternal, Infinite, Universal Self, and with all selves. God is Love, Love is God, because God is the Universal Self, and the sensing, the feeling, of this Unity, is the Love Divine, B h a k ṭ i, *Ishq-i-Haqîqî.*

Shāḍ bāsh, ai Ishq-i-kḥush-sauḍā-i-mā !
Ai ḍawā-é jumla illaṭ-hā-i-mā !
Ai ılāj-é nakḥwaṭ o nāmūs-i-mā !
Ai ṭu Aflāṭūn o Jālīnūs-i-mā ! (*S.*)
Véḍ', Avesṭā, al-Qurān, Injīl nīz,
Kā'ba o Buṭ-kḥāna o Aṭash-kaḍā,
Qalb-i-man maqbūl karḍa jumla chīz,
Chūṅ ma-rā juz Ishq nai ḍīgar Kḥuḍā ! (*S.*)

(Thrive, thrive, O Love Divine !
thy happy madness,
Sole remedy of all life's ills and sadness,
Prime antidote of pride and prudery,
Art, Science, Scripture—all art thou to me !
Véḍa, Avesṭā, Bible, Al-Qurān,
Temple, Pagoda, Church, and Kā'ba-Stone,
All these and more my heart doth close embrace,
Since my Religion now is Love alone.

Ṭā bi-āmokḥṭém abjaḍ-e-ishq,
Raqamé gḥair az īṅ na mīṅ ḍāném,
Ke ba chashmāni ḍil ma bīṅ juz Ḍosṭ,
Har che bīnī be-ḍān ke mazhar-i-Ū-sṭ.
Chūṅ ke wāqif shuḍém ze parḍa-e-Rāz,
Ḍam ba ḍam īṅ ṭarāna mī goyém,

Ke ba chashmān-i-ḍil ma bīṅ juz Ḍosṭ,
Har che bīnī be-ḍān ke mazhar-ī-Ū-sṭ !
(*S.*, SĀ'ḌI, *Mā Muqīmān.*)

(Since we have learnt the Alphabet of Love,
None other text than this can we repeat:
With the heart's eyes, wide-opened now, behold,
Whate'er thou see-est, as but form of His !
Since we have seen the Secret past the Screen,
With every breath the song springs to our lips:
Whate'er thou see-est now with the heart's eyes,
Thou know'st is but a form of the Loved One.)

One Cosmic Brotherhood,
One Universal Good,
One Source, One Sway,
One Law be-holding Us,
One Purpose moulding Us,
One Life en-folding Us,
In Love alway.
Lust, Greed, Fear, Pride, and Hate,
Long made us Desolate,
Their reign is done.
Race, Color, Creed, and Caste,
Fade with the Nightmare Past,
Man wakes to learn at last,
All Life is One !
("The Anthem of the Universal", *World-Fellowship.*)

May Peace and Prosperity return among Men,
May Co-operation unite them, Love bind them,
Brotherhood enfold them, Patience possess them,
Self-control strengthen them,
The Past be forgiven them,
The Future be sanctified for them,
May Peace and Prosperity return to them !
(Fellowship of Faiths' *Prayer for Peace.*)

Ehḍin-as-Sirāṭ-ul-musṭaqim. (*Q.*)
(May we be taught the Righteous way to Peace!)

Sarvas-ṭaraṭu ḍurgāṇi,
Sarvo bhaḍrāṇi pashyaṭu,
Sarvah saḍ-buḍḍhim āpnoṭu
Sarvah sarvaṭra nanḍaṭu. (*Mbh.*)
(May all attain the Mind of Righteousness,
May all cross safe beyond th' abysms of Life,
May all see loving eyes, good days, good nights,
May all behold the Face of Happiness!)

AUM! ĀMIṄ! AMEN!

ADDENDA

Page

61 In line 9, after '3', add: ',*SBE.*, xxxi, 255, 256.'.

62 After line 6, insert, the following:

Évam param-parā-prāpṭam
imam rājarshayo viḍuh,
Sa év-āyam mayā ṭé-(a)ḍya
yogah prokṭah purā-ṭanah. (*G.*)

(This ancient inner teaching has come down,
Age after age, from royal sage to sage;
This same have I declared to thee today.)

88 After line 6, insert:

(To those who think good, speak good, and do good,
And not to those who think ill, speak ill, and do ill,
Do I belong—saith Ahura Mazaḍā.)
(*Z.*, Yasna, 10. 16, *THR.*, p. 98.)

108 To the foot-note, add:

Gangā Prasāḍa, *The Fountain-head of Religion*, p. 12, says that Zoroastrianism has a formula, "Nést ezeḍ magar yazḍān", which means exactly the same as the Islāmic "Lā ilāh ill-allāh".

123 In lines 24-25, after '*summum individuum*', add: 'or *parvum*, or *parvulum*, or *minutum individuum*'.

141 Put in, as foot-note to sentence ending with 'all', in line 10:

See foot-note to p. 265, *infra*, (Addenda).

162 In l. 29, after 'Phylogenesis', add:
'Palingenesis',

164 As footnote to the sentence ending with 'irṭiqā', in line 16, put in the following:

Jainism knows this descent and re-ascent of the Spirit as samiṭi and gupṭi, sanchara and praṭi-sanchara, ava-ṣarpiṇī and uṭ-sarpiṇī; Christianity as Fall and Redemption, Sin and Salvation, Death and Resurrection; Sūfism as *safar-ul-Haq* and *safar-ul-abḍ*, *qaus-i-nuzūl* and *qaus-i-urūj*, *fisāl* and *wisāl*; the Véḍist systems of philosophy as banḍha and moksha, īhā and upa-rama, a-viḍyā and viḍyā, vyuṭ-ṭhāna and ni-roḍha, abhy-uḍaya and nis-shréyasa, sarga and apavarga, klésha and sva-rūpa-praṭishṭhā, pra-sava and praṭi-pra-sava, līlā and kaivalya; Buddhism uses many terms in common with Véḍism; western ethics and psychology might call the pair, 'pursuit and renunciation' or 'retirement'; and science, 'involution and evolution (of Spirit into and out of Matter)', or 'integration and disintegration or dissolution (of material form)'. A Chinese proverb says: "Heaven's way always goes round"; (Lin Yutang, *My Country and my People*, p. 189).

166 After line 12, insert:

How will the resurrection of the dead take place? To this answered Ahura Mazaḍā:—When I have created each and all of these things, would it be harder for me to bring about the resurrection?; (*Z., Bunḍehesh*, ch. 31, quoted by Gangā Prasāḍa, The *Fountain-head of Religion*, pp. 70-71).

169 After l. 28, add:

Asya brahm-āndasya samanṭaṭah sṭhiṭāni ananṭa-koti-brahmāndāni....mahā-jal-augha-maṭsya-buḍbuḍ-ānanṭa-sanghavaḍ-bhramanṭi. (*Ṭri-pāḍ-vibhūṭi-Mahā-Nārayaṇa-Upanishaṭ*, ch. 6.)

Sankhyā chéḍ rajasām asṭi
vishvānām na kaḍā-chana.
(*Ḍévī Bhāgavaṭa*, ix. iii. 7, 8.)

(Worlds beyond count, 'eggs of the Infinite',
'Of boundless Space', orbs like this earth of ours,
Each with its own peculiar forms of life,
Revolve and wander endlessly in space,
On all sides of this earth, above, below,
Like bubbles or like fishes in the sea;
Dust-atoms may be counted, not these orbs.)

Oshaḍhi-vanas-paṭayah yach-cha kin-cha prāṇa-bhṛṭ sa Aṭmānam āvis-ṭarām véḍa...Chiṭṭam prāṇa-bhṛṭsu...(ṭéshu) āvis-ṭarām Aṭmā...Purushé ṭv-āvis-ṭarām Āṭmā. Sa hi pra-jñānéna sampanna-ṭamah;...vijñaṭam pashyaṭi; véḍa lok-ālokau;...Marṭyén-Āmṛṭam īpsaṭi. (*Aiṭaréya Āraṇyaka*, II. iii. 2.)

(Herbs, trees, beasts, men—all are garbs of the Self;
And each successive form displays It more.
Man, who has mind, shows It forth most of all;
He has the introspective consciousness;
He knows, and also knows that he so knows;
He thinks of yesterday and of tomorrow;
He reaches out from Death to the Immortal.)

Taḍ yaṭhā péshas-kārī péshaso māṭrām upāḍāya anyan-nava-ṭaram kalyāṇa-ṭaram rūpam ṭanuṭé, évam év-āyam Aṭmā iḍam sharīram ni-haṭya a-viḍyām gamayiṭvā anyan-nava-ṭaram kalyāṇa-ṭaram rūpam kuruṭé. (*Bṛhaḍ Āraṇyaka Upanishaṭ*, IV. iv. 4.)

(Ev'n as a goldsmith takes a piece of gold,
And makes an ornament; and then breaks it,
And makes a finer one with it; e'en thus
The Spirit makes a body for It-Self,
Then breaks it, and shapes out a finer one.)

Vāsāmsi jīrṇāni yaṭhā vihāya,
Navāni gṛhṇāti naro-(a)parāṇi,
Taṭhā sharīrāṇi vihāya jīrṇāni,
Anyāni samyāṭi navāni ḍéhī. (*G.*)

(As a man puts away his worn-out clothes,
And takes up new ones; even so the soul,
Puts off old bodies and puts on new ones.)[1]

170 After line 17, insert:

In the first period heaven was created; in the second, the waters; in the third, the earth; in the fourth, the trees; in the fifth, the animals; and in the sixth, man. (*Z.*, Haug's *Essays on the Religion of the Parsis*, p. 192, quoted by Gangā Prasāḍa, *The Fountain-Head of Religion*, p. 65).

182 After line 26, insert:

I, the Lord thy God, am a jealous God, visiting the iniquity of the fathers upon the children and the children, unto the third and to the fourth generation. (*B.*, Exodus, chs. 20 and 34.)

---

[1] "Like the doctrine of evolution itself, that of transmigration has its roots in the world of reality; and it may claim such support as the great argument from analogy is capable of supplying": Prof. Huxley, *Evolution and Ethics*, p. 16.

193 In the last line, after 'rest', insert :

See *Manu-smṛti*, ch. xii, especially verses 71-73 ; these verses indicate that by 'births' into low, gross, animal and other forms, are meant *post mortem* states of the erring and sinning soul, imprisoned painfully in such forms, made of tenuous invisible matter, shaped by its own mentality. Some Sūfī sects also interpret the Qurānic verses, ré 'apes' and 'swine', (see p. 175, *supra*), in a similar sense.

207 In the third line from bottom, after 'wise', add : 'teacher'.

227 After line 10, insert :

Aham bhavān, na ch-ānyas ṭvam,
    Ṭvam év-Aham, vi-chakshva, bhoh !,
Na nau pashyanṭi kavayash-
    Chhiḍram jāṭu manāg-api. (*Bh.*)

(Thou art I, verily ; None Else art Thou ;
And I am thou, know well, deep in thy heart.
There is no difference 'twixt Thee and Me.
The Seers, who can see, have seen this Truth.)

257 After line 6, insert :

From the supernal hymns and harmonies
Of the celestial choirs of cherubim,
Divinity felt urge and surge for change.
It made It-Self the shape of mortal man,
To taste the joyous pain, the sweet heartache,
Of Father, Mother, Brother, Sister, Child,
Friend, Foe also, alas !, Misery and Bliss—
Till, tired of these, It pass to Peace again.

260 After line 26, insert :

Behold, I create new heavens and a new earth ; and the former shall not be remembered, nor come into mind. (*B*., Isaiah 65.).

261 After line 6, insert :

The breath of Heaven passed o'er the still sees.
And countless bubbling waves rose with the breeze ;
The smile of God flashed on the far-flung skies,
They flashed back answer in a million dyes.

261 After line 12 insert :
Loka-vaṭ ṭu Līlā-Kaivalyam.
(*Brahma-Sūṭra.*)
(As man, so God enacts gladness and sadness,
In Play and Pastime ; then, when tired of this,
He goes again into Sleep's Loneliness.)

261 In line 22, after 'Hū', add : 'Lā ilāhā illa Anā,'.

265 Put in, as foot-note to sentence ending with 'Tri-Unity', the following :

In *Z*rwanism . the dualistic view of the world was superseded by setting up endless Time, (***Zrwan***, Arabic *ḍahr*) as the paramount principle, and identifying it with Fate, the outermost heavenly sphere, or the movement of the heavens ...*Z*rwanism came to be publicly recognised under the Sasanid Yezdegerd II, 438-459 A. C. ; (Dr. T. J. de Boer, ***The History of Philosophy in Islam***, p. 8.)

274 After line 5, insert :

Who hath woe ? Who hath sorrow ? Who hath contentions ? Who hath babbling ? Who hath wounds without cause ? Who hath redness of eyes ? They that tarry long at wine ; they that go to seek mixed wine. Look not thou upon the wine when it is red, when it giveth his color in the cup, when it moveth itself aright. At the last, it biteth like a serpent, and stingeth like an adder. (*B.*, Prov., 23 : 29-32.)

295 After line 8, insert:

The unbelieving husband is sanctified by the wife, and the unbelieving wife is sanctified by the husband. (*B.*, Paul, I Cor.).

324 After *kufr*, in l. 11, add: 'error, ne-science, male-science, and multiplicity, belief in other than Self,'.

326 In line 21, after 'chief', add: 'powers'.

348 In line 8, after 'Ṛshis', add: 'Maharshis, Ḍévarshis, Paramarshis'.

360 After line 26, insert:

Pathemata Mathemata. (Greek saying.)
(Sufferings bring knowledge.)

Ḍuhkha-ṭray-ābhi-ghāṭāj-
jijñāsā ṭaḍ-apa-ghāṭaké héṭau.
(*Sānkhya-kārikā.*)

(When sorrows come, then search for knowledge grows—
Knowledge of cause of sorrows, and their cure.)

Ḍukkham, ḍukkha-sam-up-pāḍam,
dukkhassa cha aṭi-kkamam,
Ariyam ch-atth-angikam maggam,
dukkh-ūpa-sama-gāminam. (*Dh.*)

(Pain, cause of pain, crossing beyond all pain,
The eight-fold way of crossing—these four Truths,
Noble, beneficent, the Buḍḍha taught.)

411 After l. 23, insert :

Āchāryah sarva-chéshtāsu
loka éva hi ḍhī-maṭah.
Kṛṭsno hi loko buḍḍhi-maṭām
āchāryah ; shatrush-ch-ā-buḍḍhi-matām.
(*Charaka.*)

(To the wise man, who can observe the world,
The finest teacher of how to behave,
Most friendly counsellor, is the whole world ;
To the unwise, it is a ruthless foe.)

428 After line 3 insert :

A-ḍīnāh syāma sharaḍah shaṭam, bhūyash-cha sharaḍah shaṭāṭ. (*Yajur-Véḍa*, 36. 24.)

Bhaḍram jīvanṭo jaraṇām ashīmahi.
(*Ṛg-Véḍa*, 10. 37. 6.)

Pashyéma sharaḍah shaṭam, rohéma sharaḍah shaṭam, pushyéma sharaḍah shaṭam, bhavéma sharaḍah shaṭam, bhūshéma sharaḍah shaṭam, bhūyasīh sharaḍah shaṭāṭ. (*Aṭharva-Véḍa*, 19. 67. 1-8.)

(May we live, un-depressed, a hundred years ;
And even more ; and living sumptuously ;
A hundred autumn-glories may we see ;
And for a hundred autumns may we grow
In health and strength, and decorate ourselves ;
And e'en beyond the term of hundred years !)

478 Put in, as footnote to sentence ending with 'all', in line 25 :

Kalā bahaṭṭar purusha kī ; vā méṅ ḍo sarḍār,
Éka jīva kī jīvikā, Éka jīva uḍḍhār.
(Jaina saying.)

(Full two and seventy are human arts,
But two of these do hold the two chief parts:
One is, to feed and keep the Body Whole;
The other is, to find Peace for the Soul.)

480 Add, as foot-note to sentence ending with 'Meaning', in l. 25, the following:

From such exceedingly limited study and feeble thinking and public work as he has been able to do in seventy-one years, the present writer has derived the conviction that (I) *The Secret Doctrine*, by H. P. Blavatsky, studied together with five or six of the most important and best recognised *Purāṇa-s*, in the light, and with the help, of modern evolutionist science, and of Vḗḍānṭa, Sānkḥya, and Yoga philosophy, is the best available exposition, in broad outlines, of what the Divine Will or Plan is, on the vast scale, for our solar system in general, and this earth and the human race in particular; and that (II) Manu's Scheme of Individuo-Social Organisation is the best available scheme of Human Planning.

485 In line 5, after 'money-stakes', add 'within strict limits'.

489 To line 25, add: 'e. g., four kinds of pathological temperaments (or 'personal idiosyncracies') and four corresponding kinds of treatments; four types of crimes and criminals and four corresponding kinds of punishments; and so on. But it must always be remembered that these quartettes do not and cannot imply any hard and fast divisious, but that only the predominant feature or quality makes a type.'

489 Add, to para ending with 'Life-stages', in line 31, the following foot-note :

If the reader will kindly peruse, e.g., chapter 59, (which Mr. Wells himself calls "the most cardinal," in ch. 69), of that most interesting, luminous, and valuable work, H. G. Wells' *A Short History of the World*, side by side with pp. 478-489 of this book, he will probably be better able to appreciate *the contacts and contrasts* between the Vẹdist 'individuo-socialism', and the trends of modern western thought in respect of 'individualism' and 'socialism'. In the last 100 pages of his 'eutopian' work, *The Shape of Things to Come*, Mr. Wells rightly stresses repeatedly the need of "educational revolution" for "remoulding mankind"; says that "social psychology" should "become, so to speak, the whole literature, philosophy, and general thought of the world"; and suggests that "the world which had once been divided among *territorial* Great Powers" should become "divided among *functional* Great Powers", which, in co-ordination, will constitute the "World-State" or "World-Organisation". He also suggests the desirability of "a scientific classification of types". His "functional Great Powers" would seem to be, in other words, world-wide 'Guilds'. He does not scientifically classify the 'functions', but those which he indicates could all be readily classified under the four great varṇa-s, 'vocational guilds', manned by the four temperamental 'types'. (See the present writer's *Ancient vs. Modern Scientific Socialism*, pp. 69-73, 132-140, 165-209). What Mr. Wells says about 'types', shows that he is thinking of only *physical* types, suited for different climatic and other natural conditions; not of *temperamental vocational* types. And he concerns himself almost exclusively with the outer machinery of the World-State, and does not say anything about the different *psychical* types of persons, indispensably needed to discharge successfully the different (may we say, 'types of' ?) functions of the several "functional Great Powers." The Vẹdist scheme supplements the scheme of the '*outer* machinery' with a scheme of corresponding appropriate '*inner* machinery', without which the 'outer machinery' can never work successfully; and thereby makes it possible to provide, without any competitive waste of vitality, for every social work, *the right kind of worker*, who is best fitted to perform it efficiently.

There is much that seems plausible, even feasible, in this latest 'eu-topia' of Mr. Wells. His picturing of the 'things to come' may be said to illustrate concretely, how 'all things else can be added, if men achieve righteousness first,' as the Bible says. The flaw in his scheme, (as in most other 'utopias,' including Marx's and the Russian Soviet's, as the latter seems to have discovered in the actual working), is that, (even allowing full effect to the education which he very rightly stresses as all-important), he assumes righteousness achieved too facilely; does nct take sufficient account of the metaphysical Law of Duality, which works as indefeasibly in human psychology as in any other department of Nature; reduces too easily to a neglible minimum, even if he does not quite abolish, the egoistic urges and passions; and makes all human life, too readily, one round of picnics and scientific research, to occupy the vast amount of leisnre which he creates, by the magic of his pen. One gets the impression that he believes that 'pairs of opposites' are neither inevitable nor needed; that the universe can be re-manufactured, with the help of clever machinery, in terms of one only of each such pair; of pleasures only, without pains; of lights only, without shadows; of loves only, without hates; of comforts only, without bothers. Then, he provides no spiritual foundations for his material super-structure of pleasant physical sensuous life. He does not say anything about the finer spiritual domestic affections, maternal, paternal, fraternal, filial; nor about the Meaning of Life, or the soul, or 'after-life'. All the current religions are duly suppressed by his new-world-makers; but no substitute, satisfactory or even unsatisfactory, is provided; nor does he say that his new humanity has so entirely changed its psychology that it does not care for any such trifles, any more. The Vẹdic Scheme, on the other hand, makes due provision for the egoistic as well as the altruistic instincts, man's 'this-worldly' as well as 'other-worldly' needs, for spiritual as well as material bread; tells us what the Meaning of Life is; and assures us of after-life, endless evolution, Immortality. Be it observed that there is no radical irreconcileable antagonism between the Vẹdic Scheme and Mr. Wells'. On the contrary, the latter would improve greatly in balance, and therefore practicability, (as would the Russian Soviet's), if it were duly corrected and rationalised in the light of the psychological principles of the former.

590 Put in, as foot-note to the sentence ending with 'experience', in line 5, the following:

Sarva-bhūṭéshu ch-Āṭmānam,
sarva-bhūṭāni ch-Āṭmani,
Samam pashyan Āṭma-yājī,
Svā-rājyam aḍhi-gachchhaṭi. (*M.*)

(Who sees the Self in all, and all in Self,
His life is one long sacrifice to Self;
With just eyes he sees all impartially;
He finds the inner true Self-government
First; then the outer, for himself and all.)

605 After line 8, insert:

Yaḍā charma-vaḍ ākāsham
véshtayishyanṭi mānavāh,
Taḍā Dévam a-vijñaya,
duhkhasy-ānṭo bhavishyaṭi. (*U.*)

(Yea, men shall roll the sky up like a mat,
Sooner, than put an end to suffering
Without the Vision of the Self in All.)

CORRIGENDA

Page	Line	
4	1	For 'ḍaryo', read 'darégo'.
33	1-16	Read the first sixteen lines as continuation of the foot-note on p. 32.
79	16	For 'Sah', read 'Saha',
98	13-14	Read '*Mahā-vākya*' as 'M a h ā-v ā k y a'.
121	8	For 'Amriṭ-oja', read 'Amiṭ-oja'.
,,	13	For 'kathai', read 'kaṭhai'.
,,	14	For 'karama', read 'karma'.
146	1	For 'av-ékshya-māṇo', read 'av-éksha-māṇo'.
152	22	For 'as', read 'az'.
180	20	For 'Ta', read 'T.,'.
204	10	Omit 'states'.
224	12	For 'an-Other,', read 'an-Other ; is'.
236	22	For 'go the', read 'go to the'.
266	13	For 'cataclysms', read 'iridiscent dew-drops and humming-birds'.
294	29	For 'Mother', read 'Holy Ghost'.
323	13	For 'once', read 'one-'.
327	4	For '*Ṭaswwur*', read '*Ṭasawwur*'.
334	29	For 'Self', read 'self'.
336	29	For 'Jnbbaṭin', read 'Jubbaṭin'.
349	4-5	Read the italicised words as romanised.
366	29	For 'pinious', read 'pinions'.
378	8	Read '*Kṛṭya*' as 'K ṛ ṭ y a'.
417	11-13	Omit 'with compassion...his lips', and substitute ; 'a song'.
437	14	After 'religions', add 'may be noted;'.
437	18	For 'may be noted', substitute 'everywhere'.

458	11	For 'are', read 'art'.
517	15	For 'Formalism and Catchwords', read 'The Great Truth masked by the Great Error.'
520	1	After 'Danger' add '; Formalism and Catchwords'.
542	19	For line 19, substitute: 'Naught else is worth while—they indeed know naught.'

APPENDIX A

(to pp. 482-489).

Samskṛṭ and Arabic-Persian equivalents for the tetrads of the Véḍic Social Organisotion.

Samskṛṭ and Arabic-Persian equivalents for the terms of the tetrads mentioned on pp. 482-489, are given below. This book is intended, among other purposes, to be of service to workers who may have occasion to address public audiences, in India, of Hinḍū-s as well as Muslims, in order to draw their attention to thoughts already common to the two religions, and such more as can be adopted by followers of both, to the benefit of all, without in any way hurting any cherished belief of either. To be readily understood by members of the two denominations and cultures, the speaker should, obviously, be able to use words which are familiar to, and will, therefore, readily 'come home' to them. Hence, Samskṛṭ and Arabic-Persian equivalents have been given throughout the book, side by side with corresponding English words. But the following could not be conveniently incorporated in the text. Hence they are gathered here. The value of seeing the same thought through the medium of several languages, of recognising the same truth in different garbs, has been dwelt on before, at pp. 65-70 and 526.

Such equivalents, in the following, as are not established by traditional usage, but are offered newly, are, of course, tentative, and ought to be replaced by better ones, as necessary, by those who may have occasion to use them.

(1) Skt. Four prakṛṭi-s: (a) Shikshaka; (b) Rakshaka; (c) Poshaka; (d) Sahāyaka; or, (a) Viḍvān; (b) Vīra; (c) Pālaka; (d) Ḍhāraka; or, (a) Jñān-āḍhika; (b) Kriy-āḍhika; (c) Ichchh-āḍhika; (d) A-vyanjiṭa.

(The well-known traditional words are, of course, (a) brāhmaṇa; (b) kshaṭṭriya; (c) vaishya; (d) shūḍra. But they have now completely lost their very vital *functional*, *occupational*, or *vocational* (which is also their etymological) significance; have become irredeemably permeated by the notion of 'hereditary caste'; and hence are, now, much more misleading than useful, where the problems of effective social organisation, the rational division of the social labor, the training for and the choosing or assigning to temperamentally suitable occupations and means of living, and the efficient exercise-and-discharge of corresponding rights-and-duties, are concerned. Therefore the use of one or more new sets of terms has become necessary, which will bring out the *functional* import unmistakeably. There is no such difficulty involved in the Arabic-Persian equivalents. A number of other sets of terms, Skt. and also A.-P., are suggested on pp. 104-106 of the present writer's book, *Ancient vs. Modern Scientific Socialism*.)

Arab.-Per. Four fiṭraṭ-s: (a) Ā'lim; (b) Ā'mil; (c) Ṭājir; (d) Mazḍūr.

(2) S. Four vṛṭṭi-s: (a) viḍyā-vṛṭṭi; (b) shāsana-vṛṭṭi; (c) vārṭā-vṛṭṭi; (d) vrāṭa-vṛṭṭi or shrama-vṛṭṭi.

A.-P. Four péshā-s: (a) ilmī; (b) a'malī; (c) ṭijāraṭī; (d) mazḍūrī.

(3) S. Four jīvikā-s: (a) dakshiṇā, praṭi-graha; (b) kara, véṭana, bhāga; (c) vṛḍḍhi, kusīḍa; (d) karmaṇyā, bhṛṭi.

A.-P. Four mā'sh-es: (a) nazr, pésh-kash; (b) khirāj, mushāhirā; (c) munāfa'; (d) mazḍūrī, ṭankhwāh.

(4) S. Four āshramas: (a) brahma-chārī, or viḍy-ārṭhī; (b) gṛha-sṭha; (c) vāna-prasṭha, or vana-sṭha; (d) san-nyāsī.

A.-P. Four manāzil-i-umr, or, briefly, manzil-s, (staging-places of life): (a) muṭa'llim; (b) khāna-ḍār; (c) gosha-nashīn; (d) faqīr, ḍurwésh.

(5) S. Four shārīra-éshaṇā-s: (a) āhār-échchhā; (b) ḍhan-échchhā; (c) ḍāmpaṭy-échchhā, or raṭi-ichchhā; (d) vinoḍ-échchhā, vishrām-échchhā, svāsṭhy-échchhā.

A.-P. Four jismānī-khwāhish-es: (a) khwāhish-i-ghizā, or ishṭihā; (b) khwāhish-i-māl; (c) khwāhish-i-zaujiyaṭ, or khwāhish-i-aulāḍ; (d) khwāhish-i-ṭafrīh, or khwāhish-i-arām, or khwāhish-i-ṭan-ḍurusṭī.

(6) S. Four mānasa éshaṇā-s: (a) loka-ishaṇā, or sammān-échchhā; (b) viṭṭ-aishaṇā, or sampaḍ-ichchha; (c) aishvary-aishaṇā, or aḍhi-kār-échchhā, or īshiṭv-échchā, or prabhuṭv-échchhā; (d) moksh(a)-échchhā.

A.-P. Four zehnī or nafasī khwāhish-es or hirs-es: (a) hirs-i-izzaṭ; (b) hirs-i-daulaṭ; (c) hirs-i-hukūmaṭ; (d) ārzu-i-najāṭ.

(7) S. Four purush-ārtha-s: (a) ḍharma; (b) arṭha; (c) kāma; (d) moksha, or Brahm-ānanḍa.

A.-P. Four maqāsaḍ-i-zinḍagī, or maqsaḍ-s: (a) ḍayānaṭ, or ḍīn; (b) ḍaulaṭ; (c) lazzaṭ-i-ḍunyā; (d) najā'ṭ, or lazzaṭ-i-ilāhiyā.

(8) S. Four maryāḍā-s, viḍhi-s, or samsṭhā-s. (a) upā-sanā ; (b) pari-graha, or sva-ṭva, or rikṭha ; (c) kula, or ḍāmpaṭya, or gārhasṭhya, or vivāha-paḍḍhaṭi ; (d) rāshtra, or rājya, or shāsana-paḍḍhaṭi.

A.-P. Four ḍasṭūr-s, or zābiṭā-s : (a) mazhab : (b) milkīyaṭ ; (c) khānah-ḍārī, or khān-ḍān, or kunbā ; (d) siyāsaṭ, nizāmaṭ, salṭanaṭ, nazm-i-mulk.

(9) S. Four bala-s : (a) shāsṭra-bala, or viḍyā-bala, or jñāna-bala ; (b) shasṭra-bala, or āyuḍha-bala, or shaurya-bala, or vīrya-bala ; (c) ḍhana-ḍhānya-bala, or anna-bala, or arṭha-bala ; (d) shrama-bala.

A.-P. Four qūwaṭ-s or ṭāqaṭs : (a) qūwaṭ-i-ilmī ; (b) quwaṭ-i-aslahā, or qūwaṭ-i-ḍilérī ; (c) qūwaṭ-i-mālī ; qūwaṭ-i-mashaqqaṭ.

(10) S. Four sets of (duties-and-rights) karṭavya-s-and-aḍhi-kāra-s : (a) saṭ-jñana-sangraha-and-prachāra, and sammāna-prāpṭi ; (b) rakshā-shakṭi-sangraha-and-rakshā-prasāra, and īshvara-bhāva-prāpṭi or īshiṭva-lābha or ajñā-shakṭi-labha ; (c) jīvana-sāmagrī-uṭpāḍana-and-prasāraṇa, and vṛḍḍhi-yukṭa-mūlya-lābha ; (d) sévā, and bhṛṭi-and-vinoḍa-prāpṭi.

A.-P. Four sets of farz-es-and-haq-s : (a) ṭālīf-wa-taqsim-i-ulūm-i-nék, and izzaṭ ; (b) ṭahsīl-i-zarāya'-i-hifāzaṭ wa hifāzaṭ-i-awām, and hukūmaṭ ; (c) paiḍā-karḍan-wa-ṭaqsīm-karḍan-i-sāmān-i-zinḍagī, and munāfa'; khiḍmaṭ, and mazḍūrī wa ṭafrīh.

(11) S. Four karṭavya-s of vṛḍḍha-s, and of the rāshtra : (a) shikshā ; (b) rakshā ; (c) poshā ; (d) sévā.

A.-P. Four farāyaz of the buzurg-s, and of the siyāsaṭ : (a) ṭā'līm ; (b) ṭahaffuz ; (c) ṭā'm ; (d) khiḍmaṭ or imḍāḍ.

(12) S. Four vyūhas : (a) shikshā-vyūha ; (b) rakshā-vyūha ; (c) vārṭā-vyūha ; (c) sévā-vyūha.

A.-P. Four ṭanzīm-s : (a) ṭanzīm-i-ṭā'līm ; (b) ṭanzīm-i-ṭahaffuz ; (c) ṭanzīm-i-tā'm (or rizq) ; ṭanzīm-i-khiḍmaṭ.

S. Four ṛṇa-s : (a) ḍéva-ṛṇa ; (b) ṛṣhi-ṛṇa ; (c) piṭṛ-ṛna ; (d) Aṭma-ṛṇa.

A.-P. Four qarz-es : (a) qarz-i-malāyak (or anāsir) ; (b) qarz-i-anbīā (or ā'rifān, or ā'limān) ; (c) qarz-i-mūrisān ; (d) qarz-i-Allāh, (or -Ruh-ul-arwāh, or -Rūh-i-Ā'zam).

(14) S. Four ṛṇa-nir-mochana-s (or nir-yāṭana-s, or nis-ṭāraṇa-s) : (a) ijyā (or yajña, or isht-āpūrṭa) ; (b) apaṭya-pālana ; (c) aḍhyāpana ; (d) san-nyāsa (or nir-vāṇa, or Brahma-laya).

A.-P. Four aḍā-i-qarz ; (a) zakāṭ (or khairāṭ) ; (b) parwarish-i-aulāḍ ; (c) ṭā'līm ; (d) [ṭark-i-ḍunyā (or fuqr, or sukn, or fanā-f-illāh).

(a) Necessaries, (b) comforts, (c) luxuries may be equated with : S., (a) āvashyakīya-s ; (b) ni-kāmīya-s ; (c) ānanḍanīya-s (or vilāsīya-s) ; and A.-P., (a) zurūrīyāṭ, (b) āsāishāt, (c) ishraṭīyāṭ. Social organisation : S., samāja-vyavasṭhā ; A.-P., ṭanzīm-i-jamāa'ṭ.

INDEX OF BOOKS AND WRITINGS REFERRED TO

INDEX OF SAMSKṚṬ WORDS.

(English equivalents will be found beside the words on the pages referred to. The hyphen indicates the junction-point between a prefix and the main word, or between two words in a compound word. See also Appendix A, for words not included here.)

INDEX OF ARABIC-PERSIAN WORDS.

(English and Samskṛt equivalents will be found, beside the word, on the pages referred to. Some words, not used in the text, have also been included here, with their English and Samskṛt equivalents. See also Appendix A.)

Rizq, 285.
Rozā, 126, 468.
Rūh, 160, 204, 344, 381.
Rūh-i-ālam, 176.
Rūh-i-āzam, 176, 381.
Rūh-i-jārī, (See nafs-i-jārī).
Rūh-i-kul, 203.
Rūh-i-muqīm, (See nafs-i-muqīm).
Rūh-ul-quḍs, 'holy soul', 'holy spirit', 'Holy Ghost'. (S. paviṭr-āṭmā, ḍivy-āṭmā).
Rūh-ul-rūh, (or Rūh-ul-arwāh) 176, 381.

Safā, 246.
Safar-i-abḍ, 131.
Safar-i-Haq, 131.
Sair-i-āfāqī, extro-spection; 'travel in space', i. e. the outside world.
Sair-i-nafasī, 327, intro-spection; 'travel within the mind'.
Sajjāḍā, 476.
Sajjāḍā-nashīn, 476.
Salāṭ, 126.
Sālik, 278.
Salīm, 239.
Salm, 80.
Sar-āb, 252.
Saum, 126.
Saut-i-sarmaḍī, 'the eternal and incessant voice without souud and direction'; 'the voice of the silence'; 'the word that was with God, and was God'; (S., an-āhaṭa-nāḍa; AUM, OM).
Sērī-az-ḍuniyā, 129.
Shab-bēḍārī, 468.
Shahāḍat, 410.
Shahwaṭ, 325, 370.
Shaiḍā, 393.
Shaiṭān, 199.
Shakhsiyaṭ-i-aḍnā, 226.
Shān, potency, power; (pl. shuyūn, shuyūnāṭ; S., shakṭi, vi-bhūṭi).
Shānī, 109.
Shanīḍah, 335.
Shara'ī-mullā, 101.
Sharīa'ṭ, 85, 420, 422.
Sheikh, 393, 398, 476.
Shirk, 319, 320.
Shohraṭ, 323.
Shuhūḍ, 242, 263.
Shuhūḍiyah, 242, 243.
Shuṭṭahiyāṭ, 108.
Shuyūnāṭ, 266, 326.
Sifāṭ, 245, 263, 296.
Siṭārā, 474.
Spenṭa, 136. (Z.)
Subhāni, 109.
Sūf, 246.
Sūfī (sects) 392.
Sūfī, 246. (Throughout). (See Ṭasawwuf).
Sūfī-auliyā, 101.
Sūfisṭa, 246
Sukn, 365, 370.
Sūrah, 445.
Surūr-i-Jāwēḍānī, 390.

Ṭā'rum, 475.
Ṭa'iyun, limitation; (S., ava-chhēḍa, pari-miṭi).

VERIFICATION OF REFERENCES

The following, which should have been included in the Note on Texts (pp. xxvi-xlv), was not put in there, by inadvertence:

After the first edition was published, some friends wrote that textual references should have been given more precisely, by chapter and verse. The difficult conditions unfavorable to scholarly detail and exactitude under which this compilation has been made, have been mentioned before, (pp. xi, xii, xxxiii, *supra*). But the reader, who has the inclination and the leisure, will be able to verify most of the texts quoted, with the help of the following:

Jacob's *Concordance to the Upanishats and the Bhagavad-Gīṭā.*

Vishvéshvar-ānanḍ and Niṭy-ānanḍ's *Alphabetical Index of the Four Veḍas.*

Any good *Concordance to the Bible.*

Concordance to the Qurān (*Mifṭa-ul-Qurān*), by Rev. Ahmad Shah.

Manu-pāḍ-ānu-kramaṇī, a *Concordance to the Manu-Smṛṭi*, (published by The Gyān-mandal, Benares).

J. M. Chatterjee's and A. N. Bilimoria's edition of the *Gāṭhā.*

Treasure-House of Living Religions, by R. E. Hume.

GENERAL INDEX OF SUBJECTS

Deeds, good and dutiful, indispensable, 529; prove the real faith, 530; 550.
Degeneration of religions, 9, 19, 559.
Deism, 242.
Deity in image and shrine, 446-447.
Deliverance, 224.
Democratism, 58.
Democracy, method of, in religion, xiv, xviii, 18, 55, 60.
Descent, 250-252; 289. (See Arcs and Ascent).
Desire, one of the three Functions of the Mind, 85-7; corresponds to the Way of Devotion, 85, 270-333; Divine, 262; subtle self-deceiving, 280; the Primal Force or Energy, 345; men are what they, 344-345; and Desirelessness, proper time for each, 385; the Root-Cause of the Universe, 394; the Self-same Heart's, of All, 603-604.
Destiny and Free-Will, 177-180; 183-186; 380-381, 551.
Determinism. (See Destiny).
Devil, 330. (See Satan, and God inverted).
Devils, 199.
Devotees, visions of, 448-450.
Devotion, safest form of, 397; Way of, 270-420; one of three integral Constituents of Religion, 85-86; 270, 420; mutual, of each to all, all to each, 381; personal and impersonal, sterile without virtuous and dutiful acts, 529; dangers of excessive, (see Danger).
Ḍharma, meaning of, 79, 81.
"Die before you die", 206.
Dietetics, 479.
Difference, Discord, (See Agreement). 13-14, 65, 68, 79, 127, 140-142, 506, 558.
Disarmament, moral, must come first, 30.
Disciple and Master, 475.
Disciplines. (See Virtues).
Discord, spirit of, 15.
Discourse, speechless, 161.
Discovery, the Great, 232-234.
Dis-gust with the world, dis-illusionment, dis-passion, dis-taste for life, 129-132, 249, 327, 329, 360, 594. (See World-weariness).
Dissolution, 230.
Diversity, 14. (See Difference).
Divine, Bliss, (See Blessedness); Fire, periodic renewal of, 220; Heartache, 238; Union, 387; Will-and-Imagination, 412; Will, (see Will); Harp, the human body, 416-417.

"Doctors disagree", 12, 523-524.
Doctrine of the Eye, 101; of the Heart, 100; of the Page, 100.
'Domestics', 580.
Dreams, may be purified and beautified by prayer before sleep, 347.
Duality, of God's Nature, in all aspects of the World-Process, 35-50; how transcended, 42; of attributes and names of God, 44-49; of Sex, 47; of souls, minds, higher and lower, altruist and egoist, in each person, 49; Law of, 79; of the ends of life, 223, 268-269; 330-331; 353; 473; 558. (See Opposites).
Duty, varies with circumstance, 74, 308, 316-317; is neither sin nor merit, 184; the Whole, of Man, in brief, 271; difference of, 278; to rear up virtuous progeny, 288; conflict of, 312; reconciliation, 313; general and special, 314; meaning of the word, 377; means to equability, 377; devotion to, 376-379; becomes Joy, 384; necessity to know what the exact duty is, in any given situation, 479; the only right, 541; active performance of, indespensable, 538-539; 552.
EAST and West, 8-14.
Economics, 579.
Ecstatic utterances of Mystics, 107-112.
Eden, Garden of, 221, 351.
Education, relation of, to civilisation, 89-90, 568; consequences of wrong, 569; wrong and right, 586-587.
Education and the Educationist, 568 602.
Educationists, duty of, 27-33; 54 55; to teach Universal Religion, 55-59; should combine austerity and wisdom, 592-593; pure livelihood necessary for, 595; make or mar State and Civilisation, 595; right and duty of, to guide, direct, correct, reprove, rulers and public servants, 595-597.
Ego, Universal, 344. (See Self).
Egoism. xiv; and nationalism, *vs*. Humanism, xxiv; 80, 84, 127, 130, 136, 225, 321, 326-327, 349, 383, 558; hardens the heart, 131; must be dissolved, to see God, 132; the real Satan, 137; and 'personality, 148; the measure of Altruism, 303; the single root of all sins, 319; and Altruism, the only two

'm o r a l' principles, 336; 383. (See Altruism and Universalism).
Egyptian religion, views ré' soul in, 203.
Elephant, and six blind men, story of, 602.
Elixir of Life, 417.
Emotions, the chief, 317-318, 331-332.
Empires and Religion, 507.
End, the Permanent and the temporary, xxiv-xxv.
Ends of Life. (See Values).
Energism, 86, 244.
Enlightenment, meaning of, 93.
Epicureanism. (See Stoicism).
Equality, 212; and Fraternity and Liberty, 592.
Equilibrium, 41, 189, 314-376.
Eros, as Love-Lust, 134; the Prime Creator, 395; unbridled, the worst enemy, 512.
Erotic language of Mysticism, 388-389. (See Danger).
Error, always in the extremes, 44; the Primal, 319; the five 'phalanges,' 'joints', successive stages of, 352.
Esoteric teachings, 97-103; 445.
Essenes, the, 97, 98.
Essence vs. Form, 57; 153.
Essential and Non-Essential, xiii; 9; 33; 73-77; religion, 57, 301-303; in orthodox Islam and in Vẹ́dism, 126-128.
Eternal, the, Miracle, 252; Now, 546; Peace, 2, 14, 26-28, 228, 248, 250, 280, 376, 558-568.
Ethics, 270.
Eugenics, 497.
European thought, colored by Science, 8.
Evil, 50, 136, 156, 247-248; is No-Thing, 248; of nationalism, 29, 577. (See Good).
Evolution, psychical, and physical, xvi, xvii; 25; 162; 174; the ladder of, 167, 555-556, 222; 224.
Excess, the one Sin, 34-36; 38; 44.
Experiences, all, must be passed through by all souls, 374-375; 406.
Expiation, 441-444.
Explosives, psychical, the most terrible, xx.
Extremes, 34-36, 38-44.

FACULTY, Extensions of, 199.
Faith, blind, 392; without Works is dead, 535.
Fall and Rise, arcs of, 92.
Falsehood, the Primal, 319.
Familiarity breeds Contempt, 135.
Family, life of, an End, 223; the Divine Happy, 294; the whole world, God's, 295.

406; Houses of, 413; all forms His, 414 ; the pure in heart see, 449 ; the word of, 445 ; living temples of, 457; desires mercy, not murder, 471 ; live and die for, 527 ; moveth all, yet Duty must be done, 551. (See Consciousness, I, Self).

Gods and Titans, 351-354.

Golden Age, the, 132.

Golden Mean, the, 15 ; achieved by Right Social Organisation, 573.

Golden Rule, the 15, 13, 297-317, 328, 479, 481, 513 ; negative and positive forms of, 297 ; origin of dual state-functions, 297-298 ; essence of all religion, 299 ; various forms of, xxix-xxx, 298-303 ; corollaries of, 304-306 ; reason for, 306-307 ; difficulties ré, 307-317 ; how difficulties ré, may be solved, 308, 313 ; Social Organisation indispresable for working, 479-481.

Good, 31, 384-386, 553 ; (See *Summum Bonum*) ; like Evil, is No-Thing, 249 ; the, and the Pleasant reconciled, 383-385 ; and Evil, 50, 136; both created by God, 152; both in every one, 156, 157, 247-249, 350-352.

Goodness, Truth, Beauty, 31. (See Truth).

Grades of evolutionary types, 172.

Greed, 28.

Guru, the quality of the true, 594.

Hair's-breadth line between Selfishness and Un-selfishness 349, 350.

Happiness, here and hereafter, the One Way to, xix ; 84 ; 360, 390, 487.

Harmony, how secured, 409.

Hate, 28 ; extinguished by Love, not by Hate, 304, 308-310 ; 328 ; as the Un-Truth of Separateness, 331.,

Heart, large and small 72 human, throne of God, 107 ; change of, needed to see God, 130-132 ; cleansing of the, 356 ; parental, more needed in teacher than clever head, 574-575.

Heartache, the Divine, 238, 258.

Heaven, the Way of, 180 ; 199 ; 349 ; kingdom of, on earth, its meaning and nature, 590-591.

Hebrew Vēḍānṭa, 247.

Hell, 199, 349.

Helper needed by young Soul, 408.

Here, the Infinite, 51.

Heredity, 500-503, 506.

Hierarchy, the Spiritual, 6, 214-222.